MORNING STAR OVER AMERICA

The New Millennium
AD 2006-2008

Anthology of Messages
The Blessed Virgin Mary

William L. Roth, Jr.
Timothy Parsons-Heather

The Morning Star of Our Lord, Inc. is a nonprofit, tax-exempt, (501)(c)(3) religious, charitable organization that is incorporated under the laws of the State of Illinois. It has been created for the dissemination of various apologetic works in defense of the Holy Gospel of Christianity. It is the role of this Roman Catholic corporation to provide pastoral consolation to those lacking in faith, the infirm, homebound, incarcerated, deprived, dejected and those who are otherwise suffering-humanity for the Glory of the Kingdom of Jesus Christ. All proceeds from this book are being donated to other charitable causes to help feed, clothe and house the poor, and for the reproduction of Christian media for distribution across every continent of the world. If anyone would like to contribute to this worthy cause, you may do so through the following website address.

The Morning Star of Our Lord, Inc.
Springfield, Illinois
www.ImmaculateMary.org

Published by The Morning Star of Our Lord, Incorporated
Used with permission.
Copyright © 2009
William L. Roth Jr. & Timothy Parsons-Heather
All rights reserved.

Publish date: July 22, 2009

ISBN10: 0-9793334-1-5
ISBN13: 978-0-9793334-1-5

The Morning Star of Our Lord, Inc. has published eleven works to date by William L. Roth Jr. and Timothy Parsons-Heather, the initial being their nearly sixteen hundred page, two volume diary that meticulously chronicles the opening days of the miraculous intercession of the Most Blessed Virgin Mary in their lives. These two men are under ecclesial obedience to the Roman Catholic Bishop of the Diocese of Springfield in Illinois who reserves final judgement concerning their disposition.

Dedication

The Most Reverend George J. Lucas, DD

Possessor of the Faith of the Original Apostles

Archbishop
Roman Catholic Archdiocese
of
Omaha in Nebraska
Installed July 22, 2009

Bishop
Roman Catholic Diocese
of
Springfield in Illinois
December 14, 1999 - June 3, 2009

Morning Star Over America

The New Millennium
AD 2006-2008

Table of Contents

Prologue
by
William L. Roth Jr.

Page sequence continues from previous Anthology

AD 2006 735

AD 2007 857

AD 2008 973

"What shall I tell them, Master, when your enemies fall prostrate at my feet, clawing the ground with self pity, crying out that they should have believed?" Jesus answered, "...say that My forgiveness is enough for them, that they should rise and join the assembly of believers. After that, give praise to the Father that this is so."

-Morning Star Over America

Prologue
by
William L. Roth Jr.

    We possess the power to witness the origin of prehistoric events, to revive the corpses of the netherworld, hear the sunset echoing through the Andes, touch the heart of a miracle, and smell the aroma of the beginning of life as though humanity is a lone rose plucked from ancient ruins, roots and all, and placed on the Lord's high mantle. We awaken in the morning and discover that there is much more work to be done; disorder to expel, mouths to feed, wounds to dress, innocence to guard, lodes to share, and millions of undug graves; palls and anthems we may never need because Christ has discovered a cure for death. We must start digging anyway, breaking ground for His Kingdom, no longer appeasing our demands or pacifying longings that have nothing to do with the Cross. The universal question has always been about opening the human heart. Like a chick in an egg, can this be done without risking its life? Is it mature enough to free itself? Must it be seared by a firebrand of torment to prove that it belongs to God? Why do we weep and despair as though forsaken, broken, jaded, and alone? We have come to believe that Heaven is around us, though too high to reach, too far to travel, too remote to see, and oftentimes too good to be true. We need not make the case for suffering, for Jesus has already done it. We are asked to embrace it, prepare for its impact, include it in our plans, and board it like a steamer with tokens bought in advance. We must comply, defer, concede, and believe that all human endeavors are byproducts of our surrender to the providential excellence that deposited us here on Earth. We see our own worth in the elevation of the Cross because we are always living forward, always expecting more, growing older and wiser, obsessed with pruning and shearing, making something of nothing, charging the depths, surviving on unearned feasts, and crying in agony from our berth on an exiled sphere. We see the Victim by accepting our own victimhood, and we perpetuate the perfection of man by our willingness to die. Our esteem is situated in the sacrifice of the self; and this is why we yield. We look skyward like hungry foals, bedridden by lingering pain, knowing that it is in giving we receive, in humility we are dignified; we are raised by laying low; our souls are cleansed by suffering, and the matting is stripped from our eyes by our random impressions of love. The New Covenant teaches that exiled men can rise and force the dawn. We may not detain the sun any longer than it desires to shine, but we have the power to rush the ages by drawing from the Fount of Life. God ordains it, Jesus avows it, and the Archangels pray we will. Our healing begins once we recognize our helplessness, lay prostrate before the Altar, call for a deific blessing, empty ourselves to receive it, and never entertain a thought that we are unworthy of being absolved. This is when the heavens stir. Here is where God's voice resounds through the valleys below, attesting that He agrees, stooping to allay our fears, and anointing our hearts with the seeds of rebirth. We have no doubts when our spirits have arrived. We depart the shadows into the brilliance of sprawling fields. We invite every creature and stars yet unseen to celebrate our new raiments. Our confidence is hewn in stone, never again diluted or impugned, always and everywhere our strength in time of need.

We dare not deem equality with compassion so fine as that belonging to Christ or feign affection to claim it, but it is nonetheless our franchise through His awesome Sacrifice. We cannot stumble upon redemption because it usually finds us first. We mouth its praises for decades; even lifetimes are too brief; and we concede that nothing we can accomplish predates it through our hapless motivations, bereft of foresight and long too slumbered by our spiritual tepidness. For once in time, we can believe in repentance for reasons other than fear. We have new pledges to make, armaments to dispense by our suffering, heartstrings to pluck in arpeggios, and hopes to deliver like newborns. What would the Son of Man have us do?—we who are saddled by Adam's descent, reared in a failed secular world, craving to be claimed but liberated too, tied fast to societies that are devouring themselves, deceived by the conclusions of time, and who inherited the wreckage that demons have foisted on the unsuspecting children of God. Faith means knowing that enough is enough. We come of age by heralding that Christ has freed us from sin, from corruption, stain and infamy not of God's doing, but from the smokey infernos that have polluted our thoughts from knowing that not everything is precisely as it seems. We gain new birth by eclipsing the old, staring death's unstoppable dynamic directly in the face, and tanning the leathers by which we are whipped into creatures destined for martyrdom. Our spirits can tell before our minds are apprised that holiness is more than a state; it has eternity written all over it, and an order of sacred love. Once we submit to its clasp; when we suddenly realize that it reciprocally feeds on us, we are set free into cosmic wonders with tatters shed and ignorance denied. We fall to our knees slain in the Spirit, famished for all good things, with nothing else suitable for our palate. We ask in prayer, 'Lord, remake us in every way we are broken, in every apex and architecture, to untold degrees of divinity, smashing old patterns and molds, sifting and reaping, cleansing and burnishing, stripping us bare and refitting us with the counsel of the years.' And, believe it or not, Heaven will swoop down like an eagle and snatch us clean, ribs and all, hearts and minds, frost and fire, hairline and ankles, and inklings and afterthoughts. The Cross will have us swaying to tunes that have yet to be written, and we will know the right cadence despite our ill-footed posture because it is Christ dancing in us, celebrating the aeration of the heart. We will eventually discover that we made too many assumptions about the end of the world. We shall know that Salvation is befitting for us and certainly worth dying for, that the Lord's biblical yoke was like a locket around our necks bearing an image of Heaven so profound that Jesus was unable to put it into words. This is why we believe that the Eucharistic miracle is true; that Perfect Flesh is laid on our tongue from God's altar in Heaven, that we can raise our arms and wrap our palms around a chalice containing 2000 year old Blood that never congealed, never stopped forgiving, never ceased flowing from the Body of Jesus Christ. And, nothing can dam the Absolution that inundates us at that moment, for if we open our eyes, we can see distinctly the crimson fathoms that have drowned our mortality and brought us back to life.

Therefore, to ease the raspy bite of mankind's discourteous tongue and the Earth's cold-hearted winters, we find shelter in the edifice of our faith, where warehoused are our wit and wisdom in all things grand and minuscule, here and beyond, generous in thought and always about love, perpetually kind and never nondescript. When given the hour and opportunity anew, the Lord never ceases to intervene. Jesus rarely relents in piquing our hearts about the failings of the world, chiding our malfeasance, flooding our voids of conscience, and watching our spittle drool from our chins like toddlers teething on a rail. It would require epic repugnance, aggravation, insult, nails, and death to rescue us from the evil to which we are drawn in the likeness of our forbears, fallen away in sin. The Son of Man was stricken, lashed, and martyred because no one else would care. His Agony was real; His Passion was for sure, and His Crucifixion was to the depths. It is not as though Christ came driving by one day and saw a pathetic stranger named Old Adam who needed a lift from the grave. He did not enter the world to the acclamation of men like a splashed-down orbiter Apollo. And, He did not jut from under the ground like a sunflower sown by the wind. He was incarnated by God. He emerged as a bare-skinned baby boy from the Womb of the Lord's most preeminent Woman, the Blessed Virgin Mary, sacred and preserved, humble and wise, and precisely chosen to bear a child whose Crucifixion would renew the face of the Earth. Mary is as perfect as any creature can be, conceived without sin; chaste, illustrious, reverent, docile, and surrounded in holy arms. She is prepared to fight mankind's gigantomachia that has led to so many casualties whose epitaphs appear engraved in stones that would have been far better laid for a stairway to the stars. The tandem of Jesus Christ and Immaculate Mary is God's outright assault against humanity's hidden error. They have from the beginning come as Savior and Queen to reveal the purpose of life and death, to explain where we are going and where we have been, why we must seek the heavens and never look back, and to restore our sobriety from the drunkenness of our pride. Our Lady swaddled humanity's broken dreams in the starkness of the Nativity and the innocence of Her Son. She is the New World Genesis who supercedes every patriarch except the Father, and from whose Fiat has blossomed the excellence of the heart so forgiveness might prevail in places that have known no peace and little light, where angels have thus far shunned, and where the brazen dishonored among us have fled to avoid their fate. What reviving we have known! What glory we shall see! If we rise and elevate the

Cross, we will take a seat in the forever-redeeming grace of the Victim of the Mass, still lingering in our company; summoning, invoking, enchanting, enlightening, and absolving.

And, thus we transcend from the stratospheric vaults of the Holy Spirit to this wailing valley of tears wafting healing scents of Heaven to our brokenness and humbling contrast to our arrogance. The inspirations, dreams, hopes, yearnings, desires and longings of our Eternal King meld in the soul of suffering humanity. Collectively, they are the disinterring agent of His spacious itinerary that pleads from the "there" in the heavens to the "here" of our more definable and experiential moments.—Inspirations shimmering newly borne pathways raised to the magnificent equal of the cinematic visions that flicker life's eternal mystery before our sequestered interior gaze.—Dreams convoking the magnetism of magisterial divinity whose angelic dominions beckon rent hearts to fraternal participation in the breathtaking animation of amaranthine grace that sprung Creation from nothingness at the alpha-movement of God's magnificent Heart.—Hopes wailing like tear-drenched choruses of hungering babes, calling from their isolated detachment for the succoring fulfillment purveyed by the creative genius of our Maker.—Yearnings pining for each day's progress and the outcome of our existence to be as stellar in reality as the paradisial premonition welling the feelings within our souls.—Desires enticing collective humanity to fall into the rapturous torrent of beatific love flowing through the soulful colander of our interior essence, that panoramic vestibule of vision where Heaven reveals the supernatural ascension of mankind en masse toward the Kingdom of the Most Blessed Trinity.—And longings that drip like blood from assaulted wounds, aching without refrain or respite, crying that the historical breath of life would witness humanity's courageous reciprocation of this exilic opportunity to be healing Light by returning every heartfelt benefactor the complete magnitude of God refracting through the unique identity of each and every person. All we are and all we were created to be pulsates from these mystical regions within, that palatial arena of the heart where the macroscopic Kingdom of our evolving marrow flourishes with a vibrancy magnified by celestial choirs who bear Heaven to Earth behind the twinkling in every eye. Nothing has been molded into the physical through any origin save the interior of man, either from the divinity deprived essence of the darkened soul or from that royal palace where God and child became inseparably united at the baptismal ignition of divine life through the unimpedible compassion of the galactic Intendor. In honor of all that is good, we have hoped, and all became forthwith because the Creator of our advance-revelation of the unseen, He who instills and enhances the holy sentiments of His children, ordains the created world opportunistically and selfishly that we would never but commune amidst the Infinite Love of the Father, revealed to His people in time by the Crucifixion and Resurrection of His own beloved Son.

Prologue

The Holy Scriptures teach that God is aware of everything keeping humanity preoccupied, particularly practitioners and social workers who heal the sick and aid the poor. Jesus knows where we are located at all times because we do nothing that He cannot see. Heaven and Earth are sewn together by what we accomplish with the heart, stitched so seamlessly that it cannot be detected with the naked eye. Even as we internalize the ministrations of the Gospel, its effects are transferable to the associative world. A wheelwright concentrates on making spokes and tread metals, but the distances they travel, the roads taken, and the freight they will carry affect countless other people. Genuine faith transforms the energy of our convictions into sanctified acts of redemption linking us to Heaven in ways that often remain a mystery until we die. However, if we were capable of seeing them, how would they appear? Would they look like brush strokes and have color? Would they allow us to peek into the future or be polished enough to render a reflection of ourselves? We meditate upon these things to Heaven's delight because Jesus knows the power of the mind when nourished by an inspired heart. We can through our cognitive faculties construct and dismantle complex networks, initiate and dissolve intricate plans, avoid temptation, and foster good will. Every great work of art, literature, and music is routed from the heart to the mind's eye and fashioned into being. God gives us the capacity to replicate what we envision onto the printed page; great drawings and paintings of Nature and architecture, capturing a tiger's pounce, smoke rings billowing from a forest fire, lava spewing from a volcano, or spiders' silk blanketed across a hedgerow. The mind is a repository for what Jesus wants us to believe based upon the holiness of the heart to manifest the Church into the created world. Everything from the looks on our faces to the work of our hands is processed by our knowledge, perception, and judgement about our relationship with the rest of society. Having peace of mind means that we willfully accept the Truth as told by the Holy Spirit before the first Apostles, all the way down to our most recent Amen. We can calculate distances, wheedle our friends, anthologize our experiences, pore over our agonies, seize the moment, weigh our profits, and cut our losses based upon what we think about life. Unfortunately, however, the mind is also the gallery of lingering guilt. It is where the heart files its moral indictments against the conscience, where we replay our past mistakes, confront our eccentricities, and intellectualize spiritual suffering. We become placid or livid according to our analysis of prevailing conditions and circumstances, and we fight the angst and emotionalism derived from our encounters with the atmosphere in which we live. Some people abuse the intellect to manipulate others, concoct elaborate schemes, conjure ruses, and leverage material advantage. This is the reason we cannot always depend on our thoughts as the primary keyway to the Kingdom of God. Surely, if Jesus did not intend the heart to be the receptacle of our hopes and dreams, He would not have sent the Paraclete to take residence there. The heart is the focal point of every living thing, just like a hub in the wheelwright's shop. The heart allows us to purify our impressions, marvel at natural beauty, nurture our deepest secrets, assume the best, and theorize, reflect and ruminate about life. It is in the heart that we discover that if we see ignorance unaddressed, we should throw genius at it. The heart knows the origin of our frailties, while the mind can only categorize their symptoms. The heart is the driving force behind human love, and the mind archives its fruits. Our thoughts keep us entangled in barriers and constraints, but the heart breaks them all down. When human lives end, the heart goes on; and this is why battlefield warriors may fall, but their memories never fade. So we patiently await each day's revealing disclosure, shaking hands through the curtains of time with all those who have gone before, spectators and participants alike, eager for Creation to progress, to mold, to unearth and complete its purpose, praying greater things into being from Heaven's storehouse of merciful possibility; and notwithstanding and unfazed that most things in life are in the process of unfurling, loosened by passing time and faded memories, spurned by neglect and abuse, rescued from the pit and raised from the depths, used and discarded, judged and forgotten. Men know from within that the plush and luxurious go out of style; the innovative becomes obsolete, and the newly found whittled into extinction. But, we are also convinced beyond the battles of every war and the conquered rubble of every kingdom that this is not true with human love. Love cannot be unraveled, and is not subject to the contusions of the grinding years. Love in the way of God's Kingdom is perpetual; it precedes the Earth and will survive its last day. We cannot diminish love or confine it in space. All eternal power is a manifestation of love, all reason and purpose, everything beautiful and unique, and every element meant for inclusion in the afterlife. The love of the saving Messiah cannot be measured or divided, yet not a morsel is ever wasted. Applauding hands and pealing bells regale it, and eloquent prose and symphonic songs exalt it, but nothing except the Crucifixion of the Son of Mary has ever revealed so distinctly its beaming face. Through His amazing Sacrifice, the Lord God has blessed and saved us, lifted us up when we have fallen down, and redeemed our finest hopes for the flourishing finality of the meaning of human life contemplated by Saints and sinners alike since the first flash of the Holy Spirit illuminated a human soul.

And, this is what these eighteen years and a fortified allotment of faith have mystically divulged to America, and how twelve works from the Morning Star who has appeared over our nation's bountiful fields have effected the exhumation of forgotten grace from the pious depths of our fading dreams. An astral body of matriarchal divinity has impacted our lives from the veiled vaults of our awareness with the consent of the Father; consecrated and conceived two millennia ago to blast a crater of contemporary diamonds from our souls to bathe our way of life in deified refinement, to repair our falling-out with the heavens, to birth us again toward immortality, infinitely sparkling, eternal and more brilliant and powerful than any destructive retaliations that could be brandished by wayward man. The Mother of Jesus Christ miraculously, majestically, and marvelously has been called upon by Her Triumphant King to close-out the mortal ages and fulfill His unimpeachable Will to the highest degree of Her cooperative purpose in the redemption of man; to span the gap between what we see and what we are failing to bring into being, and lead us by our heartstrings from the desolate borderlands of our exile to the ecstatic epicenter of God's Kingdom which thrives beneath, above and beyond our mortal sight within the inspirited realms of every heart who has ever seen life. From that reverberating sphere of divine influence inside us all, Heaven's Queen is reaching out across our acrimony and uncertainty, and is touching our barren world at the foundation of our nobler thoughts. And, the impassioned legacy She inaugurates is that our dreams are now more powerful than our despair; our hopes tower once again above any of our mortal failings; our guilt is rescinded like being roused from a terminal nightmare, and the collective courage of the Christian faithful is jostled to reawakening like a warrior struck-down by evil, healed by a miracle, risen by an Archangel, and now advancing to reclaim God's righteous dominion by the power of everlasting life, incapable of dying again. So be warned you secular foes of Christianity, and rejoice my saintly friends, because none but the most perceptive among us realizes what Triune Majesty is about to break from the horizon of Heaven's halls! Evil would fare better staring down the most powerful locomotive whose whistle was blaring, pistons pumping, and wheels screeching on the rails than greeting this ushering of Redemptive Revelation with defiant fists raised. The powers of Heaven are about to be unleashed! No, not through failing politicians, pundits or pragmatists, but by the strength of the Holy Saints of Christendom; the Congregation of the Beatific and the Bold; the Communion of Giants and Legends; those who bear the Crucifixion of the Son of Man in their beings from exilic sabbaticals given to the tenets of the Holy Gospel as their sole reason for having ever lived! And, live they still do—a Church-Triumphant in immortal Truth!; impassioned, resilient, courageous, magnanimous and unrelenting in all the powerful righteousness of Paradise. They have claimed the providential crown of Eternal Dominion and secured the victory of the human race through a sacrificial composure in union with their Crucified King so profound that the angels have wept tears of diamonds so copiously that Heaven's crystal seas have been filled to their shoreline brims. Hundreds of millions of Saint Pauls live on high, arrayed in legions of returning purification, awaiting the thunderclap of God's justice and the command for their final resurrection into Creation like blazing space capsules of inevitability reentering mankind's turbulence upon piercing the yonder blue, falling like entire constellations detached from the heavens to fulfill their final purpose of transforming the Earth through the rewards they have secured by their allegiance to the Messianic Cross. Transfiguration will strike the Earth with apocalyptic detonation. Down will come the Holy Pontiffs in their successive splendors, and the battle-scarred Martyrs seeking their long-awaited justice. From the ruptured vaults will appear Peter and Paul, James and John, Philip, Thomas, Bartholomew, Matthew, Simon and Jude, flanked by Linus, Cletus, Clement, Sixtus, Cornelius, Cyprian, Lawrence, Chrysogonus, John and Paul, Cosmas and Damian and all the Saints, escorted by the seraphic Archangels and Dominions and Powers, borne by the holy women attending the Queenship of the Virgin who thrust them all to greatness through a submissive Fiat of Love that will never be matched. And, what will come from the lips of the enemies of the King of kings then? Terrified silence will grip their beings, blasphemy stricken from their field-dressed tongues like ripping the skin off gunned-down wild game; and then, beginning with a muffled murmur of courageous conversion in this sea of wretched humanity, a lamentation of repentance will grow from the depths of the ages into a deafening thunder rolling across the chasm of time that will sweep clean the mindless millennia of mortal men. A determined clapper of Hosannahs to God in the Highest will strike the crystal bell of Deliverance which will reverberate clarity from the Garden of Eden throughout the end of every universe that Eternity will ever conceive! Adam will witness his redemption and Eve will ask forgiveness for dethroning the dignity of man. Yea, the sunrise of legends will break Light upon this world with redeeming concussion, and we, the children of Mary, are its prophetic heralds who are ringing Christ's Mercy in warning of that swiftly approaching day! We are the children revered who have kindled the lanterns of our righteous guard from the steeples of every Catholic church, not one if by land or two if by sea, but millions by the heavens, a beacon of blinding suns that signals the clarion admonition to the Church Militant of God's High Kingdom to don the heavenly virtues and prepare for the final battle that will inter these ages of sinful mortality in the unknown tomb of the forever forgotten. Predawn, we live in the Great Advent of Jesus' Return, ominously warned of the impending Reckoning by messenger and minister alike, in union with evangelist and emeriti who plead and petition for an audience before our sensibilities so that our collective success in being human may be granted a beneficial occasion upon our depleted existence.

    Humanity is like a tiny child who is sitting upon his father's chest, giggling with the belief that he is somehow holding him down like a Lilliputian immobilizing a giant. For twenty centuries for sure, God has assumed this deferential posture with the same paternal love, leaving men of little faith unbeknownst to the subservience that the Most Blessed Trinity is showing to His creatures; and oh! what weight that lost humanity has brought to bear upon Him notwithstanding. What is the displacement in grieving tons upon the Father's chest of the flotilla of super-yachts that anchor for adoration at the festivals of celebrity; their decks laden with the dead souls of the affluent hideous, and opulent cabins adorned with the silk of kings, while the brothers of these salacious seafarers lie in destitution beneath the piers where these ships of fools are docked? How much lies in the balance of sorrow when righteous sanctity is thrown to careers of immoral fame for rotting treasure that will only be pilfered by familial buzzards and their lawyers at the final close of their possessors' eyes? What does Jesus' Sacred Heart sustain in herculean restraint having endured the plight and death of two millennia of millions of His people through diseases, terrors, famines, wars and revolutions simply because wealth was ill-gottenly gained and so predictably and savagely secured by egoistic reprobates who cared not one whit for the extended family of man? Rightly so do the Holy Scriptures state that one has no love who sees the same flesh as himself tormented and tyrannized, yet extends himself in nary a sacrifice to change the misfortunes enslaving his brothers. Look at the wealth and in whose selfish coffers it resides! These are the modern-day passers-by of humanity's Lazaruses who seek not the bosom of the Father, the spiritless progeny of the detestable damned who have driven the Earth repeatedly to the edge of the abyss in every time and through every era and age, screaming that humanity jump rather than build a bridge with their mortal riches that we might all pass unscathed. Their legacy and that of their forbears was to have been all but lost to damnation and forgotten for Eternity had not the *Morning Star Over America* appeared to offer these reckless ages of men the ultimatum which would startle them to heroic sacrifice and their own suffering that will make us one in this world and the next. The Queen of the Final Day has been called upon by God to announce that He is preparing to declare time expired; the season for the closing of the mortal ages has arrived; we have passed the mystical solstice of Redemption, and Light is on the return; and come that daybreak of fateful demarcation between the seen and unseen, the Almighty Father will take to His feet, invert His posture to the glee of the Saints and Angels, toppling humanity into submissive adulation, and altering the story of the ages with definitive confirmation in one blinding sunrise. His beneficent compassion will then strip success from the hoarding lot and deed the Earth to the meekest and most impoverished of men. One never revels in the vanquishing of any peoples, but we must rejoice in the conquering of all that maliciously labors the noble essence of humanity.

While grace from God often passes us beyond our tortured awareness like a rescue ship plunging into the watch of the night as we steam instead for material haven, it is truly a magnificent gift from our Almighty Creator that He processes His elegant Queen into the clearing of our faithful vision through message and shrine, apparition, hierarchy, Dogma and Tradition. The compendium works of the *Morning Star Over America*, beaming with power from the sacramental heart of the Roman Catholic Church, is the meadow where the Queen of Redemption is standing fully-revealed with open arms, within our sights, radiant in beauty, and welcoming to all Her children whom She wishes to gather with Her in the beatific Light that is shining from the

Throne of the Most Blessed Trinity in whose eminence She stands. Our Lady of the Reckoning is the last Heaven-sent lifeline for this mortal age before the holocausts of Divine Justice consume the Earth and purge evil in all its forms. Mankind has no future absent of wailing and pain if we do not now enlist our hearts in this most opportune of times, and believe without prideful demands of confirmation that impede us from rising with faith-filled courage to the occasion of this Maternal deliverance. We must allow ourselves to be catapulted from oblivion to Salvation at the foot of Jesus' Holy Cross which is implanted on the High Altars of the Roman Catholic Church. Our Lady speaks words that are more powerful than the greatest orators of any age because they perfectly emanate a solidarity with God in human flesh, without alteration or interpretation, with no dilution, obfuscation or mortal flaw, and nary a doubt of their authenticity in any syllable. The Mother of Jesus Christ is the "first person" witness to human Redemption required by our cantankerous age who asserts convincingly through skyborne wisdom that the Will of Her Son has reigned supreme from the beginning, and will so until the end over any philosophy or ideology that is concocted by sinful man. She cares not one tittle about the cerebral orientations and antics which self-declare as religions that worship their gods and claim their prophets and messengers. There is only one God who has appeared on Earth in human flesh; and His Name is Jesus Christ, Child of the Virgin, Victim, Messiah, Redeemer and King! The Savior of the world asks us, nay commands us, to surrender to the sound wisdom of His Heavenly Queen immediately if not sooner for three reasons. First, Her supernatural appearances and manifestations have been rendered so obvious to so many millions of people that they now bear a definitive responsibility upon contemporary humanity to respond so that God not inflict purification upon us through His just wrath in the marked absence of our humble obedience. Second, the Virgin Mary possesses the royal strength to crush evil with its most horrific head held high, a power that we require to turn mankind from the path of its now nearly inevitable fate of certain destruction. And lastly, for the very fact that Jesus' stupendous gift of allowing Her to manifest Herself to us at all demands our humble response, lest we convict ourselves on the final day as being nothing more than an arrogant lot of spoiled renegades who thumbed our noses at God's divine assistance in making something totally beautiful of the Earth at Her glorious behest. That is why it is essential that Roman Catholics, the body of faith who knows Our Lady best, rebuke in the full light of their evangelic commission those who are choking on the words, *"We don't need any miraculous appearances of the Virgin Mary."* Well technically, maybe not, if the camels that these religious dissidents are riding are the sizable dimensions of microscopic gnats which can easily pass through the holy cheesecloth of God's purifying grace. But, I humbly ask these people to consider becoming more merciful to themselves than to wander about like nomads in a motherless crucible of human life, slapping away God's generous blessings because they challenge them to be more noble and far more sacrificial than is currently palatable to their faithless pride. The vision they are disregarding in their parched stupor is not a deceptive mirage beckoning them to falsehood, but rather the true-to-life paradisial place of refreshment in the middle of this earthly desert. It is only from a monumental podium of ignorant braggadocio that one would declare that they can arrive at their final day sanctified in unequivocal spiritual perfection without uniting with the Immaculate Heart of the Blessed Virgin of Nazareth in adoration of Christ Crucified and Resurrected. It is an impossibility.

So, we are left to contemplate the miraculous gifts one would need to overcome the secular ego-stricken mentality of so many throughout our nation, and indeed, the rest of the world. The Holy Spirit implants in Christian believers innumerable questions of faith, chief among them is how to shock humanity back to life. What could be so daring, astounding, and declarative? What would startle the Earth enough to make its grounds tremble, its lakes exceed, timbers shiver, and skylines blur? It has to be something so imperative that it breaks the back of human arrogance like Angels crumbling soup crackers in their hands, an event so remotely anticipated that it grips the nations reminiscent of doomsday news. And yet, it must be desirable, demonstrative and veracious, a colossal moment that shatters world records, dissolves boundaries, upends generations, and makes the whole universe blink with jaw-dropping surprise. It requires an instant that is so unforeseen, unimaginable, stupefying, and detonating that it rattles the comatose from their sleep. Behold, we discover that it is but a word already spoken, one syllable that erased the corruption of humankind in favor of the holiness of God. The word was 'yes' from the lips of the Mother of Jesus Christ in answer to the Archangel Gabriel. Anything we might say cannot approach Her inviolate speech. She pronounced the redemption of man before the Crucifixion sentenced Satan to Hell. In all the terms and fiery speeches that humanity has ever delivered, we are unable to match that apocalypse. What a unique perspective! Our Lady is a make-or-break intercessor with a live and die proposition, and anyone who defies Her is damned. While we have been dabbling in atom bombs and bunker-busters, Heaven has been dousing hellfire in the Blood of a Crucified Man and removing boulders from the archways of tombs. This is why we must remain aligned with the Cross. God approached Mary to bear the burden of human Salvation in Her Womb, watching as the Holy Spirit told Jesus how to live and eventually when to die. The record still stands and the story is renowned. Everybody must believe it, even those who refuse to try. While Christ's disciples are down in the trenches making good of this life, nonbelievers, secularists, and feminists are standing along the sidelines without remorse, sipping their noonday teas, cracking wise about why their sense of logic does more good for humanity than the sacred residue of Our Lord's Agony in the Garden dripping from our brows. The Father sees us here unhanding our prejudices and unleashing our prayers, and the Blessed Mother looks upon our plight with sympathetic nods, knowing that human life in exile is a precious photograph that never grew old in the outdated frame of the world. She has prepared The Way for our resurgence into victory and placed obstacles in the path of our enemies like a minelayer sailing the seas. Surely we know by now that it has not been in vain. The Lord has already made the best of Her beauty and the finest of Her canticles. When Jesus' Mother places Her hands together in prayer, She squeezes evil out of our hearts and into the netherworld as if to say, 'Saint Michael the Archangel, do My Son's bidding while He doles-out His mercy to man.' It takes plenty of gall to dismiss what science cannot explain. This is the way God sees it. He almost dares us to ignore Him, calling on earthquakes, lightning strikes, floods, and constellations to make contact with our souls. And, once we realize that the Blessed Trinity has opened that door, we will fight with bare fists and elbows to keep those hopes alive.

Therefore, let us truly hope that God would hear us begging for miracles, signs, locutions, healings, and appearances of angels and the Virgin Mother herself until the pleading din is of such harmonious volume that the veil between Heaven and Earth would vaporize like a crystal glass shattering at the resonant note of a great operatic voice. Like it or not, it is as in the days of Noah with its scoffing multitudes and impending cataclysms, and Our Lady is determined that Her Son will find the Catholic Faith which He ignited in the world as inviolate as Her Immaculate Heart when He returns to the Earth in Glory. Hence, those without faith, or who otherwise reject it, should ask themselves; would they rather a messenger assuage their egos, or instead make sure their gentle hearts realize their opportunity to be aboard the only Ark which will soon pass them by? I tell you, each person with a dismissive disposition toward Our Lady is going to endure a grievous bath of scalding humiliation at the Triumph of the Queen of Heaven if they do not listen! The lights will come on in this pitch-black house of human drama and they will stand naked as the spiritual progeny of the unrepentant crucifiers of Christ before the scrutinizing gaze of the millions of Roman Catholics whose faith they mocked and scorned. These are not veiled threats, unkind assessments, or spiritual bullying for the sake of ideological conversion, so enough with the self-justifying retorts. My witness is an authentic admonition from the King of Heaven. It is loving, honest, unintimidated, piercing, and compassionate information like one would give to a teenager who drives at neck-breaking speed in the night while heading for a concrete wall he does not see. After all, what else would one have a messenger from God proclaim to those who are distracted by the world and refuse to listen while they wander toward a precipice in the darkness? The Woman Clothed with the Sun has been sent to command the attention of our contemporary era by any means at our disposal within the bounds of faith because the times could not be more grave.

Everyone must invoke their capacity to believe and then respond as if it is the last chance mankind will ever have; and when gentle persuasion is casually dismissed with obnoxious disregard as if it is mumbling from an insignificant bore, is not humanity requiring the heavens to deal more strictly with its arrogance and challenge its pride with the lancing righteousness, ominous warnings, and ultimately, divine punishment that is soon to be forthcoming? No respectable father would do anything less in defense of his children's future. There is a greater Love which impels us to cry-out the path to Glory and warn like watchmen in the night about obstacles that are lethal to our souls. Our Holy Mother has enlisted Her obedient children and the Rosary beads passing through our fingers to pry the collective foot of the dying world off the accelerator of secular humanism, moral relativism, sensual impropriety, insatiable materialism, and detestable disobedience. And, any description of the spiritual carnage inflicted by the utter selfishness ravaging the sacred beauty of the marriage bond is almost too grotesque to pass the lips of the human species. Should God be hearing us sneer, *"We do not need..."* while roaming a once-great vineyard that was left in our custodial care which has become an arid wasteland of decadence? Do we not reveal ourselves to be as stiff-necked as our Israelite forefathers who drifted the desert grumbling about their needs? Is it not the abominable cry of a pitiable narcissist who is arrogantly testifying to the heavens, *"I am perfect enough.?"* Jesus did say, "Be perfect, as your heavenly Father is perfect," or "Be perfected, as your heavenly Father is perfect." The second interpretation is generally used by those who either disavow, forget, or otherwise do not know the power of the Sacrament of Reconciliation. When we lack knowledge of the restorative nature of the Confessional, it is difficult to find logic in believing that Jesus was serious about spiritual perfection, let alone that we are obligated to elicit a healthy measure of faith to attain it. The lack of authentic catechesis has created an unfortunate opportunity for Satan to generate a perpetual excuse for us not to engage the sacrificial purgation of our sinful deficiencies. What fraudulent authority has convinced humanity that it is impossible to rise into perfection at this very moment, and therefore, to not even try? My friends, the perfection is Divine Love in the Most Blessed Sacrament of the Catholic Church. No matter the interpretation of Holy Scripture, our responsibility to ascend to the Altars into oneness of heart and being with the Most Blessed Trinity in the image of Christ Crucified is nonnegotiable; and it happens the instant the Sacred Host of the Great Sacrament touches our tongues. It is in this Holy Communion that we "become perfection" in the fullness of Heaven's beatitude, a blood red bath of divinity from the veins of the King of kings. Thereafter, we remain united with Beauty by living beautifully; we remain clothed in Courage by being courageous; we continue walking in the bathing light of Holiness by defending our restoration; and we remain impregnated with Virtue by being keenly virtuous. We must remember that being tempted is not a sin, nor does Satan's parade of thoughts through our minds soil us; rather these things should be expected as an opportunity to validate the impeccability we have received by dismissing them whether they go away or not. Attaining the perfection is the easiest part because it is God's work alone in response to our simple faith in the Holy Eucharist, His unequivocal gift through the Crucified Messiah. We are acceptable because our identity with sinful Adam is revoked, expunged, and replaced by the virgin beauty of the New Adam; this is the revelation that spontaneously generates the "Thank you" from the bottom of our beings to the top of our sky-sailing souls. When we obediently receive the Bread of Life, we are placed in Eden again where the Father hails us as His perfect children, never remembering our prodigal nature, because He sees us through the redeeming Sacrifice of His Beloved Son who has transfigured the definition of who we are by the power of His Divine Mercy and heroic Suffering. Our Lady says that when Jesus forgives our sins through the Holy Sacraments, He renders them as having never occurred. History is wiped clean, and Heaven has no memory of any infraction against divinity, no matter what any shortsighted pseudo-historians might have recorded. Is this not what made Saint Paul chide anyone who would dare hold anything against him when faced with Christ's Crucifixion? *"If God is for us, who can be against us?...Who will bring a charge against God's chosen ones? It is God who acquits us. Who will condemn? It is Christ Jesus who died, rather was raised, who also is at the right hand of God, who indeed intercedes for us."*—Romans 8:31-34. Think about this gift that the Catholic Church dispenses by the power and authority of God. While the Complete Forgiveness of Jesus Christ removes our culpability, His acceptance of our punishment in the horrors of the Cross and His descent into Hell unilaterally restores the perfection. Infinite restitution has rebalanced the scales of Divine Justice. Creation itself is purified and cleansed; and this is how miracles are granted. They are the restorative concussion of Jesus righting Creation through the power of His Crucifixion and Resurrection. And, our faith in the Most Blessed Sacrament manifests these occasions of grace to our contemporary place in time. The works of the *Morning Star Over America* are a miraculous transverberation of the Crucifixion through the Bread of Life offered in the Holy Sacrifice of the Mass which has pierced the veils of our age, lancing the conscience of humanity with both pain and ecstasy. Our part is to embrace and preserve God's unimaginable gift of perfection by emulating Divine Thanksgiving with heroic courage and enduring the sacrifice of mortality with dogged appreciation until we are called to our reward. Our Heavenly Father sees us as far more beautiful creatures than the opaque judgements of sinners would ever render because humanity has stature in the Immaculate Heart of Mary. Sins repented through the Confessional cannot be held against us because they do not exist, and anyone who attempts such judgement is nullifying the gift of the transfiguration of our souls through a lie against the reality of God's power. They are sinning against the Holy Spirit whom they do not even know. For the sake of true clarity, not a single facet of this beatific transformation occurs in anyone who refuses to partake of the Sacraments of the Catholic Church or those Communions united with the Church of Rome, because the faithful reception of the authentic Bread of Life is the consummating element of this sainted transfiguration; and that personal submission has yet to be tendered by those who reject the Original Apostolic Church. Anyone's claim to the contrary is like a woman declaring that she is with child without it ever being conceived in her womb. While the Absolution that Catholics receive is wholly unconditional, comprehensive and eternal, the forgiveness received by those who protest the Sacraments of the Mother Church of Christianity is conditional, measurable, and anticipatory of their full surrender to the Sacred Mysteries of the Church at their faithful conversion, or ultimately, their final judgement. Therefore, let us begin again on a higher plane of awareness and imitate our Father who is Love, fearlessly articulate the Revelation of His Messianic Son, accept the Dogmas of the Church, receive the Bread of Life, sacrificially bless His people, graciously receive His gifts, humbly accept His guidance, and be heroically faithful unto death. Be sure to entertain all of God's angels as your closest friends, even those who remain playfully unaware beyond your sight. The truth is, anything that is not a flourishing of spiritual perfection has its origin in the darkness of sin and is unworthy of our esteemed regard in our Father's eyes. Denying the restoration of our soul at the beatific denouement of the Holy Eucharist is part of Satan's darkness. Seamless identification with Jesus Christ throughout the entire spectrum of our humanity is our goal, a state of grace which we were created to embody from the moment we were conceived in our mothers' wombs. Does this not highlight what an abomination that abortion really is? Each person was conceived as a perfect receptacle of the divinity of God. If we confess our sins and allow the Son of Man to wipe them away, we will see our royal nature to our great joy. Our faithful allegiance to the Apostolic Church of Rome and its conservative scope of spiritual disciplines is the only way to sustain this restored identity because only there can we nourish and maintenance our perfect nature through the reception of the Bread of Life through the difficulties of time. So, are all Catholics the epitome of human perfection simply because they receive the Bread of Life? Spiritually—Yes! through the power of faith in Jesus Christ. But, the caveat is still in effect; all are subject to fail and fall repeatedly from this great state because it requires the cultivated strength, unyielding vision, and miraculous intercession of the greatest Saints to battle away the forces that rip and tear at the fabric of life, terrorizing, testing, and depleting the perfection we gain in our Holy Communion with God. Yet, on each Sunday, He looks at Creation with admiration and fatherly affection upon restoring to perfection once again His children who have faithfully ascended to the Catholic Altars to tell Him how they have spent the week working and playing in His vineyard. I tell you, the planet glows with a renewed divinity at the Consecration of the bread and wine during each Holy Mass. When we do this, break and eat, the Holy Spirit animates us, strengthens us, heightens our faith, and attunes us as willing beneficiaries of His extraordinary assistance through every sanctifying means of grace that His infinite wisdom can conceive, tailored to our unique being. We will recognize our oneness with Paradise in this Sacrament, but we must also realize that the mitigation of the suffering of our brothers and sisters comes by what happens afterward, and the conversion of the wicked will occur not at all if all we mechanically perform is our Sunday ecclesial duty and allow our testament to God's grace to fail at the vestibule door. Faith without the sacrificial works spawned by our sacramentally-initiated sanctification is dead; and evangelization becomes a rotted-out corpse. Verily I say, we must do more! If we, layman and Prelate alike, wish to change the Earth and restore the vineyard before the Master returns for an accounting of His fruits, we must purify our souls of anything of which our hearts would convict us and engage contrite rigors such as fasting, sacrificial engagement and almsgiving, and then conform our lives to Christ's divine image willingly and passionately. Our souls will then begin to float in courageous spirituality through sacramental grace accepted, and reparative self-denial employed, where we will become conformists to divinity upon the Cross by moving into solidarity with the revelatory agenda of evangelization being advanced by His Immaculate Mother through Her miraculous intercession. That is the other shoe that has dropped while so many are under the impression that it is a one-legged man. Our Lady's miraculous intercession is the centerpiece of the redemptive agenda of God to convert the hearts of humankind; we ignore it at mankind's peril.

    The purpose of our faith is ultimately about dignifying humanity here and for eternity, and of course all God's creatures, Nature, and the harmonic order of things. Every person, no matter their state in life, has inherent worth; and if we take time to learn what they endure and listen to their stories, we will discover a great deal more about ourselves. Even the unseasoned youth can teach their elders about remaining simple of heart, although there are those who believe that they should keep quiet and follow like robots the vaulting ambitions of the secular world. And, how many times have we heard that senior citizens have become too heavy a burden for society, that they should just fall off the tree and blow with the whirlwinds into history and the ages? An argument can be made that the fullest definition of a man is never really divulged until his most sacred dimensions have been revealed. We are all in the process of becoming someone greater. This speaks to the reason why we must express ourselves to others; because it is endemically perfecting to face our worst fears together, to recognize our faults, confront our weaknesses, and count our blessings as one holy ascription to the Supreme Deity. Sadly, there are people who swear that God's judgement was flawed when He fashioned us to be so interdependent. They complain about a lot of things they might have done better. After all, was it not the Creator who left too little room between the Pacific and Atlantic oceans that He crumpled the United States like tin foil to make it fit between them, forcing the upheaval of the Rocky Mountains and the sprawling Appalachians towering into the skies? And, when God painted the sea crests blue, did He not in a rare moment of spontaneity flick His brush and splatter the Great Lakes across the face of the western hemisphere? Let there be no mistake. There will come a time when we know that the Father did everything right. All good moments will converge in a sudden blast of welcome awareness, and we will see human exile for what it really is. Once our holiness matches our potential, the physical Earth will be transformed as well. Instead of storm fronts flooding the valleys, sun rays will fan-out above yonder meadows. Streams will run like quicksilver, and our votive candles will burst into crystal chandeliers. Women will be more concerned about preserving the lives of their unborn children than their constitutional right to abort them. Men will go fishing to catch fish instead of escaping the pressures of life. Employees will write their own paychecks; aristocrats will carry their water; subordination will no longer be in vogue, and the fight for public decency will cease being a two-fisted street brawl against the devil. Finally, the eximious life of Christians will make more news headlines than the cost of yesterday's oil. Let there be no mistake, the secular American media in their collective contemporary institution, yet differing forms, are the most influential, single-minded syndicate of counter-moral societal manipulation that has ever appeared in the history of man. Multitudes who lead it and compose it are walking in the darkness of the netherworld, under the influence of a Godless vision for our future. Despite any rebuttals declared from their sullying pulpits, the evidence recorded in their own media archives definitively convicts them; and the morally-sober part of America knows it, yet can do little against such a dominating conglomerate of character assassins save to continue the arduous slog to the pinnacle of Mount Calvary to be crucified in daily increments of blasphemy alongside our King. Every time the cameras roll, a minuscule retinue of morally-corrupt producers and heretical influence peddlers with the approbation of their owners attempt to lure 300 million Americans off the sacred plateau of two millennia of reasoned truth for the sake of personal profit and as a deliberate attack on the sacred bonds that God wishes we would consummate with His divinity. One fact only is sufficient to prove this indicting testament. The American secular media have approved and defended the killing of 50 million of our countrymen in the wombs of their mothers without raising a single headline in order to stop this diabolical rampage of infanticide; and there is no indication that they have any intention of rethinking their position of defending the deaths of these infant children. We need no longer ask how lost someone can be. Many will wish to accuse me of being unbalanced and grossly unfair by making a wholesale characterization of this unholy media alliance without justly recognizing the more benevolent and courageous contributions from their ranks. My response is that you cannot stand on one end of a beautiful lake and hail executives for their cosmetic development of its beaches, while their corporations spew millions of metric tons of rancid sewage every day into its clear waters from the opposite shore. What finally laps upon our feet as we recline beside that decorative shoreline? God will not heap accolades upon such calculated duplicity. We are either with Him or against Him. Goodness, righteousness, and truth must be dispensed from both hands of our integrity. Most Reverend Charles J. Chaput, Roman Catholic Archbishop of Denver, offered us insightful wisdom through his nuanced leadership when he wrote in his essay "Catholics and the Fourth Estate."

"The news media, despite their claims of impartiality, and despite the good work they often do accomplish, are just as prone to prejudice, ignorance, bad craftsmanship and tribalism as any other profession. But unlike other professions, the press has constitutional protections. It also has real power in shaping how we think, what we think about and what we like, dislike and ignore.

...When the press portrays itself as the "tribune of the people," ensuring the honesty of the other major institutions in our society through relentless critical scrutiny – then we need to ask the question, who scrutinizes the press? Who keeps our news media honest? Who holds them accountable for humiliating one political candidate while fawning over another? Nobody elected...the NBC news anchor. And readers can't impeach the editor of The New York Times...

(But) we can decline to be sandbagged by our news establishment into thinking that marriage for homosexual partners is inevitable or an obligation of social justice; or that Islam and Christianity lead to pretty much the same conclusions about freedom, society and the nature of the human person; or that the abortion issue is somehow "settled" when thousands of unborn children continue to be legally killed everyday.

Scripture tells us that the Christian citizen must "render unto Caesar the things that are Caesar's, and to God, the things that are God's." The press can't help us with that task, because it doesn't know, and often doesn't want to know, the difference. What we owe Caesar above all is honest, vigorous, public moral witness on abortion and every other vital social issue, whether Caesar likes it or not. Our moral witness needs to be formed not by the nightly news, but by learning and living an authentic Catholic faith. And when it is, we'll be the kind of citizens who can appreciate the genuine service our news media provide to society. We'll also be the kind of citizens who demand that our news media act with the sobriety, integrity, fairness and honesty their vocation requires."

We should hail and heed the wisdom of this courageous Shepherd of the Church. And, to augment his words with the mystical power of Heaven, Our Lady proves to be far more direct and explicit about their future if they refuse to reassess not only the contribution they are failing to make toward the building-up of Jesus' Kingdom on Earth, but also the daily advancement of the corrosive evil and immoral disarray that they are fomenting by their favorable agenda to wickedness and their relentless displays of personal hatred toward Christianity. The Mother of God has told me on multiple occasions, *"One of Jesus' first bold acts of justice will be to reduce the media's fallacious empire into a smoldering pile of rubble and ruins in a heap atop the ground."* Verily I say, all of us must invoke our righteous angels and allow them to conquer our lesser nature with its selfishness and penchant for willful indiscretion, or God will eradicate the impediments to His Kingdom by the fury of His own Divine Hand. He will allow us to fall into the abyss of our own making. Furthermore, we must refrain from showering illegitimate esteem on the granite visage of stoic composure as if it is some masterful commanding emanation of the Holy Spirit which deserves to be idolized and revered, for behind it cowardice and ineptitude hide, stealing deference from more noble voices who display the spiritual courage to engage these harrowing times that are withering the spirit of these worldly and faint of heart poseurs. The holier we become, the more we realize that true Christians have been fertilizing the Earth with the Lord's redemptive discipline for centuries, giving hope and foresight to the materially blind, poking holes in pragmatic theories and mechanical realism, and reframing human existence in the context of viewing the eternal side of life through God's reflective lens. Righteousness allows us to retrace the steps of our ancestors to the beginning of time with the benefit of knowing the facts, unearthing the secrets and dictating the criteria by which the accomplishments of men will ultimately be weighed and judged. In effect, Jesus hands us the Bible and vests us like jurists in our own baptismal gowns, sending us into the world to make straight the crooked, clear the path for justice, and set the captives free. Whenever we strive toward the goal of finding more fishers of men, God provides the incentive and the Holy Spirit their inducement to follow us without asking questions, not like sheep to slaughter, but as companions and counterparts in building the Kingdom that first stocked the seas, laid the foundation of the Church, freed our souls from corruption, and ignited the fires that keep our hearts warm through the cold, dark nights of rejection. Who are we to say that Jesus cannot take any action He pleases to reach his flock—in the wails of the dying, a mourning child, a martyred warrior, a blazing summer sunset, or the Sacraments of the Church? How could any man presume to know where God might send His Mother to expect our attention? She sows holiness wherever She goes, speaks strains of prudence, leads us by the hand to the Rite of Reconciliation, and prays away our sorrows with the gentleness of a dove. Our Lady witnessed the Crucifixion firsthand and knows what brings Her Son to heap copious amounts of acquittal upon anyone who loves Him. Christians must decide as Pentecostal colleagues what will bring conversion to those who are farthest from the Cross. What can we deduce, develop, and implement to excavate their hearts? Of all the volumes that humanity has ever spoken, there is one concept that captures the relationship between God and the exiled world; and it is obedience. If we do everything we are asked by Christ, there is nothing the Father will not do to help. But, no one has ever said that this is an easy task. Obedience to Jesus means believing that miracles are wrought by suffering; peace comes through forgiveness, innocence by prayer, goodness from piety, dignity by sacrifice, and healing by confessing our sins. It means being patient enough to know that nothing can destroy our hope in the heated battles ahead, and nothing short of Salvation can provide eternal rest. We must take a stand with the Church as the Saints would have us preach, realizing that we will be ridiculed by the unbelieving world. Then, we will begin to see that mainstream social thought is based more on secular fanaticism than centuries-old religious truth. And, it will become clear how patriotism and popular culture whip nonbelievers into maniacal frenzies about sexual liberation, idolatry, and material artifacts.

Assisted sanctification is the theme throughout Our Lady's intercession because the message of loving sacrifice, self-denial, penance and the requirements of holy virtue is evidently lost to a vast majority of the world's inhabitants. Ultimately, She is helping us believe in the invincible power of the Sacraments once again. No one is exempt, and no one should wish to be. If one has not periodically engaged the character assessment of their spiritual purification and risen in the strength and valor of the Holy Spirit, what message could possibly be evangelized? And, if one has never accepted the commission to evangelize, nor prepared for it, what souls will accept Salvation as the fruit of their nonexistent sacrifices? And, if there is no fruit borne from the gift of faith that God bestows upon a person, are we not logically the individual depicted in Sacred Scripture who buried the money he was given who ultimately return it with nary a penny of interest added to the sum because he was squeamish about the sacrificial demands of his benefactor? There is no virtue in loving only those who love us; sinners do as much. Loving only our families is not nearly enough; the worst of the worst do as much. Likewise, there is no moral courage in omitting the Spiritual Works of Mercy. And, since these responsibilities have proven to be such difficult tasks for contemporary humanity to accomplish, no one should wish to be presented with the sanctifying opportunity of Our Lady's immaculate grace, then reject it, and subsequently arrive at their judgment lacking the spiritual impeccability and the fruitful gifts that Jesus desired they present to Him. I can tell you personally that I did not have a chance of appearing before the Throne of God in anything other than rags and bearing any empty basket before our Blessed Mother took me by the hand and dared to confront my clandestine pride and spiritual lackadaisicalness. I have no dispensation for arriving that way, and neither does any other human being because Our Lady's miraculous intercession is burning away all of our petulant excuses. I was lost and poverty-stricken before I was found and clothed as a prince, too distracted by what the culture deemed worthy of attention, while omitting the very substance of life's meaning with too few heroic examples of faithful abandonment who would ever challenge me to sustain the perfection of my soul. The Blessed Virgin's divine assistance is all about us and how we will envision ourselves before the *ne plus ultra* of the Lord of Creation, dressed as spiritual kings or haughty vagrants, as citizens of His Kingdom who entered the narrow gate or cynical marauders who stole into the feast over a wayward fence. What justification can be offered for one's denial of supreme holiness at the moment of judgement after repeatedly spurning divine assistance from the Queen of Heaven herself? Our Lady's miraculous intercession, whether recognized or not, thrusts a gargantuan obligation upon us to allow our lives to be elevated to the pinnacle of sanctity before we see God face-to-face. Those who do not respond to this heavenly summons will ultimately hold themselves accountable to the degree of their omission. It is inevitable, no matter who declares what we do, or do not, have to believe. Each person in their soul will know. Without Our Lord even speaking a word and with the Queen of Creation standing at His side arrayed in unspeakable beauty, the human conscience will testify against its mortal legacy at the Judgement Seat, *"Why did I not accept the Virgin Mother's miraculous assistance in order to be more presentable at this grand Feast Table of redeemed humanity? God sent Her to don me in robes of royalty, and everyone knows that I said no, not once, but over and again, and still, they all love me nonetheless."* The blessed clothes in which Our Lady asks us to be attired are baptismal gowns accented and kept spotless through a humble heart that is obedient to Her words, and tendered to the spiritual inspiration and guidance that is flourishing from the works of the Holy Spirit which are originating and emanating from the heart of the Original Apostolic Church, that body of divine grace which includes Her miraculous charisms and devotional shrines within its supernatural parameters. Mary says be converted, be united and be love, which means accept a reorientation of our beliefs to reflect the Truth in the Dogmas of Roman Catholic Christianity, play our assigned part in creating worldwide solidarity at its Altar of Sacrifice partaking in the authentic Bread of Life, and share with the world the perfect Love we find there until suffering is no more. That is the beatific synopsis for human deliverance that Heaven is placing before mankind because there is no other philosophy, ideology, or doctrine that offers such beatific promise, convalescing vision, or the strength to accomplish the transformation of the Earth.

   I wish to reaffirm that I have never claimed sainthood or anything else outside the bonded promises of Jesus' Crucifixion, because without Him, I know that I would be nothing but a scandalous sinner lost in my own material and sensual ingratiation. I am fully cognizant of the depleting realms of our mortal station and know that any capacities of holiness I possess would cease to exist absent His Light—but His Death and Resurrection support me and the Pentecostal Paraclete urges me on, so proclaim the Truth I must! So accurate is the truism, the spirit is willing but the flesh is weak. We rise in strength because the heart is spirit. It dictates as the nonnegotiable authority to a flesh that would much rather scream like a coddled child to capitulate to every sensual delicacy passing in front of any of our five senses. But, consider the two thousand year old legacy of Jesus Christ; look at all of history, not just the abridged sound bites of banterers and bigots masquerading as contemporary historians who learned their satanic drivel from self-certified Catholic-haters. What has been uplifting and enlightening humanity with beatitude throughout the expanse of two millennia, and into a third, notwithstanding the mountain of millstones that evildoers have been draping around the necks of humanity in every generation? How is it possible to ignore the work of the Holy Spirit in all of this? How could hatred have grown so pronounced to have obscured such colossal goodness from mankind's deferential loyalties? What diabolical obstinance precludes humanity from seeing how Jesus has preserved for us unequivocal confirmation of the faith of the original Apostles by laying it in the custodial stead of the Roman Catholic Church? In the course of the ages, and the rising and falling of kingdoms and nations, and states and governments, through destruction and wars, and cosmic and natural disasters, what entity still exists in its original hierarchical form from the first century? Take a moment to name those institutions or organizations of convicted men that have not been toppled by the fall of empires or the cataclysms of Nature, or pillaged to nonexistence by looting hordes. None can be named, save the Roman Catholic Church, because it is a spiritual kingdom that cannot be touched by human hands, which has been brought into the current age by successive generations of courageous priests who answered the call of the King of Heaven. All other establishments have been of temporal character, created by men and felled by the sins inherent in their nature, a pathway that the democratic essence of the United States is presently doomed to tread. The Catholic Church is the only body of organized humanity that has not fallen to the tides of time because of the wrongdoings of its faithful adherents or the diabolical hatred of its enemies. Why? Because God forgives, restores, and convalesces through the immutable continuity of its sacramental essence and the sacrificial nature of His faith-filled people. The simple historicity of Roman Catholicism is the glaring confirmation that the earliest disciples were not able to rest their faith upon because the eyes of their experiences did not yet apprehend the Kingdom of God spreading out with such formidable magnitude across the Earth through time. Think of the amazing mettle of the Apostles' faith before witnessing the definitive Triumph of the Resurrection, and afterward how they maneuvered in their beliefs with such courage while facing murderous evil without a billion fellow-believers supporting them, and how they were placing themselves at odds with religious authorities by accepting the divinized teachings of One who came from nowhere whom they somehow knew presciently to be the expected Messiah. Contemplate what they were asked to believe and the stupendous dimensions that rattled their contemporary understandings. They were no more human than ourselves, and thought in ways so reminiscent of the typical thinking of sinners, so much like us in every way. Does it not seem that we now have the easier part?

Notwithstanding that it is impossible that a civilization such as ours could even exist had our Savior not yet been born, what if He had postponed His swaddling appearance until our day? Imagine an obscure story buried amongst capitalism's advertisements on page 25A of our newspaper of an outrageous claim of a virgin birth during a truce in war-torn Bethlehem, accompanied several days later by pontifications from our contemporary reproductive scientists that the whole story was an anecdotal fantasy. And, there is a report thirty years later of a healing or two in that day's edition, a couple column inches of a supposed resurrection of a dead man, a wire story about a large gathering of purported religious zealots professing allegiance to a so-called wonder worker, then an almost irrelevant reference a couple years hence to an altercation with local authorities who found the rogue leader guilty of capital crimes and executed him for violations against the state. This is followed by an equally obscure story that the religious zealots were claiming the wonder worker had come back to life, and sectarian authorities offering the more acceptable explanation that the body had merely been stolen. The news of the next day continues as before with stock market indices and blathering about whether our politicians are more corrupt than the journalists who say they are. The strike of humanity's Eternal Redemption happened two millennia ago as simply as this, and it would have been the same had it been today. We need only look at Our Lady's miraculous intercession to see the proof. God is allowing the Queen of Heaven to engage this world miraculously and powerfully, asking for the same faith of the first Apostles; yet obscure newspaper reports, mostly ignored, come out of Medjugorje, Yugoslavia in the early 1980s of the Virgin Mary's appearances to six children, accompanied by astounding claims of healings and supernatural manifestations that are dismissed as irrelevant to the higher meanderings of men. Purportedly overzealous pilgrims flock to the site in faith by the millions, hoping to experience the mystical phenomenon of Jesus touching the world in a special way, and they do! Innumerable authorities, both secular and religious, sanctimoniously dismiss the events as being in the realms of either serious caution or delusion and hysteria, each worried only with protecting their faithless reputations and their personal domains. The secular news articles that do appear are swamped with the doubting drivel of naysayers, worldlings and gnat-strainers because journalists are too pragmatic and spiritually enslaved by their corporate lords to believe religious things might actually apply to them or have any bearing on their secular itinerary for the world. Returning pilgrims, filled with renewed faith, are at odds with their contemporaries and are accused of falling hook, line and sinker into mass delirium and psychotic religious zealotry while innumerable religious leaders stand like Saul over a pile of cloaks. And, peace is finally restored by marginalizing the mystical and by passive-aggressive noncompliance with anything remotely connected to miraculous charisms or requests from apparitions until we personally see an earth-stopping miracle which would decimate our capacity to display the worthy faith that God was seeking from the beginning. This is how our Almighty Father is treated by sinners when He mercifully reveals His power on the Earth, both two millennia ago and also today. But, what made Peter say, "Thou art the Christ, the Son of the Living God!" while we cannot summon the courage to see Our Lady's miraculous blessings for what they are and proclaim to the world that we are being delivered from ourselves by God's unilateral action which is inscribing our time with the Light of converting power? It was the faith of the Rock of Saint Peter that saw God's action, the same faith that still lives as the beating heart of the Catholic Church, and the same cadence of Light and Truth that is being brought to life by Our Lady's miraculous charisms. They are a unified action of sanctification brought through time by the Father, Son, and Holy Spirit! The original Apostles and disciples were flying in a beautiful infant faith beside one whom they saw as a miracle worker who yet loved them as brothers. They had nothing but a sense from the ancient Prophets and the magnetic Love of God to convince their hearts that Jesus was the prophesied Messiah. Can we imagine their vulnerability and trepidation; yet how they ultimately threw caution to the wind through a courageous spirituality that is still our example into a third millennium hence. And, in this lion cub-hearted stature, Jesus reminded them that their flesh was weak while Peter naively chimed in that he was willing to go to his death beside Him. And, we now see in hindsight that Christ's first Vicar did just that; and with greater clarity bestowed through our awareness of the millennial rewards of the Gospel and the sacrificial history of the Catholic Church, we also recognize that if we but tender our penitential fealty to the redeeming power of Christ in the workings of the Holy Spirit, He will lead us through our sorrows, and even our deaths, to the infinite joy and happiness that exists upon our conquering of the deep antagonisms of this world. Therefore, we must answer the call of holiness as a collective people upon the Earth! Now, how much stronger, and of how much more courage should we be? How many fewer excuses do we have after two thousand years of the magnificent lives of Apostles, Saints, Popes, and Martyrs? Therefore, since we are not convinced that we are strong enough, or courageous enough, and have yet to exhaust our truckloads of excuses, the Almighty Father has been moved in His Triune Heart to assist us in these dire times with miraculous grace offered by the most beautiful and delicate creature ever to have appeared in Creation, in effect showing us point-blank the power we have always possessed through the Seven Sacraments of the Catholic Church. His sacramental graces have lain dormant in our faithless hands too long! By His unilateral Power and complete Authority, He is transcending the irrelevant agendas, scandalous doubters, the Judases and the heretics, the Sauls and the slanderers, and elevating His Truth before the eyes of men like a billboard flashing repeated nuclear detonations more brilliant than the sun, launching wisdom and conviction like salvos from a howitzer, ripping the shades off every lamp so we would declare even from the scaffold in the midst of fire, with voices thundering from the lapping flames: *Come to attention, humanity! The Queen of Paradise has deigned to appear before you at the command of God! The Almighty is calling you, each and all, to look into the skies of your heart and see Light once again! Repent and be saved for the world is coming to a close!* Our Catholic ancestors did not bequeath the Church a whiny, weak-spined message about how careful we ought to be in propagating the Gospel. They slashed, brainstormed, and barnburned their way to martyrdom because they realized that lukewarmness does not work. They detonated an explosive evangelism of the New Covenant whose repercussions are felt in our time, shuddering consciences, bowling-over bullies, and thundering through metropolises with the exclamatory words of God. They issued an ultimatum against the enemies of the Cross that they handed us to serve; and in the process, we are to include a few annotations of our own. The Saints want us to prosper their mission of clod-busting, cog-stripping, heathen-slaying apologetics for the Roman Catholic Church. And, we should never be dispirited by the baneful calamities of heretics who think they can outwit the Wisdom of the Lord. The Saints never winced, blinked, flinched, or cowered from their offices as disciples of Christ. They turned back bushwhackers and bottom feeders, fell into snake pits and hunters' traps, and fought against knives, shanks, wrecking balls, and even hemlock-laced earthenware. When fiendish dogs preyed on them the most, they never lost their nerve; they never took their eyes off the eternal side of life before boarding their final passage through the years. They proved that there are causes worth dying for that are much holier than any civil war, that confronting secular hedonism is about more than battle cries, swords and sepulchers, and that fighting for the Church has lasting consequences and eternal dynamics that cannot be seen with simple scopes and glances. They set out to give the world a brighter foundation, to make it a jewel in the skies, a place of new dawns in an otherwise lifeless night, so still that one could hear the planets breathe. Their dramatic witness of the Holy Gospel and heroic acts of self-immolation stood in stark contrast to the 'awe-shucks' concession of modern evangelists who call for calm in the face of evil so egregious that it has stained the world from the inside out, like stale blood seeping or puss oozing. They despised the damnation of souls and defied everything that got in their way to stop it. They inched toward victory against miles of pagan opposition, and they emerged triumphant in the Immaculate Heart of Mary. Nothing conceived, plotted, or devised could have dampened their resolve. They sang to the universe the joy of the Resurrection and serenaded Jesus Crucified on the Altar. Their prayers were sacred and catastrophic against the nonbelievers of the world; and they were venerable on sight, coolheaded, goal-oriented, and stouthearted in human love. We must imitate the Saints. We may be only in our infant hours, but our petitions and sacrifices will grow us up; they are the first chugs of the engine of righteousness tracking our progress to the Promised Land. The Saints rest easy now, knowing that they showed the world what grace, peace, and mercy look like when given human form.

We must confront that seemingly-undefinable "something" which is trying to convince us that religion is but a one-dimensional illusion forced upon humanity by our desperation of not being able to see the origin of life, and our time on Earth is little more than a haphazardly concocted maze of deception, temptation, contradiction, tragedy, neglect, frayed ends, misunderstanding, and errant calculations. And, after our years burn out, most of us remain face-down in the soot of anonymity, while others are quite content accepting posthumous praises, mortarboards, medallions, and applause for lives well-lived. People who view spirituality this way could not be more uninformed. Our Roman Catholic faith is the keystone in the archway of immortality; that is for sure, but it also serves a more prefatory role. If it is true that life is more about creating opportunity than treading the depths of irrelevance, then we must believe that we can become interconnected with the framework of divine omnipotence that lessens our dependence on rationality and heightens our awareness for becoming greater creatures than our mortality might suggest. The French speak about the joy of living, the joie de vivre, in terms of counteracting the erosion of the self through the efflux of time with new potentials, like eggs in an eagle's nest. We are born with the scent of Creation poised at the end of our nose, and our belief in God provides the instinct and intuition to follow that sacred aroma, that undeniable desire, to discover its source and purpose. Those who reject Christianity and that God conceived the world out of nothing are dumfounded to explain its creation, particularly since they view humanity as too much a random species among other organisms they cannot even see. For whatever motivation, they cannot bring themselves to concede that everything about the universe, all the worlds, black holes and light years, have nothing to do with the reason they were born. Never mind aging and disease; it is their curiosity that is killing them. Who cares how many suns are positioned in macrospace? All we need is one. One single light. If human exile could be perceived as a room in a larger structure, we will never leave it alive. And, we have no mandate to examine uninhabitable places any more than we owe a debt to the netherworld. We are charged with identifying with the Holy Spirit that goes anywhere the Lord desires. Orbs suspended in space cannot reveal the truth because they lack His regenerative energy. This brings us back to that one light. It is the Light of Jesus Christ drawing us closer to Heaven, the love of our redemption calling in advance of the grave. Accepting the Cross is how we pull ourselves up, calculate rightly, resist temptation, avoid calamity, and follow His Easter Mysteries to our own resurrection.

So, where do we go, and what path do we take? Where do we find our common destiny as a contentious species of humans; and how do we arrive at Heaven's door-stoop as the one family of man? My friends, we listen to the Love who speaks from the Immaculate Heart, Sacrificial Altar and Vicarial Chair, in order to unite us in the strength of God at one Table of Faith, by way of all that the Lamb of God did, to all He created, and for the ultimate end of our communal fraternity in everlasting life beyond all the ages. It is this solidarity of hearts, harmonized with each era of believers, that inspired Jesus to lay the foundations of His Sacramental Church in the souls of His apostolic witnesses with the Blood flowing from the Body of His Sacrificial Love. We must recognize that the hierarchical Apostolic Church of Roman Catholicism is the paradisial summit of the Holy Spirit's intentions imprinted indelibly upon the history of man. Within the bonds of Roman Catholicism, in allegiance to the one Vicar of Christ, we find human integrity as one heart of mankind in communion with Paradise within a factual, concrete, organized entity that prospers universality, unity and disciplined solidarity, while providing for an arena of peace where the remedy for our primal need for procreative dignity will propagate through the forgiveness of our sins. Humanity-entire will experience the confirmation of its heavenly restoration the moment we unite and enter communion with God's sacramental affections through The Most Blessed Sacrament as one people, a supernatural benefaction manifested on Earth through the Passion and Death of a Perfect Man that was so hideous that our sinful nature, along with our endlessly compounded errors, were flushed in defeat from existence the moment His Sacrifice was consecrated. The Bread of Life from the Altars of the Roman Catholic Church is the essence, the central thesis, the catalyst, the unifying element, the object and fulfillment of the Holy Gospels which in and of themselves tell us how to perfect the story of humankind in the flesh. What honestly discerning person can actually believe instead that Jesus' Church has been historically willed by the Most Blessed Trinity to being no more than a nebulous hodgepodge of infinitely propagating Christian sects, each as authoritative as any other, yet conflicted and compromised amongst themselves? Who in their right mind would subscribe to the failing ethos that proffering disjointed and unsubstantiated biblical opinions about the Will of God, each in opposition and arrogance to all others, is the path God has wished humanity to take when the Original Apostolic Church of Christianity rests before them, Dogma and Tradition intact and universally rooted in the original Crucifixion by an unbroken succession of Pontiffs while standing in faith, unfazed by its own contemporary immolation, and with 2,000 years of theological, dogmatic, pastoral, intellectual, ministerial, miraculous, structured, authoritative, compassionate, heroic and supernatural testimony as confirmation of its superiority and supremacy in the evangelization of the Will of our Creator? And, with that historically ordained resume comes the authority, responsibility and power from Heaven to fulfill its commission of converting the world to the visionary Love of Jesus Christ! That is why the miraculous intercession of Jesus' Queen is occurring with such auspicious predominance in Catholic venues, leaving Protestant leaders wailing to their intrigued flocks that Her miraculous appearances are surreptitious manifestations of the devil. You see, it is their only defense against losing every person from their congregations, those whom they must keep terrified that they would be duped should they respond to the smallest miraculous gift from God that they see. They are imitating their ancestors who charged that Jesus' power was the work of Beelzebub. The outlaw rhetoric of these false leaders is the fleece that Satan has draped around their wolfish shoulders which will be stripped from them revealing their hollow frames at the Triumph of the Queen of Heaven. What says an elevating rapture of joy is not truly about to occur, but in an infinitely more spiritual and utterly more orthodox and hierarchical way than portrayed through the preaching of Protestant doctrinaires? Who would consider that God might have designs to test their convicted expectations through the Triumph of the Immaculate Heart of Mary? Are not these people who base their faith in a celestial-defined Rapture ironically in danger of refusing to be engulfed by God's redemptive ecstasy should His emissarial Queen be the object of that flush of heavenly beatitude? What choice will they make when the realization explodes upon them that they have been fighting against their own hopes the entire time in their disregard of the Virgin Mother's miraculous intercession? What are they going to do at the Immaculate Triumph that is ordained to align the world for the Second Coming of the Son of Man, the event that is to unite Roman Catholicism and Judaism with all people of good will throughout the planet? God Himself is mercifully and miraculously witnessing to the focused reality of His Catholic Kingdom on Earth before the trumpets sound. Our Lady is issuing a call for everyone to step forward with their heart tendered at the ready because the Woman Clothed with the Sun of the Eagle's Revelation who birthed the Savior into His manger in Bethlehem is pleased to help us all understand more deeply, and quite profoundly, so that we may begin a happiness that we have never known and will never find if we reject Her. The Holy Spirit has willed the Original Mother Church of Christianity to sail like an aircraft carrier before the eyes of every New Testament generation, a mighty ship which set sail from the prophetic witnesses of the Old after its champagne christening with the Blood of the Lamb. God has desired that man mark the centuries by the birth of the Messiah; He bid the seasons be differentiated by the liturgical calendars of the Church; He preserved the legacy of His Son on Earth from being diminished by the cyclical retelling from fading memories to proceeding ages; He guaranteed continuity by imbedding His Church in an unbroken succession of Pontificates, factually and mystically secured in the solid rock of His Public Revelation beyond the intellectual whims of the willful modernizers of every decade thereafter, so that His saving Flesh and Blood could be consumed as redeeming spiritual food by every age. The Holy Spirit has known the fickle nature of mortals from the beginning of our sins, and knew better than to leave the supernatural verity of the Holy Gospel to the haphazard interpretations of any age of men. That is why the Catholic leaders of this age have no power in and of themselves to alter their declaration of Truth to being anything other than the Traditions of the original Apostles and the Church Fathers and Saints who grew from their evangelization. They cannot be modernizers and compromisers because they are solidly anchored to the irreproachable verity of the ancients. This is the glaring contrast which is the Light shining in the face of so many who believe they can secure their own Bible and decide doctrinal and dogmatic expositions for themselves, mistakenly believing they can take comfort in dismissing the witness of twenty centuries of Truth that Catholic Saints have laid before them. The Magisterial Hierarchy has no authority but to be in allegiance with the courageous, apostolic witness of bygone Saints and Martyrs because none of these holy predecessors tender them any license to reconstruct or reinterpret their factual witness to Jesus' divinity in the flesh, just as no mortal has any authority to reconfigure the witness my brother and I have locked into the pages of the works of the *Morning Star Over America*. The Truth is indelibly secured in the ages with the blood of our brothers and sisters and the sacrifice of their hearts in allegiance to Christ. Their sacrificial witness inscribed upon the pages of Catholic history and the earthen soil sanctified by their blood is the voice of God instructing and guiding our contemporary interpretation of His Will for us. That is why the custodian of His Divine Truth upon the Earth is not a detached human conscience in competition with all others, but a single Vicar who is graced to harmonize our contemporary era with the living emanation of life from a mystical lineage of men and women, each in their own time who secured and propagated the Light of Jesus' most pristine reflection, offering everything they possessed to blossom a priesthood from their own progeny to succeeding generations, commissioned with the sacramental elements of grace that all may receive a truly Living Bread, foreshadowed by twelve baskets, broken and consumed originally at the First Supper of the Church which became our Savior's last, and thereafter confirmed as sacred by Jesus' Sacrifice on the Cross. Generations have said "yes" in faith to these Sacred Mysteries, and now have peace in knowing that we will remain one with our God perpetually from this world into the next through the faith which they heroically propagated into our age.

    Until our blessed passing into Glory, Our Lady wishes us to know that the human heart possesses within itself all the strength of the heavens and the essence of Paradise in its full clarity, but nonetheless labored, strained and eclipsed by the veil of our exile which separates us from God's heavenly reign to the extent of our unconfessed sins and the acceptance of the expungement of those we have confessed. Even though we exist within this penitential condition, the Mother of God encourages us all the same to live with such pure hearts that we would fail to recognize our passage from this life into the next upon our deaths. Yes, She asks us to rise with courage and conviction, and accept this pristine state of grace through the Seven Sacraments of the Catholic Church. I know this to be possible because I can see in every waking moment a vision of God's Kingdom seared within my heart, placed there by miraculous grace at the tendering of my faith and cultivated by eighteen years of encouragement by Heaven's Queen. Now, no one need believe that my brother and I are any different from themselves, or somehow superhuman in our characters by way of miraculous gift, or that they have been deprived by God of the opportunity to partake of what is truly beautiful beyond our sights, because Christian faith is the only element required by man to which the Holy Spirit faithfully responds by offering His Pentecost to those who lift the eyes of their heart to see where He reigns. The invocation of faith is a sacrificial act of submission to Divine Truth that is executed by a humble will, a miraculous enactment that every person has the power to convoke for themselves at any moment. The heavens convene within our beings at the words: "I believe!" God's sanctifying grace is poised within every soul, waiting anxiously, yet patiently, to provide sight to the heart so that it may engage its capacity for beatific refinement upon the sacramental path of perfection. This whole miracle of deliverance occurs despite the competition leveled by our sensible faculties which survey the mortal world, generating a demoralizing obscurity to diminish our awareness of our union with God. And, it thrives despite evildoers who hackle our fears and slander humanity's salvific possibility with an agenda intent upon disallowing our visionary hearts any authority to dictate the definitions of everything we experience through the Light of Divine Reason. Prayer of the Most Holy Rosary is our contemplative weapon against those who perpetrate such devolving darkness. One need only turn on a lamp, and behold!—there is Light! When we immerse ourselves in the contemplative mystery of the Rosary, it is not primarily for the purpose of eliminating the sensible world so that we can be detached from it as if it is of irrelevant nature. The function of prayer is for the purpose of clearly observing the Definition of Perfect Humanity at its zenith, who is Christ Crucified and Resurrected, so that we can recognize by contrast the reason for our iniquitous state of being, and humbly accept that our only option for new life is to surrender to and imitate someone who can recreate us in the image of that blissful perfection, thereby giving us hope that the world can be transfigured into something more than a desolate land of sorrows. And, when we realize that that "Someone" is still alive and see Him as He is, we will recognize His infinite Love for us in the first person; then a beatific union of transcending proportions is initiated with Him which is so tender and profound that He becomes our soul and grants us the power to dictate in succession the definition of every facet of our lives in His clarifying Light. Hence, we not only see Heaven within us, we live its nature within us and are granted the ability to witness and engage the world with a transformational wisdom regarding all things, and with that, actualize the grace to heel our contemporary era in the successive lineage of generations before the Cross. We share a viable cognition of both the original nature of Creation at its inception and in its completed essence within our Christ-infused soul. The evil we see is destroyed. The sadness we experience has been made joy. The loneliness no longer knows solitude. And, death has no ownership on the future of any person ever interred. Our hearts sustain the capacity to wipe away darkness with a mere thought, just as when Satan came to the Virgin Mary on the Hill of Mount Calvary and arrogantly declared to Her that he finally killed the One whom She most loved in the world. He chided Her that he had succeeded in depriving Her, of locking Her soul in permanent darkness with no relief throughout the slow ebbing of time. But, Mary brought Her Immaculate Heart to bear and turned to him in the Spirit of God and said, *No, you are deluded; and even though My Son lies lifeless in the grave, He will rise again!* And so, my brothers and sisters, here witness the power that destroyed the dark night of the soul, the transfiguration and redefinition of mortal realms with the convincing Light of Divinity streaking into Creation from the crucified human heart! What evil has diminished, devalued and destroyed with hellish malice in the dark night of man's most vile personal agonies is reclaimed with a deific declaration of faith in the power of the Crucified Lamb who has loved humanity beyond all mortal ends, and is still alive in immortal fact to prove it. We need never fear the pains of the Earth because they are part of the sacrificial phenomenon that occurs in conjunction with the purification of our vision of the heart. In a very real sense, the veil of our exile that obscures our having an unblemished sight into Paradise is an extremely merciful commodity bestowed upon humanity. Imagine seeing Creation factually restored to perfection before our eyes, knowing it with perfect clarity in our being, and not being allowed to touch it or experience it in the fullness of our physical senses while we are still mortally exiled. Imagine carrying a vision within your soul so profound and clear, so celestially exhilarating and complete, but nonetheless having only an infant spiritual composure to compete with mankind's debilitating social agenda and hackneyed definition of human life. Very simply, perfect sight is equal to perfect sacrifice because as the vision of Love grows more clear and multifaceted, the soul is transformed and our beings experience acutely the mortal deprivation of Divine Love from this world, which becomes an excruciating bath of daily sorrow. Millions experience this sacrificial state every day, during every waking hour. There are so many beautiful childlike hearts who lie in crucified suffering. When the Love of Heaven reveals itself to a person in its many differing magnitudes of openness, the soul knows exactly what Love is in its most experiential clarity. One realizes they have found what they have been searching for their entire lives, like two harmonies finding resonance in their unity. We see clearly that Creation was made for Light and how glaring is the contrast between where we are now and the beauty that we are a mere heartbeat away from experiencing. The heart is burdened with an obliterating privation in the perfect realization that Paradise is not yet attained on Earth as God intends and wills it to be, although it is still standing readily apparent before us, being ignored like a panhandler on the street. We realize what once seemed so far away is a mere flicking of an eyelid from being manifested, like sitting at a feast and not being allowed to eat until everyone else has been seated, and then experiencing the ominous weight of being unable to get anyone's attention to take their places. The world becomes the Cross within this revelation, transfigured into a cavern of darkness that has but one source of merciful Light, which is the beacon illuminated and inflamed in the sanctified heart resting in the hands of God. In this circumscribed arena, the captives of Love are recognizable; hearts encased within shells of broken dreams and defeated aspirations, more joyful days enslaved within crippled bodies, and sorrow fed to children of a King as their daily gruel.

How can I describe what I feel and see so keenly within me? What has been placed in this simple heart, so diminutive yet beyond dimensions within? Songs carry haunting melodies that unlock visions lying hidden beneath the obscuring fog of our daily uncertainty. Too often we weep and wail, and experience the pangs of grief and the solitude of deprivation; yet the heart reserves the right to shine a Paradise like a lighthouse upon a storm-plagued shore, blazing a beacon that elicits hope and draws the most profound petitions of deliverance from the depths of our being in our most excruciating moments of anguish. In those squalls of labored darkness amidst the waves, God appears upon the crests as we aspire unyieldingly to the greatest nobility of our nature; souls come to life again, claiming a divinity through Christ by way of forgiveness that was deprived from us at our entrance into the earthen arena to play our portioned sacrifice in the return of mankind to immortality. Nothing is ever desired so deeply, save the fulfillment that unrequited love pleads to receive in the most tender places of the heart. Our hearts cry, Love me—Love me—Love me! because none weep this passion without knowing wholly what it means. Oh! how piercing the yearning of love can be; how deep is the wound incised by the lance of Heaven when inflicted to the fundamental depths of humanity's spiritual perception. Oh! the excruciating torment when Heaven allows us to see past its hallowed gates to the fount of our fulfillment, to envision and nearly grasp the spectacular consolation that a perfect Kingdom affords its children, and then have the separation of our sinful mortality reconfirm our exile at the opening of our eyes again like a boulder draped around the neck of a dove. Oh! the agony of carrying within us the beatitude of Heaven with such clarity, eyes fixed upon the most ecstatic dreams of mankind's soul, and knowing their reality lies tantalizingly and torturously just beyond the captivating ties of our heartstrings. This is the crucifixion of the moment; every moment until either time has expired or mankind is awakened and each person takes upon his shoulders a portion of the Cross out of love. How do I describe what even great poets have in vain tried to place before humbled literati in the dribblings from their masterful pens? By what method does one unveil visions that thunder like a herd of unreigned stallions across the open frontiers of a mystical realm within; eyes piercing an horizon without barriers or bounds, and nostrils flaring freedom beyond the capture of any mortal man? What are the words to describe sheer invincibility; the capacity to defeat the tyrannical ages in one fell swoop; the power to create a universe in thine image and call it your own? Where are the mannerisms and postures that would paint a convincing pose where fortune is already found and victory secured in the pages of providential care, yet still unconfirmed except in our often frail faith? What does a heart say that experiences its dreams in concrete mystical substance while the world feigns affection to dormant hopes that have been relegated to the mockery of fantasy without possibility or protection? What is it like to be a great lyricist and be able to place upon the page words of the most beautiful compositions ever regaled; ones that appear like an apparition only in the solitude of beatific moments, but then awaken to a world where futility strips the sharing of their original symphonic reality to a reproduction from a worn-out, out-of-tune ukelele? How does one endure being a mere lyricist, and not also a composer; one who is hindered in framing the score that bore the visions aloft, into the skies of that supernatural realm where beauty was plucked from the mystical vaults that descended within reach of a child, like a cloud with its silver lining flying oh so close to the ground? What is it like to be fed a burning ember that after having consumed it by the heart, one finds the flame has not gone out, but has instead grown and raged the brighter, refined the purer, scorched the mightier, and intensified beyond the realms of mortal comprehension with each successive day, and wondering with the breath of each mortal encounter when it was going to finally consume your entire being, leaving you lost to the world but to be nothing but sacrificial pain, rendering you an exhausted pilgrim traveler in an arctic wasteland without an horizon, incinerated at every trudging step by an unmatched interior inferno which ironically in itself soothes the dereliction one shoulders upon having the heart consigned with the knowledge of the depths of God's Love? What is it like to be formed by the repeated strafing of sorrows from the first moments of life, to receive the brunt of the attack, famished for love beyond the imagination of man throughout the relentless years, impaled by unappeasable grief and loneliness, deprived and starved for every definition of heartfelt affection, be they familial or romantic? How fertile is the soil of the tenderest of souls who has hoped for an image of beauty to remain inflamed from a childhood past, instructed how to lay open its heart to anguish and grief, taught to courageously bear brutality upon the softest recesses of the soul, there isolated in the grief of unreciprocated love of colossal dimensions, filled to the brim with every infliction and pain, slight and disregard, pining all the while in beatific dimensions and perfect passions for the approach of an understanding heart, for human affection of the perfect order, yearning for idyllic communion with another who simply loves in return, weeping in solitude for the single touch of a human hand upon a tear-drenched cheek on at least one night of its forlorn desolation? My sense of detachment from the heavens which seem just beyond my grasp has been brought to an incisive magnificence at times. I have experienced humanity's outcast nature acutely because I have owned it through my sins, yet through enlivened faith have been provided an interior connection to the blessed future to which we have been promised after we are finally raised by the power of Jesus' devotion to our salvation. In souls relegated to endure the commission of the night, from where does the strength come; from what source does continuity burn, by what path does Light appear in the darkness? Imagine a supernova passed ignition but not allowed to explode? Or a champion fighter submitting to brutalization because he was not authorized to land the crushing blow? Or a teacher possessing the knowledge of the Heavenly Ancients but not allowed a classroom to teach? Or simply having the grace to apply the most gentle touch and no cheek places itself within thy reach? Can agony be seen in the ecstasy? Can beatific euphoria be veiled amidst the torment? Can the Resurrection be seen in the Crucifixion? And, can humanity see Paradise in the Cross? I say it can! I see it because I experience it at every moment; and this perfect mystery of life is ours to live! We must begin understanding Love to its grieving depths; grasp it, hold it, inflame it, nurture it, passionately resolve to defend it, and when dying go to the fire and allow our beings to be consumed by its divine magnificence, whether we notice our passing from this Earth or not. We must launch our hearts into this abyss of divinity, hurling ourselves headlong into the vision and the suffering, and there expand the dimensions of our beatific composure and bring it to bear with courageous nobility upon this world like an Olympic champion sticking a landing before an awestricken world of spectators. Heaven no longer waits; the gargantuan dam between Heaven and Earth is crumbling, and the rumblings of God's universal cleansing are beginning to reverberate in the world! The restraints of our sin we must burst like chains before a resurrected Saint. Be forgiven, my brothers and sisters! Seek the Confessional and there from the heart ignite the eternal flame by rising from the occasion of humanity's sin, then place your feet on the path of Creation like a new human species of *Sequoiadendron Giganteum*. Tower over evil and spread a canopy of deliverance from the shores of your heart! Assail the darkness with the Light! Refuse to placate the ego-stricken hordes and clap your hands with glee when you see their plots to destroy you become manifest! Take your place in the ranks of royalty and don the power of the Cross. Engage the world with nothing but Divine Vision and obliterate every sinister agenda with the Light bestowed by Heaven in the blazing radiance of your most burdened heart. Reach-out, strike down, lift up, remake, rebuild, purify, dream larger than this life, hope beyond fading hope, trust like it is the first day of your childhood, thrust your heroic hearts into the stormy skies and blow away the rain, and beneath the glistening rainbow write a legacy of love for humanity that will be complimented by Christ on the last day upon the backdrop of the heavens with colors that mankind has never seen! Prepare to pass the threshold of Heaven with your heart lacerated like history's greatest warriors, but still radiating and shining beatific Light from every cut, your jaw extended squarely into the wind and eyes laser-fixed on the beaming horizons of the Sacred Heart. Inhale the confidence of the King of Creation upon His first breath from the Easter Tomb. Tell Him that you have come before Him to claim time itself, that you are going back into the night to reclaim the ages and storm again through earthen history with vindication written upon your mantle. Inform the Lord of lords and King of kings that your heavenly duty before entrance into Paradise is to visit every hovel in its decrepitude, take center stage on every theater of war before the holocaust has ensued, intercept every arrow launched at a human heart, deflect all misery before its impact, enlighten every shadowed alley and illuminate every darkened avenue in advance of their tragedies, and announce to every ear ever deprived of the intoned word that they are special and that the dignity, grace, and eternal life in their dreams has arrived in a Messiah, and His Name is Jesus Christ!

Spectacular visions loom in the pleats of our prayerful contemplations; and they exceed the dreams of all the romantic men who have experienced the painful march of time, scratching to preserve the beautiful; those storied realities where our bleeding beings recline in yonder realms beyond the sad inflictions of doubters and doppelgangers. The heart beats a knowledge of yearning poets and relentless patriots, hoping the tomorrows we have seen in the forlorn mystery of our interior passions will become the todays in which broken humanity might revel in carefree joy, while our prayers tell us it is but a fleeting moment in time away. A welling dream of deliverance flourishes within, excelling past the defeated illusions that lie in the surreptitious shadows of our afflicted minds which have too long distressed our pining hearts whose cardiac might has overwhelmed the ages with an eminent artistry of suffering, learned from the royal gracefulness of the heavens who have been so kind as to stoop in condescension to our wasteland of shattering defeats. Oh! how powerfully the heart can pledge itself to the sanctity of man, the defense of dignity, and our final paradisial destiny that beckons from the eternal brilliance of Divine Light itself. It is beyond mere envisaging what breadth the beatific vision of the human heart can conceive of the eternal reality of Heaven. How much must be endured and by what precision must the concise realism of Divine Love saber our interior essence, should we be granted a glimpse beyond the veil? Can we envision the seeming impossibility of seeing Heaven from where we stand and yet be unable to shed the flesh and unite completely with its essence either in our mortal senses or the constructs of our mechanical day? The soul can be sorrowful, beaten, driven and tired, and thereafter left standing upon the icy stoop, knocking with no one opening a door, but it still lives with a grace that cannot die. It is oftentimes exhausting engaging the lonely battles against the depleting forces of this life that poise themselves at every advantageous turn to decimate and destroy our hopes and any opportunities that would provide relief to our wearied being. But, the shining Light of God within us e'er raises our heads because we know the final sunrise is always prefigured by His delivering glints on our interior horizon, portending the inevitable daybreak of our dreams.

Our Lady told me on the first day of the second week of Her miraculous intercession in 1991, *"Satan is the darkness, the devil, the sinister one, and the doer of evil. It is very prudent that I make you aware that your Salvation is in danger if you do not pray to My Son to defeat him. Satan is a heretic and a rebel. As I have told you everything that My Son is, Satan is not. Satan is the undoing of justice, sanctity, life, peace, and happiness. You must pray, My children, to shut Satan out of your hearts, souls, and lives. Satan cannot help you get to Heaven. He will never do one good deed. He is against every good domain that My Son died for - the Savior of your souls and promise of Eternal Life in Heaven."* The Devil is a definitive, discorporate, spiritual personage, no matter how many supposedly enlightened people attempt to obscure this fact with their pragmatic rejection of the truth. He is not simply a religious metaphor for evil. He is a supremely-intelligent creature of pure demonism that humankind cannot fathom who preys, even though futilely, upon our mortal existence, attempting to obfuscate and harass every good intention and better sense we possess, pining to subvert any earthly hope left to lie within his reach that might provide a soothing caress to our scars, and seeking to inflict lethal carnage against God's earthly vineyard at any flash of an opportunity left open to him by man. All the evil we witness in the world is wrought by his diabolical hand. Many people have been seduced by the Antichrist and do his bidding without conscience, especially those who wreak unmitigated terror across the world in the name of neo-religious indoctrination and the lot who are suffering from the secular plague of atheistic liberality who have legitimized, allowed, and cooperated in the killing of fifty million unborn children, while peddling their cartloads of deranged hubris that is destroying the benevolent fabric of our peaceful communal identity. Our allegiance to the Mother of God requires that we recuse ourselves from these heinous acts and selfish enticements, and instead patronize with each breath the alluring flow of Divine Life gushing-forth from the Sacred Heart of Jesus. She wishes us to submit our loyalties in their totality to the triumph of the human race in the Glory of the Most Blessed Trinity. Fear not becoming an outcast for choosing Eternity in Divine Love over the farcical facade of this failing world! Fear not being deprived of the emotional support of your family or friends, for in the end, they will follow your example to the heights of Glory. Be unafraid to turn your back on false ideologies that have enslaved humanity in the darkest recesses of the ages. Seek not the healing caress of a doting wife, the scampering innocence of adoring children, or a life of prestigious success, if it means forfeiting your dedication to the One who will redeem you into Paradise. Revere not social advancement, achievement or recognition from the secular world because the American media culture does no more than create pottery heroes that they feverishly will to destroy for entertainment the moment one claims victory. Dispense with the need for the respect of your fellow faithsians, their morsels of admiration and affirmation, or the comfort of friends who might realize the privations that your soul endures at each minute of every day. Sense the more noble journey of love, and place your feet upon its path, leaving God to provide you with succor. Embrace your destiny in Light and savor the trials that will take you there! Oh! how noble God allows us to be by way of His grace to generate heroic virtue with every mortal step and revel in the tornadic winds of our metronomic dailiness in the flesh. I do not have the words to describe the Love that rages for mankind at every moment, an overwhelming conflagration of beauty that scorches my present awareness, engulfing me in a seclusive elevation where God refrains for a time to reach below me and ordain the projection of my heart upon the Earth so that it would meet the dreams that my soul wishes to experience. Oh! the things that I can see without words to paint them on a page, the possibilities that lie just beyond our grasp, behind the wisping veil of erratic decisions and the terminal obstinance fronted by those who refuse to enlist the heart and believe that they are the healing conduit of consolation for humankind. I cannot create dreams, but I have them nonetheless. It is a holy burden and an annihilating existence to witness a Love so grand, yet not be allowed to touch, consume, immerse, experience, embrace or unite with it in the totality of my senses because I have yet to complete the sanctification of my heart in the Holy Sacrifice of Jesus. Litter and debris imply waste; shards and fragments incriminate destruction; and suffering and death intimate redemption. All the songs of serenaders delivering the yearnings of the lovelorn, the recitation of all soul-wrenching verse spilled onto the scripts and scrolls of the ages, and the collective pool of blood shed from the passionate existence of faithful men, are the testament to Jesus' promise to dispense yet untold Glory upon those who have wept for Love. Therefore, I ask mankind to cry with me for just one moment; shed a tear, experience the longing desire for Divine Love as a collective heart; intone one Our Father as a united species, and embrace the almost surreal presence of the heavenly city that beams with its own unique ethereal presence from within each of us. Let that beckoning of finality to the story of redemption and resurrection well-up with you, that Love may be the complete composition of our existence, seen and unseen. Can the heart of humanity be forever broken open in one glorious instant where the omnipresent universe of the Heavenly Hosts washes over our mortal existence in one cleansing bath? I say it can! And, that rapturous moment is almost upon us!

Our hopes and dreams are the power of the Holy Spirit animating our human frames! Nothing can escape its destiny in our hearts. We wage a brutal battle with the forces of Hell while we are in this place of mortal exile, being consigned to a frail position of deception and angst against the human anatomy through all the sensibilities by which it is molded and buffeted. But, our spirits remain of the same invincible mettle as the spark of the Third Person of the Holy Trinity from which we were created. Oh! how many dreams have been inflamed in human hearts throughout the millennia!—all of them composed of hopes to be at peace, free from suffering and indignity, others returning the love that was extended, and able to manifest in physical reality the visions one has seen in the heart. I too dream, and I know everything that I have wished to experience to the last smile, but has passed me by instead, is being held as a treasure by God. Therefore, I am not afraid to lose in the moment because the final tally is being accrued nonetheless, and its bestowal upon my heart is inevitable. Hence, I am overjoyed that I was placed in this arena during such an awesome age of sacrifice! In time, rising to the occasion has meant everything because I know that nothing can alter the legacy that Our Lady has generated or change the manner in which She has assisted my brother and me in engaging the subtleties and sorcery of this age. My heart is love, unique in its creation; and it has lain for decades within me, tenderly gazing at Creation as one betrothed to ultimate peace and fulfillment. Oh! the hearts of God's people who have pined for love and have been deprived its emollient succor while on Earth. What privations they have sustained! What sacrifices of graceful endurance they have splayed before the ages! What an image of divinity that all the heavens will marvel at for Eternity! I tell you, kings and commanders are kneeling before paupers! We wage our altercation with mortal life amidst the fraudulence generated by the Devil. His froth and the breadth of his reach can be somewhat astounding at times, yet it is temporary and of no real power or lasting definition. He has only the moment in his ability to lie, which is always trumped by divinity in time; his wiles are utterly defeated in every sense, while he exhales nothing but gasps against an invincibility that has crushed him with the weight of his own iniquity. Lucifer is truly a coward who despises all that is good about humanity with demonic ferocity, like a spoiled child kicking his feet and arching his back on the cold, hard basement floor of Creation; bluster with no lasting dominion; an angelic misery who forfeited Infinite Love for a prideful arrogance that refused to submit to the Godhead which doomed him to everlasting fire. The fall of Adam is not the true tragedy, but a consequence of angelic wretchedness that engendered a pride so profound that the Light Bearer from the Kingdom of God waived his essence and plummeted from the highest rank of Heaven to the deepest waste pit of self-annihilation, and is attempting to take all mankind there with him, with the shot at Eve being his first volley. That is the true calamity, but also a great irony, because mere human creatures, once flawed and broken, now have more power than the former highest Prince of Angels; and women who submissively imitate the grace of our Holy Mother have become the most powerful agents in bringing the eye-apparent transformation of the Earth into Eden once again. This Father of Darkness can throttle our flesh and intimidate our spirits in the wake of our weak faith, but he cannot impede Love from being inflamed in any human heart, nor can he succeed by saying, "Come to me instead," once Jesus Christ has revealed the Love of His Sacred Heart to man. The Devil is helpless before compassion, virtue, heroic self-sacrifice, and humility. He cannot touch a soul who is given to Jesus through the Immaculate Virgin of Bethlehem. What could he possibly do to a person who walks with the Love of God within them while the Virgin of Calvary stands guard? When he barks, *I will make you suffer*, we tell him to put forth his best effort because we do not want to be seen as cowards by the Holy Martyrs. When he tempts, *I will bestow upon you all your mortal desires*, we respond that we already possess our heart's desire in the Love we carry inside. When he says, *I will make you famous, and the world's elite will worship you if you embrace me; and you will feel the warmth of the adoring crowds if you follow me*, we say that we already feel the loving warmth of millions of Saints and are already famous before them for the sacrifices we have embraced in order to imitate their grace. When he says, *I will nip at your heels every day of your life, and pursue you to your death with as much sadness and grief as I can heap upon a person*, we declare to him that we wish our lives to be centuries long, and remind him that the only sadness that will last has already fallen upon him! Every time Satan raises his head against us, we retaliate with the spectacular vision of the Holy Cross in our conduct, in our demeanor, our comportment, in our hopes, in our thoughts, and in the flashing of our eyes, making him wish he had never turned his gaze against a child of the King. We feed him gruel through our faith. He is force-fed defeat at our hands! Yes, we boast of our Father's prowess that we have inherited in Christ because the Love resurrected by the Virgin's beckoning Heart is now on the offensive! Let the legions of Hell know that intrepid warriors have now placed their feet upon the battlefield, upright and invincible beyond the reckoning. We bring everything to the fore, all the powers of our spiritual being to the absolute pinnacle of devotion that God could generate in the human heart, His crucified image imprinted in us at the conception of our creation. We are supernatural creatures, asked to sacrificially experience the captivating boundaries of this exilic arena for a mere flash in the eons, but are able nonetheless to don divinity like battle-hardened veterans and transcend in spirit an entire Creation by the power of Love within us. An entire fruitful world has been created for mankind to subdue, conquer, conform, share and sanctify to its likeness in

Heaven. And, we see the beatific domain of God's supernatural reign within us in our most sacred of moments, those instants when the Light overwhelms our being and the magnificent appointments of a Paradise that only a heart could know explode with clarity and reality in our contemplations. It is no fantasy or delusion to herald an everlasting reality yet unseen with human eyes, but experienced every second in the fantastic universe of our soul. God placed Himself within us and called it Heart! This divine receptacle of Heaven is our connection with our true identity that wells vision, hope, expectation, success, prosperity, happiness, and anticipation of an unconquerable destiny beyond the temporary phantasms of our seeming defeats. We are unvanquishable creatures. Nothing can stop us from rising to the dreams we envision except our lack of will to confess our sins, accept the forgiveness that is ours, embrace the recreation of our beings in perfection, and rise with conviction as a new creation, sanctified in the powerful image of Christ Crucified, all for His glorification! No force of Hell can claim even an instant of our lives, notwithstanding Satan's preying upon our lack of knowledge of this truth. In the flushing midst of this exilic deception, he paints a picture of life before our mortal eyes using the sinful weaknesses of lost mortals who conform to his lies, who then prod us incessantly through every imaginable venue to believe we are insignificant creatures who have appeared by chance in the cosmos and will pass unknown into nothingness the moment time is extinguished from our eyes. If our penitential sojourn in the flesh seems an endless sacrifice without merit or purpose, we need but turn our thoughts to the Eternity of Light that exists once our frailty passes. We will reign like gods, subordinate and in union with the benevolence of the Most Blessed Trinity, our God in Three Divine Persons; creating, doing, being, and experiencing anything our hearts could conceive now, along with the limitless panorama of eternal livingness that will be inflamed within our same heart the instant the eclipse of exile passes from before our spatial awareness. Our hearts are now the size of all the oceans, but contain a mere thimble of those beatific visions that will soothe us past this life because sin has dammed up Heaven within us. Our dreams lie there in the darkness waiting for the Light, some crushed, others unfulfilled, most dormant. But, take heart because Our Lady proclaims that none of our hopes are lost; nothing has been experienced in vain; nary an aspiration has been defeated, and no sentiment has faded past the certainty of its fulfillment. All will come flowing back to us as on the first day we envisioned their comely revelation, exactly the way we dreamed them being and more, showered upon us in their pristine nature before their fall—all the victories that eluded us, the joys that passed us by, the shots that would not fall, the relationships foiled by happenstance and the haranguing of evil, and the triumphs that were consumed instead by horrors. Imagine a nondescript day in Texas when Mission Control headsets suddenly crackle, and a radio transmission wafts across the airwaves from out of man's broken dreams, "*ssskksssst.... Houstsskksskkst..... Houston, this*

Prologue xli

is Columbia. Vehicle secure. Vectoring eastern seaboard, altitude 37 miles, 18000 feet per second... Visual on Challenger confirmed; two o'clock position. Touchdown at Cape 16 minutes." Or standing on the National Mall during our annual Memorial Day ceremonies, when out of the distance the whopping of rotor blades ripping the air strikes the ears of everyone present, and from the sky like locust descend squadron after squadron of battle-scarred vintage Hueys which come to rest in prideful formation on the grassy Ellipse. Before the awestruck crowd of holiday mourners, the military olive-green doors of these choppers slide open and, one by one, out climbs every soldier whose name is engraved on those sullen granite monuments, with no one left behind. And, from the rolling hills of Arlington, Virginia, a roar of ovation cascades across the waters of the Potomac like from a crowd in a giant stadium; America's risen warriors standing beside their vacated tombs in honorary rows saluting their comrades, hailing their brothers in arms and restoring the dignity lost to the nightmare of mankind's Viet-nemesis. Or the commanding admiral of Pearl Harbor rising on a crystal-clear Sunday morning, and over a cup of coffee peers out over Battleship Row, and suddenly sees a Pennsylvania-class battleship, the USS Arizona, majestically upright and afloat, ready for battle with her military appointments polished and glistening in the sun with all 1400 of her seaman standing at attention on her decks, and the realization flooding his conscience that World War II lies rendered but a dream. Or huge crowds along the eastern shores noticing in astonishment an early 20th century steamship plunging through the waves, passing the Statue of Liberty, about to enter the safety of New York's harbor, waving passengers lining its rails, and horns and whistles blaring as if it were some special port-of-call that had been awaiting them for nearly a century. And, as the magnificent ship turns in the waves to prepare for its docking, the name "Titanic" appears emblazoned across her bow before the eyes of the incredulous throngs. Or a mother in Oklahoma City sitting in the midst of her sad memories, suddenly startled from her grief by the ringing of the phone, and upon picking it up, hears a woman on the other end say, *"Yes, this is the daycare center downtown at the Murrah Building. I am calling to let you know that you can pick up your child anytime before 4:00 pm. Just a minute, somebody is just a little too impatient and wants to talk to you.......Hi mommy, I can't wait to show you what we made today in art class!!!!"* This is the Power of Resurrection; impossibility drawn forth to reality by the omnipotent Hand of God! Apostles reclining around a table in grief, traumatized by the events of the execution of their beloved Master only hours before, when the inconceivable occurs: women disciples barge through the door with elated joy, *"We have seen the Lord! He has risen, just as He said!"* And, just assuredly as Jesus rose from His Tomb, we will see His Glorious Return bearing the resurrection of human history and all its inhabitants from the sepulcher of death with equal triumphant bearing and as hopeful as the parables I have just plucked from the possibilities of God's creative genius—*"...in hope that creation itself would be set free from slavery to corruption and share in the glorious freedom of the children of God."-Romans 8:21.* Perhaps Berry Benson, the legendary Confederate soldier and romantic author, painted the most beautiful picture while attempting to describe his hopes regarding the horrific Civil War battles that he experienced when he wrote in his great work, *Reminiscences,* "*Who knows but it may be given to us, after this life, to meet again in the old quarters, and to again hastily don our war gear while the long roll summons to battle? Who knows but again the old flags may face each other while the cries of victory fill a summer day? And after the battle, then the slain and wounded will arise, and there will be talking and laughter and cheers, and all will say: Did it not seem real? Was it not as in the old days?*" No matter what glory God has planned in His ultimate act of Deliverance at Jesus' Second Coming, Satan will nonetheless experience a complete, intricate, infinite, multifaceted defeat in everything that brought even the slightest shadow to a human heart. Victory wrested from the fangs of sheer disaster. Rebirth drawn from mortal wreckage. And, the high noon of paradisial light ignited after the perilous strike of an enduring midnight. The Evil One will be the most humiliated thrust-down creature ever to have experienced consciousness for what he has perpetrated against the Kingdom of the Most Blessed Trinity, and so will those who serve his evil. Beware you who defend abortion; your defeat and punishment is imminent. None of you has yet to truly contemplate or understand the just fury of the Godhead. It will rain down like incandescent fire at the final Resurrection of the dead when Satan's kingdom of darkness will be stripped from him as he is dethroned and destroyed. All Glory has been bestowed by the Almighty Father upon the Lamb of God who died so that Heaven may become a perfect realm of united love amongst all the creatures He conceived, the lion even laying down with the lamb. Every facet of Creation—absolutely everything—has been conferred like a precious jewel into the hands of the Savior of the world. Jesus Christ is to credit for every smile, each handshake, all the acts of good will, our talents, treasures, accomplishments, our prayers of devotion, every inspiration, and all the noble and holy sentiments that have been lifted by humanity in every age; and He is personally glorified as the creator, inspirer and caretaker of mankind's dreams. And, not only that, but Christ the King has also claimed the forsaken, the wretched, and the desolate; and atop of that, has taken for Himself every sin in all of history; every harsh word, every sinister glance, the mistakes, all the inflictions, the atrocities and hellishness, the diseases and destitution, the disasters and the wars, and even death; and He has rescinded them, revoked them, conquered them, and removed their definition from the history of the world by a Triumph so spectacular that Creation has been recreated, redefined, redeemed, sanctified, and glorified by the power of His Passion, Death and Resurrection manifested through His mystical Sacrifice propagating through time. The Lamb of God has snatched unimaginable victory from a seemingly irrevocable historical cataclysm and has left Satan with all the humiliation in defeat that a creature could ever know. The Despicable One has lost in every way that can be conceived; even the sinister victories he thought he gained in each moment of humanity's exile have been stripped from him by Jesus' redemptive genius. God intends to vanquish Satan and his hordes into oblivion beneath a heap of total abasement that is Creation deep and human history wide, there to page through the Book of Life containing the meticulous history of their defeat in the Redemption of Creation wrought by the Power of Jesus' Cross. The Prince of Demons will choke and heave on Christ's mastery of human divinity, spiritual invincibility and the magnanimous creativity of His Father for all eternities to come, and will be humiliated that humanity imitated and now shares life with the Father in ways he rejected outright. Satan is going to be deprived of the faintest hint of satisfaction that he could have gained from any moment of darkness which obscured the pages of history and the blessed vision of the human heart. Every horror we see emanates the Triumph of the Lamb of God. All punishment is going to come down upon one angel, just as the Cause of Redemption came to rest in the flesh of one Man. Evil and all who cooperate with it are doomed. Yet, we must hope that all will be forgiven by the Most Blessed Trinity in the most blinding act of mercy that the heavens could ever conceive. We have been told without equivocation that Hell is a tangible reality that is reserved for those who reject the Divine Mercy of the Crucified Messiah. Eternal Damnation is real and permanent, but Judgement is being withheld until the scope of Jesus' Divine Mercy has been fully defined by the redeeming Holy Sacrifice of the Mystical Body of Christ yet in time; this is why we pray so deeply and passionately during our beatific communion in the Holy Mass, and sacrifice and do penance for those who are far from the Truth of Christianity. Creation has yet to have Salvation conferred upon it in its manifest essence, and time still exists for all to be saved; and this is why the *Morning Star Over America* has appeared!

    The heavens have launched a battle to reclaim God's vineyard from the wickedness that has consumed it, and it is the Immaculate Mother of the Lamb of God who has been commissioned to mount that heavenly offensive. Her artillery and legions are being moved into place. She asks us to call upon Saint Michael the Archangel who is God's perfect retaliatory strike against Satan's personifications of wickedness. This Prince of the Seraphim will never fall and has been vested with avenging power and liberating authority over all reigns created by the Lord of Creation. Saint Michael has been called to serve the Triumph of the Immaculate Heart of Mary. Yes, the Heavenly Father has definitively risen to the challenge of the Prince of Darkness in our age. The Most Holy Trinity here accents and defends His paradisial dominion in Heaven, on Earth, and even to the bowels where evil has been driven to its eternal demise. Redemption is not a defensive action by God against an all-powerful wickedness who competes with Him; it is instead an act of offensive obliteration inflicted upon an arrogant evil through the powers, graces, moral excellences and promises of Christ as an act of the Father comporting Creation with His Divine Will, which is perfect Love in His Messianic Son. We are the royal children of that Holy Dominion by virtue of His Calvarian Sacrifice consecrated on the Altars of the Holy Mass, and are willed to thrive in love within His virtuous domain and transform the Earth through our acceptance of the Cross, and our witnessing to God's power which will place us upon it. As a child-prince of the heavenly Kingdom, and in honor of my Father by the power of the Resurrected Messiah, and through the Voice of His Holy Spirit, I hereby petition: *Against the Prince of Demons and his diabolical horde I summon Heaven's power, light, and divine fire through the mighty intercession of the Archangel, Saint Michael! The endurance of the spirit of humanity has come to perfection in the suffering of Christianity's Saints while in the midnights of their hidden mortal desolations. Oh! angelic Prince, forage history's interior battlefields and retrieve the tearful treasure of unrequited love that lies upon those indwelling altars, and from these sacred shards that witness to mankind's broken dreams, coagulate their tears into an impenetrable mettle; smelt anew their ancient hopes mixed with the newborn engagements of the Church Militant! Languish no more suffering humanity, but rise to spiritual arms! Oh great winged benefactor, forge the vindicating sword of God's liberating fury against audacious evil, form it in the inferno of your divine righteousness, sanctify it in the Blood of the Crucified Lamb, polish it with the intentions of the Communion of Saints, christen it "The Saber of Resurrection," and lash it in my clenched fist against all the nefarious agents of the netherworld and their legions who have dared to inflict such indignity upon God's most precious creatures whom you have defended throughout the ages. Advance your determination now for the day when humankind en masse finds final dignity and peace beneath thy commissioned protection. Grant this mystical weapon its appearance for the transformation of helpless submission into avenging resurrection. Let hinges be ripped from their fastened moorings at its beatific strike and stones displaced from the lintels of evil's falling gates! Let the dawn blaze from its shimmering blade, oh! great Archangel, and blind the demonic reign back into the oblivion of its own eternal night. Bring to light this Age of Messianic Resurrection and laser strike it in the facades of the four corners of the Earth, across the peaks of Gibralter, upon the brows of Rushmore, on the cascading slopes of the Tetons and the crags of the Rockies, upon the soaring brinks of the Alps and hewn into the spires of the Himalayas; let white clouds of obliterated chalk billow from Dover's cliffs, inscribe the walls of fjords and the sheer faces of every canyon grand; make every escarpment your canvas; etch the doorposts of governments with judgement, and the threshold of every nation with conversion. Drive the Saber of Resurrection from pole to pole that the Earth may spin upon righteousness once again! Issue forth the power of the Conquered Cross! If there be a dark night upon the soul of a child, retaliate indeed! If there be an indignity or depression heaped upon a creature, be it upon the beast, be it upon him, complete and everlasting; he who defied the Godhead of Divine Love and has so crucified your beloved humanity! The Almighty commands that liberty be declared and granted to His captive children, thus liberation comes from one who has conquered! From the haunting* *nightmare of broken dreams, awaken to your freedom! From the gnawing inadequacy of gutted hopes, believe them all again! From the cowardice of inferiority, be crowned with superior nature! From the agonizing fires of worthlessness, be quenched with deific dignity! From the pulverizing depletion of despair, be lifted to victory! From the mindless midnight of mental carnage, be enlightened with the genius of the Holy Spirit! From the icy loneliness of ignominy, be warmed with the inevitability of kingship! From the deprivation of being unloved, receive Infinite Love in thy being! From the deceptive shockwaves of abandonment, be enjoined in the fraternity of the coming Eternity! From the unrelenting fear of a vacuous future with no delivering end, be redeemed into the Triumph! And, from the darkness which obscures the only Light that can soothe the human soul—the Light which is Love—bathe in the Love of God, Our Lady and all of the Heavenly Hosts who are coming with the returning Messiah! And, out of the celestial vaults, a Voice reverberates from the Heavens—"**Hear Me! You are not forsaken, My beloved humanity**—and will you never be. I am the Resurrection and the Life! My Name is Redemption and you are My Redeemed! I authorize you by the invincible Power of My Cross to rise from the night and grab the darkness by the throat! Toss it to its demise beyond the sight of My omniscient gaze. My Sacred Heart has hoarded every hope you have cried from your most disconsolate gloom, and I bring your dreams back to you fulfilled! I answer every desire you sought from Me, all that your hearts ever yearned, every sweetness you pined to savor, and cast down every villain who brought even the faintest shadow to your happiness. Beneath your feet and in your hands, I place 'Triumph!', and upon your head the Crown that you always possessed in My sight. The Time of times has arrived! I say—Rise! I declare My benisons upon you, My faithful, upon your age, and every age and universe that has passed before My eternal sight. I answer history's souls lying in the auld meadows of humanity's strife, strewn in their heroic mortality before the apse of My mystical Kingdom, their dying breaths sighing their last. They are even now looking through dimming eyes across the ages to the hilltops of My Reign, bleeding hopeful passions that the cavalry's legion would answer the heart-rending notes of their retreating love; and I am the King who comes! Upon My stallion of Righteousness and with the fiery gaze of My Crucified Love, I peer down from the overlook of Paradise into the glistening reverie dying in their tear-drenched eyes. I flash the enfiladed fields of corpus-dreams stacked in time past the fading sunsets, there resting dormant and defeated in the captive darkness of approaching death—there awaiting Me! The Lion of the tribe of Judah is now here and I bellow across the lands, 'The Earth's Reckoning has arrived! Victory has appeared! Let the Trumpets of My Justice sound forth! My victorious Saints, now let your sabers be drawn! You, Archangels and Legions, launch the battle and unleash all the Powers that My Father anointed in Thee!' And, from the headlands, like an ocean loosed over a mighty falls, I lead the rain of Deliverance down from the redeeming seas on high. Into the desolate valley of death I thunder—'To Life, To Love, To Eternity! Spare no darkness, grant inhumanity no quarter, conquer and destroy all that portends defeat to the grave, wipe My Vineyard clean; plant and restore, build, create and grow, embolden every spirit broken, awaken every dream snuffed out, raise every* *soul beaten down, and bestow victorious majesty upon My Saints—Resurrect the Dominion of My Love—because it is I, the Christ, who declares with the Sign of My Cross that Love comes to conquer! It is I alone who have subdued the ages! And, I prove My Power by preserving everything from the heart of My precious humanity for the halls of the Kingdom of My Father! Heaven is a Paradise indeed because you will be there!'"*

To these lyrics we look into a world of Earth again with childlike hope renewed, strength restored, expectation resurrected, vision inflamed, prowess engaged and ability determined. Satan would have us believe that the years have tattered us, that they have given us sullen images that cannot be dispersed, that we are no longer capable of the valor with which we were born, that we can no longer see, let alone hear, and that there is no hope for us as these days are utterly spent. But, Satan is a liar and a deceiver, while we have been made giants before the Father by Christ our Lord. We are the Children of Mary who cannot be vanquished, whose hopes and dreams are as intact as upon the first day they glimmered in the eyes of our hearts; they will come to us now, and they will transcend the final ages of the created world. My brothers and sisters, it is Jesus who anticipates our victory with sureness and confidence, and sustains its inevitable appearance with His Omnipotent Will. Along the way, we have heard His reproaches of the millions who spurn Him, ridicule His Crucifixion, and slander His Church. We have listened to the haggling of the lunatics who have nothing invested in their own future because of their idiocy, because they do not believe that there is a future outside of time, or even one within it where they would choose to love. The wicked and wretched only haunt themselves, dwelling on their own pride and materials, wondering how they will pilfer their next buck, ignoring the plight of the poor and neglected, especially their progeny of today's societies who are being torn from the promises of their mothers' wombs. My friends, Satan would have us believe that sunsets and new dawns do not mean anything to the Church or the faith by which we are led to our final acquittal. He does not see artistry along the horizon at sundown, but instead another opportunity to take advantage of the coming darkness to spread his own wickedness, to emerge from the shadows where he has cowered from the light. He would have us believe that our best days are gone, that our youth has been spent, and nothing we can do will ever make us happy again. I am speaking of the Father of Lies who is terrified by the Mother of God and vanquished by Her Holy Offspring! Please come to this majestic Lady of comfort; stand with confidence beneath Her Holy Mantle, obey Her every word, draw light and strength from each of Her sentiments, and pull yourself, kicking and clawing if need be, to the foot of the Cross where Her Son's Blood will fall upon you like a gentle rain of new enlightenment and encouragement. Jesus Christ has saved our souls there, and He has enlivened the spirit of our hearts, our heart of hearts, to convince us that we are anointed by His power to rise above our fears, and with blazing eyes of love, drive evil from the parameters of Creation. There were many days before today when our Virgin Mother would liked to have related these things, but it has come to this finality through years of penance and sacrifice, and we are being made poignantly aware of Her deepest sentiments now. We are shoulder-to-shoulder with the Saints who themselves were racked by the horrific onslaughts of evil against their prayers and dignity, against their wisdom to survive in a world of ignorance, in a nation that despises the beneficial auspices of the Apostolic Church of Rome. America was built by a college of pilgrims who protested against Catholicism, and their hatred for the Holy See has never died. But, they will die as all men die; and they will be called before the Truth which will appear like a spectacular mountain range before whose glistening beauty they will begin to weep as humbled men for the first time in their lives! They cannot outlive the genuine perfection of the Holy Sacrifice of the Mass that has saved this country from certain annihilation on more than one occasion.

The Father gives us the dexterity and creativity to embroider our most comely aspirations into the fabric of everyday life, but we must confide in the Cross our deepest passions and dysfunctions, delinquencies, anxieties, backwardness, and trepidations. Confessing our sins is as specific to our redemption as the Crucifixion itself, for unless we disavow our corruption, we will not quit the darkness in favor of the light. We will remain like vultures devouring the carnage of our own transgressions instead of ducklings feasting on bread. We cannot permit our impudence to fester; it is utterly mandatory that we comprehend the cost of saying no. Through the Holy Cross, the Lord rescinds the epitaphs of the dead, evicts pain from our memories, reinstates the life that Adam stole, remolds us into perpetual creatures, annuls our inequities, harvests our sacrificial tithes, excavates us from the depths of sorrow, and crowns, adorns, commends, and inducts us into the Kingdom that He was conceived in Our Lady to sustain. Ever since the self-awareness of mortal man began, we have searched for intelligence that is both foreseeing and farsighted, elucidating, relevant, intuitive, justifying, and evocative. We have huddled in caves, shanties, bungalows, and castles; and we have communicated by hieroglyphics, percussion, flames, tongues, and radio waves. But, through it all, the most important matter to the Church has been keeping Satan slithering away to his grave. If we as a nation do not stop placating him, the loss will be ours and the shame upon us. It would require only a few popular, high profiled, strategically placed Americans with a penchant for decency and posterity to rise against the tide of evil that is ripping apart our national flesh, and the public would respond. Infidelity is stalking what remains of us; and when we finally succumb to our own self-destruction, we will leave behind an appalling-looking corpse, one that is emaciated, decayed, consumed by lawlessness, morally bankrupt, and infested with parasites. If we do not change course now, history will record that we poisoned ourselves with sin, that we died of suicidal trauma caused by the collision between our freedom to make choices and our unwillingness to do so wisely. We are walking our children to the gallows one piece of legislation at a time and summarily executing their future. We seem to forget that we are created beings, not self-constituted; and we will soon discover that the air of permissiveness that we spread across our landscape turned out to be our deathbed, that it was a fatal mistake to turn our backs against God. The United States of America used to be celebrated as one of the most preeminent societies in the world when it comes to religious virtue, but due to the suppression of our common piety, Washington's left-leaning extremism, atheist litigation, liberal judges, and anti-Catholic opportunism, we are now hardly in the running.

If Americans are the composers and wonderers we have always claimed to be, surely we know that the Earth still pangs in anger and the skies are starved for new anthems. There must be better ways to demonstrate that we are more dimensioned than our compulsions might imply, that we are connected at the soul to God through the miracle of Jesus' Sacrifice. We are responsible to prove to one another and the whole world by word and action our oneness with the Trinity, and stop obsessing about false numens and prognostications that have nothing to do with the Cross. The mind-bending Spirit of the Father to whom we owe our conception resounds through Creation even louder than Hiroshima; and the reason we do not hear it is because we have not made the connection between the sound of repentance and the sight of ourselves in Paradise. Humanity throughout the ages has dedicated whole dissertations, treatises, and manifestos to the effects of being mortal, but rarely do we ponder what comes next. We hypothesize about what we see, touch, dissect, scrutinize, and infer based on history and its continued making. We have created comprehensive frameworks for evaluating human endeavors, but only little about where they will lead. In effect, we are in the process of always looking backward, measuring how far we have come, extrapolating how far we can go, lending to life no more significance than our experiences might provide. One of the most foreboding concepts of our years in exile is the idea of reckoning. We loathe being held accountable for our missteps by anyone else or at any hour. Our patriotic zeal would have us believe that we are capable of circumventing every kind of judgement that could reproach our way of life. This is the American way; it is the product of an inanimate Bill of Rights that says that all men have guaranteed choices in personal conduct that supercede the jurisdiction of the Church. Put simply, flag-waving westerners are at liberty to dictate their own morality as long as it does not infringe upon public law. There have been occasions when these morals contributed wisely to democracy; the elimination of slavery, granting suffrage to women and minorities, and socializing programs to address inner-city poverty and crime. The Church would have done as much. On the other hand, when the definition of morality leads to the breakdown of the traditional family, the plague of infanticide, culturalized homosexuality, assisted suicide, secular elitism and embryonic mortality, then democratic freedom suborns human sin. We may be free to believe whatever we choose as private individuals, but not at the expense of exploiting the afflictions and weaknesses of our fellow countrymen or forcing Christians to sustain the perversions and transgressions of liberalism. The authority of the Church may not have any standing in the courts, but when the reckoning comes and we are forced to justify our compulsions, those who have defied the Cross will be left groveling on their knees with no more in their hands than the evil remnants with which they squandered their own redemption. And, when the brilliance of Easter blinds them to the world and opens their eyes to the lives they should have led, there will be no articles to protect them, no fifth amendment to plead, no constitution to shield their insolence, and no way to appeal their condemnation. This is why they must enter the Church. Sinners require time to think about the effects of their pride, and their fate, misery, and detachment. Have they been engaged in conduct that is unworthy of intelligent beings? Is their momentum away from the Crucifixion that they must impact with the full weight of their sins? Common physics says that they will not change course unless they are affected by an outside force, which in this case is the Lord's redeeming touch. Even if they have committed no harm, they are still pagans in His eyes. Jesus will reinforce their better acts, but they have no intrinsic goodness without His Holy Sacrifice. And, this is why we should pray for them, not always with earthshattering homilies in thundering convention halls, but humbly from our homes with Providence breaking across our thresholds and calm breezes through the air, listening to the cardinals flutter, the faint voices of pedestrians passing by, and children playing next door. It is part of our consequential faith, and the whole world is changed by what we petition from our quaint domestic quarters. Thus, Our Lady speaks to us today about remaining determined to succeed. We are riding in time and headed for the regal chariot whose wheels will clap down streets of gold in a land far above this one. We will see the Heavenly Hosts there, and the Immaculate Virgin waving to us with Jesus in Her arms, welcoming us into the beauty of Paradise, if we but follow Her now.

  I have never recorded until this moment the most profound experience of these nearly two decades past. During the initial years of Our Lady's intercession, there was a time of deep sacrificial darkness in my emotions resulting from the diabolical onslaught against my heart by others for claiming to be a recipient of this miraculous charism. My being was being ripped away from this world and all the sensible elements that held comfort for me. It was an emotional infliction that lasted years in the tenderest places of my heart. One evening in the midst of this despondence when I thought I could endure it no longer, I was taken definitively by the Holy Spirit before Jesus' Throne. It all seems just a magnificent dream after all these years, but I stood before His majesty, one step down, staring into the glistening beauty of His eyes, taking-in all that He is in His Glory. The Beatific Light was unimaginable; the dominating resplendence of human perfection, Glory beyond all glory, an obliterating Love that had always existed throughout eternity, personified in the Man in front of me. I could write for years trying to describe it and never exhaust the ages. I experienced an omniscience of being and omnipotent vision, and a complete silence of will in the midst of it. All the greatness of human history emanated from Him in an undescribable way; the rolling of the ages, the rising and falling of times; not like looking through a portal or seeing a vision, but as a substantive unity of beingness, similar to contemplating the world and seeing Our Lord through our faith or peering at the Most Blessed Sacrament and seeing a human being. I looked at our Messiah and saw every aspect of Creation from end to end in reality and substance in a single moment, and felt its redeeming drama singing to my being. Somehow, I was united in experience with the most minute facet of every consequence of history through Him, with Him, and in Him. I saw the beauty of every sunrise and sunset that had ever split the horizons of time from every longitude and latitude of the globe, compounded and multiplied together in the same breathtaking collage, along with witnessing the sentiments of every soul who stood in the fading or expanding light of each one of them. I engaged a melding oneness with the heart of every person ever given the breath of life, experiencing and enduring each individual instant of their lives as if we had somehow been conjoined, spiritual twins the entire length of the ages; all the dreams torn asunder and the tears that fell, the joys, and the relief of being released from the pains of mortality. I heard all the symphonies that were never penned into their scores and the comprehensive opus of humanity's hidden visions which described the riveting essence of aspirations of every precious child. I saw the origin of all the refinement of Creation, the perfect pedigree of God's children, the lineage which produced divinity from nothingness, the bell of liberty which rang a single time and resonated a universe of souls, each sounding their unique tone of trembling beauty, consuming them, each and all, with the most magnanimous dignity that could ever have been consigned to the domain of sacrificial flesh. The summation and totality of all Beauty consumed the essence of my creation and revealed itself from its very Source, through every sense a spirit could possess, all in the same moment; so much that my meager mind now faintly has the capacity to move near its greatness, let alone the faculties to circumscribe such beatific magnitude to discern it again. I am simply left with the blessing of its mystical afterglow and the hope of someday being consumed by it for all ages with the contents of my heart reveling a unique beauty of its own in that revealing Eternal Light. It was the comprehensive dream of a Heart so sacred that an entire universe of life emanating its divine image had to be created, populated, redeemed, and sanctified to unveil its infinite nature to the realms of Eternity which would bask in the enshrined beauty of a God who would condescend to mortality to unite His Creation with Himself because He loved it so much. And, then standing before Him, He extended His hands to me, palms up, and rested them gently in my hands which I spontaneously extended as the response of my extinguished being. Hear me now humanity! As I looked down, my eyes fell upon the Sacred Wounds that have saved the world, that innumerable Saints throughout the centuries had pined in their contemplations to see, there lying right in my hands, glistening like diamonds, emanating a sensible detonation as if it was the moment of ignition of a weapon that could blink the vaults of the universe from blackness into the daylight of a new Creation. No power on any world can compete with these Sacred Artifacts of God in human flesh. I felt a mystical pressure to cry for the rest of Eternity, but only peaceful tears of gratitude trickled down my cheeks because His tender presence would not allow my composure to fall into that self-flagellating pit. I can still feel His hands resting in mine as I write this and see myself looking down at His gaping scars as if it was for the first time. He smiled at me so gently and approvingly through the sparkling of my tears, and without having to speak a word, told me to love and obey His Immaculate Mother no matter if the cost be scars such as His. He then tenderly and slowly withdrew His hands, still gently smiling, and assumed His position in the unimaginable Light that emanated from His Being. I just stood there gazing at Him, my soul fleeting peacefully through the revelations of human history. And, without knowing how, I found myself in this world again, still able to see the "all" for a moment before my vision was quickly dispersed like the scattering of a flock of feeding doves at the approach of a rambunctious pack of kindergartners. The vision of Glory became an eclipsed memory because my mind could no longer sustain the peaceful purity that consumed it only moments before. So easily it slipped away, and only on the pilgrimage of deep contemplative prayer does this exiled traveler again catch a glimpse of that glorious realm. In those moments, it comes out of the fog with concrete, glistening beauty, descending like a jeweled city that I only wish would allow me permanent citizenship in the ages to come. It is the memory of our sins in the flesh that disturbs the soul which then disallows the perpetual continuity of our participation in these glorious realms at every moment of our exilic lives.

    Hence, from that day onward, I have continued with the Holy Spirit "in residence" within my being, infused with a spiritual strength united with my memories that has sustained a fortified resilience I never possessed before those moments. So, from 2:45 a.m. on February 22, 1991 until the falling silent of Our Lady's words as the *Morning Star Over America* a short time after 2:29 p.m. on December 28, 2008, the Almighty Father has allowed humanity to witness openly what His Queen really means to the Church; Her hierarchical station, Her ecclesial authority, Her magnificent feminine grace, how She has been with us every moment since the beginning of human Redemption, and how She will remain in our midst nurturing our dignity until the battle is won and our arrival in Heaven into Her arms is secured. Let no one believe that Her miraculous intercession has in any way been diminished or that She has departed from any of us even the remotest distance simply because She has chosen to publicly enter a more contemplative state in relation to our position in exile. She truly would have wished to continue speaking volumes to Her American children, and will do so in more nuanced ways within the boundaries of our personal faith as time progresses. Her motherly care will continue. But, She was required by our human processes to demarcate a fixed point of closure to this particular revelation before She would be taken seriously in a more universal way and allowed access to Her children through the machinations of discernment by the Church. This is as it should be because the devil can cause great damage and disarray, and She wishes this work to be granted permanent protection within the great bastion of Her Son's Church. Our Virgin Mother wishes not that this great gift flounder in obscurity through the flailing faithlessness of men, or to be treated as the personal spiritual aberration of an eccentric, but rather that it be heeded as authoritorial from Her Immaculate Heart, but not authoritarian by any man's standards nor those of the Church. The work is not to be relegated to a private bin of personal grace in an attempt to disregard it with clearer conscience or dismiss it through ecumenical compromise which would serve only to placate those who would attack it with reckless pride upon its supernal truth gaining solid footing in the hearts of God's lost children. The *Morning Star Over America* has revealed with clarity Her ecclesial station within the Church as our Heavenly Mother; and She prefers nothing more, although Queen of Heaven and Earth, Co-Redemptrix and Mediatrix of All Graces, and Woman Clothed with the Sun are very profound and august titles to hold within Her Son's Kingdom. She has validated every sentiment and teaching that the Apostolic Church proclaims infallibly to describe Her, along with every affectionate moniker each Saint has been inspired to place before men in Her honor. And still, we have not spoken ample strains worthy of Her regal beauty. Through eighteen years of miraculous grace that shall continue for each of us in more personal ways to the ultimate conversion of the Earth, Our Lady has appeared in Light as the Roman Catholic Church has factually portrayed Her since the Apostolic Age. Therefore, my brother and I are happy for this final era of men and humbly honored to have been burdened with this sacrificial transcension of grace into our midst. We will continue to bear both the brunt of those who will never believe and the relentless mystical attacks that Satan will level against my brother and me personally as punishment for our obedient faith. He will create a cross for us because we love Jesus and Our Lady with the Christian power that he has been seeking to destroy since the sounding of the original Fiat. This miraculous revelation has really been nothing more than being told where to unearth a treasure whose beauty has lain buried in plain sight within the heart of the Roman Catholic Church for 2000 years. Mary, our Mother, has been with each of us our entire lives, and soon Her pedestal will come into full bloom where God will reveal with complete disclosure just how intimate that personal relationship has been; and the joyful weeping will begin. Until then, I extend to you the love and the trust that Our Lady has placed in my brother and me. These years have been a story of our love for humanity which shall wax to a crescendo of triumph. We love you. We have always loved you. And, we trust you to stay the course with us and let nothing diminish the faith to which you have dedicated your lives. This is why together we are able to rise in the morning and know that we need not remain frail or faulty. We have committed no infraction that cannot be forgiven. We are not weak in the face of the worst evil and darkness that has ever tried to lay a pall over our eyes. Satan will be able to lie to this world only a few moments longer. Then, he will be cast to irrevocable defeat, screaming why he ever stirred the sleeping giant in our Roman Catholic hearts. God is about to show him what humiliation really is. Now, I too thank you for having responded to the call of the *Morning Star Over America*. Her tender reveille of Wisdom will resound with clarity and compassion in the pages of this apocalyptic work through the end of time.

> **Hail Mary, full of grace, the Lord is with Thee.**
> **Blessed art thou amongst women,**
> **And blessed is the Fruit of Thy Womb, Jesus.**
>
> **Holy Mary, Mother of God, pray for us sinners,**
> **now and at the hour of our death. Amen.**

MORNING STAR OVER AMERICA

The New Millennium
In the Year of Our Lord
AD 2006

* *On December 5, 2004, Our Lady began revealing names of some of Her children from Christian history who are presently Saints in the Kingdom of Heaven, although they have yet to be canonized by the Magisterium of the Roman Catholic Church. One purpose of this delineation is for everyone to realize that the Church's official recognition of Saints is an authoritative declaration of fact regarding the citizenry of Heaven, rather than a conferment of deliverance. Our Holy Mother wishes the world to know that millions have achieved the blessedness of Paradise who will never be recognized by the Faith-Church on Earth. Therefore, none should fear exclusion from the Kingdom of God because they will not be hailed in the eyes of the Church. These Saints' names have been denoted with an asterisk.*

Sunday, January 1, 2006
Solemnity of Mary, Mother of God
1:33 p.m.

"Dear little children, the calendar has turned another year, but the Love of God remains the same; yesterday, today, and forever. I am with you again to say that Jesus' Sacrifice heals the brokenhearted, converts wayward sinners, emits His Heraldic Light upon the ages, and gives you direction to manifest fairness among yourselves. Today, I exhort you to live dutifully, with the same hope by which you have encountered the past. While humanity groans and disagrees, feel the peace of the Holy Spirit guiding you to a simpler life as you practice your faith. Conduct yourselves honorably, letting go of the disquietude that creates such negativity in the secular market. My angelic ones, I invite you to embrace this stillness of the heart especially during the new year. Ignore the tongues of sarcastic sinners, and pray that they will soon repent. If you do not, My dear children, you may become embittered and impatient; you may not be receptive to the assurances that Jesus places in your hearts. Where there is Christian piety, celebrate it. When you see suffering, ask the Lord to end it. Where there is heresy, stand upright against it. Remember that you can live diversely in the world, and even motley, but you are not permitted to deviate from Divine Truth. I am responsible for shaping your interaction with other men. For nearly fifteen years, I have taught you to rebuke reprobates who are luring innocent souls from the Lord, and you have complied. What I am seeking is not a form of surrender, but choosing the better path in the struggle against godless men. I am not asking you to relinquish your voice about the injustices you see, but to view them from the perspective that they are near an end. Be more hopeful about future events, and understand that My having taught you about admonishing lost sinners since February 22, 1991 has been a sanctifying blessing. Beginning this year, I urge you to make an assessment of the Earth as it should be. It is fitting for you to find the lost while espousing the pleasance of the Holy Spirit from within. This is My request for 2006. I offer My intercessory prayers and pledge that I will ask Jesus to touch you in all ways, discernable and beyond your senses. These are grand and glorious times you are living in service to Heaven, and God knows that you work sacrificially for Him with steadfastness, honesty, and humility. When Jesus numbers the Saints at the conclusion of the Earth, you shall stand among them. Also today, My angels, I wish to speak about what your purification means. In your spiritual communion with the Lord, you know that you are called to an endearing holiness that takes you to the arches of righteous action. The years have taught you hard lessons, that you must enter the fight for Christian virtue, choose your battles wisely, pray fervently to preclude the transgressions of humanity, and understand that your hearts and souls are the profits of My Son's

Holy Sacrifice. Jesus desires that you accept His Crucifixion and Resurrection, knowing that your faith brings the realization of every hope you have ever espoused. Do not become exasperated about the painstaking process of reaching lost souls because time cannot delay the eventualities of Truth. God knows what is occurring around the world, and He is often disheartened by what He sees. He depends on the intercession of the faithful to shepherd these sinners into His presence. Your petitions are bountiful because they amend the errors of humanity. I am aware that it is agonizing to witness the desecration of the relics of the Church, and that you are offended by the unforgiveness of secular idolists. I wish I could announce that everything will change overnight, but you know that it requires more sacrifices to mend the ills of the world. The self will of humanity is rarely commandeered by God because He prefers His creatures to convert of their own volition. As I have said, what kind of love would there be if the receiver extorted it from the giver? Therefore, we welcome 2006 knowing that Jesus will destroy His enemies with one awe-striking manifestation, which He may do soon. I beseech you to believe that you are making a difference, that your contributions to the Kingdom of Heaven are meaningful. Please trust Me and know that I am nurturing your eternal exculpation.

It is with good tidings that I come on this first day of the year, especially filled with thankfulness that you have remained before Me in prayer. My Special one, My earlier request does not imply that you have not written a useful essay to reproach the media for their support of abortion. By all means, give it to them. You should issue such reprimands because this is not the kind of negativity I am asking My children to avoid. I am attempting to reverse the vexation of the spirit that comes from encountering the indifference of pagans. My purpose is to seek in you a renewed sense of solace that springs from the Holy of Holies. There are insufficient means for Me to state how gratefully I wept while you were creating your text about the media. The Truth cannot be proclaimed more clearly than this. Your writing is filled with soul-searching eloquence and inspiration. This is what will be reflected by your manuscripts as the future takes its course. You should feel this fulfillment inside, knowing that the Holy Spirit is working through you as you form your thoughts. I ask that you place the letter to the media in one of your books because it emits intense converting light for those who are trapped inside the dungeon of their own disobedience. Grace, Truth, Wisdom, peace, and hope are exalted from the love at the center of your heart. Your brother is correct in his assertion; you have a brilliant heart, you glorify the excellence of God. And, this is another wonder that will bring My children to take your work seriously and accept their Savior. I remind you time and again that you do not realize the good you are accomplishing, praying with your brother for so many years. This home is a flowerbed of spiritual conversion, the magnification of the teaching, Passion, Crucifixion, and Resurrection of Christ Jesus. I have no doubt that you know this. I ask you to feel confident that the decades have sustained your honor, that the knowledge you possess about the Kingdom of God will prove good counsel for humanity. I am so appreciative for your life, your gifts to Jesus, your sanctity, valor, vision, and eagerness that I cannot place it into words. If there were times when you seemed less than patient, let them depart your mind because you have more than overcome them. Hold to the promises Jesus made, that His Truth is within you, His Sacrifice is your relief, and His Wisdom is your way of internalizing Heaven's plans for human redemption. As for your brother, he is aware of the burden he is placing on you, and the guilt he feels is overwhelming. He is but a humble child, and is afraid of many things. He worries that your work might be abbreviated. *(Timothy recently had gallbladder extraction surgery with serious postoperative complications.)* Yes, he has studied 2,000 years of history and seen that countless disciples of Jesus have been sacrificed too soon. He wishes to proceed toward the conversion of lost sinners for many more years, but he fears that he may not live to do it. It seems apparent that your lives have special meaning, and he does not want it to end. Thank you for having such compassion for him. I promise that Heaven will repay you a hundredfold. It is proper that the Queen of Paradise be honored on the first day of the year, as I was accorded the blessing of first knowing the Salvation of the exiled world. I stand at the pinnacle of the universe and survey the landscape of human endeavors, and I am warmed by the determination I see. The pits of darkness surrounding you are forces against the Kingdom of Divine Love that are exacerbated by the hatred of unconverted men. You view them as evil because you live above them like an eagle escorting a rainbow. Please share My intentions with the Church, realizing that there are battles still being fought by heroic Christians. This Feast reflects the hope of the Mother of Jesus, and I am honored to know that you have given yourselves to the conversion of the lost on behalf of My Son. When you venerate Me, you open-wide the sentiments of humanity to reach for pure faith, to grasp the bastion of righteousness that God has laid before you in Jesus in the manger, on the Cross, and at His right hand in Heaven. My children, I will never abandon you. I shall pray for you and proclaim to God that you are worthy of Absolution. And, according to the Father's Will, I shall procure the answers to your petitions. Thank you for accepting your part in the renewal of the Earth, and thank you for responding to My call."

Sunday, January 8, 2006
Saint Emeritus McCann [1566-1604]*
1:46 p.m.

"Wellness and good wishes I pray for you, My angelic ones, that you may know the intensity of God's charitable peace. Today, I have come to speak to you about the facets of love that give you strength, perseverance, and comfort. I offer My guidance and support as you battle the forces that attempt to weaken your faith. If you allow, I will lead you to a categorical comprehension of your role in the redemption of sinners; and it is obvious that your heartstrings belong to Me. I am confident that you as My children have placed your suffering and sacrifices in the context and sanctuary of the Sorrowful Passion and Crucifixion of Jesus because you hold to the virtues of Christian Truth. There can be no diminishment of your participation in the cultivation of the Earth, and no rescinding of your desire to succeed in exalting the Kingdom of God through your prayers. What is revealed as the Church observes the Epiphany is that the whole of humankind has been irrevocably touched, converted, healed, and sanctified in Jesus' birth, ministry, and Sacrifice on the Cross. You are aware of the signs that foretell the objectives of your faith, that you are fighting a triumphant cause for the transformation of humankind into the likeness of the Son of Man. What is transferred to you is a concise perception of yourselves in His image and in the Divine Glory by which you are vindicated and sought to embrace. Charity and goodness are integral parts of this faith, My children, because they are themes that run concurrent with your acceptance of God's Will. The Church's loyalty to Him is of old, and you are successors to the gracious calling of its heroic disciples. Speak among yourselves about more ways to concur with their assertions and comply with their requests, begotten and dispensed by the benevolence of the Holy Spirit. It is within such meditation that you comprehend the true purpose of your faith, your role in the unfolding of Salvation history, and the means by which you may lead your lost brothers and sisters to a full appreciation of the preciousness of life. We pray that My words fall upon welcoming ears, and that those who hear will comply with all they know to be the redemptive beckoning of Christ. There are so many missed opportunities for His people to speak on His behalf because they are distracted from the Light of Heaven. Graces flow copiously from there, and My children see them as such. How difficult it is to concentrate upon the Sacred Mysteries of the Salvation of humanity when there are so many other digressions. This is why you must ponder wisely and discern from among many influences which ones are worth your time and effort. I speak not only to My messengers, but to the millions who live-out their lives on faith alone, who are business owners and employees, those whose vocations include working in the Church, and young people who are designing ways to build their future. I promise that God will provide the answers to your prayers because He vows the sanctification of His Creation. He yearns for you to place the element of time in proper priority, realizing that it is deceptive for those who do not know the meaning of life. Heaven does not ask that much from you, My children. Jesus does not coerce you into becoming statesmen or Doctors of the Church, nor does He demand that you enter religious orders. He simply asks that you surrender your hearts to Him, no matter your walk of life or chosen field. This is the essence of the belief Jesus would have you invoke. My Son does not call for your martyrdom on your journey of conversion, but there can be no doubt that you must crucify your self-will to confirm your compliance with His Gospel. Let not your words fall silent when the Earth wails for your voice in the struggle to enlighten faithless men. Do not cower in back alleys and boweries when Jesus asks you to command corporeal purity from those farthest from Him. You must rise above the vexations that torment you, the temptations that would have you look another way, and the delinquents who attempt to dissuade you from finishing your work. There may be incalculable hours remaining in this world, but you do not know which is the one when the Son of Man will return and conclude the mortality of the Earth.

My Special son, I see that your spirit seems much higher than a week ago, and you are entertaining the hope that conditions are changing for the better. I wish to respond to your question about your workplace by saying that your doubt as to whether you are doing what God desires is ill-founded. You are too self-critical if you believe that He does not warrant you to pursue other opportunities. I assure you that you are close to Me, and you are accomplishing the Will of the Father as intently as ever. Please do not feel so dubious about your contributions to the conversion of humanity. I promise that the Lord is pleased with you, and I am elated that you are praying with Me for the dispensing of My messages. To be sure, you have placed them in public fora for the Mystical Body of Christ to peruse. This is the purpose of your mission, and they are responsible to listen. As I have said, the Holy Spirit will guide their consciences to the work we have done together; it is not a matter of whether you have been sufficiently effective in propagating them. Therefore, be at peace knowing that your efforts will achieve the results that Jesus intends. You have entered 2006 with questions about your Apostolate, the future at your workplace, and other important issues. I call you to remember the apsis you have reached to incorporate My weekly messages into several published manuscripts that you never thought you would complete. Offer thanksgiving to God for the good we have done, and know that Jesus is cognizant of your life with your brother, heralding the Gospel. Please welcome the days with higher hope and less despair. Your heart is reacting to the negativity around you in ways that attempt to dampen the tranquility in your life. I have helped make you more religiously strong than to permit these things to wear you down. If you trust Me as you have in the past, you will recognize that transitions are what you make of them. I have told you to seek a different career, and you have been praying for one. If it is the Will of the Father, you shall secure it. If it appears that it could be later, it will be because He has more work for you to do. Indeed, He may wish you to remain only a little longer while there are other critical events preceding your departure. In other words, pray for guidance and patience, and God will prepare the way He knows best. You must remember that you reside in a rural region that offers little opportunity for gainful advancement in areas other than politics, so your position of employment is a blessing. However, this is not something that should bind you to a location in which the atmosphere tests your spirit every time you enter the door. There are countless things more valuable than money, and peace of mind is chief among them. Working toward another sensible project will require a great deal of practical planning and completion of goals that will strain your resolve even more than now. If you believe that is justified, then you should proceed with your preparation. There is a surrender of privacy when someone opens himself to secular-capitalist ventures. My little one, please do not become frustrated by thinking that you are not evangelizing the Word of God, for I have told you that you are doing so. I believe the origin of your stress to be your occupation. It is the sole reason for your desire to strike-out on your own. It has nothing to do with going where you can more easily relate My messages. I understand your position about becoming self-employed so you can reserve more time for your writing. I am telling you that your Apostolate is a body delicately formed with prefigured purpose. I have heard your prayers for change; Jesus knows about your wishes; your brother offers his daily holy hours for your intentions, and God the Father sees best how you can serve His earthly vineyard for the conversion of lost souls, the exaltation of the Cross, your veneration of Me, your invocation of the prayers of the Saints, and the purification of this world that cries-out for holiness. You are blessed in ways that will not be abundantly clear until you have made a wholesale reorientation, in future times when you look back upon these months. If that fulcrum comes during Easter, then this is the Will of God. If it occurs later, it does not imply that you have done nothing to assist it. I am asking that you abandon the frustration that exposes your heart to turmoil and causes you to turn away from the hope that Jesus has been giving you since you were born. How else can I express the infinity by which you are loved? I only ask that you be pleased that I have come with words of encouragement, knowing that you pray for peace and purity for the world, that you are a staunch opponent of the antagonists against God's Kingdom, and that you will never surrender the fight that the Saints of the Church sustained during their mortal years. Thank you for your trust and vision, for rising in strength and courage to travel the sojourn of human exile the way God has deemed. I will stand beside you in your endeavors and ask Jesus to bless you with success."

Sunday, January 15, 2006
St. Mariana Sagredo, Mystic [AD 844-893]*
1:43 p.m.

"The dearest days occur when I speak to My children who prayerfully kneel beneath My Motherly Mantle. If you allow Me to accentuate the intentions I have come to accomplish, your hopes and dreams will be fulfilled. I wish to effect the cultivation of the heart in the perfection of Triune Love so the toxic repugnance of human sin can be eradicated from the Earth. I desire your prayers on behalf of the forsaken, for the millions worldwide who are enduring gross neglect, illness, poverty, and oppression. No matter what the adversaries of the Cross attempt, they cannot hinder Christians from reciting their prayers. They cannot nullify the heart by anything they do. They cannot steal faith from the conscience, and they cannot inhibit the beatific vision that is granted by the Almighty Father unto the inspired soul. Today, we assemble for your blessings of freedom, health, piety, goodness, and peace. We pool our petitions with others who are reserving this Sunday in supplication for their needs. We share and celebrate your Christian faith with gladness, knowing that your belief in Jesus lives in perpetuity. My messages are brief, My little ones, but the Divine Truth is eternal. I appear with good will to bring you peace. My Immaculate Heart overflows with admiration for My cherished ones who are obedient to God. I know where the Holy Spirit resides, deep inside your hearts of miraculous love. My purpose is to teach you to be aware of the ill-conceived motivations of the enemies of the Church that are sired by illegitimacy and reared in an environment of corruption. The human species must always remember that there is no harvest in smoldering ashes. Calm meditation neutralizes the effusive verbalizations that devalue your poise. Your Mother is aware of the adversities you face in your lives. Believe it or not, there is sophistication in your suffering, even as you toil every day for righteousness, sweating your veins' crimson dew onto the earthen floor. Jesus is your sustenance in all ways, your pillar of resurgence when you feel suppressed. Remember that a well-grounded Christian authenticates his beliefs when he is scrutinized, under pressure, or in the heated throes of persecution. God alone is the arbiter of Truth, and His Wisdom is a savory gin for the deficits in your knowledge. This is why He sends Jesus to teach you, and His Mother as your eternal Advocate before Him. The poor are evidence that there is much more work to be done, but too many sinners seem unaware of their suffering because the reckless are blinded by their own errors and excesses. Those who have only little endure a hostile, obnoxious, insulting, and degrading existence. And, even when men in foreign lands promise food and water, they are often unable to pay the cartage to deliver them to the needy. This is why I call you to invoke the Lord's intervention. Jesus was born to a people of sound Mosaic practicality, and He requires the Church to embrace His Messianic principles. My children, you foster the emergence of your friends from the depths of despair. While knowing that they are frail, acknowledge that not every mistake is a scandal. Moreover, do not demand your honor when doing the Lord's work; and especially do not covet fiscal rewards. My Special and Chosen ones, you are living your profession of faith with distinction. Wherever you go, the Love of God attends you because you possess His Grace within you. Let the future be bright by expecting His salutary blessings. Anticipate your victory in the Sacred Heart of Jesus, and He will take you to the Kingdom you seek in Him. My Special son, I know that you are enjoying My messages from the turning of the century. It is through your faith that you have received them. I offer everything in accordance with the Will of God, and I assure you that I present your intentions to Jesus. I wish for you to enjoy the day while easing your mind. It is important that you employ patience while your brother recovers from his surgery. It will be difficult for him to leave home on many days. I urge you to pray that his health returns to normal. And, thank you for trimming his hair, feeding him, giving him shelter, and tending to his emotional needs."

Sunday, January 22, 2006
33rd Anniversary of Roe v. Wade
United States Supreme Court
3:06 p.m.

"Creation is altered every time you pray, little ones. This is why I come to you with My request for you to be persistent in your ardent supplications to God, that you will seek from Him the blessings that will ultimately change the Earth. I tell you that you are partaking not only in the transition of the old world into the New, but the transformation of the one humanity who shall inhabit it. Today, we observe the grotesque anniversary of the American decision to legalize infanticide, where already more than 50 million unborn children have been killed. Were it not for the prayers of the faithful, the number lost to the scourge of abortion would far exceed the population of the entire United States. While this is no consolation, it is proof that your petitions have great power. Please do not stop praying for the end of abortion until it exists no more! I call you to the intensity of the heart that will cause you to be moved by the Holy Spirit to be perseverant. Even though you cannot yet see the beginning of immortal life, surely you must envision the Love that is bringing it before you. Also today, I beseech My children to call forward the Holy Angels, and especially the Guardian Angels, to preserve and protect the moral conscience of each expectant mother, that they will give birth to their little children. After all, it is the judgement of the child-bearer that determines the fate of her unborn progeny. We shall ask the Lord to touch them in heartening ways, that they will recognize the gift of life that He has given them. Please call on the intercession of the Holy Innocents to safeguard their young counterparts who are enwombed in earthly mothers. I promise that grave Justice will be heaped upon America for the sin of abortion, which I have foretold and about which you have written in your books. The call of the Christian conscience requires the tenacity of prayer, that you will speak to God in ways that few before have done. Seek in Him the peace and reverence that will tender your hearts to mutual forgiveness. Perceive in the Love of the Father the sacrificial balm that takes your spirits to perfection in the Crucifixion of Jesus. And, know that you are blessed beyond all imagining to be part of the redemption of men, that you already anticipate the end of the world. You are not cowards; you do not fear the howling of the wolves; you approach Me with piety and wishfulness, and I return to you the Gospel of Jesus as your enlightened faith. The great battle for souls continues to rage, oftentimes clandestinely around you. The search for moral goodness is an interior calling for every man, woman, and child. You instill in them the vision to see Heaven more clearly when you pray from the heart for them, when you allow the Holy Paraclete to permeate your thoughts and actions. This seems a simple prospect, little ones, but many in your company are too distracted by workings of their own making to heed the call. They cannot be satisfied in their station in life because they refuse to permit their spiritual motivations to grow. This is why I am speaking to you. We are making their consciences fertile ground for the seed of righteousness to be planted in their hearts. I assure you that you are prospering a worthy mission, one that will purify the Mystical Body of Christ for the Final Judgement. It is with admiration that I tell you that even though you cannot see with your eyes, the people you were meant to affect through your prayerful works are being touched, and they are now converting to Jesus' Sacrifice. I invite you to accept My words as Truth, that you trust the Will of God in the knowledge I am transferring to you. These are more than auspicious years, they are revolutionary times during which the veritable stature of humankind is being reconfigured for the ages. This is why your success is so crucial. You have My gratitude and the benefaction of God for staying the course, not surrendering to temptations of the flesh and materialism, and keeping your hearts focused on the culmination of the Earth in the Sacred Heart of Jesus. My Special son, your devotion to Me makes you one with Jesus and causes Him to look upon you with appreciation. I cannot reveal how some matters might evolve, but I assure you that Jesus' Love will be with you during the remainder of your days. Thank you for taking such good care of your brother, as you know the problems he has faced. It is imperative that he follow a strict diet while his body is convalescing because the associated symptoms have a mortality factor. Also, *Supernal Chambers* is an extremely beautiful book in that it teaches humanity how to become more holy in a preemptive way. I am overjoyed to speak to you! Thank you for praying for the end of abortion, that the unborn will be given the gift of birth. It is the delight of Heaven that they should live."

Saturday, January 28, 2006
Saint Thomas Aquinas, Doctor [1225-1274]
1:24 p.m.

"My Most Immaculate Heart is a lovely dwelling place for your souls, My children, because I nurture Salvation for you there, My Son in whom your trust is worthily placed. I appear here knowing that you pray for this broken world, that you envision the moment when all Creation will be one. Today, we remember the distinguished Doctor of the Church, Saint Thomas Aquinas, whose perception of deific hypostasis was sculpted by the Holy Spirit in extraordinary ways. It is not necessary that you be his likeness in Christological intellectualism, but it would be fitting that you imitate his devotion to the Lord in the Eucharist. You desire the conversion of lost sinners because you are striving with Me toward that goal. We shall not concede the fight for every soul we can convert to Christianity, that all will accept the Holy Cross, the Blood of Jesus, as expiation for their sins. As we move forward, know that you have My sacred blessings to accompany you on your journey of faith. You need not be concerned about the fashions that attempt to distract you or fearing the enemies of God's Kingdom. There are manifest ways for you to elevate Jesus in your completion of the work He has given you, and the most honorable is your obedience to Me. Our peaceful correspondence means the difference between beauty and unsightliness, freedom and slavery, perfection and corruption, Salvation and condemnation, and springtime versus nuclear winter. I will guide you to safety in Jesus' Sacred Heart because I am the Mother of Love, Matriarch of the Blessed Sacrament, and Queen of Heaven and Earth. It is with enhanced hope that you seek in Me the intercession that provides the benisons from God for which you have longed. I have reproached humanity to ensure your moral integrity and the meticulous infusion of Eternal Wisdom for the Earth, and to see that your contemplations are tapered toward a more refined atonement for your spirits. I anticipate your attentiveness during your strenuous degrees of self-immolation in the darkest nights and the early morning golden skies of autumn. I encourage your vision of happiness because you are capable of achieving love, that you must beware of the devious motivations of partisan schemers and those who are morally primitive, cold and heartless, unclean, impious, and devoid of any semblance of righteous spiritual direction. Since I have come, you need not speak of hope in glimmers, but in deluges, starbursts, and rainbows. Jesus knows your grief and the torments that haunt you. He can see the apostleship of the Church in your weary eyes and the expressions of mourning that emanate from your faces. When you are bereaved during your laborious sanctification, the Son of Man is your consolation. If you stand firm in faith, I promise that Jesus will reward you for your achievements in a universe filled with infinite unknowns. Satan has told Americans a tale about the exercise of freedom that includes acts of sin, ones that are so abhorrent to the Father that they defy every sense of decency. This is why the Holy Spirit reorients your thoughts and actions whenever your desires and preferences are not aligned with the teachings of the Church. If you were to hear Jesus' voice today, He would insist that you do not suspend your conscience, even for a moment, because your acceptance of the Lord's Will is a natural reflex to the committed Christian. He will touch you if you let Him because the heart is highly absorbent; it deflects very little that impacts it in a spiritually reparative way. The message of the Gospel is clear and cannot be hidden in the thicket of humanity's indiscretions. When you attend the Holy Sacrifice of the Mass, you witness the expelling of human arrogance, ridding the Earth of the parasitic influences of hatred and indignity. Thank you for calling on Me, and please know that I will always be here for you. My Special son, I am heartened that you are writing your books here at home with your brother, and that you are planning to reach-out to others with the Sacred Word of Truth. It is imperative that your spirit not become stagnant while pursuing our mission. Each day is another opportunity for you to see humanity anew, to admire in the Church the pious goals that you share with Heaven. As I have said, I speak during these days of 2006 with every intention of completing the transformation of your prodigal brothers and sisters. Thank you for receiving Me, especially today, because it means so much to the Salvation of the world. Creation is a holier place because the Lord birthed you here, and His Kingdom is advanced by the dedication you have invested. The Father will bless you many times over for your goodness, piety, and servitude. Please remember to pray for the intentions of Pope Benedict XVI on behalf of all the peoples of the Earth."

Sunday, February 5, 2006
Saint Agatha of Catania, Martyr [d. 251]
4:55 p.m.

"Today, little children, I pray with you in the hope that humanity changes, that everyone whose lives are aching will be consoled by the piety of the Lord, and that their conversion to the Holy Cross will be comely. It is true that it takes their contrition and willingness to accompany the Grace of God on their faith journey. We also pray for the mitigation of sin, for the eradication of pestilence, poverty, disease and suffering, and for all the petitions My children are raising to Jesus. There is intense Light in the offing today because the Church is poised to accept His peace. The faithful are prepared for the consolation of the Holy Spirit in ways that are unparalleled in history. Can you sense the anticipation of the world for something new, a better and brighter future? We already know the comprisal of that dawn. It is obvious that the Will of God resides there. When you rise for your morning's work, you realize that the unfolding of His Kingdom grows ever wider. Therefore, it is with joy that I speak to you in preparation for the granting of the miracles you seek. Let us pray for the unborn, for those who are contemplating self-injury, for the unchurched, for the committing of all human hearts to the Most Sacred Heart of Jesus, and for the remaking of the face of the Earth to reflect the beauty of Heaven. There will be varying discourses in the next months about the urgency of the ages, those spectacular historical moments that are often repeated where wars are redeemed for peace, where injury leads to pardon, where breaches are repaired by forgiveness, and where the seed of brotherhood is sown for future reunions. I am hopeful, My little children, that humanity will collect all its finest hours into one day of charity, hope, and love. Let it be true that they come to Me for Wisdom and blessings from Paradise. I carry the Child Jesus in My arms for that reason. If only the bitter and sorrowful will call upon Me, I will soften their hearts and make them satisfied. I will decide tenderly in their favor and approach Jesus on their behalf. Indeed, I will intercede in levels that are overwhelming for these times. My Special and Chosen ones, I speak briefly today, but sincerely. It is imperative that you remember that Jesus inspires you, that He instructs you about living in ways that you have never thought. God loves you and wishes you to live abundantly in Him. While this seems difficult at times, His Will is best for everything you shall ever learn, teach or avow on behalf of His Kingdom. Thank you, My Special one, for addressing your brother's medical needs. It is clear that it will require intense efforts to stabilize his health, but each day is an opening for the doctors to tend to him. There are many beautiful things that God provides for you, such as the gifts you have received, the blessings from Heaven that offer you foresight, and the Glory by which your souls are nourished and perfected. It must be obvious to you how supernatural is God's Light. Timothy is receiving the medication he needs, thanks to your generosity. And, as for your holiness, you have never been in need of change because your spiritual heart has not seen a moment's diminishment. I adore the way you pity your broken brothers and sisters, those who suffer and the innocent, and the devotion you extend in your life for Jesus. Should all the world have your faith, it would be healed. Please pray again for the intentions of the Holy Father in Rome this week."

Saturday, February 11, 2006
Our Lady of Lourdes [1858]
2:04 p.m.

"With sincere elation, I speak to you about the Sacred Mysteries of human redemption and enjoin you to pray for the conversion of lost sinners. I am the Immaculate Conception. My holiness is the origin of your blessings, My Grace the template for your relief. It is the Eternity of all souls we seek, that they will reside in Heaven with Me and Jesus, the Angelic Court, and the Hosts who have celebrated the anagogy of your prayers. Today, I speak about your own spiritual obedience in the wake of the persecution you endure. Remember the great Saint Bernadette, that she was never deterred from her work by those who ridiculed her. She is an influential intercessor for your intentions before the Holy of Holies. Her simplicity, honesty, and meekness are lessons for Christians today. What I asked of her would have humiliated the proud, but she was pleased to respond to My request because she knew that her life satisfied an important need in the Plan of God. After seeing Me, she never denied My presence. When she was asked to convey My messages, she did so with innocence. And, when she was called to suffer torment and endure physical pain, she did so with thankfulness that such unity with the Holy Cross was willed for her. It is crucial that you remember the response of Saint Bernadette as much as the miracle of My apparitions. Thus, I seek humanity to invoke her memory with gratitude. Her example is unmatched in your time. Therefore, as you pray for the conversion of the world and the gifts you seek from God, imitate the life of Saint Bernadette as your model. Some of My seers have approached Me saying that it must have been easy for Bernadette to be unassuming because she was so young when I appeared to her. However, simplicity and humility do not discriminate in Christian hearts. You are called to be like little children in your allegiance to Jesus, and wise in matters of Truth as the Doctors of the Church. This is not an insurmountable mission as you live-out your faith. You have been given plentiful examples in the lives of the Saints, in the sacred priesthood, and through the Holy Spirit inside your hearts. Also today, I exhort humanity to pray for the solidarity of nations around the world who are facing warring religions. Belief in God is a blessing for His flock, but to harbor discord is a damaging occurrence for those who practice their faith. Hatred and violence do not address the question of how believers should interact. If only the millions around the globe who believe in God would more outwardly display their duties in honoring Him, there will be no conflicts between them. I implore you to engage the fight against the real enemies, that of unchecked evil, indifference, exploitation, and impurity. Pray as one humanity under Heaven, one body of goodness who prevails upon the Lord for the blessings you need to grow in faith, live in peace, and inherit the awareness that you will soon see His glorious Face. Indeed, fight against the antagonists of the Church by praying for them, asking Jesus to intercede with strength and prudence. Beseech Divine Truth to inhabit the hearts of your adversaries who would rather see you fail in your noble works than convert a single soul. I assure you that God listens to your supplications. He understands the descriptions of your plight in your litanies. Heaven is eager to cease your sorrows, supplanting them with paradisial joy. Nothing of ill-favor is wished upon you by the Heavenly Hosts; they desire your perfect union with the Most Sacred Heart of Christ. There is a great deal of debate about whether the Gospel is relevant in the 21st century or if it has become antiquated by the passing of time. Anyone who maintains that the New Covenant of Jesus Christ no longer applies to the exiled world is under the influence of Satan. You must pray for lost sinners who advocate false choices that suborn sin. Abortion is a manifestation of evil, and same-sex unions spew directly from the mouth of the devil.

 I wish for My children to be delighted knowing that the Truth of the Holy Gospel has won. Do not despair that you do not seem to be making a difference because you are adding to the Kingdom of God gifts and graces that you cannot see. Know with sureness and satisfaction that the universe is being reshaped by your prayers; the ascension of humanity is being returned to its proper course, and Satan is breathing his last gasps. Everything you see that seems contradictory to the Kingdom of God is in its last throes. Eternity will bear-out what I am saying. Just like those who persecuted Saint Bernadette, they will arrive at the conclusion that they are on the wrong side of immortal history. I assure you that it is difficult to see this sometimes, and it may seem as though the Lord is taking a lifetime to respond. However, if you are persistent in the ways I have told, you will partake of the Victory of Eternity with the Angels and Saints, knowing that the battle was worthy of your efforts. In the aftermath of human exile, you will see that your life was the beginning of your journey to infinity and permanence. Every day you live is another opportunity to ask Jesus to endure it more intimately with you. His presence is enhanced by your lives; His Spirit flourishes by the opening of your hearts. While you are unsure what the future may bring, know that it is filled with added struggles, more petitions to lift, great suffering for many, and the marching of an untold number of souls into the arms of Jesus because of your willingness to succeed. I am with you to help carry your burdens. My prayers are forever your support. My Special son, thank you and your brother for receiving Me in this place. There is a mighty Grace that showers upon you every day, not just as we speak. Love emits from this home like light from a beacon. I cannot tell you that there will be no more difficult days. However, I would never give you false hope that the future will be anything other than that which God has deigned. He loves you with an affection that is unparalleled in the annals of Creation. His timeless divinity is the breeze behind your back. There is no doubt that you already know these things, and that nothing will befall you that is not ultimately for the good of the conversion of the wicked. Thank you again for taking such wonderful care of your brother. His health is susceptible to fail if you do not remain on course. His body is in a precarious state in that his condition could go either to the better or continue to deteriorate. It is by your saintly care that he will not pass into Heaven on February 22, 2006. Therefore, you must remain on guard that you not take for granted the progress he has made since we spoke last week. I have spent fifteen years telling you to be prepared at any moment for the culmination of time. You know when to act and what to do based upon the wisdom in your heart. If a particular venture seems insolvent in time and material terms, it is best not to enter into it. The Holy Spirit allows you great latitude to discern what avenues to embark and which to avoid. I have seen nothing to suggest that you are doing anything unworthy of a messenger or your station in life. If you are forging a sword with a hammer, and you hear that a ship is docking at a nearby seaport, knowing that your sword is necessary for the protection of the crew, would you drop what you are doing and watch the ship enter the port? Then, do not worry about Armageddon unless you hear that it is not such a ship, but Jesus' Almighty Judgement at last. Yes, whatever you do on Earth in accordance with your prudent discernment is fitting preparation for His return. Your actions will lead sinners to My messages. Thank you for being strong in faith and Truth, for fighting the good fight of Christian reason, for promising Jesus that your life has become the begetting of millions of converted souls, and for taking care of your ailing brother with such saintly accord. If anyone should inquire, he is in guarded condition."

Sunday, February 19, 2006
St. Germaine Hernandez [1867-1924]*
10:08 a.m.

"With edifying splendor, I speak of the loving relationship between My Son and your wounded souls. Today, we pray for beatific sight to find lodging in every heart, that all will be comforted by the Providence of God in ways they have never known. Little ones, you carry a tremendous responsibility of faithfulness every day, and you must be perseverant in remaining true to your cause. How awful are the attacks you endure from others, from the elements of the Earth, and from your own self-doubts. God wishes that you will strengthen the trust you have placed in Jesus so your existence in exile will be more sustaining. He has given you the power of prayer for your struggles and the vision of the Cross during your plight. When shrouds of darkness attempt to dampen your faith, remember to summon His Divine Light as your courage. There is no monotony in human life if you see every hour as a gift from Him.

When the dawn breaks, you are given yet another venue to grow in holiness in reflection of Jesus' tenacity and the Truth that is now consuming Creation. I urge you to encounter the years with renewed fervor, with an awe-inspiring reverence for Wisdom. This is why I implore you to preserve the dignity of the unborn so they can be given the birth they deserve. It is also the reason I requisition your prayers to end famine and disease, and afflictions of all kinds. My dear ones, your spiritual lives are the framework of your virtue. This is what you will bring to Heaven soon to live with the Angels and Saints. If you remain steadfast in knowing that your deliverance is at hand, you will see a bright future ahead; you will accept that your lives have higher meaning. Thank you for praying for all the intentions I have asked you to support. The prospect that you are imploring God for His intervention is welcomed by the Hosts of Heaven. Today, I beseech you to pray for the waiting Bride of Christ, that the Church will remain strong in hope throughout the closing ages. There is no question that the faith of humanity is being tested during these difficult times, and the viability of your trust in God must be made clear to those around you. It is true, My children, that others will emulate your Christian conviction if you practice it loyally, knowing that Jesus is beside you every moment, shepherding you to righteousness. You sometimes stray because you do not always trust Him; it is this simple. When in your meditations you remember My faith, your spirituality becomes more clear. I have brought humanity through centuries of wonder and inspiration by My advocacy and intercession. My little ones, it is My intention to continue these gifts in the present hour. Let the whole world see your Christianity in action! Be clear in your commitment to the Holy Spirit, in your communication with Heaven through your petitions, and in the framing of the New World that the Father has provided through My Messianic Son. Be peacemakers who foster the end of wars. Govern your individual lives with piety, allowing the Grace of Heaven to infiltrate every chamber of your being. Let the Holy Spirit make of you awesome creatures of courage and enlightenment; and then you will know what it means to be holy. Hence, I expect you to be receptive to the Will of God in ways that you have never afforded. Sense the peace of His living Kingdom in your company, the peace that cannot arise from the temporal world. You shall forever be liberated from the confines of mortality by the perfection that the Lord plants in your hearts, if only you will let Him. Why do I ask you to trust the Father without knowing His plans in advance? Because it is you who are effecting those plans by your prayerfulness. If you become like Jesus, you will shape the Earth into the likeness of Heaven with charity and love. Your souls will know that they are bound for the Glory of Paradise before your flesh is ever abandoned. I promise, My children, that your holiness is the making of these enduring miracles. Your prayers suspend the laws of Nature and neutralize the insults and injuries imposed by the ravages of time. Please believe what I am saying, and you will see these things come.

I have asked you on a number of occasions to read the Sacred Scriptures for guidance, consolation, and Wisdom. You have recited the Penitential Psalms to aid the purification of humanity. I urge you to remember that the transformation of the hearts of men is made possible by your sacrifices. What people learn of the Lord is manifested by your lives in Him, especially in this new millennium, with its swift means of communication. Everything you have given Creation for the Salvation of your brothers and sisters has been recorded in the annals of Eternity, put there for veneration by the Angels and Saints. The gifts you have accorded My Son are glistening in His Crown like the sweet fruits of the vine that have been transferred from Earth into Heaven in advance of your souls. Please go about the business of redemption in your everyday lives, being the forgivers that Jesus has sought you to become. Bear the cost of absolution in your likeness of Jesus, and in the end, God will recognize Him in you. My children, when this comes to pass, there will be no greater blessing you could receive in this life or the next. I have told you that I cannot ensure your happiness in this mortality, and that there are many crosses to be borne, countless stumbling blocks on your path, and untold periods of darkness over which you must prevail. This is God's design for those who follow Jesus because living as He commands mitigates the corrupt nature of humanity. As difficult as it may seem, you will someday thank Him for allowing you to serve so sacrificially. In what numbers does the Communion of Saints pray for you! They approach the Throne of God on your behalf with supplications that resound your prayers because they love you; they understand the depths of your suffering. These are the dignified warriors who found their eternal home through lives of personal charity that portend auspicious blessings for you, that stand as harbingers of defeat for the enemies of the Church. Truly, I beg your humility for everything you wish God to provide in life, and I remind you not to be deceived by the element of time. Like the essence of your hearts, the Divine Love that lives in them cannot wane and will never desist in the cultivation of the world until the Second Coming of the Son of Man. If you wish for grander things than those that have transpired, God will give them to you when His people submit their faces to the Light of the Cross. Somewhere deep inside you, My cherished ones, lives the bounty of the eternal ages yearning to emerge. The Scepter of Jesus seeks to burst into His Kingdom on Earth with such profundity that it would rival the explosion of the sun. I have declared that there is a manifest awakening about to startle the conscience of mortal humanity; and that moment is near at hand. The prophesied signs at My Marian shrines will soon be unfolding in prefigured sequence to the surprise of countless unsuspecting souls. I have wished for lost sinners to come to Jesus in advance of these occurrences, and they have been walking toward the Cross with their hopes in hand. I promise humanity that He will spread His arms and receive them. Jesus loves you with such intensity that it would be impossible to place into words. The emotion by which you live, your struggles and passions, the determination of your faith, and the belief you espouse of your passage into Eternity are connected beneath the Cross of My Crucified Son. If you trust Him through lifting your prayers, you will know the relationship between every sight and deed ever dispensed from God to His people on Earth. You will discover how many hairs were counted, where every sparrow fell, and with what true excellence those innumerable rainbows and sunsets you have pined to touch were fashioned beyond the celestial shores. Give your hearts to the Son of Man, and all these gifts will be yours. My Special and Chosen sons, it is with gladness that I see you so dedicated to your labors for Jesus. I ask that you never cower from the requisite fight because of external pressures or undue burdens placed upon you by anyone else. You have received only little ridicule over the years because I am protecting your anonymity. You will someday realize what a gift this has been. My Special one, you are living the holiness I have prescribed with truth and goodness. Thank you for praying the Holy Rosary with genuine compassion for those who suffer. My Immaculate Heart is filled with love for you, for the faith you embrace, and for the awesome approach you take to ordinary life. You are the embodiment of honor that is lacking in many people. I wish for you to enjoy your day with your brother knowing that I am with you, praying for your well-being. Remembering that you love Me, open your mind to peace, and your heart will be consoled. Thank you for the concerns you have placed in your writing for Jesus. When you pen your thoughts, the Holy Spirit is always with you. Please do not overemphasize the passing years. You know that there is much more work to do. However, God is intensely grateful for the fifteen years you have given Him. The Earth is more blessed, and the Kingdom of Heaven is enhanced."

Sunday, February 26, 2006
Saint Principia Cheyenne [1744-1798]*
2:23 p.m.

"Glory abounds when you offer your prayers for the healing, protection, and sanctification of humanity in the righteousness of God's Kingdom. My children, the power about which I speak is unmatched by any force in Creation. When you appeal to the Almighty Father, His attention is trained on your requests; His Glory is centered upon the wishes of His people. Today, we have the mission of seeking His blessing upon you for help in gathering humanity at the foot of the Cross. I wish you to remember that your prayers are the beginning of your conversion to His Truth and the culmination of your souls' destiny in the Most Sacred Heart of Jesus in the Promised Land. I call on you to repeat the prayers of the Angels and Saints in unison with Mine. We ask Jesus for the alleviation of pain and suffering, for the end of infanticide, for feeding and sheltering the poor, and the cessation of everything in contradiction to the Holy Scriptures. I have already said that the cultivation of the world is a process, one in which there are multiple steps toward the journey of righteousness. If you grow weary on this journey, you will find rest through My Son. These are times of change that you know to be important in the impending arrival of Jesus in Glory. Please do not defer to anyone else for the supplications that you are supposed to lift. Let no hour pass that you do not heed your call of conscience, that which keeps you in union with Me. Your hearts echo the clarion of Peace and Justice throughout the world, and your petitions signify your agreement with the Will of the Father that they come to pass in your age. It gives Me hope and anticipation knowing that you have decided for Him, that your eyes of faith are focused on His Kingdom. I assure you that you will be blessed with a joy that cannot be darkened or dampened by any sorrow or regret when you make your lives the perfect emulation of Jesus' Love. Indeed, the road is often difficult to travel, but the Holy Spirit tells you that your labors are worth the effort. Little ones, it is better that you counsel yourselves in the Holy Spirit now, while there is time to seek the Lord. Remember that your responsibility as Christians was manifested at the outset of the spiritual enlightenment that God accorded you in your youth. There can be no true Christian devotion without that initiation of the heart staying with you during the remainder of your years. I desire to teach you to be like little children assembled around Jesus' Cross and beneath My Holy Mantle. While there is no greater Love than that which impels someone to lay-down his life for his friends, it is also a Love that is encompassed by the Mother of God. I have seen the entirety of your years on Earth, and I have nurtured you from the bedside of your birth. I hold fast to the designs of Heaven so you will enjoy its Light when you pass from this world. If you wish to be happy on Earth, remember that these are days of preparation, months and years during which you are learning the essential meaning of supernal peace. I have given you countless graces, signs and wonders that lift your hopes in expectation of your deliverance to Eternal Salvation. Remember that I lived on Earth centuries ago, and I know your apprehension about the uncertainty of the future. When all else fails, Jesus will never abandon you. When you weep beneath the palls of despair, call upon His healing strength for perseverance, consolation, and perspective. Know that My Son has borne your grief and carried your sorrows before you were conceived in your mothers' wombs. I promise that the Lord cannot fail you because His Divine Love has already conquered the enemies of the Cross. If you seek in Him the awesome omnipotence by which He reigns, He will confide in you the secrets of the ages and vest you with the prescience of the future. Knowing Him imbues your sanctity from those youthful moments about which I have spoken, those formative years that gave you such inspiration learning that He is alive. The signs you witnessed are still living in you; they are the catalyst for the conversion of your friends in the same way they first led you to the Truth. I assure you that these are important days for the whole of Creation because your fate and God's Providence are intersecting at junctures never before known to man.

Therefore, My children, I beseech you to become even more dedicated to your work for Jesus. Live with confidence that He holds you in the palms of His sacred hands in such a way that shields you from the malevolent elements of the world. He provides you peace of mind, comfort of spirit, and consolation of the heart. When you speak of the relevance of Christianity, you refer to the inevitable reconciliation between God and man that is closer to you than ever before. You have been given the dutiful commission to live this great hope because it is you who are experiencing the benefits of His spiritual Grace. The fruits of your labors and the gift of your lives are sweet to Jesus' taste because He knows that you have accepted Him as your destiny, that you embrace His Kingship as your purpose for breathing. Imagine how His Most Sacred Heart is enlivened to acknowledge your loyalties to His Paschal Sacrifice as expiation for your sins! Christ Jesus is a grateful Man and appreciative God. He will dispense the graces you require to remain one in Him with valor, appreciation, atonement, and renewal. These are especially auspicious times because you comprise His Faith-Church on Earth to whom His beatific affinity is drawn. Pray to understand how important this is to the Hosts of Paradise. Grow profusely in the Wisdom that has been implanted in your hearts, thriving and blooming with the Dominion of the Lord that cannot be expunged. Garner the persistence of faith from the knowledge that you belong to Him, that He knows your every word and action before you commit them into history. These are the calling of the Holy Spirit for you, and they have become the appealing awareness of people who have been too long asleep in indifference and sin. Should anyone ask who told you that Jesus commands your concession in the reproaches of humankind, tell them that you heard it from the Mother of God. The shy and tremulous existence of the innocent is itself sufficient reason for you to wish to become successful in the lineage of Jesus. You are their servants as His disciples, the source of their sustenance and survival. When you give your love in support of them by transmitting the Light of the Holy Spirit to be their guide through the perils of darkness, you will live the perfection of the divinity of God. You will procure from Heaven miracles unknown to transport the Earth past the obstacles of time; and gone will be the galls, traps, and snares that tempt you to surrender to distraction, diversion, contemptuousness, and despair. It is for His Light, My children, that you have been given life and the sublimeness of moral reason; and it is for the decorum of deific adulation that you have been accorded a Christian conscience. I implore you to ponder the brilliance by which God has fashioned you in triumph and given you spiritual fervor for the acceptance of your acquittal. If you aspire to know more about Him, revel His Justice through time and space as though you have already walked into Heaven. Destroy the barriers to your faith that keep you from recognizing the prophecies that have come to fruition in your age. Most of all, My little ones, be not afraid! Answer the bugler's call for courage in such a way that there is a triangulation between Heaven, your souls, and the brothers and sisters you are commissioned to amass! The existence of the world is near its zenith, and yours are the petitions that will determine the success of the Church in these crucial times. Jesus' first Apostles are depending upon you to finish the work that their own mortality disallowed them to complete. You are their extension in the contemporary world, the agents and representatives of a beatific age of sophisticated men. Unfortunately, however, to some people, sanctity and sacrifice are only theoretical terms and abstract concepts having little meaning. They may have heard about the Holy Cross, but they lack the initiative to move toward Jesus' Crucifixion with any semblance of conviction. Together, we must convince them that it is as urgent as life over death and important as the empowerment of Eternity over the brevity of their years.

    My Special and Chosen ones, I come to you in great happiness that you are still together, working like warriors for the Kingdom of God to reclaim the Earth. When the Angels celebrate man's nobility, they refer to your lives; they speak to the sincerity in your hearts. Eternal bliss is fitting the Earth with the garments of your work, and I have come to revel in your success by continuing My miraculous messages. It is true that you become tired, but your spirits are never broken. It is My ardent desire that you begin this year to refocus on the joyful part of your Christian mission. The negativity and darkness that you concentrate on is going to destroy your hope if you do not attend your spirits to more lighthearted things. You have done nothing to bring this upon yourselves, but the heaviness of seeing little response by humanity to the Church, to the call of My messages, and to the simplicity that the Holy Scriptures dictate casts a burden upon all My children. I cannot carry the weight of your concerns for you, but I can help you prioritize them. I have asked God, My children, to bless this year of 2006 for you, that you will grow in your trust of the Holy Spirit and in your desire to bask in the Light of His peace. Indeed, there are still too many inequities, too many unanswered questions, too few who are willing to risk their stability to reach-out in faith, and so little time for the remaking of the face of the Earth. If you must know, I have stood with you in seeking a new blessing upon humanity so all people everywhere will rise together in unending belief. God has told Creation that He has dispensed plentiful graces to captivate His followers. His Grace alone, He says, should be enough to inspirit the hearts of the lost. The faithful who have already accepted the Crucifixion of Jesus are an extremely fortunate lot. Your own genius is seated in the Wisdom of the Salvation of the world through the Son of Man whose gift of compassion is flowing into your lives. My children, My message is one of staying the course, being strong in the face of your adversities. You have come to Me in prayer for over fifteen years, and God will never forget the blessings He has promised for your loyalties and faith. This is a simple home with two beautiful companions. What else could Heaven ask of anyone than to bless the work you were sought to submit? Your work is Heaven's delight; it is the labor of love that the Holy Spirit has summoned. Nothing has made Me happier than to turn to Jesus and tell Him that you are two of My most favored children. This alone should make you smile with glee. My Special son, I have given you another portion of this message that you will enjoy because it has an overarching strength of vision. You can see that your brother still tires at the end of the day. His body is struggling to recover, and he has a way to go before he can be considered beyond danger. It is imperative that you realize that any recovery he has known is directly attributable to you. I can sense a new peace in your heart that you have not known for months. As you enter the Season of Lent, be thankful for the gifts God has given you. I ask that you make this cause of joy your purpose for Lent, that you work toward easing the tension in your mind by remembering how much you are loved. If you choose to give-up something during Lent, please make it the negativity that I have spoken about because you can vent your frustrations by showing the world that it cannot harm you. You are stronger than any opposition; your heart is more valiant than any cowardice that may attempt to keep your happiness at bay. With all My Heart, I wish for you to remember that you are more than special, more than the simple child on Monument Avenue who happens to be My messenger. You should resume your prayer group at your leisure, whatever you believe will emit the happiness of Jesus into more lives. There seems to be no end to the gifts you continue to give Him. I have chosen you because you are willing to fight the good fight of faith, to enlist the Truth in every situation, to extol the Salvation of humanity to anyone who will hear, and to enjoin your peers to do better things in their lives. It is amazing how this makes you the likeness of the Saints. I am happy that you visit businesses for your meals and enjoy atmospheres where you express your good will to others. Whenever strangers see you and your brother traveling the streets, or when others watch you walk in, they see two people who are fashioned by the propriety of God. They see gentlemen of stately spirits. I am pleased that you are looked upon so appreciatively by people you do not even know. I am more than thankful for your expressions of love and for saying you belong to Me. This makes My Immaculate Heart sing with joy. I will continue offering messages about the redemption of humanity as long as God allows. For now, continue to work as though your lives will ensue for years, hoping that everyone whom you are praying to convert will make that change before the world is through. Let your heart remember that Jesus holds you deeply in His care."

Sunday, March 5, 2006
St. Matzo Sheng Ziyang [1837-1878]*
2:19 p.m.

"My children, I address you with a joy that is more brilliant than a thousand diamonds. The evocative attentiveness that you give My messages bodes well for the conversion of lost souls and the blossoming of the eternal beginning they will discover in Jesus. I hope you live this gladness with Me and pray for everything I have shared. There is no question that the world requires your petitions for its healing because your supplications usher the foundation of Heaven's response. Given everything you have learned about Christianity, you surely understand the importance of your relationship with God through the Holy Spirit. Some of My children have said that they are aware of the changing mood of Christians. While you live in perpetual expectation of the Coming of the Lord, you recognize that you play a crucial role in receiving His Kingdom. My work cannot be completed without your help. The people I am attempting to reach see you in tangible ways; they observe your stewardship and purpose of renewal. If everyone around the world emulated My holiness, there would be no sorrow. Your closeness to Me, and therefore to Jesus, displays a miraculous presence of divinity. I daresay that no other people on the globe have matched the dedication to the Sacred Heart of Jesus as those whom I have summoned with more specified faith. I am a grateful Mother whose mission flows into this century, as broad as its future comes to be, so that all nations might appeal to the Cross with faith and articulate contrition. This is an achievable goal in your time! Therefore, please join Me in the elation that I feel for the conversion of those whom you have never met. The Lord knows who they are, and He realizes your redemptive gifts to the Church that make such a difference in propagating the Gospel, the Good News of the Salvation of men. I beseech My children to avoid the spiritual fatigue that plagued the earlier ages. This is not a time for reticence, and is certainly the opportunity for stupendous courage in the reenforcement of the virtues of your faith. I have wished the best for you in episcopal terms, that the Prelates whom Jesus has chosen to guide His flock will be as excellent as their counterparts from the past. I call on My children to pray for the Church, for the Holy Father, for the Cardinals and Bishops, and for priests and religious servants everywhere. They have taken on an enormous task of defending the Church from the onslaught of mediocrity that has defined the beginning of this millennium. As I have said, these are frightening times for dedicated parishioners who are awakening to the grotesque persecution of the Roman Catholic Church. You must admonish those who are critical of the Hierarchy and be professorial in teaching the ignorant about the righteousness that the Mother Church espouses. When you refer to human love in catechetical terms, you speak in the context of the

Paschal Banquet where God's disciples are fed. Remember the words of encouragement from the Saints who heralded that God is Truth, and He cannot lie. Your souls mean more than the whole world to Him; greater is His Love for humanity than all the universes combined. Indeed, My little ones, God's devotion to your Salvation transcends the physical elements of Creation in ways that you will not understand until your footsteps are recorded in Heaven. I plead for you to sever your ties with materialism and idolatry. Hope with sensitivity in your hearts that the world's citizens will turn to Jesus for the eradication of their obliquity and the elimination of their vices. These are not just attributes of humanity's error, they are too much pressure for your souls to bear. Pray to accede to the sound morality that is pursuing your hearts with pardon and mercy. Return to full communion with God through your honest repentance in the Penitential Sacrament of the Church. Where your hearts go, My little ones, your conscience follows. There is no doubt that the pilgrimage on which you are traveling in the Holy Spirit is worth the cost of your struggles to engage the Earth through the merits of your faith. I would not ask you these things if they were not your testament to Christian holiness in the sanctity of the Lord.

I ask you to commit to your daily examen through the sincerity of your lives. Remember that sin is deeply offensive to God because it separates you from the fullness of His Grace. There are grave consequences that accompany those who refuse to give their hearts to Jesus, the unfortunate number whose obstinance is the millstone around their necks. The cruel and catastrophic future that faces the unrepentant is entirely avoidable by their acceptance of His Crucifixion on the Cross. You are the ambassadors whom He has dispatched to people you know and other lands far and wide, seeking-out the lost who are wandering aimlessly down errant paths. The most charitable gift you can offer them is your prayers, and thereby fulfill your oath by asking Jesus to enlighten them. Remember that you were commissioned upon your baptism to amend your lives and follow the righteous course, telling the world about its absolution in My Son. You have been ordained into a priesthood of service to Heaven, and are given the sacred seal of conviction about which the Holy Spirit spoke in the early times. Your hearts have been immersed in God's mystical zeal and a holiness that will outlast the ages in apostolic hope. Can you see why it is so important for Me to encourage you with Motherly Love, with the urgency of the times that require the transformation of prodigal men? Your role is to console the persecuted through the affiance of your faith. Be gleeful in accepting the rejection that the world hands to you at the tips of swords and with biting tongues. Yours is a promise of deliverance not only for yourselves, but for the sinners whom you call your enemies. This is what prayer is for, My dear children. Remember that no person is born unable to comprehend moral Truth because its intuitive potential is inscribed on the conscience of every man. You realize that there are mitigating factors that diminish the severity of unintentional sin. Our focus today, however, is to amend the lives of those who live in wanton disobedience to the Commandments of God. I ask you to pray for them like you have never prayed before. The austerity you have embraced is a beacon for millions worldwide who have never heard of the supremacy of Divine Love. Someone failed to teach them the lessons of piety amidst the labors of their fears. They have been too lacking in sight, and much too poor in spirit to seek it on their own. Your faith lends you to becoming the wiser and nobler followers of the Kingdom of My Son, and you are expected to perpetuate the blessings of the Holy Gospel where your forbears could not go. Let this age be the inundation of the leagues of nations in the Blood of Jesus' Sacrifice. I call on you to wield the fortune of hope you have been given and share the virtuous vision that permeates the essence of your souls with the Wisdom of the Lord. Let not a hint of human pride lead anyone to bow to lukewarmness, indifference, or rejection of the Cross. The gift of faith is a favor that is absolute, and is founded in the miracle of God's Love living in the eternal beyond. What we share, My children, is the begetting of your unity with Him, the restoration of His happiness into the center of your hearts, and the transference of supernatural Glory that absolves you of your sins. Rejoice and be glad that this is ongoing. Revel in your freedom to be harmonious with the Will of the Father in whose Providence you are about to inherit the Land of Promise. I pray that My words will be well received not only by the ears of My messengers and seers, but by the untold masses who are only now turning their faces toward God. Let their awakening be a cause for celebration on Earth and in Heaven! Be jubilant that Christ Jesus has never abandoned them, that He has not given-up the fight for the retrieval of their souls. We pray here together for the overwhelming sanctity of His Most Sacred Heart to become their new reason for living and their peace of mind in the middle of life's storms.

  My Special and Chosen ones, these are hours of unprecedented Grace for you and your brothers and sisters. We pray not only because we adore Jesus, but because we realize that your work is making a difference; it is touching lost souls around the globe. I admire and appreciate your dedication to your manuscripts. They are permanent records of the sublime perfection of God, of the refurbishing of the collective human spirit in ways that are unparalleled in these modern times. These things you feel in your hearts and sense through the intensity of your trust in Jesus. You know that He supports you, and He guides you so you will not feel abandoned during difficult periods. The Holy Paraclete is the sanctification not only of yourselves, but of everyone with whom you come into contact during your mortal years. I ask that you remain with the Lord while the masses are only now acknowledging the sovereignty of Heaven over the universe. If only you knew the goodness you are manifesting, you would be willing to wait another million years for the conclusion of time. And, depending upon one's perspective, it is either fortunate or unfortunate that there is not that much time left before the

Glorious arrival of the Son of Man to end the world. I offer My support in everything you do, in the works of your hearts and hands, and in spiritual succor when you feel forsaken by men and fearful of their naked sins. If you placed your lives along a continuum and were able to see the breadth of your labors across the expanse of time, you would see that it connects societies and republics in ways that they have never foreseen. You are defying the perceptible elements of the created world by making Salvation so imperative that they are shedding their other goals. This is what we set out to do in February 1991. My Special son, My joy eclipses anything you could imagine for the opportunity to appear before you. You kneel in this place to pray with Me because you are the reflection of the Love of God. Through Him, you understand the difficulties that are inherent in persuading mortal men to take up their crosses and follow Jesus. You are feeling better because your new writing is a gift to those who are seeking a closer relationship with Heaven. Many have cited that your parables are deep, symbolic, and valanced with overtones of meditation and rumination. Others say that they are pedagogic and admonishing. This is true, and thank God that you are writing this way. You continue to ask the question why you speak with such pageantry and beauty. It is because you said yes to Me on February 22, 1991. This implanted in your heart the sacred vision by which you have lived and has vested you with the Wisdom of Truth never before known to you, thus allowing you to write with the esteem that is worthy of your faith."

Sunday, March 12, 2006
Saint Alma Johnston, Virgin [1711-1768]*
1:09 p.m.

"These are among the most miraculous, progressive, holy, and prosperous days you shall live. Despite the perceived ill fortune and difficult times, you will discover that you are revealing a holy light to humanity; you are helping Creation bask in the Glory of God's Providence, and you are establishing a means for your pagan brothers and sisters to comprehend the meaning of spiritual sacrifice. My children, I come with deep happiness and joy, with empathy and understanding for the harshness of your years, with support and prayers that you will lay these moments across the landscape of Heaven's finest lines. Within you is true charity for the healing of the broken. You have become like Jesus because you know that His holiness is sacred, merciful, honest, receptive, and perseverant. Please do not surrender to the darkness that is trying to take away your joy! I am the Mother of God who is telling you that you are proffering great benisons to the Earth by your willingness to withstand the buffets and insults from the netherworld. Evil cannot vanquish those who are given to Jesus Christ! I promise that He is aware of your agonies. He knows about your struggles because He is living them with you. My children, these are not just pretty words to keep your hopes alive. I speak to you through the verity of the Cross so you will recognize that your identity is found in Christian discipline, not in the fashions of societies and the whims of other men. You are evidence that the justice of God is reigning, that heavenly jurisprudence is overwhelming the Earth. Remember that if you are not opposed, you will not be successful. The remainder of your years must be dedicated to this justice, and I will help you because I am your Mother. Please live as Saint Paul asked, to fight the good fight and finish the race because a crown of Glory awaits each of you, a vindication so profound that it defies description. Your strength is fashioned by the knowledge that the Church is God's one final Covenant with mankind, that He deigns your success over evil forces. As I have said, the tenacity of your faith and the genuineness of your prayers assure your ultimate victory in the Sacred Heart of My Son. My children, your lives are given to the retrieval of prodigal men from a world that lures them from their rightful exposure to the sublimity of the Cross. The Father asks you to pursue them with candlelight, prophecy, Gospel, and bell. Ring in the crispness of their loyalty to His omnipotent domain by the invocation of His peace, showing them through the piety of your lives that their dignity can be restored. They are suffering from the intensity of self-imposed guilt, unaware that such a proficient Absolution awaits them in Jesus. Heaven is asking you to herald their victory over sin and death in the Triumph of My Immaculate Heart. Give them hope, little ones, for the resurrection of the innocence they lost when they could not resist temptation. Guide them to the presence of Divine Grace in the Mysteries of the Church, to the expungement of their sins through My Son's Crucifixion. They are having difficulty seeing beyond the awkwardness of their fears well enough to recognize that they can regain their spiritual perfection in the Holy Sacraments. If you lead them to the path of reconciliation with God, He will repatriate them into His plenteous Grace and convert them by virtue of your love. Therefore, I beseech you to invest in them the gift of your lives in ways that reflect the memoirs of the Saints. Let no one turn away from you believing that they are unacceptable to God. And, while this may take months and years, you will see at the culmination of time that you participated in the awakening of Heaven's most prodigious patriots. Your prayers are catalysts for their conversion. Anything you do to lead them to repentance, you do for the Seat of Wisdom. If you must invoke more courage to accomplish these things, then stand on the highest mountaintops and remind Creation that you belong to Me. Go forward in your contemplations with the expectation that Jesus will ratify your words and deeds on behalf of the sinners He came to save. These are the actions that revel the distant stars to shine more brightly in the heavens and dispatch the Angels to celebrate the invigorating conscience you are enlivening in the sons and daughters of the New Jerusalem. Certainty, fealty, Truth, vision, and austerity are found in the gifts you offer Jesus through your faithfulness on Earth.

My angelic children, I wish for you to pray for the inflection of everything beautiful to grow from the hearts of contemplative men. Urge them to pen their thoughts about the purpose of life in spiritual terms. Tell them of the redemptive value of their prayers, of their songs and inspirations, and their patterns of global charity that they have afforded the poor. Convey to them through your writings the unique blessing they have been to Jesus on the Earth. You have been told that Jesus is present in innocent victims, in the plight of paupers, and in the revelatory acclamations you are making to teach the ignorant about the magnificence of the Cross. Always remain aware that My Son is your guard in whatever you do for the exaltation of Heaven. Just when you believe that there is no conceivable way that Jesus could bless you more, you discover that He has more blessings to dispense. We have spoken about tenacity and perseverence in the context of the Holy Cross, and you have accepted your part in initiating them. Many have asked why it is so difficult to effect your participation in the conversion of humanity, and God has given you the answer. It is all about proving your faith, My children. It is more than the ancient blessing that God gave Creation 2,000 years ago; it is about the contemporary deliverance of an authenticated people in the Incarnation of Jesus in Bethlehem. And, it refers to the expiation of every form of human sin from the eternal record, so permanently expunged that not even God has memory of them. These are times of unprecedented Grace for mortal humankind. There are untold miraculous manifestations flying in the face of obstinate people who cannot turn their backs quickly enough to ignore the presence of God. Everything Heaven is giving you is for the completion of His Plan. This is the reason He trusts you to commend them to Jesus through the recitation of the Holy Rosary and your other daily prayers. What happiness comes to those who walk with Him interiorly! The distinction you harvest during your journey of life is one of the noble heart, one that blooms from your genuine anticipation that the end of the world draws near. I urge you to never concede to your enemies whose bantering has no effect on the integrity of your faith. You know to listen to the calling of the Holy Spirit in every instant, during every moment you are placed in the company of antagonistic men. If you could understand the gift you are to Jesus, you would seek new ways to evangelize His Crucifixion to the far corners of the globe. You are given venue through your petitions and holy acts, and it is in your votive meditations that a clear faith is dispensed to you. I again offer My suppliant intercession before the Son of Man. My Special and Chosen ones, I wish you could know how close you are to Me, that you are living-out the promises you made to Jesus many years ago. The sublime newness of Creation is alive in you, and you are pitted in the world against the adversaries whom the Lord has asked you to rebuke. I assure you that only your own negativity, your mediocrity in adversity, can make you unhappy because Jesus is the Eminent Victor through My Immaculate Heart. These are pungent days, but they are no worse than those faced by the earliest Saints. Your spirits are being accosted by the darkness of the Earth, a darkness over which you are already prevailing. If you will stand farther back from the picture, you will see what I am saying. I come with compassion and guidance to comfort and console you. I wish for you to realize that Paradise is on your side. I am pleased because I have seen the success of your work. There could be no soul alive who would not be overjoyed by the sureness of your lives in Jesus. My Special son, I am praying that humanity will open its eyes and see the manifestations that God is bringing into being. This is where I desire you to be focused, on the changing world from its horrible depravity into its enlightenment in the Holy Spirit. This is why today is a blessed day. It is good because you and your brother are living it. It is good because you said yes to Me, and you live-out the meaning of your fiat. Things will improve here at home, and you will notice it. I come to bring you hope that Jesus remains with you. Please get more rest and elevate your spirit to the peace you find in Him. I will pray for you to do so. Thank you for remaining with Me! Next week, I shall speak of Saint Joseph!"

Sunday, March 19, 2006
Memorial of Saint Joseph
1:39 p.m.

"Your diligent holiness is recognizable in Heaven as the precursor to your sainthood, My children. Your love is hailed as the initiator of perpetual blessings for humanity, the begetting of a bastion of sanctification being fashioned in the Sacred Heart of Jesus. Please do not be dismayed by the egregious errors before you, but rejoice that they are dying with the tragedies that cannot bind your hearts to despair. My dear ones, living in each of you is a consecration to survival and hunger for light. Whether you can see Heaven from the Earth is irrelevant to your capacity to perceive the perfection that is gestating in your faith. To most of My messengers, there are more questions than answers about what the future may bring. You are tested more than others because you have been given a venue that few have been accorded by the Father. When Heaven asks you to extol the Truth of Christ, you are expected to strike a chord of atonement for humanity through your holy lives. This is why My children are so indomitable; you do not fear the wolves in the night or threats from violent forces, and you certainly do not fear the inevitability of death. Indeed, it is not an ending, but the beginning of the rest of your life. Most pragmatic thinkers try to strike fallacious parallels between the Glory of Paradise and issues based on secular opinions. You must search for the supernatural presence of Salvation in ordinary times while seeking opportunities to manifest the forgiveness of God in the ways and means of your behavior. Both peace and ecclesial affirmation are profits from the investment of your trust. Since you have 'seen' in ways that few have observed, you are aware that a miniscule number of acts and factions in the Earth's domain pertain to the expertise of redemption, and you should be happy knowing about the gifts that enhance your ability to magnify God's Deific Light. I realize that you are grateful for My having called you to propagate His Love, and you are equally as thankful by multiplying your prayers to purify humanity. It is for these reasons that you are instruments for the conversion of the lost. You are observing the anniversary of a war in the Middle East that fulfills My prophecy of September 16, 2001. How sorrowful that such anniversaries must come. Would it not be better for families who have lost loved-ones in these battles to observe the creating of pacts of peace, rather than erecting memorials to the dead? Instead of invoking the great Saint Joseph on this date three years ago for guidance, America turned to its armaments of war, their instruments of death and destruction. Let us call upon Saint Joseph anyway, that he will ask the Lord to end every conflict around the globe, heal the broken spirits of the grieving, and comfort the victims whose lives are shattered by such senseless fighting. I have told you of the powerful intercession of Saint Joseph, even more intense than the protection of your guardians angels. I join in praying for the cessation of all wars, wherever they are fought. I seek a renewed sense of unity in My children that has been absent for many centuries. Allow the Prince of Peace to infiltrate every fiber of your being, to lead and assure you that good things come from prayer. If you heed My call, if you humble yourselves before the Cross, Jesus will heal your lands. I beseech you to heighten your awareness of the plight of indigents around the globe whose future is in the hands of sinners who will not care for them. They are oppressed by secular regimes that disallow the honoring of God and the Church. Please ask Jesus to set them free from bondage and call their captors to reconcile with Him. If you persist in My requests, little children, the nations will coexist in social accord.

Today, I also ask you to ponder the many ways you approach and evaluate your lives. It is obvious that you are living in a seminal state of transition on the Earth. Beneath the guiding hand of God, you are moving through time with the scrupulous expedience of Christian goodness. Can you not see, My children, that these are your moments of excellence? This is your time for action and reflection, pondering the days when Jesus walked the Earth in human flesh, wondering what He must have thought about the same things you worry about today. He knew men of great sincerity and promise who espoused the righteousness about which He was speaking. He also knew many who rejected the piety of the heart that He seeks in you, those who could not readily understand why the definition of Love includes such physical and spiritual sacrifice. My precious ones, God has poured Himself over the souls of humankind through Jesus so you may be immersed in Wisdom, Truth, and Salvation. When humanity was parched and separated from Heaven, Jesus submerged you in the peace of His Most Sacred Heart, that your thirst for renewal might be quenched in the splendor of His Crucifixion. I call on you to comprehend this in contemplative terms, that you might bring yourselves to believe that you are sought to be the nourishment for the famished souls of lost men. There is an adequate supply of satisfaction that offsets your mortal sorrows, one that keeps you strong during difficult times, one that warms you from the cold hatred of these modern decades. Your world is no less caustic than that which confronted the first Apostles and disciples, but you are given the power to defy it by the Holy Spirit who opened the hearts of the early subscribers to the Church. I wish to offer you the gift of consolation for the daily routine that you must face to survive in the material world. It is obvious that too many in your midst see no recourse in the spiritual Truth that has kept your hopes alive. I beseech you to never surrender to the repetition of the days, and to stay the course for Jesus while you pray. Your perseverance is tested because the Church is so despised by the secular void. Do not relinquish the dignity you have inherited from the Almighty Father by comparing yourselves with others who appear to be only temporarily happy, for theirs will be an inauspicious awakening at the end of the ages. Your humble petitions, pleading, supplications, and intentions are your communication with the future. They represent your desire for humanity to esteem the perfection of God in real terms. Knowing this, it is imperative that you lift your hearts to the Light of Truth and convey to the heavens your sense of good conscience about the course of events that is unfolding around the globe. It is obvious that humanity questions the validity of true justice when perceiving the inequities that riddle the Earth with such hollow deprivations. I exhort you to remember that these are the makings of mortal men, and not the designs of God. His Will is that all Creation should become the likeness of His supreme Love, that every breathing being will embrace the stillness of His beauty like the mountaintops basking in the sun. The natural human instinct is to seek the consolation of the heart from things that are irreversibly connected to Heaven; this is the beginning of your understanding of love. If you grow that longing into a sanctified desire for holiness, God will sustain you not only in what you seek of Him, He will expand your insights and reconstruct the entire Earth from the realms of your fondest dreams. My children, I call you to allow this kind of joy to come by tendering yourselves to everything in Christianity that matters—the alleviation of suffering, the protection of unborn life, the eradication of poverty and disease, the sanctity of the human soul, and the gifting of humanity to the Sacred Heart of Jesus. There is Mercy aplenty in Jesus for the untold number of sinners who cannot deign to forgive themselves. I assure you that there is an encrypted awareness in the consciousness of every Christian to know that their spiritual contrition is worthy of God's Divine Absolution. This is why Jesus told you that the Almighty Father is happier with the conversion of a single sinner than the praises of a hundred righteous men. No mortal is too far from that Grace to be resurrected from the grave. Everyone alive and who passes from mortality is worthy of My Son's Sorrowful Crucifixion; and He has founded the framework of your kinship in the shedding of His Blood. You need not fear the world, My children, or that only peril and darkness lie ahead.

    My Special and Chosen ones, it is with intense gladness that My presence here is made, that God permits Me to speak to you with such eloquence. You are the bright spots in Creation that make the Angels leap with joy, that allow Jesus to smile through His tears that somebody as dedicated as you is listening to Him. I know that you live-out your devotion to the Communion of Saints; you offer your lives to the apostleship of the Church. Great days lie ahead, My little ones. I have told you before about the signs of the times, and you have wondered which events are reminiscent of them. Your faith informs your spirits about the impending return of Jesus in Glory; it is as sound as the foundation upon which His Sacred Truth is laid. I have said that I cannot assure your happiness in this life, but you will be happy nonetheless if you give yourselves to Christ Jesus, to His patience in waiting for the transformation of His Mystical Body into the perfection that will reside with the Lord in Heaven. You have often wondered where time has gone, and you will one-day ask where it went altogether. This is why these years are so important, so crucial to the conversion of humanity. My Special son, you have stated that God would never allow the past fifteen years to go unneeded. In His Divine Plan, there are specific purposes for every minute of your life. Every word, every thought, the passion of your writing, the messages I have given, the untold hours of your prayerful labors, your gifts of time and treasure—all of this has been encapsulated in the Glory of Jesus' Resurrection. Will you see it occur? The petitions that you and your brother are reciting are holding the attention of Heaven. God sees man's desperation, and He hears the essence of your desires. I know that I have told you that certain books will awaken the conscience of people in America, and they will do so. However, your new *Supernal Chambers* book will attract them like a lightning rod. All your books will lead the United States back to your original *Morning Star* epic. I am more hopeful about your patience than ever before. Your work is moving through Creation much more quickly than you know. Please remember that it is you who have made the past fifteen years possible. Let us see what God has planned. Indeed, let us hope that Jesus returns before tomorrow. Whether humankind is prepared or not, your work will implore them to accept His Divine Mercy. Thank you. Your faith is fostering many miracles."

Sunday, March 26, 2006
Saint Vesuvius Hart [1911-1976]*
1:59 p.m.

"Now comes your Mother to express My endearing love for you, dispensing Heaven's accolades upon your holiness. We pray for the unfolding landscape, one shaped by the forces of cultivation for the hope, destiny, and designs of the Lord's chosen people. I wish you could know how fortunate are those who have decided to receive Him, to follow the Way of the Cross with allegiance to Jesus. I urge you not to fear the probative events you will soon face, for they are meant to awaken the sleeping hearts of lost sinners. The pining you harbor for the transformation of the Earth is about to be fulfilled, but you must employ faith and know that God is working to destroy the corruption of mortal men. I ask for your valor and trust in the times ahead to remain determined with Me, and stay with Me when all else seems to fail. There is no room for bitterness in the acceptance of the Will of God, and you shall observe on an intercontinental scale the need for patient endurance. Therefore, let us pray for Christians everywhere and commend them to the Grace that Jesus inspires in His disciples. It is time for the end of abortion; it is time for those who have been responsible for the infanticide that has plagued the West to pay for their transgressions. If you pray as you were taught, you will recognize the hand of God configuring the Earth into the architecture of holiness. With all My Heart, I wish you the best of everything having to do with love. Here, where you live in exile, you know it to be a manifestation of sacrifice, servitude, humility, and insight. Jesus desires you to subscribe to all these so you will better learn how He lived on Earth, that He taught lost sinners about the Love of God for the ensuing generations. Jesus generously blesses modern believers who are practicing His legacy of righteousness. And, with your help, the Church will succeed; the faithful will march onward in the anticipation that the revelations given through the Holy Spirit will arrive in your day. It is for these reasons that I requisition your prayers; you understand that the Kingdom of God is flourishing around and through you. It is imperative that you internalize what it means to have a heart dedicated to the sanctification of humanity. This is derived from your remembrance of the paschal goodness in your own lives, knowing in truth everything you have done to further the divine profits of repentance. Your reconciliation evolves from the eyes of your spirit recognizing the timeless purity of your actions that reflect the kindness of God. Each time you bless your brothers and sisters in prayer, good will, material aid and social liberation, you imitate the harvest of Jesus' Crucifixion. Beyond all things, those who inherit Heaven are dedicated to the elevation of human dignity. This is why Christian outreach is firmly rapt in compassion, servitude, sacrifice, empathy, trust, and charity. People who hold to these principles are wrought from the piety of Jesus into the begetting of His peace and destined to be His spiritual Martyrs, if not Martyrs in fact, for the consecration of humanity to the Cross and the purification of the Earth beneath the guardianship of God. My little ones, the definition of courage is not necessarily one of raging against the darkness through blind allegiance, but one that sees well, one with a perspective to seek perfection, to extend Divine Love to prodigal men in ways that include their holiest attributes in their transition beyond the physical Earth. What aches inside them is not the contusion of death, but their immortality struggling to emerge. This is why I have come. My messengers, seers, and visionaries are activists for their conversion to the spiritual realms; and others can best be enlightened by seeing you extol the Holy Gospel. Indeed, they will join you there; they will assume the facets of your compliance with the tenets of Christianity into their personal conduct; and this is gratifying to the Creator in Heaven. I have implored you to live patiently and in hopeful expectation of Jesus' glorious return to retrieve absolved humanity who is rightfully His. Again, I summon you to pray to comprehend the universality of His Most Sacred Heart, inundating yourselves with the joy of your redemption, and perceiving the forays and burdens of the physical world as being small when compared to the jubilation you shall know in Paradise.

You should realize that human life proceeds in moments, phases, eras and epochs; and there are multitudinous issues, fads, and fashions that tempt you to go astray. Your spirit searches for permanence, for that which is everlasting and transcending of human endeavors, for the synergy of the irreducible Truth of God and humanity's thoughts and actions. As My children, you know that the source of infinity is the Love of Christ in which your relationship with Eternity subsists. When you dwell upon His Resurrection through everything else you see, hear and touch, your conclusions mirror that Eternity. The meditations of your hearts, the words of your mouths, and the structure of your life's labors are products of your understanding of the purpose of Jesus' life, Death, and Resurrection. And, when praying during the Season of Lent in anticipation of the High Feast of Easter, you should remember that your rise to holiness sustains your ascension in His Grace. The gifts you offer 'the least of these' are your ways of enhancing God's Kingdom with the prevalence of human obedience and gratitude. Your predecessors Adam and Eve desired to don the power of the Father in accordance with their own will, not caring about their perfection; and they risked being separated from Him with advance knowledge of the consequences. They severed themselves not only from Heaven, but they fomented a fissure between their hearts, jeopardizing the bond they shared in a Garden so conducive to their purity. Hence, they became clothed in error; they required shielding from the shame they brought upon themselves, and their conduct caused the beginning of humanity's corruption. I have come to remind the

Earth that Jesus has reversed all this. He has eradicated human sin, expunged the record that stains the annals of the universe, and provided humanity recourse to be transformed from the crass rigidity of indifference to the pluvial deluge of Supreme Love. Will you permit your Mother to train your focus on the sublime and supernal Salvation that is awaiting you outside the temporal confines of this world? I pray that you will comply with My wishes for your own good, and for the enhancement of the New Jerusalem in whose census God intends you to be counted, to whose pristine palaces you are recommended. I thank My children for remembering the Annunciation of the Archangel Gabriel yesterday with such ardent petitions. Even as you are observing the Season of Lent, you understand the efficacy of declaring 'yes' to the Father in deferential ways. By all means, Lent is a period to respond affirmatively to the entreaties of Heaven with deep fervor. You will soon find that every decision having to do with sanctifying the nations involves denying the self. These are intense moments for changing the world! My Special and Chosen ones, I have come speaking to ask that My words be given to humanity at an hour deigned by God. He will release this message in accordance with His Plan, and there is nothing you need do to hasten the process. I hope, My Special son, that you will discover new ways to accept the peace of the Holy Spirit, to rest unto yourself in that peace, to rid annoyances from your mind, regain the crest of self-confidence that you had in the past, decry the despair attempting to diminish your faith, and live with anticipation of ultimate victory. I fear that you are losing sight of these things because of the heaviness of life. You are having physical difficulties because of your urgency to rush the future into being. And, when I make suggestions to tame your thoughts and console your heart, you look at yourself too critically instead of with compassion. Please remain optimistic about My intercession because I have dictated to you an important message for the world."

Sunday, April 2, 2006
Memorial for Pope John Paul II [1920-2005]
2:58 p.m.

"We pray in the splendorous Love of God for remedial peace to overcome the Earth, for the conversion of hearts to the Cross that redeems humankind. It is considerate that you have welcomed My intercession, that you give yourselves to the cultivation that is making Saints of ordinary men. We remember Pope John Paul the Great on the anniversary of his entrance into Heaven. As you know, he is a tremendous gift to Creation and a meaningful intercessor for the faithful. The royal simplicity of holiness that he espoused is living in you; it is growing in you. What many refer to as conservative Catholic values are precisely what Jesus asked Pope John Paul to exalt through his papacy, and they were concise reflections of wholesome Wisdom, meriting no such reference to any conservatism or liberality. Truly, they remain edicts of the Church. Anyone who strays from the teachings of John Paul II and Pope Benedict XVI is not living according to the Will of God. These holy men have called Christians to walk the path of holiness and denounce the relativism that has eroded the morality of the masses. My children, I pray that exiled men will long hold the pontificate of Pope John Paul II at the center of their conscience because he replicated the piety of Christ. Here, time allows you to march toward your own immortality with swiftness, with the beatifying of your souls to bless. What will the future hold for America and the other regions of the Earth? I have told you that the response to this depends upon the prayers of the faithful and the good works of missionaries and the laity worldwide. How do My children reach-out to the needs of the impoverished and those lost in the perils of darkness? These questions must be answered before discerning the texture of the coming years if the Earth has not been transmuted into Eternity before then. The spring of 2006 has broken, and there are still many issues that need to be resolved. The poor require your riches; the famished need to be fed, the naked clothed, the homeless sheltered, and the sick healed. If My children heed My call for Christian accountability, these matters will be redressed. I call you from life's complexities because I wish for you to ponder the Passion of Jesus during these latter days of Lent. Even though His suffering was grotesque, His courage was based on the principles of His Sacred Love for the Children of Light. He came to redeem the Earth, every person descended from Old Adam, the many who would take upon themselves the raiment of holiness for which He died. It is true that a fallen grain creates new life, and the Crucifixion of Jesus manifests the Salvation of every man who offers himself to the Cross in repentance. Christianity is a commitment of sacrifice and purpose, speaking truth when one is surrounded by lies, professing allegiance to God whom has yet to be seen, and addressing the errors of humanity whose pride has filled the world with dying souls. If you believe in Heaven; if you accept the expiation of human sinfulness that impaled Jesus onto the Cross, then you must realize that the conclusion of mortal life is the beginning of your station in Eternity. I have called upon your help during times of distress and jubilation. My Immaculate Heart has beseeched you to extract yourselves from beneath the ruses of the guileful and elevate your spirits to Paradise. There is no denying that your faith is often tested. You have been called as peace-seeking ambassadors to find the best in other men. Were it not for God's intervention, My dear ones, you would have no reassurances by which to live; you would be lacking in the graces that are appreciably afforded to refine humanity in the Sacraments of the Church. God in Heaven stands with anticipation that you will join Him in the City of Light and bask in His beauty in the presence of the Angels so you can look back at time with valedictory poise. I have taught you about invigorating your conscience with such detail that you no longer pursue the fashions of the world. I have asked that you bring your sincerest hearts to the Altar, embrace your brothers from whom you have been estranged, and stride confidently down the nave of human life with both purity and modesty as your flanking guards. I remind you that I would never lead you into something that you were incapable of achieving.

I often speak about happiness, My children, because you yearn for the sense of joy that the Holy Spirit sows in your hearts. The faith of your fathers has been bequeathed to you as a gift, and what you do with it has a profound impact on the closing ages. Will you be memorialized as Jesus' disciples of the 21st century? Do you have the mettle to reach outward in supplication and heal the ills of the world as though it were about to end at dusk today? Such urgency is not beyond the call of your Christian priorities, and it is reasonable to assume that Jesus may return before you take your dying breaths. There is still much work to complete, a great bastion of hope to inspire in the lost and lonely around the globe. You do this at the peak of your bent, the charities you offer the poor with pity in your hearts, and the prayers you raise all hours of the day. The Almighty Father hears you because He anticipates your call for help, and He knows you as among the one in ten who has come back to thank Him for graces previously accorded. My Lenten message is a clarion for you to imitate the brilliance of Jesus' Most Sacred Heart, even after the Easter Mysteries have been celebrated. Be willing to live in a perpetual state of openness about what I am saying, contemplating your own reconciliation with the Holy of Holies that you will witness someday. Most of all, My children, I urge you to be unafraid of things to come by bathing yourselves in the Light of Jesus' Resurrection when you are submerged in your darkest emotional hours. Let your lyrics, phonics, and intonations echo the ancient Psalms through which the Lord emboldens your posture for the End Times. Recite the Stations of the Cross on Good Friday, depositing your pain inside Jesus' Wounds, imagining with sincere devotion what He suffered to sanctify your souls. I join Him in blessing you for everything you are doing to advance the spiritual conversion of the world. You are entering a new era of awareness that will bring many good things to bear upon the actions of My people. Too many of My children still walk through life wondering when the final bell will toll or when the last trumpets will sound. Others are much too concerned about counting the offenses of their enemies or who has tread on their feelings. Such are manifestations of vanity and have nothing to do with the Cross of Truth. I call on humanity to remember the way Jesus was rejected, the Cornerstone and Foundation of the Apostolic Church. Believers whose spirits are dejected by such treatment who hang their heads are not fondest to Jesus; they are slaves to their own pride. This is why I seek messengers who are not affected by such matters. My summons is to charitable sons and daughters who take-on the wicked without complaint, who know that the only verdict worthy of the heart is the Final Judgement. My angelic ones, there is no rejection of good souls there. When everyone I have asked to assist in the conversion of lost sinners understands that it is for Heaven that you are living, you will walk hand-in-hand with peace so profound that little else will matter. These are joyful, historic times for the Church and the entire world. Movement is being made to manifest the modern miracles God has promised through Me. I fear that My people have placed themselves in a self-induced depression because they cannot avoid the deception of the element of time. Life is short; this is what I have been assuring you for many generations. If you cannot recognize anything else in your experiences, you surely must know about the brevity of time. My Special and Chosen sons, your Mother is pleased because you do not subscribe to the negativism that is overwhelming your peers. You delight in God's promises, in My words of encouragement, and the changing seasons of humanity's spiritual welfare for which you pray every day. I know that you maintain your loyalty to Christ Jesus because you have proven it on countless occasions. My Special son, I am happy that your new book will be published this summer, and that so many will enjoy your writing. It is a gift to Heaven from you, one that humanity will embrace on their way to see the Beatific Light about which I have spoken. It is obvious that you are tired and have been resting accordingly. Thank you for reciting the Litanies in the wake of your brother being healed. I also pray for you to have clear perspective about the feminine gender. I have said that American women can be selfish, but you decline to adjust your view accordingly. This is not a problem with you, it is a problem with them. American women who submit to abortion are grossly sinful, arrogant, possessive, and materialistic. I wish someday you will look back at My messages and see how many deal with the issue of American females. I have safeguarded you from their meanspirited ways. You have spoken about wishing that your female friends would be more like princesses, that they would prefer flowers and chiffon over liquor bottles and leather pants. Sadly, most of them will not listen to reason; they decline to remain effeminate because they believe it remands them to servile roles. This is one phenomenon that your work addresses. You have knelt to pray as a befuddled man, fallen victim to something lacking good deeds and the air of victory you shall soon relish. I am not blaming you. I am blaming them. I hope you will accept the consolation you find in Me. I am your source of comfort because I give you Jesus. Thank you for remaining steadfastly with Him."

Sunday, April 9, 2006
Palm Sunday
1:58 p.m.

"The melodious strains of righteousness that touch your hearts are coming from beyond the stars, raining down upon you with Providence and thanksgiving. Heaven is filled with gratitude that you are praying for the conversion of humanity to the Cross. I bless you for your professed loyalty to Jesus because it makes My intercession complete. Without your response, you might concede that the world would continue to broil with hatred. We have manifested increased hope by our prayers! We have wrought countless miracles for faithful Christians throughout the ages. If you trust the Will of God in obedience to My messages, you are given wonders to elevate your faith and strengthen your resolve to go on. Should God allow you to see the previously unseen, plant seeds of revelation in your hearts, or dispense upon you Wisdom you have never known, it is for the furtherance of His determination to convert the unrepentant. I come in adulation because millions of Christians around the globe are honoring Jesus' desire for your sanctification. It is in this prudence that He reestablishes you, not for the longings of your pride, but that you will recognize your importance to His Kingdom. While it is true that He came for the Salvation of your souls, it is you who must finally change; every wayward sinner must approach the Holy Cross. There is no doubt that this is an urgent decision for those who have denied the existence of God. As you know, however, everything is possible through Him. The sense of imminent victory is real; it is the foundation of the hope of the faithful. It is satisfaction, fulfillment, ratification, and justification for those who live steadfastly in the Church. I assure you that My messages are only the beginning of the knowledge you shall receive before the years are through. I ask you to pray for the reuniting of the races, for the special intentions that I hold for My children around the world. If only you could sense the opportunity that I see, reaped by the Crucifixion and Resurrection of My Son to redeem your souls, you would pray without ceasing. I summon you to the invocation of spiritual peace, that you may understand the true meaning of the Gospel for which you are living. Your membership in the Church is more than perpetuating goodness in this life, but also the broader expansion of your piety thereafter. There is no diminishing the importance of your lives in Christianity beyond the cries for fairness you witness here on Earth. My call continues to be for forthrightness while you live according to Jesus' excellence until the end of the ages. When you look for the beauty of life, see with the perception of the Angels the last bastion of Divine Glory that is equally your inheritance from God. You have arrived at a time when the peoples of the Earth are struggling against a more pervasive evil than that of the two World Wars. Satan has mutated his infamy to infiltrate modern cultures by utilizing methods that were unavailable in earlier decades. He is deploying the use of electronic technologies to corrupt the minds and hearts of adolescents. He tempts families to become victims of consumerism so parents no longer have time to teach them right from wrong. While mothers and fathers are working for the value of the dollar, they ignore the impiousness of their children. This is why Jesus asks you to shed the material world in favor of Biblical Truth. There can be no true goodness or allegiance to God in those who focus only on the calculated broadways of wealth. There is agony and disquietude at the opening of the 21st century, products of the bloody massacres of the 20th. And, as important as human freedom is, where are the rights of the unborn? This is the supreme question that is being ignored by industrial societies. Jesus is the Sacred Avenger for God in matters of morality, and it is certain that justice will be meted to the guilty because the vengeance about which I speak belongs to Him. My children, circumstances need not be this way. You can pray for Jesus to abate this punishment, but you must foster the revisions He requires. If God were an unmerciful Father, I would not be speaking to you now. I call upon you to fight to the utterance with all the imperatives you can muster for the conversion of lost men, asking for appropriate amendments that will elevate the weakest among you to their long-sought dignity in Christ.

You can imitate the compassion of Jesus in profound ways by the holiness about which I speak. You can stand tall in the universe as fashioners of peace and good will through venues your forbears could not imagine. You reach the summit of life's meaning in the Holy Gospel of Jesus. And, this is much more than meets the eye; it is absolute spiritual insight, attested by your sacrifices. With this faith, you see Me in the midst of the anguished world, calling My children to the Glory in which you were first created. I pine for your allegiance to Jesus because I know that His Sacrifice is your Salvation. You are unable to comprehend righteousness without Him, and you are helpless to reach the New Jerusalem unless you bathe yourselves in His Sacred Blood. My cherished ones, this is accomplished by your prayers. Ask Jesus to give you sanctity of the heart in the Cross and bestow upon you the newness of life that is found in His Paschal Resurrection. I beseech you to discard your fears about the way the Holy Commandments are enforced as a means of purifying you. The annals of history should clear your doubts about the demands God makes of His chosen flock. Heaven perpetuates in your hearts the explication of His Divine Will to the far corners of the globe. And, you must open your lives to your countrymen so the exile of humanity will have a meaningful ending. It cannot be overstated that you must seek the intercession of the Angels and Saints to help define your stature in the fullness of God's Kingdom. If you are unable to envision the happiness that He lends you, then surely you can anticipate the Light of Paradise in the Creed you profess. I remind you to beckon the power of the Holy Spirit to flourish through you, and call on My intercession as the days unfold. I am not leading you to some remote kind of divination that springs from unknown origins. My goal is Truth in the human heart, the bonafide affection for God that the Holy Spirit has sown within you. And, no one should take this faith lightly because it is the source of communication between you and Jesus. If you ponder the wholeness of Salvation in everything you are taught, you will sense the connection between the requirements of the Cross and your reaction to the words of its Victim. You will glean from life's experiences the measures of devotion that inspire you to learn more. When this occurs, My children, you will recognize your hearts coming to life. If you peer into the faces of the poor and see Jesus standing there, you will realize that you have reached the summit of holiness as His mortal creatures. Everything I have taught humanity since My first apparitions has been about elevating the Cross through your lives. I have told the world for generations about embracing the reciprocal aspect of redemption by your faith. The more you evangelize Jesus' teachings, the fonder you will be seen in the eyes of the Father. God has never forsaken you, and He will never leave you orphaned. These are the reasons I have come. I am hopeful that billions of sinners on Earth will welcome My Son's Easter Mysteries, especially during Holy Week. This is a special year because it is another opportunity to elevate Pope Benedict XVI. Please know how jubilant he will be when you pray in unison with him for the sanctification of the world. My Special son, it gives Me hope to speak to you and your brother. Even though he does not hear Me at this time, I know that he appreciates Me speaking to you and sharing My sentiments. I am mindful of your gifts to My children who return to the Roman Catholic Church. Thank you for taking such good care of your brother, for safeguarding his health, feeding and sheltering him, and for being his spiritual brother in every sense. You are like Jesus; you are like Heaven in his eyes. His body is still making adjustments to the extraction of his gallbladder, but thanks to you and his medication, he is doing much better. I can pronounce him healed. Let us pray for those who are suffering from ailments, and for all who are physically and emotionally abused. I will speak to you next week on the Paschal Feast."

Sunday, April 16, 2006
The Paschal Feast of Easter
2:36 p.m.

"My children, today is the celebration of the new beginning of Creation, of the restoration of the life of humanity, and the refurbishing of hope in the hearts of all who believe in the Messianic Resurrection. How many ways can someone describe eternal joy? With what elation can a man understand victory over death? You celebrate the Sacred Mysteries of the Easter Triduum with the awareness of our loving God at the center of your conscience. He gives you faith to believe, the ability to know, and the presence to act through the Grace of Heaven. It is indeed a mystery to realize the implications inherent in the Resurrection of Jesus for the whole of humankind. When you feel the overwhelming nostalgia of comfort and peace in your lives, you are tangibly reaching the heights of Jesus' Resurrection. In your hearts and minds, when you sense the wholeness of life and the fullness of Truth, you are likewise basking in the Light of His Resurrection. Warmth and goodness are bountiful in My Son because He wraps you in His care. He elevates you to the heights of Triune Love where you see firsthand how beautiful is your Salvation in Him. Today, we remember all these holy blessings, and I ask you to reach deep within yourselves and understand that they are found in you every day. The material world attempts to push you away from feeling the refreshment of the Lord. Life on Earth is a tremendous burden, but your spirits are encouraged by your vibrant faith. This is how you comprehend the Paschal Feast. Christ Jesus conquered your sinfulness on the Cross, and He has given you eternal life by His Resurrection. It would seem that you hear this same message during Eastertide every year, and it is honorable that you welcome it. It is more important that you realize that it is timeless, and so are the years, and that the resilience of your faith to march kindly toward the horizon of immortality is showered by God's holiness. Every parish hails the Church by acknowledging the destruction of death during Easter. However, the more striking connection with Heaven is made inside each heart. You ponder what Easter means for you by assuring God through the Death and Resurrection of Jesus that you belong to Him as a person. This, My children, makes Him pleased! The mission of the Church is fulfilled at Easter; and during the Octave that follows, you are asked to meditate upon the world renewed, on your position in it, what Jesus expects of you, how you will respond, and why you are asked to help convert the multitudes. Without telling your intentions to the Apostolic Church, you would not understand its function from its beginning to its Triumph in Heaven. Thus, you know that Christ the Messiah has been raised from the Tomb to be instituted as the Lighthouse of unending absolution for the entirety of the world. You find great solace in this, and tremendous responsibility to follow Him with the loyalty of the Angels. There is nothing you can do to earn Salvation, My children, but live for God through Jesus; be the servants of the poor whom He came to be. Wrap yourselves in the cloak of Wisdom and learn from the Holy Spirit how to grow the faith of your brothers and sisters by what you say and do. Instill in others your own desire for purity, for true justice, and for seeking the integral communication of Christian fortitude that keeps humanity struggling for heartfelt peace. You have seen the condition of societies today. You have heard Pope Benedict's call for greater clarity of faith around the globe. He has warned My children about the influences of Satan, of people who follow the luring of evil, and of those who are utterly indifferent about the scourges that stand against the righteousness of the Church. I assure you that the Pope speaks on behalf of God; he is the inspirited messenger of the Holy Paraclete to humanity gone awry. My children, there is a pristine essence of Providence calling you. There is a presence of heroism and greatness waiting to come alive at the center of your being. Jesus will take you there; Heaven will open this gateway of excellence that cannot be obstructed. I speak of a new Easter rising within you, a dawn of hope so brilliant that it glorifies the Father who gives beatific reason for your birth.

The workings of the Holy Spirit are the conjunction of the sublime Passion, Crucifixion, and Resurrection of Jesus living deep inside you. Your hearts are to procure the active reception of His Grace upon you, that you become not only the reflectors of His Love in the world, but servants who are resplendent in His Glory. He implores you to join Him on the Cross and sail with Him on the high seas of eternal destiny in His rising from the Sepulcher. Jesus is the Way, the Truth, and the Life; and you are deeply seated in Him to effect the sharing of His Kingdom through the precincts of the globe. The legacies of your Christian predecessors are living with you. Their success is the seed of your progress. God has grasped you, enfolded and possessed you, elevated you, enlivened you with Wisdom, and delivered you to the fore of the Promised Land where the Saints bask in the glow of His Light. He calls you particularly during Easter to become engulfed in the deluge of His eagerness to purify the Earth, to close the cleavages between men, enlighten those who govern, console those who mourn, and enlist the aid of the millions who are wandering other paths. Verily, Easter is about the instillation of knowledge and Holy Wisdom to the depths of the human consciousness, so much so that those who hear of the Incarnation, Crucifixion, and Resurrection of Christ cannot keep from believing it to be true. The Holy Spirit wishes to create a sense of urgency in the hearts of mortal men, one that takes you to the dawn of every morning anxious to pray for the conversion of all lost souls. God deigns to bless your efforts to do this; He gladdens when He sees the world rejoice in the Paschal Mysteries of Easter. There is no doubt that Creation glows in emulation of the Heart of the Father on the Easter Feast. Little children are more giddy, their elder counterparts search for better ways to make peace, the animals rejoice, Nature blooms, the winds and rains bless the Earth, and the wholeness of the universe resounds with the strains, *He is not here. He has been raised, just as He said!* My children, the divinity of hope for which you pine is extolled at Easter; it is your rehearsal for the Eternal Resurrection that will deliver your own souls to the Face of God. Streams flood with miracles; the accord of the heart that is so lacking now is being structured and renewed in the raising of Jesus from the dead. I wish I could convey the happiness this brings. My Immaculate Heart yearns for your comprehension, that you will understand that your existence subsists in Jesus in ways more sanctified than you have ever believed. He will wash the feet of men until they utterly disappear and your souls stand safely in the heights of Paradise. Through the Church, in your trust and the Profession of Faith, by the oath of the Apostles, and in the calling of Divine Absolution, you are asked to be steadfast in the goal of entering Heaven someday. Just as sure as you are given to the Son of Man through your baptism, you are given to God by Jesus who was Crucified, He who has cleansed the souls of humanity by His Blood on the Cross. My children, the Salvation about which I speak is wholly more than symbolism and objectivity. It is not about magic or interstellar travel. Your redemption is a manifestation of ultimate victory so powerful that you will soon be stationed in Paradise, looking back upon the Earth, wondering how the concept of time eluded you. This is real Salvation and true deliverance. It is Grace abounding through your good fortune. It is Truth conquering lies. It is the mightiness of confession over the fragility of fear. When you ponder the Paschal Mysteries for the rest of your years, remember that Easter lives in you every day. It is the holiest acts of your families, the loyalty of your friends, the coming of every new beginning you could possibly conceive, and the power given innately to you to alter the course of human affairs. Easter is the certification of your faith in Jesus, the afterglow of your acceptance of His Sacrifice, your vision of all eternal moments, the refreshment your spirits seek from the insolence of the world, and your tangible message from God that He has finally decided to take you home.

Do not desist, My children, in taking Jesus' Resurrection as simultaneously yours! Wait no longer to believe! Cast aside the shroud of darkness that makes the days seem so repetitive. Never mind the sentiments of mortals who embrace the defeatist attitude that time is taking too long! Harken your childhood; feel the inner-sense of inevitability that you are growing closer to God. Inhale the incense of Glory that is flowing through your veins. See the smiles of your brothers who have already been raised in the Sacrifice and Resurrection of Jesus to the other side of time. My Immaculate Heart is aloft in hope for My children on the Earth. My feelings of jubilation cannot be bridled. The intensity of My intercession will never wane. Today, nothing else matters but the promise of God to take each and every one of you to Salvation in the Crucifixion and Resurrection of Jesus Christ. This is chief among the principles of Christian charity that give you clearer vision to tend to the poor, condole the brokenhearted, counsel the wicked, and move boldly and carefully through the fabric of time with an ennobled sense of purpose. I bless every child of God with these things at Easter. I pray that you will emerge from your suffering like true champions, rupturing and conquering anything and everything that tries to hold you back. You have been told that you are more than conquerors in Him, and the time has come for you to discover what this means. You have the confidence of heart that your conquest of the ages is nigh at hand, that your vanquishing of pride has begun, that the benevolence you promised on your Confirmation is being fulfilled in this age. God has asked you to stand firm, tall and upright; not in some vain way, but inside the posture of His Heart, with a stately presence, so He can fashion your Crown with princely designs. Take the happiness of Easter with you when you go to bed, and rise anew wearing it like little kings. Thank you, My Special son, for allowing Me to speak to you. You are strengthening the meaning of righteousness for many who will follow your path. Whatever you suffer, whatever you think you are suffering, is not a matter of grief solely for the rise of torment. It is your way of telling God that you love Him. The intensity of your life is witness that you hope for His Kingdom to succeed. The writing you shall release at the end of June is further evidence that He will prevail, that hearts will open like spring flowers to receive His bountiful Grace."

Sunday, April 23, 2006
Feast of the Divine Mercy
2:42 p.m.

"You seek My maternal intercession as you pray for Jesus' Divine Mercy for yourselves and the whole world. I respond to your petitions because I love you. I wish for you to know that My Son is always absolving. Whatever you hold within your hearts, what good things you pray for, the healings and blessings, all of this is yours through the Love of God. Today, I ask you to remember the intentions of His Holiness Benedict XVI and all who pray in cloistered communities for the conversion of humankind. You have long known My desire for the sanctification of humanity, and I implore you to remember My intentions as well. The Diary of Saint Faustina makes clear that you must overcome the hardships that accompany Christianity in the way of Jesus. He looks upon the Earth with pity, and He seeks from its inhabitants an honest pursuit of spiritual health. God knows all about the wars that are ongoing, the separation of families, and every sin by which Heaven is offended. Remember that Jesus is present, especially in the poor, and that you must be comfort for their lives. Compassion with awesome magnitude is sought from those who follow Christ because it is reflective of His Divine Love. And, in order for you to effect this compassion, you must accept and remember that the holiness in your own lives is your sacrificial love. Each time you think of the poor, let this be an enabling of your desire to ameliorate their poverty. This is how the Divine Mercy of Jesus is spread through the nations. Creating new ways to end the injustices that plague the lands is an invitation for Jesus to help His Creation to merciful degrees. You have the power to dispense great acts of goodness, and He asks you to make them gifts to His weary ones, those who are not included in the world's prosperity, the mentally and physically afflicted, and the many who do not know the path to inner peace. We pray for them; we ask the Lord to be their blessing through the dedication of your lives, and we lift them up before Him for healing. This makes your prayers immensely important not only today, but in the future. My little ones, the Feast of the Divine Mercy is more than asking for help for yourselves, and it is larger than the parameters of a single day. This Feast is for the final journey because it gives you vision that remains well beyond the ages. Imagine the changes you would make to the social environment if you owned that kind of power. Ask Christ Jesus to help everyone living around you. Pray deeply for those changes to come, beginning with the personal amendment that He asks of you. He does not call you to grasp every emotion that flows through the minds of other men. He has not summoned you to be counselors without the guidance of the Holy Spirit. He urges you to be consolers in His image through the power of the Cross! There are often solutions to problems that do not seem obvious, that are illogical in human terms. There is holiness and wisdom in people whom you never expected to possess them. If you believe that Jesus has the ability to reach all hearts, pray that they will be spiritually slain by His touch. This Feast is about heightening your devotion to the Holy Cross, so much so that you combine your sacrifices with Jesus' Passion and Crucifixion. It is about contemplative prayer, such supplications that seem extraordinary during other times of the year. And, it is fitting that this day is celebrated the Sunday after Easter because the Divine Mercy of Jesus is about the resurrection of the human heart from the smoldering wreckage of man's corruption. It is about hope and Glory, miraculous Truth, and the beauty of the soul that is not found elsewhere. This Feast is about absolution and forgiveness, and of opening the heart so wide that the Angels can see in. My dear children, there has never been a person who lived without hope because it is natural to the human intellect. It is about bringing the future into the present by giving the spirit to God while still in the flesh. The hope about which I speak is not for fair skies tomorrow or good luck in the games, or meeting that special companion. It is a transcending instinct that reminds you that the union between Heaven and Earth is real, that warms you from the inside when your friends seem so far away.

The Feast of the Divine Mercy is your call to heavenly arms. The Spiritual and Corporal Works of Mercy emanate from this Feast. It is about teaching the ignorant about the Divine Truth of the Father and seeking the brilliance of Jesus' Resurrection as the Fruit of the Cross. You are empowered beyond your remotest dreams to bring comfort and healing to those who are broken. And, as I have told My American children, it is about breaking the backs of the haughty who believe that patriotism is the seed of liberty. Quite the contrary, My little ones, patriotism is seen by your countrymen as license to sin in the name of secular choice. I have told you that Jesus came to conquer the relativism that has enchained America in the dungeon of materialism. The Lord will have mercy on the United States when its people lay-down their possessions, take-up their crosses, and follow Jesus to the Rite of Repentance by their Christian baptism. Then, My special children, to follow the promises of that Profession of Faith! Who among today's Americans will say that they rebuke the provocations of Satan? How many among you will rise and attest that unchecked Western capitalism stands in diametric opposition to Christianity? Only those who see God's Grace with the sheen of dignity! Only the Children of Mary who have been taught to impart Wisdom through the Gospel Truth! I offer you the Divine Mercy of Jesus in reflection of the Grace and Truth to which I refer. Your response, as always, is to give your fiat of obedience to the Commandments of God. In doing so, you make every day one of Divine Mercy. When someone utters the words, 'Our Father, who art in Heaven. Hallowed be Thy Name, Thy Kingdom come, Thy Will be done on Earth as it is in Heaven,' they enlist the God of your fathers to look upon His Creation with pity. They are deeply devoted and thankful for everything He has done to elevate His people to the Salvation granted through the Prince of Peace. They say, 'Give us this day our daily bread, and forgive our trespasses as we forgive those who trespass against us. And, lead us not into temptation, but deliver us from evil. For Thine is the Kingdom, the Power, and the Glory, now and forever. Amen.' I say, come to your Mother, humanity! I offer the immortal cleansing that makes you pure again! I give you Jesus, the balm of Divine Love for the broken children of Adam! Please do not desist in your desire to be healed and raised from the darkness of the abyss. Do not fear the challenges that will come, the cultivation of the ages for which you have prayed. Ask God to grant unto you the Light of Heaven, to inspirit you with gladness and joy that knows no end. Be of kind heart and open mind about the finishing of the generations in the service of the Cross. Bring the aspirations from your youth to these moments, and prepare to see the God of Abraham and Isaac with tenderness. If today you hear His voice, harden not your hearts! I beseech you to perceive your lives through this Glory, through the prisms by which your loyalties have been hewn, through the rainbows of peace that give you strength for the sojourn of life. There is no room for despondence in the Christian heart because you are closer to the culmination of the world than ever before. There will be more days of darkness, both spiritual and spatial, but you must allow your love to carry you through. Those who are close to Me will be spared the gruesome horrors to come. They will kneel around Me and pray for the Mercy of the Christ, for His guidance and assurance that every last whimper of the brokenhearted will be heard. He has told you through the life of Saint Faustina that He hears them. He restores your confidence that builds up your strength in His Eternal Kingdom. Always remember that no power or principality can steal you from Him.

    Thank you, My Special and Chosen ones, for praying on this Feast of the Church. I know the intentions of your hearts and the lives of peace that you have invested in the Kingdom of God. You have been making these clear for more than fifteen years with Me, for the ushering of humanity to the threshold of Everlasting Life. We not only hope together, My children, we see together. I have taught you about the perception of Love through which every other envisionment is threaded. I no longer preface My messages by saying 'If you love God' or 'If you love Me' because I know you do. By all means, I begin by saying 'Since you love God' and 'Since you love Me.' I cannot exaggerate the greatness of this seemingly simple concept. I do not speak to some of humanity in these terms because they claim that I am being presumptuous about them. I know your hearts, and I certainly know theirs. When your lost brothers and sisters become like you, the fullness of God's prevalence will arrive. Regardless of how distant this seems, it will happen in your lifetime. No matter how strongly you disagree, you will see this moment before you walk through the Gates of Paradise. I promise that everything I have told you is true. The question is always the same. Will you be patient? And, you have often thought that it is a rhetorical one because you have no other choice. Today, I promise that your perception of the conditions of the world must not be contingent on what you see, but on the ones you wish to see. One day, as I have said, you will wonder what happened to an obsolete element called time. You will wish to go back and undergo certain suffering again, knowing that you conquered it in the end. Those who have despised you will approach you in the Afterlife, and you will have no recollection of their offenses. I am speaking about a miraculous reconciliation, the true presence of humankind, fully redeemed and transformed in the Light of Heaven. My Special son, I am elated that you believe in the Divine Mercy of Jesus. I am grateful that you call on the intercession of the Angels and Saints for the sanctification of lost sinners. We pray for your intentions, for the prosperity of your holy works, for the gift of your lives to Jesus, and everything you have laid before Him on this Feast of the Divine Mercy. Please remember that you are but a young child in a body that is growing older by the day, but not one that has been afflicted in ways of many around you. Let us thank them for fulfilling their role in the conversion of the lost. Be of light heart and kind spirit while you endure the years. The Holy Spirit that gave such eloquence to your predecessors is enlightening you. I have with Me today a great Roman Catholic homilist who lived on Earth for 90 years, Father Frank O'Hara, who is jubilant to be with Jesus. His tenure was long and dignified, and he is pleased to defer the platform of the Earth to you and your brother, that you will follow in his path of heralding the Gospel. Your book *Supernal Chambers* rings with the same tenor with which he spoke. *In America, they even have houses for their cars!* Let his legacy of humble profundity be a gift to you and your brother. The world will soon be reunited with him and the Hosts of Paradise, and you will see unveiled the purpose of the Faith Church and the fruits it is carrying into Eternity. Jesus has heard your appeals for Divine Mercy, along with the millions worldwide who have embarked on the journey of faith to commend their friends and loved-ones to Him. Summon the intercession of Saint Faustina often, as well as Saints Pio, Bernadette, Augustine, John Paul the Great, and all the Saints. We shall soon meet in the daylight of Heaven where you will know that everything for which you have prayed has been warehoused for you. And, I tell you especially today that you will see Me again before you come to Heaven. Thank you for taking such good care of your brother. He tries not to be a burden. Your charitable care places you among the greatest of the Saints, of the Doctors who led humankind through the most perilous times. Saint John has said on many occasions that he wishes he would have been the sweet consoler to Jesus that you have been for your brother. There is truly no way to describe the inexplicable comfort you have given him over the years. Your reward in Heaven will be great, and you shall see there every soul for whom you prayed, that they would reside for Eternity in Paradise with God. Feeding the poor, clothing the naked, and freeing the captives have been the fruits of this day! I am thankful that My children have listened."

Sunday, April 30, 2006
Saint Pius V, Pope [1504-1572]
2:01 p.m.

"I speak to the brilliance of your hearts, that you will receive the Holy Spirit openly. This day is filled with joy because you resolve to follow Jesus, to emulate His Love and fashion your words and actions from the purview of the Cross. The God of your fathers has wrought miracles of faith to enhance your desire to pray. If you ask Him for help, He will provide it. We seek from Jesus the blessings that will convert the wayward world, a humanity seemingly bereft of the vision to see clearly the pathway to holiness. I have told you that conversion is a process, that it is a product of the granting of forgiveness to those who have never known the benefits of the heart. Thereby, they will not only follow you, they will live the joy of God's daring, leaving their inhibition behind. This is a special Sunday because it is another day the Lord has made;

it is another opportunity for you to see past the present hour into the perpetuity for which you hope. How many ways can the Mother of your Salvation examine your intentions and refocus your vision? I will persist until all My children have received the Word. Many have asked how I can be so diligent, and the answer is plainly simple. I have prayed for your conversion since the days of Gabriel, since I watched Jesus grow into adulthood, since His ministry awakened those around Him, and since His Passion and Crucifixion first cleansed your souls. You know that all time is one in Heaven, and yet ultimately timeless and flawless in beauty and sublimity. You are called to become disciples of the Glory of Paradise, to allow the Holy Spirit to bring the Church to perfection while you live on Earth. Where there is hope and charity in your petitions, there will be the cultivation of men. You are serving a Master who deigns your dignity to be uplifted in moral Truth. I promise that He will prevail by every means, and Creation will be reshaped for the betterment of all souls. Please remember in your meditations the continuity of your lives with your Christian predecessors who are praying for you in Heaven. Each and every Saint has your interest at heart. My Special and Chosen ones, I have great gratitude for your lives in Jesus. I speak to you briefly today because I wish for you to practice your composure in everything I have taught. There is cultivation in your lives, and peace, justice, Glory, and Providence. Everything you have sought from the Lord will come to pass; all the righteousness for which you have asked in prayer will be manifested. I intended for today's message to be brief since I first came speaking to you. You live and grow in the Light of Heaven with compassion for your suffering brothers and sisters. Christ Jesus acknowledges your contributions with His own loyalty to your work. Can you see His gratitude as He dispatches the Angels to prosper your goals for the future? Now, you are being given their intercession because you endure the Earth; you conduct your lives with discretion. My Special son, please do not allow anything to distract you from the mission you have been given. I have told you that you are a creature who has paced himself with a quick mode of living since you were a child. When there seems to be a lack of peace around you, it is because your perception is skewed. The greatest Saints of all, the honored Doctors of the Church, never allowed their poise to escape them. They saw the darkness and pursued the Light. They wept for the sinners of the world and called God to enlighten them. And, like you, they prayed profoundly for the arrival of the Son of Man to redeem the temporal Earth. Has this not been the vespers of the Church for 2,000 years? I beseech you to be fair in your judgement of the proud. I have seen many pious Christians, followers of Me, who self-destructed because they were unwilling to acknowledge that Jesus is in manifest control of His Kingdom. Their exasperation and impatience took them backward from blessedness, onto a course that paralleled goodness, but did not fully complement it. They became self-serving and autonomous from the call of the Holy Spirit because of their pride. In essence, My dear son, they left Me. And, I was unable to control their penchant for becoming first in everything, even to the point that they rejected the capacity of the Father to finish the Earth with their undivided humility intact.

My message today is the same as always. Please know that you have power that is untold in the history of the ages. You are forming an alliance with Jesus, with Heaven and all its Hosts, and with like-minded Christians around the globe who are pining for the ecstasy of Salvation. If you only knew how God wishes to close the refrains of time, you would rise at this moment and ask it to be done. Remember that His kindness is of old; it is brought from the innocence of Gabriel to the power of the Resurrection. Somewhere between your fondest dreams and His determination to claim your soul stands today, not lost in time, but blooming from it like a valorous flower, too bold to cower to the smouldering cauldron that evil has made of the Earth. I seek this beauty from the spirits who live, from the compassion that My Son has instilled in His chosen ones. These are not random days on some anonymous continuum, they are select times of choice, made by the Church and Heaven in unison with Truth to ensure that the Sacred Scriptures are fulfilled as they were first dictated to man. You are not seeing provisions for the deliverance of the Earth, but the actual core of Redemption being given to your souls, the essence of pardon and absolution. There is no man who will ultimately live somewhere between Heaven and Hell, but in one place or the other. This is why Jesus enlists your total commitment to the sanctity of the Gospels. He asks not that you receive the fragrance of one flower to live-out the piety in your lives, but an entire collection of bouquets, the veritable field of beauty that He has given to His people. Seek not just a portion of Heaven, but all of it, complete Glory in its fullest. There is no such phenomenon as partial redemption. Having told you what I have said, and knowing that you accept it, the same does not apply to your daily lives; and this is the source of your unhappiness. God did not Will from the beginning that there would be an explosion on Earth and His Kingdom would instantly form. He knew that it would be the work of converted men, millions of them, during centuries that would upend their lives. He willed that your forbears would participate in the making of goodness in the face of horror, and that they would hand you not only their tools, but the profits of their faith. You hold them in your possession now. And, while there is no reason to believe that Jesus will not return by dawn tomorrow, He asks you to bequeath to your own successors everything you have learned about Heaven from your pious interpretations, the contemplations of your heart, the legacies of the Saints, from innocuous little children, from Nature and the cosmos, and especially from Me. He wills that you maintain your dignity in this procession of things, that you see your place in history as having been the bridge from the past to the future, regardless of how long that may be. The Holy Spirit is helping you make your final imprint on the cultivation of the world and instill in you the willpower to pen your renditions of Love and Truth. This is the process that is happening today. It is the effect of your faith in places outside the Holy Mass. It is the intersection of your mortal existence and the Eternity of God. It is the blooming of Grace and Peace through you, a vessel of Light and Wisdom into places where no one else will go. If men continue to struggle seeking the meaning of life, let them come to you. Let them learn from you all the miracles that God has brought through your dedication and hard work. Let them read your thoughts that have blossomed from your patient endurance, through the tears you have shed while lacking understanding why things seem so grotesque. Yes, let them see the record of your toils for God that you have left for the children of the Earth, for they who seek only a share of the Providence of its Creator. My Special son, I see your life in a different context from your point of view. I see the thread of human perfection sewn carefully by Jesus through the corridors of time, unharmed and unfazed by the contusions of mortality living within you. I see a child of Heaven who worries deeply about his friends, who weeps silently inside to stop the negativity and secular injustice that make the headlines every day. I assure you that they are ending as the Kingdom of Salvation is opening, and I urge you to see them in this perspective. Know that public movements and historical events are simply that—actions of mortal men living in the physical world. I expect them to be holy and seek the Lord with the innocence of eager little children, sharing their wealth and time with those who wish to be one with God. You have been told about Leviticus 19:34 in preparation for tomorrow, and I ask you to look with the perspective of God's Domain peering through your eyes, with awe and wonder, while Jesus looks along with you. There is insufficient reason for you to view the element of time as your enemy because it was divided by God when Jesus was born. It was a Friday when your souls were redeemed. Time is a subset of Eternity, and this is why you should know that your everlasting life in Paradise has already begun. You are embracing the Light that has always been there. Your brother has commended you to it before God. He must know that he has a reason to live, that he has given himself to the Lord for the purity of the Earth. I will always be at your side. I will intercede for your needs. I will offer you the consolation you seek, and I will ask Jesus to comfort your heart."

Sunday, May 7, 2006
Saint John of Beverley [d. 721]
2:44 p.m.

"Now comes the Mother of Jesus to speak to My darling children and give you comfort and strength in your struggles with life. It would seem easy from My heavenly vantage to urge you to be more happy, but your happiness is what I seek because your faith is the exemplification of humanity's future. Your holiness and obedience perpetuate the seamless intercession of the Blessed Trinity in Heaven and on Earth. No matter what you anticipate from God, know that He loves you beyond all telling, and His Will is attuned to the Salvation of the world. Today, you are given beautiful weather to accompany the clemency of your hearts. We pray that the collective spirit of mankind will grow as does the springtime toward New Life, toward the everlasting Love of Jesus. It is true that some have said that God has not made Himself sufficiently prevalent, and this is why He is not known as well as He might by nations and peoples around the globe. I remind you today that your faith is evidence of His presence, as well as the Church through which you exercise it. The most endearing blessing in all Creation is the faith of true believers. Nothing else of any measure, origin, or space is as commendable. You must know that your good faith is not only the exaltation of the Father, but your assurance that you accept Salvation in the Blood of Jesus on the Cross. Therefore, we pray with the conversion of your unbelieving brothers and sisters in mind, that the fullness of repentance will consume their conscience. This is a decision made by man. I am pleased because My children kneel in honor of their Mother during the month of May. Indeed, the changes that will overwhelm the Earth are at hand and unfurling. The reconstitution and awakening of the world are being made in degrees and at levels that are difficult to discern. Each of you is given his work by the Lord, and you are not always told at the fore what role you are playing. I ask you to pray for My messengers; take to heart everything I have said, and open your lives to accept My Son's Crucifixion on the Holy Cross. Heaven bears great gladness for you that can begin here on Earth if only you will recognize what your sacrifices for God really mean. My Special son, O how you make My Immaculate Heart overflow with joy. It is obvious that you battle many obstacles in your life. It is also true, however, that you comprehend what this means to the Kingdom of God. Your brother is undergoing a period of darkness in a way you have known, but he will arise from it. He has no choice. There are no words to describe the gratitude he has for taking such good care of him. I invite you to remember that what you say is true; the Mother of God did not come for no reason. And, I ask you to stop speaking about your victory as though it will come only in the next life. You will indeed be sought in the same way while you live on Earth by the millions who hunger for the consolation of God. As you say, I am protecting your identity so you can live as normally as possible. Your words are profound when you opine that you must be careful what you pray for. Indescribable disarray will come upon you when you are recognized by humanity as emissaries for God. You truly do not know how well you have it. Therefore, when your brother says that he feels as though his life is futile and irrelevant, you must impress upon him that this is not the case. I predict that you will one day turn to the Lord in prayer and seek these days back again. This is another reason why I wish for you to invoke your sense of satisfaction. You are blessed and permitted to see and hear words and images from Heaven that are not widely known by your counterparts. Why has this come about? Because I have foreseen that you would not surrender to the squalls of daily life, and that you will not allow your thoughts to become burdened by the contrast between what I have said and what you actually encounter when you survey the exiled world. The promises of Jesus' Kingdom and the scenes on television have little in common. You are witnessing the widespread perversion and desecration of almost everything Christians hold dear, and this should give you reason to believe that your writings are crucial to these times. I shall bless the little children as you have asked. Thank you for standing for Jesus as you live and never abandoning Him, keeping Him company in the Holy Eucharist."

Sunday, May 14, 2006
Mothers Day [secular]
2:54 p.m.

"Prompted by My undying Love, I speak about your deliverance to Heaven and the amendments to your lives that Jesus expects from His disciples. Today, it is important to pray for everyone you hold dear, all who have supported you through the ages. You are the product of painstaking hours of devotion by your friends, parents, schoolteachers, and helpers of all kinds. It is necessary that you remember them to the Lord in your novenas, and ask Him to bless them. The miracle of My Motherhood is so overwhelming that you can scarcely take it in. I am grateful to those who honor Me this month of May, and I assure you of My intercession before Jesus on your behalf. My children, while I will never exhaust the phrases and images with which I celebrate His Kingdom, it is an inexpressible new beginning for you. The Plan of Salvation for humanity is revealed in Jesus, and you share in His Sacrifice with eternal gratitude. I beg you to feel warmed in His sight, and loyal and simple, loving and obedient. As I stated centuries ago, do whatever He tells you. If you knew how pleasing you are to Jesus, you would wish to live ten thousand years more, accomplishing the goodness you have been according His earthly Creation. Obviously, no one lives that long; most remain in this exile only a few decades. Masses of people will see His Sacred Face before sunset this evening. This is why your work is so crucial, My little ones. Many are the hours when Jesus depends on you to enlighten your brothers and sisters, not only about the Holy Gospel and its message of Redemption, but maintaining a course of conduct that is worthy of His teachings. These are critical times for the Church and the reestablishment of good will. It is clear to you by now that few are the number who take to heart the feelings and well-being of the hurting and impoverished. Millions of mourners around the globe are grieving loved-ones lost to war and famine and disease. I assure you that anything you do for them is a signal that the Holy Spirit is present in you. I ask that you not become immersed in the debate about Satan's attacks against the Church. This is what evil followers want you to do because it consumes time during which you would otherwise be speaking about the propagation of Christianity. Tell the world about Salvation in the Holy Cross without legitimizing any fallacious alternatives. Do not waste your breath assigning pronouns and descriptions to the ilk of Satan. Remember from My first messages that I asked you to concentrate on the message of Redemption, not stopping to stone the devil's dogs. When you dwell upon evil, you will not be emphasizing righteousness. I do not ask you to ignore evil in your midst as if to lend tacit approval, but rise above the commotion and retain your dignity in the Resurrection of Jesus from the Tomb. The debate you should begin publicly and privately is why so few are heeding the warnings of the Gospel Evangelists. Never mind the informal and institutional ways sinners evade the mission of the Church, but present the case for the Crucifixion. I am confident that you understand My intentions. Moreover, it is clear that your best battles against evil are won by your prayers in substance and simplicity so the Lord will reroute the course of human history in favor of His chosen flock. It is not that He has lost sight of the last day in time, but He strongly desires that you help inherently, that you become factors and fashioners of that momentous event. Your strength is your communication with God in prayer, and He flanks you with countless Angels to protect and guide you, to be your friends in good times and bad. It is clear that you know they are there because you have the giddiness of children in their company, and this is your means of emulating them. They shield and advocate for you, striking at your enemies' heels to keep you close to Jesus. Along with your purity, the Angels will remain with you well beyond the Apocalypse.

  My Special and Chosen ones, thank you for remembering Me this Mother's Day 2006 and for taking to heart My messages that I have given in love. The fact that you are still praying with Me is sufficient evidence that your allegiance to Me from the beginning was authentically real. Indeed, the more time that passes, the higher your grade of blessings and the greater is your power on Earth. My Special son, you have written with such profoundness over the past fifteen years that there are hardly words to describe it. Why have you done this? Because you endure. You live your days like a candle, pouring-out your soul for Jesus like His priest-sons. I need not remind you how fortunate is the Church for having you here. I urge you to remember what you wrote this week about living a day at a time, with patient expectation for the return of the Son of Man. There is nothing wrong with living for the moment as long as you know that the entire collection of moments will yield the blessings of Jesus in the end. This is what you have been doing with wholesome success. I am honored that you receive Me to speak to you. I cannot achieve anything without the response of My children. You need not move mountains to please God or create reliefs of artwork, but be holy in the things you do. Sometimes Jesus weeps happy tears instead of sad ones, like when you smile at a stranger, give an extra gratuity to a bellboy, or say a prayer for someone you do not even know. Surely, it sometimes feels like you have conquered the ages when you just place a photograph of a little orphan on your desktop that makes the heavens tremble with joy. You really do not know how much good you are accomplishing, but you will see."

Sunday, May 21, 2006
St. Beaumont of New England [1801-1886]*
2:24 p.m.

"With overwhelming admiration for My children of the Cross, I have come to speak to you about the longing of God to see your souls in Heaven. Why would the Lord of such magnitude seek the company of His people? Because He needs you like the Earth needs flowers. He desires the seamless reunion of Father and child, of Divine Truth and your prefigured innocence. Your presence in Paradise is summoned so your joy will be complete and Creation will be entire. Today, I ask you to pray for this and all the intentions that are being raised worldwide for healing and enlightenment. It is not difficult to see that the prophecies of old are occurring in these days; even the predictions that were given in recent years are beginning to unfold. My children, God has been handing you miracles since the inception of time to tenderize your hearts. He not only speaks to you through the elements of Nature and the Wisdom of the Holy Spirit, but in silent and invisible designs. We join in prayer of thanksgiving for everything the Almighty Father has given humankind throughout thousands of years. I am always prudent to tell you that His greatest blessing has been Jesus. When men stood on mountaintops and asked for the meaning of life, He sent Jesus as the answer. The purpose of the life of man is to become like Jesus, to be the personification of His Holy Love. Many who are weak say that this must be an impossible task because they are unwilling to sustain the sacrifices involved. Others cannot surpass their own penchant for falling into temptation and sin. Still more are confident that their acts alone are the keys to a perfect life. I have told you that human life is a process toward such perfection, a journey on a pathway of encouragement and dispensation. The Holy Spirit guides you to the way stations of time where you are given more knowledge about the changes that arise over the years, naturally, physically, emotionally and intellectually, so you can tolerate them and adapt according to your own spiritual awareness. Indeed, your life on the Earth is about the welfare of God's Kingdom, helping others overcome the adversity Jesus faced as a Man walking the ground. And, your exile is about manifesting goodness and joy in matters of the spirit, not of the mechanics of the world or the type of sensualism that worldly men gravitate to with such distraction. This joy is about transcending the veil between God and man in the indelible beauty of the heart, in the acceptance of tragedy with grace, and in mentoring your brothers and sisters in the requisites of morality. This joy is about character given flight to the deliverance of the impoverished from pain, of leadership that renders the whole world a holier place. It should make you happy that Jesus fosters your repatriation and redeployment into Heaven that is rightfully yours in your inheritance from His Passion and Crucifixion. He wishes to make models and artistry of your souls so Eternity will be appointed by your innermost sanctity. The Father asks His children to pursue these things because you will eventually see yourselves as worthy of the Salvation you are seeking. He calls you to be aware of the deific purpose of your redemption, your repositioning into the heights of celestial freedom at His feet in Paradise. He asks you to yearn for the sweet melodies of the Archangels and the harmonies of the Communion of Saints. There is no need for you to fear the destiny of man, no reason to cower beneath the clutter of materialism or addictions to chemicals and matters of the flesh. Be heartened by your growth in holiness, and you will have the perspective of saintlier men who know that the abundance of Wisdom is at hand. I promise My benefaction and intercession to help you unite with Jesus in everything that will bring you to purity. These are the defining moments of your priesthood, the crucial times for which you have pined during the entirety of the Earth. I ask you to live in patient anticipation for the Coming of the Lord, always acknowledging that you are more powerful in Him than you ever believed.

 My Special and Chosen ones, this is an especially auspicious time for Me because you are about to release another of your powerful books. My Special son, your Christian writings make people weep with gladness and inhale a fresh breath of conviction. You will someday look back on these days with such elation that you will wish to live them again. Nations will seek your counsel and empires will replicate your awesome life. It comes down to a phenomenon called vision, not one by which you see other people or the process of making benevolent decisions. Yours is a vision about the reunion between humankind and its Maker, between humility and conviction, and between the greatest power ever told and the essence of humanity-redeemed. Your vision transcends the distant portals of outer-space, invoking the Holy

Spirit of God to infiltrate every molecule of the Earth. My son, this is the definition of courage and tenacity. Some get it from inheritance, many from their peers, and yet others from speaking Truth to power. Yours comes from obedience and simplicity, and your devotion to Me, the Mother of God. And, Jesus has been the source of romance for many poets, the strength of valorous conquerors, the Bread of Life for those starving for dignity, and the hearts of war heroes and visionaries, including the invincibility of Saint Joan of Arc during her conquest. He has been the mystical and mysterious source of courage for untold numbers of men and women throughout the centuries. And, this is another reason why you and your brother have remained devoted to Me. Hence, when you pray, ask God to bless all whose lives have been strengthened by their own genuflection before the Cross. Yes, pray for all the women whom you know should rely on their gentle side for survival, for them to examine their consciences at the beginning of the day. If you put yourself in the minds of the millions who will come to Jesus because of our work, you will have better focus not only on the immediacy of your life, but on the horizon of blessings that are coming to humankind. Imagine the heights of freedom, liberty, renewal, and jubilation that new converts are feeling. This is the initiation of peace as opposed to the reprisal of vindictiveness. I come to make My children holy, and I will not cease until My goals are accomplished. Jesus will speak soon about His happiness and the power you are wielding on His behalf through your writing, through your willingness to endure, and through the primacy of your vision for the present and the future."

Sunday, May 28, 2006
St. Senator, Archbishop of Milan [d. 480]
3:34 p.m.

"O how joyful I come, My children, to apprise you of the closeness in which you are held by the Hosts of Heaven. I pray for the arrival of every wish you hope to see during these days and the beginning and flourishing of the Eternity you are yearning to reach. Today, I tell you that God remembers your personal sacrifices on His behalf, ones that not only mitigate the transgressions of humanity, but also make yourselves more holy. You become better examples of Jesus every day, His humble envoys who spread the Gospel of Truth throughout the globe. I beseech you to never allow the despair that has caused so much darkness in other lives to envelop you. Jesus remains true to His promise of rewriting your history so you can soon savor every good stride that should rightfully be yours. I have spoken about remembering that your exile is not etched into immortality because God reserves the right to fashion your future however He pleases. When a converted person dies and appears before the Cross, that sinner can ask Jesus to expunge his record from

Creation; and in doing so, the history of the world is amended. While this sounds impossible to you, I promise that it is factually true. Therefore, when you sense the longing of more auspicious conditions to prevail during your life on Earth, this is your petition for God to intercede in the ways I have described. And, when you say that this is little consolation for those who are suffering at the hands of the unconverted, you must take your thoughts into the context of the Afterlife, knowing that the sacrifices of dutiful Christians make these alterations possible. Please accept that this is among the sacred miracles by which you live in faith as you pour-out your lives for the redemption of humanity. I told you fifteen years ago that there is one Salvation, and it is imperative that it be nourished perfectly while you live on Earth. I assure you that Jesus' perfection is not only flourishing through you, but will continue to grow in the hearts of all whom you are touching by your response to Me. You speak of obedience leading to sanctification; and this is true, but it also leads to freedom of the soul. No snares or sorrow can keep you from endless jubilation when you remain in love with Me, with the Mother of your resurrected Messiah. This weekend is a time when you remember those who have died, especially people lost to wars and violent events. I ask you specifically to pray for the consolation of the mourning family members who survive them. Americans of old referred to this as Decoration Day because the families of the deceased would travel to cemeteries and place flowers on their graves. Whatever you do to memorialize them is all right by God because He knows that your love did not die when they passed-away. Be happy for those who have seen the Face of Heaven! Pray that they intercede for you in ways you readily see. Offer them your cares and sorrows, your grieving and sadness, and they will seek comfort for you from the Consoler of Souls. Embrace the Wisdom that teaches you about the Divine Mercy of Jesus, about the peace given your loved-ones who have entered into His Kingdom. Especially prefer your own lives to His commissioned care, knowing that His Providence will lead to your reunion with the ones you mourn. I hope that you pray for the poor souls in Purgatory, that they will see the Light of Heaven by your petitions. Condole the parents and children of the victims of battle, those who fought as warriors, and the millions who died because of social unrest and physical abuse. Pray for the untold millions suffering from depression who are pondering bringing themselves harm or taking their own lives. There is nothing short of your heartfelt prayers that will restore their spirits to the Light of God's joy. If you hasten your novenas for the suffering, He will tend to them; He will offer them the succor they need for their torments. Indeed, He will charitably eliminate their problems by taking their hearts into His Paternal embrace through My Immaculate Maternal Love.

  My Special and Chosen ones, I wish you could know how joyful I am to be in your company. To speak during your Sunday prayers is an honor; it is My way of enjoining the Heavenly Father to mend the world. Together, we have rectified many wrongs, healed broken hearts, reunited divided families, ushered sinners to the Rite of Reconciliation, and given new reason in life to millions who could not find their way. You realize that the conversion of humanity is a process, that it takes time to effect God's Plan. And, you know that we are enjoying great success as time marches forth. You are giving endearing love to the Earth by offering God your Christian lives. You are not seekers of the limelight or practitioners of social elitism. Like Me, you only wish that the world will change, that your brothers and sisters will turn to Jesus in record numbers for the conversion they require to be loyal to the Holy Cross. As the month of May draws to a close, I hope you have the feeling of ascension that I spoke about before, the sensation that imminent victory is yours in the Sacred Heart of My Son. Through the past fifteen years, you have stirred a momentum of triumph that will last beyond the end of the ages. There is no doubt that you will have good days and ones that seem not to be; such is the course of human existence. However, at last, you will permanently taste the perfection in Creation for which you have prayed during the entirety of your lives. If this were untrue, I would have told you. You realize that faith and Christianity are indivisible gifts from My Son to the temporal Earth, conjoined by the intensity of your trust in His Sacred Word. I am with you not only to guide you to that end, but to offer My Wisdom and Grace along the way. These are miraculous times in which you live. The book you will complete in two weeks, *Supernal Chambers*, is another of those wonders. While it would be inappropriate to suggest that any of your books is better than the others, this is one of the Lord's favorites because it is filled with vision and eloquence about the divinity of His Kingdom and the role humanity plays in shaping the end of time. I promise that it will propagate these things with the advocacy of the Angels. Thank you also, My Special son, for the unprecedented gift you gave Jesus eleven years ago today, for allowing God to meld you and your brother into a coalition of exemplary faith. As you see, the Angels have called him to remain inside the parameters of their intercession. The reason is because they do not wish him to depart their influence into the physical realms. I assume that you understand the meaningfulness of their ways. You have known your brother over thirty years, and your endurance and spiritual willpower have fed his own resilience. All the messages you have been given are the product of your love for God. Please never forget that you are the reason the Lord is able to convert many Americans to the Holy Cross. Do you recall that I told the Medjugorje visionaries that I could do little without them? It is the same with you. I have spoken about beauty, supernal Truth, princely conduct, and receptivity to the Holy Spirit. You embody this virtuousness, and you comfort Me when I see only few others willing to carry their cross for Jesus. You appear unfazed by the burdens of sacrifice, and you realize that God has accorded humanity reason to persist in the ways Heaven has touched you. Let Me refer to the picture on your brother's bookshelf *(There was a picture of my brother and me next to his Bible)*. I will tell you what I see, as opposed to what mere mortals might see. I envision the uncontested beatification of the human soul, the surplus of God's pardon, the vastness of His creative genius, the Triumph of My Immaculate Heart, the deliverance of lost sinners to the vestibule of justice, the ecstasy of the Angels, feeding the poor, freeing the captive, enlightening the ignorant, and everything that God will achieve in the annals of men. Why do I see these things? You can tell by your faith. And, this is why I have been so appreciative of you and your brother, that you give your hearts to Jesus by living without the anxieties that kept your trust in God partly reserved in the past. You see the impending completion of the world because your sight is in advance of the end of your life. The creativity in the religious faith of men is unsurpassed at this juncture in time. It would be beneficial to describe to your brother what I have told you about the picture in the frame. He sometimes struggles with what he sees as a contradiction in his vision and the Kingdom of God. When we speak again, it will be the month of the Sacred Heart."

Sunday, June 4, 2006
St. Antonio Vicente, Martyr [1773-1804]*
2:58 p.m.

"With what awakening do My children adore the Cross! It is with gemstone clarity and keen atonement that the human soul pines for Heaven once the heart is inspirited by the Third Person of the Most Blessed Trinity. It is a phenomenon like no other, a reaction to a sublime impulse of Divine Love that pierces the heart with peace. Wisdom permeates and infiltrates the 'being' of the converted person, so no more does one live for the world. I urge My children to pray for the infusion of God's Wisdom into everyone on Earth, that lost sinners will come to Jesus for consolation, knowledge, and Salvation. Today, I ask you to remember to pray for the intentions of the Most Sacred Heart of Jesus and especially for the spreading of the New Covenant Gospel during the weeks of June. Ask God to touch the calloused and cold-hearted with compassion and understanding. Remember, if you will, everything for which I have asked you to pray throughout the years. It is for the grander purpose of Creation that humanity should live, and not only for sustenance for today and tomorrow, but for the inclusion of all souls in the Grace of God, for their participation in the refinement of the Earth, and the shaping of the world into the likeness of Heaven. We pray for the cessation of abortion and suicide, and the eradication of suffering, disease, poverty, and oppression. And, we pray especially for the precipitous end of all wars. There are so many victims from these horrible scourges that their numbers would seem impossible to count. Each serves the Cross with a brilliance that they cannot see. We include everyone for whom you have petitioned to heal in our supplications as well. Thank you, My children, for understanding the power of prayer and asking Jesus to restore the simplicity to the Earth that it needs to turn to righteousness. This is My message for you today, a privilege that I take seriously. It is My call to Christians, that you will undertake the heavy burden of living selflessly and sacrificially toward the just conclusion of the world that Jesus has promised. My Special one, this is a day of importance because I speak at this urgent hour about human holiness. There has been no greater need for the conversion of humanity because the Earth is closer to the end of time. You see it with your eyes and sense it with the beauty of your heart. You are shielded from the throes of violence in your life, but you witness the darkness of others' indifference. I assure you that the spirituality for which we pray will come, and it is being manifested through the Church. I do not make idle promises to keep you attuned to My intercession simply because it seems the kind thing to do. Your life with your brother has a designated purpose in God's Plan. There is no questioning your part and that of your sacred work. Please remember the perspective about which I have spoken, and how precious is your anonymity. Once your messages are examined by secular doubters, the tone of their passages may appear to lose their impact because they will be taken out of context by those who do not believe them, while others will discard them to assert their autonomy from the Church. You have been living a particular peace of urgency by realizing that you have sufficient time to complete your labors for Jesus. Even though this may seem contradictory and paradoxical, it is nonetheless true. Please remember to pray for those who have lost loved-ones to death and for the survivors who do not understand the concept of going to Heaven afterward, especially small children. I will ask Jesus to bless your lives in Him."

Sunday, June 11, 2006
The Most Holy Trinity
3:01 p.m.

"We wait in joyful hope for the coming of the Lord! My dear children, you celebrate the Feast of the Blessed Trinity and simultaneously your enlightenment, conversion, sanctification, and Salvation. I know that you call out to My Son with your prayers and supplications, and you worship His Holy Name throughout the land. I am with you to speak about encouragement and piety today, and the New Covenant that has brought the Good News of Redemption. You are living inside a tidal wave of spiritual transformation, a time when you are being given countless graces before the end of days. Today, however, I urge you to focus on your work for Jesus because the passing of time is taking care of itself. Let each moment be one of joy, an endearing reality of your Eternal Salvation in the Blood of the Cross. Remember the liberation you have found in Jesus and the vibrant beginning you have inherited in His Resurrection. I beseech My children worldwide to reject the stagnation that comes from secular negativity because it is only a vexation to your spirit and an inhibitor to the trueness of your faith. See the expiring years like the tolling of bells, like the beat of Jesus' Sacred Heart against your palms. I ask My messengers and seers to initiate a new movement of Christian joy that cannot be dimmed by the darkness of the world. By the time My message today reaches the masses, it will be obvious that human conflicts do not procure peace, and that you must call your brothers and sisters in every region and of all beliefs to find unity anew. There can be no true peace in the heart when bitterness abounds. This is My call, that you cloak yourselves in the peace of the Holy Spirit that lasts beyond the ages. Do not inject ill feelings where none exist. Look for the goodness in others that is hidden beneath their mistakes. And, live one day at a time! I have spoken of the urgency of the Gospel of Salvation for many years, and today I am asking you to resist the temptation to force the hands of time and the Will of God. Redress your grievances through prayers and accord. Negotiate honestly between yourselves about the disbursement of material wares, but do not compromise the principles of Divine Truth! During this month of the Most Sacred Heart of Jesus, it is crucial that you remember His Divine Mercy that flows from Heaven. Give yourselves to His Absolution and bow before His sacred presence wherever you go. Recite the Holy Rosary in reparation for the sins of the world. It must be true that your bodies will return to the dust when you die, but this does not imply that your souls should perish with them. As contradictory as it seems, the Earth has never been plagued by so many quagmires, but I have never been more hopeful about the effectiveness of the Church. The Holy Spirit to whom Pope Benedict XVI has commended you is nourishing and strengthening you! Jesus is teaching His flock through the Roman Catholic papacy. Sinners are being admonished, servants are giving their humble best, those with vocations are perfecting them, there have never been more Christians than there are now, and children are being fed the spiritual energies they need to encounter the future they will inherit. Let there be no mistake; the Mother of God is filled with elation about the faithfulness of the Church. God shines His beatific Light on your lives to aid your journey to Paradise. These things are certain, and just as certain is that My little children are leading the charge against the dangers in Creation. On this great Feast when God has Thrice given His Truth to humanity, you must understand that you have the power to bend the course of human history. It is in the recitation of your prayers! I assure you that He knows the suffering of the least among you, and He is aware of the abuse of power that is terrifying the Earth. Nothing committed in the dark will remain there, for everything unconfessed that humanity does will be exposed by His Triune Light. Henceforth, I beg you to retrieve the hope you have lost by the erosion of time, by the battering of your spirits from the physical world. Be still and know that I AM is Lord, and He will give you blessings untold!

My children in this sacred home, I promise that your Mother is not unaware of the length and breadth of your suffering for Jesus. It often appears that days are long, but they seem to have gone with uncontrollable haste. It is your duty to find solace in the context of these two, and to live in peace from the break of dawn until you retire for the night. I have said this previously. I implore you, I beseech you, I beg you, and I pray that you will disallow the commotion of the world to destroy your joy. It is a shameless pity for someone claiming to be a Christian to allow his enemies to shape the architecture of his life. In the Name of God, I ask you to stop living with such instability. If there are problems causing your joy to cease, solve them. If it is a brash environment, leave it. If your sorrow is brought on by others, depart their presence. If your sadness is caused by the same routine, change your plans. Do something, do anything to escape the relentless negativity that is bombarding you from the secular world. Your lives should be a confident prayer about forgiveness and contrition. You were not sent to conquer the devil; you have been asked to live the victory of Jesus, for He has vanquished the power of Satan from the face of the Earth. If you are insulted by those in your company, shake it off like a puppy shedding bath water. Laugh in the face of misery. Smile when you see the enemies of the Cross falling into the pit. Ask God to give you joy, and He will do it. Thank you for everything you have done on His behalf. I have every intention of interceding for you beyond the institutions of time. We will sit together in the shade of Heaven where it is always cool and gently warm. We will look at every sunset that God ever placed on the horizons of the Earth like picture shows, and you can tell Me which ones you like most. Truly, My Special son, these are times of change. You sense it in your dreams when your vision is clear. It gives Me hope when you live one day at a time. Considering the urgency of My messages the past fifteen years, I fear that I have left you with the belief that each day is not precious. The insistent hours remain, but God has asked Me to impress upon you that every day is a gift, and you must not place your sights too far into the future. These times are precious because you do not know the day or hour when Jesus will return, and you must be prepared. If He should claim His Kingdom tomorrow or next week, or unknown years hence, He will be pleased with your ascension toward Heaven because of the stature of your heart."

Sunday, June 18, 2006
Feast of Corpus Christi
2:42 p.m.

Ave Verum Corpus, natum de Maria Virgine. Vere passum immolatum in cruce pro homine. Cuius latus perforatum, unda fluxit et sanguine. Esto nobis praegustatum in mortis examine.

Hail, True Body, born of the Virgin Mary. Truly suffered, wracked, and torn on the Cross for all defiled, from Whose love-pierced, sacred side flowed Thy true Blood's saving tide. Be a foretaste sweet to me in my death's last agony.

"Today, My little children, I ask you to remember your vows to Jesus in the Blessed Sacrament, that you have promised to venerate Him in His loveliness, to ensure that He is preserved from desecration in the Sacred Host, and that He is adored by the faithful who come to Him for strength and purification during the Holy Sacrifice of the Mass. You have long known that the Holy Eucharist is your source of peace while living on the Earth because it is the power and Wisdom of the Holy Spirit becoming present in your mortal soul. Thank you for reserving your greatest moments to ask Him to help you in all ways. You are My obedient children who have taken to My Son like ducklings to water, not like others in your company who boast of warlord abilities and social influence. They see themselves enhanced by their vaunted pride before the masses, but you have abandoned the world for the sake of the sanctification of humanity inhabiting it. With this Truth present in you, I call you to pray for the strength of fathers and for their guidance and development beneath the Cross of Jesus. Ask them to help you in areas where they are wise, and counsel them if they stray from the path of righteousness. Call on Saint Joseph to be their intercessor in times of strife, when they are tempted to forsake their duties or are under the attack of evil legions. As you know, Saint Joseph will remedy their predicaments, both temporal and spiritual, because he owns the favor of the Lord. Saint Joseph would tell you to remain faithful to your fathers, to care for them in their elder years, and make sure they know that you respect them. My Special and Chosen ones, I speak briefly today to pour-out My Grace upon you. I do not have a lengthy message because this is sometimes what I do. Please pray for the families of the casualties of war, and especially for their children who are grieving that they have no fathers to hold them. Pray that God will do so as their Father of Love, that He will support their spirits in ways that are miraculous. It is true that supernatural events throughout history have been the source of faith and solace for millions of broken hearts. I continue to be elated about the completion of your new book in ten days, and I assure you that it will be fruitful for the conversion of lost sinners to the Holy Cross. You speak between yourselves with confidence that this is true because it will come to pass before the conclusion of the ages. My Special one, it is obvious that many folks you have known during your course of life are growing older, but their hearts still belong to Me. Everyone you speak to is aware of your grand oratorical works and written manuscripts. It will be a bright future for them under your leadership to My Maternal Heart as the future unfolds. I beseech you to always remember that My Love is invincible and inviolate. I have the greatest admiration for you as your Mother, and sincere compassion for you when you suffer. This is how the Lord makes good of conditions that appear to be less fruitful than one might believe. It will be in the Afterlife that many will see themselves as Saints of the Church. If you fail to remember some things, please never forget that anything is possible with God. He will make the best of human endeavors that place His Kingdom before everything else on Earth.

I extend My gratefulness as you share your friendship with your neighbors. I was saddened earlier last week when you questioned yourself about addressing your adversaries, but I am feeling better as you regained your self-confidence that you have done the correct thing. Please do not go searching for circumstances where it is necessary to admonish such people, but never feel guilty once you have done so. I asked the Angels to see if you would pray about all the inmates who remain in prison cells that measure eight by ten feet square for 23 hours per day. They have no contact with outside societies and little fresh air or natural light. They cannot leave! It would be appropriate for you to ask Jesus to set them free. There are millions of children missing their mothers and fathers today who are locked inside prisons around the globe. They cry to see their papas, but cannot because they are caged behind concrete walls and barbed wire. Some of them will be put to death by wardens in state-sponsored executions. Please include all these sinners in your prayers for the captive."

Sunday, June 25, 2006
St. Sorenthia Contreros, Martyr [1441-1464]*
3:17 p.m.

"While the secular world is broiling in its own apathy, we are praying for the spiritual conversion of humanity. My precious children, I ask you to understand that yours is the time that is awakening Creation to the early fulfillment of God's promises. You cannot be distracted when you remember to bless Heaven with your inundating supplications on behalf of the poor and brokenhearted, the lost and forsaken, and those who are suffering their final agony. My faithful children are seeking Jesus through Me; they are pursuing the perpetual life of Salvation that is found in His Holy Crucifixion. There is no common landmark of human existence in any parallel lives because you were created from the singular Truth that is the Divine Love of God. When you recite your daily litanies, remember to pray for all those who have strayed from the narrow pathway of righteousness. There is no alternative to Christianity that can purify and chasten you. Jesus is the origin of the sanctification of the soul. Therefore, remain sown to the Holy Spirit in His Kingdom for guidance and protection, for nourishment and peace. Today, I call you to remember not only the great Saint whom I have mentioned when I came, but also please pray for all the believers who have assembled at the Marian shrine of Medjugorje. My messages there have been the seed of hope for many millions of aching souls who wish to know Redemption through the Cross of Jesus. Awakening, awareness, and purification of the heart are taking place between the mountains of Medjugorje; and it is a place where many in America have learned to obey the Will of the Father. I have prayed for you there while speaking to My messengers and seers. It is only by your faith that many have believed, that countless souls have turned to the Most Sacred Heart of Jesus for consolation and enlightenment. The Church will ultimately announce the great favor of God that can be received at the holy site of Medjugorje, where priests and laity alike have poured-out their lives in veneration of their Mother. We pray on this special day in history that millions more will go there to receive the Sacrament of Penance and participate in the Holy Sacrifice of the Mass. Jesus awaits everyone across the globe in their home parishes in the Most Blessed Sacrament. I pray that every soul on Earth will live the fruits of Medjugorje in their personal and public lives. When you offer your daily petitions in the future, please remember to pray for the pilgrims who are traveling to My shrines around the world. And thank you, My Special son, for writing a published letter in defense of your Mother. I wished to mention it only after Sister Bernadine from Sacred Heart Convent called you. Yes, she was congenial, and your affirmation of My part in human Salvation and the nurturing of My precious girls was eloquently spoken. There is no doubt that you have furthered the cause of My intercession at home and in other nations. All the Saints in Heaven are pleased to see from the other side of time the awesome contributions that you and your brother are making to procure the conversion of humanity. It is a wondrous prospect to ponder, My Special son, that each of you plays such an integral role in Jesus' Sacrifice. We pray that the sentiments of your parish priest come to pass, his utterances during his homily this morning that confirm that God has a purpose for creating every life for the propagation of His Glory. This does not imply that He is a selfish God with vanity or pride. He loves His creatures so much that He has made you part of the evolvement of the universe as the conclusion of time nears. As I have told you, these are years that are crucial to the coming of the Kingdom of Omnipotent Truth not only in temporal terms, but in the hearts of men. When you say your thanksgiving prayers, please remember to include your gratitude for the gift of faith and for the actualization of that faith into good works.

Jesus is profoundly grateful for your commendation of loyalty to Him. Now, you have arrived at the epilogue of *Supernal Chambers*. You have written such a beautiful book because you endure mortal life. This is not some accidental offering that you are giving God, it is the manifestation of the conversion of the same humanity whom Jesus died to save. It is the opening of your heart to all the possibilities He has laid at your feet to succeed through Him. It is the pinnacle of salvific thought and the spreading of the Good News in oratorical terms that have never before been seen in this age, scripted onto the printed page. And, you have selected a beatific cover for your book, one that will grasp the attention of all who see. Yes, I have told you about watching the sunsets, zeniths, coronas, and the like when your soul has been reposed in Heaven with Me and the Angels and Saints. For now, I need not repeat how important your work is for the Lord. I have concluded today's message. I simply wished to offer My thankfulness and congratulations on completing your book. It is obvious that you feel affectionate toward this one because it reflects your years of devotion and dedication to Me. You have the unique vision that God has accorded you because you said yes to Me in 1991. There is no question that you are My beloved Special one and brother of Jesus in whom He has deposited His Spirit. One of the great miracles for which you will thank God when you come to Heaven is that He has given you many years of anonymity. There are spectators in the thousands who would recommend how to record and publicize My messages, and I am unsure that you understand the degree to which this stresses My visionaries. Also, one of your brother's prayers is that you will give all the glory to the Father for everything he means to you. He would rather live unsung because he knows he offers little to the world. Unbeknownst to him, Jesus has plans that are similar to yours; you have yet to deliver your speech at Chandler Cenotaph. Let us see what the Lord has planned. There is no doubt that He has provided the supernal expanse of His Triune Love. Thank you for keeping peaceful in the changing world by remaining one in Jesus. I shall speak to you at the opening of another new month."

Sunday, July 2, 2006
St. Joyce Ellen Foster, Martyr [1813-1871]*
2:47 p.m.

"My dear ones, thank you for praying with Me for the glorification of God's Kingdom before you, that you will rebuke the cynicism and sarcasm that mark the temper of your brothers and sisters who discount My intercession, and that you will rise in hopefulness for the opening of Eternity upon your souls. I urge you to plead for the clemency of the condemned and everyone being held against their own volition. Pray for the cessation of substance abuse and the millions who are enslaved by materialism. We seek a world that is free from the slavery of lust and licentiousness, and unchained from the bonds of sloth and gluttony. Even as these moments transpire, there are untold sinners in the world who cannot sufficiently break themselves from temptation or seek the simple piety they once espoused in their youth. Christians should renounce all forms of negativity and thoughts that lead to despondence and depression. Most important, My little children, everyone should strive for purity of mind, heart, and flesh so that you are chaste in all ways in the judgement of God. He seeks you with compassion and understanding, and in the tenor of reconciliation. Regardless of what some in your midst believe, God wishes not to be the wielder of punitive Providence, for He embraces His people with pity and consolation. He is swift to take you into His care and confidence, to support you in the battles of mortal life, and heal you through the power of the Cross. It is imperative that you accord Him the faith that He has instilled in your hearts so you will believe in Him and call upon His justice, knowing that He has blessed your lives. I also ask for your intercessions for the end of infanticide, for the curing of fatal and crippling diseases, and the eradication of poverty. Living inside every Christian heart is a sacred dignity that must be given room to thrive. Reject the phenomena that are vexing to the human spirit, arising from the secular realms. By seeking a closer relationship with Jesus in prayer, you will be guided to the Light of understanding, to the center of salvific belief. Whether you choose to acknowledge it or not, these are miraculously induced days in which you are cultivating the globe, giving the Holy Spirit the opportunity to reach lost sinners. My Special and Chosen ones, this is perhaps one of the briefest messages you will receive. I have plenty yet to say on future days. It is not that you are unprepared, but I wish you to ease your thoughts and feelings in the Wisdom that God brings, in the sublime and evocative Providence that has been your comfort and bastion of hope. You have given so much to Him that it is beyond your comprehension. Creation is being exposed to *Supernal Chambers* where the Love of the Almighty Father resides, where He presides over His Kingdom with authority and power. I offer My appreciation and blessing on behalf of the Holy Spirit by whom you are led. You have lofty goals to pursue with the thousands of words I have given for your next books. Indeed, you are in many ways just beginning, but have already established a record of achievement that is preemptive of most others. It might seem easy to rest on your laurels, knowing that you have offered an overwhelming sacrifice to the Triumph of My Immaculate Heart. I lack the terms to adequately describe the impact you are having on humanity's purity. Creation is basking in the spoils of your victories, and you will soon recognize your personal touch in the architecture of the redemption of the world. I am not asking you to boast about the laudable holiness you espouse, but realize that you have been contributing to the realignment of the future of exiled humanity who is consistently inhibited by the distractions of the present.

Every messenger with whom I have interacted has asked the same question, 'why is the Lord taking so long?' And, My response has always been that it is humanity who is dragging their feet. The free will given to Adam and Eve is the same diversion that the contemporary Earth is deploying to decline God's overtures. Please do not worry, He will not desist in granting signs, wonders, and miracles until His people recognize His signature. Thank you, My Special one, for the focus and dedication you have afforded Me. I remind you that your sentiments are true, and you must not take too seriously the buffets that the world imposes against you, such as the breaking-down of lines of communication and the disrepair of material things. Not everything that happens is the influence of God; some are the simple correlations between the fragility of your machines and the obsolescence that consumes them. Thank you for praying and taking such good care of your brother. Bless you also for your petitions to heal your family and friends."

Sunday, July 9, 2006
St. Ancestria Largesse, Hermit [AD 817-866]*
2:54 p.m.

"There now, dear children, you are praying in My maternal presence once more for spiritual nourishment and guidance, and for comfort and consolation. I wish to remind you anew that infinite Wisdom keeps you pure, and My words accord you the ability to judge properly the things of the world during your age, that your lives will remain dedicated to the holiness of Jesus in your obedience to Me. As you wend your way to the pinnacles of virtue, I assure you that the Grace you need is with you always and everywhere. It is true that you are a humble people who do not require the immediate acclaim that accompanies other men. You do not demand the affirmation that secular competitors savor because your labors are larger than this life. I offer My intercession and gratitude on your journey of faith, your parenthetic sojourn through time toward the affable pleasance of Eternity in Heaven. Will you remember that Jesus hopes the best for you, and the Angels and Saints are your companions in your quest for Christian piety? There can be no doubt that you are living in times that stress the mission of the Church and the lives of your fellow Christians. Many things you see during these years are not unlike the days of old, with all the wars and calamities befalling the human race. You are aware of the deceit and destruction trying to undo the goodness you have sown through your lives, ones that place a terrible burden on the wishes you have nurtured through time. I urge you not to despair that the failures of secularism do not appear to recede overnight. The free will of men is a stubborn force to amend. You have already achieved your mission in Jesus by fully accepting His Will, and the signs and good omens you have embraced since you were children are now coming to pass. If you remember the pledge God made to your ancestors and forbears, and the blessings He passed to you, your anticipation of success in the Light of the Holy Cross will be well-placed. God has told you through Jesus that He will never leave you orphaned to the perils of the netherworld. The Word of God is the promise of divinity, and you can trust in everything the Holy Spirit commends. My Special and Chosen ones, you have seen that your friends and peers are hungry for righteousness; they have proven this in their curiosity about your new book. This is a precursor to the future when the entirety of the world will come like hungry seagulls to the Wisdom I have imparted through your holy works. I assure you that everything I have told you in the past fifteen years is true and unfolding. Today, I also ask you to pray for the Marian Movement of Priests, and all who have accepted My messages to Father Gobbi. Due to the unfortunate misinterpretation of My words, the followers of the MMP have arrived at a drastic misunderstanding. *By virtue of the year AD 2000, the Triumph of My Immaculate Heart is assured.* The new millennium represents a fulcrum of the ages; the Lord has fashioned the final measurements of the Earth around its current inhabitants. Everyone believing in My intercession should reserve judgement about those who do not, and pray for the ones whose lack of trust disallows them from accepting the miracles of God. There is no doubt that everything humankind needs for the Salvation of sinners is located in the Sacred Scriptures. My messages contain no dogmas that are not promulgated by the Faith Church on Earth. I have come to uplift your faith, to sanction, ratify and strengthen your trust in the supernatural power of the Love of the Holy Spirit. I do not weep because people do not believe in miracles, I weep because they will not relinquish their pride. I mourn because they decline to carry their share of suffering for the conversion of lost souls, that they cannot see their way clear to recognize the purifying graces in Christian prayer, contrition, and sacrifice. I shed tears because too many reject My intercession as though I cannot help them nurture the seeds of righteousness. Time is changing them, and I must remain patient for the wait.

  My Special son, it gives Me pleasure that you have been so kind to all the people you have known throughout the years, especially since I began speaking to you. You have given an entire third of your earthly life to Me. God will reward you with the riches of Heaven. Those who have seen *Supernal Chambers* from your workplace are taking another look at their impressions; not that you need it, but as an act of reassessing their ability to judge other men. You speak correctly when you say that this book is different. And, it opens the door for reviewing your previous works. Even in light of the revelations you made in *Morning Star Over America*, one of the favorite books in your sequence for those who have seen it is *At the Water's Edge*. However, your other books, including the three you have yet to publish, are ones that will eventually change humanity. The support you are according the Lord God cannot be valued in monetary sums; it cannot be calculated in anything other than the magnification of the Glory of His Kingdom. In light of this, your life has become a beacon of knowledge for the masses, a venue for training the soul in the Absolution of Jesus found in the Holy Cross. Is there any way to repay you for the gift of your life to Him? Will your redemption be sufficient to elevate God's thanksgiving for your dedication and devotion to the heights of human awareness? Indeed, you will receive this and more; you will see the faces of untold sinners beside you in Heaven that societies everywhere have already condemned as unsalvageable. You have been the one who has not given up on them, who has held-out for higher grace for the dregs on the Earth whose hearts were opened by your tenacious faith. This makes you a champion in the lineage of the Popes who have led the Catholic Church through Creation's most tumultuous times. Finally, I wish you to tell Mary Jane that she need not worry whether she will have a happy death because Jesus will provide it. As far as the day and hour, tell her that such things are irrelevant in the Plan of God. She will be happy to have lived as long as she has, and glad to join the Angels and Saints in Heaven. And, tell her that God will allow her to speak to you when her soul arrives in Paradise. This will be a special time for her and the entire world. She will see how she has shaped your strength during these years, that her prayers mitigated the gall of human sin, that her presence at My shrines was a blessing to her peers, and that the gift she made of her life to Jesus during her Holy Hours gave Him consoling peace. Remind her that God loves her beyond all imagining, that her paintings of Saint Joseph and Saint Padre Pio gave the Angels reason to rejoice, that her comfort of the afraid and lonely was the Holy Spirit thriving in her. And, please remember to tell her how devotedly I love her; she has been one of the reasons for the dispensation of My Son's Divine Mercy upon this wretched world. Please tell her these things, My Special son; and tell her I will see her in the Light of Heaven soon. Remember the promises Jesus made to those who suffer. I do not want you to see Me as a Mother who is always asking you to look tomorrow for better days. They can be these times if you will let them. In all the themes you just mentioned, let happiness prevail."

Sunday, July 16, 2006
Our Lady of Mount Carmel
2:52 p.m.

"My praying little children, I call you to remember that Jesus listens to your pleas and suspends the laws of Nature to calm the Earth, making the environment for your petitions placid for your souls. I beseech your intentions for the cessation of wars that are breaking-out with ferocity around the globe. There are too many innocent victims who have fallen prey to the armaments of rogue states, and they are agonizing in their homes and on streets from the destructive forces of modern weaponry. These people wish for the peace of Christ to saturate their homelands, and that God will heal their nations with His sublime consolation. And, we pray that they will be given support by their Christian friends and comrades on whose side the Son of Man remains. My children, I call upon your heartfelt compassion for everyone who suffers around the world. I summon from you the contemplative presence that the Wisdom of the Holy Spirit infuses into your hearts to be their comforters during times of struggle, strife, and duress. The most important thing you do is pray to God, that He will send them help. Today, I ask My children to recite the Holy Rosary with fervor for the purity and chastity of humanity, and to emulate the faith of Saint Simon Stock. Give the Lord every facet of your mortal being, that He may envelop you in His care. We do more than pray for those who suffer when we urge Jesus to intervene; we give them to the Love of the Father in every way divine and benevolent. The charity of your Christian hearts rests in the conviction by which you pray for your agonizing brothers at home and in foreign lands. I tell you with the confidence of truth that their lives are softened by your good wishes for them. This is why I ask you to pray and make yourselves holy so humanity becomes the likeness of Jesus, the Prince and King of the Cross. I call out to Christians everywhere and of every origin to inherit in your hearts God's bequeathing genius so you will decide on His behalf for the least among you. The Paschal Paraclete would have it no other way. Please pray with Me for these things, little ones! Thank you, My Special and Chosen sons, for heeding the call of piety that you hear every day. My gratitude and blessings are yours because you have given your lives to My Son. Can you see that you are adored by Him? Every beat of your hearts represents the approaching Dawn of Morning that will bring closure to the ages, ushering the fullness of God's Domain to the ground on which you walk. These are auspicious days whereby you are completing the work to which you have been given. Your walking staff is your upright conscience, and you are traveling the noble paths of righteousness here in the mortal world. There is great reason for you to rejoice in the ensuing days. Creation is becoming more aware by the moment of the power of Jesus to heal the lives of His disciples, to bless you in your honorable loyalty to the God of your fathers, and touch you in ways that reflect the beauty of Heaven. Jesus beckons you to remain aloft in His princely peace, and He seeks in you the ability to serve steadfastly in your works for justice. As I have told you, live each day to the fullest in His likeness. Never lose sight of the purpose of your life; always remember that your goal is Eternal Salvation. Remain true to each day by giving your best, expecting with the same contemplative prescience about which I speak that the rising of the sun in its final hour might happen tomorrow. All the Hosts of Heaven are your conveners and admirers. You live among a contingent of Angels whose intercession before the Throne of the Father cannot be annulled. The Communion of Saints pray for you with a pious ethic and enthusiastic zeal that cannot be dismantled. With these advocates pursuing the favor of God on your behalf, your future looks bright. You are entering a period when the years will take a toll on your friends, counterparts, and family members. You will need to remain strong during the transition of the ages, the times when many people whom you have known your entire lives are called to their rest in Jesus' arms. My Special son, you know that your brother has been permitted to bring a defensive weapon into your home to deflect assailants who would interrupt My messages. You will be allowed to see this sidearm, but it will be stored in a secluded container where it will never be shown. There is no imminent threat at this time, and I wish not to give you the impression that you have any reason to fear. It is another door I am closing that Satan might walk in. There is no need to mention the weapon after Tuesday, and I beg you not to dwell on its purpose. I assume you understand why this has become necessary. Many who have opposed you are teetering on fear and admiration right now because they are seeing a growing number of works from you, and they know that you have been taught to always tell the truth. You have had an enjoyable summer, regardless of how things seem. Someday, you will see from the purview of Eternity how blessed are the days you are living. Your lifelong friends have spoken of your contemplative intellect and bowed their heads in prayer for you. My Prelates are hungry for spiritual comfort, and your books provide it to them with overwhelming abundance. Hence, yours is praying for discernment. I know that you are aware of what this means to Me. He has opened his heart, and he reaches to the sublime elements that his parents taught him about Me and the Hosts of Paradise. It does not require a theologian to open *Supernal Chambers* and see that it is the inspirited work of God. Thank you for being that contemplative soul. Please offer thanksgiving for the miracles Jesus has afforded you in the past fifteen years. Your brother has always stated that if there is good will in the world, there is room for the inception of love in the lives of lost men."

Sunday, July 23, 2006
St. Brigid of Sweden [1303-1373]
3:01 p.m.

"Now comes your Mother from Heaven to speak about the future of exiled humankind. I wish for you to listen carefully because My words contain crucial urgency for those who are far from God. Let us pray that this message reaches the ears of My spiritually famished children who are in need of His Grace and Peace. It is clear that we must tell humanity about the Salvation of souls in the Cross of Jesus and about His call for world accord, for the eradication of suffering of all kinds, and for the purification of the spirit and body of God's people. This does not imply that you must display today's message across the vast placards of the continents, but pray with Me that it will reach all lost souls before the expiration of time. Jesus is extremely patient with a world that is obviously undeserving of His pardon, but His Divine Love prevails over the aberrations of humanity that draw the Earth away from embracing the common piety that has been handed-down by your early counterparts. There is a pace to human existence that keeps you attuned to the inner-workings of Jesus' Most Sacred Heart, a rhythm of life that allows you to know His Will with clarity and sureness. Your faith leads you to the knowledge and understanding of God's Plan for the finishing of the Earth, and I come among you to strengthen that faith for the conversion of the nations. Thank you for heeding the call of the Mother of God, for praying devotedly for the sanctification of your friends, and the Christian obedience that I have summoned from you for centuries. Today, I am heartened to know that God's creatures are turning to Him in large numbers. It is no secret that the broiling of humanity's pride has led to worldwide war during these modern times. I promise you that My Son will not permit these things to fester for many more years. If you stand with Jesus during these difficult times, He will reciprocally remain beside you in your darkest hours of fear, suffering, and despair. He will deliver you to the vestibule of jubilation where you will rejoice with all the heavens in your compliance with the requisites of Holy Love. Thank you, My Special son, for everything you have done to complement My efforts in your day. Thousands of readers have seen the notice of your book released to the public that appeared in today's newspaper. Even though this may not translate into immediate contact from the secular world or even from your faithful peers, it is an event that has been etched in time for the Triumph of My Immaculate Heart. I have told you that no souls who are bound for Paradise will get there without reading and internalizing the entirety of your works, even if at their moment of being laid bare before the Judgement of Jesus. I call upon you to trust My prophesies, knowing that the public is not knocking on your door as we speak to hear what I have to say. I confirm that it is better this way. If you received early citation for your service, I assure you that My messages would have been disrupted. You would have been thrust into poverty, and there would be no way to live in true peace. I am protecting you more than you realize. However, there will come a time when you will be acclaimed for your completion of My anthologies, for the preeminent way you have recorded My messages, and to respond to those who are curious about what makes the Mother of God so holy. I know that there was once a time when you would toss a ball into a basket to the applause of throngs of spectators lauding your talent. And, this was part of your interior balance, the social approval that kept your competitive spirit alive. Being a messenger for the Mother of God does not work that way, but you are inherently and unwittingly expecting it to. Please feel gratified that the Lord is maintaining the ordinary facets of your daily life with your brother so our work may continue; you can publish new books unimpededly, and you can travel your city without the complications that follow others who are seen with distinction by large groups of people. God knows what you are doing; your Bishop is aware, and you and your brother are building-up My Son's Mystical Body as you live each day. This makes your lives an indispensable part of the excellence of Creation and the manifesting of the Eternal Kingdom that humanity will come to see. I am pleased that you are making good progress in distributing My messages, and you will see that they will reach the secular world at the precise moment prefigured by God. Everything is unfolding as it should. Please pray for the two 37-year-old men who took their own lives. Committing suicide is blasphemous against the Spirit of the Father, and it makes parents feel as though they have been unloving. Pray that such self-destruction will end. I assure you that I am aware that many of My children are petitioning to change the world of sin and violence."

Sunday, July 30, 2006
St. Peter Chrysologus, Doctor [AD 406-450]
2:46 p.m.

"The Grace and Peace of the Holy Spirit are with you, My angelic children, and so is the miracle of My intercession. I wish you gladness and joy during these summer days of 2006, a year in the transformation of the world anno Domini, that you will promise to adhere to the Gospel of Jesus to the depths of your souls. You know that His Love is the reason for your holiness, that justice and righteousness are fashioned by your attendance at Holy Mass, and that the passing generations have evidenced the Will of the Father to usher you to undying purity in the Blood of Jesus on the Cross. I call upon you to be diligent in accepting your part in the welcoming of Eternity, to do what is willed for you in the Plan of Salvation, and to greet the future with valor, happiness, vision, and hope. My Love is with you always, extolling the tenets of your faith, teaching you about the Virtues of Truth, and elevating you before the Holy of Holies as a sanctified people, worthy of Jesus' blessing. Let it be known that your Mother is your greatest Advocate in His eyes! Today, therefore, we pray for the uplifting of suffering people everywhere, and for the final purification that will prepare your souls for the highest Redemption God has to offer. These are perilous times during historic years for the Earth and for the Church. If you could see the conclusion of the ages from your position in that history, you would feel confident that you are doing God's work with a prescient proficiency that you never knew you possessed. I assure you that the universe is maturing with grander meaning than you might realize before your passage into Paradise. The mission of the Church is prevailing. My goals for your conversion are being accomplished, and the firelight of the Holy Spirit is keeping warm the elements of faith that must be nurtured until the ages are spent. This is why I come, My children. I call you to sustain your inner-confidence that these days are a reciprocal blessing from the Lord because you are obedient to Christ in all that is worthy of the last sunrise you shall ever see. When the glow of Heaven comes to replace it, you will bask not only in the abundance about which I speak, but in the hailing energy of the Earth, personified by the legacies of all the holiest souls to ever live. My Special son, how happy I am that you are with Me again to pray with your brother for the cultivation of the world and the finding of lost sinners. The relationship that you have shared with Jesus is more than one of trust, but of mutual companionship that transcends the veil of your own mortality. He asks Me to request from you that you remember to keep your heart, soul, and mind trained on the times in which you are living. Focus your effort on the moment at hand, knowing that the Lord will take care of the Eternity that will soon come, the Glory that will appear before your consciousness ever knows it has arrived. You have spoken of life's changes, whether good or inauspicious, as though they are the opening of doors. This is a meaningful metaphor to keep steady watch on the uncertain future. It is an appropriate way to anticipate the unexpected. You will garner strength for your continued journey with this vision. By all means, you will recognize how important every chapter of your life has actually become. You can dwell upon today and Life Everlasting with concurrent urgency and still be single-minded in your thoughts. I have come today to thank you for your many prayers past, for the years you have dedicated to the Salvation of men, for your piety and gentleness, for your invocation of the presence of the Paraclete of the Resurrected Messiah, and for the many other benisons you have bestowed upon His Creation by the goodness in your heart. When Saint Martha served with optimism the God of Abraham, she knew to gather herself around the miracles of His Son, My Jesus, whose gift of raising Lazarus from the dead manifested the spiritual awakening of countless unbelievers. When Saint Martha visited yesterday to assist the work in your home, it was reminiscent of the greeting of the Spirit of God to guide you, give you new strength for your labors, and help you face the rigors of everyday life. There is something you will be asked that you must begin thinking about regarding your body of contemplative works. Which is your favorite? And, you know this forces ajar the passage for you to make difficult choices. How will you fashion a response to this question? How would you develop a hypothetical comparison of the ways your books differ? And, how would you react to a formal inquiry about areas in which My messages have changed from 1991 to the present? *(I gave Our Lady my early thoughts about how I would answer these questions.)* My goodness, that is a wonderful response! Will you remember to employ it at the correct time? Your Bishop has noticed this subtle progression of My messages, and also as an academic, the evolving of your personal writing to rival the Mystics of the Church. Whatever your plans, they will be bound in Heaven as you bind them on Earth. I commend you for staying the course in the work I have requested you to do."

Sunday, August 6, 2006
Feast of the Transfiguration
3:24 p.m.

"Today, My dear ones, I bid you peace in ways you have yet to fathom, and hope through the vastness of your contrite hearts. I bring you God's gratitude for your faithfulness and His profound uprightness while you struggle to emulate the perfection of the Cross. The Feast of the Transfiguration is the celebration of the Glory of the Son of Man, Glory that He had within Him long before He ascended Mount Tabor. He chose to reveal to His friends the majesty and dynamic that He possessed from the moment He was conceived in My Womb. This was more than the revelation of Jesus as the Glory of the Father Incarnate, it was humanity's time to hear the voice of God proclaiming His pleasure in His Son's life and teachings. ...*With whom I am well pleased* is the testament that all souls should seek from Heaven, a blessing that can be bestowed upon mortal men long before they shall die. This Feast reveals to all creatures that spiritual faith is a manifestation of the heart, greater than the eye can see on any ordinary day. Therefore, I wish for My children to remember that Jesus lives inside you, transforming you into Himself, granting you peace, and giving you hope that cannot be procured from anywhere or anyone else in Creation. My children, what the Apostles saw on the Mountain was the same Divine Light shining upon you now, My Jesus who lives and reigns in a Kingdom with the capacity to reverse the effects of time and alter the course of human destiny. Christianity is never a covert discipline, but a kind and loving tenderness, cultivating seeable righteousness in honor of your birth, sustenance, learning, awakening, conversion, and redemption. Let it be true that all men will come to Jesus in their humblest hearts and cling to the Gospel in word and deed. Heap your sorrows and burdens upon the King of Love who was transfigured on Earth the way you shall be recreated in Heaven. Pray for the cessation of war so indomitable good will can flourish in its place. Ask the Lord to bless the world with prosperity and irrevocable joy. If you petition for these gifts, you will see the blossoms of goodness grow where they are now being trampled by lost sinners. My Special son, I am extremely thankful that you and your brother continue to be about the work of the Church. I have come speaking only briefly because I wish for you to relax in the way of your choosing. Thank you for your innocence in a world riddled by the guilt of human sin. The days you are living are blessed with purity, integrity, and esteeming grace. Thank you for sharing My messages with others through your manuscripts and in the life you have accorded Jesus as your legacy to men. This past week was difficult for many Bishops who are explicating their initiatives to stop the priestly abuse in the American Church. Even as your Prelate appears burdened, his heart is consoled and his spirit at peace because the Collations in *Supernal Chambers* give his diocese more reasons to pray. He loves Me dearly and has been expressing his devotion to Me in charismatic terms. Your writing complements his understanding of humanity's hope in their Immaculate Mother. Therefore, you must appreciate the benefits of your closeness to Me. You will see these things before you come to Heaven, and especially upon arriving. And, your brother is building a relationship with the baccalaureate college you attended so there will be another citation in their newsletter about My appearances. All of these issues are adding to the exposition of your work to the nations and to those whom have known you for years. They are among the hundreds in your hometown who are aware of the gift you are to the Church. It is obvious that you do not require their accolades at this juncture, sufficing the point that you must still work for Me with relative anonymity. As long as this exists, you will know that our messages have not reached their fulcrum. Thank you for reflecting the intentions of the Pope in Rome and calling for prayers to foster world unity. There has never been anything righteous in the United States' invasion of Iraq. It is the fulfillment of My predictions of September 16, 2001. There are collateral victims dying from injuries, children starving, thousands of homeless refugees, and countless others whose hearts and spirits are being vexed and violated by the scourge of war. You are fortunate to live in America. Let us work toward the conversion of the hearts of humanity."

Sunday, August 13, 2006
St. John Boniface McCarthy [1121-1166]*
2:51 p.m.

Diatessaron: harmony of the four Gospels arranged to form a single narrative.

If your brother does wrong, correct him; if he repents, forgive him. If he sins against you seven times a day, and seven times a day turns back to you saying he is sorry, forgive him. [Luke 17:3-4]

Peter asked, 'Lord, when my brother wrongs me, how often must I forgive him? Seven times?' 'No,' Jesus replied. 'Not seven times. I say seventy times seven times.' [Matthew 18:21-22]

"Dear children, on this fortunate occasion, My desires are coming to pass because we are speaking directly about the reorientation of the collective human spirit so all in the world will hear about the necessity to accept the Holy Cross as your source of Eternal Salvation. We have been afforded a unique opportunity in these times because of the urgency of the sanctification of men. Thank you for heeding My call and responding to your Mother. Today, I have come specifically to My Special and Chosen ones because I know that it is oftentimes necessary to renew your hearts in the Light of Jesus' Sacred Love. I have offered testimonies of Americans who are growing increasingly impatient about their everyday labors and whose minds are at the point of breaking from the pressure of tending to their lives. Why have I done this? First, because I want you to know that you are never alone in your struggles inside the temporal realms; and second, so you will realize that your misconception about others having more productive lives is inaccurate. It is obvious that you are working for the Lord at an unprecedented pace, but the burden placed upon you by Jesus is light. Indeed, the physical world has not laid upon you an egregious weight that your religious faith cannot sustain. At various stages along your passage through time, especially during the past fifteen years, you have paused to wonder why humanity is not answering My call. This is not an attribute that is reservedly yours as pilgrims in the Church. Imagine the deep frustration of Catholic leaders and other clerics who watch the same news you see every day. They furrow their brows in disbelief about what they see affecting the condition of humanity's soul and the precipitous breakdown of its moral values. They have bequeathed polemics and diaries in their estates that have bemoaned the atrocities of a people they felt helpless to convert. My Special son, they have never been alone in their frustration. You and your brother have joined them in speaking and writing about the ways they have been treated in the secular arena by holders of wealth and members of the other gender in whom they placed a high degree of respect. These have been learning experiences for you. As with all My messengers, becoming visionaries, seers, and locutionists does not exempt you from formulating opinions about the endeavors of human existence. Some are centered in the same issue as before, that your brothers and sisters and fellow faithsians are not deferring to My messages, choosing instead to continue living as though Jesus is not trying to reach them. This is a wholly different kind of frustration than you hear from many with whom you work that are confused about the suffering of good people in most every setting. Thanks to your openness and candor, you have helped your superiors see more clearly about how their subordinates grieve. They are overwhelmingly grateful for your honesty. More than twelve years after I began My messages, you wrote a meditation titled *Rambling*. It is an indication of your deep concern about the conversion of the human family, a document that Jesus has taken to heart, just as your workmates were moved. I have little way of proving that the changes you seek are occurring without transporting you to the future to show you. However, doing so would detract from the elation you will feel about how My Son has provided for you. In the context of a metaphor you mentioned since we last spoke, what would be the purpose of playing thirty-two minutes of a basketball game if it ended on a last-second shot? Why not play until someone scores and conclude the contest at 2-0? Indeed, why not have the racing cars you watch every week travel one lap and award the trophy to the winner? My point is that these things consist of a process, not unlike life itself, by which you refine and perfect your *reason* for competing, not simply whether you are the best in the end. Your life on Earth is like a link in a chain with which men connect the past and the future for Jesus to elevate the weight of the world into the heights of Paradise. I previously said that this is a process, one that is not only painstaking, but of fulfillment, excitement, agony, torment, grief, jubilation, emotion, and so on. These sensations do not leave you too weak for the fight, they inspire and prepare you for the last shot and final lap. You are legitimately concerned about why more people are not heeding My messages, as have tens-of-thousands before you. What we must do today is reassess your view of victory so you will know that the Triumph of My Immaculate Heart is comprised of the rendering of humanity to the Passion of Christ and His Triumph over the Cross.

The parting subject I will discuss today is the inspiriting of the Apostles and writers, especially the Gospelers and Saint Paul. Consider the passages I offered at the beginning of this message. You are aware that four men recorded the Holy Gospel using varying and sometimes contrasting words. Do you know how many theologians have mulled whether Jesus meant seven times or seventy times seven times in fulfilling the responsibility of forgiveness? How would you advise them? Historians inquire which transcription was clearer. What did Jesus say? He said both, and the Scriptures reflect it. The reason I bring the idea of *diatessaron* to your attention is so you will understand that

Jesus spoke panoramically to the heartstrings of His followers, just as He does today. This is how My messages to you and your brother in the United States complement My apparitions around the globe. I tell you this because I see the curiosity of your faith, and I sense your willingness to retain the originality by which I have brought you the joy and brilliance of My Immaculate Heart. I know that you are devoted to God, and I am grateful for your prayers and sacrifices for Jesus and the Cross to which you are so consecrated. While you did not see Octavia at the fairgrounds last evening, you saw his friends who will give him your regards. *(Octavia was a huge draft horse that I had seen at the fair previously, whom upon the first time I saw him began staring at me and became very animated and whinnying at me as if he was speaking to me. On that occasion, I began imitating the sound back to him which caused him to continue for the longest time as if we were "conversing" back-and-forth. Many people were standing nearby watching the phenomenon with amazement. I was tickled by it, and as we finally walked away, I told my brother that I wondered what I had said to the horse.)* The horses love you because you recognize their brawny elegance, resounding the mightiness of our Creator who conceived them. Your heart is fascinated by their strength. They are poised, stately, collected, and befitting of the power by which they pull for the Kingdom of majestic Truth. Most of all, they are gentle in ways that giants are meant to be. And, your ballroom dancing is beautiful. Thank you for staying the course, for praying as the Saints have prayed for you, for your allegiance to My Immaculate Heart, for your compassion for suffering humanity, and for espousing the patience that I have sought from My messengers and seers. These are times that do not try your soul as much as they test your faith. And, you are faring well in that examination; you are helping Jesus in every way He requires. Thank you deeply for remaining true to Me. The Lord is with you every moment of your life."

Sunday, August 20, 2006
St. Bernard of Clairvaux [1090-1153]
2:48 p.m.

"Worthy are you, My children, of the benediction from Heaven that gives you complete knowledge of God's Triumphant Love. I bid you joy and holiness on the Feast of Saint Bernard, and I engage your faith to accept the Will of the Father for the purification of the Earth. You do well always and everywhere to praise Him for His goodness, and I ask you to heed the Wisdom of the ages, for soon the world will pass away, and you will be with Me in Heaven. Today, I have come to urge you to pray with the Saints for the transformation of humanity into the image of Sacred Love, to the perfect reflection of the compassion of Jesus, and the beatific spirituality that makes you so admirable in the presence of God. I call you to gain the sense of Truth that leads you to the pinnacle of prayer and service for the Lord while you live in this world. You must never surrender to the forces that lure you into temptation. Vanity, pride, and excess are enemies of your piety because they inhibit the movement of men toward the Grace of God. When you pray, He enters the location where you kneel. He will bend Creation according to your wishes and heal your land. Henceforth, I seek in you the austerity that He commends for you, for the enlightened heart, and for the Kingdom to come. Your intentions should include everything for which Pope Benedict XVI is praying, and for the cessation of war, the end of poverty, the alleviation of suffering, and for the end of abortion. These are among the plagues you should ask God to dispel from the Earth. There are multitudinous reasons to ask Christ Jesus to bless your lives in unprecedented ways and close the divides between parents and their children. Seek from Heaven the convalescence of everyone confined to hospitals, nursing homes, and sanitariums around the globe. The Almighty Father hungers to bless you by every conceivable means, and you are the people chosen to receive His undying compassion. As the latter days of August approach, please remember to observe My Queenship prayerfully, and I will bless you and present your petitions before Jesus. I am your Intercessor and Matriarch who holds you deep within the bounty of My Immaculate Heart and beneath My Holy Mantle. I intercede with urgency because this is a time for prayer. My Special son, if you can see your way clear to be more patient with your weekday chores, I will ask My Angels to protect your heart from harm. You are being tormented by Satan and the physical world for the explicit purpose of inducing you and your loving brother to surrender to the doldrums of everyday life, thereby ceding to evil the spoils of the victory Jesus has handed you. I beg and beseech you never to let this happen, especially while the fullness of My messages is being prepared for release to humanity. This is a crucial period you have entered. You are correct, My messages are beautiful, and humanity will love them. The only factor that will impede their presentation is your perceived strife and subsequent exhaustion. I have told Jesus that you are suffering, and you require His intervention. Heaven is aware of your struggles. When Jesus asks the question about the origin of your dismay, humanity should never admit that it is from simple boredom. This is insufficient reason to beg His advocacy. You have an entire world to convert to Christianity. Ask Him instead for the eradication of evil and for the sanctification of the lost. The Gospel says that you will prevail at His behest; you shall survive and succeed in everything Jesus asks you to bear because you love Him. There is neither an hour nor moment when He does not perceive your plight and agony. The Father in Heaven watches over you every day, and He wants you to believe that He is present. Human exile is not an imprisonment that you endure, or a depravity, but often the impugning of your dignity and sense of self-worth. Jesus is deeply concerned about these things, and He has said that anyone trying to take them from you is guilty of egregious transgression. You are suffering for the Cross. I told you in times past that this would happen. However, it is not an unending torment; it will come to an end like the rising of the sun. Please take life one day at a time because, as you have said, you do not know what unexpected doors the Father will open, fracturing time into individual pieces. I have completed My message for today. O' I hope you liked it! Your Morning Star anthologies will be massive volumes of charity, peace, Wisdom, vision, and Truth. Your collection is growing so elevated that it will take flight of its own accord. I have implored the Son of Man to heal your spine. Thank you for taking such good care of your brother. Twenty-two years ago at this hour, he saw his mother's mortal remains lay in state at the funeral parlour in Ashland. His heart has never forgotten it, but you and I have brought him comfort. I wish the best of life for you with splendorous miracles and good health."

Sunday, August 27, 2006
Saint Monica [AD 332-387]
2:58 p.m.

"This is where you are brilliantly blessed, My little ones, where you hear the call of Love from the Mother of Jesus. I wish you well on this day of rest because I know that your spirits often tire from the concerns of daily life. In Jesus, you are never lost; your souls are uplifted by the strength and courage of Divine Wisdom, that of the magnitude of the decades readily ushering you toward the end of time. I speak with happiness because you are with Me to pray for the conversion of lost sinners. This is your gift to God and to the Church, and it is your commitment of conscience to yourselves as servants of The Christ. Please always remember My intentions inside your sanctuaries. I know about the hurting in your families and those who are suffering in places that no one sees. My Immaculate Heart is filled with empathy for the masses of My children around the globe, and you would be surprised to hear how many petitions are from people who would be considered to have no spiritual inclination at all. Thank you for finishing your work as it has been assigned and according to your stations in life. Your charities, penances, contrition, humility, servitude, prayerfulness, tenderness, and compassion are the building blocks of mutual friendship and absolution; and this is the life Jesus is asking you to adopt. Please accept My heartfelt gratitude for everything you are doing to enhance His Kingdom, for the ways you emulate His graciousness, and for the long-suffering contributions you have made to the broken souls longing to see His Face. Today, it is important to pray for those who are lost in accidents, fires, natural disasters, acts of violence, and by self-inflicted wounds. And, please remember to pray for the strength and consolation of their families. I have spoken on previous occasions about living prayerfully, offering your guardian Angels the opportunity to embrace you physically and spiritually in a dangerous world. It is true that you must never live in paranoia, but you are given the gift of intelligence to know when you are in harm's way. If you are sown to the Spirit of God and not to the flesh, you will be safeguarded by your good judgement; you will know when there is peril nearby. My Special son, it is ostensively My purpose to speak to you about conditions around the world because I know you are of a state of mind to pray for them. Your supplications are reflective of the poetic awakening that God seeks for the Earth, and your service to Him in ameliorative ways has long been the staple of your life. Therefore, I urge you to pray for My little ones around the globe who are lost, those who are taking others for granted by their greed and self-aggrandizing tempers, and the prodigals who refuse to obey the teachings of the Church. I summon My children to seek all that is holy in your homeland. I came to America where your forbears once lived, where they played as children among the fruit trees beneath the blessing of the sun, where they sowed the future with new seeds of hope, and where they built their sons and daughters into caretakers, visionaries, and statesmen. I have led you to the Cross to turn your burdens into opportunities. What you perceive to be mediocre, careening, and destitute can be transformed into farseeing faith if you trust what I am saying. You are afflicted by offensive trauma and by pains that draw you into new dimensions never before known to men. I call you to the larger reason for your birth, to recognize that the Earth is but a skiff on the seaways of Eternity, so you will open your hearts to the accessibility of the Truth taught by the Holy Spirit. You need not reject your own heritage to pay homage to God, but incorporate its best aspects into your holiness in the Church. Once you understand what it means to be saved, you will never be lost again because it is impossible to unring that bell. We must pray to end all wars and famine around the world. The Lord will answer your petitions as you raise them because He wishes humanity to know that He is listening to you. You represent the seamless unity between Heaven and Creation-redeemed."

Sunday, September 3, 2006
Pope St. Gregory the Great [AD 590-604]
3:02 p.m.

"I speak to My esteemed children on this late-summer afternoon to bolster your strength, faith, vision, and hope that the Light of the eternal ages shines on you auspiciously, and to say that these times shall live forever in your hearts. You are seeing the days, weeks, and months that are shaping the Earth to complement the beauty and standing of the universe. Please know with sureness that God has favored you with My presence, giving you the blessings of Truth and Justice from His Countenance so this year will be encased by the peace that has fashioned your resilience in Jesus since before you were born.

It is clear that your march toward Heaven is a grand procession, and this year is framed inside a past and future that wills your unity and participation in the Salvation of men. Thank you, My little children, for leading such exemplary lives for the Holy Cross. Whether or not you realize it, the unfolding events that led to this moment were ordained prior to the founding of the Earth in time and space. Your souls and those who are destined for Paradise are situated precisely where God wishes them to be, defending your faith, finishing the work Jesus began 2,000 years ago, exhibiting the piety that the world must don like a raiment, and giving Heaven that lasting distinction of grace in anticipation of your arrival there someday. Where your forbears have spoken of eloquence, sublimeness, perfection, inner-peace, sanctification, and endless jubilation, they referred to these hours of your lives in this place, where you have stood firmly in favor of and bowed humbly before the Son of Man. Never fear that the blessings you have garnered for the world, Nature, life, and purity will ever be lost, for they are irrevocable gifts from the Father of Love. Henceforth, proclaim your dignity in the New Covenant as a reverent species, created only a little lower than the Angels, and forever as stunning as their holiness. Hold high your heads alongside the Holy Cross that has elevated you as a re-commissioned people who belong not only to the ages, but to the timeless Father who has given you life and breath. Built into your future is the beatific perfection to which you have been called since the Christ Child's first infant cry resounded through the dark corners of the globe. Indeed, these are the times of commencement for the redeemed, the hours and moments of reconciliation between Heaven and Earth. Save the ages remaining in the temporal world, you would already be there. My Special son, I dignify not only your trust in Jesus, but the faith you preach among His people. You live not a mechanical or manufactured existence in a place where the heavens deign to tread, you give meaning to the artistry of Creation, willed by the Creator of every good thing. I would be remiss if I did not remind you of this, and ensure that you are worthy of accolades fit for a champion. Thank you for your humility, persistence, and righteousness. Most of all, bless you for taking such good care of your brother who is not your equal in matters of piety and wisdom. You have been given to each other through the passage of mortal time for co-reflection and companionship, not unlike the seventy-two were sent to the farthest corners of the Earth to teach, heal, admonish, console, and enlighten. As I have indicated to the rest of them, you surely must realize that time is wending its way around a bend that it shall never pass again. Please be at peace with God and believe that what He wills for you is best for your service in His vineyard, best for the ullage about which Saint Paul spoke, and best for the emitting of the Light of the Cross from your position in this room. It is true that I have spoken with My dear children in metaphysical overtones that serve to rekindle the connection between 'being' and 'accomplishing,' but you are manifesting a record of achievement in Jesus that is somewhat unprecedented for your age. Where the Lord sees foyers and vestibules filled with converted sinners returning to the fold, He also sees you as a revolving beacon summoning them. Please be gracious in His sight the way you have been since the days of your youth by envisioning the lost coming into His arms slowly but definitively, and thank God in Heaven that He gave you and your brother this indispensable role to play.

You know that God is the Master of timing, and we shall see what He has planned for your holy and persuasive work. Finally, please pray for your war casualties and the thousands who have died on battlefields, and for their survivors. History and eternity will remember the repugnant invasion of Iraq by the United States of America as one of the most grotesque injustices in the annals of human experience. My Special son, I will help, but you are responsible for guarding the work you have invested in My messages for over fifteen years. You must be cautious and wise, protecting yourself spiritually and physically, and engaging others scrupulously in all ways."

Sunday, September 10, 2006
St. Nicholas of Tolentino [1245-1305]
2:26 p.m.

"The awesome wonder of God bathes you in Beatific Light as you continue depending on Him. Jesus provides every hope, every reason to espouse Christian goodness and lend yourselves to His Mercy before the ages have passed. My little ones, today is a time for rejoicing in the impending fulfillment of these promises. I am with you to pray for the awakening of Creation in such a way that vanquishes the enemies of the Blessed Trinity and converts lost souls to God's Absolution, to find them wittingly seated at the Table of Plenty of their own accord, and to ring-in an era of trust and heroism as the evening of the world has come. And, for what do we search on their behalf? It is obvious that global peace has been elusive to humanity; and for such unity, we approach the Heavenly Father. You have never doubted that those far from God can be converted; by all means, this is why you are listening to Me. And, you have long praised the aspirations of the Archangels who have given you enlightenment through the power of the Holy Spirit. In turn, you are heeding their calls and admonitions in matters of faith and sacrifice. God is forcing the repentance of His wayward people in ways unknown before these times because many of them are ignoring the inevitable justice of His Kingdom. If these years seem too long for His lost sheep to obey His commands, they will never concede to spending eternity with the Saints in Heaven! The latter is a gift of lettered genius and inexplicable ecstasy. Therefore, we pray to end all wars and create a new age of clarity for the human conscience. And, we pray for the end of abortion and contraception, for the renewal of the bonds of good will that have adorned the ages with indescribable currents of sublime peace, and we pray for the flames of righteousness to consume the whole Earth, as surely as Jonah was swallowed by a whale. Please be My humble petitioners, preparing for everything that Jesus wishes to dispense to His brothers and sisters. Give yourselves over to the singing of joy and composure in the symphonies of the Holy Spirit. These are the blessings for which we pray. My Special son, I shall speak more briefly today because this is sometimes what I do. I promise that you and your brother are complying with the Will of the Father, and you recognize His signs of approval in your actions on His behalf. I wish for you to consider some of these gifts to be reparative in nature, that you are exacting Heaven's justice in your native land in ways that exalt the Cross for the spreading of the Holy Gospel in your day. Please remember to pray deeply for America, that your fellow countrymen will find their way into the Church with apostolic poise. They agonize in a writhing, shadowy hesitance when they are called to believe, but they seem unaware that their lack of faith is the source of their inhibition. I call them for Jesus not because they are perfect creatures, but because they need Him to ascend that holy mountain. They must be reminded that every Christian is fragile in the beginning, but it is better to make a novice mistake now than commit a veteran's blunder later. I have said that spiritual conversion is a process of new beginnings. I call the children of God through the heart. You know that the heart is a more sacred repository than any museum, archive, vault, or ossuary. If someone's self-confidence is freckled with doubt, they should turn to the Holy Spirit for courage. And, humanity must stop infighting and disagreeing about issues that have no eternal bearing. How many times have the deafening thunders of battlefield bombs given way to the clopping cadence of horses hooves? It happens every hour before the sight of God, not only when a president is slain, but every time another pauper dies while society turns away. It is such things as these that prove that the United States has undergone a vulgar deformity of character that is unworthy of your national renown. Your citizens must answer the call of the heart with valid belief in the Providence of the Father. And, My children, you must do this with joy. Anyone who lives their faith grudgingly would do better not to practice it at all. If My children respond to My call, the world will inherit many cherished memories in the months and years to come.

I have also said that some people behave recklessly when going about their work and leisure without levying the consequences, ignoring the danger and their protection. Pagans do as much. Many have complained that God must not have taught guardian Angels to swim, otherwise drowning men would be alive today. Such statements as this are heresy. The Angels stood on the banks, calling them to quit the waters for the safety of the shores. The Angels' warnings rang through their ears, but millions around the world surrendered to their own demands for exploration. It might seem difficult to realize, but such people equate their talents with the invincibility of God. And, what occurs?

They perish because they have not permitted Him to lead them on the supernatural, beatific, salvific, spiritual pathway to deific surety and destiny. This is the essence of My messages to you since 1991. And, until humanity understands that being godlike means becoming the seamless image of Jesus Christ, more will die, and millions will be buried after having succumbed to their misguided addictions to human pride. Your potential is centered in the creative Love of God, not in growing your prowess in the art of physical exertion, but in the excellence of reparative holiness. Your placement on Earth has been misinterpreted by some of your ancestors who were blind to the definition of eternal triumph, choosing lesser victories instead. I have called you beyond this world, to the realms of celestial majesty, and to the pinnacle of holy sacrifice so you will become not only disciples of Christ, but living relics of His holiness that provides the ability to ford streams without getting wet and dive into the depths and tame such stingrays as the one that sent the Australian zoologist to his death. I am not rebuking humanity for being curious about the constructs of the world, I am saying that your emphasis and priorities should be placed on the Creator of that world. This is what I am asking you to tell your brothers and sisters before your work is finished."

Sunday, September 17, 2006
St. Robert Francis Bellarmine [1542-1621]
2:19 p.m.

"My dear little children, I remind you that nothing in linear time can inhibit the Wisdom of the Lord from reaching deeply into your hearts. You are praying with Me today because humanity remains in great peril, distracted from holiness by matters having nothing to do with their Salvation. They are preoccupied with syndromes, fashions, scurrilous perceptions, and false impressions. Vileness spews from their mouths that is unworthy of a people destined for resurrection. Why do they shout sordid epithets against the sanctity of the pure of heart? Why do they disparage those who have given their lives to God? Because they have yet to do so; they will not close their eyes to the world and open them to the Glory that is yet to be seen. They look at poverty and neglect as though they have no cause. While squalor and vagrancy imply personal intent, the poor do not choose to linger in the darkness of the night without food and shelter. The inconceivable air of hubris that many Americans show toward the less-fortunate is directly from the mind of evil. Your nation has shown a propensity for this; it is the substance of your history. This is why I have come to pray with you. We must touch the hardened of heart and convert them to the compassion of Christ. There is such error in their judgements! It must be made clear to humanity that once you accept the Wisdom of the Lord, you will have reached the antiquity of human miscalculation, rejecting the anarchy of impiety and ignorance. You will be open to Heaven's stupefying Grace, and you will sense God's Light and no longer tend toward the darkness. I have come to accommodate your transition into this holiness and help effect your first factual rebellion against the obstinance of your enemies. This is why I summon you to attend the Holy Sacrifice of the Mass with regularity. When you enter the sanctuary, you can feel the matrimony of your spirit with the Divine Love of God. You take leave of your doubts and inhibitions about what Jesus requires of you, and it grows more obvious that the purpose of your lives is to become renewed in His Crucifixion. The Earth beneath your feet is also His footstool, and you can peer into the skies and almost see His Face. What do you suppose His expression to be? If He sees you bearing a heavy heart about the conditions of the world, He will help you carry your burdens until they have all been rectified in Him. He will raise you like the waters lifted Noah, bringing you the satisfaction that Heaven supports you not only from On High, but from the foundation of your existence that keeps you fasted in mortality. My children, you will someday shed these bonds. You shall break free from the snares that entrap you in the mayhem of Creation and the forced habits that define you as creatures in need of atonement. My Immaculate Heart is a basin of opportunity for you to be cleansed by the Blood of the Cross of My Crucified Son. We love you in ways yet untold by the prophets of the past. The Father reveals His miraculous Truth in messenger and Word, by Apostle and disciple, in the morning and at night, and through the fuller awakening of your conscience in the Holy Mass to which I have referred. My little ones, I beseech you to approach your Mother with innocence and pining because the Son of Man evokes it from you through the confession of your transgressions. Hence, you are sanctified by being purged of everything that stands contradictory to your holiness. My Special and Chosen ones, I particularly request that you pray for the millions around the world who are suffering from illness and disease. Remember the indigents for whom you have prayed for many years, the new ones that are cast into suffering because of the greed of the rich. I have castigated humanity when its members do not reflect the mandates of the Gospel, but I also commend you when your actions match those dictated by Jesus through the Holy Paraclete that have always been present in Him. By edict and example, He has taught the world that Prudence and valor grow from your own faith-sacrifices, from the benefit you gain in eradicating injustice where you can best serve His cause. The Christian heart is your clarion to do more, to receive the sacred knowledge and Wisdom from the Father that the Earth is still broken. Would that every heart open to receive Him, this shall no longer remain. As the Fall 2006 descends upon you, I invite you to remember the harvests yielded by the many who labored so dutifully in the Spring. These times are yours for planting new seeds of hope in the lives of your brothers, while simultaneously reaping the reward of converted sinners whom you have led to the Sacred Heart of My Son. With trust in your success, you must march forward with your Rosary at the ready to battle against the adversaries of the Church, rebuke those who impugn its holy name, prepare your best heart for the Messiah to enter, be advocates through life for those who are dying, comfort their afflictions, and remember with confidence that your passage into history will reveal your noblest intentions. I have prayed for you, My children! How long I have asked the Lord to be your sustenance, and that the Saints will come to your aid in numbers sufficient to encourage you. We know that your exile is a burdensome task, but you are never alone; you have the faith, intuition, and creative instincts to stand for what you believe. Jesus will help if you welcome Him. My Special child, I have concluded My message for today. I assure you of My intercession for you and your brother's needs. I remain with you at all times and offer the warmth of Heaven's Light that emanates from My Immaculate Heart. I will come next week with a message to reconfirm that these are auspicious times for you, but ominous ones for prodigal humanity."

Sunday, September 24, 2006
St. Augustine Brookhart [1538-1569]*
2:29 p.m.

"Today, I dispatch the Light of Heaven to bless you in peace and goodness, and offer God's consolation for everything you endure on behalf of His Kingdom. Please pray with Me for the cessation of war and the uplifting of broken humanity. It is clear that there are not only clashes of cultures around the world, but a lack of communication between religions. Through all this, My children, I call you to remain steadfast in your faith in the Cross. In the context of warring peoples and colliding ideologies, remember that you are Christians in the lineage of the Saints and Doctors of the Church. They fought battles against Paganism and relativism, and they knew that the Gospel would be assaulted by the enemies of the Church. Hence, as you proceed into the future, do not be concerned with your opposition. Any echoes of adversity are intended to draw you away from your focus, to distract you from preaching the Truth of Christianity, and to bring you sorrow during the wait for the conversion of the wicked. Please remember that the Lord is on your side, that Jesus supports your efforts to prosper the Good News of redemption in Him. Also today, I ask you to pray for those who have been affected by cold wars and natural disasters. Do not forget to pray for the unborn, for those who do not have medical care, for the impoverished and diseased, and for the outcast and abandoned. Most of the manifestos being positioned before the consciousness of humanity today are rife with heresy and the desecration of the Traditions of the Church. If any man claims that these Traditions cannot be justified by Sacred Scripture, tell him that the 2,000 year old Roman Catholic Church is sufficient justification in itself. You carry by your faith the edification of the human spirit in all things pragmatic and sublime. The Roman Catholic papacy is the primal source of piety and catechesis on Earth, and the Holy See has been the Vicar of Christ for all men throughout the ages. This is the beatific fortress of Truth that was situated in Heaven before the Ancients were giddy little children. I summon the faithful to pray for purity in Creation, for the introduction of the mightiness of the Holy Spirit over the flesh. I beseech you to choose wisely the things of life, overcome your weaknesses through daily prayer and meditation, contemplate the priceless morality that God has given you in the Wisdom of Jesus Christ, persevere through your engagement of that Wisdom, see beyond the trials that darken your days with temptation, and yearn for the overwhelming presence of His Dominion in all you say and do. I ask you to be simple Christians and holy people, and give one another your blessing of peace and justice by your exemplary service in pious humility. These are not burdensome manners to offer God; they are not heavy to carry through the world. They represent your gratitude to the Son of Man for His Sacrifice by which you shall be taken to the Throne of the Father. Whether you realize it or not, these are good days. They are times during which you decipher the difference between just causes and worldly whims, between eternal vision and casual sight, and between genuine forgiveness and expedient dismissal. Whatever this day in 2006 means to you and finds you doing, and whenever this message from the Mother of God reaches humanity, open yourselves to the contrition that Jesus expects from you of your own volition so you can attest that you have made a contribution in refining the Earth, purifying the hearts of lost men, clearing the fields with the harvest of souls, and binding-up the wounds that have divided your brothers and sisters with centuries of hatred, prejudice, and disdain. Become a part of the solution that tenders the Earth to the Divine Mercy of Jesus, making yourselves participants in His charge, and opening the future for the mending of ways and the melding of hearts, all to the purpose of uniting the creatures of God beneath the Cross of His Crucified Son. These are the ingredients that perfection is made of, My children. It is here that you find the meaning of existence and the fulfillment of the hopes that have seemed so elusive to you. Thank you for praying with Me. I will speak to you next week with another message for the Church. Let us proceed in joy. Yes, let us strive to maintain the dignity of the soul."

Sunday, October 1, 2006
Saint Therese of Lisieux [1873-1897]
2:54 p.m.

"On this blessed and beautiful Sunday afternoon, I have come to pray with you for floundering humanity, for the purification of My children, for the opening of closed hearts to the Divine Mercy of Jesus, for the sunlight of joy to flourish in your souls, and for the realization by the world that God has dispatched Me to call you to holier lives. It is not enough just to know about the omnipotence of God, My children, He asks you to act on your awareness of His Kingdom in obedience and compliance, to eradicate everything in your lives that fosters selfish pride. We pray for your unity in Jesus' Sacrifice because, by the Cross, all are one in Truth. Today, I ask you to remember the servant of the Child Jesus, the Little Flower, the Saint who gave so much to God's desires in the brevity of her years. It is not too late for everyone to give their soul over to Jesus; and I ask through this message that anyone who hears it, even if near their death, to know that God awaits their willing conversion to the Crucifixion of His Holy Son. The days pass oftentimes slowly, and at other times quickly; and you wonder where they have gone. They are slipping into a history that cannot be relived in your lifetime, but they can be regained in the infinity of Heaven if it is your wish. The mentors who shaped you from the cradle, the ones who nurtured you in your youth, who taught you about the Kingdom of God, who listened and responded to your pleas, and who support and pray for you even now are one in the Mystical Body of Christ to which you are called through the Lord's invitation. If you remember that you are fruits of Jesus' Crucifixion, you will preserve yourselves in heart, mind, spirit, soul, and flesh for presentation to the Father at the end of your exile. Jesus offers the continuance of everything that God has brought to perfection in you, especially the virtuous life that has been implanted in you and given to the Earth in the image of the Saints. You have tenacity and wherewithal in the power of the Holy Spirit through your words and actions when you espouse the temperance that has been so profoundly fashioned into your thoughts. When I tell you that God is grateful, I refer to these things that you do so well in His name, in reflection of the teachings of Jesus. My Special and Chosen sons, I come as the brightness of hope and the consummate Mother of Holiness while you forthrightly proceed with your lives. You give the freedom of the Resurrection to the aggrieved who are oppressed by the worldlings that persecute them. You admonish lost sinners who are steeped in self-interest, lust, materialism, and secularism. Yours is a vision that is not unlike the Doctors of the Church who have passed into the Light of Glory. And, you persistently ask when your time will come to take your case to humanity. The response is that you are irrevocably doing so now. You would not wish to climax your work too soon, at a time when millions are pursuing other matters. They will become desperate to hear My messages, hungry for My Most Immaculate Heart, and starved for the mandates of the Gospel through which they shall be sanctified. I have said that your hopes are well-founded in the outcome of Creation. This is My immutable narrative while Jesus reveals to the world who you are in grander terms. Until that day, I promise that every word you say and every prayer you recite is recorded in the Book of Life where they were inscribed at the founding of the Earth and the beginning of time. The last age will unfurl into the basking bay of contemplation for men from all walks of life, leading them not only to accept their Salvation in Jesus, but to pursue it to the heights of their souls. God looks upon you as you see the Saints, orators, and visionaries who opened the eyes of humanity to the true intent of faith. He acknowledges you as servants and prophets, foot-soldiers who are waging the fight for righteousness with His other chosen children. It has been said that one problem with life is that it is so everlastingly daily, until you look at the calendar again and see that the years are passing away. Please do not feel as though you are not accomplishing anything while remaining committed to your daily responsibilities. My messages magnify your Diary and will lead masses of unconverted sinners to the Holy Cross.

I have said that I would refer to the words of the Holy Father in Rome, Pope Benedict XVI. First, I would like to ask what you believe the motivations of Pope Benedict to be. *(I told Our Lady that the Holy Father is trying to purify all people and lead them to Salvation in the Church.)* Yes, he has done these things to show other religions and the entire world that he is unafraid of speaking the truth. And, his purpose has been to call on peace-loving people to rein-in their rogue brethren. How better to cull peace from others who are prone to violence than to condemn their violent actions? The Pope shifts the burden of keeping the peace onto those who are breaching it. Yes, he knows precisely what he is doing during his homilies, and he anticipates the reactions beforehand. While Pope John Paul II had a charismatic papacy, Pope Benedict XVI is blessed with a deep ecclesial intellect. He was the centerpiece of counsel for his predecessor, and has awaited this hour to lead the Church into the final ages about which I have been speaking for fifteen years. He has lived eight decades of grace and wisdom to reach these times. Non-Catholics around the globe have requested to visit and stand beside him, not because they wish to complain about what he says, but to prove that they are not as violent as their radical counterparts. And, he has welcomed them with outstretched arms, with compassion, understanding, inclusion, and unity before the sovereignty of the Lord's sight. There is genius in what he does, and long will live his legacy of striving for an end to the violence that has plagued humanity for centuries, perpetrated by the enemies of the Church. Pope Benedict's words are easy to understand, and they go no harsher than to place those enemies on notice that the Church will preserve itself. And, thank you for sending a communique to the editor of the newspaper, prompting them to publish your brother's letter about the activist in your diocese who is impugning the reputation of the Church. Please read the paragraph that begins 'Understanding Catholicism...' How could any writing be more conciliatory? Roman Catholics across the nation have been led to this; and priests, deacons, bishops, and cardinals will learn more about the absolution and redemption of men. As I have said, you need not see this occur, but please know that only goodness comes from the gifts you offer the Church. I have watched with gratification as Catholics have wiped away tears of thankfulness and encouragement, knowing that they are not alone in the struggle to dignify the Sacraments of the Church. Mothers and fathers sent their children to markets to purchase copies of Saturday's edition to give their relatives at home and abroad. Elderly men and women used rusty scissors to cut the piece from the newspaper and place it in the indexes of their Bibles and on their altars at home. Copies were laminated and stored in bookcases and lock boxes. This essay is one for the ages, a monograph to be read to the redeemed on Judgement Day by Saint Gabriel because it echoes the Gospel of reconciliation between the Father and His creatures, emphasizing the preservation of everything good about humanity. Just as sure as there are three threes on the clock at this moment, know that God is heralding your literary art with confidence, taking to heart everything you say with jubilation, Providence, and Love. Thank you for responding to My call."

Sunday, October 8, 2006
St. Angeline O'Hara, Martyr [1556-1603]*
2:51 p.m.

"Through your charitable prayers, the conversion of humanity is manifested with compliance and devotion, and the spirit of friendship reigns across your land. Let us pray for these blessings to appreciate during these final years so Jesus can claim an open flock that is anticipating His return. I will help you, My children. I will intercede before the Messiah and foster your nourishment in your struggle to prevail. I shall usher you under the Light of the Ages by which you can see the future with entrancing beauty. And, I will sustain you during the darkest hours when you are lonely and afraid, when Satan tries to take away your innocence, and when you give-up hope of seeing the dignity that the Lord wishes you to enjoy. I have said that I am always with you, each and every one of My children, to give you comfort and consolation as you carry your crosses for Jesus. Surely you must know that I have seen many sacrifices and sufferings by My children through the centuries. These modern times can be ones of peace and positivism if you allow them to be. They can instill in you the ardent desire to reach across the expanse of your differences to coalesce in the Divine Love of God. Beneath My Motherly instruction, you attain that unity; you live in that unprecedented peace. Reading into human life things that are of no significance is a waste of your time. Follow and perpetuate the Gospel message of the Roman Catholic Church, and you will be on your way to Salvation. Pursue innocence and benignity in all things; yearn for goodness, and search for purity. Give of yourselves as you know Jesus offers Himself to you. Be reconcilers instead of dividers, builders rather than destroyers, and shields instead of assailants. If you call on Me for everything you need as the Mediatrix of all graces, I will ask My Son for the benedictions you require to make your lives whole on Earth. All this is a product of your simplicity, humility, and austerity. Pray that the Lord will place these virtues in your hearts, that they will grow and flourish on your march to sainthood. My Special son, as I promised last week, I have come to speak on this day which is filled with the beauty of Nature and the goodness of your obedience to Me. I know that living in accordance with My desires is not taxing for you because it is the fulfillment of your hopes in Jesus. There are many issues being addressed in the public arena, too many debates that are irrelevant in the mind of God. It seems that you do not become engaged in them because you are aware of their insignificance. Your efforts are on the Holy Cross and the unification and cultivation of the Earth in Christian Truth. After you have published My messages to the current date, things will unfurl rapidly. You received forewarning of this during the past week when you and your brother were criticized by some philosophers professing to know all there is to learn about Stephen G. Brady and the malevolent enemies of the Church. Surely you recognize that hatred is working through them. The Holy Spirit lives in you, not vengefully, but with enlightenment for your brothers and sisters. Where there is justice, the kind of justice that flows from God, you will know the uplifting of the Sacraments as its sweetest fruits. If someone demands vengeance against a penitent sinner, they are under the marked influence of evil legions. I realize that I am addressing a matter about which you are fully aware. I am warning Jesus' disciples to be on guard against nonbelievers who would pillory your faith in the public square as a scolding for your allegiance to the Cross. Remember that Satan is lethally adroit at causing cataclysmic destruction to the exclusion of any hint of relief. However, he is incapable of impeding found souls from being drenched in My Son's Blood of the Cross. Humanity's part in keeping your promise as Christians is to present yourselves as Saints; strive to reach the upper registers of holiness, and pray as though your eyes are rapt by the magnetism of impassioned love. If you cut ties with your old habits, you will be free to make these choices. The Supreme Deity is one, inseparable constant. The Blessed Trinity is the Truth; Divine Wisdom is the Way, and the Lamb is the Life. It all comes down to your willingness to make yourselves poor to enrich the mission of the Church. I realize that this is difficult in the United States, a country built on the profits of private enterprise. Wealthy Americans safeguard their assets with vicious arrogance, and most of them do not know the difference between bare necessities and redundant conveniences. They do this while mortgaging their children's ability to care for their own generation. It is no wonder that so many people have said that the future is not what it used to be. My Special son, next week your brother will make connections to enhance the dissemination of your work. He will enjoy seeing his friends from long ago, the classmates and teachers he met in August 1972. There appears to be such a swift passing of time that three decades has been no more than the expiration of a day. Esquires do not disavow ameliorative piety, and memories are shaped by what affects the heart. Thank you for your receptiveness in inviting Me to speak to you. Remember that the physical world will come sprawling around you in good and bad terms once you are recognized as a messenger of Messianic faith. You will need a different kind of protection by then, but you and your brother will never soldier alone. Your critics cannot reach empire status against the Church. Last week was a foretaste of this."

Sunday, October 15, 2006
Saint Teresa of Avila [1515-1582]
3:19 p.m.

"Today, I have reached into the created world to touch My little children who yearn for the Holy Spirit of God with monumental resilience. If you pray with Me for the conversion of humanity to the Blood of the Crucifixion, everyone will know themselves as catalysts for change and advocates through which your lost brothers and sisters are purified in their hearts and minds. In these tumultuous times, God anticipates your prayers. He expects your desire to touch the Cross with urgency. Jesus completes your communion with the Heavenly Father, and He wishes you to accept His Sacrifice with the opening of your lives, invoking the Divine Love of Heaven in ways never before known in the temporal realms. I have spoken of the longing of My Son to become one with you, to nourish you with Wisdom and healing, and encompass the spirit of humanity with celestial intervention. The Lord has given each of you work to complete while you live and become a part of the Kingdom through which you have been blessed. As you see, there is much more praying to do, much greater reparation required to be offered through your attachment to and application of the tenets of the Sacred Scriptures. In essence, God summons you to be united with His Truth in indivisible ways, and fashion your discipleship in the elements of holiness that Christ Jesus delineated centuries ago. When you ask yourselves whether you are suffering with patience and living in grace, you are coherently taking your religious faith into alignment with Jesus' Passion. A daily examen of the Christian conscience is inclusive of the litany of perceptions by which you apply in scrupulous ways the mandates of the Gospel. You might ask how you have tendered yourselves in faith to aid the poor around the world whom you have never met. Such charity is the mainstay of the Christian heart. And, the core of your Messianic values resides in your forgiveness of those who have offended you, for this is the reason for the Crucifixion that has reunited you with our Creator in Heaven. At last, if you harbor unforgiveness in your heart for anyone you have known, you cannot be in perfect unity with the Son of Man, your Savior and Redeemer. My Special one, your Mother speaks with profundity during a time when your lives are opening further with peaceful awareness. Your compliance with God's wishes shows you to be one with His Will, attuned to the blessings that He has bestowed upon His flock through His followers' lives. Can you sense that you are saturated with devotion to Jesus in the Holy Spirit who is speaking through Me? Miraculous are your works and faithful are your intentions when you disseminate My messages to your wayward brothers and sisters with humble attribution. Releasing My 2000 through 2008 messages in three separate anthologies with respect to the New Millennium is what Jesus prefers. You and your brother have internalized all of them to date, and My words are the seeds of your sweetest dreams. My 1997 through 1999 messages relate to the formation of your Diary and the way I sustained you during its preparation. One example is July 10, 1998 that will touch many Christians with new beginnings, as brief as that message is. Thank you for facilitating your brother's visit with his classmates at MacMurray College. He saw his lifelong friends with broken lives and wounded souls, and he knows that your manuscripts and My blessings will heal them. This is what he is most grateful for. The future will bring many opportunities for the dispensation of My messages through these formal outreaches. I am gladdened that you have chosen to partake of the holy life you are leading, and that you place yourself in transcendent joy pursuant to your prayers, anticipating the gifts of God to come streaming into the world. My cherished son, I have said that you cannot imagine the depth in which Jesus loves you, in ways that no power or principality can match. Thank you for calling on the Saints, some of whom were canonized by Pope Benedict XVI, because they are your intercessors. I have sought you to implore their aid, and I have revealed their identities during My messages. Thank you for taking such good care of your brother. He finished the task of attending his class reunion, completed the requisition and dispensing of the cemetery deed for his brothers and sisters, and can now concentrate on the problems of the world. Your brother believes what you say about your detractors, that it is their unchecked pride, but he does not allow it to counterproductively affect him. He pities them because he knows the outcome of the universe. Let us pray for sinners who do not see how offensive they are by their stubbornness. In the epitome of irony, your brother has been accused by atheists of being deluded because he kneels in homage before the God of their fathers. Please pray for all Christians who are persecuted for venerating the Cross. Timothy's sister Patricia in Heaven will touch your hearts on her birthday tomorrow."

Sunday, October 22, 2006
St. Chantel of Nevers, Martyr [1911-1949]*
1:36 p.m.

"Now, during these propitious moments, I bring Jesus' benediction for your good works and holy achievements in appreciation and admiration for everything you are accomplishing on His behalf. My children, once I establish dialogue with My visionaries, I never leave you, even if My appearances are unbeknownst to the rest of the world. I could never ask for your heart and then say nothing more until you enter the magnificence of Heaven. In the meantime, we shall speak about the Cross for the benefit of humanity and toward the pursuit of holiness for all men, for the intentions that God laid-out for the centuries, for the healing and mending of hearts and ways, and for the Light of Divinity to broaden the horizons of your hopes to the halls of Eternity. Today, I bring you vision and inspiration for these things because I join My prayers with your petitions. I seek Jesus in you so God will know you when you die. Please remember of the Father that His eminence breathes through your love for others. He desires not only your commitment to your faith, but consistency in practicing it. You are no longer compartmentalized in a world that seems distant from His Grace, but are woven and incorporated into His Kingdom like threads in the fabric of His handiwork on the Earth. In this, you are participants in the sanctification of your brothers and sisters in much the same way that Jesus is your source of conversion and forgiveness. Why? Because you teach them about their Salvation in Him, about the cultivating and purifying Wisdom of His Dominion over the world and all created beings. If your goal in embracing Christianity is peace, then you must realize that such is the product of self-immolation and sacrifice, that it is a goal achieved by allowing yourselves to be overwhelmed by the power of the Holy Spirit in ways that only those who will enter Heaven can understand. Many of you do not already know because you are distracted by ordinary days and material things, by the burden of avocations and capitalism, and by the struggles that carry you through the years into the vestibule of your impending mortality. However, your forbears reached Heaven because God loves them the way He did when they walked the Earth, giving them the gift of edification through the blessings of the Saints who preceded them. You have entered the latter part of AD 2006, and there are still many prayers for you to lift. I have spoken about the deficits of Creation many times, and you know what your personal needs are. I urge you to blend these into a universal prayer fashioned by your love for everything good that God has given the world, for your intentions that mean so much to your families, for healing and sanctification, and especially for the conversion of the wicked. I have told you that where there is darkness, you must be hope for the world. You must be healers and wound-dressers, teachers and advisers to even greater men who seek you for consolation and support. This is what will make you giants among them; it will place you in good stead below Heaven and bring you to the summit of beatific vision in all things that touch the Heart of God. You must rest and rise again with this vision, and in the knowledge that each day is counted as your posit of virtue to the Earth on behalf of the Savior of humanity. In so many ways, My children, you are like Jesus, and you emulate Him when you exercise the holiness of which you are capable. If you wish, you may refer to the possibilities that are dispensed from God as the divine potential in every living thing; that all you see, hear, and experience has within its grasp the ability to facilitate the growth of His Kingdom where you live and breathe. And, in doing so, Eminence breathes through you; it flourishes and abounds through the charity inside your hearts. I promise you, My little ones, that this is what the Lord asks of you; it is what He is waiting to see before the end of the ages arrives. If this were not possible, He would have already come. Therefore, I beseech you to turn this potential into true love, that you will respond to Jesus with affirmation to the Holy Gospel through your dedicated actions of faith.

    My Special son, I offer the Lord's accolades and benisons for remaining at your brother's side and continuing your long journey of labors on behalf of Jesus as the months expire. It is not easy for you to see the movement of time without others offering you the decency that you know of Heaven and the Hosts who love you. It has been the same for all the centuries since the Son of David ascended there. He promised that He would never orphan you; this is why the Holy Spirit is alive and thriving in your heart today. These are not only crucial times you are living, they reveal the need for prayer, for remaining steadfast in your devotion to Me and the Angels who have guided you in matters of faith and the Will of God. You have seen the corrupt works of heretics who oppose the Vicar of Christ, but you have the insight and allegiance to the Cross to know not to fall prey to their lies. Why would anyone be concerned about the status of the Church when such error comes from incipient revisionists claiming to be so knowledgeable about the intentions of the Holy Spirit for these modern times? And, to exacerbate their gall, they seek My help as though I would endorse their wrongdoings before the Son of Man in Heaven. I need not remind you about the workings of evil around the world and in institutions claiming to be friends of the Church. Some of them are like wolves in sheep's clothing who are attempting to defame the Church so as to elevate their pluralistic relativism before young people who are more impressionable than them. God has the right to choose whomever He pleases to succeed Saint Peter in the twenty-first century without any diatribe from false apostles, especially those whose credentials are limited to the fanatical ideologies of social science. The Roman Catholic Church is not a democracy, and those who believe otherwise are doing more harm than good in the mission of the conversion of lost sinners. We have in the past used the word 'amazing' to describe situations and people, and that word is applicable here. I am pleased that you are accomplishing your goals and have not allowed others to dampen your thoughts or force your spirit into darkness. Thank you again for taking such good care of your brother; and know that he is remorseful for offending you during the past few days. You and Jesus are all he requires in this world, and he knows this from the center of his heart. He will mellow as he continues to age. I will ask Saint Chantel to intercede for you in extraordinary ways before the day is through."

Sunday, October 29, 2006
Saint Krystyn Izaak Karol [1844-1903]*
1:39 p.m.

"Enter, My children, into the loving concession of My Immaculate Heart where I offer you rest. I protect you from the disingenuous forces of the everyday world that try to dampen your faith and lessen your expectations of achieving the holiness to which you are called. Please pray for everyone whose hearts are vexed by those around them, who prey upon their innocence and lead them down sinful paths. I bear true witness on behalf of My Son by affirming and confirming your good standing before the Cross in the shadow of His Sorrowful Crucifixion. You are worthy children who have earned His blessing over the years, not unlike your forbears who suffered with distinction to propagate the Sacred Scriptures, that the entire world will be brought to the Church. It is imperative that you pray with Me during these latter ages for people in every land to turn their hearts upward to the enlightenment of Divine Truth that is given through the power of the Holy Spirit. For all your research about the beginning of the Church, its structure, hierarchy and mission, nothing is more important than sharing the gift of Christian Love. One need not practice a religious vocation to understand God's desire to redeem you, to embrace and enfold you in His patriarchal care. Where would the world be without His providing? For every complication that befalls humanity, there is a single solution to them all, and it is the childlike innocence of Heavenly Love that the Lord plants in your hearts like a flower. Indeed, He wishes that you will be nourished and grow by the Wisdom and peace that are profoundly given to you when you open yourselves to the ingenuity of the Most Sacred Heart of His Son. My children, you are greater conquerors than you believe. Your vision is broader than the parameters of time and the constraints placed upon you by space and the timid years. I have spoken to you about transcending the elements that hold you fast to the Earth by praying and becoming involved in the contemplative lives that aided the Saints in knowing God to the highest degree. This is no different from the First Century Church; it bears the same cause for the conversion of the lost to the Gospel and eternal Salvation in the

Blood of Jesus. Today, I also speak to you about the Saints because you are entering November. Please remember all who have died, especially those for whom the Church summons special prayers. Give God your best supplications for those in Purgatory and the many whom you have never known that have fallen asleep in Jesus. They are and shall become willing intercessors for you from their station in Paradise. I remind you that you may someday seek the same assistance from your families and friends on Earth. The intercession of the Saints, those canonized by the Church and the billions who have yet to be named, is the greatest charity you will receive through the Mystical Body of Christ. It is a grace surpassed only by the Divine Mercy of Jesus, and one for which you should pine all the days of your life. With the blessing of the Saints, you can overcome any illness and vanquish any enemy. You can regain the vast framework of innocence that you have long dreamed to restore, for yours is a place that has been reserved beside them with God. Imagine any form of error or any lacking on the globe, and the Saints will intercede during your prayers. Even from whence you were babes in the days of yore, they have welcomed your petitions on behalf of the material world. Through blood and treasure, they have given to God in ways by which you are taught, by self-sacrifice, humility, contrition, servitude, and prayer. Some became accidental Martyrs by mustering courage they did not know they possessed, to the extent of laying-down their lives for the conversion of their friends. My children, the prophecies of ancient days are being fulfilled in your time. You are the achievers of righteousness about whom Moses spoke, and Abraham, and all who preceded the Messianic Crucifixion. The revelations of the mystics who wrote so presciently and succinctly about the world today are coming to pass in your words, deeds, intentions, and motivations that augment the work of the Holy Spirit in dedicated men. Christians devoted to My Immaculate Heart are the Children of Mary for the End Times, and are witnessing the conclusion of the Earth that God planned from the moment He suspended it in space.

Therefore, I come with hope and inspiration that you will dispense My holy messages to the whole of Creation about God's Love so Divine that it supercedes internationality and global wars; it heals pandemic strife and epidemics; it pales the genius of extraordinary men, and it blossoms from the finest of palaces, the human heart. I speak of power never known to the many whose consciences are deceased and poised for the grave. Mine is a message of freedom and release, of the beauty of Nature in spiritual form, of the grandest themes of forgiveness that any nation has ever imagined. I draw you into the Light of Christ for reasons far-flung and hailed by magistrates and magnates, by Archangels and principalities, by royalty and paupers, and by the incalculable women around the globe who are heavy with children that God deigns to be born into the fullness of life. I take you to the Truth, to strength, majesty, agility and confidence that is of old, from days when the winds blew torrents across the Earth to calm restless hearts of solemn alarm. And, in this

Truth, you will discover the only bastion of hope you will ever need. You will stand at the center of perfection and upon the summit of peace. My Immaculate Heart yearns for you to approach Me, your Mother of Perpetual Help, so I can avail you to the limits of healing and happiness on the avenues of trust and sanctity, that you will know why you were born and where you are going. If My Motherhood has taught you anything, I pray that it has convinced you that you have dignity in the Holy Spirit, in the fire that warms the heart and lights the night. I pray that you will hereafter know Me as your advocate and stewardess of the Divine Mercy of Jesus, accepting Him for everything you shall need at the end of time to be raised from the crypts of your death to the Glory of Everlasting Life. Once you have fully accepted these things, you will know what human pain is for. You will comprehend the mandates of physical frailty and the veil behind which you are serving Jesus with honor and privilege. You will gain a renewed sense of vigor for the tenets of your faith, and a greater appreciation for the multitudes of blessings you have received. You cannot reach the climax of life's purpose until you have traveled its trails. Then, My children, you will remember not to forget; you will recall the reasons God created you with tenderness and care. And, you will see from the other side of time why the Archangel Gabriel came to Me with such hope for you. He spoke in the night for the Dawn of New Day. I responded affirmatively with gladness and allegiance because I love you, My children. I have always loved you with the intensity of God. I have dreamed the same dreams that young men were given. I have prophesied the success of Christian disciples, and I have offered My Being—body, soul, Heart, and will—that you shall forever be immersed in the same blessedness that gave Me the breath of perfection. My little children, I beg that you remain dedicated to the Roman Catholic Church through your veneration and reverence for Me. I ask you to treat it gently and pray for one another. Be loyal to those in whose care your future has been placed. Be sound witnesses for the Traditions that have been shared through the centuries, the ones holding you fast to Truth and peace as you complete your lives with such joyful hope. Your Salvation is Jesus' Blood on the Cross, which is the sustenance and nourishment of the Faith Church on Earth. If you do these things, My little ones; if you answer My call for consecration to Me and the Cross, you will capture those dreams about which I speak. You will know that your faith has a worthy reward. My Special son, thank you deeply for allowing Me to speak to you. I say this to My two children who are given to Jesus in ways that you may have never known in your younger years. And, your collection of written works is a body of truth for the conversion of the lost. Someday, millions will see that their journey to Mostar has led them to The Morning Star. I am confident that you can carry through the dread of winter with ardent desires for the bright future ahead."

Sunday, November 5, 2006
St. Althea Wilson White [1756-1800]*
2:55 p.m.

"Today, I come into your presence to shine the Light of Divinity upon your souls and give you the benefit of My holy intercession to build your strength in Christian Love. I assure you that God holds you dear to the Sacred Heart of Jesus; you are the beneficiaries of His Mercy through ways yet unrevealed. We pray for civility in the public arena and fairness in the marketplace that have been lacking in America. We implore the Lord to preserve life through the good works of His followers, and peace to prevail where there is war. We seek in your brothers and sisters the desire to ask Him for the gift of enlightenment in matters of faith and morals, and in finding cures for crippling and fatal diseases. In essence, My little ones, I beseech you to live according to the dictates of the Holy Gospel and the Church's reciprocity through the Holy Spirit. I wish you knew how intense is My compassion, given that you live on Earth that is separated by the veil of your exile from the bounty of Heaven. It is not impermeable, My dear ones, no thicker than a curtain of air! I understand that you struggle to comprehend the meaning of life and cope with its difficulties. I ask God to save you from the schemes of evil men and the entrapments that surround you, fomented by malevolent spirits. If you knew how I pity you, you would seek My intercession to greater degrees. You do not see the pulverizing forces that attempt to minimize your hopes for Salvation and fulfillment. Things are sometimes not as they seem, and many judgements are rendered prematurely in personal and global affairs. It is not always true that familiarity breeds contempt, especially in Christian societies where you need one another to succeed. Even though history rarely reveals its alternatives, you know that your life in Jesus is the one you shall live in Heaven. It is imperative that you comprehend the meaning of the Sacred Scriptures with reference to the final days and latter times. I have prepared you not only to withstand the arduous journey of life, but to recognize the Face of Divine Truth by whom you shall be judged at the end of the world. My Special and Chosen ones, I have come to speak briefly because I love you, and so you will be uplifted by My Wisdom for another week. I bring the solace of Jesus that overcomes your aggravations, and I advocate for you before Him in matters of faith and trust. I hope deep within My Immaculate Heart that you realize that you have already begun to live anew. As I said, if you live as I request, you will not recognize your passage from this world into the next. What does this mean? It is acceptable that you assume that this implies that you can see the Light of Heaven from Earth. What it says is that you must keep Jesus so close that you feel His presence now as much as when you will enter the Gate of Paradise. There will be no debates or debacles there, no lacking or overages, no demands to concede, and no feuds between light and darkness. You will bask in the perpetuity of Triune Love and endless streams of eternal bliss. God knows that this is the miracle that is most difficult to foresee. I have told My children in other nations that I cannot make you happy in this life. However, I can with your help seek a yearning for your happiness, born by your acceptance that Salvation within you has already begun. The concept of time seems stressful not because you lack the ability to endure, but because your brothers and sisters are unwilling to embrace the Kingdom that you hold deep inside your hearts. I have made clear that the physical world is a vacuum of secularism and relativism. Christianity is the succor of life and spiritual reason, founded in the Catholic Church as it was created on Pentecost. Since then, faithful human creatures have been spreading the Good News of Jesus' Crucifixion and Resurrection with the hearts of lions and tongues of angels, with clarity and intensity, devotion and adulation. Thank you for being united with the Saints who discovered eternity in the Cross. My Special son, you must remember that I came because you asked this of Me long before February 22, 1991. Jesus controls the dissemination of My messages that have been given to you and your brother. When your anthologies are published, please do not go your separate ways. Pray for the Will of the Father to be done. Could you be near the Great Battle to conclude the Earth? We shall see what God has deigned. You will soon look into My Immaculate Heart with jubilation and see that the words 'we win' will be the next to issue from My lips. It is only a matter of time. Thank you for lifting the petitions and intentions that humanity requires for reparation, reconciliation, and repentance. Thank you for praying the virtue of purity into being and acknowledging that God is not only the Master, but also the Master of timing. And, bless you for remembering this month all who have died in His friendship."

Sunday, November 12, 2006
St. Pierre de Charlemagne [1622-1683]*
3:01 p.m.

"Welcome to the solace of My Immaculate Heart where the dark devices of the temporal world are repudiated by the brilliance of Divine Love. With the same hope in which you live, we pray to the Son of Man for His affirmative response to your petitions, for the Father's blessing upon your souls, and the intercession of the Angels and Saints who give you reason to lift your hearts in joy. My children, the greatest mysteries and challenges are not always fixed in the seeable traits of existence, but in your acclimation to the spiritual life you find by complying with the Sacred Beatitudes. The Sacraments of the Church, your obedience to the Will of God, and the intermingling of Heaven and Earth beget your movement toward Salvation. This has been an unfolding process since before you were born, when the Holy Spirit established the Church with Wisdom in tongues of fire. What we have done over the course of generations complements the litanies of the Angels so Heaven can be broadened to include converted souls in its preeminent designs. I have implored My children throughout the centuries to augment these designs by responding to My messages. Even though I cannot foretell the precise day when Jesus will return, and I lack the commission to promulgate dogmas reserved for the Mother Church, I do have the capacity to reveal the thoughts of My Son. He is a precious Absolver of your sins! His pity and empathy are of a magnitude that you can scarcely fathom. You pose questions about the art of living every day of your lives, each time you tread the ground as if to know where you are going. All the interrogatories concerning where, why, and by whom you were created are answered in your interaction with the Kingdom of God. Why would the Lord not give humanity the breath of life when you are so beautiful to behold? How could Heaven not call you to the innocence in which you were born infants from your mothers' wombs? When all is said and done by pious men and women, it will be evident that you were fashioned to reflect the beauty of Love; you are Love in the image of Christ Jesus, and your 'being' is part of the perpetual divinity that brings such hope into your dissertations. In effect, you concede to the Will of the Father by your exquisite works of faith. The holiness to which He summons you is an insightful framework, including the thoughts and actions that you generate in His honor. He seeks your prayers and praises not because they add to His Glory, but because it connects you with Jesus in supernatural ways. It should be known that collegial formality does not always imply piousness, although it is acceptable in God's sight. Quite the contrary, the Father wishes you to gather at His feet like children who are unique unto yourselves. The fact that you are united makes you one with Him, and this pleases Him infinitely. Your holiness, goodness, sharing, prayers, invocations, petitions, compassion, and all other things are products of your love in Him; they are facets of your constitution in the Sacred Heart of Jesus. I behold and accept you for Him as My contrite children because My Motherhood espouses inclusion and consolation for the lost, sympathy for the brokenhearted, and advocacy for the helpless. You have entered an era when it is becoming more clear that the recklessness of sinners remains a lethal force across the continents. When the spiritual awakening about which I speak takes root in those who hold sway over the rest, this recklessness will recede. Hence, I will reiterate what I said in 1992. The recent elections in the United States have barely changed anything. Matters of the Christian conscience are not dictated by partisans and politics; it is the reverse. Without the doctrines of Christianity that Jesus issued to Creation, there is no life beyond the polling place or the sepulcher. I commend you to the Divine Mercy of Jesus regardless of your ideological persuasion, and I command your compliance with the Gospel for the betterment of the Earth. Holding fast to these things, you will feel the warmth of the Light of Truth shining upon you with magnified intensity.

My Special son, I realize that you have been battling with too many issues to which you have oftentimes referred as a thousand cuts. You do not suffer these pains without purpose. God hears your every devotion. He concedes nothing in ensuring that you are at every moment bearing closer to Him, understanding the Passion of Jesus more wholly, and defining for your fellows around the globe the meaning of righteousness. When the Paraclete inspirits men and delves deeply in their hearts, the troubles of the world try to drive God out. What frustration this brought into the lives of your Christian predecessors! Every time you entertain a reparative thought about your life and the cruelness of mortality, you are praying for the return of the Son of Man. This is your readiness; it is your life of perpetual expectation that I told you about in previous years. Therefore, you are fulfilling the Will of God in your age; you recognize the need for His clemency to redeem the Earth and reclaim the souls of christened men. Please do not feel as though negativism is inevitable. It is part of the darkness that enveloped the first Saints who ever lived. What made them remain steadfast in their beliefs? Their sense of levity and their ability to see beyond the events of any given day. They gained perspective knowing that no accumulation of ill-giving can offset the Glory of God that has ensued in the lands where you and they walked, served, and poured-out your hearts. There are seasons inside the human psyche, just as they are inherent to the Earth. However, in the final analysis, it is the same Earth that revolves, and the same human spirit that weathers the storms of life in your valley of tears. You are stronger for the fight, and the happiness you seek is manifested through your remembrance of the Crucifixion and Resurrection of My Messianic Son."

Sunday, November 19, 2006
St. Suzette Cartier, Mystic [1856-1903]*
3:56 p.m.

"Heaven is filled with joy not only because Eternal Life is blissful there, but because everyone who sits near the Throne of God anticipates your entrance. My good wishes are with you, My little children, as you progress toward the AD 2006 Advent Season and your praises for Christ the King. Today, I appear in this place to allay your fears about the uncertain future and remind you that your spiritual faith is your security and protection against the throes of temptation and anxiety. You must remember that your faith is a gift emblazoned upon your deepest love. You must nourish, foster, and grow your faith in the ways given by Jesus, with the Cross of Truth as your focal point to redemption. I remind you that God looks for genuine faith, more than a belief system informing your decisions, but a faith that is the substance of your memory, your existence as the prescient followers of the Gospel as Jesus sees you examining the parameters of life. Your trust in Him and your loyalty to the Holy Spirit must lead you to the Wisdom they provide. How is this done? By abandoning your self-will in deference to everything that is from God, to the righteousness that is known to all the Saints, and to kindness, justice, congeniality, and fairness through every facet of the Catholic Church. When your peers speak of honorable men, let them refer to the Light of Love that shines from you, allowing Creation to see you for what you are in the New Jerusalem to come upon the Earth. Your souls are provocative to God when you accede to His Will. And, your works are evocative to all the nations when you declare that His Will is the eternal destination of the mortal world. Your lives in Christ Jesus espouse this destiny. Your petitions usher-in His Kingdom so that everything blessed by Him will prevail beyond the end of time. There is no lacking of matters about which you should pray, My children. There are plentiful issues that need to be resolved. Please take this opportunity to remember that the masterful purpose of human life is not simply to succumb to the burdens of the years, but to transcend them by living outwardly in the Most Sacred Heart of Jesus. His is the life that cannot be destroyed. My Special son, I am elated that you have welcomed Me to speak this Sunday afternoon. It seems that time passes too quickly for you to comprehend the diverse thoughts and actions of the physical realm. I have told you that they are deviant in range and scope, and most of them are irrelevant in the larger plan of God. Yours is the sacred focus about which I speak; you have the desire to see the conclusion of the Earth according to the Holy Scriptures so that all the goals of Heaven can be fulfilled. A week from tomorrow, the Church shall celebrate the Feast of a Saint who is your forbear in faith, and there are many other Saints who have aligned themselves with your cause. You are brothers in arms against the same evil that befell Adam, and you are united beneath the Holy Cross that has led prodigal sinners to become Christians. My Son's Mystical Body has suffered intense growing pains and horrific strife through the passing of time. However, humanity is healed by Jesus' Love, remade by His Grace into greater beings than you have ever known, heartened by the integrity of the faith that I have spoken about today. No human intelligence can supplant the genius of the Father, even in its keenest hour. And, the Archangels share this vision with tenacity, not unlike you and your brother, to teach your fellow men the difference between knowing about God and accepting Him. It is imperative that you remember that I love you beyond your ability to grasp. I relay your prayers to My Son for the conversion of lost souls, for the dignity of the Church, the nourishment of the hungry, and the realization by all humankind that all paths to forgiveness begin in the Divine Mercy of Jesus. Next Sunday will be the Feast of Christ the King, and He will bless you mightily for the goodness you have shown."

Sunday, November 26, 2006
St. Juan Alejandro Torres [1592-1673]*
2:49 p.m.

"I join your healthful, invigorating supplications for God's blessings upon you on this day when you remember with emphasis that Jesus is Christ the King. I urge you to call upon His infinite Mercy for straying men, for the many who do not accept Him, and for your friends and loved-ones who are in need. Today, I appear with deep joy because of your awareness of the power of My intercession. I proceed to call upon Creation to enlist My aid in the conversion of sinners and the cleansing of the Earth of everything that stains it. Those who live in America owe the Lord immense thanksgiving for the gifts He has bestowed upon you. No other nation has access to the benefits of life that you enjoy in the United States. This places upon you a tremendous burden before the poorer regions, to peoples around the world who lack your lavish lifestyles and possessions. I speak of the latter in terms of your Christian responsibilities. Even though you have adequate food, shelter and clothing compared to impoverished nations, you are yet starved in many ways for the spirituality that keeps you close to the Most Sacred Heart of My Son. If you perceive the tenets of the Holy Gospel through the faith you have been given, you will recognize that Jesus is most prevalent where men are dying and suffering. This is how you see Him in the lives of broken souls. It is possible for someone to live-out their days knowing about the mission of the Church, but completely isolated from its intent. Clearly, the baptized prove their charities by embarking on sojourns that lead them to dark quarters of the globe where paupers huddle, shiver, starve, agonize, and die. When this is impractical, it is necessary to provide ample resources to missionaries who do. The Mystical Body of Jesus is plagued by many deficiencies in the lives of the abandoned, lonesome, afraid, disenfranchised, persecuted, imprisoned, and exploited. I call you to remember them in your intentions and actively seek new ways to touch them with your time, talents, and treasures. This is a means through which you can emulate the life of Jesus more intensely. My children, when all is said and done, your persistence in Christianity is measured by how well you dealt with this pressure and whether you sought understanding in others' suffering with that of your own. True disciples of My Son are dissatisfied when they see the agony of people who have only little with which to sustain themselves, even strangers whose identities are unknown. When you look into their faces, you see the suffering of Jesus that is reflective of the Holy Cross in the contemporary world. This pressure is also a result of human greed to the extent that those who hold great wealth decline to share their plenty with the least of these. My messages are about dignity and purpose in the lives of people whom you do not know, but there are no strangers to honest Christians.

Since the Lord deposits within you the conscience to know right from wrong, you must be able to discern excess from negligence. As countless Americans wish to be known as heroes and legends, let us require from them the desire to prove their integrity by living-out the promises of their faith. Only self-sacrifice and service, matched to true courage, has allowed any man to become a hero. Only simple piety and outward humility take you to the greatness that makes for giants to lead the charge against the pall of the cumbersome ages. If you think of poetry where every line rhymes with its predecessor, or if you can envision an American dream so profound that the simplest writer can grow the vision of an entire race, then you are poised to receive the Wisdom that will take you to Heaven. You will win the battle and finish the race alongside Saints Paul and Timothy; you will be elevated before the Father with the elegance of the Angels. If you daresay that you are of one and the same conviction that took the Son of Man to His Crucifixion on Good Friday, then you are prepared for the battles of freedom and courage that cannot be vanquished on your adversaries' best day.

I beg you, My children, to let your hopes carry you across the threshold of trust in new beginnings, that allow you to believe in miracles to unprecedented degrees. I call on you before it is too late. When you see droplets of rain falling on rose petals, imagine this as God's metaphor for His Divine Truth enlightening the souls of men. If you dream of accomplishments that have leapt entirely above anything ever achieved by mortal man, then you are on your way to foreseeing the Spirit of God perpetrating defeat upon the enemies of the Cross. When you lift your eyes into the heavens and cannot train them on anything you see, your heart has reached beyond the bonds of time and entered the foyers of Everlasting Life. I am the Blessed Virgin Mary, the Mother of Jesus Christ, the Mother of God; and I am calling upon all creatures great and small to unite in a universal mission of Messianic Light that was first planted in the hearts of humanity on the occasion of Pentecost. You have been set aflame with prescience and impassioned peace to the point that you cannot turn back. There is no avoiding the chores you have been given by Almighty God to teach the ignorant about the Kingdom of Heaven that will overwhelm them with invincible Love. All that is of God that lives within you is indelible and irreproachable, and this makes you the heroes and warriors whom you have long yearned to become. It lifts you higher than the mountain peaks you have tried to ascend. And, it makes you mighty conquerors in the Plan of God for finishing the Earth, the same end about which Jesus spoke so painfully from the Holy Cross the day He died. Whereupon you are prepared to enlist your strongest faith to overcome the dailiness of the world, He will declare your earthly commission perfect. When you see fires of valor leaping higher than the world's smiting hatred, you will be near the Second Coming of the Son of Man. When in your prayers you elevate the Cross, Jesus will draw humanity to Him. My Special son, thank you for allowing Me to speak to you.

I am grateful that you subsist in the Grace of Jesus so My messages to you and your brother can continue. I promise that you will be rewarded, and rightly so, for inviting your friends to come to believe in your work. The year 2006 is passing into history, but this does not mean that your hope should do the same. Remember that for all you have done for Heaven, for all that is rapturous about your life, there remains one simple message, that of the Triumphant Cross. I am with you to say that you are spreading the Holy Gospel with clarity. Please pray for the poor souls in Purgatory, especially during the Season of Advent."

Sunday, December 3, 2006
St. Dietrich Annenberg, Martyr [1811-1842]*
2:51 p.m.

"Welcome to the sanctuary of My Immaculate Heart, dear little children, where you are nurtured on your life's journey toward Heaven. It is the Will of God that I speak about the graces and benedictions that He bestows upon those who love Him. I offer splendid wishes upon the arrival of Advent, hoping that you will reassess your lives in light of Jesus' Nativity in the Manger at Bethlehem. I come as a manifestation from the Father to teach you about your future as Saints in the aftermath of His revelations. The Holy Paraclete infiltrates your hearts so you will propagate God's eternal Kingdom to all nations and peoples. It is through this indoctrination that you see the purpose of life, and that you wish to evangelize the Salvation of humanity in the Blood of the Cross to your friends and their families. There are untold sinners who need to be touched with the awesome awareness of Christianity, and you have been assigned to be messengers for Jesus at this hour. Whoever is affected by the stark constraints of secularism and materialism must learn about the liberating force of Jesus' Sacrifice and Resurrection. To this end, I pray for the conversion of the lost, freedom for the captive, healing of the sick, comfort for the dying, and for the enlightenment of the many who reject the call of the Holy Spirit to awaken to the Wisdom that is engulfing the entire universe. Our prayers are never in vain, My little children. Like your hopes, they are living prophesies of everything you have wished your lives to become. Speaking to Jesus is humanity's way of predicting the outcome of the world because He responds to your petitions. I realize that you are still trying to understand the commingling of suffering and happiness that composes the passing of days. You wonder what it means to shed tears with God's Light shining on the darkness of the Earth. You perceive your compliance with the Sacred Scriptures as a contradiction because you know that to be blessed implies that you have made yourselves poor on behalf of the poor and rich in kindness to a world that hates you with impunity. Please remember that the logic of the Earth is not as it seems in the Kingdom of Love to which you are called. We speak of greatness many times during My messages and enduring the element of time while joining your hearts with the Eternal Now. There is no question that you are fighting with a level of courage not exceeded by any previous age. Human life is not as benign as it used to be; there are too many distractions for your children and grandchildren. Impurity has been idealized as an acceptable price to pay for modernism, which violates the Commandments you were given centuries ago. I assure My children that the Mosaic Commandments about purity and chastity remain in place; they are to be obeyed as in the days of old. Truly, greater temptation does not mean that there should be less discretion on the part of those being tempted. You are fighting against forces that were not prevalent in the years of the original Apostles and disciples. Yours is an age of relativism where modesty is being desecrated by the enemies of the Church. The larger humanity grows, it appears that there is an aversion to the moral distinction by which you are supposed to live. This is why our prayers are needed, My little ones. Heresy and atheism are diminishing the core beliefs of democratic leaders. Even in America, the spirit of Christmas comes not in the form of holiness or self-sacrifice, but under the facade of materialism and consumerism. Why else would one hear holiday songs an entire month before the Feast of Christmas? It is not because corporate America loves to tell the story of Jesus' birth, it is to persuade patrons to buy more material goods. This is the hypocrisy that is so damaging to the faith of the Western world. My Special son, I offer My blessing and assurance that I intercede for your needs. I see that you are writing a narrative about your countrymen. What are your intentions for this essay? Are you attempting to say something in greater terms than that to which you have dedicated the article? *(I told Our Lady that I wanted to speak my piece about the way our country is sinking into moral decay.)* Have you relegated it to any single offensive acts? Please write until you have said everything you wish to cite. It seems that all problems are concentric in the topic of your essay in that their solution is found in self-sacrifice rather than selfishness. I am pleased that you embrace your Hispanic friends who came to America seeking a better life. Your companionship with them makes Jesus extremely happy. My messages will continue as long as God allows. Let us pray for His Will to be done. I include within My intercession everything for which you are praying. There are serious problems that you have known about for years, not the least of which were discussed by the Supreme Court Justice on the television you watched this morning. It is clear that many issues could be resolved by the Court, but they believe they are collectively above the laws of Christianity. The freedoms of choice and privacy must not be exercised in violation of the Gospel Truth. Please keep track of the Saints' names that I have given you over the years, especially ones you have never known. I urge you to live with patience, and be kind to those who persecute you. Ask Jesus to grant peace to those who are angry and afraid. There are crucial and auspicious events in the offing that will augur the capitalization of your mission.

Please do not worry, we will embark anew once all your manuscripts are finished. I am pondering an appropriate response to your imminent inquiry, *Holy Mother, is there any way you can make us anonymous again?"*

Sunday, December 10, 2006
St. Emily Boyce Goldblatt [1743-1805]*
2:59 p.m.

"Descending upon you now are the Grace and Truth of God in Heaven, and peace that the world cannot give or take away. I am the Mother of that peace, the Queen of Love, to whom you come during your every waking moment for Wisdom and instruction, and I call you to fervent prayer for the success of Jesus' disciples the world-over, for the Holy Spirit to be welcomed into human hearts with greater surety than ever before in the annals of history. Today, as you pray for yourselves and loved-ones, please remember those you have never known; ask God to bless the billions whose faces you will not see until the Earth has been encapsulated by death. These are Advent days when the world is at war with itself, not against any extraterrestrial, but within the unfriendly confines of the college of nations. It has long been said that there is nothing wrong with humanity that cannot be fixed by everything right about humanity. This is true only in your response to the Will of Jesus Christ, My Sacrificed Son, because He is the essence of perfect humanness. If you are aware, or wish to become aware, of the purview through which Eternal Dominion examines the acts of men, then you must realize that only through your Messianic Savior can you join the everlasting procession of sainthood as people united under God. Therefore, you should muster true humility in your hearts, and unity and continuity in your relationships as diverse individuals cast across the Earth in different regions and of multiple tongues. You should have the strength and vision to look with pity at your sisters' grief and brothers' pain and know what glory resides there, the interior genius that is released beyond its potential by your Christian love for them. I have said that I am a simple Matriarch of a complicated world. I have spoken, and you have listened. You have searched for the ingenuity to become self-sufficient in every way known to man, and you have discovered it in the dignity and diligence of your Christian faith. I implore you to pray that the world will open like a jubilee door and receive the benediction from Heaven that will keep your redemption on course. I ask for your petitions for those who do not know God, and for the many who do, but defy His Will. Raise up the multitudes who are only now learning about the virtuousness of piety, chasteness, contrition, reconciliation, and rebirth. My Special and Chosen ones, I have been speaking to you in private endearments about God's Triune Love for several years, and the purposes that have come from your messages have had positive results around the globe. Please know that you have been placed here in America to supplement the Christian conversion of the whole of the nation, to touch its people in states that must become even more united, but not in a secular way. There is no means of measuring your progress at this point because the process is ongoing; you are still living-out the reason for your birth in the flesh. You both have exquisite qualities and attributes that align you with the heavens. When the Lord surveys the world in search of evidence of His Kingdom, He sees you as the likeness of the Son of Man, Jesus, to whom you have consecrated the culmination of your mortal years. Your souls and actions are replete with characteristics of the miraculous life to which you have been drawn. In you has been deposited a resurrected heart, the supernatural presence of our Holy God for the masses of men who must turn to Him or suffer the consequences of failing Him in this, the final age of the Earth. I am not implying that you are worthy of worship or that any man should idolize you. I am simply affirming that your Christian discipleship is laudable before the Hosts of Heaven and the throngs of men who still inhabit the physical world. You are God's voyagers in this last era of Creation before He calls His flock to Himself as one Mystical Body devoted to the holiness in which He created Adam and Eve. Hence, I remind you to will into being the desire to approach Him, and ask your brothers and sisters, if only in your prayers, to emulate the righteousness of Christ Jesus while you await the final hours before He comes in Glory to judge the living and the dead. My Special son, your statement is precisely on target when you say that I have given you messages for good reason, real goals with definitive objectives for the conversion of lost sinners. There is no way to express how intense is My admiration for you, and how glad Jesus is that you are His friend. You are justifiably offended by matters that run contrary to My teachings, and you are often indecisive about how to cope with them. There is nothing lacking in your spiritual eyesight. The constructive discussions that you and your brother have about current events are good ways to see what is unseeable, where decisions must be made to convert as many lost souls as you can reach. The league of nations has been destabilized by the Iraq war that you have accurately heard described as the greatest strategic blunder in the existence of the United States. Now that it has been committed, the problems must be addressed. Contrary to some beliefs, it is not Christian to suspend what America is doing and allow hatred to commit suicide because there are too many innocents who will die, all collateral damage of a Western foreign policy that has been a shame for years. There are children who must be protected and nourished; they must be given the opportunity to live in peace, even if they are transported to other lands by the millions in military airplanes. Once this is done, the fanatics can exterminate one another at will. Do you sense, therefore, that I do not see you as blind? You are much like many Popes and Bishops of the past, and simple lay-persons as well; you are practically and politically helpless to do anything about the errors of your elitist public officials."

Sunday, December 17, 2006
St. Mahalia Charlton Burch [1841-1910]*
2:58 p.m.

"With the expansion and immediate influx of Grace by which all men are baptized, My children, I reach-out to you. The Lord Jesus calls your attention and loyalties to the Heavenly Throne where the Father of Light awaits your hearts and souls. Today, it is My joy to announce His favor and the blessings of the Angels. I seek from you the righteousness of Christ Jesus to worlds known and unknown, everything you can gather from the depths of your hearts that advances the Glory of His Love. My cherished ones, I seek greater holiness from you than you could imagine in a million earthly lifetimes, and yet My call is so simple that a child can understand. Blooming in you is a righteousness that is so profound that it cannot be hidden in the annotations of history or even the shadow of its echos before the finishing of the Earth. You are capable of emulating Divine Love through your exemplary piety, the same holiness about which I told you from the moment I was named your Immaculate Queen. Yes, I search for more than you realize for all the reasons you shall be finally redeemed in the Sacred Heart of Jesus, to reveal to the Celestial Hosts all you were intended to be the moment you gave yourselves to the Cross. Therefore, I urge you to give Him what I seek; offer the heavens the core of your existence, and you will know peace. I seek love in you, My little children! It is this simple. In every way you can discern its uniqueness as prescribed by the Scriptures and the revelations dispensed by the Holy Spirit in your hearts, I seek love from you! This is the reason for your prayers and the purpose of My calling. Every moral ethic by which you practice goodness, faith, virtue, dignity, fortitude, generosity, and service is unified and ratified in God's hands. Hence, remember during Advent and Christmas that you can be perfected by the Law of Truth that is perfect, the words and earnestness of the Son of Man. He was born to humanity to transform you, to shine on you the Light of His Kingdom never before exposed. He asks you to be wedded to the wishes of the Father, to be infused with Wisdom in ways you could not have anticipated before His coming as the Prince of Peace. In all ways, My little ones, I bid you that peace at Christmas because the Earth is filled with fear, terror, darkness, and indifference. One week from today, you shall celebrate the Eve of Christmas in a world that is breaking by the hour to the Dawn of Eternal Love. All around the globe, Christians will kneel to pray and stand to sing, and they will rejoice that Heaven has chosen them to be with God at the end of time. How happy this should make you; how anticipatory you must be to know through faith that you will be a united family in the City of Everlasting Life. The first, foremost, and ultimate gift the Father gave humanity was His intention to raise you among the Angels through His newborn Son, to fulfill and supplant the Old Covenant with the Messiah of the New. Christ Jesus transcends all time that incorporates every human act deigned to Him through the righteousness in which you are saved. The entirety of Creation, the Ancients, the gift of Judaism, and the present and future are eclipsed by the birth of Jesus from My Womb. Linear time has been redefined as a parcel of the infinity of the Incarnation of Divine Love in the King named Jesus Christ. This, My people, is why God can restore you in an instant; it is how He can remake your lives by offering the benefit of living again. It was in His power to light the nighttime skies of Bethlehem with warplanes and fireworks that had yet to be invented. He can suspend the laws of Nature, retrace the pathways of the planets, reverse the tides of growing old, and elevate you from paupers to princes in the blink of an eye. The birth of Jesus is this overwhelming; it is so unique to humanity and Creation that you cannot imagine anything given to the world, past, present or future, that can match its blessing. This is the same Man-God who was transfigured on Mount Tabor and Crucified on Mount Calvary. His is the same Spirit working in you for the resurrection of the greatest centuries ever passed. And, your souls wait for them now, while you pray in anticipation of Christmas, a seasonal Advent inside the Great Advent before the Second Coming of Jesus in Glory. I ask you to ponder the night Jesus was born in poverty, but in desire and with plenteous magnitude that makes Him everything humanity must become. You are fortunate to answer the call of the conscience to be at His side and remain in His presence, with the Holy Spirit shining from Him through the expressions of peace He offers. What these holy hours in Bethlehem mean to man is greater than the ferocity of all world wars and its weapons of mass-destruction. The Virgin Birth of Jesus Christ prophesied the Salvation of the world that would never come again or in any other way. His Nativity was the precursor to the Holy Spirit who keeps you apprised of the destiny of all sinners. He is the Incarnation of The Word! Therefore, My children, I urge you to not stop seeking Him while He can be found. Heed the Epistles of Saint Paul to the letter! Imitate the Acts of the Apostles and internalize the demands placed on you by the burdens of the Scriptures recorded by the Evangelists. This is Christmas, My children! It is time for awakening, new and intensified by your celebration of the birth of Jesus inside the constraints of the galaxies from the infinity of Paradise. You are perpetuated spiritually and mystically in your observation of the Eve of Joy, and the globe on which you stand is lighted like the sun in the pit of the night. This joy cannot be expelled from your presence because it is the endlessness of absolution seeded in your hearts. Pray for the release of the souls in Purgatory this Christmas so they can enter Heaven that has been waiting their arrival. Ask God to allow them into His house. Offer your Christmas Masses for the Poor Souls in Purgatory!

My Special son, it is 3:33 p.m. and I am speaking about the sublimity of joy that supercedes all time. I have been with you all these years to bless everything you have given Jesus. There is not a moment when you failed to comply with My wishes. Now, if you could only seek from your brother this same obedience! You are good for him; you are his example of Jesus during this life. I am overjoyed that AD 2007 will bring the publication of My New Millennium anthologies for your brothers and sisters. You are witnessing signs and wonders of the prevalence of the Lord's Will. Every day and hour you live, you see with your eyes and envision in your heart the shaping of the human collective, the Mystical Body of Jesus, that brings you to have new hope in the transformation of Creation. We have for many years prayed together, and I have told you that the return of Jesus is near. I have said that there are omens aplenty to prove that your future will be provided. It is important for you to remember that I am not speaking about false hopes. There will be difficult times and dark days ahead, but bright is the countenance of the Cross and the success of your work. We pray for the same thing from God and for men; we request that His blessing and humanity's faith will lead to the banns of Heaven and Earth. I have said that I cannot reach My goals without My children. This is more true than you know. Thank you for being so kind to the laborers in God's vineyard, for supporting them, taking to task those who persecute them, and lighting the path for the many who cannot see where they are going."

Monday, December 25, 2006
The Virgin Birth of Jesus Christ
2:51 p.m.

Jesus was born into the world to herald God's Love, perpetuate Heaven's Light, manifest human Salvation, heal the afflicted, liberate the captive, and to create headlands, landmarks, and milestones by which mankind from all generations and walks of life would discover the meaning of Truth.

—The Dominion Angels

"The Feast of Christmas brings new opportunities to align yourselves with the intentions of Heaven and avail your souls to the miracle of Salvation. Brought on this anniversary, heralded by the Angels' repertoire of songs, is your awareness of the grandness and divinity of the Lord, present in the Anointed One laid in the Manger. My children, I pray with you for those who agonize over the darkness of their sins and the millions seeking the Light of Jesus to emit His Kingdom into their hearts. We pray clearly and perfectly in beseeching God for His presence in your spiritual exile. Yes, we ask Him to respond to the wishes of Pope Benedict XVI whose Christmas homilies resonate from the lips of Christ Jesus. There is no question that humanity is in need of this; the world requires Salvation through the Cross. Jesus is the

Savior about whom multitudes of visionaries have spoken for centuries. He reigns among you disguised in the poor, and His Spirit infiltrates your hearts and gives you Wisdom in thought and action to eradicate suffering around the globe. The archways of Heaven hover above the Earth like cantilevers of supernaturalism, calling you beyond the immediacy of life into the miraculous presence of Jesus in Word, deed, and Sacrament. Christmas is meant to be a holy time of reflection, renewal, reconciliation, and inner-peace. I assure you that you are given these things for the unification of peoples and nations, for the cessation of war and hostility, and for making the Earth the seamless and timeless reflection of the bounty of Heaven. I have reminded you to seek Jesus in this life so you will know Him upon the culmination of the ages. Be My little children of Abraham's bosom (Luke 16:22) so your hearts will open to the sanctification of your souls that Jesus foresaw when He was born in Bethlehem. My children, on prior Feasts of Christmas, I invited you to look at the world with all its pretenses and pretexts in light of the Love of God. He calls you to a better understanding of Truth; and in this, you will decide for Him and tender yourselves to His Love, away from the distractions behind which you are hiding your motivations. Anything that is not about Christianity comes from these diversions. If your words and actions are not founded in the Holy Gospel, you are living an existence of falsehoods. You must remember that the world is maturing; it was finished by Jesus on the Cross as your redemption in Him was granted through the Grace of the Father. Jesus was born in Bethlehem as the Child-King, destined to be slain for the expiation of human sin on Mount Calvary 33 years later. History and Eternity have recorded that He did these things for you because, as God Incarnate, He could not bear the sorrow of seeing you absent from the highest mansions in Heaven. I have said on many Christmas Days that His Kingdom is unparalleled by anything in the universe or beyond it, and in whatever context you scrutinize and decipher the elements of space and time. Jesus is perfect in all ways He calls you to be, knowing that you are capable of emulating His righteousness. As this Christmas message touches the hearts of many in the years to come, I pray that it inspires all to recognize that Christian piety is more than the ends I have described today; it is a procedure that is ongoing. The lives of men are replete with princely actions, from forgiving the offenses of others, lending relief to those in need, dispensing the Corporeal and Spiritual Acts of Mercy, and the untold number of other blessings that bring you into compliance with the Holy Commandments and Sacred Beatitudes. Wherever there is a man who declares that he has fulfilled these oaths to the satisfaction of the Father's Will, you will see a man who is about to die. Why is this so? Because life is a process of filling the ullage where Jesus wept, served, suffered, and died. And, it is one that will proceed until you see His Glorious Face.

My Special son, it gives Me hope that you are praying during this Christmas Feast, realizing that you shall never surrender your desire to make everything of life that Jesus expects from you. Whether you know it or not, these are revelatory times, even more than the days of My opening messages in February 1991. Every week, month, and year that passes takes you closer to understanding the insights, visions, and prophecies that I told you about back then. This is why you should be happy at the core of your being that we are effecting the Will of the Lord in this decade in human history. My Love for you has never waned or faltered, and your obedience as My child has been as intense through the passing of time as when we first began. Christmas is a time for forgiveness. Hundreds of thousands of souls have been released from Purgatory into the Light of Heaven because of the prayers of the faithful and the Masses offered on their behalf. The Nativity of Jesus is a current event that enlivens your petitions to grant Eternal Light unto the redeemed, and for good will to flourish on Earth inside the hearts of families and friends. It was an act of kindness for you to visit your brother's family last evening on the Eve of Christmas. They all admire and respect you. We are grateful to God that your brother appears to have recovered from his surgery and can continue your work in 2007. As I said before, it is imperative that he remain with you so you can issue your manuscripts to the Church. You are important to My mission because I cannot convert lost sinners without the assistance of messengers like you. Please exercise prudent judgement in distributing My words. Jesus is with you as you attend your workplace, even though it may seem unobvious. It would be unfair to ask you to consider the plight of the unemployed, homeless, starved, and suffering when speaking of your daily chores because it seems an impossible way to lift you from the oppression. I pray deeply and dearly, however, that you will not subject yourself to undue criticism at the end of time when you see how others have been forced to live. There is no dismissing the persecution to which you have been subjected by those around you. I have compassion for you, and I am with you in Spirit and Love to bring you peace. I intend after the publication of My anthologies from AD 2000-2008 to propagate your work in ways previously unknown. You will have an awe-striking deposit of writing by then, too evocative to ignore. I hope you enjoyed the quotation that the Dominion Angels recited at the beginning of My message. I will speak to you at the opening of another new year. Please remember in your prayers all who are living in seminaries and convents."

MORNING STAR OVER AMERICA

The New Millennium
In the Year of Our Lord

AD 2007

Monday, January 1, 2007
The Blessed Virgin Mary, Mother of God
2:33 p.m.

"My little children, today's intermittent sunshine is an advance blessing on tomorrow's skyline brilliance. We gather in your home of prayer to begin another year of petitions to God on behalf of the broken world. I yearn for My children to know and accept Him, and exalt and revel in His unprecedented, perpetual Light amidst the dawning of the final ages of men. Today, you observe the Feast that reminds you that I am the Immaculate Mother of Creation, and you are sought by Heaven through My Eternal Grace. It is here that we begin 2007 with hope in the success of the Church and with high expectations that the lost among you will be found by the Holy Spirit. There is a vast difference between living on Earth and accepting true life. If you assist in converting the multitudes who yet do not know Salvation in the Cross, you will be flanked by holy Angels who also adhere to the principles of Truth and peace. Men will study war no more if all societies become united in the Sacred Heart of Jesus. My children, do you remember when I told you that it is impossible to draw milk from a picture of a cow? Too many sinners believe that Eternal Life can be gained by subscribing to earthly things, that they can reach the Afterlife through something attached to artifacts of the Earth. As you know, this is untrue. If they asked to receive a photograph of a loved-one and were given instead a photograph of that photograph, they would feel as though there is another dimension separating them from the one they love. They cannot hold-in-hand a photograph of a person if they receive only its reproduced image. This is not unlike the distinction they recognize once they understand that human Salvation is not of this world. Their conversion leads them to seek the spiritual Truth of the Holy Paraclete sent by God to live in and among them. The tangible reality of Heaven is not a contradiction in terms to those who practice Christianity because you realize that Paradise begins in your hearts; it is with you as you travel the broadways of the Earth through the authenticity of your faith in God. Hence, we assemble to pray for billions worldwide to search for Him while He is in your company, and seek redemption while it can be found. And, as I have said, thank you for responding to My call. This will be another year of grave consequences and drastic events because human sin makes it that way. Modern technologies and ideological differences contribute to the calamities and battles that divide My children one from another. As in the past, transgressions of all stripes will darken your days; there will be horrors and gruesome onslaughts against human dignity around the globe. This happens not because we have not prayed well enough, but because your brothers and sisters who are lost in darkness are walking around with stones in their chests instead of human hearts. Greed abounds throughout the nations, and gluttony, vengeance, envy, sloth, and licentiousness. I wish that I could attest that these grotesque violations have been wiped from the face of the Earth like tearing a page out of history, but ill-leaning American lifestyles do not make it possible. We shall prevail in the justice of the Lord! The years that pass before you, the annae of human vindication in which you are living, are leading you away from the horrid remnants of mortal existence gone wrong, and into the Light of Living Truth. While I realize that this sounds like promising something too good to be true and far in the distance, it is occurring now; it is blooming like the rising of the sun while unwary sinners are asleep in their beds. When I put My assurances before you, I beseech you to believe My words as much as you accept the Will of the Father. These days are like links in a chain that began in ancient times and will extend to the final generations of the world. You have neared that future where it connects to the Eternity that has already commenced. Your lives, allegiances, and legacies will close-out the ages of humanity on Earth; they will assist Jesus in making way for the lasting peace that He promises those who love Him. I call My children to be consistent in faith and more persistent in patience, and Creation will culminate before your eyes have had the opportunity to focus upon what has already transpired. My Special and Chosen ones, I have given you signs and wonders to lift your hopes that your works are of true significance in the redemption of humanity. The year 2007 will be crucial along with the messages I have given you since this day in 2000. I know that this is difficult for you to see because you are traveling a continuum of time that has not seen many changes since February 1991. I remind you that all things come to an end and yield to new beginnings, and this is what 2007 will bring. I am not suggesting that you will be separated for a length of time, I am saying that you must be prepared for change. There is renewal in everything that God wills, and His is the perfect judgment that has situated the Earth beneath His feet. I ask you to remain together in the same way you have in past years. Be courteous and respectful, and ensure your safety when you are in different locations. Your three books of Millennium messages will be astounding and evocative; and joined with your other works, they will be a force for the positive good about which I am speaking. Can you sense that this is beginning to happen? I tell you these things because they have purposeful perspective and designs that make you humble and holy. Thank you for your prayers beginning this new year on My Feast Day."

Sunday, January 7, 2007
The Epiphany of Our Lord
3:12 p.m.

"How holy you are called to become, My dear ones, and willing to accede to the sacrificial demands of Divine Love. I know you accept your daily crosses willingly because you can see through your faith that the Land of the Living lies not far from here, very near to the imaginings that help keep you strong during your darkest hours. My children, Jesus does not command that you become so instantaneously pious that you lose your simplicity in the process. His lessons and teachings take time to be internalized by those who hear Him. You are given mortal lives to make this occur. And, He does not require that you become strict doctrinaires in matters of faith and morals, but that you approach His Love as little children seeking the Wisdom and consolation of their loving Father. Today, therefore, I invite you to remember that your love for Jesus is based upon and fashioned through your simple understanding of God's hope to deliver you to His side in Heaven so that Creation will become complete and replete with genuine holiness and true good will. The Holy Spirit warns you to avoid the perils of the material world and its false prophesies and empty promises. Always remember that atheism and secular humanism are no more than cruel hoaxes against the human spirit, and they are distractions from the Truth of our sovereign God. The Lord wishes only good to come from you, and that this goodness will prevail over everything else you encounter during your earthly years. It is all about Divine Light, My little children. Your search for Heaven implies that you have already accepted it, that you yearn for the Eternity that has been implanted in your hearts by God like a seed of righteousness. I beg you to never forget that the genesis of your growth in Christian piety is prayer from the heart, and to understand that your lives in Christ Jesus are only now blossoming into their greatest relevance in your pursuit of His Heavenly Kingdom. I have come here to foster your growth in everything you know to be associated with your Christian conversion and your emulation of My Sacrificed Son. Thank you for allowing Me the opportunity to be of service in the Salvation of humanity, and thank you for having responded to My call. My Special son, I speak to you on this blessed day that reflects your own epiphany in the genius you have come to know about your spiritual faith and the Everlasting Life you have been accorded by the Kingdom of God. I have told you many times that human redemption cannot be earned, that it is a gift from Jesus for those who follow Him. What is rewarded, however, are the efforts you have perpetually given Him by all the gifts you bring to the Feast Table of Love. You make such great reparation for sinners who defy the Will of the Father that Saint Paul has trained his eyes on you in grand appreciation. This new year 2007 will amend the future that would have come with dismal regrets by many of your friends, and even those whom you do not know. I implore you to remember that I never make empty promises or levy burdens upon someone simply to satisfy deific vengeance. We are praying together because we make a positive difference in transforming humankind from lost sinners into faithful warriors for Jesus in His vineyard of the Earth. It should please you to know that you have participated in immeasurable degrees toward the purification of the world, ridding it of vice and corruption in ways that you may never see until you depart from this life. The gratitude that God holds for you is beyond description. And, what I see of your writing is beneficial to all who still do not comprehend the meaning of change for the better, not simply for its own sake, but to augment the pieties and reverences that deliver the human spirit to Jesus like fine pearls and jewels. You oftentimes garner a sense for the overwhelming in your sojourn through life as you see the greatness of the Doctors of the Church, the heroic sacrifices of common people everywhere, and the signs and wonders that the Lord is manifesting around the globe. Indeed, your experiences with Me are part of them. And, you are coming to view the illusion of time as serving only the purpose of keeping your brothers and sisters on the path of preparation for their last day of mortality and first in the presence of God. I remind you again that My work here is not yet concluded, that the Earth on which you live is in need of deeper cultivation."

Sunday, January 14, 2007
St. Louis O'Halleron, Mystic [1722-1768]*
3:01 p.m.

"We prayerfully gather in this humble place to join in beseeching the Lord to bless humanity in all its vastness and limitations, no matter where His people are, and regardless of their stations in life. We cherish our moments together on behalf of Heaven from which I come into the world of such need where you live. My children, we are not only creating memories of humanity-refined, but forging changes that will render your brothers and sisters holier for our dedication. As I have told you, your work for Jesus is all about the enlightenment of humanity in matters of Christian faith and sustaining the good will between men that Jesus came to establish. You serve at the pleasure of God through the intercession of the Holy Spirit as advocates yourselves, little paracletes who understand that the meaning of life is the transformation of the soul into the dignity you gain in the Sacred Heart of Jesus. My message is always about spreading righteousness to peoples of all origins and vocations through your enduring commitment to God. This has never been an easy task, not only because the veil of mortality prohibits you from seeing with your eyes, but by reason that you are opposed by enemies of Divine Love that lurk among the multitudes. They practice a covert agendum of anti-Christian adversity by embracing a faithless indifference, persecuting the Church in every way conceivable. You can defeat these perfidious adversaries by your devotion to Me and the prayers and Sacraments to which you have been led by the union of your hearts through the Providence of God. My commitment is to you, reaffirmed by My presence beside the Angels. When speaking about the power and awesome wonders of Jesus, please remember the beneficial advocacy that I offer through My intense love for you, and through the splendorous efficacy of Saint Joseph's prayers. Even when it seems that you are defenseless in this life, never forget that your power rests in your belief that your forbears in faith, the Angels and Saints, the Omnipotence of the Father, and the blood of the Martyrs serve as sources of strength for your journey through and freedom from the bonds of mortality. It is imperative that you view the ensuing year as a new opportunity for reclaiming from the material world the dignity you once lost because of others' misdeeds and hateful acts. You are children of holiness, not of the netherworld where antithetical nonbelievers go. Salvation is real; your absolution is a tangible, captivating redemption through the Crucifixion of My Son. And, equally real is your relocation to the City of Light where God resides, calling you to His presence for all eternities to come. When men speak of the outcome of the world, they are implying a sequence, that the finishing of Creation has had earlier endings. The completion of the Earth is the pardoning of all people by their reconciliation with Heaven, and the outcome is the Eternity that has already proceeded. This sacred timelessness has commenced, and you are passing through your tenure in exile. Your existence is more than tangential because you have given your fate to Jesus' Resurrection. With the transference of your spirit into the Wounds of Jesus when you pass from this life into the next, you have determined your own fortune; you have assigned equifinality to the reason you accepted His Crucifixion as expiation for your sins. My precious ones, I wish you could know what lies in His Glory and Providence; and through your vibrant faith, you can foretell it. This is as much a blessing as life itself. We imagine what your joy will be when you see My words carved in stone. You will have a grand entrance into the Afterlife as one humanity assembled before the King. You will be one family in which every soul who dies in Jesus' favor lives. These are the moments that lead to the blessings by which you shall be rewarded for the goodness you have espoused.

      My Special son, I pray from My Immaculate Heart that you will extol the gladness that lives inside your being, begging to emerge. Indeed, I ask this not only from you, but from every child whom I deigned to adopt on Good Friday, all who call themselves signed through the Wisdom of the Lord. This is not an easy prospect because of the dailiness of life and those who are vexing to the soul. You must consider the suffering of this life as worth the Glory you are about to inherit in the Son of Man. I bid you to remember the writings of Saint Paul about all the temptations that attempt to imperil your relationship with Jesus, and that you have the power and capacity to defeat them at the utterance of your prayers. The greatest temptation that Christians endure is that they might surrender to mortal sin or be drawn away from the Sacraments of the Church. Another temptation is to retaliate against Jesus' enemies in inordinate, undignified ways, or surrender your composure in upbraiding the enemies of the Cross. Trusting that God has vanquished the adversaries of His Kingdom is part of the conquest that you have achieved over the darkness of the Earth. There is hope in this, and advancement in morality, and your reckoning that the return of the Son of Man cannot be much longer in the offing. This leads all believers to the inevitable conclusion that these are preordained times because previously revealed prophesies have reached the point of fulfillment. Physical and supernatural manifestations promised by God through His messengers and seers are not irrelevant provisions that may not come true. They have been given for specific reasons, ones that will further advance the perfection of men in the themes of sacrifice and righteousness. Hence, you will see that God keeps His promises, and many will be the beneficiaries of His oaths to purify the lost. And, My Special son, I extend My gratitude for your allegiance to your work here, for remembering that I have never once said something that will not come true. It is to My honor that you have prayed, and in My honor that you shall pass in My arms to Jesus with your brother to the accolades of the Hosts of Heaven. I see that you have encountered the operatic aria by Giacomo Puccini that is sung with such artistic heartiness by Luciano Pavarotti. His renditions of the Nessun Dorma replicate the glorious vision of Jesus from the Cross on Good Friday when Jesus proclaimed *I shall win!* as He delivered His soul to the Father, making reparation for the sins of humanity. He saw Himself as the Champion of the ages, the Conqueror of human weakness, the Creator of Saints, and the delight of millions of widows and orphans who would place their hope in Him. You have a heart worthy of the Divine Truth that has found solace there, and you can see where the Holy Spirit moves common men into serving roles and creating acts of uncommon valor. Thank you immensely for taking such good care of your brother, for forgiving his wrongdoings, being patient with his imperfections, and remaining at his side as messenger during these critical modern times. Your lives have augmented Jesus' work to an infinite degree. Thank you for your holy petitions. I assure you that your brother's birthday will be more a celebration of his devotion and commitment to God than a reflection of his passing years. I urge My messengers to pray for the thousands who have died at the hands of the American government. Pro-life? I am not sure this is true."

Sunday, January 21, 2007
Saint Agnes, Virgin and Martyr [AD 291-304]
2:59 p.m.

"I have come addressing My Christian vessels who receive My messages on behalf of humanity, that all will accept Salvation through Jesus' Crucifixion for those who love God. I wish you could comprehend the satisfaction that is felt in Heaven and the rejoicing that abounds over one converted sinner. Be confident that your reward for giving humanity your gift of faith in tune with the Gospel will be immense. Today, we pray for the grace Jesus promises to inspire in your brothers and sisters to aid their transformation to the pinnacle of spiritual holiness. I wish deep inside My Heart that they will live for the intentions of God with increased devotion, and that lost souls will have a sudden qualm of enlightenment toward the righteousness of Heaven. It is for these reasons that we join in prayer in this room where, for several years, you have heard and contemplated about matters of human absolution. It is true that this has not been an easy task for you, that you have been forced to endure substantial hours of social isolation. I have said that the currency for humility and holiness are love and sacrifice, and that yours have been especially more accented as messengers and seers. When the Lord speaks about deific gratitude in the Sacred Scriptures, He is mindful of the thankfulness that all Creation has for your dedication to the sanctification of humanity. It is in your steadfastness that you are made stronger in faith, and in your piety that you uphold the virtues of peace. Where there is belief in God, there is the presence of the Holy Spirit. My children, thank you for having responded to My call. And, thank you for aiding the God of your fathers in the cultivation of all peoples in this age where there are countless distractions to the avenues of holiness down which your ancestors traveled. You see before you in word and deed many good people who are battling the obstructions to the enlightenment about which I speak. We ask Jesus to bless their efforts with His touch and intercessory power. We should anticipate that He will help them as He assists in your grand labors which expand His Kingdom before you that is growing ever-wider by the hour. My Special son, My Immaculate Heart is moved with thanksgiving that you are praying with your brother here in this home that has been made holy by My presence. All you have come to understand about fashioning a world of purity and justice is growing to fruition, a deposit of spiritual artwork that brings compassion and healing to the Earth. These may not seem to be monumental times as you live-out the common days known to ordinary life, but they are crucial to the unfolding of God's Plan for the culmination of the exile of men. You have seen moments of intense glory and victory with your own eyes, and you have likewise known periods of sadness and spiritual darkness. Can you not see, however, that the Light is always much more prevalent? The joy of the Holy Spirit resounding in your heart is invaluable as you proceed into the future because it overcomes the shadows of previous times that have nothing to do with the Providence of God. You have grown in your capacity to recognize the presence of the Holy Paraclete in everything you experience, and you have become able to discern where the thud of secular indifference impacts the floor of the netherworld in the errors of the enemies of the Church. When we speak of the call of the conscience, we refer to anyone's ability to see through their spiritual vision the workings of the Holy Spirit in the actions of men and the fruits that are born of their hearts. I am pleased that you have matured in wisdom and poise, that you are one with Jesus in struggling to capture the lost from the things of this world that have nothing to do with His invincible Truth. There is no doubt or question in faith, and yours is filled with trust and goodness, a genuine respect for the Will of the Lord to cleanse His people in preparation for the end of time. I promise that with His help, you are living according to the Commandments and Beatitudes that He so profoundly dictated to His disciples.

You realize that your movement through time is yielding untold benefits for the least and weakest among you. This is not a matter for which you have pride, but graciousness and thankfulness. You are wholly capable of writing heartfelt dissertations about the Glory of God as evidenced by your thoughts yesterday and today. Defending the concept of orthodox religion by citing the term 'organized' is brilliant. You are reclaiming a term from your lexicon that has been previously used to disparage the Church by revealing that Jesus came to establish the orderly transformation of sinners into new creatures in the Cross by extraordinary ways. If this is organized, then why are the adversaries of Christianity complaining that the Church lacks a clear mission and goals? They constantly refer to the wars that religions have allegedly caused, but they refuse to admit that they are the origin of the wars they oppose. They wage campaigns of lies and deceit against Jesus to deny the sanctity of the human soul, and then claim that the error rests with the followers of the Cross. You have come to know in your lifetime that they practice doublespeak and profanity against the Kingdom of Heaven that they have never taken the time to comprehend. And, this is to their diminishment; it is to their undoing. They are sinners who remain in darkness, who will descend into the pit of condemnation that they made for themselves. It is clear that we rebuke them, and feel for them; but it is more important that we teach them about Salvation in the Blood of the Lamb before it is too late. This I have also told you many times. There are no extrapolated sanctions to force them to respond, just our prayers, our sincere intentions for those who are distant from the Mercy of the Lord. This is the focus of our appeal. I am thankful that you have given the purpose of your life to help My Son succeed. You and your brother are having a good year thus far because you are maturing in understanding My messages. It is not that you will see the grand finale of

Creation in the next hours or few days, or even before you die, but you can sense the crescendo that is building for the return of the Son of Man. Of all the years I have been speaking before you, 2007 is crucial because of the Millennium messages you are about to release. They complement *Morning Star Over America* and represent My commitment to the rediscovery of My lost children. It is obvious that My 2000-2002 messages that you will publish this year will have a tremendous impact on assuring the multitudes that God's miracles are real, that He cares about the plight of the forsaken and the future of the faithful. Added to your other works, the books containing My Millennium messages will be laid in good hands where they will suffer no indignity. The passing of 2007 will bring the dissection of your manuscripts and scrutiny from sinners of all walks of life. I will guard your anonymity while these events ensue. I cannot describe how painful your lives may become once theologians release their content analyses of My messages. It will mean the strangulation of your personal, private lives. This is why in past generations the Lord allowed such interrogation of His messengers' works only after He raised them into Heaven. I cannot overstate the ugliness that becoming messengers brings to those who have been faithful to His Word. I wish for you to think about this on occasion and remind yourselves that I have said that My messages will be heeded by everyone who lives as a prerequisite to their final absolution. Hence, time does not matter; it is irrelevant for the achievement of everything you are accomplishing for God. I wish to make clear that becoming publicly-known messengers in America is different from those in other countries. Here, you become the property of the calculating multitude. Your lives are levied against the perfection of Jesus, and your private records are laid-out for the whole nation to see. You will have scarce moments to yourselves when you will not have to fight the exhaustion of your spirit. There will be few public dinners and quiet evenings touring the countryside because of the danger to your safety. Do you understand everything I am saying? This does not imply that you will not be able to appear at novenas and cenotaphs to deliver the speeches you have planned for humanity to hear. A mystical presence will surround you during those times, and you will know that the Son of Man is poised to make His glorious reentry into the mortal world. I repeat that this could occur during your natural life. Thank you for welcoming all the things I have told you. You need not dwell on them with apprehension or fear, but use faith and reason to understand what the future may bring. Nothing in this world can expunge the good we have done. I again refer to the Nessun Dorma by Luciano. His rendition performed in 2006 is the precise implication of victory about which I speak; it is a valedictory presentation in the likeness of the Saints. My work through you is somewhat the same kind of aria, a spiritual song. We are in the interlude that precedes the far-flung Triumph that you will inherit. I realize that this is difficult to see in the awkwardness of life, but I ask that you hold in your heart the expectation that throngs, cheers, and tossing of tassels and fists in the air are inevitable from your place in history. Thank you for accepting your part in awakening the Earth for Heaven. When Jesus was about to finish the world on Good Friday, He had a purposeful composure, reflective of the past and His role in its fulfilment, and confidence in what the future would bring."

Sunday, January 28, 2007
St. Thomas Aquinas, Doctor [1225-1274]
3:01 p.m.

"It is by God's Grace that I speak to you when the outside air is wonderfully cold and the warmth of Divine Love is alive in your hearts. My little ones, I wish that you not be preoccupied with the vain attempts of sinful men to imitate the power of God, but embrace them when they reflect His holiness. Give them your affection in the likeness of Jesus, knowing that they are growing in the themes of Christian Truth as their faith continues to blossom. I have spoken in admonition and warning many times in the past, and also given high praise and accolades for your exemplary conduct in the likeness of My Son. It is good that you should do this; it is imperative that you embrace the decency in human affairs to which you are guided by the Holy Spirit. Disavow the evils of Creation; avoid the snares of the devil that are indicative of apostates, traitors, and false apostles who are trying to bring humanity to ruin. I promise that I offer My guidance and protection in matters of human conversion and Eternal Life. Today, therefore, I come to ask you to proceed, knowing that you are given shelter in the Sacred Heart of Jesus. Offer your prayers in confidence; bring to the Altar your assurance that you trust in the Lord and all things benign. You have lived with hope during the years and have followed the Light of Heaven as the Earth basks beneath its brilliance. By all means, never relinquish hope that everything for which you pray will come to pass. This is the hope, or esperance as known in earlier centuries, that keeps your strength in Christianity healthy and true. It focuses your vision and hones your judgement. It must become your nature to remain alive in hope, in the perpetual expectation that I mentioned in the past. We aspire to the coming refinement of men in all things glorious that flow from the Throne of the Father. And, we seek from your brothers and sisters not just virtual belief in something extraordinary when planning the future, but a virtuous faith that helps them realize that God's Kingdom of spiritual riches is now at hand. My Special son, I see that you are yet enjoying your religious writing that is offered through your openness to Jesus by the power of the Holy Spirit. All knowledge and foresight come from Him, as do reverence, spiritual romance, leniency in personal accord, and the better factors of life that lend your heart to cheerfulness and joy. I cannot overstate the efficacy of your writings because they leave in history an accounting of your relationship with God. They are in response to My prayers for your contributions in finishing the Earth and the purification of exiled humanity. Let there be no question; you are penning the final acts of Christian charity that will bring lost sinners into the fold on the last day in time. You have said quite aptly that there is something beatific about music, that it tenders the heart and comforts the soul. The reason it does is because all Creation can be heard in a song; it can be described by its lyrics and explicated by the harmonies by which humanity is called to live. It is this concurrent blend of unity and harmony that your soul feels when it hears music that is consoling, that does not cross the grain in the way you mentioned in your Diary. The Angels exalt the Lord in their songs; the masses regale the history of the Church in hymns and anthems, and the lonely and frightened are encouraged by the promises found in the stirring of the human spirit with strings and trombones, trumpets and harps, and cymbals and drums. Each plays its part in the same way that the diversity of humanity calls the one, single virtue of Love from Heaven to Earth in the Man-God on the Cross. There are untold melodies and unwritten lyrics that the Archangels will provide for the flourishing conclusion of the world in the ways you have dreamed. And, thank you for being so nice to your friends. It is these kindnesses that are recognized by God the Father as the representation of eternal greatness in you. Even though the tremendously visionary Saint Thomas Aquinas is celebrated today, it is clear that even he was resigned to the simple acts of love. He called them futuristic because he knew them to be among the culminating acts of the human species that would beget the arrival of Eternity onto the surface of the Earth. Hence, My message is one of gratitude and support, one that I hope will instill in you a new motivation to recognize that you still have great gifts to give the Church by your expertise in miraculous issues. When you greeted Bishop Lucas at the Pax Christi Mass in the Saint Joseph parish, he was touched to see you because he is aware of your unity with Me and your devotion to Jesus. Your Bishop searches for signs of Jesus in everyone, traits and attributes that assist him in seeing the Most Blessed Trinity in his flock at home. He saw in you the towering presence of the Father, the kind reflection of the Son, and the inspiring genuineness of the Holy Spirit. All of this, and the only thing you did was shake his hand. As for your brother, well, suffice it to say that he saw a spiritual son who wanted to say hello to his papa. These are auspicious times for Me because you are making the work of My messages the chore of humanity, to embrace and obey them, and nurture them with the fineness of gold in those who chose to believe. Thank you for taking such good care of your brother, for being kind to him, joining him on the occasion of his birthday, and keeping him safe from harm. Compared to most people you know, he is quite younger than them. He knelt before his bed before retiring last night and thanked God with the strength of his heart that he was led to you. You have compelling reasons to look anew to the future and see the valiance of your spirit of hope."

Sunday, February 4, 2007
St. Madeline Goffe Bixby [1813-1844]*
2:26 p.m.

"I come into your company to offer graces and blessings, and assure you that the Holy Spirit wills that you expose your lives to the ecstatic light that lends meaning to the years. When you perceive humanity's more honorable history, you are heartened by the acts of holiness that usher the Kingdom of God to the Earth. Like Me, however, you are dissatisfied by the suffering that engulfs the lives of the innocent and the predatory practices employed by those who remain opposed to the reign of sovereignty that Jesus holds over humanity. Unscrupulous sinners pursue an existence shaped by fiendish initiatives, addiction to impure pleasure, suspense, ignorance of Truth, and ruses by which they appear as the only heroes. Many mock and impugn the spiritualistic attributes of the human conscience; and when called to task for their lack of compassion, they are quick to flash a Crucifix or cruciform as if to convince their peers that they are consecrated to Jesus. I have warned against these kinds of villains, ones who use gadgets and gimmicks to distract you from the real problems of the world, and who elevate themselves as though deserving of the spoils of the battles of war. Indeed, My message today is to be wary of these hollow creatures because they are lying to themselves and those around them. They are scoundrels whose destiny is in peril when their lives are laid alongside that of the Son of Man. Thank you for praying for guidance and discernment in this and for your allegiance in faith to the Roman Catholic Church through which the Salvation of humankind exists. It is imperative that you pray for the people who are traveling in precarious places, for the unemployed and ill-educated, for the rescue of those facing danger to their health and safety, for the millions who have insufficient food and shelter, for the end of abortion, and for the intentions that are pertinent to your individual lives. God holds in His hands plenteous gifts to dry every tear, and relief for all who agonize for the conversion of humanity to His Kingdom of Glory. It is mandated that you pray to remedy everything that runs contrary to His ordinances. My Special son, please never forget that My Love for you transcends the origin of the Earth and the framing of the universe. I speak the reverent Truth with the knowledge that your faith is your wisdom and the Crucifixion is sufficient redemption for your soul. We have chosen to do more because we share the miraculousness that brings healing, sanctity, enlightenment, and chastity to your brothers and sisters in unprecedented ways. These modern times are of wonderment and advancement, and are indicative of the End Times mentioned in the Sacred Scriptures. I once said that even logic instructs that the Second Coming of Jesus is closer now than 2,000 years ago. I am blessed for more reasons than humanity will know before you fall asleep in death, and I desire to reveal the salient impressions of My Motherhood to those who will benefit from My kind succor. You are a wise child, My son, for never doubting the Will of God or the effectiveness of My messages. You are faithful for never turning your back on the supernatural facets of man's relationship with Heaven. How can I express My gratitude in ways you will understand? By simply promising that everything for which we have prayed is nigh at hand, in terms that your brothers and sisters will recognize in Nature, communication, the prosecution and cessation of wars, and the uncompromised capacity of Jesus' Mystical Body to hold dominion over the animals, birds, and fishes. While this does not diverge from the beginning of the Church, yours is a more peculiar commission than centuries ago because you are living closer to the end of the world. Jesus is the Author and Finisher of your faith, and He scripted these ages in the final chapter of the Book of Redemption. Thank you for grasping this with your heart and never surrendering to what might lead you down errant paths. I have spoken today so you can enjoy the bountiful life that My Son has accorded. It is not inappropriate for you to watch the debates that are being conducted in America and around the world as long as you do not become as cynical and sarcastic as those who are engaged in them. I wish you only the best of all possible blessings in the patience you have shown while God uses you to reach the hearts of the faithless and lost. Never mind that some Christians are banished from their families. Saint Michael the Archangel flushes-out those who worship their own children as gods instead of the Son of Man. Blind allegiance to one's sibling relationships in matters having nothing to do with the Cross is shallow and disreputable. With what shame they will find themselves guilty of standing in violation of the Gospel! What was Timothy's sisters's answer to his having rebuked her for elevating her offspring as idols? What was her reaction to your brother on whose behalf Jesus deigned to teach her? That he is deluded because he will not condone her unchecked pride. She crossed a line that your brother will never forget; she assailed you, she took-on and accosted a person whom your brother has often described in his prayers and contemplations as the reflection of the deity in Heaven, the living essence of human perfection, and the empowerment of the Crucifixion in contemporary flesh. It may be difficult to bear the emotional aspects of these issues, but I assure you that it is worth the price to defeat the pride that infiltrates the lives of someone's family and friends. In fact, it is nearly undescribable how your brother feels vindicated in light of his sister's terseness, and he feels more gratified to learn about the Gospel in real-life terms rather than reading it on a page. You will receive a particular blessing from Thomas the Patriot on Wednesday, the anniversary of his admittance into Heaven."

Sunday, February 11, 2007
Our Lady of Lourdes 1858
2:51 p.m.

"Through the peace and grace of our awesome God, I make Myself known to the nations, for I am the Queen of Love and your Intercessor in Heaven. I wish you goodness and happiness all your days, that you will clothe yourselves in the piety that the Gospel elicits from those who adore Him. Creation is made more whole by your prayers than yesterday because you are connected with the purity that makes your life complete. Awaiting your death is a supernal diadem that will place you among the chosen people, fit for all who have given themselves to the Messiah of Bethlehem and Nazareth, the Victim who draws humanity to a new birth of freedom. My little ones, you oftentimes speak of the legendary artworks of the Saints, and rightfully so. However, their gifts to redemption are more than legend, they are contributions to the miracle of your sanctification that are given only by the followers of My Son. There is no doubt that you live in their shadow, that you have stood upon the proverbial shoulders of giants to make your way to God, and that you have offered your good offices for the glory of His Kingdom on Earth. This is why I am pleased to speak to you, and persistent in calling you to the perfection of Jesus. Your emulation of His Truth is what makes you part of the permanent future of the Creation about which I speak. You call yourselves to higher nobility in your internal conscience and references to everything holy you have cited in your speeches and writings. Truly, the Holy Spirit finds its way into the hearts of the many who are dedicated to the cultivation of humanity in veins that are articulated by the mind of God. When you hail Jesus' Holy Name with accolades for His courage and justice, you are recalling the surety of His nobility in you as well. I learned as a young Maiden that the Father is serious when He speaks not so gently to the Earth about remaking its face through the perfected human conscience of His people en masse. The Roman Catholic Church is the only place for achieving charismatic faith, and it is your duty to become one in it, the Mystical Body of Christ whom God will redeem in the fullness of time. My dear ones, we celebrate the Feast of the Shrine in a country far from you, but the fluency of My presence is as profound where you live. You have heard many lofty oratories about unity and vision, foresight, accountability, social responsibility, and inclusion. I remind you that eloquence has its place, but it is misplaced if it fails to exalt Jesus Christ in all its purpose. There is no such thing as correctness without morality. When people come and go with surprising succession, they are heaved over the cliff with the anonymous ones if they decline to evangelize the Christian faith that is calling the heart of everyone alive. I join with you to see that this is done, for we seek an America that is not only filled with hope for peace and good will, but one that is saturated with these blessings for the right reasons. We urge public servants to resist the temptation to proclaim their leadership in mending differences between peoples and societies by covering them with short-sighted ignorance and remnants of the same old injustices. The newness of God's Kingdom calls you to a future based on the time-tested values of Truth and Love, not in the sense that you love someone enough to allow them to live as they want, but to require them to live as the Scriptures command. Deep seated differences between people and societies are the result of a percentage who refuse to accept Jesus as their Salvation. I realize as His Mother that the changes about which I speak cannot be achieved in a day, or even in the span of weeks or years. But, this does not mean that humanity cannot try. Through the historical accuracy of the Gospel, with the advocacy of the Holy Paraclete as your mentor, and with Me as your Mediatrix of all Graces, it is possible for the Earth to utilize the Crucifixion of the Son of God as your spiritual compass.

My little ones, I impel and implore the nations to turn themselves over to Jesus, the Son of Man, for everything required to set the world aright. There is no poverty in this that cannot be explained by the tenets of His Word. There are no reasons to defer to any future age the responsibilities that have fallen upon you. Your ancestors and forbears handed you a world with unlimited potential to do good, to see Light for what God made it to be, and open the future far beyond the horizons you see with your eyes. They passed to you a torch of spiritual vision that cannot be supplanted by the brevity of crescendoes by which you spend the hours. They saw in you what you refuse to see in yourselves. They recognized that you were more than capable of seeing the conclusion of Earth's realities in the Resurrection of the Messiah, faced and devoted to the purification of every man, woman, and child who would inhale the world to come. I pledge to you the promise made by the God of your fathers, the God of Abraham and Isaac, the God who has at last and finally dispensed to you the power that has made your sojourn to Eternity filled with majesty, simplicity, vision, Truth, and the only joy you will ever receive in this life. I witnessed centuries ago your years and decades filled with a hope that only your faith in Jesus can procure. You are the operatives and actuaries of His twenty-first century miracles, the fulfillers of His own dreams that were oathed by the prophets to foretell the end of the world. My pledge is more than hope, My little ones, but altogether to prepare you for the inevitability of the Final Judgment of mankind before God who deserves the fealty of the people to whom He gave life with providence and mercy. Why, then, did He dispatch His Mother of such Grace to awaken you? Upon what condition does He place your absolution for everything you have done to offend Him? He commissioned Me to remind you that He loves you beyond anything you could possibly imagine, and to say that you must provide your unconditional allegiance to His Son who died on the Cross that would live forever. I spoke to Saint Bernadette of Lourdes about sacrificing and suffering on the part of humankind in the likeness of Jesus. I did not refer to any gangly lawyer in Springfield, Illinois in the way a certain aspirant for office did while invoking the name of Abraham Lincoln. While the latter was speaking that year about a house divided, I was a world away talking about the divisions between humanity, socially and spiritually. I was referring to the gaping hole where men had abandoned purity and truth that in effect would soil the Earth before the face of Heaven. It is in this tone that I speak to you now, that you will perceive the intentions of God reverently, that you will accept His civility with open hearts and single minds, that you will walk in the Light of His righteousness, trusting that He has already chosen for you the path that will lead you to lasting peace. When visionary men speak about the unity of all the diverse peoples who comprise a nation, they stand at the brink of encountering without boundaries the vastness of God. They only need to mark one more step that will take them there, to realize for themselves and communicate to the people that the God of their fathers to whom I have referred invokes every whit of knowledge and wisdom to lead humanity to the Roman Catholic Church. If peace and justice are to rain down like a mighty stream into a river of understanding, they must be fed by the presence of the Father living through the Church. There is no other means to comprehend human life than through the Sacraments of the Catholic Church; for anything else, secular or otherwise, is only a temporal distraction. My role in Salvation has been more than to give birth to the Son of Man in Bethlehem, to teach Him the ways of life at Nazareth, and to pray alongside the Apostles and disciples when His time had finally come.

I was commissioned to be Mother for His chosen flock, to everyone who ever pined to know the truth, to the little people who had no one to elevate their dignity, to unborn babies whose cries cannot be heard from the womb, and for everything else beautiful that ever begged for a chance to live. My dear children, please make no mistake, I will uphold My oath to God. I will deliver you to Jesus with your loyalties intact. Whatever it takes to convert the Earth, whatever means must be employed to retrain humanity's vision on the future world, replete in the Glory of God, I will use it. If miracles are not enough to arouse the sleeping consciences of man, I will redouble and treble My efforts until My presence is utterly inexplicable by the sciences of the Earth. I will pray so profoundly that those who yearn for new birth will come wailing to Me to discover from whence such beauty has come. I will make the four winds blow, strike the Earth with the Father's Scepter, and raise from among you again those giants about whom I have spoken today. I will cull from your ranks new heroes for Jesus, ones who will fight not only to the death, but to their resurrection from the carnage that the Triumph of My Immaculate Heart will leave behind. I will deluge the Earth with Angels' tears and set before you the Feast of Sovereignty that Jesus, Saint Joseph, and I have been preparing for you for the past 2,000 years. I will harken the Saints of old to muster in you a belief that is so unique that you will take to your knees and beg God outright to see His Face before sundown falls. I tell you, My dear children, that I will sustain My pledge to Jesus that I gave Him on the day He died. I shall stomp under My heel the evil that makes you have doubts, and I will prevail over anything and everything that ladens your hearts with heaviness and sorrow. I will beckon the gladiators of the ancient times to return to Earth as your defenders and supporters, in armies so mighty that the darkness of Hell will fall even further into the pit of the night. The ferocity of My intercession cannot be put asunder by any creature or even the thought of one. My Special son, I bid you the best of all things, in all times. I pray for your convalescence of everything that ails you. I inspire your hope in the new tomorrow that stands in the offing, one where there is no lack of the peace of Jesus, one where you sense the victory of His Love more fully, and one in which you can finally proclaim to Creation that Salvation has come presently and permanently into your midst."

Sunday, February 18, 2007
St. Etienne Marseilles, Martyr [1772-1813]*
3:01 p.m.

"With high expectations for the conversion of prodigal men, I have come to speak to you while your prayers are presented before the Trinity in Heaven. It is an auspicious time to raise our pleadings during this period of openness, during the days prior to the Second Coming of the Messiah. While spirituality is not the province of any one person, I call each of you to a deep relationship with My Son. You are tasked with helping Jesus convert His enemies to the Cross because their decisions will someday be condensed into one moment of self-judgement. Prayer domesticates the human spirit to be fit for residence in the Father's house. You must approach complete strangers with the Gospel message as though you have known them all your lives. But, to be sure, speaking and hearing, and writing and reading, do not imply that they will accept your counsel. You may be treated with flagrant disregard by those who are against the concept of self-immolation. Their obtuse conduct, behavioral abuses, and lack of discipline are indicative of their proneness to avoid the difficult choices in matters of faith in favor of their secular-oriented freedom of expression. They are entrenched in this, My children. You are trying to persuade them to enlist in the army of Christian disciples while they are engaged in a dramatic convention of ideas that have nothing to do with God. And, they will deny as patently untrue that they are unwilling to listen. You, however, already know that they will eventually stumble over themselves. While they are steeped in convivial fraternity, the true disciples of the Lord are suffering for His sake. Your hearts are insignias of His peace in a world that is embroiled in destruction. What meager provisions they give to the poor are insufficient to keep alive the insects and trees. I join in your prayers that humanity will become a vessel fit for the righteousness that Grace Incarnate has chosen as His transfer into the farthest portals of Creation. It is clear that there are millions who are not yet there with Him. Too many are causing humanity's morals to list and careen from the stalwart goodness that God expects from His people. Therefore, I come seeking your petitions to open their hearts. It is never too late to pray for them. And, during these months when the Earth has laid its harsh winter upon you, we embrace the warmth of the heart as an innovative lifeline to their spirits, that they will opt for the Light over the darkness of their unconfessed sins. I am filled with anticipation because you are witnessing the revelation of many prophesies that have been foretold through the years, and now announced as part of the history you are making. It is saddening that so many are methodically wasting the ample opportunities to witness to God's presence. If only they would invoke the faith in their hands, they would see the unfurling of the Providence that He has fashioned as signs and catalysts for their spiritual rebirth. Yes, hundreds of millions of your wayward brothers and sisters are overcome by the hysteria manufactured by the entertainment industry and the cultural elite. We know that they must be wise in the things of holiness, but they seem unaware because of the distractions blinding them from recognizing the signs of Heaven's eternal peace. It is entirely possible for modern men to see and replicate the pious sacrifices and honorable modesty that made Saints of your fathers. It is our prayer that their goal of attaining this will resume in earnest, from whence they were children running playfully in their fields of innocence. Indeed, it is imperative that the refining of the conscience of human hearts opens like a flower and receives the Lord's benediction. My Special little son, you have given the United States a tremendous blessing by your recently published article about the last great hope for world peace.* Jesus is appreciative that you repeat His provocative message about the redemption of humanity in the Cross. Due to the ease of communication in this age, thousands of sinners have read your essay. This makes you happy as a child of God, but it makes Him even happier. He allows you to take advantage of the venue that you have heretofore criticized as part of the problem, the American media. God is putting in motion the gifts of love given by His people around the globe because He knows that the time is ripe for the conversion of your peers. These are obvious attributes of His signature across the landscape and a means to ensure that your efforts are not in vain. I have said that time is of the essence, but it is a nonissue for the temporal development of the Earth. We are prepared to wait as long as required for your brothers and sisters to turn to Jesus for assistance as an act of their own accord. Your gifts are of the fruits of His Crucifixion, and your patience is an even grander virtue derived from His Paschal Resurrection. Can you see these things from your purview in exile? And, you are capable of knowing that to everything there is a season, and the momentous advances you are achieving in the Triumph of My Immaculate Heart offer plentiful opportunities for those who oppose the Church to repent of their sins. There is unbridled hope in this, ways for you to discern the motivations of Jesus as He bends Creation. After all, this is what your faith is for; it is why we are praying together. My greeting you with compassion and foresight represents the prescience of the Father to know in advance how His people will respond. It is with this anticipation that I seek from you a broader perspective of what the future will reveal. Please realize and accept that your life is seamlessly connected to the mission of the Church and the upending of the Earth. All the prognosticators that could possibly be assembled could not make this more clear than at this moment. It is beyond the thoughts of humanity what Heaven holds for those who serve God. My Special son, I reflect Jesus' thankfulness that you are taking such good care of your brother. You are reshaping the Earth into the fineness of indomitable purity. I shall always be here at your side. This did not just begin at the inception of your messages. Thank you for befriending My American children working in restaurants, cafeterias, and marketplaces. They sense in you the companionship of the Lord."

* Our Last Great Hope
The Onslaught Against Organized Religion

I recently was listening to a distinguished veteran recollecting his memories of the above-ground atomic testing in the southwest United States after World War II, and how at the time he had learned of a test to occur in the New Mexico desert. Although he was stationed on a ship nearly 200 miles away, he thought he might witness remnants of the explosion during his scheduled watch at the time of the early morning event. In the twilight hours before dawn, he trained his eyes toward the horizon, intent on seeing the flicker of the blast, when suddenly the sky lit-up in a spectacular burst, illuminating everything around as if it were crystal clear on a bright Sunday afternoon. He remembered an extremely ominous feeling overcoming him as his minuscule expectations were suddenly and irrevocably overwhelmed by the astonishing reality of such unimaginable power.

This vignette comes to mind whenever I read or hear about people boasting of their reluctance to recognize any benevolent or redeeming qualities in "organized religion," while simultaneously pining for its demise. I find it rather disingenuous that the generic term "organized religion" is even employed by those disparaging someone else's faith, as if Christians, especially Roman Catholics, would be surprised or offended to know it referred to them. The phrase "organized religion" is merely a pejorative indictment used by the Church's detractors who believe all they have to do is pronounce the epitaph and their peanut gallery of partisans will join them on queue with boos and hisses, believing they have some semblance of credibility beyond their own peers. I contend that it is beneath the dignity of any educated person to attack an institution of faith when every authentic perusal of human history distinctly reveals that the progression of Christianity and its contributions to civilization are of admirable influence. It is neither laudable nor commendable for anyone to appropriate an informed air about the topic of Christianity, the transcending scope of faith, or its twenty centuries of courage, sacrifice, and virtue when they are armed like children with nothing more than a scant collection of sound bites whose true realities have been lost to the obscuring fog of socio-religious bigotry of the past 500 years. These disoriented people fail to realize that the intellectual foundation of organized religion encompasses far more than the limited parameters they reserve for it in their ill-informed world views. That's why the story that began this letter is so appropriate. The adversaries of hierarchical Christianity are looking at its structured competence, believing it to be no more than an ignited firecracker that is gone in an instant, when in actuality, it is the super-colossal concussion of miraculous events that preempted human existence two millennia ago, which are presently reverberating through the corridors of our station in modern time. The Crucifixion and Resurrection of Jesus Christ is the climactic detonation of God's revelation of Himself on Earth in human flesh, replicated or usurped by no man since. The events of Good Friday are the luminous spectacle whereby infinite love was unleashed into the desert of our history in an awe-inspiring display of valorous human perfection that is yet aspired to by word and example within the hallowed chambers of our sacred basilicas, cathedrals, churches, seminaries, convents, workplaces, schools, and homes, now into 2,000 years and counting. Hierarchical Christianity is nothing less than the beatific tradition of Heaven's sacrificial genius rocketing through mortal time like a massive blast wave propagating away from the epicenter of an explosion, leveling evil at each expiring nanosecond. Indeed, Mount Calvary is God's ground zero, and his deific love has raised recurring generations of faith-filled people to their feet in allegiance to him, offering devotion, unity and sacrifice, and setting them free as one royal family upon a salvific plateau that no person can deign for themselves. The accolades belong to no one but the Sacred Messiah who was sacrificed there, indelibly dressing his global theater in unprecedented glory and righteousness. He wishes to effect eternal redemption upon us in an orderly, peaceful, and unifying fashion, reflective of the Church that his spirit has raised. The organized traditions that Christians extol are the only hope humankind has to understand what love is, and how we may live in lasting peace. Henceforth, let the false caricatures of the hierarchical Church and the hatred by which she is pummeled expire so our civilization can be something more than rogue protestation, disunity, immorality, vilification, and war.

Sunday, February 25, 2007
Six Tibetan Children, Martyrs [d.1963]*
3:01 p.m.

"With urgent kindness, I bring Good News for the fractured world of men, where there is healing of spirit and body, where Jesus' Love permeates your lives. My faithful ones, a great deal is made of legacies and fortunes where estates may prevail, but I call your attention beyond these things. The superiority sought by benevolent men resides in your capacity to confess your helplessness, of being unable to see through the blindness of your transgressions, and offering them to God through the Crucifixion. At this hour in time, you see the Earth as much in turmoil as ever, with as much destruction in its own right than has existed during the entire history of wars. Today's evil attacking you is of the same origin as that which corrupted Adam and Eve, but is mutated by the manipulation of modern deception and the desecration of previously sacred manifestations. It is true that this has happened because lost sinners have forsaken the Lord for whom they are to serve, and the righteous among you have remained silent in the presence of this condition. While there are accidental sins on Earth, most of your error is from a premeditated plot by Satan to neutralize the Church. The onslaught of indecency against the chastity of the world's youth is unprecedented. Simple piety is rapidly diminishing because the global culture of impurity and death is overwhelming the senses of the young generation. Today, therefore, I call upon you to increase your prayers for the conversion of the hearts of the wicked, for the conquest of the indifference that is eroding the spiritual conscience of your children, and for the extinguishing of everything that has nothing to do with Jesus. My people should teach their offspring that Salvation in the Blood of the Cross is their birthright, their sacred endowment given by God in Heaven. There is little doubt that they cannot learn this on their own because they are distracted by lust and materialism, and their innocent discernment of life is plundered by the neglect they face every day. Yes, it is all about the children! My emphasis on reaching the hard-hearted and gently treating the least of these is based on the responsibility handed to you by My Son. When you accept the Cross, you are supposed to instruct the ignorant about faith, to the purpose of furthering their knowledge about the Beatitudes and Commandments that have preceded, overcome, and will ultimately supplant your existence on Earth. When visionaries and seers impress upon pilgrims around the globe the sacred commission to be perfected as Jesus is perfect, they resound My messages to an unwary people, one that underestimates the determination of God to purify the land upon which they live. I have told you that there are auspicious times in the offing for those who worship Him, for the millions who walk in faith toward the end of seeing His Kingdom with more than physical sight. You must see with eyes of trust. If anyone asks the essential goal of the Mother of Jesus, tell them that it is that Her children must defer to the Son of Man in all ways, to do everything He says, and become like saints in wisdom, contrition, servitude, and integrity. The latter of these implies that you do not question the motives of the Church, that you embrace God's Will in the shadow of Abraham, and that you stand tall in prudence and seek from yourselves and your friends the most noble holiness you can muster. I am not speaking of a nobility that places you in the company of kings, but one in which you sacrifice in benevolence everything you are and have been given to the refinement of the human experience, for exalting Jesus' Kingdom, and for healing and elevating the grieving and dying. I speak of nobility that inspires you to uplift the dignity of those for whom no one else will stand. My dear children, I am referring to a nobility that would have you slain as martyrs in many places around the world.

Thank you again, My Special son, for bearing your suffering for Jesus, for your reward of Salvation will be great. There are reasons yet unknown to you that are driven by your patronage to Heaven, by your loyalties and allegiances to your faith, and by your ability to see Creation as it should be. You live in wonderment of the awesome power of God to shape and heal the universe, and you know that Jesus does everything to perfection. I ask you to pray for the consoling of hearts in the families of the victims of wars, for the thousands who are lamed by the heat of the fight, and for the heroes who bear their battleground scars on the inside where no one sees them. This is the kind of anguish that you have many times stated to be more horrid than physical pain. My Special son, if you tell My people nothing more, remind them that Jesus is aware of the brokenness of humanity. Tell them that He is trying to sanctify them through miracle and message, by the forces of Nature, and in the framework of torment that darkens millions of lives. Indeed, if you tell them little else, remind them about the Divine Mercy awaiting them at the uttering of the words *Jesus, I Trust in Thee*. You have laid plentiful wisdom upon the plateau of human existence to keep magnates and magistrates in awe for the remainder of their years. They must busy themselves in the things of redemption, disavowing the tyranny through which they govern, implementing peace-filled initiatives where the fires of destruction are devouring the sheer heart of their highlands and meadows. If you show them the way of Divine Love, they will come forth. You should always believe that I have not given you hundreds of messages in vain. Your life has been an apologetic for the Grace that is dispensed to men from God, and you know the epilogue of this story. Your faith and that of your brother have been gifts to the Church, even as this was unbeknownst to you prior to February 22, 1991."

Sunday, March 4, 2007
St. Leopold Motiva Darsette [1613-1678]*
3:11 p.m.

"The Lord has made My mission the retrieval of His disciples who inhabit the Earth, and I pray with you to that end so you will have sufficient strength and perseverance to evangelize His Holy Word. While these days augur hope for the conversion of millions of souls, there are many who yet live in agony and torture. It is our desire to touch them with the Spirit of God, with the gladness of old that is manifested by their acceptance of the Cross, and through the enlightenment they gain by summoning His Wisdom. Hence, My brief conversation today will herald the Gospel that brings solvency to life, that changes everything in the world not solely for the sake of change, but for the heightening of the righteousness of humanity, an awakening they can discover nowhere else. My children, you are aware of the resurrection of the conscience that Jesus instills in those who accept Him. Their spiritual rigor mortis, their stiffness behind their death of hope, is not permanent. With this hope in hand, they are renewed in faith. Anyone can begin again through the Light of Love that Jesus gives in Christian faith. While I realize that these are mystical things that occur on the inside, the fruits of this conversion are overtly obvious. What happiness you procure, knowing that you have played such a crucial part in the opening of the future world! I tell you again that these are the latter days of cosmic spheres; these are times when the moral imperatives of your spiritualism must be internalized by the many who are far from the Divine Truth of God. To be sure, we do not do this alone. You are engulfed by the Grace that has saved you; your souls are protected by the Legions of Angels, your hearts are nourished by the poetry of the years that extols the holiness of the Saints. You need not worry that yours is an age that serves only to close the parade of loyalties given by your predecessors. Each person in his day gives a unique clarity to the Love of God through his gift of life. I assure you that this mark of destiny brings you to the foot of the Cross where Jesus sees you individually, with all your faults and failures, and with every treasure you have deposited to advance His Kingdom and propagate the Church. You are the Mystical Body He claims for transference into the Glory of Eternal Day. My Special son, My Immaculate Heart is aglow in this same hope that makes your smile so beaming. We know what billions have yet to learn, that the purpose of life is far greater than the sum of its years, that its meaning is to approach the Cross with dignity, respect, contrition, and humility. While I have said that this requires a grand awareness never before known to this age, it revolves around the radical reorientation of the heart so the Holy Spirit can enter. While this seems like a concession that most men are reluctant to make, it is one that finds the beginning of Eternal Life. It is not only a surrendering of the will, it is the restructuring of priorities so the will serves at the pleasure of the Creator of all things. In this, the meaning of life takes on dimensions greater than ever discerned by those who are novices to the Gospel of Christianity. Why, some inquire, is this so opposed? Because it stands in diametric contrast to everything the secular world believes. You are lambasted for upholding the sacred principles of the Lord and the virtues by which you live, but you are prophesying the demise of those who decry His Kingdom when you remain firm in His defense. You are living a time when war is a casual response to offensive action, when negotiation and diplomacy are spurned. I am happy, My Special one, that you do not become burdened by this; it is clear that you see them for what they are. God has blessed you with this vision and will reward you for trusting that everything about which He has spoken will occur. When I use the word auspicious at times, My intention is to employ its meaning in the strictest terms. *Surely goodness and Mercy shall follow you all the days of your life.* You have given your existence to Jesus while on your earthly journey. In return, you will inherit an inexplicable joy that no one can hamper. The exhilaration that you mentioned in *Morning Star Over America* is unfurling as the months expire."

Sunday, March 11, 2007
St. Juniper the Benign [AD 416-453]*
2:29 p.m.

"Wellness abounds in you, My angelic people, because you implore God to bless your homes and families. Jesus is listening. He realizes that you subscribe to His call to prayer. Today, we remember the ailing and infirm in a special way, asking Saint Juniper to intercede for them. There is goodness and charity in your works, and high praise from the Son of Man who commends you to strengthen their lives through the blessings of His peace. Please also invoke the Holy Spirit for the souls whose hearts are torn into tattered shreds and mangled wreckage by human hatred. We must assure them that Christ Jesus stands with them, that He provides for their healing and well-being, and that the Angels and Saints pray for them during their personal distress. You understand that life brings suffering, even though it need not be, and that your compassion evokes the pity of the Lord. This is the gallantry of your Christian trust and the working of the Holy Paraclete throughout the physical world. Please do not allow the distractions and schemes of your enemies to bring you any disappointment in the procession of events by which you serve the Church. Let no one persuade you that your faith is in vain, that your petitions do not matter, or that Jesus cannot hear you from Heaven. His Wisdom, power, and influence permeate time and space. His genius guides you on the everlasting path of righteousness. Soon, you will see firsthand that the

Will of the Father has come to you in ways that are unparalleled for these times. New avenues of Glory and the enlightenment of men are eclipsing the Earth, and you are the fortunate souls who are participating in edifying the masses. While I have told you these things before, you are capable of seeing it with greater clarity. The supplications you have offered the Lord are answered in His good time, and your devotion to Me has yielded immeasurable graces for humanity. My dear Special son, you have been writing an introduction for your next book that is befitting of the intelligence of those who believe. And, for those who do not, many of them will reconsider what it means to be a messenger for God in this new century. No one has said that your contributions would be easy, but you are proving that the blessings overwhelmingly outnumber the liabilities. Thank you for your vision, loyalty, faith, trust, and love. I shall speak briefly today because sometimes this is what I do. You are feeling better now from a cold virus, and your foot is on the mend. What does the Holy Spirit say in describing how My messages are received? Their conveyance is as inexplicable as Jesus' Ascension and My Assumption into Heaven. The term is 'transcension.' It is a beatific phenomenon that is prehistoric to your semantics; and it addresses how earthly concepts interface with the sublime, spiritual, and super-miraculous attributes of Salvation. I am pleased by the prologue of your new book, and more pleased that you are receptive of the Angels. Your discussion of the transmission of My messages is appropriate. I assure you of My dedication to your enlightenment and the transference of the Wisdom of the Lord into your heart."

Sunday, March 18, 2007
St. Breighton Chillocothe [1869-1924]*
3:39 p.m.

"Welcome to My Holy and Immaculate Heart. It is My joy to pray with you for all who are in need of Jesus' blessing, especially the millions who are far from the Cross. In this Lenten season when you recall Jesus' temptation in the desert, you are expected to remember your brothers and sisters, and the temptations they fight to overcome the evil that brings them to despondence and surrender. I need not remind you where they live because you know about the pandemic stress by which humanity cries. When My messages of peace and prayerfulness take hold, the Earth will be unified in Jesus' Crucifixion. It is a contradiction for someone to say that their existence lies stagnant when all they need to do is open their eyes to the righteousness that blooms from the hearts of My children. I have formed a Christian vibrancy in you that is unforeseen for these times. And, you must be mindful that God's commitment to the New Covenant of Jesus is one that He has kept to His death and resurrected life.

The Holy Paraclete cannot be stilled. The gifts of God's Love cannot be negated. It is with this confidence that you should march forward as My children, that you should forge into the future with greater trust than that espoused by the first disciples. For all the piousness, charm and hopefulness they embraced, they did it for you. They built the Faith Church as instruments of Christ's legacy. And, from the Pentecost that birthed the Church into being, you are living-out not only the faith of the original Apostles, but your inheritance as their heirs. I have called and collected you before the Holy Cross as your beacon of hope and lighthouse in the darkness. It is your spiritual vision that guides you to manifest a universe of good will whose fruits are seeable with your eyes. A man who lay in death was raised by Jesus in the sight of his friends, and the stench of that death could not overcome the joy that was replete in their hearts. In everything they believed about their Lord Jesus, they realized upon the resurrection of Lazarus that the Son of Man was in their presence. Your evidence need not be in the raising of your friends from the sepulcher, but your knowledge that the power vested in Jesus is given to you to heal, nourish, teach, guide, bless, and unite. God views these things as preeminent to bringing a dead man from the darkness of the grave. It is apparent that these kinds of miracles are difficult for some to believe because they want to witness the other one first. My sons, how many Thomas's have you met in the last sixteen years? These individuals live in the fog of their inhibitions; they are unsighted because they refuse to see. What is it about Christianity that is so repugnant to them? How many more cures and unexplained events of Nature do they require to know that God is communicating with them? The Holy Spirit will not desist in bringing redemption to the core of His people's hearts, but they must let Him in. Jesus is more than a fair-weather friend. He remains with you during the calamities of life as well as your victories. He manifests the aid and assistance of the Father in ways that have yet to be told by the millions receiving His blessings. My message all along has been that the willingness of Heaven to intercede for you is as prevalent today as it was in the first century. If this were not true, I would have told you. I wish therefore that My children would teach your brothers and sisters about what Jesus would have them do with their stagnant lives. People who spurn the Wisdom of Heaven, those who ignore its overtures, and the billions who reject the Cross violate their own sense of belonging. They are isolating themselves from the affirmation they seek from immortality. They are lost, and must be found. Thank you for praying for them as their lives end, as they are apprised of the perilous conditions that call them to disavow their callousness. This, My little children, is among the blessings we are seeking from Jesus. My Special son, I know that you are receptive to My message of conversion, even when I repeat it. We shall not cease to open the hearts and minds of those who reject the Gospel. You and your brother are holding-up well for all you have endured. As you know, you are each other's greatest gift. By the power of the Cross, I will dirk the acts of your enemies and the nefarious motives of nonbelievers. You will be pleased to present your new book to humanity because it represents a large deposit of your messages since the turn of the century. Thank you for taking such good care of your brother. You are his hero in more ways than I can describe. You bring out the best in him that no one else sees."

Sunday, March 25, 2007
The Annunciation of the Lord
3:39 p.m.

"My children, this is an emerald day in history, for the voice of an Angel has pronounced Good News from God, and the whole of Creation has been restored. I pray with you for the overwhelming transformation of humanity into the likeness of the Son of Righteousness, that this will occur in your day. There are plenteous reasons why you should look to the future with anticipation, with an envisionment of the Glory that has come through the Messiah and the Paraclete. I remind you that billions of people around the world have yet to accept this sublime Wisdom; they still do not understand that Jesus Christ lived and died for their redemption. The fortune you shall inherit is more than the land of milk and honey that is cited in the journals of men, it is the Paradise which all humankind has been seeking since the first mortal was footed on the face of the Earth. Reality as you know it must become the scrupulous transference of your souls into the presence of God in the spiritual heights. This is not magic, My children. It is not karma or sleight of hand; it is the return of humanity to their belonging in the Grace of the Creator, of the Almighty Father who deigned to breathe 'being' into something that had never existed. All of this is a manifestation of His Providence. It is by His hands that you are willed into substance, sustained in life, raised upon your death, and stationed in His company for all eternities to come. This is why what we do is so important for a world in which there exists such dire consequences and depravity of the heart. We reach-out to foreign lands from this humble place in America to remind them that they were created to leap higher than the physical frame allows, all the way beyond the stars and universes, completely and totally in union with the New Kingdom that will soon eclipse the Earth and all existence as you know it. There has been proof of this Glory in the Savior who came to absolve you, to remake and remold you, whose bloodshed has cleansed and purified you, and whose Paschal Resurrection has launched you atop the towering pinnacles of the years. Your faith, My dear ones, is the seed from which all this grows. I speak of the Archangel Gabriel because he deserves it, and humanity requires it. I draw your attention to God's salvific contact with exiled humanity because you are prone to ignore any sense of the miraculous due to the blindness you inherited from Old Adam. Jesus is your new vision. He is the enlightenment you have gained in the eloquence of His passionate oratories while walking the Earth in sinless flesh. He is your majesty and propriety in a perfect Man, in the Spirit of God who hails you above the stars and in the Most Blessed Sacrament from the altars of the Roman Catholic Church. Therefore, I announce to you a gift of joy, that this Man of Love comes seeking you in every way conceivable so that you might garner your own conception of what the next life must be. Faith hails from this curiosity, and it is a productive use of the human experience to stare-down evil with righteousness, reminding the netherworld that you shall forever reside both high and beyond its demise. Your spirits are cleansed by the steely pumice of Jesus' Sacrifice, and you share in the magnetic joy that He has instilled in you through the Glory of Easter. If you imagine what this Salvation is like; if you release your grasp on the material world, and if you leap by faith into the embrace of God by trusting My words, you will be freed from the bonds of everything you have ever feared. You will know that it is possible to fly untethered, to soar with the eagles as leaders in truth, and to bask in the Light of Heaven that is shining down upon you now. There will be sacrifices and the bearing of undue burdens that seem inordinate to you, but you shall know at last that everything willed by the Lord satisfies His purpose; it is all in alignment with His master plan for the redemption of the world. My children, you have learned from the Annunciation of the Archangel that the proper response to the intervention of God is prayer. Your conversion is all about prayer! Without conversion, there can be no sanctification. Without both, there is no elevation of the soul to blessings unknown. It is true that the world is upside down. To walk in the ways of Jesus, you must close your eyes upon Creation. You can see more clearly when you perceive the Will of the Father with your hearts, rather than your glances. This has been true since the inception of time.

    My Special son, I sincerely wish you happiness and contentment in your labors on My behalf. There is no question that you are in full compliance with everything of God, and that if the human heart were an incendiary device, yours would have already blasted the Earth into awareness to make way for the parade of Saints walking in your midst. These days are about the Glory of which I speak only because God's visionaries are seeing in the spiritual sense, the innate ability to anticipate His motives with the predominance of the heart. You are one with this accord because you have given yourself to Me. Thank you for everything you do, especially waiting in joyful hope for the coming of the Lord. And, bless you for expiating the infidelities of your brothers and sisters by your petitions in your altar room at home. Please remember that prayer is a mystery; it is a sacred one. It is remedial and salubrious; it is salutary and beneficial to the dawning of God's Kingdom. When you pray from the heart, the excellence of the Trinity is brought into the temporal world to destroy the effects of evil. It is emphatic of the Second Coming because it chases the devil from any place you deign when you recite the Rosary. Thus, you wield the power of Jesus' Crucifixion. Look at the blessings you have given the Earth! What grand and miraculous gifts you have forged into being by remaining steadfast in faith and strong of heart. I assure you that you will comprehend this with precise clarity when you see your existence alongside the grandness of Heaven in the fullness of time. I wish not that you have fear, but always be brave when I say that the Lord does everything right. We will soon prepare your armada of books for launch in the places that will remove the cover beneath which you have lived for several years. Thank you for your holy petitions. They are deadly to Satan, but healing and reparative for humanity."

Sunday, April 1, 2007
Saint Ira Scarborough [1873-1934]*
3:02 p.m.

"With every assurance that you are living in God's good graces, I appear to you with His kind regards and pleasant wishes. You are entering Holy Week with the anticipation of little children because you know that it is the precursor to the moment when Jesus returns in Glory and takes you to Heaven. My dear ones, we have solemn petitions to lift to Him prior to that occasion, ones He receives with dispatch. We seek from the Holy Spirit the Wisdom that will change the hearts of sinners here in your midst and on continents where many have never traveled. Our earnest supplication at the break of each new dawn is that the Church will be united, Heaven and Earth, with the Mystical Body of Christ intact, leaving no one behind, and benefitting all who have searched for the meaning of life since they learned the capacity of reason. There is an uprightness and oneness to which you are called as Christians; some people refer to it as a kilter in which things that are wrong are made right, where darkness is scattered by God's Divine Light, where sickness and disease are finally eradicated, bringing health of mind and body to everyone. You must recall, My children, that you are summoned to a holiness that cannot be revoked, and one you take to the final day of your life. Holiness should never be offset by a backlash associated with many secular movements in civilized places, ones where the majority rules, and where there is a plurality of approaches to studying the existence of God. Anything less than complete righteousness is lukewarmness in Jesus' eyes. Once you have garnered the strength, foresight, and grace to avoid falling into temptation and sin, you must never believe that there is a balance that must accompany your actions so you are not seen as fanatics by those who do not share your faith. There can be no diluting the passion by which you live or the tenets of the religious conviction you profess in the Apostles Creed. Therefore, I call you to ensure your loyalties to God through frequent confession, attendance at Holy Mass, and remembering everyone in your petitions who is in need of Heaven's intercession. This is an hour of celebration because you are growing near the completion of life. You are a pilgrim people who espouse order and pacivity compared to those in estranged nations. While this is an honorable way to live, you must do more to pray for solutions that only come from God. You should call on the Holy Spirit to give you wise judgement in public affairs. I know that this is not an easy task in the Unites States where you are plagued by rampant materialism. My messages all along have been about seeing beyond the temporal Earth, looking where only few eyes have seen God's Glory in the lives of the poor and the millions who are in agony from the ravages of neglect. We must pray for them, My children! This is the thesis of your having given your lives to Jesus, that you will by your Christian works end the suffering of the poor, and by your prayers seek the advocacy of Heaven to lift the downtrodden and provide for everyone in need. This is the most effective way to bring miracles to displace social depravity, justice to overcome inequality, and good health to heal the wounds of the broken. When you speak about nurturing the seedling faith of those who are still learning about Christianity, they see best when they are shown the giants among you who are hailing Angels to the Earth in droves, who look like seers and prophets whose lives have been touched by the fairness of God. Jesus asks you to feed His lambs and tend to His sheep, and these are the years when your affirmative response is most imperative. The gravity of world suffering is grotesque, and Christians bear a responsibility to do something about it. The Heavenly Father holds true that your response to the gift of faith is to exercise it. Prove that you are worthy of the inspiration that the Holy Paraclete has given you.

My Special son, I love you! With what Grace do I descend from Heaven to speak with appreciative overtones, honor and respect, and devotion and care. It is clear to you how crucial are the days because you have been anticipating them. Regardless of what anyone might tell you, the element of time cannot deceive you or prohibit you from seeing the conclusion of the Earth at Jesus' hands. There is a debate ongoing in secular circles about the existence and relevance of religion, and you know that it is a moot discussion. Anyone who disbelieves the presence of God is under the influence of evil. Anyone who claims that the Holy Eucharist is not the Body and Blood of Jesus Christ is committing blasphemy against the Kingdom of Heaven. We share more than our prayers, My little one. We together own the future of the world as it sits in space, waiting for the Second Coming of My Son. The Crucifixion has done more than redeem the souls of humanity, it is the centrifuge of reason through which all elements of your existence are refined, like cream to the top of a barrel; and anyone who does not believe in the Messiah will be thrown to the underworld to be lost. The rotation of the Earth is not unlike the spinning about which I speak; it offers humankind the opportunity to see that everything about you is in flux, fluidity, and motion except the immutable Truth of God.

If Nature could speak in refrains; if wildlife could intone your language, and if the sun could bear upon you an epitaph before setting the final time, they would all repeat the strains from the songs of old that remind you that God is the Wonderful Counselor who has come to reign in your midst as the Incarnate Jesus. They would hail Him as their Maker, elevate Him before the nations as the only ambassador capable of uniting them, and lift Him high enough for everyone who has ever lived to see with their own eyes. My little one, you have yet to hear the forests tenor such choruses or flowers sing out loud. You have seen the smiling sunsets, but have not heard their last crescendos. All of these things are measured by your love for God in your heart, by your faith, and by the intensity in which you anticipate His tenacity in maintaining His Kingdom over anything that may try to impugn it. Thank you for permitting Me to speak to you. I am pleased that you remained at home to rest this morning, and that you so kindly prayed with Me today for the regeneration of the spirit of piety that engulfed the lives of your ancestors in this pretty land of yours. Lastly, thank you for praying with your brother with such intensity in your altar room. Many dark places are being exposed to the Light of Heaven."

Sunday, April 8, 2007
The Paschal Feast of Easter
2:58 p.m.

"Dear children, you have mourned the suffering of Jesus on the Way of the Cross, now you bask in the brilliance of His Paschal Resurrection. And, with this renewal in your hearts, I come speaking this day about spreading the Gospel of the New Covenant worldwide, to the far corners of the Earth, so the billions who are yearning for Salvation can be found in the Sacrifice of My Son. Little ones, My mission has been to speak to the prospering of your divinity. I have urged you to the perfection of Heaven in the way that Jesus has shepherded your souls. Pay no regard to the malignance of the secular void; turn instead to the Divine Love of God for purity in your lives. I call on you to speel the mountains of righteousness where you can see with the eyes of your souls the conclusion of time and the Glory awaiting you in Paradise. This is a vision about which I spoke to your fathers, the ones for whom the Martyrs surrendered their lives; and it is the capacity to see the future that has been foretold by seers and messengers through the ages. Now, My children, this vision is yours to wield in miraculously orthodox ways. We pray on this Easter for the swelling tide of human holiness to lift your poor brothers and sisters from poverty, and we ask God to intercede by the Resurrection of His Son to end all wars. The Vicar of Christ, Pope Benedict XVI, hails the presence of the intersection of Heaven and Earth in the human soul for the remedying power that heals the lives of the brokenhearted, and for the Holy Paraclete to take residence where God has been unwelcome. I pray that the whole world will heed the call of this Pope for the conversion that is required to the tenets of Christianity which are so ameliorating for Creation. This Paschal Feast is about new beginnings and the convalescence of the mind, heart, and spirit. It is about resurrecting everything about humanity that complies with the Will of God. My Special and Chosen sons, it gives Me satisfaction knowing that you are still together receiving My messages, that you understand that the goals you are accomplishing through the passage of time are greater than time itself. This is an unselfish faith that you are offering, and your reward will be liberating. Thank you! I speak in the knowledge that you are looking forward to releasing My messages from the beginning of the century, and that you recognize their relevance in the spiritual domain of these times. If you should be told that there will be twenty more anthologies, I am convinced that nothing would prohibit you from completing them. I have confidence that you realize your station in time and space, that you comprehend the purpose of your lives precisely as they have been prefigured by the Providence of God. This must give you pause and comfort, and a sense of endowment as you ponder the events of history and your place alongside the Saints. It must allow you to see the future, completely beyond the expiration of time and the obsolescence of the Earth to know that your existence has been fashioned by the necessity of the human family to commit to repentance. You accept that it is for Christ Jesus in you that you are living yourselves. Hence, I seek in you the profession that you are heartened by your compliance with the wishes of My Son, that you understand your fostering and nurturing of the spiritual conversion of your brothers, and that you see your place in God's Kingdom by whom you were conceived into your mothers' wombs. This is the preordained meaning of your lives. It is not that you are unworthy of being in Heaven already, but God needs you in His vineyard for the restoration of His peace in a world gone awry. You walk with companions like Saint Paul in completing Jesus' Crucifixion for the reparation of human sin.

You have become the emeriti of holiness for Jesus in your time; your works and sacrifices are poised to alter and amend the face of the Earth into His likeness for your successors. And, why should this not be true? After all, it is you who said 'yes' to the Mother of the Lord; it is you who have preserved your lives for Jesus; you have declined the distractions of secularism and rejected the temptations of the devil. My son, it must be a good feeling knowing that you have placed inside the parameters of mortal time the vehicles through which so many lost souls will be led to the Sacraments of the Church and before the Son of Man for purification and Salvation in His sanctifying Word. You are the epitome of human obedience in matters of faith and morality as a member of the Church. Easter is about this; it refers to the elevation of humanity from the darkness of their lives through such wonderful gifts that you have accorded on behalf of the Almighty Father. Please be reminded that it has never been My intention to heap undue praise upon you. I am only telling the truth. Your persistence has wrought the contemplations that will raise the hopes of millions and augment the power of the Holy Spirit to bring happiness to so many lives. You speak about seeds and of fruit-bearing acts that effect positive change. Can you not sense the blossoming of the eternal presence of international concord growing from your faith in Jesus? And, it is not only you; it is all My children who are praying and acting as Jesus would have them live that are stirring His Sacred Heart to enter and bless places that are dark and desolate. This is what Christian faith is for. It leads to your own redemption, and it moves your lost brothers and sisters to embrace the Holy Gospel and live according to the Scriptures as a way of joining the great commission that will make one world out of many nations. If ever there were a manifest destiny, it is this spiritual one that the Lord commends. I extend My gratitude for the writing you composed for the preface of your anthology of My AD 2000-2002 messages. It contains adequate explanation of the theoretical and contemporary aspects of your thoughts, as well as their content. And, the eloquent symbolism that you included at the end of the piece is touching to the heart. I hope you have enjoyed Easter weekend thus far, and I know you will look forward to summer when so much will be accomplished after your Bishop receives your new book. I am praying that you will feel better physically and emotionally. It is ironic that you told your brother a year ago that he had many things ailing him, but you see a record of your own with your back injury, your weakened leg, poor eyesight, abdominal issues, nervous condition, and irregular heartbeat. Additionally, I tell you from Heaven that John Daubard is grateful for your years of friendship. He is with Jesus in the Father's house, and he wants you to know that everything the Church teaches is true. He is so joyful that he is unable to put it into words. John is with your Grandpa Roth. They were friends, and are perceiving all their years in the perspective that they could never have known during their decades in exile. When speaking about human decency, these souls emitted the holiness of Jesus, of gentleness Incarnate. It is important for you and your brother to rest while cataloguing My messages. You see by his weary eyes that it is taking a toll on him. He asks the Dominion Angels to tell the Lord that he will never give up. He wants to complete the mission for which he was born, and this is why he was so emotional last year when he was nearly on his deathbed. It was never about being afraid to come to Heaven, but that he would leave you alone and his work unfinished. Next week, we will ask Jesus to dispense His Divine Mercy upon all who seek His forgiveness."

Sunday, April 15, 2007
Feast of the Divine Mercy
3:01 p.m.

"Exultant and forever inspirited, we pray with the ecstasy of the Angels for the conversion of the world to the Holy Cross of Jesus, to the Divine Mercy that gives you the reprieve that is willed by God for His creatures on Earth. I assure you that He desires to bestow the prestige of His eternal redemption upon you because He is the origin of the deific offices by which you live. He has fashioned your return to innocence in the Crucifixion, and you are summoned to obey Him. You are called to the summit of holiness through the Holy Paraclete living in your hearts. My children, there will be plenty of time for other things once your future is fasted in Jesus' Sacrifice. There will be time for dancing and rejoicing, and for mourning the deficiencies of the past. You will not relinquish your right to travel the globe, seeking the elements of Nature, and creating arts of your own. There is plentiful time for every mother's son to die on the battlefields of Earth, but you are called to the core of Divine Truth first. Do you reckon that many of the former things that will pass away will not matter as much anymore? I am speaking about the arrival of your vindication, your exoneration, from the sins that bind you to death, even as they are the reason you were cast from Paradise. It is not that you have not sinned or failed to avoid its pitfalls, but you are found not guilty of them by their expungement from history in Jesus' Blood on the Cross. Hence, as we pray today and you invoke His Divine Mercy, remember all who have asked you to pray for them. Recall the millions who are far from God, those who reject Him, the endless legions who are defying His message of Salvation, the scores who are working against His Kingdom in the media and other baneful conglomerates, and the unwitting masses who have become their prey. I speak about Jesus' Eternal Heart, the Sacred Heart through which you are given the wisdom to pursue the purifying Cross in which you shall live beyond your death. Even though Eternity is timelessly transcendent of the ages, it lasts an extremely long time. I urge you to think in these terms when you bow before the Son of Man, when you wonder what Salvation is like, and as you rise at sunup to engage your vocations. Today, I ask you to seek Jesus' compassion for those who have been victimized by evil to the point that they attempt to replicate it. I told you long ago that My children do not know enough about hatred to hate, and I repeat it today by asking you to realize that evil is not inherent in men. It is heaped upon them by the venomous factions of the netherworld. Your innocuous hearts are exploited by promises of power and wealth, of elitism and untold prosperity. I assure you that any of these that contradict the Will of the Father are illusions; they are subtle devices for the destruction of weak and impressionable souls. My prayer in this Hour of

Divine Mercy is that the Holy Spirit will plant in you the knowledge that you are greater than anything in Creation that would restrict your movement toward the Cross or repeal your desire to be sanctified by the Eucharist. This day is about upholding your oath to your faith. God has given you a New Covenant to which you are to pledge your loyalty of honor, holiness, contrition, and sacrifice. You are saved by God's Grace, and you must realize that this Grace calls for your concession to His Will. What fortunes and fame lie ahead for you in this world are irrelevant in the grand architecture of humanity redeemed. If you see yourselves as one people in Him, Jesus' Mystical Body, you will recognize that there is no goodness separate from other men; there is nothing worthy of pursuit that omits their concerns. This Feast is about purging yourselves of anything contrary to the Sacred Scriptures, especially regarding your stature of piety and holding open your hearts for the enlightenment that falls like rose petals from Heaven. If daily life seems grim and toilsome, it is because too many sinners are anchored in materialism and matters of the flesh rather than the artistry of the Father's works. I seek in you the humble submission that takes you to the foyer of that Grace in which you are granted the Lord's infinite Mercy.

My Special son, I have heard your prayers this afternoon for the healing of humanity and the propagation of My messages. It is obvious that I hold the same wishes. I have asked for the intercession of Sister Faustina today because she has unparalleled venue in Jesus to dispatch His Mercy upon needy souls. Thank you for praying for Pope Benedict XVI on the occasion of his birthday and for the success of his book. You recognize many of the same themes in his book as you have written in your volumes, especially *When Legends Rise Again*. This will not go unnoticed in the future. And, I offer the veritable essence of My Immaculate Heart as you proceed, for I understand the burdens of mortality. I am mindful of the cares of human life. I have served as the comforter and benefactor of billions before you who advocate your success from the house of the Father. Will you not receive from Me the gladness of My trust in which the Son of Man was conceived? I tried My best to be a model of perseverance as I reared and taught the Messiah who has rescinded the errors of the world. There is no question that your life is difficult, but God wishes that it not be that way. You have expounded upon these issues in your writing. You hail the same plenary vision that gives you such hope. And, it is with this that you claim victory in Jesus. I promise that He is with you. What would He ask you to remember? Of course, the many who are scandalized by the wrongdoings of sinful men, and those who commit such acts. Please recall that He did not come to applaud the righteous, but to convert those who do not know God. I have long cherished you as a facilitator of that goal, a principal of His teachings, one in the midst of thousands who understands His message of ameliorative piety. In this, you are part of the Divine Mercy given to your friends from Heaven, and all will see this in time.

Thank you for your kindness to Jesus' brothers and sisters. He reminds you that you have accomplished His peace with distinction. And, bless you for your openness and attentiveness to the prayers of the Angels, for being so receptive in the presence of your agonies of life. You are fulfilling the prayers of Saint Francis of Assisi. You are Heaven's brilliance in the darkness of night; you give hope where there is despair, and you enlist the virtue of Jesus' Wisdom to eradicate the pandemonium that is rampant in the workings of other men. As you see, I reserved this moment to speak about My Son's Divine Mercy in the context of your gifts to humanity because a large share of His Mercy is reflected by disciples like you, by all who are devoted to the Most Sacred Heart who ever lived. Please reinforce your own patience by identifying and sympathizing with the suffering of others. The spring has come, and you will see its fairness in a matter of days. Thank you, My Special one, for being who you are. Do you recall that I told your brother that he is fragile to Nature? My words refer to the fact that you are both maturing through time and will mellow in your later years. You are placing your writings in proper sequence to introduce your next book, and the paragraph you penned last Sunday about receiving Heaven's peace was spawned from your projection of God's sublime integrity. If you recite the prayer that your brother mentioned, it will help the people about whom you have worried during the past several months. Regard this as a mystery and prophecy."

Sunday, April 22, 2007
St. Arianne Beauvais, Virgin [1712-1764]*
3:11 p.m.

"As it were, if you will, and so to speak. These are among the interjectories used to accentuate the parables of life both verbally and in writing. My children, you oftentimes struggle to find the means to glorify the Lord in communicating the Gospel of Salvation, but the Holy Spirit complements your speech when you open your heart to His Wisdom. Some say very little; others plenty, and many are too awestruck to testify on behalf of the Son of Man. This need not be a difficult process. You are not required to solve the mysteries of the universe to practice the tenets of your faith. Holiness is not hidden in algebraic expressions or scientific formulas; it is a precursor to the rebirth you are seeking, and which is looking for you. It makes no sense to impose a new narrative on a Salvation that was written long before your forefathers were given the breath of life. I come to address this holiness and seek in you the willingness to safeguard it against everything that is attempting to diminish it. I wish to teach you about human cohesion through the Sacred Heart of Jesus, and help you rebuke those who are intent on destroying the Church. We pray for this because God ordained prior to this age the finishing of the faith of your children yet to be born. Your courage and tenacity are derived from your knowledge of sacrifice, in knowing that your self-denial is the basis for your earthly exile. Does this sound redundant to the children who have heeded My messages? Is the mantra of immolation too repetitive that it is seen by many as yesterday's news? If so, I implore everyone to remember the circle of life, that you are born as children and shall die with the same innocence in your hearts with which you were brought from your mothers' wombs. The degrees of your success as Christians who are legitimized in the Cross reside in what you do for God. My presence here is His intention for you to know that He cares deeply that you offer your lives to the unconverted. My Special son, I have come briefly today because I wish for you to enjoy the wonderful weather. I know that you are excited about releasing My AD 2000-2002 messages, as you should be. You observe the element of time carefully because there is nothing you cannot accomplish for Jesus during your life. The spiritual images you have formed are sacred relics to reorient your brothers and sisters to the Divine Love of Christ. This has been the crux of you and your brother's friendship for the past three decades. Therefore, let not these sanctifying impressions be your last. The Lord accords great blessings upon His people because He loves you. He sees your reaction to His intercession as a gift to His flock, to lead them to the precipice where they can see beyond their own mortality. I urge you to be of good cheer because of the pathways you are blazing for lost sinners to discover the Holy Cross. You and your brother are serving as the Lord's compasses to direct them; you remind them to be careful about the rhetoric they hear and the malevolent intent of atheists. Jesus hears your prayers for the victims of wars and mass-murder. He understands the Church's desire to end every conflict and degradation. Every heresy and desecration of the traditions and repute of the Catholic Church is being stopped in places like this home where My children are praying. Healing and amendment bloom from the Holy Sacrifice of the Mass, and the reparation God seeks in the shadow of the Cross is made by souls who are suffering in Jesus' likeness. It is obvious that you realize what these things mean for humanity and the multiplication of His Kingdom. You appear surprised that the spring leaves on the trees have frozen, died, and turned brown. This is a seasonal occurrence in the northern states and along the eastern seaboard. I will close by saying that these years are inciting the adversaries of the Church to fight more stringently against it, so your intensified prayers are needed. Will you continue to help Jesus fight for the conversion of their souls?"

Sunday, April 29, 2007
St. John Claude Sargent [1929-1974]*
3:03 p.m.

"My children, your faith is keenly sublime, and the wonders of your agonies have wrought untold blessings to the Earth. I include you in My prayers because you are Children of Light; you foster the repentance of humanity that leads them to the Cross. To believe that one can envision the creative genius of God without touching the garment of Jesus is errant and pretentious; it defies the purpose of your exile. I urge young men to lead and serve the Lord like princes. And, I call women to embrace motherhood with the same nurturing instinct through which the heart is fed. They must pursue purity and dignity by yearning for flowers and perfume instead of tobacco and alcohol. One of My greatest demands is that the role of motherhood be elevated to its rightful place. Each of My children sings his own aria in the symphony of life; everyone has his part in the begetting of peace. Today, we pray that the cultivation of the heart is grown by the broadened vision of humanity in matters of temperance. Virtue and piety are aspects of the spirit that can be captured in time, and they are the reasons you have faith. My angelic ones, you are archers aiming for the hearts of the lost, like little cupids, to make them fall in love with Jesus. If you could pull a single arrow from your quiver that would truly make a difference, it would be to seek humility from everyone, gentle contrition that extols Jesus' Crucifixion through other men. I am speaking of an achievable goal. My words refer to the tangible, manageable attributes of your existence that make you seem almost supernatural to those who lack good faith. Your Christian profession and the fruits of your lives are installments toward this end. As I have said, this is why there is time and the reason you are in it. Hence, I urge you to remember in your prayers all who are struggling to understand the mandates of Christianity, and that they will take the initiative to seek Jesus while He can be found. It is not too late for this to happen. There are malformed and obtuse spirits circling the Earth that are attempting to weaken your faith and lead you down errant paths. You conquer these predators with prayer; you defeat them and see your way past the obstacles to your love. It is intrinsic to the practice of Christianity that you hail from lands far above those you can see with your eyes, that you embrace a stature with your belief in God that elevates you beyond the ordinariness of life. You are precious in the sight of Heaven, and God recognizes your call for assistance in miraculous terms. The Saints I have mentioned number among the Communion of Saints whose commission is to help you, to uplift your ability to become one with them in ways that you cannot yet see. Unfortunately, many of your brothers and sisters place too little emphasis in their intercession. When you ask them to venerate the Martyrs and

Saints, they look dubious and affright; they seem unwilling to admit that the dearly departed can be of any aid. The Church teaches that they should call upon the Hosts of Heaven and ask the First Apostles for help, and all who have fallen asleep in Jesus. The world is but a fraction of Creation; it is a parcel of the collection of universes among which you are situated. And, even as the beauties of Nature are blessings to behold and you pledge allegiance to your homeland, you must strive for the Kingdom of God in a sacred province that is beyond your sights. I have come to teach you about the multifaceted and manifold traits of life that change, that lead to the perpetuity of your coexistence with the Lord. What Divine Light is shining upon you now! His Dominion and Domain are your right and left guards as you pass from this world into the next. My Special son, thank you for the awesomeness by which you have embraced My maternal intercession. You enjoy such distinction before God that you are the envy of your predecessors. This week will bring the beginning of May and fair skies. You should remember that I told you that My Angels will help you remain strong during these times. Your work is on course, and My messages will reap their desired effect. I will speak to you again in the new month dedicated to all mothers, and I will always love and intercede for you."

Sunday, May 6, 2007
St. Nikita Vichniakov, Martyr [1924-1937]*
2:17 p.m.

"My reverent children, I bring a message of perspective, deliverance, purity, and eternal exculpation. My cause is benign, to offer My intercession before Jesus in whom you enjoy a future beyond your mortal years. Today, I come specifically to seek your prayers for unborn children, especially in Mexico where many of the Catholic faithful live. We must ensure that God hears your petitions for them, and that He intercedes to rebuke the consciences of those who are responsible for the scourge of infanticide. You know that the Earth stands in the midst of the battle between goodness and evil, and that the preservation of human life in all stages must be guarded through the reciting of your prayers. You must remember that My obedient children are praying in the ways they are asked, and God is listening and responding to them. But, what does He make of a world in which only a few hundred in locations of thousands of people seek His paternal instruction? You are surrounded by heathens, some of them outwardly cruel and susceptible to the corruption and error that secular fiends heave against their judgments. This is why we pray, My children; it is the reason for the urgency of My messages and the eagerness of God to answer. It seems not enough, as humanity would have it, that I have appeared in places around the globe to messengers, seers and locutionists, declaring that Christ Jesus is displeased about the immorality of sinners who are serving in governments. I have the terrible task of telling you that there is a great need for change; the condition of human hearts must be upgraded from dire to good. It is with high hopes that I appear to you, praying that you will disseminate My message of repentance to those who are responsible for the transgressions of uncivilized societies who exploit their own children. Woe unto those who would lure one of these little ones into sin! I promise that the Day of the Lord will never end, but human sin will end, and the process of its eradication has been effected through Jesus' Sacrifice on the Cross. If His lost brothers and sisters will not stop offending Him by their crass indifference to the Gospel of their own volition, He will stop it Himself. My Special and Chosen ones, it is a privilege to speak to you on this day and honor a young boy who spoke prolifically about Christianity in a land where his voice was unwelcome, where he was martyred for his faith in Jesus. You must remember how fortunate you are to live in a place where your religious zeal flourishes without the constraints of censorship. I assure you that this is one of the reasons why I came to you in America, to eliminate the possibility that your right to speak freely would ever be infringed. Imagine what it would have been like to write a diary in a country where it would have been forced underground for hundreds of years. This is a mystery of time and eternity, and one that you have allowed to flourish because you hold in your heart deep love for God and the Church. We must be in agreement that you comprehend the nature of this miracle by virtue of your holiness. My Special son, I will clarify the distinction that you and your brother possess by describing your testament to the Holy Gospel as Jesus has deigned through your earthly existence. Your brother takes his strength from the inspiration that comes through his prayer with you. And, you exalt the presence of Jesus and the Holy Spirit to avail humanity to this same type of courage. This is indicative of what the Lord sees as you pray; and your willingness to forego your leisure to evangelize His Covenant of Salvation is the origin of untold graces for America and the western hemisphere. Your capacity to write with the eloquence of the Angels is wrought by this piety; it is given flight by God's response to your voluntary extension of the spiritual blessings of His Kingdom to the captivated Earth. It is not that humanity inadvertently stumbles upon the Cross, but that you introduce repentance to their conscience through your righteousness. There, they discover the truth whether they like it or not. Their compliance with what they see is a matter of their free will. You take them to the water's edge and immerse them in an inundating flood of Wisdom. This is why you are so adored by Jesus. You must surely realize that I see in you and your brother the awakening of Christians to join the march against the world's evil and the inexorable defeat of the enemies of the Church. It is My honor that the Lord has permitted Me to speak to you for so many years, and that you have responded by your consecration to Jesus and Me."

Sunday, May 13, 2007
Feast of Our Lady of Fatima 1917
3:01 p.m.

"My children, majestic and stately is the prudence that visits upon you the goodness of Heaven, and long is your awareness that God seeks you as disciples of these times. My Immaculate Heart is given to your redemption by prayer and miracle, faith and trust, and by your dedication to the Crucifixion. The Kingdom of Paradise is manifestly exalted by your desire to see it blossom across the Earth. Please remember in your prayers, dutiful service, and industry that the Holy Spirit implants graces in you so you will look at your lives with the satisfaction that God beheld when He created you. Today is the Feast of Fatima where I came to speak to humanity about holiness. This was to become an inward impeachment of your conscience, one that would portend the awesome power of the Lord to alter the future, steer His people away from war, and spare you the sorrows of disabilities, destruction, and disease. I sorrowfully report ninety years later that the world did not take seriously My Fatima messages, and humanity has paid a terrible price. It is a simple prospect for ordinary men to understand that there is a cause and effect relationship between God's demands and your faith. If you decline to heed His summons for purity, sanctification, peace and conversion, He will allow you to endure the hellish years to come. This is a new day because the answer of men must be different. Jesus has taken a comply-or-perish approach to the conversion of the Earth by which humanity shall be purified. There is no need to witness its destruction from your nucleus of existence because Jesus has already preserved you in His Sacrifice on the Cross. There, He has dismantled and rebuilt the world from its inception to the Eternity that shall last beyond His Glorious Return. In that process, He redefined your role in the Kingdom of Light. He gave you a new beginning and a fresh perspective from which to engage our Creator in beatific terms. Indeed, this time, humanity will respond to My messages or mankind will endure the wrath that is rightfully God's to wield. My little ones, this is not an idle threat; it is not just a passing storm that will inconvenience you. This is the Truth that has been spoken by God for thousands of years. My requests at Fatima are not complicated; they require little more than your piety and devotion to the God who breathed life into your ancestors. I called for prayer, penance, fasting, peace, awareness of the suffering, and the refurbishing of the spiritual conscience of the masses from all continents. I reconfirm that these same components are crucial to the finishing of the world, and I pledge that the Lord remains as serious about your compliance with the Gospel. He calls on your veneration of the sacred relics handed-down through the ages, the intoned aspirations of the Angels and Saints, and the echoing homilies of the First Apostles that can yet be heard by the loving of heart. Do not worry that your brothers will not respond in this new millennium because it is inevitable that every heart bound for Salvation will hear. However, while My messages are urgent, you must remained focused on the suffering of the innocents, each and every person who is precious in God's sight. You are His sun rays and moonbeams that are called to shine your love intensely on their plight, to alleviate their poverty by becoming followers of the Cross. This, My children, is how God sees the culmination of the years. Jesus has hope even though He has seen the annihilation of the world. He reigns with dignity because you have lifted Him up. And, His sovereignty remains in His gifts of justice that pour upon the Earth like monsoons. You are encompassed by His brotherly care, consumed by His generosity; and your Salvation is wrapped in His Sacrifice for the Eternity in which your absolution has been preserved. All He seeks is your fiat in reflection of Mine. Then, Jesus will send not only the sun plummeting to Earth with great light, He will dispatch a million more to embrace and embolden you. My Special one, it is a fruitful day in your Illinois city because I have come seeking the hearts of men as your Christian allies. You and your brother are living a well-deserved happiness; you are worthy of the Holy Spirit dwelling within you. This is a peace that cannot be gotten from the temporal world; and life cannot take it away. You will see before the passage of the next eight weeks the publishing of a manuscript of messages that will take humanity by storm; and so will the book to follow, and the one after that. I am pleased that your kindness and deference to Heaven has led to the unification of your brothers and sisters. How profoundly they are being moved. I remind you how beautifully you have updated your website to enhance its appeal. You can sense during these days the arrival of another period of grace as you complete your book for AD 2000-2002. You are the reason your brother is helping us because you are his sustenance and friendship. Thank you for taking such good care of him. History will prove that he was likewise spoken about with prophecy in Philippians 2:19-24, and that his prevalence in this century has been provided by your faith in Jesus and obedience to Me. Thank you for responding to My call. When you release this message to humanity, please remind them that I am aware of the occasion of Mother's Day that is celebrated every year. Tell them that I am grateful that they chose to give birth to their children in their wombs in defiance of the evil that has produced so many abortions. You can see that the Holy Paraclete enlightens Pope Benedict as he speaks stoutheartedly against infanticide and other affronts to human life. How pious and humble is this man! How willing to defy the scourges of hatred and relativism! You were told by many on April 19, 2005 that his would be one of the great papacies in modern times for reasserting the primacy of the Roman Catholic Church. This Pontiff is Heaven's response to the millions of petitions that were raised in April 2005 by those who are consecrated to Me. As I say, the Lord is in control of His Church. Thank you for remaining so faithful to the Cross and to Me, and for standing upright in Jesus for the conversion of sinners."

Sunday, May 20, 2007
Saints Olaf and Dexter, Martyrs [AD 943]*
2:54 p.m.

"I appear before you filled with grand aspirations for the conversion of lost sinners, for they are wandering in the void of darkness made of their indifference toward Christianity and fostered by the vacuum of secular idolatry. I have spoken about the urgent need for their conversion not only because Jesus may return at any moment, but because their participation in building-up His earthly Kingdom is crucial to the mission of the Church. You must remember that every soul who is converted to the Holy Cross represents one less enemy of human redemption. Today, I call you to contemplate with fondness Jesus' Ascension, to cull from your memories your sweetest rhymes that you learned as children about His elevation to the right hand of the Father. This is why the faithful look up to My Son in more ways than the universe provides. He lived among you as a sinless Man and also God Incarnate as Christ, who is your Salvation. The Holy Spirit dwells within you now, and whomever Jesus permeates He also perfects. This is the reason for our prayers, My little children. I offer My promise that I have taken your petitions to Him for generations last passed. I have supplemented your daily prayers with My intercession because I know your needs in this exile. Please realize deep inside your hearts that time is pressing for the purification of humankind, and there is timeliness in accomplishing it now. When you seek for yourselves some share of His Kingdom in your meditations, you must remember those for whom no one is praying, the millions who do not know how to pray, and the uncounted numbers who have never requisitioned the help of the Lord. Your mission as Children of Light is not just to be saved, but to pursue the evangelization of the whole Earth and unify Jesus' Mystical Body before the end of time. Why is this so important? Because you are incomplete without your brothers and sisters accompanying you to Heaven, not those who are unworthy, but the Saints in whose number you shall reside for the annals of all eternities. My beckoning is sincere. My purpose in this world is not mocked. I cannot be impeded in My goal of touching the hearts and souls of My children. Thank you for helping this happen in your day. My Special son, you and your brother are esteemed beyond all imagining. There is a sense of peace here; there is hope and anticipation that will last beyond the ages. I see in you the same expectation that kept the Apostles strong during some extremely difficult times. I pray that you will accept My heartfelt wishes because I speak to you from the flowering Wisdom of My Immaculate Heart. You and your brother are beginning to sense the greatness that comes in releasing to humanity another series of messages because you are encouraged by their content. Once they have been set into history, My Special son, they cannot be removed. I have assured you that every soul to enter Heaven heretofore and hereafter has and will see the entire deposit of work that I have given to you since we first began. Your humility takes away any boasting of this, but I ask you to be confident that you are as wise as any of your predecessors in matters of faith and morals. The Lord has welcomed into His Kingdom your deceased family members to the accolades of the Angels and Saints because they were dutiful warriors for the Cross on Earth. They asked to be blessed by the hand of Saint Peter and christened by Saint John the Baptist as members of the redeemed who are praying for you before the Holy of Holies. As this decade comes to a close in three years, you will see a number of your friends and relatives who will pass into the arms of Jesus; they will bequeath the world to you to liken it to the Paradise for which they pined all their mortal years. You are aware that there is a ribbon of sanctity that stretches from everyone's birthday to their death, one that binds them closely with Divine Truth from the moment they are reborn in Jesus. There is no happier destiny for man than Heaven, and this is what we seek; this is the reason I am speaking to you now. Memorial weekend will come next Sunday, a time for reflection and commemoration about the lives of all who have died by natural passing or other consequence. It is a secular feast for the forgotten, and you should hail the bonds of all who have died in Jesus, not only the Saints of the Church, but known to all as having shared the Gospel of the New Covenant. Remember them with satisfaction because they are now with Me. I brought them to the Wonderful Counselor from whence they were babes in their mothers' wombs. I blessed them with the peace of God through the Sacrifice and Resurrection of Jesus. Now, I nurture them in the presence of His Kingdom, not that they are lacking, but that they commune beneath My Mantle with all who are given to the Sacred Heart of My Son."

Sunday, May 27, 2007
St. Geoff Krzyzewski [1853-1902]*
2:32 p.m.

"Bringing you to the counsel of the Crucifixion is not a vain effort because you are becoming aware of God's Kingdom that is open to receive you. What will it require to win the affections of humanity for Him? Surely you can see that the sacrifices you have made are for this, as are the people you have Christianized by the prayers you have said. Today, I remind you that being memorialized on Earth by the survivors and mourners of the victims of battle is not enough; they must be mentioned in your novenas, and their intercession should be sought by believers everywhere. I speak on behalf of the tens of millions who have died in wars, and for their widows, widowers, and orphans. I call you to deep compassion for their agony. Where does loss of life in wartime fit into God's plan? Why does He allow such atrocities to occur? These are among the questions people are asking during Memorial Day in America. My children, the Lord does not sanction war that is not fought for the Cross, nor does He approve it. Casualties of these campaigns are victims of the sin that felled humanity from the Garden of Eden. How many times has Jesus asked your hearts to be filled with the diplomacy and discretion of the Holy Spirit? On how many occasions have world leaders refused to obey? The Father does not call for unprovided deaths, and He deplores the conditions that perpetuate suffering. He asks for your return to sacred unity, the immutable desire to live in holiness for the sake of Jesus' Sorrowful Passion. The Son of Man died in violence so that humankind could live in His peace. This is the obedience to which you are called; it is the reason you have confessed your sins before the Church. There is no means to describe the sympathies that the Lord has for those who are maimed and deformed because of the brutalities of war. Losing one's life is egregious for families, and being shorn of mobility can sometimes be an awful task. My cherished ones, if the conversion about which I have told you has taught you anything, I hope it is better vision, one that allows you to see the conspiracies behind human error, one that is founded in knowing that noncompliance with the Gospel causes every kind of violence. How many artworks, factions, motivations, and innuendos can be counted in a day? To what degree of insult are the victims of greed subjected at any one time? It would bear heavily on the mind to calculate these things. Hence, rather than force an answer, they must be thought about in terms of their collective impact upon Creation as a whole. Once the origin of sin was destroyed, the future of humanity commenced. I am speaking about an event that has already transpired. The redressing of every grievance and the resolution of every dispute is found in the Crucifixion of Jesus on the Cross. Every healing, reunification, resolution, and consolation in the whole of the universe comes from His Sacred Passing. Anything that contradicts Jesus' Sacrifice is a manifestation of the devil that is perpetuating such suffering around the globe. If someone says that he is a healer of men, but in the same breath denies the Son of God, then he is a fraud and prevaricator because all healing comes from Jesus, given to the Earth from the Father in Heaven. Let this be the criterion by which you judge public officials and practitioners. Lay their actions alongside Jesus' life, and let them repent. These are crucial years of discernment for humanity. I have said on more occasions than you care to count that the means of deliverance for the world from its present predicament is prayer—prayer from the heart. You cannot be just until you pray; you cannot live and breathe the freedom of vindication unless you reach for the heights of Heaven through compassion for man and beast alike from the center of the heart. When I speak of exceptional forces, I refer to the extremity through which you invoke Jesus' Sacrifice for everything you need.

My Special and Chosen ones, this is a particularly pleasing time because I appear before you with gladness for your lives in Jesus. I defer to you when you humbly beseech His aid because you request His consolation with the innocence of children. Even when you watch your enemies who are complicit in denying the Grace of the Lord, you pray for them as He requires. This is the precision of your love; it is the Holy Spirit thriving through your hearts in ways that were taught on Mount Calvary by My Son. You have heeded the call; you are running the race, and you are remaining steadfast in the righteousness that is eclipsing the Earth with God's omnipotence. You are moving into June, and will complete the latter preparations for the publishing of your New Millennium messages. I need not say that their like has never been seen because you have made this declaration already. It is a matter of time, and strictly so, that you will see their fullness across the spectrum of the ages. You will know why Jesus has asked you to live for Him. Make no mistake, your messages will affect the lives of those who will follow you down the pathways of miracles, and they will command their own holiness during their mortal years. It is inevitable that they will bear fruit before you are taken to Heaven. You have foreseen this; you can feel and predict it, and you are prepared for the conversion of the sinners I came to teach. Is this a redeeming reward? It shall be for the millions who will scurry into My bosom for relief. No one man or woman can suffer the Messianic Crucifixion that took Jesus to His death and the Salvation of the human race. However, your consecration to Me, your devotion to Jesus' Sacred Heart, and the endearing practice of your Christian faith—all of these augment the evangelization of His Sacrifice until the end of the Earth. This is your retribution against evil. Your holiness is God's vengeance against Satan. Thank you for having responded to My call."

Sunday, June 3, 2007
St. Charles Lwanga and Companions
Uganda Martyrs [1885-1887]
2:54 p.m.

"Today, I celebrate with you the concentric concordance of the Most Holy Trinity, and pray that the Spirit of God remains inside the hearts of the neophytes who come to the threshold of saintliness by their newfound faith. My children, there is mystery and glory in everything deigned by God; it is His intention that you seek Him for the answers you need about living, about the unreasonable and inexplicable divisions between men, and for the grace to speak your piece about your mission in His Kingdom as creatures redeemed in the Blood of the Cross. It is with this sentiment that I ask you to pursue justice around the globe through your efforts to make peace. Jesus knows that you are blessed in this, and you are aware that He is close to you as you live-out your promise to be true to His Most Sacred Heart in benevolent ways. In My message today, I also ask you to pray for My Jewish children, the chosen people who have deeply embraced Mosaic Law in which I was reared. How they are loved by God! How they must be honored, elevated, protected, and admired for their courage and steadfastness in the ways of the Pentateuch! I ask all Christians to defend and lift the dignity of their Jewish friends, and that they will provide for them the gentleness and Wisdom that Jesus ushers into the world. Ask the Blessed Trinity to touch their hearts with the gift of Salvation in the Blood of the Cross so they may be open to everything the Holy Spirit would have them accept. The temple is a place of God. It is the precursor to the cathedral of the heart in which you have yourselves enriched humanity by your faith in Jesus. Make peace with those who believe differently from you; offer your hands and intentions to the unity of all peoples, and Jesus will touch them with the Cross, proving to all that He is the Messiah for whom they have waited. Peace is about these things, My little children. It is the prevalence of Heaven on Earth that is affronted by secular antagonism, pluralism, and religious bigotry. You have given yourselves to the Church to eradicate the differences that separate so many of your enemies from the Lord's forgiveness. My Special son, I wish for you to realize that the offing is as you are describing it. God has provided that I come to you for a unique and specified purpose, to the edification of lost sinners and their conversion to Christianity. My message is about instilling in you more than hope, but true confidence that you are accomplishing this goal. I have said more to you today than will appear to have been told. You are fortunate to hear the substance of My messages that I have given during the years, any of them quite profound in addressing the needs of your day. I would like for you to think about how My messages have been dispensed, that they were dictated as you heard them, and with their entire text revealed through time. This is how the Lord is reconstituting the universe, by recasting time itself according to His agenda. You have seen that weariness, exhaustion, and frailties cannot obstruct the mission that He has planned for you. My son, every day is a good day. Even when you cannot see past your own difficulties, you are moving toward Divine Peace and Eternal Love. There are too many tragedies around the globe because of people's lack of prayerful living and faith in the genius that Jesus brings. I have said that being a good Christian is a process as much as a vocation. Therefore, you should be pleased while seeing the tremendous progress you have made over the years on My Son's behalf. I have used the concept of unhouseled in My messages to lead humanity to the Holy Eucharist. If anyone disagrees with My choice of terms, either here or anywhere else, please tell them that what I have said, I have said. All the miraculous content that you have been receiving and are revealing in your New Millennium messages is God's response to you and your brother's receptivity. I stand beside you at all times. I never leave your side, and I know when you are praying. If you believe this, then you will also realize that I have done this for everyone in Creation who has ever called My name."

Sunday, June 10, 2007
St. Horace Marquette [1848-1909]*
2:59 p.m.

"I have found in you the followers of the commission of humanity to come forward with courage and trust in the Lord, accepting your part in the reshaping of the Earth into the likeness of Paradise. This is the Kingdom of Love for which you serve as soldiers against His adversaries; it is in you that the Holy Spirit has come to rest. You have been told about seeing it raining fire from the skies, and you have carried the flaming torches of Truth with word and deed, spreading the message of Salvation in the Blood of the Cross over the Earth. My children, you cannot yet know how you are blessed for your obedience because God's gratitude comes in such magnitude that you scarcely take it in. Today, you are reminded about the indescribable gift of the Most Holy Eucharist. I have told you through the years that the Body, Blood, Soul, and Divinity of Jesus is your Bread of Life and your spiritual food on your sojourn through exile. This is important to you because your souls need nourishment as much as your physical bodies; but even more, you are given wisdom of the heart and mind that your flesh cannot contain. The Blessed Sacrament is the living presence of Jesus in you, and gives strength and foresight from the purview of Heaven that cannot be gained anywhere else. I have offered plentiful reasons to be receptive to Jesus in all ways, and especially in His Eucharistic Sacrament. What predominance in the themes of holiness is opened to you when you receive Holy Communion as you are elevated to heights where non-Catholics cannot go. This is why your attendance at the Holy Sacrifice of the Mass is mandated, and it is the reason you must receive the Most Blessed Sacrament worthily. Jesus-the-Eucharist is the supernatural intervention of God through His Son into the present day in physical form. Where you are expected to effect your faith in the Sacraments, this is one that you can see with your eyes. Jesus is with you, before you, and persistent on your behalf within the confines of time in the Holy Eucharist. There is no question that the souls of the redeemed know that the Eucharist is your deliverance to Salvation, the pricelessness of your Christian conscience, and the antidote to the poison of secularism that you fight every day. My little ones, the Blessed Sacrament has provided the rectification of ills, the cessation of wars, the prevention of an imminent 1962 nuclear holocaust, and the feeding of millions the nourishment they need to undergo plight, disease, pestilence, and degradation. Jesus-the-Eucharist has fed the Lord's disciples for twenty centuries the Wisdom, courage, and vision to overcome their weaknesses and vanquish their enemies so their vocations could be completed. The flame of Truth in the Holy Eucharist has given rise to the annihilation of entire societies at odds against the Church, of whole nations that would have otherwise caused intense destruction to the Mystical Body of Jesus. There would be no Christianity in the world without the Holy Eucharist; there would be no Salvation; there would be no contrition, and no other Sacrament to enliven the faithful. My children, the Holy Eucharist is your faith, the reason for your faith, and the culmination of your faith. How can this be true? With what does the Lord do with those who protest against the Holy Eucharist? He urges you to lead them around because they are blind. Only through the Holy Eucharist can you see the redemption of men with your eyes. When you genuflect before the Tabernacle or kneel in Adoration before the Eucharistic Son of Man, you are acknowledging that Emmanuel remains with you corporeally, the Child born of My Womb in Bethlehem and Crucified on Good Friday. You are proclaiming that peace is with you in more ways than God should allow, given the scandalous indiscretions and grotesque conduct of modern man. My message today, My children, is that you remain true to the Eucharist, that you comprehend its sanctifying Grace during your lives. I remind you that this is why it is crucial that My children attend Holy Mass, receive the Rite of Reconciliation, and approach Jesus with humility while His Eucharistic Body is in your presence. Thank you for having responded to My call.

My Special and Chosen ones, I need not remind you about the tremendous responsibility bearing upon you during these days, even though you are suffering only little. You know the awesome sacrifices you have had to make to proceed in finishing your work. I wish for you to understand unequivocally that your Mother is not unmindful of your sorrows and regrets, of everything that causes you to see darkness instead of God's monumental Light. I have compassion for you during this, but I say that you are too near your work to have a true sense of perspective about it. You have said that God sometimes opens new doors that allow you to see with keener awareness, and He will do so if your despondence becomes too great. He will not allow His call for help to cause you anxiety. He will not bring any burden that will force your feelings into the ground. Today, for the first time since February 22, 1991, I tell you that He is so compassionate that He has placed you under a special state of observance. If you feel heavy inside, He will lighten the load. If life seems too repetitious, God will give you a new vantage to begin each morning. Please remember that Jesus is the Savior of joy. God is the Father of Love, and Salvation is a matter of dignity. You are entering the latter stages of your work. I wish for you to consider this a happy time because you will rearrange your schedule, especially on days like this one, to suit your convictions. You will increase your circle of friends and travel to places that will remove the sense of stasis that you have endured. How does the Lord God thank you for all you have done? He bequeathed you to Me. He saved you through the Crucifixion of Jesus, and He has told you that you will never be orphaned as evangelists of the Cross. Jesus' Sacrifice has absolved you of your sins, and your faith is your healing. I will remain here and dictate My messages as long as the Father allows, but you must know that Jesus has a conscience that cannot be diluted. He will not permit your work to cause any depression. My Special one, you are poised and strong; you have a firm sense of who you are, and you lead life dedicated to Me. These personal and spiritual qualities are indicative of an extremely saintly person. Your brother needs your example. His sentiments are erratic; he is afraid that Jesus is going to take you away from him, and he has no means to sustain himself other than your labors and charities. He expects no immediate response to your Catholic Apostolate by secular societies, which is why he does not pursue any goals in self-preservation; he knows that he contributes nothing to the immediacy of humanity's problems; he is aware that others view him as unwilling to compromise, and he feels that social and religious prejudice have kept him from securing employment. However, in light of all this, there is nothing that Satan can heap on him or the world spurn him to make him quit. He is like the thoroughbred you saw in June 1973. His spirit is running like a tremendous machine. He knows that there is little he can do about humanity's indifference, and this is his greatest cross. Remember, if you love someone, it is hidden unless you say so. You are making remarkable progress on your most important spiritual work since your first Diary. There is sufficient substance in My words to take you beyond the span of your natural lives, and I care so much about you that I will not allow you to live in irrelevance. I realize that you would never lay-down your crosses or the mission you have set-out to do. It is not the weight of your labors that bothers you, but the perversions of the secular elite. You cannot avoid secularism as long as you require gainful employment to sustain yourself. This is the paradox that your brother sees, that puts pressure on him. You should tell him how you feel. Never suspend your communication to spare him of this reality. He is praying for everything in life you desire. Without your kindness, there would be no roof under which My messages are received, no place to prepare them out of the elements, and no way to preserve or archive them for the eternal record. Christian conversion could not have been accorded the American people if not for your willingness to help."

Sunday, June 17, 2007
Saint Georgiana Dobson [1821-1890]*
2:49 p.m.

"With firm allegiance, you are giving yourselves in the service of Jesus by whom you are sanctified, and you see with the vision of His Sacred Love that the Earth must repent in order to become more like Heaven. I see in you not only the desire to be holy, but the determination to take it to your nation's citizens before the hour is too late. Today, My angels, My prayers are with you as you count the gruesome casualties you endure from accidents and catastrophes in which your friends, countrymen, and loved ones lose their lives. I have told you that you must live prayerfully for the power of your Guardian Angels, and that your motivations must agree with the preservation of life that God commands. Everyone who lives can speak of someone who has been lost to recklessness and carelessness. These tragedies are avoidable. Divergence from prayerfulness causes them, and you will hear more of them as the world's population increases and their prayers decrease. My children, too many are suffering and dying from curable diseases because they are not given adequate health care. They lack the food and provisions they need to counteract their poverty. Will you provide for them through your petitions and good works, and see Jesus in them, and be their mentors and best friends? I have spoken about the egregious inequities that exist in many poor countries, and in developed ones too. It comes down to human compassion, seeing others through a viewpoint of pity and sympathy. It requires the envisionment of a world that is saturated with Christian Love. Therefore, it is My request today that you pray for all who are facing neglect because they are your brothers and sisters in Jesus; they are one with you as His mystical species. Throughout the ages, there have been innumerable souls who have been long suffering and impoverished because few would care for them. The early Saints stood by them, offered them food, shelter, clothing and medication; and they have inherited the Kingdom of God as a result. However, these Saints served the poor not only to achieve their own sainthood, but because they recognized the Son of Man standing before them in the presence of the suffering. Their faith told them that it was Jesus they were feeding. He was apparent in the least among the nations, and Christians worldwide answered the call to give Him aid. I offer you due blessings for accepting the awesome task of pursuing social justice where there is unfairness. This is one of the mainstays to believing that there can be refreshment where the world's evil has caused decay. The compassion in your hearts grows the seeds of dignity from within those who are incarcerated and rejected. Many have asked how it can be possible that young children are sold like livestock into slavery and sexual prostitution. It happens because Satan's forces are not being opposed by secular activists. Remember that the deafening indifference of some people perpetrates as much malevolence as the meanness of villains. My weekly messages have always been about uplifting the lame and poor of spirit, rescuing them from victimhood, and giving them a share of the Lord's plenty. The virtues of community, caring, and empathy are gifts of the Spirit of God that shape your lives; they give you reason to practice your faith on practical terms. Thus, My little ones, your sainthood awaits at the end of your labors for the Cross. It sits in awe-striking wonder in God's Paradise of freedom and unification, basking in anticipation that you will walk through the gate. How much hope you aspire in foreseeing the beauty of Salvation! I come with gladness because you are listening to Me; you are heeding the summons of the Holy Spirit to muster the courage to battle the devilish waves against your redemption. I told you in the beginning that your work would be cast-out, ignored, impugned, ridiculed, and discarded. However, those who opposed you then and the ones who are against you today do not have in their grasp the ability to obliterate your gifts to Jesus for the advancement of His Kingdom. No act of righteousness offered in His name will go unanswered. I have made definitive promises, My children, and this is one that is good for any number of eternities you might imagine.

My Special son, it is My privilege to speak to you on this occasion, and I see that you have offered special prayers to God on this earthly father's day. We hold fond memories for the years you have given Him, for the untold sacrifices you have made for the conversion of men. These are revelatory times not only because you are fashioning more works on My behalf, but because you are seeing firsthand how they are criticized by the adversaries of the Gospel and the detractors of the Catholic Church. I have told you that I have sheltered you and your brother from the onslaught of calumnious attacks by which you are subjugated when you place articles in the local newspaper espousing human morality and social truth. Even though you are Americans whose skin is white, you are hated just as defiantly by those of your own race when you attempt to elevate the dignity of people of other colors. It is not your color they oppose, but your sense of fairness and pursuit of the inclusion of all the Lord's disciples beneath the Cross. Had you any idea that a simple narrative written by your brother for the newspaper could generate such disdain? Yes, they are delusional about the purpose of human existence, and they are reluctant to accept anything having to do with the mystical and charismatic. Can you see why I have shielded your identity for so long? I shall proceed while you are finishing your next books. Do you sense that you are in physical danger? You must be extremely careful in any way that might give your enemies a venue for assault, and this should be done sooner rather than later. Jesus is insistent that you take the necessary initiatives to ensure your safety against anything that is a threat to your well-being. With the exception of giving the Rosary to Saint Dominic and providing your shoes with which to walk into Heaven, humanity has rarely seen Me pass anything physical through the veil of your exile. The books you are publishing are manifested on the earthly side of the veil with My beatific intercession. Therefore, you are heros and conquerors who have allowed My work to prosper from this venerable abode."

Sunday, June 24, 2007
Birth of Saint John the Baptist
3:28 p.m.

"I beseech you not to allow the shrill of life's aggravations to take away your peace, My children. Pray with all your might to disperse the darkness with God's Holy Light. Today, you are called to remember the Holy Spirit that accompanied John the Baptist during the Baptism of Jesus in the River Jordan, and tender your thoughts to his meditations at that time. How profound for Saint John to know that he was preordained to reveal to the world the grace of baptism, the exultant feeling to sense the Will of God in such an ethereal way. I have asked you to tread lightly upon the ground and be reminded that Jesus is with you through every trial and temptation. Walking the straight and narrow path does not mean that you are always balancing yourself on a taut wire or tightrope, but knowing what is worth pursuing as you contribute to the advancement of the Lord's Kingdom. Realizing that you will be tempted does not imply that you will fail. Wielding wisdom and truth ensures that you can avoid the pitfalls that plague faithless men, those who shut God out of their lives. This is the reason I speak to you so imperatively about the Sacrament of Penance; you accept that you are forgiven for your failures of the past. I wish for you to acknowledge that weaknesses are not necessarily sins, but attributes that can lead you to yield to temptation if you do not overcome them. Likewise, your faults do not inherently mean that you are prone to commit certain sins, but you must suppress them so they do not lure you from righteousness. My children, most sins are the result of poor choices; people decide to do something that is contrary to the Word of God. Accidents do occur, and sinners make honest mistakes. While you must confess your offenses against God, you should realize that you are products of your environment and psychological upbringing. Jesus wishes that no one will walk through life believing that they are unworthy of His forgiveness. It is impossible for a person who defers to Jesus in every way to be blasphemous. You must examine your spirits to comprehend His overwhelming desire to take you under His care and absolve you of your sins. My children, we have spoken of this concept before. How much premeditation is present in the transgressions of men? When do they begin to understand that they are willingly committing wrongdoings, and when do they become unwitting victims of a larger framework of error? To what degree have they internalized the corruption that is intrinsic to the environment in which they were reared? What about the forces of psychological pathologies and acquired habits? All of these matters are taken into account by the Lord when you confess your sins, and how justice is meted-out in time and at its conclusion. God asks you to try your best; walk in confidence that He will guide you to the nobler way, and always call on the Holy Spirit for help. Here, you progress toward His Kingdom, rather than in stagnation or shunning Divine Truth. You will not become perfect in one night or a week, or perhaps in your mortal lifetime. Jesus is looking for your capacity to stand before Him at the moment of death and say that you did your best against unimaginable opposition, that you fought the worthy fight, and that the weep-holes in your conscience are where you cried-out for His help in your darkest hours. My Son will absolve you, My little children. He understands the allures of the world. He knows about the ways secularism pummels you with temptation. Indeed, you have come to Him for this reason, that He will embrace you with forgiveness when only few on Earth would. Living inside each of you is the power to bless one another with goodness and light in the name of God, in the same way that Saint John baptized Jesus in the Jordan. While Jesus was not in need of God's absolution, He knows that you are, and that you would follow His example in christening your souls to the Father through your baptismal oaths. Yes, He realized that you would come to Him by the millions with your baptismal gowns as white as snow through your holiness, manifested by the Sacraments of the Roman Catholic Church. My Special son, I speak on this awesome opportunity to regale your service to humanity. The next weeks will further ratify your office as miracle worker on behalf of Heaven. I urge you to be patient with your brother because his spirit is tired. It is not broken, but it is aching. My child, I am overjoyed by the preparation of your next book! If you allow yourself the proper discernment of the nature of things, you will recognize that I can do nothing without you. Your heart is consecrated to Me, and your manual labors and those of your brother make the entry of My messages into the world possible. Getting them past the veil into your earthly domain has been our goal since February 1991. There is no doubt that we have had extraordinary success. Your books have been part of God's preordained Will since before you were born. They were endowed upon the foundation of the Earth. It is only now that you are publishing them because this is your time during the history of the ages. It does not seem such a burden when you place it in this perspective."

Sunday, July 1, 2007
St. Nicolette Demuthe [1702-1754]*
2:53 p.m.

"Honoring the creative genius of the Lord to brighten your days, I pray with you for all that ails humanity. Today, it is My joy to remind you that Jesus is with you. His Grace and Passion are your courage and strength during these grave and perilous times. It is not too late to pray for the things you need, for the remaking of the Earth, for the reversal of tides and the rewriting of history, and for healing, longevity, good health, and redemption. I tell you that the story of human life that was finished by Jesus on the Holy Cross is still being scribed by His emissaries. Modern men would do well to heed the call of the prophets who have remained devoted to Him. The Love in His Sacred Heart is the invincible power by which you have already succeeded in vanquishing the enemies of your faith and casting evil spirits into the Abyss. Where would you be without your faith, My little ones? This is the gift that God has dispensed to you! You have dreamed of new days to supplant those that are inundated with suffering and pain. You have envisioned better years filled with gladness and celebrating, times to come when you can bask in the victories of Truth over the lies of the netherworld. It is in this battle that your faith is hewn because you are warring on Jesus' behalf; you are followers of the Holy Gospel and leaders of the sons of men. I beseech you to trust in Him, to invoke the power of the Crucifixion during your daily struggles against evil and indifference, and to hold fast to the indivisible grace by which you are sustained in Jesus' Wounds. Surely you realize that life as you know it is being refashioned into the Glory of the New Kingdom you have inherited by your obedience to My Son. There is no doubt that your prayers are heard by the Father, and that He has willed for you imminent success over your obstacles. I am confident that you can see as well today as you will through the infinity of Heaven that your Salvation is assured because your trust in Jesus is irrevocable. How does this affect your faith during times of distress? It makes you stronger for the fight; it magnifies your capacity to endure anything that tests you in these final ages. I pray with you that millions more will join in this cause, that your petitions given to Me this day will reap untold numbers of converts for God. Thank you for having responded to My call. My Special and Chosen ones, many have been the months and years that we have prayed for the alleviation of suffering and the repentance of lost sinners for My Son. You have no way of knowing that there are measurable results because you have no faculties by which to see from your station on Earth. There is a finite number of people living in the world, but your ability to convert them to the Holy Cross is infinite; it is of the holiness and eminence that comes from Heaven. You are deploying incalculable graces for them by your intentions and spiritual labors. Therefore, I extend the Lord's gratitude and affection. Please stay the course that is raising humanity above the fray of dark works that are attempting to keep your brothers and sisters embroiled in the indignity of sin. I appear here before you to speak because I realize that you are working diligently through the days preparing for the release of My AD 2000-2002 messages. In effect, you are harboring another miracle in this place that you will spring upon your brothers for their own good, as much as it chastises the guilty and lauds the righteousness of those who have remained with the Sacred Heart of Jesus. You are God's envoys and catalysts for bearing admonition to those who reject Him, while you are heaping due praise upon the disciples who do His bidding in His earthly vineyard. As you are within a few more weeks of bringing your latest book to closure, please enjoy the process. Take into account the magnanimous oracle that you are giving the Church and the faith you are instilling in millions. You know how close you are to Me and to what degree I have come to educate you. My intercession is more powerful than you can discern, and this is why I exercise My Maternal influence before the Holy Cross. I have told you that Jesus hears our unified prayers, and we shall proceed in the knowledge that we are amending the fate of mortal men by lifting them to the plateau of Christian righteousness.

Yes, this is the final month before the release of your AD 2000-2002 messages, and you are gaining the sense of confidence that arrives with such gifts. You realize that this book is awesome because its content is appreciably from Me. I promise that My messages will be taken seriously by the faithful, but not to the point that you will become distracted from publishing My messages of 2003-2008 in two separate books. Imagine what it would be like to attempt to accomplish the work you are doing in this place with the door being constantly opened and the telephone ringing incessantly every day. You will see what I am saying in the future, that you will yearn for these kinds of days to return you to the simplicity of life. Indeed, it is imperative that you know that most every miraculous manifestation that the Lord has ordained in private revelations was not publicly manifested until those seers came to Heaven because their work would have been inhibited by the commotion. This is not how your years will play out, pending the measure of your progress. It is important that you and your brother remain united and try not to dispute immaterial issues. We have shared a great unity over the years from which you must build the framework of your trust in Jesus on behalf of the sons of your fathers. I am pleased that you are feeling well and that your focus is upon your labors, not impatient or begrudging because you are not seeing immediate results. I say this only because hundreds of My messengers before you have neutralized all the hours they invested because they quit the fight; they could not withstand the wait to be lauded as victors for Christ. Your success is championed as much by your patience as by your labors. Yes, the Communion of Saints who read your works hundreds of years before you were born have utilized My Wisdom in their intercession to those who called upon them from the Earth. Thank you for staying with Me. Let us pray that this month is filled with peace as you pour-out your lives for the Church."

Sunday, July 8, 2007
St. Dominique Kelly [1752-1804]*
2:37 p.m.

"My children, I appear with you to lend another installment of My messages of human redemption in the Blood of the Cross, to lift you to the Wisdom that has delivered you from the vacuous gutters of ignorance, and to give My blessing for everything you have accorded God on behalf of His Kingdom. You are enriched when you pray because your endearing petitions usher His presence to the Earth. Today, it is My joy to complement your prayers for the conversion of the lost; and you have seen how lost many of your brothers and sisters are. However, the Holy Spirit has given you power and venue for deific Truth to prevail. In this, I rejoice; any mother would rejoice. How could any matriarch remember her dolors when her children are obedient as you have been so faithful to the calling of Jesus? And, as I pray with you, I offer His commendation for your visionary perseverance, for your persistence in withstanding the burdens of the physical world, realizing that the human spirit is mightier than anything that may attempt to dilute the strength of your faith. It is not a simple task to endure the oppressive adversity that comes with being Christians, especially in America where no religion is widely accepted in the public domain. I have told you that the United States is dying from its own indifference, from the relativism that has drawn so many away from the Church. Salvation cannot elude them if you pursue your mission for them to be redeemed. You became more openly spiritual for this reason. I appear here with visions and messages for this same reason, and your far-flung labors are succeeding for this reason. My children, it is easy to perceive the miracle of your lives in the Church. Your stature as the Lord's creatures has been enhanced; your dignity is broadened before every venue where you recite His Holy Name. This does not imply that you have not suffered, and it does not mean that your days have not been infiltrated by darkness and anguish. I call you today to remember that conflict never implies defeat, but declining to engage the fight certainly does. You are victorious in the Triumph of My Immaculate Heart that is now proceeding. Therefore, it is not necessary for you to linger near corners where the Gospel message will never be heard. Do not loiter with those who despise you. Realize the futility of engaging in political arguments with brinkmen who have already impugned the message of righteousness that has flowed from your lips. You need not chase them down or force them to partake of the Holy Gospel because, as I have told you, it is you whom they will seek-out at last. There is a magnetism living in your holiness that will raise them when they are about to die from spiritual thirst because you have already partaken of the Living Water of God's Grace and Peace. We pray together not only that they will reassess their lives, but that they will take the initiative to amend them through the Sacred Christ who was born in Bethlehem, reared in the holy confines of Nazareth, Crucified on Mount Calvary, raised from the Sepulcher, Ascended to the right hand of the Father, and dispatched into your hearts as the Holy Spirit, the same God whose voice you hear in the content of My messages. When you speak in terms of victory being imminent or about days to come when you will see the sweet fruits of your labors falling from the trees of your faith into your brothers and sisters' hands, know that it is presently happening. I have long told you that human conversion is a process; it is a living, viable, vibrant, growing seed of goodness that is springing forth into Creation. Every time you think about this, you are punctuating another place in that continuum. No one can vanquish your hope for the conversion of humanity; there is no creature living or dead who can suspend its progression. Therefore, how much time is remaining before the hour when the Son of Man returns? Soon, and very soon; and this is why we must be constant in our prayers and good works on His behalf. Whether you consider your life in Jesus as a labor of love that is reminiscent of a wall to keep evil away from your souls, an excavation of lost sinners from beneath their transgressions, erecting a towering beacon to show them the way to their absolution in the Cross, or whatever you might see your purpose to be, know that it has God's blessing and Heaven's intercession. My Special son, you are living splendorous times, and your heart and soul know it. You are given signs and wonders during this period prior to the publishing of your new anthology. The manuscript itself is sufficient evidence of your 07/07/07 miracle. Another is the action of Pope Benedict XVI. However, the greatest is that Jesus came to your door yesterday begging for help, and you answered the call of the poor. This was more than lending assistance to a neighbor; it was a mystical phenomenon that God placed before you. Oh, My Special son, do you realize the miracle you are about to give humanity? It is sacred because you are praying it into being. Your anthology is a blessing that is unprecedented in the history of the world. This is why yesterday was such a time of grace. We shall see what Jesus deigns to happen on August 8, 2008. Because of your employment, your brother has only so much time to spend with you formatting My messages so they can be incorporated in the full deposit that will impact humanity in the ways we have discussed. Please try to remain in the spirit of calm confidence by which you have been living. Trust Me always, and know that Jesus is with you through the entirety of your lives."

Sunday, July 15, 2007
Saint Orpheus Vochez [1613-1688]*
2:51 p.m.

"While your secular counterparts are deeply involved in the world, seeking fine stones and precious metals, you are kneeling here in prayer, attempting to intercept them on their way to perdition; and this is the blessing that the Father has given them. My children, your petitions are never in vain. Humanity whom you are touching are embracing their redemption in Jesus because God knows that you care for them, and He understands your desire to institute world justice. Therefore, we seek them on His behalf. I wish to remind you that I have been in your midst longer than your forefathers lived, long preceding their birth from the hand of God. I have seen your actions in Christian faith and everything you have accomplished and hoped to achieve for the furtherance of the Cross. Time alone is evidence that you are succeeding; it is the element that ratifies your decisions in reflection of My Son. You know that I have called you many times to persevere. If anyone asks you about remaining steadfast in your goals, you may tell them that your Mother has pleaded with you over and again to never desist in your witness for God's Kingdom. Never surrender to your foes, and always extol the things that you know humanity must believe. For those whose habit is to archive acronyms, tell them that I have made a consistent call to My children to embrace righteousness, divinity, acclimation, and consecration, RDAC. Long have I lived for humanity in ways that cannot be calculated in hours, days, or years. My Love is as eternal as the Lord; it cannot be measured by anything at the hands of men. Like My Son, I am aware of your untiring contributions for the betterment of the world to foster assistance in addressing issues like poverty, oppression, freedom, purity, holiness, virtue, faith, charity, and humility. With certainty, each of your days could be captioned with something you have afforded Jesus through your trust and belief in Him. And, you have done this in the face of awful opposition. You have survived volatile situations here at home and abroad against your holy works. Even yet, many parts of the globe are like a tinder box, prepared to ignite into full-scale war because of religious bigotry. Pope Benedict XVI has reiterated the primacy of the Roman Catholic Church, and God expects those who hear him to convert. I have told you previously that it is only because of the Martyrs and Saints and through Jesus' Mercy that others are saved. Today, My Special son, is of auspiciousness because you and your brother remain together as many yet travel the Earth two-by-two to disseminate the Gospel message. I cannot repeat too many times how grateful the Lord is for your earnestness in upholding your pledge of faith. Now, you are weeks prior to releasing My 2000-2002 messages that are directed toward many. Some of them are lengthy and arduous to discern, but they are forward and sufficient, never irrelevant or superfluous. I have come to remind you of God's appreciation for your generosity and deference. I shall be brief today because I realize that you need rest. I will have more to say to you and your brother next week. He will have ample opportunities to report to humanity everything I have said to him at the same time I have been speaking to you during My Sunday messages. This is a memoir that none have yet known about, but will eventually be dispensed to the world. His consciousness and presence have been with you, but his spirit, soul, and heart have been listening to everything God has revealed. I am encouraging him today, teaching him how to gain the strength in humanity to reverse the horrible tides of atheism and relativism that are affronting the dignity of the Church. You will know in time what I am saying to him. All of this will be part of his visionary parlance. I am pleased by your prologue to your book, and that you have made a simple dedication to the unborn innocents of the United States. Thank you for your kindness to Mario, Cristian, Santiago, Martin, and all the others. Your lives have become a prayer that they have resounded. I bless you and give you the Lord's peace."

Sunday, July 22, 2007
St. Ingmar Philadelphus, Martyr [1398-1436]*
2:54 p.m.

"My beautiful children, we are finishing God's Sacred Will that was laid on the Earth's foundation, *quod erat faciendum* (which was to be done) in honor of your predecessors' faith, their charismatic contemplations, and their heralding of hymns and anthems of exaltation to proliferate His Sovereign Kingdom. I offer My rendition of your prayers to Jesus so your petitions can be presented before the Father. I cannot overstate My advice for you to pray honestly and incessantly. I refer the intentions that Jesus harbors for humanity, and My Immaculate Heart overflows with compassion for your suffering and pity for your helplessness. My children, no single moment can capture the miracles that surround you every day. The concepts of peace and sanctifying grace cannot be denoted by a certain date or hour because they are perpetual; they are wholesome and overwhelming to the consciousness. This day on which you are receiving My message finds you lifted from the boundaries of time into the Eternal Divine. Yes, you can see the world as you have always known it, and you are aware of your collateral environment and physical constitution. However, Jesus has taken hold of your spirits, raising them to the Throne of the Father, extracting them from the dangers of the Earth, and vesting you with the righteousness that you seek from your Christian faith. This does not imply that you are more beautiful in the presence of God than any other day, but you are pulled beyond temporal kinetics into beatific rest.

Hence, you reside in Heaven and on Earth while I am speaking; and during the days in between, you aspire for Salvation by your prayerful work in the Lord's vineyard. My Maternal Love is so intense that I weep trying to describe it in terms that you will understand. No suns or moons can capture it; no phraseology can describe it; no crescendo can eclipse it, and nothing short of the Providence that sends Me here can come near to reflecting its sincerity. You are the recipients of My Love, the object of My sights, and the subject of every sentence that is predicated in the mind of God. I come to bless you, My children, for all you have done to remain true to the Church and your brothers and sisters with whom you are united in the Cross. The mysticism of the human heart is cultivated by your vision of Jesus; it is enhanced by your willingness to let go of the world and take hold of His Spirit. You are unanimously chosen by the Hosts of Heaven to take residence in Jesus' Most Sacred Heart and in My arms where He teaches and guides you. You have come far on this journey of faith! I wish never to look upon you and see that you have become stilled in any negative way, that you are no longer making progress toward the Kingdom to which you have staked the outcome of the future. As long as you are praying for the world to change, you are treading the path of liberty. When you ponder goodness and virtue; when you see in your mornings the hope that springs from Jesus' Resurrection; when you look your enemies directly in the eyes and tell them that they have already been defeated, then you are moving as I would have you walk toward Heaven. Such things are made of prayer, and they simultaneously comprise your prayers. This is a summer of the progress about which I am speaking. From your purview that transcends time and space, from the paramount fineness of your religious faith, you can see the end of the ages; you can sense the Triumph of My Immaculate Heart. When you live according to this blessing, and when you elevate your hearts knowing that everything I am saying is true, you will live-out your fullest allegiance to Jesus. The years come and go, so many hours, and too much testing, pulling, retrieving, mourning, and enduring. All you can imagine has come to you by way of your earthly moments; and you have relished some and grieved others, but you have usurped the sorrows that beleaguer you with dark thoughts and desperate responses. The Holy Spirit springs forth in you to lift you from the throes of life into the joys of living. I have been with you during all of this, since before your mothers' painfully birthed you from the womb, while you have labored for the faith you have chosen. And, I am poised to welcome you into Heaven, the land of infinite jubilees.

My Special and Chosen ones, I pray that you will never permit your lives to perplex or tempt you into believing that the ordinary times between your close encounters with Heaven have nothing to do with your invocation of redemption or your worthiness to be in God's service. You outshine any diamond with which lost sinners might attempt to persuade you to abandon your work. No winds of change, either good or ill, can amend the fact that you are the Children of Light; and you are called as little suns in the darkness of the Earth to rescue the lost from the perils of death. When the Lord's people pray for His help, they are not aware that we are His answer. What we do in His name, everything to which we have been devoted since the announcement of the Archangel Gabriel, and all to which My Son has been dedicated is to reap the harvest of souls for God. This makes your lives and My Immaculate Conception one with Jesus' Crucifixion and Easter Resurrection. If anyone sees a lacking in their spirituality, they can discover the Father in Him. I am a determined Mother who will not surrender My children to their own devices. I will never deny a sinner who is consecrated to Jesus. I will not turn My back on a believer who is approaching Me for help. If it requires My repeating this affirmation every hour for the remainder of the world, I will do so, and no man can stop Me. You may be helplessly exiled, but you are not shorn of assistance from the same God whom Adam and Eve betrayed. Through everything that has befallen humanity, in all the egregious errors of which My children stand accused, in the face of any opposition to your redemption, I stand tall and fearless in My promise to raise you to the Salvation that Jesus has won for you. You live on an Earth of bearings and a lack of them, of persuasion and deception, of dearth and plenty, fear and courage, darkness and light, and clemency and punishment. Never mind the expletives of these things. Pull yourselves beyond their attraction and inexorability. Be one with Jesus, and you will know, you will see, and you will walk past the horizons over which you have yet to travel. Thank you, My Special one, for the opportunities you have accorded your Mother to humble My children before the Cross. I ask you and your brother to remain united peacefully for God, and never be petty or bicker about unimportant things. The megalithic works you are publishing will foster the conversion of multitudes during this century. Once they are released from your hands, they can never be expunged. My messages will have a devastating impact on the wicked. I am grateful, and Jesus has unprecedented blessings prepared for you. You will receive no less than you have given to Him. Thank you for having responded to My call."

Sunday, July 29, 2007
St. Boniface Juliana [AD 611-658]*
3:02 p.m.

"We remember in our prayers all who are yearning to know God through the awesome Glory in which they were created, to the infinitude where your hearts are melded together by the unity of the Holy Spirit. I have summoned you to lift your petitions to the Father not only because He hears, but because you realize that He responds. Prayer is the music that decorates the centuries with sanctity and gives you a supernatural understanding of life.

You have in your power the means to destroy your enemies from your kneelers more comprehensively than lances on the battlefield. You can stop your adversaries' aggression and refute humanity's unlettered polemics against the sacredness of the Cross. This is why I seek your petitions, My little darlings; and to that end, I have appeared before you with the Lord's peace and blessings. Today, it is My honor to remind you that you are well beyond the goals that modest men would have made for their journey through life. You see skirmishes and debates that rage in the secular realms about the faith of Christians, the purpose of religion, the facility of virtue, and the gaining of future blessings through lives of sacrifice and renunciation. These are prayers, such that your very existence is your means of speaking to Heaven by your sacred desires. If you inhale anxiety and exhale confidence, you undergo the transformation that takes you closer to Heaven's unerring perfection. There are no wasted moments when you offer yourselves wholly and completely to the Son of Man, that He may utilize you in any way He desires for the cultivation of the world, that the Lord is glorified as He deserves. I urge you to meditate upon these things when you pray. We magnify your faith and it becomes emboldened when you realize that Jesus is listening. Pray for the end of abortion, the arrival of justice around the nations, the eradication of famine and disease, the alleviation of poverty and suffering, and the enlightenment of sinners in the decrees of the Gospel. If you complete these objectives while under the blessing of the Father, you will be given strength that you never knew you could have. My children, I have come speaking today to offer My endearing support in your contributions to the Kingdom of God. I remind you that every moment is filled with His Grace, and you are forever beckoned to open wide and receive renewal from His forgiveness, from which all reunification is dispatched. If you could measure your success in milestones, you are well on your way to this destiny. My Special son, how pleased can your Mother be? With what elation do I perceive your life! You have moved within sight of August, the month when you will release to humanity My messages for this new century. And, as has been recorded, My first greeting to your brothers and sisters is 'yes.' This is My response not only to the Archangel, but to everyone who comes to Me for God's Wisdom, comfort, intercession, and consolation. I could not deny the Will of the Father. I have always accepted His determination to absolve His creatures, and I will never spurn My children who are redeemed in Jesus' Crucifixion. You have known this for decades, and you are working diligently for all things redemptive for those who will be saved. I need not remind you that you have been blessed in degrees beyond others, but you have made great strides of your own, based on the authenticity of your faith. You believed when many others turned away; you stood firm when it might have been simpler to take another course; you refocused your vision with the precision of the Saints, and you never once questioned My motives through the sacrifices I have asked you to make. Most important, you have stood by your brother who has walked by faith and not by sight the perilous roads of this Earth with the timidity of a child. A quarter-century ago, you embarked together on a journey for the Florida sun, now you are placing the finishing touches on a manuscript that will chastise whole societies of men.

I have watched your reaction as you heard My new millennium messages, and you have thought of the ofttimes-cited strain, 'wait until the world hears this.' None of these thoughts could come to you without the presence of the Holy Spirit in your heart. Just seven years after your Floridian holiday, our work began; your transaction with Paradise ensued in which you lent your lives to God in exchange for the conversion of humanity. Will this end in the ways I have planned, with the anticipation through which you have hoped? I assure you with the intensity of the Cross that it will. Your love has been timeless since before you ever knew who I was. I watched over you with your crayons and the pagoda at your grandfather's house. I have known all along about your pleading innocence through good times and bad. I prayed when you felt violated and during the high moments when you were hailed as a champion before admiring throngs. I have held you beneath My Mantle since you were conceived and cheered your progress every step you took. I was above you when you peddled for doughnuts and struggled to balance your bicycle when delivering the newspapers. I knelt beside you when you hid behind the door, and caressed you when you slept so silently in your bed. Why did I do this? Because Jesus led Me by the hand and through My Immaculate Heart to your home and into your life while saying, *This is the one; this is the child I wish you to bless. This is Maximus, William the Conqueror, who will be My warrior through the end of time.* I wept for you when you were afraid, stood up for you when you were scorned, and never allowed any creature in the boundaries of time to believe that you would remain on the ground. I knew that you would raise your spirit and your sword for Jesus during your tenure of years, and this is why I am speaking to you now. Mercy will come in many fashions because of people like you. It will arrive in time to rescue the lost who are about to fall into the pit. It will grasp errant souls about to descend into the fires of Hell and convert them to the Cross. Brave and eloquent kings will stand upon your deposit of works like children on soap boxes to see beyond the horizons of time, to take a peek of Glory that awaits them in the end. There is a sense of inevitability in everything I have told you from February 1991, one that unfolds like a flower in slow motion, but one that is nonetheless occurring despite the opposition of men. We have heralded the Salvation of the world, Jesus born of My Womb and present in your heart. We have sanctified the corruptible, glorified the rejected, beatified the blessed, and lifted the Mystical Body of Christ to the holiness for which He was slain on Good Friday. We have made progress in places that were so stagnant that nary a heart would stir. We have moved mountains, scaled peaks, filled valleys with the Lord's good will, and shed light into places that have laid in darkness for thousands of years. And yet, we have done this as delicately as a breeze might blow, as quietly as the sun rises, as deftly as the flight of the Angels, and as proficiently as all the sentinels who have ever stood watch over the charges in their sights. We have sung harmony together, My little one. We have been help for the sick and comfort for the dying. We have given new meaning to suffering where men saw no other cause. And, you have Christ's endless accolades; you have His benediction and gratitude. We shall go on from here knowing that your home and your life with your brother have been benevolent places in an otherwise nondescript corner of the world. You will soon see with eyes of certainty what you have dreamed with visions of the heart."

Sunday, August 5, 2007
Feast of Our Lady of the Snows
2:49 p.m.

"With confidence in the awakening of your peers, I pray for the Living Will of the Father to become the intentions of humanity, and that healing will pour over your spirits during these crucial hours of the world. These are prevailing times for your consciences to be stirred with the Truth of Jesus Christ, to rise above all things normal into the supernal dignity that you have inherited in Him. My little ones, I promise that God will never forsake you. He will not remand you to the darkness of the ages or permit you to lie fallow as the soil, hungry for the seed of righteousness. He feeds you Divine Love and the Manna of Life, and sustains you in the Sacrifice of His Son. No one can escape His scrutiny; not a child can hide from Him. If anyone tries to conceal themselves in the deepest fathoms, He will part the waters of the seas and flush them out. We must work to ensure that the souls of the lost are found and nourished in their lifeblood of repentance and absolution. This is My message today, My children. I summon you to take leave of anything that lures you from Jesus, anything secular that rings contrary to your Christian faith, all that leaves you perplexed in issues of morality, and everything that accosts your purity. As you live these times, remember that there are endless distractions. The enticements to which you could be drawn are seductive, and they are the work of the devil. Anything by which you feel pressured to follow any other life than Christianity is directly from the bowels of Hades. If you pray with Me, My doves, if you hold to the manifest principles I have taught for 2,000 years, you will be blessed by God and your lives will be replete with joy. I beseech you to invoke the intercession of the Angels and Saints so they will hear your petitions for the healing of the nations and peoples who lie suffering from the effects of spiritual blight and lawlessness that are rampant in Europe and America. Look around you and see how your brothers and sisters are agonizing over their broken lives. See how the world's wealth is hoarded by only a few, which in itself creates an atmosphere of insurrection. Place yourselves in their shoes; walk more than a mile beside them, and recognize how fortunate you are to have freedom, food, shelter, industrialism, and mobility. These simple but vital elements are absent from millions of lives worldwide. My Special one, I promised this week to speak on a Feast of the Church based upon a miracle that the Lord has reserved for His people. Such manifestations will not end until the Earth has been concluded in Him. Heaven has fashioned a finale for the ages in which all redeemed souls will play an integral part. Hundreds of visionaries have already participated by writing contemplations from their hearts, and have assisted Jesus in penning the thoughts that complement His teachings that have been dispensed through the ages. You are among these disciples, and your brother is your helper. Thank you from the center of My Most Immaculate Heart for taking such good care of him. This is a bright and blessed time for humanity! I am overwhelmingly impressed by your kindness and obedience, that you would never stray from My presence, and that you realize that you have a stake in your sacrifices to protect Jesus' Mystical Body. You have done plenty, more than your share, as God knows, to apprise wayward sinners about the condition of the Earth and My advocacy for the grieving among you. These are miraculous times because Jesus has granted forbearance to those who are indifferent, giving them sufficient years to amend their lives and join the homecoming ceremonies for His glorious return. These are not just ordinary days, they are each and every one the dawn of a new era toward the awesome waxing of the refinement of men. I assure you that the terms grand and noble do not adequately describe the stature that you hold before My Son. The faithful are widely anticipating your unfolding Apostolate, reading with care My messages, and growing stronger in their trust and knowledge of their role in the Catholic Church as pilgrims beneath the Holy Father in Rome. I invite you to be heartened by the expiration of time because My work through you and your brother is proceeding exactly as Jesus said. I ask for your prayers for My children, especially seminarians who commend themselves to the Divine Mercy of My Son. Please remember the obedience and selfless contributions of My locutionists who have been My witnesses where so many have been taught the perseverance of your faith in a nation that often ridicules it. It seems a long time since I told you about the seeds of new beginnings, about the Lord never leaving them unsown, even for a moment, because humanity must bloom and grow the designs of Christianity every day. This is My goal and the desire of Jesus as well."

Sunday, August 12, 2007
St. Ancienne Pulchella [1369-1430]*
3:49 p.m.

"It is worth investing hours of prayer to seek the rehabilitation of humanity in the ways of righteousness. It is the Lord's desire that you comply with His Will in making the Earth like Heaven. My children, I call you to pray for the world's brokenness, for those far from the Grace that has saved them, for the many who misconduct themselves when they should pursue holier paths, and everyone who is suffering, especially the victims of the hatred of those who manifest evil and ill will. You have been handed the power to make all things right. Please utilize the gift of prayer to change Creation, to restore what has been plundered, and to unite everything known to man that has been put asunder by the legerdemain of the devil. Today, I remind you to cherish your faith through the Church, and travel every avenue to purify and bless your brothers and sisters in Christian goodness. Embrace and practice the edicts of the Pope, and defend the Traditions of the Church that are handed-down through the ages because they are sacred heirlooms by which you are guided and informed. The human conscience must be nurtured by God's Spirit to be viable. Prayer gives this sustenance, My children. It is clear that My motivations are to direct you to offer your petitions in matters that will convert lost souls to the Cross. It is often a simple correction of course that fosters their repentance. If you offer your prayers for these souls, they will be capable of saying 'I know what to do' instead of the helpless acclamation 'I know not what to do.' Christians have lent great appeal to this cause from many centuries past. You have joined the grand experience of exchanging ideas about how to approach your brothers who have strayed from the narrow path. You are lauded in Paradise for this. There is no time for idling as you wait in joyful hope for the coming of the Lord. There are sinners who require your supplications to be transmuted into the piety in which they will shine when Jesus takes them to Heaven. This is why we are offering our prayers to God, and it is the reason you are enlightened by the Wisdom of the Holy Spirit. Pray for the victims of oppression and genocide, for the thousands in places like Serbia, Kosovo, Ukraine, Darfur and the other lands where poor people suffer at the hands of ruthless tyrants and those who would see Christianity fail. They shall never succeed because Jesus will forever prevail. My Special son, it is particularly My honor to speak to you at this time when you are outlaying the final pages of your new anthology. When it is completed, you may contact your Bishop to meet with him. During that conference, please be sure to tell him that I have instructed you to remain within the modesty through which I came to you, that I have asked you to live as though these are My first days and weeks. Offer My collectanea to him with humility, with childlike happiness and dutiful faith. Remind him that I speak of him with affection, to the extent that he understands that even though he is a descendent of the First Apostles, he is a little child. Assert that humanity depends upon him and his fellow prelates to lead the Catholic Church as Children of Mary, especially in this Diocese that is dedicated to Me. Give him My affirmation that the Holy Spirit embraces him with Heaven's superior countenance, protection and confidence, and that he stands esteemed before the Communion of Saints. He will understand these things if you say them with deference. It is important that you tell him that these are the messages from 2000-2002 that I asked you to wait five years to release (since 2002). Concede that you are unsure of the significance of those five years and that I will explain it in the future. Hence, My 2003-2005 messages are planned for publication in 2008, and the final three years in 2009. He will understand that this has been prefigured to give you time to write and present your previous books to him and to the world. Finally, please offer him comfort and consolation at My behest for the burdens that he bears in fighting against secularism during these times when the enemies of the Church are at demonic levels. Yes, it is exciting to know that you are another book closer to laying My intercession upon the world stage. It is a matter of exemplary piety. Commercialism is only a ruse, but our work is the factual truth about the conversion of men; not of profit for the person, but for the deliverance of the wicked to the foot of the Cross."

Sunday, August 19, 2007
St. John Eudes, Missionary [1601-1680]
3:14 p.m.

"My little children, today I invite you to pray with sincerity from the heart so that your petitions do not become rote exercises when you think blandly about the needs of humanity. Remember all who are seeking reconciliation within their families, those who are not gainfully employed; and please pray especially for the end of abortion and social animus. You have within your power the capacity to bring transcending good will among men through your communication with the Lord, for He hears you and touches their hearts according to your intentions. It is My blessing for you that He should do this; it is a manifestation of My undying Love for your Salvation. Call upon the Saints who have been raised to the Honors of the Altars to be your intercessors before the Throne of God, for it is their joy to respond. I have told you about the ills of humanity near and far, and about the illusions under which many people live, their oppressions and deficits, and their need to come to the Living Water of God's Wisdom through Jesus' Sacrifice on the Cross. If our work is to have any bearing upon their future, we must apply every sacred principle at our command to convince them to approach Him in contrition. They must learn that repentance is a dignifying and purifying process; not one in which they are dismissed or castigated, but elevated through their sanctification. What else shall we do with your valuable time on the earthen floor? To what other end could you lend your hearts than to the propagation of the Kingdom of God? The individual, particular needs of each region and location are wide and varying; they are expressed by your family and friends in their suffering and frustration, by the changes they seek for spiritual renewal in their lives, the sustenance of their offspring, and the friendships that lather the Earth in benevolence for the cutting edge of Jesus' omnipotent discipline. If we were to recount all these, My children, we would speak well into the night, beyond the dawn, and past the latter hours of tomorrow. I simply ask you to recall that there are problems aplenty that burden your brothers and sisters for which you should ask God's mediation according to the articles of His Will. My Special son, it is My unending happiness to speak not only to humanity through your messages, but to the future as Jesus has shaped it by His heritage and Sacrifice. You have spoken about not allowing your brothers' suffering to be wasted on the pages of history, and that all the new mornings you shall know until the return of the Son of Man will be saturated with purpose in the redemption of all who are born. Christians who do not pray for the enlightenment of the lost are negligent in their offices; they are not upholding their promises to remake the Earth into the likeness of Heaven. You have also stated that nowhere in Creation have I spoken to My children so comprehensively, even effusively, as I have to you and your brother. I do this because God's Kingdom is at hand, and because of your unique interest in confirming that it be completed to the benefit of every man, woman, and child. This is the source of My thoroughness, not only that you have broached these critical ages, but that you are willing to functionally take the urgencies of the Gospel to the masses through your talents and resources. You have devoted untold hours in the preparation of your books, the release of My messages, admonishing and instructing lost sinners in matters of righteousness, and offering them the perspective of Heaven from your purview on Earth. How could Jesus ignore these praises? What would Saint Paul say to the Messiah for whom he suffered if the Lord did not grow your efforts into a magnifying grace? You are intensely appreciated for your good works, unprecedented faith, a lifetime of dedication to Christianity, and taking care of those who have no way to fend for themselves. The Church as a spiritual institution would be remiss if Jesus did not acknowledge everything you have given Him in your adult years. Hence, I stand with and before you during these times, these crucial hours, weeks, and months that are so revealing to the millions who are searching for the true meaning of life. The hundreds of thousands who accepted the Holy Cross years ago in your nation are learning anew what their consecration to Jesus implies. And, they are elated to see that it is as much about miracles as walking by faith.

Vast numbers of Christians have known about Salvation in the Blood of the Cross, and they realize the purifying efficacy of physical and emotional suffering. What they have not known, however, is that such things are more liberating than incarcerating. They have ironically fought to become free from the very freedom that is sanctifying the Earth! It is the same as someone who does not know how to dip a pail into a rolling stream to get a drink of water. Together, we are helping them understand the simple connection between Love and Redemption, about sacrifice and preservation, meekness and courage, and the many other virtuous distinctions of mortification that come from your allegiance to Jesus' Crucifixion. Where ironies abound, the revelation of the human spirit flourishes, surpassing the breach between witnessing and participating, and between acknowledging and propagating. I have mentioned that this is the anniversary of your brother's mother arriving before the Lord in Heaven. She has been with us for twenty-three earthly years, but forever in the sight of God. What she left this world is the gift of the one who is praying at your side. I promise that your life with him has been to the Glory of God in more ways than you can know. It is obvious that this week is the time for which you have been waiting, that you finally completed your next book of My 2000-2002 messages. The clock expires more rapidly than you wish, it seems, for all the gifts you are handing Jesus by your integrity and underlying determination to be obedient to Me and responsive to the Holy Spirit. I understand your point about the dailiness of life. This has been a burden upon Jesus' Mystical Body for centuries, but the repetition allows you to work carefully on magnanimous volumes such as the one you just produced. Please pray for your adversaries because they will soon become your most ardent supporters. God blesses you during your daily prayers."

Sunday, August 26, 2007
St. Teresa Jornet Ibars [1843-1897]
3:08 p.m.

Night is little more than a shadow cast by the departing day, a wedge of darkness poised between the recurring dawns, a place of freedom and protection beneath the blanket of stars.
—The Dominion Angels

"I see My little children as having charity, hope, intelligence, and foresight in Christian piety. I join your petitions to My prayers and offer My intercession because this is the way we touch other lives. Thank you for remembering in your novenas everything that you have previously raised that will ensure humanity's trust in Jesus. It is by the graces of Heaven that you are healed and given wisdom to prophesy the upending of the Earth, brought to justice through Jesus' Sacrifice on the Cross. Bless you for teaching your brothers and sisters right from wrong by exposing hatred for what it is. I made this clear in Medjugorje yesterday, that hatred is a vile sin against the Kingdom of God and the dignity of your religious faith. I concur with your visionary monographs that you address to those in your company who will not heed the call to holiness, who live only for themselves and those they hold close. I commend your allegiance to My Immaculate Heart, and Jesus gives you the disciplinary expressions to reprimand anyone who persecutes the Church. It is often difficult to witness for the Holy Gospel because too many wear their pride and emotions on their sleeves. They are unwilling to climb from the pit of indifference where they live to scale the walls that will allow them to see beyond their ignorance. I have offered you the vision about which I speak. I have given you manuscripts to obey the mandates of the Holy Spirit, and it is you who must respond. It is humankind who must react to the mystical overtures from the Lord and answer for these final times, knowing that everything about your mortal lives is reconciled in Him. We have tread far on this journey, My children. Many daybreaks and moonbeams have come and gone while you have waited for Jesus to return. However, you have never relinquished your determination to see your faith through. Your devotion is intact; your perseverance is wholesome, and your holiness is undeniable. In the waning days of this summer, you must remember that everything for which you have struggled is another season closer. I have long taught humanity about the benefits of patience, the strict determination to kneel with confident hearts shining brightly so you can anticipate the answers to your prayers. Jesus has placed the words of redemption on your tongues and lips to be spoken at this moment to convert your prodigal brothers. If there can be impious syllables stricken from them, this is the work of God. Know that He sustains you as your advocate, and He avows your orations on His behalf. This is the speech of the Holy Spirit. Knowledge of Jesus' Sacred Heart is appealing to those who shall live in Heaven. Appreciation and gratitude are fruits of the converted soul, sweet to the palate of the Angels who are proclaiming the Good News before men. My messages follow this line of thought for everything you have accomplished to evangelize Christianity and elevate the Holy Roman Catholic Church. Let no one hinder you from honoring the Seat of Christianity, the Holy See in Rome. Let no man from the Protestant apostasy make you believe that the primacy of Messianic Christianity resides anywhere but the Chair of Saint Peter. I declare this with pity for those who oppose the Catholic Church, for they are denying the foothold of their own Salvation. Jesus says that the Holy Eucharist is their redemption, and they must convert and be made worthy to receive the Most Blessed Sacrament so they will have the fullness of life in them.

My Special son, see why your consecration is so blessed! Turn to any page in your new book, and you will see a miracle. How unpretentious is your vigor in assisting the Gospel to prosper, and how pleased is Jesus that you have done so. Your ardor is not only applaudable, but extremely revelatory to millions of people worldwide. You have helped Me bring them to the realization that you and your brother are not living for casual purposes. This will beget the process that shall lead to the downfall of their animosity against the Church. And, thank you for the prayers that you and your brother offer every day. Do you remember that I once said that the credibility of your beliefs should be solid as a rock, like gemstones instead of fraying fabric? This is what you have been, effectively one indomitable force against evil, unflappable for the purpose of manifesting your seamless unity with the Crucifixion. Humanity must build upon this prayer, knowing that they have the wisdom to avoid evil without being scandalized by Satan. It has been a hot summer, but you have remained inside and finished a profound new book for your native homeland. My 1997-1999 messages will be in a separate book of their own; they will appear chronologically as your anthologies, and they will express My sentiments about the conclusion of the 20th century, and how believers, the underworld, publicans, and all other creatures having self-awareness should have prepared for AD 2000. The Second Coming of Jesus Christ is threefold—Spiritual, Corporeal, and Glorious. You are living during the age when humanity must prepare for the reaping of the Earth upon which time all human flesh will be shed. In other words, Jesus has come, but not yet. *(I raised a perspective to Our Lady that the world has been on the cusp of the Second Coming of Jesus many times, but Our Lord extended His Divine Mercy to sinful humanity because of the declarative witness of His Saints. In other words, each of the Saints who proclaimed that Jesus' Return was imminent in their time was correct at that moment, before the Father relented in bringing Judgement to the Earth as a result of their witness. There have also been times when the Father was an instant away from giving the command for Our Lord to return because He saw how holiness and sacrifice had grown to such a beautiful crescendo, but was nonetheless forced to remain patient out of His great love for the few who were still unprepared to accept His Son. There have been surging and receding phenomena in relation to the moment of Jesus' Second Coming throughout the ages. Those in the Bible who believed that Jesus' Return was imminent were correct, although they never saw their witness fulfilled in their time.)* Yes, you pose the possibility that Jesus is closer at times than others, and the evidence is in miracles like the Stigmata of Saint Francis and Saint Padre Pio. These were converting events and censorious warnings to humanity that the conclusion of the old Earth is near. Now, to your point about acclamation. Saint Vincent Ferrer was correct as you have said, and I have spoken about the ebbing and flowing of universal knowledge and the peaks of holiness that have come through the lives of Christian men and women. Indeed, if everyone uttered the Our Father simultaneously, each and every living soul, then the world would cease to exist as you know it and the heavens would open to the New Jerusalem. The closeness of the Flesh and

Blood of Jesus to which you refer is manifested by His presence in the Holy Eucharist. God wants you to know that His blessing is in the actions of the Church in all good ways."

Sunday, September 2, 2007
St. Danielle Simoneaux, Virgin [1667-1713]*
2:49 p.m.

"My children, I come with the gladness of old to bring you the counsel of the Trinity and offer My supple kindness as your guide to daily life. Christ Jesus knows that humanity is suffering. He is heartened by your affinity for the Cross during these crucial times. There is no question that He asks for your allegiance in good times and inopportune ones, when you are smiling and when in tears, and as you age in years and wisdom like statesmen. You have braved the darkness of night, now go and herald the gifts of redemption where the sunlight and breezes bathe you. Remember that there were more fatalities on Good Friday than Jesus. Not only did He surrender His life for human Salvation, He simultaneously put everything evil to death. Jesus died on the Cross of Mount Calvary, and He took Satan down with Him. The men beside Him were collateral casualties of Satan's corruption, but one was shown the Light of Absolution for his own awakening at the dawning hour of Resurrection. As I speak to you, there are untold streams of wholesomeness that have sprung from the Crucifixion; there have been billions of conversions and incalculable actions of courage in the image of the Victim on the Cross. Purity has been restored to those who have forfeited it; peace has been brought to warring factions; wedding bells have chimed for matrimonial love, and intercessions have been granted from the Saints in Paradise. It is My request that you ponder anew the meaning of your faith; measure your virtues alongside the holy deeds of your forbears, and inhale a new breath of the breeze about which I speak. I have said that your hearts rest at the outer perimeter of Creation, that you stand at the End Times, the concluding ages of the physical Earth. Why God has placed you here is important because the Holy Spirit has specifically prepared you for these days. You have been given ample opportunities to anoint the world with your religious zeal and deposit onto the Earth your sacred impressions of what it means to be Christians. You have not only become the servants of God, you have retread the courses that your ancestors fought to be blessed. They who will follow you, many in their elder years, will depend upon your strength of spirit to help the Son of Man clear the pathway for the conclusion and fulfillment of the Scriptures according to the Will of the Father. My Special son, you have devotedly listened and responded to the Lord. It is the earnest gratification of Heaven that you have understood the reason for your birth, for the extraordinary way that you survey the actions of men, decipher their motivations, examine their ulterior intentions, and plead for Jesus to set them right. We have shared lengthy conversations about the prophecies implied through your works, their facility in converting your brothers and sisters to the Crucifixion, and the beneficial outcomes they will have on the collective human conscience. These manifestations came because Jesus visited you through Me in 1991, and you have said yes, as I said yes. When someone asks what it means to hear God's voice, you know what to tell them. They must not harden their hearts! It is not enough to establish a relationship with Heaven for the purpose of one's own sustenance; you must witness to your conversion before the masses. It is the same principle that asks the question about whether you love your brothers and sisters, and if they know it. The one to which I refer is that you accept forgiveness in Christianity, and does everyone else believe you? You have proved the latter during your decades in exile. Choosing Jesus and witnessing for Him run concurrently; humanity must expand the faith given by His Sacrifice to lands near and far where Christianity is hardly known. You must avow your fealty to the Cross through service, suffering, guidance, prayer, devotion to Jesus' Sacred Heart, allegiance to the Beatitudes, hunger for the Fruits of the Holy Spirit, and aptitude in the Catechetical Acts of Mercy. You realize that everything about man begins somewhere, and the origin of your life is begetting the harvest of souls for God's Kingdom in this age.

    I pray that you are well, and it appears that you are. Your brother set out on this journey with you, placing your lives in the context of spreading the Gospel. While this may appear to take a long time, the Angels harken your hearts to the Resurrection, and you will sense what I have said in more comprehensive tones during the immediate future. While this is specific to you, I have also through the centuries spent much time encouraging My messengers and seers about surviving the struggle for happiness and remaining focused on the outcome of the universe with patience. The largest share of what I have said to humanity is being placed into your texts in America to be broadcast. Yes, it will be incorporated into more works if you allow it. You are young enough to do this and willing with undiluted trust to withstand the wait until I have said all I came to say. Your brother does well when he sees that he is making progress, and this is what those little prayers are about he recites along the way. He has milestones and guideposts serving his patience, and they permit him to see the finish line without yet crossing it. This is the heart of a child who asks his parents when they are traveling where they are going. You will visit your Bishop soon and take My New Millennium Anthology. You may literally interpret My suggestion of praying in the sunlight to bathe you. This will aid the progress of your work. Thank you for being so kind to your new neighbors. They are trying to be peaceful for you. You have prayed for them, and we pray even more that they will practice their faith. I promise that everything you have done for this world will be repaid a hundredfold. Someday soon, you and your brother's joy will burst into Creation like an atomic bomb. You have held this hope from the purview of a childlike mind. The Hosts of Heaven are praying for you. The heat of summer will soon pass, but you will have many days to sit on the porch before winter. If you need a sabbatical from your work for a week or ten days, then by all means do so. Remember that life is a redefining process. This is what you do for Jesus, for your daily examen whose product may not be known until seen with eternal perspective."

Sunday, September 9, 2007
St. Cicely Belle Conger [1816-1843]*
3:17 p.m.

"How well you have understood the efficacy of prayer; how prettily you have responded to My call, and with what fathoms you are consecrated to Me! My little ones, I bring you peace through My presence and promote the Truth to which you have devoted your lives and the constancy of your hearts. I realize that you do not do this without sacrifice. Many of My messengers are persecuted by doubters and chided from the pulpit as being holier than thou by people who commit grievous transgressions against the sanctity of the Church. There is no question that you lend your hearts to Me respectfully and truly, and you pray to stop holocausts on the Earth during moments when you would rather be engaged in something else. However, you know the priorities of the Father. Together, we have leapt across oceans to reach the poor and disenfranchised, the oppressed, diseased, and dying. You have made a difference by responding to Jesus in ways that most men would never afford. If you think about reestablishing good will, amplifying the humble beginnings of sincere faith in the hearts of meek people, and nullifying everything contradictory to the Kingdom of God, this is the crux of your existence in these final days. And, you are doing this with poise; you are not searing the continents, telling your brothers and sisters that the sky is on fire. You have learned precisely as I have requested that the purifying of humanity is a protracted procedure with lasting results and irretractable consequences. I revealed the meaning of holiness by bearing Jesus from My Womb, and we ask Him to bless your apostolic mission and the Roman Catholic Church through which you are fed. What may seem like events of randomness are signals for people you will never meet in this life. The universality of Christian prayer finishes God's Will in such a way that all suffering culminates in His Glory. I offer His remembrance for you today and always, His sublime intervention when you feel alone, and Heaven's crowning victory in the Triumph of My Immaculate Heart. There is unconstrained spiritual imagining in offering your prayers for lost sinners, much more than you might realize from Earth. Those you consider your adversaries in Christianity are defeated by your petitions to

Jesus and Saint Michael the Archangel. Your visions and prophesies are comprised of this; your hopes for divine human reconciliation are brought into being. You may seem able to ponder this without your relationship with Me, but it would scarcely be possible. I am the Lady Crowned with Twelve Stars to whom the Apostles turned for maternal advice. I am your intercessor in this age, for all the ages, so you will know Jesus like those with whom He broke bread centuries ago. People who never knew Him are meeting Him now. His Glory is revelatory for all times and seasons. His laws are obeyed by every sense of immortal being. And, I assure you that His advocacy is among you during this new millennium as you sweat in His vineyard, waiting for the hour when He pronounces your years complete. The idea of a smidgeon has no place in the comprehensive framework in which you have embraced Him, and He floods your hearts with peace for the growth of the Church. Will you remember how you are appreciated for this? My commendation is that the Lord will make you instruments and disciples of His Kingdom so all the world will be illuminated by the refrains of Salvation that are setting the Earth aglow. I seek your petitions to end infanticide, to propagate moral reason, and lead all sinners to baptism through which Original Sin is expunged. Give your intentions to Jesus in these ways, and He will look upon you with pity. His Countenance will shine upon you, and all the hours when you have prayed for the wicked will be redeemed. My Special son, all this goodness comes from your perseverance, faith, prayer, laboring of love, and trust in your Blessed Mother. And, it is the Lord's way of proving that He accepts your sacrifices to cleanse humanity. The Sacred Mysteries of the Rosary are the reason you are completing the objectives to which your life is given. I have spoken about the practicalities of the days, the preparation of your previous manuscripts, your worries and concerns, and the satisfaction of your overwhelming needs. However, all this has been worth the effort you have invested to lead to these months during which the finishing of your heart's desires come. Let every sign you see in the future convince you that My intercession is on course. Your confidence is your vision. No outside pressure can defeat you unless you allow it. Thank you for uplifting everyone you have mentioned. We will remember them, asking Jesus to touch them in ways consonant to the Will of God."

Sunday, September 16, 2007
St. Frieda Donee Settles [1737-1816]*
2:49 p.m.

"My dear children, the sweet motet 'Ave Verum Corpus' with which we have begun our message today is reminiscent of the melodies of the Angel Choirs that touch your lives and give you warmth, tranquility, and plentiful consolation. You enter this peace with Me; you are able to abandon the clamoring world and feel the softness of the Holy Spirit caressing your hearts. The Spirit of the Lord takes you to places unseen by your perceptions of earthly existence because you have approached the floodgates of Glory as your reason for living. You see many sights and listen to the voice of God, all the places where you believe His presence to be, in the actions of those closest to His Kingdom, and where His creatures scamper and play. It is as though you yearn to hear the lowing kine of the farmlands and birds chirping in the treetops on command, whenever you feel the need for the comfort of Nature and the intercession of its Creator. I bring this tranquility, My children, in prayers and words, through My constant intercession on your behalf as Queen of Heaven, and by the innumerable miracles I offer those who are open to receive them. Thus, I appear before you this beautiful September afternoon in AD 2007 to bless and teach you about the Love of Almighty God. My little ones, I seek not great things from you, but temperance and confession, and compliance with the tenets of your faith to which you would have conceded even so. And, I pray deeply that you will know that My visiting is to justify your undertakings in Jesus, to assure you that you are binding new manifestations in Heaven that were previously unrecorded on Earth, and promise My true allegiance as you proceed to the hour when you will join the Saints in Heaven. I come simply and nobly in spirit, wishing and pining for the hearts of My children, perceiving a future when all will be surrounding Me, singing the strains of Jesus' Paschal Resurrection like doves cooing an infant. I am a gentle Matriarch in all ways, and I seek a contrite humanity to defer to the Will of God during your sanctification and preservation. Thank you for having responded to My call. My Special son, please realize that these months and years are your vindication before many; they are times during which your consecration to Me is taking on tangible overtones with those in your midst by whom you have refused to be defeated. As you receive the Spirit of Jesus in your heart and offer your consistent valor to the Trinity, please believe that the call of the conscience and the 'Hail True Body' that began My message are your salutation before the nations. There are certain plateaus in everyone's life when you see more clearly than others, when you know that something has proverbially clicked that allows the events of the past and hopes for the future to take-on new meaning. This is one of those eras in the history of men that regales the justice that you are fostering across this land and around the precincts of America. I bid you to cherish these times while you are yet capable of traveling anonymously, when you can relax at the portico in relative ease without being impacted by the curiosity of those whose intentions are to accost your mission instead of accepting it. It is not only by lack of conveyance that Jesus traveled so few miles from home, but because He knew that the annals of His life would resound across the globe through the Glory of the Easter Triduum. This is you and your brother's benison from Him as well. It is not the same as tossing a basketball through a hoop and receiving a standing ovation. I did not come to preach to the choir. And, you are being brilliantly perceptive. You are seeing occurrences that you could have only dreamed about ten years ago that are proving to the continents that My role in the Salvation of humanity is powerful; it is inevitable, and it is to the benefit of those who will hold out until the end to convert. Hear wise counsel that Jesus has plans for America that will allow everyone to share the suffering of the Cross because it is in this acceptance that you are taken into Heaven. It is through such emulation of the Passion and Crucifixion that you are re-created in His likeness. Indeed, it is for the purification of the Church that it be taken to the pinnacle of sacrifice for the reparation of human sin. All corruption must die this way. I have also come to say that you remain popular with some of your friends, and this is comforting for you. They know what you have believed for almost 17 years, that I have come to touch your hearts in such a way that you will be consoled for eternity beyond your entrance into Paradise, beginning now and on this Earth. Hence, let us proceed as we have before, daily approaching the hour when your work will be complete, praying for humanity's conversion, world peace, the end of abortion and famine, and all the intentions that God's faithful take to Holy Mass every day. I was present when you and your brother became acquainted in 1974, and I have seen the progress you have made for Me, your Mother of Perpetual Help. Your brother began his employment in Beardstown 30 years ago today. He was forced from office fourteen years later when I enlisted his help for the conversion of lost sinners. Like him, your heart remains the same; you are focused on the precision of Christian atonement and the bringing of humanity en mass to the foot of the Cross."

Sunday, September 23, 2007
Saint Pio of Pietrelcina, Stigmatist [1887-1968]
3:22 p.m.

"Your prayers are received high in the cynosures of Heaven, and your lives blessed, actions perused, and eternity ensured. I bring you the true essence of the Lord's Providence to hold you to your promises to Jesus because this is His Will for humanity. You may not yet know what lies in the Afterlife, but it is shaped by your consecration to the Cross and the prayers of the intercessory Saints. I pray with you during your assemblies, hoping you will remember that My Immaculate Heart is engorged with your petitions that I deliver to Jesus. His Sacrifice is your bastion of strength, your light of days, and the Wisdom by which you procure your Salvation. Your sanctified hearts are the sweet hope of this midwestern autumn, and your prayers are psalms of praise for the Creator who shall answer them. You have longed for the coming of fall and the harvest of the seed, for the anticipation this brings for winter, and the arrival of another spring. You have dedicated these cycles to building-up the Lord's Eternal Kingdom because this is the reason you were baptized. His happiness is contingent upon your obeisance. I have told you that whenever you speak His Holy Name, you are guided and nurtured in ways the Earth has never known. For My part, I certify your place alongside the Hosts of Paradise through Jesus because this is why I consented to the Archangel Gabriel. I have said that My messages resonate the call of Heaven in much the same way, seeking your compliance in the Order of Truth by which humanity lives, tending to the articles of your faith in righteous accord, and raising your hearts wholly to the sacrifices that Jesus seeks from you as Christians. Once you proclaim that you belong to God, you have surrendered the leisurely life. Jesus has told you that the poor will always be among you, but this does not mean that the ones you lift from poverty will be among the final lot. My Son has commissioned you to be blazers of new paths and broader inroads in leading the modern world to the faith of the old, and this you do by cherishing the Traditions of the Church with emphasis, fondness, piety, and purpose. My children, it is possible to place your hearts in future times by elevating humanity in the present. The conclusion of the ages and the finishing of the world have been provided for you, and I commend you to the words of the Holy Scripture, Revelation 2:26-28. All the prophecies that have ever been told are fulfilled in the Rosary. One Hail Mary can commence the rolling of the seas. Therefore, I implore you to keep praying for the sanctity of men, that all people will be reunited for the cause of human Salvation in the Messianic Cross. When your perceived enemies visit your native shores, greet them with bouquets; show them your gentler side, and take their hands in brotherly love. I assure you that you will be blessed by the Lord. It is My intense desire that you ask God to make you all one in Him, feed you from the One Loaf, give you consolation in the Most Holy Trinity, lay you to rest in the knowledge that you have been redeemed, and awaken you when Jesus comes again in Glory to the flowers and horns of the Resurrection. You cannot lose your hopes for awesome forgiveness when you do this. All the pomp and circumstance that you could possibly imagine bloom from your hunger to be freed from hatred. The Saints of the former ages, your forbears, ancestors, teachers, writers, and mentors are calling from beyond their graves to today's humanity to let go of your biases and prejudices, and refuse to allow fear to foment any discontent. If you do this, My children, you will be complementing the work of the Saints and completing the Will of the Father. You will fashion for yourselves and the future a promise of peace and protection for all whom you love and their children. I speak about Divine Light during the darkening of early fall so you will keep your hearts ready for change, conducive to the reconciliation of neighbors and nations, sufficient that Jesus will look upon you from Heaven and proclaim that you belong to Him. My Special son, I speak today about the lofty Paraclete living in your heart and feeding upon your kindness to God and His people. Of all the beauty of Nature that you will see in the next weeks, none is as grand as the rainbow of peace that lingers above the life you have devoted to Me. I know that you love Me; this is why I am speaking to you. You have reached out to your brothers in ardent admiration; you have shown pity for the rejected and despised, and you have taken the brokenhearted by the palms and delivered them to Jesus for healing comfort. Indeed, you have accomplished the good work that the Lord asked you to do. I know that you are not finished, and you understand that this is what the passing of time is for. You have finally comprehended the art of patience because you are seeing where you are being led, where humanity's eyes are focused upon My work with you. If you watch the universe unfold as it was meant; if you tender your motivations to God's plan for the redemption of humanity, you will hear My voice proclaiming 'Morning Star Over America' to the world. These are consequential times because the deposit of knowledge that you are pouring across the Earth is configuring the conclusion of human events that I spoke about earlier this millennium. Jesus has imbued His disciples with the courage to look forward with inclusion, one that is unprecedented in these times. You hold a grasp on the edification of millions of souls who need to discover the path to repentance. You once said that My praise for you is high, that it is lavish and abundant. My intent is that you will remember the prudent compliance that you have accorded God as His child, and that you will keep safely in your heart the harbored hopes that you told Me about in the early hours of February 22, 1991. It was much too vast for you to comprehend at that time, but now you are seeing your life alongside your brother with the benefit of over sixteen years. It is clear that you can see what it means to be in Heaven ten thousand ages, and yet just a day. I have come here in joy. I have spoken the intonations of a grateful Mother, and I have concluded My message for today."

Sunday, September 30, 2007
St. Kiev Digamma, Martyr [1674-1723]*
2:56 p.m.

"My presence is your means of comprehending the lightness of heart that becomes you, that makes you the Christians that Jesus has summoned to be His companions. He asks you to be courteous to your brothers and sisters, and to be strong. It is possible to be scrupulous without appearing introverted. It is clear that your reticence and diffidence are only temporary because the Holy Spirit will enliven and strengthen you in evangelical ways, giving insights and confidence to take the Holy Gospel to the wicked. Please accept My intercession in this vein. Break free from the isolationism that divides you in favor of the unity of believers beneath the Holy Cross. This makes Me joyful in this world and the next where I concurrently reign. Today, I urge you to pray for peace in ways that have been previously unheard because violence is spinning out of control. Immorality has never been as rampant, even compared with ancient times, because this age is one of venues through which lust and impurity are readily transmitted. Little hearts, minds and bodies are being violated, and impressionable adolescents are being led astray by sinners who are preying on them. Is this not how every advanced society begins to fail? Is this not the making of destruction in ways that are worse than those that have preceded you? Once you depart from the virtues of sanctity about which I have spoken, even as many in your midst discard and disrespect the importance of My call, humanity's moral compass becomes broken; you lose your path to the Light because of the darkness devouring your souls. I have called you to prayer because God will respond in redressing these matters. Never before in history have so many behaved so wretchedly because the Earth's population is larger than ever. Tragically, this does not imply that a proportionate percentage is finding its way to conversion. While we are not losing the battle for lost souls, we have a great deal more to accomplish to persuade others to join in our prayers for the transformation of the Earth into the likeness of Heaven. God deigns that there be life here, that you become enrollees of His indomitable contingent, and that you accept His peace with the gentleness of lambs. I command My children to rise above the partisanship that beleaguers so many republics. Politics is the pettiness of fools, unfit for those who practice the righteousness of Christ. While it is imperative to choose leaders who comply with the teachings of the Church, it is wrong for Americans to become so enthralled by the particulars of campaigns that your holiness is lost. Every time you celebrate the quadrennial leap year, the bissextus of February 29, you seem to ignore the reason for your freedoms. You become embittered and argumentative; you set aside the key elements of holiness that have fostered the grace that brings you to true social liberty. Hence, I call My children to seek Heaven because it is inherent to your faith. Know with truth and loyalty that God desires your espousal of prudence through Jesus, and you will all be free; you will find your liberation from every form of wrongdoing that could possibly be conceived. This is My message for the final day of September 2007. It is the reason I have appeared before you with the majesty of God's brilliance shining on your hearts with approval and admiration. The people you cannot see with your eyes, the Hosts of Heaven, the Angels and Saints, the celestial oceans and winds that beg you to imitate their eloquence implore you to look through life with perspective and at life with assurance. O' how the Angels have pursued your allegiances! That you would join them in heralding the Glory of God would be a blessing for this broken world that is unprecedented in this sapling millennium. My Immaculate Heart opens for your hopes and dreams to come, for your healing and maturity in the Truth of the Lord. I will be with you throughout the whole of Eternity beginning now, so I plead with you to join Me in ushering your souls to the foyer of Heaven. Thank you, My

Special son, again this week for being strong during your workplace trials, for thinking things through with spiritual logic, and for being consoled by recalling thoughts of Me. It would seem that an entire wall is missing from your prayer room since we last spoke! It is nice to modernize in ways that will make you more comfortable at home. Oh! Yes, you went to the Commitment Ceremony at the Motherhouse, and to Holy Mass in the Church. The Lord is grateful that your brother wrote a newspaper article about pardoning George Ryan who spared the lives of condemned prisoners. 'Watch what they do to him now,' were My words from January 2003. Please, think about this. The pardoning of the 171 inmates was a world story, and the call for his pardon will reach as many shores."

Sunday, October 7, 2007
Feast of the Holy Rosary
2:49 p.m.

"My children, as you age, you perceive the world more clearly, analyze it more accurately, describe it more appropriately, and avoid pitfalls more adeptly. You have grown in unison and faith according to your investment in the Gospel, and the future has been reconciled by your comprehension of God's Will. Today, we celebrate the accomplishments of those who venerate My Immaculate Heart in a special way. I have spoken about the facility of prayer, its power and purpose in the conversion of men. It is clear that My messages are a clarion to induce you to kneel, to clutch Jesus' hands with your hearts, and search for peace and justice according to your life's stations. There have been multitudes of innovative people who have lived before you, and others still among you who are inspiring humanity in issues of rapprochement. There have been teachers and prophets about whom I have spoken, and researchers, doctors, and excellent men and women who have advanced the world in their own peculiar ways. God even gave you the insights of a young man who discovered the cure for cancer, the long-dreaded scourge that has caused the death of so many people. Tragically, he was killed in his mother's womb on September 11, 1974 by the mortal sin of abortion that was legalized in the United States, the son of a legislator in a nation that would have advanced his research of eradicating this ruthless disease. It would have taken one Hail Mary by someone who never prayed the Rosary to save his life. This is the power of the Mysteries, My children. I have come to remind you what might have been, what could have grown from a country of genius had opportunity and righteousness been given venue. The senseless scourge of infanticide has killed countless healers and peacemakers who would have transformed the Earth and spared the suffering of so many who have died and the grief of their mourners. The Holy Rosary could have stopped every war and attack on innocent lives from bunkers to jetliners, and the surface of the Earth would have remained undefiled. It is not that another soul in the world will not discover the cure for any disease known to man. Let us pray with fervency that a second researcher will be chosen to reveal the discovery of the cures for cancer and diabetes, and all crippling and morbid sicknesses. It is possible to reverse the tides of time and make known to the nations that prayer to the Father is reciprocally rewarding. If you respond to His call of the heart, you will understand the necessity of entering a unique relationship with Him whereby you bless His creatures and comply with the Commandments. The heart will take you on a journey beyond the distractions that inhibit your sight of the origin of all things, permitting you to witness the confession that exiled the first beings. This call defies the mortal ages and makes men young again by certain benevolence, in everything graceful and true, and by every conceivable inclining. There can be no separating the heart from conversion because its beginning is found there, and its power is generated from within. Jesus' Sacred Heart makes Him the greatest teacher, the most compassionate and forgiving, and the most feeling in matters of human sorrow. He calls you to embrace the Cross with the heart and trust that everything He has revealed to you comes from the Father in Heaven. My prayer today is that you will also pray. These are My words from years ago, and they are applicable now. With the benedictions of Paradise, I offer My encouragement to strengthen your faith and heighten your hopes. Please seek all who comprehend the exigency of human spiritual conversion to help evangelize the Holy Gospel to the lost, to those in trouble, the throngs who are raging against organized religion, and the millions worldwide who lie in-extremis.

My Special son, there is no question that you know of the salvific value of the Holy Rosary because this is how we met. You called Me saying 'Hail Mary!' and I appeared. It has been for the betterment of the United States and the larger world. You sought a flicker of light in the darkness, and the Lord God gave you the Morning Star. Thank you for your faith, your true faith and loyalty to Me and all whose intercession you have requisitioned. Saint Joseph helps you perform the carpentry in your home and intercedes as the Patriarch of the Holy Family in ways that evoke the virtues of Salvation in the hearts of your brothers and sisters. You are capable of knowing where evil lurks and goodness lives. You can distinguish between Jesus' Truth and Satan's lies. Your conscience allows you to discern the false prophets from the real ones who are capable of fostering your understanding of the Kingdom of God. Even as you are wise in the redemption of man, there are some things that you are too young to know, and this is why I am teaching you. In ancient times, a prophet was also known as a mantis, and it was necessary to decipher his message and presume by whom he was sent. In later centuries, you have proof who is sent by the Spirit of God. Conditions and nomenclatures have changed, some to benefit the Earth, while others have deceived many. Anyone that comes to your door evangelizing Jesus' Sacrifice and Glorious Resurrection who states that he does not believe in the Most Blessed Trinity is an imposter. He is not representing Christianity. He is a false apostle and fraudulent mantis. What causes such men to behave in ways contrary to the Gospel? The same thing that makes men criticize the Roman Catholic Church. Their self-will stands in direct contradiction to the Kingdom for which you are destined. These creatures feel autonomous from the Apostolic Church and practice their own prejudices and raw ignorance. Most, however, are randomly meanspirited, such as when a pit bull attacks a child or a cat devours a bird. You must remember that the instinct about which we speak cannot be completely separated from discernment. Some men are vindictive even to their own demise. One would think that they would run for cover when they see the well-grounded faith of Roman Catholics. However, in their blindness, they stand firm because they are deluded by their error. When Saint Francis spoke to the wolf to leave the people alone, he was appealing to its capacity for discernment. Its instinct was to kill and devour, but it had the ability to choose another way. Praise is the greatest motivator. I have heard you say this before. To whomever you direct the love in your heart, the most beneficent results will be achieved. Some things occur by physics and happenstance, others by instances where the environment such as gravity affects creatures with living cells. Without the need for nourishment, would wolves attack their prey despite their ability of discernment? Their struggle for survival is like weight holding them down, playing a role in their sustenance. Your spiritual faith is comprised of everything that serves to inform you that you are human, that you were created by a higher being, that you have definitive needs set in corporeal and aesthetic contexts, that you have the faculties to judge right from wrong and good from bad, and that you are fully self-confident that there is something outside the world that nullifies the effects of death. If you thought that you would never die, would faith have any purpose? How would you define it? How can you overcome something if you do not know it is there? I am the Immaculate Conception, and I was born without sin. I am perfectly human, but it must be made clear that I am not part of the Most Blessed Trinity. Further, there has never been a hint of concupiscence in Me. Like Jesus, My life on Earth was spiritual perfection in a sinless organic frame. I have spoken about hunger today, but what kind of hunger? Spiritual hunger. This is how you judge matters of Earth before the tapestry of Heaven, avoid temptation, make sacrifices, commit to fasting, remain chaste, and offer God anything that would tempt you in physical ways. Always believe anyone who says that I had no concupiscence. Discernment should precede your actions; it makes straight the path to faith and keeps you aligned with the Will of God. I was born to My parents for no other reason than to give birth to humanity's Savior. I am aware of the temptations you face without having fallen to them. This is why I understand the failures of My children. How could Jesus have been tempted by Satan if He did not have the capacity to be tempted? Being born in the flesh does not imply any lack of knowledge about the effects of being human. Every sinner will eventually die, but God sent Jesus to lay down His life as a sinless Man. I never died because I am not the Redeeming Victim. You will never meet another woman like Me, but there is good news, all will be as pure as Me in Heaven. I have watched the benefits of holiness through the Lord's Hosts of Angels, Jesus' Joyful Nativity, His Sorrowful Passion and Crucifixion, and His Glorious Resurrection. Yes, the Most Holy Rosary is the Feast that you celebrate today, and it is through the Sacred Mysteries that you become like Jesus. Thank you for praying with Me and for safeguarding your brother. You will be rewarded a thousand times over for taking such good care of him."

Sunday, October 14, 2007
St. Autumn Isaacs, Virgin [1373-1402]*
2:56 p.m.

"The Father of the ages loves your souls timelessly and seeks from you the righteousness with which your ancestors exalted Him, whom they lived for during their years of praise and honor. It is not more than you are capable of achieving that is sought from you. Some in America have asked why faith is best expressed through the Church, an organized institution of orthodoxy. The reason is because your sense of Salvation comes from your unity in Jesus; your willingness to coexist for the single cause of natural love subsists in your common faith, and the Truth that has set you free from every sin and deficit comes through the Roman Catholic Church. You pray as one people in Jesus' sacred name, and the Holy Spirit invites you as one Creation to laud the redemption that you have been accorded through His Sorrowful Crucifixion. As I have stated, every semblance of decency you will ever display is a fruit of the Sacred Heart of Jesus; all your good works spring from there, your future and everything you have ever asked from the Lord are procured from your faith in and allegiance to the Messiah of My Womb. Hence, this is why I come seeking your prayers to Heaven and your loyalties to the Father. Whatever else you believe about life, you must accept that you are His people, that you are My children given Me on the day Jesus was Crucified. You are asked to reconcile with one another as sinners and with God, our Maker. Why prayer? Because this is your expression of repentance to Him, seeking His approval of your obedient sacrifices and holiness, recognizing that He has given you life and forgiveness, and remaining true to the Gospel that has been handed down through the ages. It requires a simple heart to defer to Him, only a childlike demeanor to exemplify His Grace. While you are unassuming in your faith, He protects and guides you, and nourishes you with the Manna of Life. You could devote every hour of your lives to His honor, and you would be as productive as His Will induces you to be. His Kingdom is glorified by the way you tend to His sheep, make peace between enemies, clothe the naked, shelter the homeless, heal the diseased, and perfect every other act of goodness that He requires. The Holy Paraclete invites you by scrupulous discretion to emulate Jesus, to rid the Earth of every form of evil, peril, and blasphemy. If you heed My messages, you will succeed in miraculous ways. Thank you for responding to My call. My dear Special son, how awesome is this year of our Lord in which you live! With what grace are you given the Wisdom to reach into the hearts of your lost brothers and sisters and take them to unseen heights of divinity. For what reason do you do this? Because you are the Lord's sacred creature like the Angels and Saints. Your inner-being is manifested from the perfection that has wrought every ameliorative thing into the world, and all the vision, fortitude, power, reason, and patience that will bring a happy conclusion to human life. My Immaculate Heart is touched by your consecration to Me and My Son, and Heaven is exalted by your years of service for the propagation of the Church-Militant in earthly exile.

More close to home, your hours of construction and labor are helping make your dwelling place more amenable for you and your brother. I am deeply sorry that he did not employ better judgement that would have precluded the egregious injury to his back. His effort would have been such a boon to your modernization project. He is embarrassed that this has happened, and he is paying the price for his mistake. He is uncertain whether to enter the hospital and have surgery to suture his torn tissues because he is being inconsistent in taking care of himself. If he does not stop walking across concrete surfaces, this could be a lifelong de-habilitating event from which he will never recover, meaning that he will have to use crutches the rest of his life. He can begin later this week seeing his personal doctor to renew his medication and secure a prognosis. In the olden days, this kind of injury was irreversible because men were required to maintain their chores to feed their families. Since this is not the case with your brother, he stands to benefit from remaining more sedentary. This much he has in his favor. Time alone will heal him if he does not persist in abusing his movements and posture in ways that aggravate his condition. The surgery about which I speak would further lengthen his immobility, so the options must be weighed one against another. For his part, he does not know. The sutures would promote his healing, but he can make a full recovery if he does not continue making the harmful motions of his body. What happened is unfortunate; it was simply an unforeseeable accident. It is one of the most grotesque injuries he could ever suffer. You are not to blame for this injury. That would be an erroneous position for you to take. He is hurt because he did not do what he was asked on February 22, 1991, to live carefully and prayerfully, and remember that he is fragile to Nature. While your compassion is admirable, he appears to be most in need of your patience and assistance. And, he should remember that circumstances for you both are not as they would be for others. Satan is looking for a way to impede your work. By the time your kitchen is finished, he will be healed, dependent upon his actions, and the matter will be pushed into history. You must reprimand your brother later as a means of warning him about maintaining proper protocol to effect swifter healing."

Sunday, October 21, 2007
St. Holta Blue Fair [1413-1456]*
2:59 p.m.

"With good measure and holy orchestrations, I hold your petitions safely in My Immaculate Heart to offer Jesus, knowing that He will respond according to God's Will. My advocacy is His answer, and your deferential reaction is to follow the Holy Spirit in everything you do for the Church. I find joy in acknowledging your perseverance that is untold in generations; so many years have you knelt to pray in My company. No tumult or turmoil can blur your focus from the outcome of life; nothing can distract you from achieving your Christian aspirations. All the temptations of the devil could befall you today, and your intuition will remain on your obligation to the Cross. This is how you love Jesus and hear Me; it is the way you have chosen to finish your lives beneath the sunlight of Easter. Hence, I offer a message of hopefulness and purpose as you sense the dawning of the dominion of Jesus' Love in hearts who have never known Him, and even as you learn more every hour about the unlimited need for God's unreserved discipline. I seek your prayers for the faithful and the unfaithful, for paupers and sufferers, and for little children in the womb and walking the streets. There is no question that you live in a world of spiritual darkness that is much more perilous than the voids of night. It is through your acclamation that the Father's Holy Light brings sanctity to your brothers and sisters and gives them cause to know His Love to the betterment of their future. It is true that if we convince them to pray, they will be like Jesus. He taught humanity to pray by worshiping the Father. This is what we accomplish through our work, to foster your relationship with Jesus and intensify your prayers to God in Heaven. We will implant in your friends the seed of righteousness that will grow their piety and tender their lives to the advancement of peace and good will. Why must we do this? Because unborn children are being killed by evulsion from their mothers. Civil war and unrest plague the hemispheres. Neighbors and families disagree about the meaning of life and their responsibility of sharing the world's wealth. We do this because we want them to embrace Jesus on the Cross and His Paschal Resurrection. My Special son, this message is brief because I am with you in other ways, offering guidance and strength. Much good is being done where you stand, sit, kneel, pray, rest, and deliberate. Upon this holy location in the world, the Lord is manifesting the conversion of His lost children through My messages because He needs them. You are personifying the instrumentation of righteousness that Saint Francis hailed for the purification of the Earth, for the enlightenment of races about the truth of Divine Love, and for the transformation of mere humans into spiritual giants while you wait for Jesus' return. It is untrue that I unduly dote upon you for your brothers and sisters to hear. They should be as blessed to possess your spiritual insights. Nothing is impossible with God. He will touch them before their lives are through. We have built a formidable arsenal. Before God completes His mission with you and your brother, all your adversaries will say 'I am ashamed of myself, and I take the blame.' This is not vengeance by the Holy Spirit, it is gentle apprising. Remember that Jesus tells sinners that the human will provides the ability to welcome their Salvation. No one has ever been dragged into Heaven against their volition. They seek redemption because they foresee their place alongside the Saints through their personal sacrifices and their awareness of the Judgement of God. If left to His chosen preference, there would be no one condemned. Individual sinners make this choice because they decide that they are unworthy, that they have shunned His Grace so egregiously that they cannot accept His charitable Absolution. We are working to persuade them that any sacrifice for Jesus is worthy, every holy intention, anything that lends to their exculpation before the Christian Cross of human deliverance. There are wide and varying solutions to life's issues, but they must not come at the expense of human morality or the diminution of someone else's dignity. This is what the conversion of the heart is about, showing lost sinners that there are false competitions in the secular void that turn people against others. What divides nations and separates enemies are unnecessary comparisons drawn by rogue secularists inebriated with power. Jesus calls humanity to be one beneath the Cross and through Him in all ways spiritual. He forfeited His life to prove it! I implore you to remember that He stands beside you, and the Holy Spirit lives within you to restore the unity that is lost to unmitigated sin. There is no doubt that you understand, that you have an appreciation for the fullest reconciliation between God and humanity and the reception of anything that eases divisiveness between your brothers and sisters in Jesus' Sacred Heart. Always prosper the Light of Feasts that is celebrated by the Church during the Liturgical Year. We are effectuating everything we planned in February 1991."

Sunday, October 28, 2007
St. Pella Kohlbecker [1774-1829]*
2:14 p.m.

"We pray to reprise the civility that was once part of America's mainstream conscience, and redress the portly greed that has brought such poverty upon those with little means. My children, please do not live as though there are no solutions to these things. We are making a difference in ways that are seen and unseen; we inspire invisible forces for good to be rooted in the hearts of proper men, and we shall prevail in the achievements for which you have prayed during your years of heartaches. My entrustment as your Mother is not only to nurture and teach you about holiness and social justice, but to ensure that you know the consequences, good and bad, that accompany the human response according to the poise of the individual. We strive to open and motivate the hearts of your brothers and sisters, many who have only cadavers where they should have living consciences. While prayer is the key to holiness, it is enhanced by your trust that God hears you, and that you are to believe that change for the better is occurring beyond your sights. Please remember that it is by faith that you walk. I have high hopes not only that humanity is being brought to the Holy Cross, but that each person will recognize Jesus' Sacrifice as the redemptive grace that has enlightened their thoughts about the conditions on Earth and making peace with the Father before they die. Why should we entertain any positions to the contrary? What would be the reason for surrendering the dreams you have spent years to build? Upon the foundation of Christianity is the repentance of your lives constructed, and you must believe that your heart stands there, shining like the sapphires of Heaven. The reluctance of your enemies has no effect on the outcome of the universe because their purposes are riddled by irrelevance; such is the epitaph of the secular world. Christian hope is the most powerful force known to man, next to faith itself. This is because you are given it through the Kingdom of Love, the Father of Jesus who is the Patriarch of Truth. What about this power? How do wise counselors and gentlemen speak of such prophetic genius without being overcome with righteous emotion? The fact is that they do not, and this is evidence that the Holy Spirit is touching them. Today, I have given you a vision for the future that is not unlike that spoken about by Saint Paul in his letters, to all who hear and understand the truthfulness of the intervention of the Lord in your earthly domain. When speaking of the Pauline Epistles, I have said that they are from a man who once persecuted the Church for which he died. Paul is exemplary of the conversion that must come to all men and women, that should flush from the world all nonbelievers so the Wisdom of Heaven glows into every dark corner. Lost sinners must choose for once in their lives something righteous that is based on the Lord's Triune perfection that they cannot see with their eyes. It is an envisionment whose source is the heart, the open field where God plants the seed of holiness for the cultivation of the globe. It is true that every person must become Christian to be in the constant Grace of God, and that the collective society of these souls composes the Mystical Body of Christ. This is why I have come to you, My children. I am through My messages attempting to build-up Jesus' Mystical Body so the world will be reunited in and through Him. Whatever barriers divide you, never mind differences in language and dialect, Jesus hears you quite well through the intentions of the heart. Prayers for peace and healing are universal; they are directed toward the High Priest who speaks intelligibly with every created being. Inviting Heaven to engulf the Earth with purity is not something particular to any single nation. Hence, I appear in America to call you to a higher decency and request from you your finest effort in looking beyond the harshness of the years and nautical miles from distant shores. My prayer for My children is that you will remain in Jesus to enhance the purpose of your birth because you were created out of Love, and you must return to this Love with your baptismal garments unstained.

My Special son, what an appropriate occasion to speak on the anniversary of your brother's Confirmation into the Church. And, you see from abroad that Pope Benedict XVI has made today a cause of celebration by the beatification of an impressive number of Martyrs. This has been an historical day for the Church throughout the centuries for blessings to humanity from the Throne of the Father. I urge you to remember the resplendent papacy of Pope John XXIII. With all that has been given you, through everything you have suffered and brought to the Altar in sacrificial gifts, you have always been pleasing to Jesus. You and your brother have been oriented to God and willing to sustain the brashness that discomforts messengers and seers. Many things have run their course, and others prepare for the future. Even more, your prayers for those who have died with the Lord's proviso have yielded untold numbers of new Saints in Heaven, freed from their suffering in Purgatory. You are instructing your brethren about the wishes of Christ through your manuscripts and personal witness about Me, the Queen of Love. All this has happened because you have complied with the commendation of the Holy Spirit in your heart to the Salvation of the contrite. You often speak of finest hours and noble causes, and rightly so. I refer to the manifest beauties that live in your heart and bloom into the material world like gladiolas, like the expansion of grace in uncontrollable redundancy to people who are broken and alone. My accomplishments in 2,000 years pale to that achieved by My messengers because you operate on faith and deference. Do you remember when Jesus said 'Go, your faith has been your healing?' This is how He mends the spirits of the anguished. He abates their suffering because people like you pray and trust that His compassion is greater than His Justice. Thank you for your generosity. I shall speak to you next month when we remember all who have died."

Sunday, November 4, 2007
St. Evan Chesterfield, Martyr [1634-1691]*
3:04 p.m.

"Bringing wondrous piety to bear against the unholiness of the wretched, we lift our prayers to the Father for His lost children; not forsaken, but wandering aimlessly in the world's secular wilderness. With My blessings, I shall accomplish My goal as unifier of Christians because My empathy has brought wisdom to the faithful. Today, you call forth the presence of all the Saints known and unknown, remembering them to God, enlisting their intercession. By marshaling the forces of goodness against the evil assaulting your faith, you conquer the enemies of the Cross. I urge you to welcome the destiny that the Holy Spirit has given humanity since Jesus' Crucifixion liberated your souls on Good Friday. He is your Savior and the only one to die for the deliverance of man. It is by His Blood that you are forgiven. Jesus is your final pardon before the Father. Whatever you do for Him; however you choose to elevate His Kingdom and sanctify His flock, you do this for the Glory of Love. You approach Jesus in silent prayer, and He hears you. By taking the Gospel to the masses, you perpetuate the message of sacrificial life. By sharing your writings and oratories extolling the Cross, your word-smithing stirs the incandescence of the heart. I help define the virtuousness that informs your faith in the ways of Christianity, and I offer Jesus your lives while you magnify His Kingdom. What must you say to America? Would you travel from hilltop to valley and reconfirm that the United States is lost in the lust and materialism that I have denounced so many times? Do your young people need to hear again the call of holiness, purity of the heart, chastity and virginity? What makes them holy comes not only from our prayers and the Lord's response, but your example of the words of Jesus in your day. Indeed, by telling them that they are your spiritual heirs; by reminding them that they shall become the keepers of the faith and custodians of long-hailed traditions of loyalty to Jesus, are you not speaking for God Himself? Since the Christ lives in you, it is imperative that you urge them to exalt Him in your stead once your generation has expired. My Special and Chosen sons, with the Father's blessing, I speak in this sanctuary to the charity of your spirits, to the thoughts and acts of selflessness that you are giving Him. These are the ages to which I have dedicated My Queenship, calling with heartfelt anticipation on My children upon whom the Lord has shed His Light. I am your Immaculate Mother who lived among the Apostles during Jesus' earthly time, and I remain with you today through His Spirit. I beg you to never concede a sinner to the netherworld; know that God will find the lost through the depths of your faith. The lame shall walk, the depressed will dance, the dead will rise from their crypts of oblivion, and everyone will see the Living Christ through your dedication to their conversion and love for the Cross. Presidents will speak of the mysticism by which you have been led. Writers, poets, and singers will dream about your sacred charisma and describe the beauty that breathes in your hearts. Strangers you have not met will walk miles to your door; the obstinate will be humbled, and child-bearing mothers will petition the American people to annul the laws of abortion. You must believe this, My children. You must know that the Earth is in transition, that inequalities will be negated, that poverty and disease will become obsolete, and that atheistic intellectuals are at this moment on the road to Damascus. The Lord will give you these miracles, My sons. Dearly, I pray that you will live in joyful expectation that the Good News will be received by those who do not accept Jesus as wholly as I took you as My adopted children on the day He died. Please do not dwell on their failures, mistakes and weaknesses, but on the awesome progress they have made. I will speak more about these lofty ideals, tolling bells, the emancipation of hearts, and everything majestic that places the potential they possess alongside the dignity of Christ in this new century."

Sunday, November 11, 2007
St. Phoebe Dutchess, Virgin [1557-1604]*
2:33 p.m.

"My dear faithful children, we pray for miraculous solutions to man-made problems, ones that will heal and reunite societies composed of fragmented souls. It is with more than daring that you face-down the malevolent forces that attempt to demean the proprieties in your hearts; you employ courage that is fashioned for you by Jesus which you exert with apostolic zeal. I bring Wisdom to fight against humanity's ignorance. I offer unparalleled evidence to bolster your trust that the Lord has come looking for you, and I pledge that in the fullness of time, your lives in the Cross will be repaid. You do nothing for Heaven in vain. Even though you may not see the fruits of your labors firsthand, they are there; they are forged into being by your prayers, faith, and good works. These are exhausting ages because you must live every hour for Christianity in the face of the Earth's opposition to the Church. The errors of moral relativism and secular humanism comprise one of the two-headed beasts that are preying upon your holiness. I urge you to defy their skewed perception of social equality and justice, for they have nothing to do with either one. All are equal beneath the Cross and before God's eyes. We pray for the reproaching of those who have beliefs that are contrary to the teachings of the Catholic Church, who stand in contradiction to the Sacred Mysteries, and who disobey the mandates of the Gospels. God did not create man to suffer; you were born to glorify Him. I have told you that God enlivens Creation so He can boast with righteousness that you reflect

His Divine Light, and it is for this reason that He sends Me speaking to you. Today, we pray for those who spurn His Will, that they be repatriated along with your brothers and sisters who have passed into the Promised Land. This should evince from you heraldic thoughts that you have something to strive for that is greater than life or the death to which you will be subjected. Everyone has a given mission. Mine is to counsel and console you, to intercede on your behalf, offer Jesus' hands in comfort and brotherhood, and lead you to Mount Calvary. Your years are fundamental sequences that help open your hearts to the Holy Spirit, repent of your transgressive ways, amend your actions, accept the sacrifices that God asks you to endure, love your enemies, and appeal to Jesus for forgiveness, refreshment, peace, and the bountifulness of life.

This is another beautiful autumn day, My Special and Chosen ones. It is fair, clement, and inviting as your motivations should be. You pray with intense compassion during the Holy Sacrifice of the Mass for the conversion of the lost with the assistance of the Archangels. These petitions are sound ways to amplify the intentions of God because Creation is healed by your desire to be with Him. Yes, leaders of other religions are converting to Roman Catholicism because they realize that the Seven Sacraments of the Original Catholic and Apostolic Church will never die; they have always been the defining essence of Jesus' life, death, and Resurrection by which you are healed, uplifted, and reconfigured. These converts know that the Catholic Church will never yield to secularists who are calling for the redefinition of the family in defiance of the sacramental expression of procreative love. You are seeing the beginning of these conversions because Catholics supply the example they need, and the Holy Rosary is having illustrative effects in changing hearts and minds. As you pray, your petitions provide the framework of light that gives new sight to those about whom I speak. The older you grow, the better you can see eternal redemption as a process that leads to the unbridled jubilation you will have in the Salvation Jesus has won for you. This is why you must praise and glorify Him, and lift Him up before nonbelievers. It is the reason I am speaking to you. He dispatches Me to remind the world that He will return in Glory, along with the Angels and Saints. My Special son, it is heartening that you walk with majesty and integrity, and you have not given up on the purification of humanity. After all you have witnessed; after undergoing what seems a lifetime of hope, you have held your confidence that Jesus knows what He is doing. Do you remember that I have at times sought your feelings about matters of faith and morality? Do you see the evocativeness of your brother's letter to his friends? From their place in the Middle East, they encounter what your brother has been saying. They see broken lives, victims, paupers, orphaned children, and refugees. Human life is never easy; you have felt this in recent months. However, it is not inevitable that it be intolerable, and you know when paranormal situations occur. There is intense desperation in the lives of the Koreans for whom you pray, and they will be freed. God will do this because you have asked Jesus to intervene. They will enjoy the liberties you have known. Please be more patient with yourself and lenient toward matters in which you may be lacking or failing. You are one of God's messengers, not unlike those who have preceded you, and I ask that you never downplay your relevance. Jesus commands that you recognize your own righteousness because it is His gift accorded to His Kingdom by the commitment of your heart. Thank you for the beauty that makes Me weep in joy. The Lord pronounces justice among men. Bishop Lucas admires you for deferring to his episcopate, offering your prayers, and defending humanity's unborn innocents. You will be remembered as a deliverer of truth and practitioner of the faith. Please pray for the intercession of Saint Phoebe when you feel spiritual darkness."

Monday, November 12, 2007
Visitation of the Archangel Saint Gabriel
7:51 p.m.

I had returned home earlier in the evening and was resting in my prayer room before my altar reciting the Rosary when the Archangel Gabriel appeared in the Glory of God which radiated throughout the room. My entire being was startled with rapturous wonderment at his presence, and a great anticipation consumed my soul. I wondered what his appearance could mean, then he began to speak.

"Hail, full of valor! The Lord is with you! The Lord be with you! *(I responded, 'And also with you.')* May the Lord bless you in the Name of the Father, and the Son, and the Holy Spirit. Amen. On this sublime occasion, I the Archangel Gabriel, who broached the news of the Salvation of man, have come in peace and the Glory of Christ with the strength and purity of Divine Love, and with the superlative dignity of Jesus' Baptism, the courage of His Passion, the sorrowful agony of His Crucifixion, and the glorious paschality of His Resurrection from the Tomb in which you, God's chosen one, have been raised. This night, twelve November, twenty o' seven, given by the Providence of the Father, is threefold: to give you Wisdom, encourage your strength, and seek your Fiat. We do this in emulation of the Handmaiden of the Lord whose Fiat has begotten the Redemption of human people. Thus, as I have said, the Salutation is joined by man. *'Hail Mary, full of Grace, the Lord is with Thee. Blessed art Thou among women, and blessed is the Fruit of Thy Womb, Jesus. Holy Mary, Mother of God, pray for sinners now and at the hour of their death. Amen.'* We ask that you be at peace, that the Holy Spirit may engulf and enrich you, comfort you, and console you so your heart will be light and empathetic for the millions who support the grand mission of the conversion of men. Greetings from the Almighty Father, and in this silence comes His blessing."

(Saint Gabriel became silent and bowed his head, and an overwhelming sense of tranquility enveloped my soul. My being was caressed by great grace for an extended period of time.)

"Now, to the Wisdom. Dear Special one, you are living a mortal life that is circumscribed by your Eternal Life. All the blessings and dreams, and penchants and drives, and energy that you have captivated in your heart are being realized through your faith beyond the realms of this world. You live simultaneously on the Earth and in Heaven, and you are given Grace because you are the Lord's beautiful creature. When the Son of Man was crucified, He said 'It is finished,' and He wrote the final chapters of world history and the opening resolve of Eternity that shall last without end. In this Wisdom—It is finished—you are given everything for which you have hoped. You will live this life; every hope will come true; every act, every pursuit, every enriching dogma and doctrine for the complete, utter, and profound sanctification of humanity. All these things are happening now. Yet, you do not remember because you are in mortality. The veil is your gift. You are given the Truth and Wisdom of the Lord one day at a time; for if not, you surely would falter in understanding your mission with exiled creatures. Let not your heart be troubled; this is your Wisdom. You will record this date at a later time as a juncture in which you ultimately learned to embrace complete peace in your heart. At your young age, you are given many gifts and are called to few sacrifices. The intensity of your labors for the Mother of God is unprecedented. She calls you blessed! And, in the Divine Wisdom of the Lord, you cannot fail. *Maximus! William the Conqueror!* Be healed of all that darkens your spirit. Be in love with the destiny you are helping humanity yearn. Resolve to let nothing steal your peace away! O' how beautiful you are! You live beyond parameters; you carry a pontificate upon your shoulders that is worthy of John Paul the Great. You are proceeding his mission and enlivening his flock to journey toward his successor, the Vicar of Christ, Pope Benedict XVI, the year in which you live. This is Wisdom; this is the teaching that the Lord sends you through me, the Archangel Gabriel. I have seen the Lord. I have been to the mountaintop. I have touched His Face and felt the warmth of His Light; and it is beaming upon and within you not light-years away, but by the Grace, the Wisdom, and the power of the Holy Spirit. You are called to reside in this conviction, in this consecration, and in this knowledge. You have never wavered in your belief that Our Lady is speaking to you. This is Wisdom, and this is strength. And, in the simultaneous lives in which you are living, and the only one that you can now see, you are blessing the broken, feeding the hungry, administering the Works of Mercy, spreading good will, flooding the Earth with kindness, encouragement, and enlightenment from this shrine, this monument to Holy Christendom in which you have been poised for the Lord. You are one with Christ!

Second is vision and strength. And, with what vision and strength should you approach the dawning years? You are obedient to the Holy Paraclete in every extent. Your pursuit of what made the Saints dance is the clemency that the Lord is offering your enemies. November the twelfth, twenty o' seven is not a day to divide; it is not a means of moving your intercession with the Holy Mother in any new direction, but to seamlessly unite it with the bygone past and continue reaffirming it to the last day of the world. You will see why this day; you will see why with the blessings and greetings of all your predecessors and forbears and the loving blessing of Father Lumen. And, you will wax nostalgic about his glorious blessing! The benediction of the Lord is upon you! And, in this comes your Fiat."

The Archangel Gabriel then made God's request for the ultimate act of my faith and the sacrifice that would testify before the heavens that my devotion to Jesus Christ, Our Lady and the salvation of humanity could never be struck down. It was a test with spiritual and material components, a reality that I was asked to accept that would otherwise have permanently paralyzed the very nature of earthly men. I could see the heart of Abraham upon being asked to sacrifice his son, Isaac. I could see Our Lady's Immaculate Heart upon knowing Jesus was going to be crucified. I peered across Jesus' brow in the Garden as He faced the terrible onslaught of His Passion and Death. And, I realized with transcending peace that saying 'yes' was the only path to Heaven for the lost millions who would never find their way to Paradise. Warriors are called to battlefields. Hearts are thrown into the breach. Heroes engage the enemies of beatific destiny. And, Saints are raised to Victory! Be it done unto me according to your word. 'Yes' rings throughout my being. A child of God answers the call. A life now exists by the strength of the Father and the Blood of the Son, and animated by the Light of the Holy Spirit to be launched against the powers of this darkened world.

"The reason this is brought is because it is the final and ultimate opening to the sacrifices in strength and power and Grace. Remembering as I have said that you are living simultaneous lives both here and in Heaven, you can dream and it will happen; you can wish and it will come. Jesus will not fail you. Should this life give you such happiness for no reason? Providence comes to you! You may share a record of my appearance as it must be recorded in the history of man. Does the Lord seek in vain your happiness? Does this Glory go untold? Surely these rhetorical questions have touched the ears of those who are one with the Messiah. How blessed are we! The Hosts of Heaven, the Archangels, the Orders of Angels, Saint Augustine's Order of Loves. How blessed is the Communion of Saints to receive such Providence in the world they left behind, tendered to such caring hands and obedient wills, and aspiring hearts to towering heights, and people of sentiment!

Our chosen one, you are now with your brother working on a tremendously powerful and important text; the one subsequent to your current work will bring you to date, and your life will change. The Lord seeks most in you humility because it is there. He thanks you for encouraging His prelate, Bishop Lucas. Upon your Apostolate has he founded his Episcopate. Nay, I repeat. Upon your Apostolate has he founded his Episcopate. In the sequence of time, you are his Christ. A descendent of the Apostles comes to you, not unlike Saint Francis, a mystical, charismatic lay person with such vision, with such heart and dedication to Our Lady, to the Most Blessed Trinity, to human Salvation, and to the Light of Heaven. And, you are blessed beyond any reason that you might know at this hour. You are blessed! Do you recognize and realize with what awesome faith and trust you have received me here? Do you realize this gift to the world you have accorded humanity? *(I responded, 'I will do the Father's Will. I have believed, I do believe, and I will continue to believe.')* Then, men shall be saved! Then, men shall be saved! And, so it is that it has come to this. I will speak to you again before you come to Heaven. I will not remove the Light that is cast upon your soul that you reflect into the depths of the darkness of the Earth. I will let no harm befall you. I will call upon my brother, the great Archangel Saint Michael, and he will lend to you the invincible power of the Sword and the Cross. Make this mandate your mission! Give of your heart to yourself; be gentle with yourself. Our Lady begs you to be gentle with yourself. Be righteously proud of your service to this world and to humanity, and to the Father, to Jesus, and to the Spirit of Love. I depart, but I do not leave! And, I bless you in the Name of the Father, and the Son, and the Holy Spirit. Amen."

Sunday, November 18, 2007
Saint Janis Meliaceae, Mystic [AD 716-780]*
2:20 p.m.

"My dear children, there are times when I pause to share My feelings about your North American nation, its culture, and your battles against the secularism that has been such a curse to so many lost sinners. I will speak about the contrast between goodness and evil that men see as the difference between the broadness of day and the pitch of night. You live in a country of freedoms, for sure, but you are also subject to a patrician form of social elitism that excludes commoners from sharing the assets of your coffers. As Christians, you not only observe these types of discrimination, you must do something about them. All peoples everywhere must comprehend the concept of morality from the origin of human life, the God of your fathers, who sent Christ Jesus to redeem you. It is through Him that your belief system must be founded. One thought by Jesus is greater than the entire deposit of human intelligence. His hand raised in blessing creates more force than all the labors of mankind in the whole of history, including the construction of every skyscraper, bridge, road, tower, warship, and space machine. Jesus has intercepted your inordinate plunge into the darkness by the Cross, and your daily prayers are your application of esteemed grace that has saved you. You stipulate to a moral code that is more concisely affirmed than any other kind of behavioral parameter. Thus, you cannot conceal your secrets in your hearts like a strongbox because it is the first place that the Holy Spirit looks. Amid the bewildering sea of opposition, your Christian faith must survive. You will learn at the end of time that it has always been the singular path to true human genius. There is only one melody in the world, and it has taken millions of people through innumerable generations to sing it. It is heard in the tenor of sacrifice, and the Cross is the key that opens the door to Eternal Salvation. Civilizations for centuries have lived by unwritten social contracts, but the Holy Gospel is the record of the Father's Will for your personal, familial, and public intuition. This is why I have always called you to renounce the blustery, absurdly immature acts of secular nonbelievers who have their own revisionist retrospect. It is an unspeakable tragedy that American moral values are being devoured by neopaganism—a cold, strange, calculating, upheaval against the spirit of decency. To exacerbate this matter, Christians who defend moral Truth are often accused by the secular left of radical intolerance. Secular psychologists have created an entire discipline categorizing humanity's high crimes and misdemeanors, but they have never once drawn the connection between antisocial behavior and the Fall of Adam. Secularism habitually crosses and blurs the lines of acceptable conduct and identity, fostering an agendum of liberalism that has seeped its way into the Church. As a result, Satan has left in his tracks a world that is littered with shivering skeletons, trails of deceit, and unforeseen tragic endings. Once your conscience has been tapped by the Spirit of the Roman Catholic Church, you realize that something is amiss, the feeling you have when you see a horse laying on its side or a dog barking at a statue. The human soul knows when things have gone wrong because the Spirit of God has led you to believe in everything right. This is how your faith grows from the size of a mustard seed to the highest boughs of a national forest. You become more mature and know what the Lord expects from you; it is the same reason your elementary school room and childhood home seem so small when you return to them as an adult. This holiness gives you an orchestral posture with which you play-out the remaining days of your lives with purpose. Turn to the Church; heed the edicts of the Pontiff in Rome, and you will know what Heaven expects from you. Jesus has deposited His entire Resurrection speech in the hands of the Holy See, but it is embargoed until humanity's hearts are opened wide enough to listen. Abolishment, appraisal, durability, turbulence, disquietude, revolution, conflict escalation, temerity, and lechery—all these things matter in your examination of mortal life. And, promises of grander magnanimity can only be believed when the human conscience is predisposed to hear them.

My children, the citizens of the United States have become disillusioned by the dilapidated morality of your most notable public spokesmen. Do you realize what America's national social-sphere looks like when seen by intelligent eyes? While ordinary people seek lives of refreshment, ventilation and exoneration, their future seems instead lost beneath the wreath-laden depths of their broken hopes and dreams. And, the gluttony of your democratic leaders has caused them to be stricken numb from their ulcerated craws. They have a proneness to vice, sloth, and catastrophic global destruction. They boast about a proverbial city on a hill that stands shimmering and never dulls, but your country has never been plagued by as much indecency as it practices today. Truly, it is being glossed-over with brainless political oratory, academic palaver, superficial comparisons, unprovided largesse, misplaced interpretations, and misspoken vows. The American people have contracted a pathogen whose etiology is the atheistic tactics of their leaders. It seems as though Western capitalism cannot survive on its own without selfish, claim-staking venturism. Your financial crises will abate once you begin to hear of such concepts as world-working and the Americonomy, but these will not arise until there has been a total breakdown of your patriotic isolationism. Surely your bellies are full of being the consumers and braggarts of the temporal world. Your unremorseful surfeit has placed you last in the line of souls whom the Lord calls His most benevolent creatures. My message today is one of forewarning. Go and make peace with God and look into the future. Most people prefer a surface of life that is millpond smooth, glazed, clean, and still. Christianity will deliver you to this peace; even though your faith is not optical, it is nonetheless that farseeing. Walk boldly in the night and rescue your muffled dreams! There is still hope that your democratic experience can yield holier results than it has before now. Your finesse in the arts of spiritual love must become your new way of life because your freedom to pursue it is ageless.

My Special one, I come to speak about your mission, and you may reveal to humanity whatever you deem appropriate. You gave God in Heaven your fiat on February 22, 1991, and this is the day He asked Me to discuss the gifts that you have manifested, the conversion of sinners, the release of tens of thousands from Purgatory, the healing of the sick, and the peacemaking that you have accorded the Earth by your compliance. I will tell you about God the Father, the Patriarch of all created things. All paternity begins in God. He is its formation. In order for Jesus to come to Earth at Bethlehem as the Father Incarnate, His only Son, it is necessary that the Father be patriarchal. When you spoke with the Archangel Gabriel, you told him that you would make-up for your brothers' failings in much the same way that Saint Paul spoke of ullage. You have seen the slow attempt by rogue theologians to emasculate the

Catholic Church and humanity's perception of God. In other words, ecclesial heretics have tried to neutralize His sovereignty as Patriarch of Creation and the Church. You know from the Catechism that the Blessed Trinity is this same Patriarch in Three Persons. The Son is the Father Incarnate, and the Holy Spirit is the Wisdom of the Father. With what profound obedience you and your brother have consented to personify this Triune Deity! You have been called as have other Marian messengers to evangelize the Father as Patriarch, and you must believe that He tends toward excelling the advantages that reaffirm His paternity. Do you see that you have comforted Him, knowing that His disciples are upholding His Paternal Truth? This is His way of spearheading the Divine Kingdom that lauds His name. Just in recent weeks, you brought Him to shower rains on parched fields that had not seen moisture in months. Thousands of paupers were saved from death by thirst. And, their soil was soaked, their crops grew, and their children thrived. Can you see the enceinte moments bearing your faith and God's actions? My Special son, you have written the strains of some of the most eloquent wisdom known to man, and it is your gift to the world. You have chosen to participate beside the Son of Man to sow the Earth with the Word of Truth, and this is the blessing of your faith. It is the same whenever I touch My children's hearts. You have helped wash clean the inequity of humankind's faults and transfer impulses into lofty speeches glorifying the Father who waited so long to place them on their speakers' lips. Now, you welcome further self-denial. This is priceless, even more prescient than you have known because it extends in your time the ability of God to feel His Kingdom bending toward Him. While it appears drawn-out to you, it is eternal in His eyes. You are given burdens to lift like the suffering of the Saints, employed throughout the centuries by giants among men, at least those who were healthy enough to endure it. This is what helped the Apostles remain strong and the Saints who wished for more meaningful ways to pray. The force of misguided humanity to desecrate the Church is being defeated by sacrifices known to Jesus and the Father. And, this is why My messengers are praying today. How can you be sufficiently thanked? Six days after you spoke to Saint Gabriel, as long as it took God to finish the world, you offered another gift to Jesus. How strong and commanding you are, how filled with vision! True Christians suffer for the Lord's Kingdom because they see that it purifies the human spirit. My child, you know that this is about the sanctification of humanity, the conversion of the heart; and it is about obedience and clarity, providence, and pealing the sounds of Glory to the republics. You are embracing a valiant invincibility and disdain for evil acts. The purpose of your petitions is to unify the world, and they will. And, they are about committing and submitting humanity to the Grace by which they are redeemed. Prayer is a deeply meditative state that leads to absolution for those about whom I speak. All to the Father's Glory! All to His Patriarchal Spirit overcoming the Earth! You have learned about the path of your works and deeds on behalf of the redemption of men."

Sunday, November 25, 2007
Our Lord Jesus Christ the King
2:44 p.m.

"You surely see that you are worth the price paid for your redemption, that Jesus' Crucifixion reveals that you have become one with the Father through Him, that you have the potential to forfeit the prowesses of the Earth and reside in the favor of the Creator who fashioned it. My children, with what grand joy does My Immaculate Heart overflow with appreciation for you! Your celebration of Jesus Christ the King witnesses that you are precious to Heaven and present with the Angels and Saints through your faith. God has chosen you to share in His Light because you have been true to Him. The Sacred Scriptures say that God knows everything about you, the number of hairs on your head, when you sit and when you stand, and with what adulation you approach your Salvation. As I told you on this date six years ago, the Lord knows precisely where you are located in time, and He is forging every step. Hence, you attest to His kindness by honoring the King. I seek your prayers for those who ignore their absolution in Jesus, the many who would remain fatherless and graceless at the end of time. Their hollowness and obstinance are of the devil because they reject the Kingdom of God, and how unfavorably they will view themselves upon the occasion of their death. Do you remember what you have been taught? What does it profit a man to inherit the world and lose his soul? Why do they gamble their future on the false proposition that God does not exist? The answer is in their hardness of heart, the corruption of their views, and their desire to seek only what is available to them without the sacrifices that make the world a holier place. I have told you about the deceptive element of time more than a half-dozen occasions because it is possible to be so focused on the present that one loses sight of the future. This is what Christ the King was born to teach. He has visited you for your Salvation and the betterment of human life. Your position in exile is more than an experiment in inter-social development, but the making of your spiritual conscience in alignment with the priorities of God. You can do this, My children. Everything about you that lends to greatness comes from Heaven. All your attributes that make you heroic in the eyes of the Father are present in you now. Today, I call you to ponder what Christ the King would ask of you, and what He has dispensed so you may have life to the fullest. The Holy Gospel is your blueprint for sainthood. When you comply with the evangelical tenets and Pauline Epistles, you are tendering your heart and soul to the reason for your deliverance to Glory. Jesus seeks your prayers in humility, servitude, the conveyance of the Grace of Paradise in your conscience, and your willingness to defer to whatever He asks. In return for this, My children, you are reciprocally rejuvenated by Him. You are knighted, ordained, and absolved into holier creatures than you ever thought possible. My Son provides this for you. He protects and defends you, and He spares your feelings before the brashness of the wicked. He stands erect in the darkness with His cloak of guardianship wrapped around your souls, that no harm will befall you. He gives generously His Divine Love to uphold your dignity, that helps you see the horizons of perpetuity in the ordinary aspects of today. Not only that, He lends you His compassionate ear to listen to your pleadings when others stalk you or threaten to bring you harm. My little ones, this is why I urge you to pray with such intensity. Deep inside Jesus' Sacred Heart is a flourishing Salvation that He anticipates with joy to spread over you, even as much as you pine to receive Him from your place in recorded time. If you yearn for wisdom, He will make you instant geniuses. His Prudence and Truth console and advise you. His sustaining forgiveness is the prefiguring of holy wherewithal that sanctions your days as long as you tread the mortal Earth. Indeed, Jesus does what the King of Creation should do by nourishing you in everything just and true, by healing your maladies, sharing the graces by which you hear Him, and stripping away your sadness. In the midst of all the relativism, desecration of the Church, and impugning of your religious faith by nonbelievers, Christ the King raises you up and takes you to the pinnacle of perfection.

My Special son, where does the Mother of this King begin to describe His admiration for you? I wish for you to never tire in anything you do on His behalf because your efforts augment the teachings of the Gospel and the intercessory blessings of the Holy Spirit. You are laboring hard and remaining strong. Like Christ the King, you are providing for your brothers and sisters by teaching them through word and example; you are rendering a legacy that will take them to the foot of the Cross. It is My privilege to speak to you because you have never said anything to make the Father believe that you would surrender under any pressure in service to His vineyard. His Kingdom is enhanced in unconstrained ways by the years you and your brother have devoted to the propagation of the faith. I am righteously proud that you have accepted your mission on behalf of the Church and the Salvation of man. And, as I told you on this day six years ago, the Glory of Truth belongs like a seed inside your heart, as the Light of Heaven illuminates everything that will brilliantly lead lost sinners to overcome their errors. Why is it true that it often seems of men that casual projects lead to traumatic experiences? Somehow in the future, I hope that you learn that perspective is a phenomenon that is much more serviceable than rhetorical figures of speech. Yes, your petitions have been and will be the impetus for the conversion of untold numbers of lost sinners, but I need not tell you this because you are aware. There is opposition by evil factions to what you are doing because you are throwing defeat in Satan's face. For your edification, he is taking steps to attempt to cease your progress. However, you are sufficiently innovative to confound Jesus' evil adversary by becoming more powerful in the Wisdom of the Holy Spirit. How worthless Satan is! Does he realize that you can vanquish him at any moment? Does he forget the profound gifts you give the Father when you pray like a gladiator? The fact is that he takes his evil to humanity a day at a time for the purpose of stealing souls from Heaven, and you live a day at a time to win them back. Never forget that evil is no match for you because the Holy Spirit is on your side. Jesus' Sacrifice empowers you to overcome any obstacle or repugnance to reap the harvest of converted souls. This is why I am so happy and the Trinity is so pleased. You invoke mannered ways to deepen your resolve to uphold the sovereignty of God's presence in the actions of your lives. And, I wish for you to know that I am not unmindful of your artful and skillful works. Please remember that Christ the King reigns through you!"

Sunday, December 2, 2007
St. Maria Javier Izquierdo [1740-1813]*
3:19 p.m.

"My children, when the Lord's peace overcomes you; when the Holy Spirit saturates your hearts, and when the words of the Holy Gospel envelop you, there is no doubting your future. I have articulated the criteria through which your faith is defined and how Christianity transforms you into purified beings. Jesus refers to this as your spiritual indoctrination that leads to the sanctification of everything about you that will be admitted into Heaven. This does not imply that everything mortal is without merit, but mortal things do not redeem you in the way of Divine Love. Today, I wish to begin sharing your journey toward Christmas so you will be more aware of My presence throughout the whole year. The Sacred Scriptures speak about your refinement on Earth and your transformation into Saints. As you realize, this is an ongoing, concurrent process that requires heavy sacrifices and sacramental poise. I have for centuries spread God's Wisdom over the Earth in the form of locutions, visions, apparitions, and inundating spiritual gifts. When you respond, God reacts to you. My Queenship is the catalyst for your conversion because of My advocacy and innate desire to greet My children in Heaven. While nonbelievers make this difficult, the piety and prayers of My faithful people make up for their deficits. This is the way Martyrs and Doctors of the Church are made. We are subscribers to the Kingdom of Love, and nothing can separate us. I refer to the biblical declarations of Saint Paul. Hence, you should see your lives as the shedding of the imperfections you inherited from your ancestors who tried their best to teach you right from wrong, but whose own inherent means were flawed. Perfection according to Christ entails your comprehension of the unseen City of Light to which your lives are committed, the Church Triumphant of which you are a predestined part amidst such devotion. It is not visible because it exists in the Glory of Eminence that you strive to reach by the faith we have discussed. My children, you risk nothing by trusting God, and you have everything to gain. When you receive My blessing, you invite the Holy Spirit to enlighten you about your final assimilation into the Triumph of My Immaculate Heart. My Special son, what can Jesus' Mother say that would exemplify the gladness that overcomes Me? When Mary Jane Kerns only two hours ago left a message that said, '..and your book, oh...well, I just can't explain it,' she speaks for the whole world. You have taken seriously the mission that has restructured your life, and you understand clearly that obedience to Jesus is paramount above every human act. Do you remember when I once proclaimed, 'Do whatever He tells you (?)' This is the Holy Wisdom that I am dispensing to humanity through the ages; it is My concession that I do not adjudicate the Lord's Will or apply methodologies that affect His sovereign decisions. Your compliance is reminiscent of the Saints, mystics, and charismatics who suffered in their own right so humanity could see the uniqueness by which God has visited His people, and through what extraordinary acts of truism sinners are converted. My Special one, these are miracles in themselves, and you have known this for an extended period of time. You lived with common piety for the first 28 years of your life, but you have now been transfigured by the Holy Paraclete to propagate the universal mysticism through which Jesus' Mystical Body is taught. And, you have never entered into seclusion to do so! You have not become a monk or other religious; you have dedicated yourself to My intercession in such a way that Christians will eventually know everything that has occurred between Heaven and Earth in this home that is relevant to their eternal exculpation. I do not speak superfluously to commend you because there are millions of people I would rather reprimand. My compliments are not mildly given. I take seriously the condition of the Earth and the souls of My children. You see with what honesty I have offered My messages to you for nearly seventeen years.

Yesterday was one of those parametrics of mortal time when you battled evil face to face and won, just as the Angels said. Why did you win? Was it because you plunged into the fight as though you had no foreknowledge of the outcome? Certainly not. You took arms against Satan knowing that you would be victorious, and the coward ran from you, unprepared for your determination. This is how he has been for 2,000 years when giants among men demand that he take leave of other lives in the name of Jesus Christ. This is the Light by which you walk, the marshaling that sustains your valor, and the implications with which you took the oath of the Apostles Creed. You would do anything including the destruction of misspent life to maintain your obedience to God. My child, you would not have done this back in your days of simple piety; you have deigned this by the power of love imbedded deep inside your heart. You have not only studied sacrifice, you have actualized and magnified it through your own pious acts. Your identity has been transformed into a greater person than you ever thought you could become because you have extended the boundaries of your faith into a new conviction that cannot be reversed. You are more capable of communicating God's intentions to humanity because you have experience manifesting them. You accomplished all this without being dubious or having repugnant feelings. Please be reminded that this has been voluntary on your part. You are not required to do anything except comply with Jesus' Sermon on the Mount and live your life as any other Christian. However, you decided to do more; you echoed the clarion that emblazoned your conscience with the prospect of victory, and humanity is blessed by your decrees. There are signs and wonders aplenty so you know of God's unbounded providing. Can you see that Jesus is behind them? There is eternal profit in your response to God that cannot be matched by tepid men. Sinners are being led to the Living Waters, marriages are blessed, offspring conceived, the sick healed, the lost found, and the lame cured. And, in the matter of one day, your brother's writing to the newspaper caused the high school to remove the word 'iconoclast' from their marquee to be replaced by the word 'integrity.' This is the effect of righteous terminology on the indifferent secular void. I told you in February 1991 that you would prevail, and your brother's feelings about coming into prosperity are not out of the question. This is why I commend you for taking life one day at a time. Thank you for allowing Me to see with more than spiritual vision a world that is changing for the better, in the direction of the Cross and the Salvation that Jesus offers."

Sunday, December 9, 2007
St. Thomas Wilmer Heather [1914 -1988]*
2:58 p.m.

"Millions of people would hope that they could utter a word to the Mother of God, and She would reply audibly. This is your miracle because your lives in the Sacred Heart of Jesus took new meaning when you responded affirmatively on February 22, 1991. My children, it has made all the difference in the world. My Grace and your courage are lethal to Satan's evil because you dare to envision life without it. My repentant children are gathering, replete with their commitment to God, hoping on their own that they will be the recipients of His supernatural presence. Let there be no mistake that their faith is stronger than your locutions. Even in this, I call upon you to persist in your sacred duties because their faith is strengthened by your witness. Even the vapid, lifeless consciences of those who have rejected spiritualism altogether are being moved to Heaven's sights by your urging them to convert to Salvation in the Holy Cross. As I have said, this makes your devotion to Jesus timeless and priceless, and your spirits will feel warmed in the Father's arms. This Advent is your premonition that 2008 will be ominous for obstinate sinners along the paths of mortal life. They will be shamed by their lack of holiness, and they will endure the same callousness that they have heaped upon others. Fate and misfortune will take swift retaliation upon them, and Nature will unleash its fury against their valuables. There will be collateral victims, and you realize that their sacrifices are to the sanctification of humanity. Even as the Holy Father Pope Benedict XVI is warning the young about the perils of consumerism, Americans are picking and choosing material wares for themselves in a heretical way to observe Jesus' Nativity in the stark quarters of Bethlehem. Let us pray that they will see the brilliance of His birth as though a flash of lightning has impacted their conscience. For all you have written about pluralism, moral relativism and atheism, societies and cults everywhere will become aware of God's intention to lead His people to the single Truth of His Divine Love in His Messianic Son. My little ones, auspicious is the moment when the heart awakens to the welcoming Kingdom of the Lord. This is the supernal recognition when lost sinners realize that they are such, that there is a chasm between the present and Eternity that can only be closed by the conversion of the soul. It is the realization that the hour of death is calling, and what will the future hold beyond that? We have prayed for humanity to understand the genuine faith needed to connect the heart with the Holy Gospel and the ageless beauty of Heaven. You live and breathe during these times; your lives change by the minute, and days can seem like years. This is your anticipation of the Eternal, of the forgiveness that comes to you in the Persons of Jesus Christ and the Holy Paraclete. When you offer your petitions to the Father, He sends His Son to nurture you in this faith and give you the belief, temperance, and conviction that will make you productive Christians, and to uphold your sense of hope that you will soon depart this world into better consequences than you can imagine. My children, the most important matter is that He offers this faith as a gift without violating your free will. When the Holy Spirit takes residence in your heart, it is because you welcome Him there. In the healing warmth that embraces you from Heaven, you are wrapped in awareness and spiritual acumen that cannot be stolen away because it is infused in you from the inside. Even the destruction of your physical body cannot remove the Love of God living at the center of your being. Therefore, I applaud you for building-up His Kingdom on Earth because you are constructing an inviolate faith that comes from above; your own contrition and servitude foster the repentance of lost sinners who hear your testimonies and share them with their friends. When this occurs, you see the miracle that the Lord tenders His children.

My Special child, how awesome it must feel to be you! Wild dogs surround you, and you vanquish them by your visionary heart. Evil strikes at your heels and you remain undaunted, prepared for the fight, adaptable in the battle, and willing to censure whatever is foisted upon you. Thus, the concept of manifest abruption, the unexpected and immediate reversal of course based on sudden circumstances, data, input or impulses is nothing you cannot sustain with faith. The point more importantly is whether you understand why it occurs. What can you tell Me about Satan's dismal attempts to dilute your power to destroy him? Is it not true that he seems to poison the circumstances to gain control? He is capable of pressing his evil into multiple places at once, but he is locked in time. And, you have become definitively aware why you and your brother have been having such difficulty the past ten years getting your messages into the secular media; they are managed by atheists. Atheism is not simply a benign form of indifference, it is a collective evil that wants the Church to fail. They are enemies of the conversion of men. Given this fact, you still have success reaching the masses with My messages. You are seeing an admission by them that is almost unprecedented because your brother is bombarding them with so many questions about their lack of holiness. And, you sent them such a brilliant essay about reconstituting morality in the United States that they felt overwhelmed by your righteousness. I am impressed by your ability to write like Saint Thomas Aquinas with the courage of Saint Joan of Arc. My benison comes from the Father, and He gives it to those who call His name. This is the power that blooms through your trust that I am speaking to you now. It is the genius that makes you vex Satan at every turn, and he runs like a coward. The way to defeat the evil that mocks people of good will is to remain committed to defeat it. This might take weeks, months or years, but it is your way of proving that your emulation of Jesus' Sacrifice is timeless.

Now, you are moving toward the end of 2007. If you look in hindsight, you are reminded that it has been an extraordinarily favorable time for your Marian works, for sharing My intercessory gifts, for the kindness of your Bishop, and for many other purposes you hold deep in your heart. Most crucial is that you have moved another year closer to entering Heaven with the Saints and achieving the Salvation you have sought with every dawn and sunset. Your hope is sturdy; your mission is on course, and your aspirations for the cultivation of humanity are well placed. The restoration of human decency that you wrote about in your essay to the newspaper will happen without them; it will come to pass in your time. The Lord will not violate someone's human will in His appeal for them to accept Him. He has the power to manipulate the will, and He reserves the right to exercise it whenever He deigns. However, can someone's love be authentic if it is procured against their will? This is why He calls on the help of humble men like you and your brother to induce sinners to accept the Christian life and give themselves to Jesus by their own engagement. Our entire initiative since 1991 has been about persuasion. With all your works, you have put forth the case for His Kingdom so endearingly that the Cross cannot be denied. As you enter 2008, you will confront the human will. You cannot prosper the harmony of the Earth if you expect God to place your enemies into some sort of trance. That would not reflect their true motivations. We are trying to amend their will. I know that you understand,

and I am convinced that you are prepared to fight. What we are planning will include some crass, humiliating behavior from them, the likes of which has not been seen in ages. This is the conflict between goodness and evil that began in the Garden of Eden. The reason you continue is precisely because of the power of manifest abruption. The Holy Paraclete can change hearts in an instant. You are appalled by how defiant some people are because you may not have seen this side of them. I am not surprised because I have witnessed it for centuries. Even some women feel subjugated because they are lent to the pains of childbirth, and this is what radical feminism and abortion are about."

Sunday, December 16, 2007
St. Jude Choennes, Martyr [1382-1421]*
2:52 p.m.

"I urge you to offer your Advent petitions for those suffering in poverty, and especially ask God to intervene with condoling solace where widows and orphans endure the hollowness of someone's death. My darlings, you see the easiness of life in the United States; you have savored the sweetness of comfort and lived where there is plentiful provisions for your daily needs. This makes you blessed, but no more special in Jesus' eyes. If you harken to your childhood, you will recall moments when darkness engulfed you and the harsh reality of facing the Earth's oppression impacted your senses. The Lord has provided for you in ways that are unprecedented in the history of man, and extreme responsibility falls on you to care for the poor, the sick, and dying around the globe. I tell you these things not only because you approach the celebration of Christmas, but that you will come to believe that Jesus' poverty lives in everyone given to self-sacrifice, to the many whose renunciation suppresses their deepest longings. I have spoken of spiritual wealth in the past because this is the richness to which you are called. How can someone comprehend the meaning of sacrifice if little is taken from them? Your perfection evolves from your determination to see the world to the righteousness dictated in the Bible and your inheritance of wisdom that apprised your forbears about Jesus' prescription for modesty. How many times must the Mother of God reprimand America about materialism? While I will never become breathless or lacking in words, you must eventually understand that true holiness springs from your desire to imitate the lives of the Saints, discontinue your pursuit of artifacts and the flesh, and seek the Kingdom of Truth that owns the Earth and makes way for your resurrection from the grave. How can you be holy if you do not practice these basic laws of Christian discipleship? It is cold and wintry outside; there are snowdrifts around your homes, and the skies are overcast with storm clouds. This is not the main concern of your survival, rather you must concede to the burdens of righteousness that echo from the valleys and through the trees with the urgent voice of God. Will you heed this call? My Special son, My gratitude overflows this place. My Sacred Love shines like a beacon in the night. As you pray the Rosary at this moment, lives are being amended and estranged family members reunited. Another one of your loved-ones has come to Heaven, and as a gift to you, she has decided that her prayer in honor of your sacrifices is her nobility for today. I have said that long will be the hours when the final battles of the Earth ensue. Those who have preceded you in death will see them from Eternity, and they will be your supporting advocacy before the Throne of the Father. You are looking at a world that is about to conclude; you are seeing your own life with valedictory poise, and you must be elated that you have accorded Jesus the opportunity to enlighten His people. There is true florescence in your heart. You have legitimacy even in your accidents; you will do no wrong in the eyes of the Lord. And, when you and your brother reproach the enemies of the Crucifixion, you do so with gentleness and Christian etiquette. When you turn to an atheist and say, 'May wellness and good fortune be your providence,' you are showing signs of the Divine Mercy of Jesus. This implies that the generosities of love can be prevalent in all hearts, and you wish this goodness to inspirit them with faith and hope. Their consciousness may not be aware of this seed planted in them, but their mind and soul certainly know. Your prayer for their conversion is more than peripheral; it is uniquely obvious as they finally accept that no mortal could touch them without the power of the Holy Spirit in them. I have told you about the demise of your detractors, and it is happening quickly. I need not restate your knowledge of the victory that has come in the Triumph of My Immaculate Heart, but I wish to remind you that it is through your loyalty to Jesus. You can see how the Angels helped your brother comprise another communication to his elder as a mirror before her face, and she said, 'please do not turn away from me again.' This is the pleading of someone contrite, offering her concession. Your brother asks her to speak with civility and not anguish, and with peace instead of divisiveness. It is amazing that it takes the intercession of the heavens to make this come to pass.

My Special son, your receptivity and patience make this an attractive place for the Angels, like the Dove of Peace lighting where there is calm. The Dove of Peace is the Lord's capstone above good Christians to honor the resilience of their purity of heart and restore benignity to the order of things. It is very much like a trophy that God hands you for remaining true to Him. Indeed, once someone has won an award, they are not likely to reverse course when pursuing that for which they have been feted. I wish for you to remember the incident about your brother speaking to his dying mother, the one about the boxers in the ring. This is a good parable. What would a child think when seeing them hitting each other so many times? They have no way of knowing that it is a professional sport. It is vexatious to the spirit to entertain such conflict when the heart is given to the peace of God. This is why your home is such a place of comfort; there is no abrasion or division, there is no callousness or negativity, and meditation and prayerfulness compose the hours of the day. Even in your weaker moments, you are admirable in Jesus' eyes. Your next book is on schedule; your workplace atmosphere is having more cordial overtones; you are anticipating the Feast of Christmas, and your journey through life has you deeply invested in the completion of your goals. You should remember that there is a difference between being evangelical and evangelistic. The former is of Protestant fanaticism, the latter is the esteemed character of the Roman Catholic Church. I am not parsing syllables when I say this because the distinctions are notable. Yes, you have said it correctly. The former is a sectarian division, the latter is based on universal Truth. *(The term evangelistic emanates from a life in accourse with the universal Truth of God, while being evangelical is little more than babbling about a life which the speaker truly refuses to accept. Protestant ministers will never fulfill the Scriptures because they refuse to lead their flock to the Eucharistic Bread of Life upon the Altars of the Roman Catholic Church; therefore their evangelical rhetoric is hollow.)* Strangers are reaching out to you because they see your sacrificial piousness emanating from your service in the Church and your soft demeanor calling for their repentance. Thank you for permitting Me to speak to you, which I will do twice more in 2007. I shall identify one more Saint this year, and your 2008 messages will be dedicated to popular passages from the Scriptures."

Sunday, December 23, 2007
St. Marguerite Compass [1671-1733]*
2:43 p.m.

"My children, you cannot understand perspective until you gain a sense of inevitability that your conquest over evil is on course. Holy and awesome are your acts and intentions, and you are pleasing to God. I have come to pray among you so your petitions will be magnified. Thank you for bringing your holiness to bear upon the Earth's indifference. My good wishes accompany you during this holy season when you commemorate Jesus' Nativity in Bethlehem. We know that He is your resurrected King and compassionate Savior. He is aware of your mortal temptations, but He also knows of your potential to be His likeness when you set your fears aside. I have seen your lives since you were born. I have known of your heroism and trueness to the preferences of God. He cherishes you as the Angels, and Jesus leads you to the Sacraments so you will be reborn, refined, and remade. Thus, I have Good News for humanity that I share in charity and peace. I bring Emmanuel because the Earth needs an ending. Please join Me in praying for the end of sins, those of omission and commission. If it seems too difficult to avoid making mistakes, please address your committed sins first. It is better to tell the Lord at the end of time that you tried not to do something wrong than to say that you are excusable for not having done everything right. Intentional sins usually affect others, while sins of omission reflect a lack of concentration. All sin is sin, this is for sure. I urge you to demand from yourselves and evoke from others the willpower to find your lost brothers and sisters to the best of your ability, never grudgingly, and soothe the spiritual and physical suffering of the brokenhearted, starving, ill, and lonely. If you refer to the Spiritual and Corporal Works of Mercy, you will travel the byways that will take you where they are hiding. In all matters, you must be honest and pure while implementing everything Jesus tells you to do. In addition to your conversion, sanctification and redemption, this is your plotted course, to conquer human impiety. My Special son, each week makes you more admirable. Your presence with Me is your happiness; your servitude dignifies the Earth and bathes it in beatific peace. I know that you are tired today, so I will be brief. You have performed splendorous acts, and God holds you in esteem. You have listened to Me long enough to believe that I have no hesitance in telling you what to do better. However, you are behaving well. You are touched with a Holy Love that is likened to Me. Hear the Saints compliment you! I have been helping them. No stone has been left unturned, and only goodness will prevail. You have stared-down the world and repudiated evil. You have elevated the Cross and stirred the conscience of men. Most of all, you have loved them; you have emitted the Light of Heaven into the remotest places on Earth. I will speak to you once more in 2007, and we shall start another year anew. Thank you for your faith and holy heart."

Sunday, December 30, 2007
The Holy Family - Jesus, Mary and Joseph
2:54 p.m.

"My dear children, of all the actions, desires, motivations, and inspirations that comprise your faith, your adherence to My wishes is most important to Jesus. You have the wherewithal to withstand the negativism that impacts you every day because you are determined to see your lives to the fullest, to reside within God's Providence through your indomitably sacred holiness, and never lose sight of the Cross situated before you in the Gospel by the Holy Spirit. Today, you have knelt to pray for humanity in a world that remains roiled in controversy, injustice, lack of peace, sinfulness and darkness of heart, and rife with famine, disease, impurity, and every other manner of transgression against Jesus' Kingdom. When the Earth passes away, you will discover that His Divine Mercy has been God's sustaining peace; the Holy Mass has been your Christian ordination, and Jesus' Resurrection is your deliverance from the dead. We must beg the Father to bring an end to the scourge of abortion and its horrid affront against the sanctity of life. With all the euphemisms that are employed to describe abortion, from freedom of choice to medical procedure, the fact remains that it is unmitigated murder; it is infanticide under any name. You would be amazed to know the Holy Wrath that has befallen humanity from the Throne of God over the destruction of unborn life, so much so that many disheartening failings of human endeavors are the result of the world's reluctance to shield the unborn from death. I have often said that I do not bring doomsday cautions or speak of cataclysmic chastisements to bring the guilty to justice because My messages are heard by people of faith; and it is your progress toward righteousness that must be elevated. Indeed, you know many of Jesus' evil adversaries living across the nations, and you avoid their demonic clutches. My messages have raised your hearts to the joy of the New Jerusalem and urged you to reprove the enemies of the Cross. Your compliance will result in multitudes of conversions and baptisms. What can be said about AD 2007? What descriptive terms can encapsulate the tremendous achievements you have made for the Lord? Surely ideas like consistency and adequacy apply in defining your devotional lives. Where would the Church be without your eagerness to propagate the legacies of the Saints and herald the salvific graces of the Seven Sacraments? You inherited the faith of your fathers; you are building a bridge between your forbears and your successors. When the Church Doctors crafted their pastorals and penned their memories, they thanked God for putting your faith in place so their dissertations would never die. Are your hearts not the archives where their inscripted holiness still remains? My oath to the Father is to assist your understanding in matters of faith and morals, to complement the papacies of His Vicars, and prove that I am the Mother of Eternal Triumph. While this is simple for Me, it is difficult for you in exile because you are distracted by your environment and tempted to depart the path of holiness through influences of the flesh. After reexamining My children's labors through history, I declare that there is no deprivation in your decency; there is no deficit in your desire for Jesus to enter His Kingdom with eager anticipation. Next to affirming that He loves you, His favorite proclamation to the human soul beyond the element of time is 'well done, good and faithful servant.' Once these words pierce your spirit, you will surpass the majesties of kings and queens. You will join the ranks of the greatest people who ever lived, and the Angels too. You will harken the hour when you first became aware that you have lived not for you, but for Christ. And, upon the stroke of midnight tomorrow, you will pass another annum toward that revelation.

My Special one, it is too brief a passing, it may seem, that you kneel before your prayer altar listening to Me speak one word at a time, touching your humble heart in encrypted terms, painting images and implications that foretell the future of man. By remaining beside your brother in all things merciful and dutiful, you have emboldened Christians who would not have known that Jesus' Crucifixion is so personal, and that His Easter Resurrection is so relevant in their time. You know that life is not ended at death, it is changed by the Sovereign Glory that has overwhelmed the universe. You have dispensed more than piety to the cultivation of men, but a wholesome awareness that brings peace to the heart. The essential content of Heaven has been altered, and this is the Will of God. All the accolades I could possibly place into terms would fall short of describing how grateful I am that you serve Him with maturity and humility. You are aiding the transformation of the Earth into the image of Paradise with ecclesial expertise. The words 'thank you' are insufficient to express My feelings. Hence, you shall enter AD 2008 with grand hopes for the glorious coming of Christ the King. There will be moments of unexpected gladness, extraordinary satisfaction, and sound confidence among your ordinary periods of darkness and confusion. Such is the drama of life. Upon fuller analysis, there are always more good days than bad; there is higher purpose to your promptings than you may know, and you will feel beset with paradoxes to rival the most remarkable in memory. You will prevail through your faith in Jesus above everything gratifying or vexing. He has bequeathed to you a happiness that the world cannot give or take away. My Immaculate Heart is your repository of joy where you must come for Wisdom. Let there never be a day when you do not turn to Me for assistance. God provides signs for you, just as you see 3:33 on the clock at this instant, to ensure your trust that your works are on course. The way you pray is a sacred mystery itself; it promotes the cohesion of Christians and the consolation of the heart because you remain resolute in this trust. You know that the protocols which are in place, your writings and the protraction of God's desire that you esteem Him, and your own initiatives that exemplify Jesus' Sacrifice are present through the sacred appeal that is claiming the lost for the New Jerusalem about which I have spoken. There is nothing complicated about this. God will sow peace everywhere there is an opportunity given on Earth. It is man who must decide these things, and I believe that your righteousness can be expressed with the Lord's blessing in whatever ways you wish to pray. I have told you about the requisite of holiness in your obedient response to the call of the Holy Spirit. This is what the vocation of matrimony is about, and it is the inspiration behind the sacred priesthood and the other Sacraments. I am elated to know that you live with the confidence that the Holy Spirit is always more powerful and preeminent than any other force or prescription in Creation. Without accepting Jesus in your hearts, you and your brother would have separated by now, and My messages would have been incomplete. Can you see that you thrive by prayer, how empowered you feel, how united with the Cross you are, and with what great discipline you address each new day? You must protect and preserve My messages at all costs. Do not draw any premature conclusions, and welcome the future with trust. You have learned your lessons well."

MORNING STAR OVER AMERICA

The New Millennium
In the Year of Our Lord

AD 2008

Sunday, January 6, 2008
The Epiphany of Our Lord
2:57 p.m.

"My children, brandish the Crucifix against evil forces around you! You see by Jesus' Holy Sacrifice that atheism cannot impede the march of the Cross that stands tall and is perpetually undaunted. We have spoken about awesome things during seventeen years, heightening the hopes and insights of modern humanity, addressing ways that you can transmit God's message by whatever medium or method of conveyance seems appropriate, and how to invoke an urgent response to My call for holiness. I promise that should you ever stumble by accident or fall through exhaustion, every grace and blessing from Heaven will arrive even so. The Lord desires your Salvation and assistance in the conversion of His people. He has no other agendum. As 2008 opens, you recognize that there is a criminal element to the American government and an animosity toward Christianity that has never before been seen in the history of men. This is why it is necessary that I come to you, that Heaven opens its arms to embrace your goodness during these times of perverse cultures and social degradation. I told you six years ago that My appearances during your prayers are part of the hyper-extension of God's Truth. This lends to your enlightenment because you accept the Holy Spirit within you; the future is expanded in your consciousness, in the context of your existence, and by your receptivity of the Eternal. My children, Heaven's designs are only meant to purify you, not to punish your mistakes or castigate you for the deficiencies you inherited from your fathers. And, you have seen that this purification consists of many kinds of sacrifice that enable your spirituality. This is faith, My little ones; it is the only way you will survive the awful reckoning between Heaven and Earth. What will you do this year to give encouragement to your lost brothers and sisters? How will your thoughts and actions cultivate meaningful communication between people of different races, religions, and partisan persuasion? Christianity is about building bridges that lead non-Christians to the Holy Cross, and your support for them through kindness and compassion is always a greater motivator than force and isolationism. Also today, you are seeing multiple influences attacking your public institutions and trying to drive religion from the secular discourse. Anyone who says that there should be a separation between Christianity and the public debate is under the influence of the Antichrist. They are of evil intent and in dire need of confession, contrition, conversion, and repentance. How can America be spared the poison dividing its citizens one from another if they do not ingest the antidote? Jesus is your common unity in everything about you that is human. He opens your hearts and heals you. He informs you in every way about obeying the Will of the Father in your personal and private affairs. His Sacred Heart bears the Wisdom that will heal, lead, and comfort you to avert wars and undue dependence on materials and the flesh. He is The Way by which you shall be sustained during the ensuing years of disquietude. Indeed, by His sacred teachings are you given the genius to know what is worth seeking, and by His Sacrifice are you cleansed. Your commitment is tested in the fires of Wisdom to purge you of everything that opposes the revelations of the Scriptures. By these flames are you forged, and all that stands between you and holiness is incinerated. It is you who remain in the Grace of the Father, wholly sanctified in Jesus' Crucifixion. And, like the burning bush, you survive the conflagration by not being consumed by the fire. My main request as your Mother is that you see anew the Lord's intentions for this world. Raise your awareness about the future of empathy and charity that He has called you to establish for your heirs. Induce your enemies to embrace you by revealing the Spirit of Truth living in you, taking you to heights you never knew possible. Then, you will realize the true power of humanity; then the Light of Heaven will shine from within you into the darkest dungeons of the Earth. If it is healing and good will that you seek, you will find them in that power.

My Special son, I speak with compassion and conviction because you have entered AD 2008 with your focus on the Triumph of My Immaculate Heart. There are many goals that I have set for you this year, one of which is to seek from you a new approach in communicating your ideas at home, at your workplace, and in your writing. I wish for you to avoid the caustic style of speaking that is known in the media and people who know nothing about the kindness of God. This can happen without your knowledge because you live close to these things. Another issue is that you have more appreciation for who you are. I have said that you are distinct among your peers, that you have allotted your life to God's Kingdom in ways that have been unknown to those with whom you were raised. There are no words to describe your priceless spirit as you are seen by Heaven. Nothing of any earthly value can match your worthiness in Jesus' eyes. I am proud that you are My son. The swiftness of Heaven's justice is always with you because you have deferred your life to the sanctification of lost men. No prince can replicate your goodness; no light can compete with it. You will next month complete seventeen years as My messenger, and you have grown accustomed to My intercession in a way that prohibits you from realizing how other men see your work the first time. Turn your memories to the first days of February and March 1991, and you will sense what it means that the Lord has removed the barriers between His Glory and your heart. You were acclimated by small acts that you knew to be miracles because they could have only come from Me. However, your friends to whom you are giving your books are receiving the full impact of My intercession when they open your Diary or New Millennium messages. Be happy for them because their lives will be forever changed! All this is possible because of your genuine faith and your love for the Most Blessed Trinity. The Church is strengthened by your loyalties, and humanity en masse is moving closer to the Cross. You have learned that there are many symbolic acts that open the hearts of people in families and public life, but your dedication to Jesus is real. It is not a symbol of allegiance to Him, but your veritable oneness with Him for the Salvation of the whole world. If you were the Son of Man, how would this make you feel? Indeed, He is pleased that you care, that you permit Him to perfect His earthly people through the piety of your heart, the submission of your will to His ways, and to the growth of virtue on an Earth that rarely knows its meaning. You are seeing with eyes of faith what it means to walk in righteousness without fear and apprehension. This is how your Christian prevalence treads water through these crucial years in the finishing of the lives of men. You have risen above the depths of the universe to stand tall with the Christ. Please do not allow your brother's eccentricity to annoy you. We have through seventeen years so taxed his mental strength that it is impossible to place into words. Your remark about hearing his voice thunder from podiums and before lecterns was a kind thing to say, but he is becoming weary because of his compliance with the requests of God. He will speak; there is no question about that. But, it is yet to be seen about the amplitude of his voice. Your brother lives every day in a constant state of apology because he feels such a burden upon you. He is wholesomely sorry for causing you any grief, and he asks Jesus that he not become a liability for you. You know that he is goal-oriented; we have mentioned this before. As for your speeches, remember the simple and confident oratory of Pope John Paul II. He described speaking personally or to an auditorium filled with people as though he would see them only once. Do you remember when I asked you to be gentle with yourself? One never becomes angry with himself to the point that any thoughts of self-retribution come to mind. If you fall into this, your presence to others appears callous and bitter. This is not the way of the Holy Spirit. Furthermore, when someone speaks about a quarrel or circumstance, it is better not to personify the imperatives of that instance. In other words, if you repeat someone else's upbraiding of a condition in the world, you should deliver your message without the inflection of other speakers. This is the case with entire societies. It is why violence manifests violence between people who are otherwise disinterested parties. This is how mob mentalities are derived, simple imitation that becomes internalized. This matter is one that I would like you to address in 2008. Thank you for your kind promptness to My words and compliance with the Will of the Father."

Sunday, January 13, 2008
The Baptism of Our Lord
2:57 p.m.

"This is our time, little ones, to lift Creation to the Father and remember the forsaken and brokenhearted, to appeal to Jesus' Mercy for the redemption of the lost, and mend the divisions that have long divided world enemies and estranged families. Be thankful that you have this power and that I am with you to assist in your interaction with Heaven. It is true that you pursue the wholesomeness of humanity and the restoration of your brothers and sisters' innocence, so profound that it seems another lifetime ago. Your artful imaginings of the refinement of history and the legacy of your forbears is possible; it can come in your time. You can rewrite the patterns by which the Earth has evolved and set the record straight for the ages. All things are possible with God. Today, we concentrate upon the weaknesses of your companions so they will have the adequacy of your strength and virility in matters of faith and morality. Only by prayer can this be done, and only by opening their hearts can it be accomplished by them. When you perceive in your mind's eye a better world where there are no dying children or persecuted Christians, where the globe's plenty is dispensed to the hungry and homeless, and where equal access is allowed for every form of righteousness known to man, you are seeing with the perfection of the Cross. Truly, you do not realize the goodness inherent in your prayers, for if you could see the amelioration that they bring to just one life, you would pray without ceasing. You would move swiftly to kneel in adoration before the Blessed Sacrament and thank the Eucharistic Jesus for past prayers answered and future petitions accepted. If His call to prayer was not urgent, I would not be here speaking to you. If the Lord did not hope in seeing that His people are capable of conversion, My messages would have never begun. Thus, we pray for your intentions in accordance with His Will, and for everything good that comports with Jesus' commendation that you shall have life, and life to the fullest. As sure as day turns into night, and the dark to morning, you are part of God's creative desire to touch humanity with lightness of heart and sincerity in your judgements. His intent to heal and sanctify the world has never been more prevalent than in this age. My children, you have labored long and feverishly to help your lost brothers and sisters understand the purpose of miracles. I am your miracle; the Holy Spirit is the fosterer of miracles, and the changes that happen on the Earth are other miracles on the journey of cultivating faith and virtue. You are aware from the Scriptures that divine intervention has been the basis for the repentance of men. The Archangel Gabriel has attested to this, and so have many in his likeness who woke your predecessors in the night and on their travels to give them wisdom to seek the Kingdom of God. The Archangel

Michael wields the most powerful Sword ever known to man. And, the Archangel Raphael ratifies your healing of mind, body, and spirit that the Father has willed for those who love Him. Thus, do not allow anyone to tell you that no miracle can convert them because they have no comprehension of what they are talking about. Humanity has the strength to endure any hardship on Earth for the Christian conversion of lost sinners. It is surely extremely dark in the belly of a whale, and blindingly brilliant on the summit of Mount Tabor. The point is that you are all instruments when you place yourselves in the hands of the Lord. And, anything breaching the restraints of time can offer you a sense of the dignity and Providence of Heaven's beauty and eloquence. I once told you that upon seeing the Resurrection of Jesus on Easter Sunday, I heard the strains of symphonies sounding from instruments that had yet to be invented. You have been to the mountaintop about which Saint Martin Luther King Jr. spoke, even as you walk in human flesh. And, you are beginning to learn that being mortal does not imply that you are also violable; you have simply not died to the world and witnessed the Face of God. I implore you to trust in Him, that He will send you every good thing from Heaven, along with the Most Holy Eucharist of the Catholic Church to keep you strong while you wait in joyful hope for the coming of His Son.

My Special one, we have determined together that nothing will stand in the way of your progress in nurturing your lost brothers and sisters to spiritual health. When humanity has prayed during the centuries since the Descent of the Holy Spirit, they have uttered the phrase 'surely goodness and mercy...' I attest to you and all Christians that these are with you all the days of your lives. Even in your darkest hours, there is *The Morning Star Over America* to guide and comfort you, to take you over what seems unconquerable summits to the dawn of another day. We have spoken about all the books that could be written about how this has been accomplished by the billions of people who have lived. Indeed, it would take reams of paper just to testify to the glory you have known in the past twenty-four hours. With My determination and your faith, we shall succeed in everything I came to do. Nothing will inhibit your progress toward enabling humanity to be mobilized in the power you have gained in Jesus' Crucifixion and Resurrection. No impedances can stop the flow of Divine Mercy from reaching penitent hearts. No darkness can prevail against the Light of Truth. When in this day, anyone who turns to the Father for Wisdom, he shall have it in the mighty waterfalls of enlightenment that come through Christian faith."

Sunday, January 20, 2008
2:47 p.m.

"Wisdom sings her own praises. Before her own people she proclaims her glory." [Sirach 24:1]

"My children, the only sinless Woman in Creation has come seeking your assistance in converting the world's lost sinners to Jesus, to the Holy Cross where their sins are expunged from the eternal record, to the Grace and Peace that have overwhelmed the facets of human life that are both obvious and undiscernable to you. Today, we remember the precious unborn in their mothers' wombs, and ask God to guide the consciences of these mothers to furnish absolute opportunity for their offspring to be born. I have said that the Earth is your precursor to Paradise, and that many virtues you learn during your mortal years mirror the Glory you will soon come to know. However, there is no law of opposites or centrifugal balance in Heaven like on Earth because the Glory to which I refer is impeccably unified and tranquilly still. While you will enjoy unbounded bliss in the Light of Paradise, you will notice that there exists no reason to prioritize motives and impulses the way you do here. And, while Salvation will bring you rest, you will have all you wish to accomplish for endless millennia adoring the presence of God. Unlike the Earth, you will not feel the urge to conjugate verbs in your spare time or count backward from a hundred in threes. There will be no need to decide what to wear on any given Sunday because you will be clad in the raiment of Divine Absolution. My little ones, without Jesus' Crucifixion, this would not be possible; and without My having accorded My Fiat to the Archangel Gabriel, you would not have known Jesus. I am a Mother to whom My children cannot say no. I bring you Wisdom, Truth, tenacity, perseverance, dignity, humility, and conversion. Through My Immaculate Heart pass all who shall enter the Gates of Heaven. If you wish to emulate the kindness of God, imitate Me. Come to Me, pray with Me, adore the living Christ with Me, and call out to every race with urgency to apprise them of My messages about these latter times. When you wish for greater things to come, always tend toward the perfection that I give you in Jesus, and you will reach the pinnacle of human success. When the disciples of the Gospel speak about divine reason, they refer not to the cynosures of logic to which refined men and women aspire. They speak about sacrifice and self-denial before the Lord's Kingdom, the supernatural Providence that has made you aware that Jesus is present here and now. And, in this, you are expected to discard the pleasures of the flesh, defy the temptations that would lead you into sin, and dignify the inherent proficiency of your heart to remain steadfast in the righteousness of God. Since there is reason in divinity, it is a fruit of your acknowledgment of the power of the

Most Blessed Trinity to refine humanity by any means and to all degrees desirable by Heaven. Truly, this includes amending your ways before you get there. My messages have always summoned you to be people, but to be divinely inspired by God's Glory to not only wish to be absolved, but to seek the forgiveness of the Lord as an act of your free will. This is where your actions and His reason converge because He does not wish for you to descend into eternal perdition. As the Handmaid of the Lord, My mission is not only to intercede for you while you pray, but to teach you how to pray as you ought and complement your knowledge so you know what is important to pray about. The Holy Spirit of God speaks through Me, and if you accept your part as missionaries of human conversion in the material world, He will speak through you by your contemplations, meditations, blessings, acts and intercessions. It is imperative that My children comprehend the unprecedented immortal power you have in your petitions. I have said this as many ways as you can understand, and it is the thesis of My apparitions around the world. Without prayer, you have no relationship with God; you will never see Heaven if you do not ask Jesus in prayer to take you there. I beseech your compliance with My wishes as a matter of divine reason. My Special son, I gladly dispense My blessings upon this home and you and your brother because you are living in accourse with the calling of Heaven. You are aware that there is no law of opposites there, only the singular Truth for which you have labored your entire mortal life. We share more in common than you know because the same Holy Spirit who inspires your heart sends Me here to speak to you. And, you yearn for the refinement of humanity in spiritual terms to awaken them to the Paschal Resurrection in which they inherit their Easter joy. I speak about timeless issues even though you are encased in the collection of hours. You have received a hint of what the future will bring with many who will eventually believe. Thank you dearly and devotedly for your cheerful heart and dedicated service to the Kingdom of God. I will speak to you again next week, and we will pray for the conversion of lost sinners to the Glory of the Cross."

Sunday, January 27, 2008
2:49 p.m.

"There is an appointed time for everything, a time for every affair under the heavens." [Eccles. 3:1]

"While the hoarfrost lays heavily on the evergreens, I come with a message of peace to awaken the spirit of humanity in the stillness of winter. My children, you know of My desire to convert lost sinners to the Blood of Jesus on the Cross. Thank you for helping stir them into action for God. Today, I offer a message of unity and reconciliation, virtue and enlightenment. Christians have many graces for which to be grateful in the Divine Light of Paradise. The Blessed Trinity will not stop interceding for your souls' sake, so that all men and women can gust the sweetness of Heaven when their earthly years are through. I also bring a message of warning about those who would see your mission fail. Yes, beware of the false prophets and evil-mongers doing Satan's bidding. As I told you four years ago, there is a certain peril that comes with choosing and changing leaders in nations as powerful as the United States. You hear the prattling of prevaricators who will not keep their promises. They seek power for the purpose of self-enrichment and the plundering of other nations' wealth. America has built an empire on naked aggression and a social framework of deception and imperialism. Others will stand before you and promise the Moon and stars to lull you into complacency about your spiritual responsibilities to Jesus, citing a group of sinners who in the 1700s posed a freedom that was lacking in Apostolic Truth. These men will come upon you like thieves in the night, promising change for the sake of change, and opening you to being hoodwinked by their arsenal of errors. They are articulate in talking empty bombast to deceive you into believing that their intentions are based in the Omnipotence of God. (2 Peter 2:18). This is why I forewarn you that you must choose wisely the things that affect your nation and your personal lives so you will remain in the Lord's good favor. I once told you that the United States of America is the least generous country on Earth. Even as we have been working and praying together since then, little has changed to eradicate the selfishness of America's leaders. My dear ones, it is imperative that you realize that you can live in the spiritual realms of Christianity consummately, even as you conduct your daily affairs as mortals. Although it may seem to be a contradiction in terms, your existence on Earth is a transitory station, meaning that while you are tethered to the flesh before you die, you are spiritual beings who are inhabited by the holiness of God. This is from where your moral goodness evolves. This is how you have dominion over evil. Indeed, it is from where you gain the wisdom to come to the waters of righteousness to be absolved of your error. Jesus' Crucifixion has ridded you of every sin, and you are incontrovertibly preserved and preconditioned for deliverance into Heaven because of His Sacrifice on the Cross. Nothing of the flesh can contribute to your enlightenment about matters of faith and morals. By all means, it is your physical suffering and withering bodies that throw open the passageways of your conscience so you can feel Heaven before you die. There is limitless potential in this, My children. Everything you have ever been taught by God through Jesus and the Gospel is based upon the fact that you are capable of becoming spiritual creatures situated on the face of the globe. And, in this, there is no contradiction. With this truth, you comprehend the beatific nature of Divine Love as newfound beings in the eyes of the Father. If you believe that you have been complicit in corrupting the world, then know that you are more than capable of rectifying it by accepting the purifying Sacrifice that helps you sanctify it again. This is the power about which I have spoken for nearly seventeen years, and it is the season of hope that is bringing forth the change for which you have prayed all your natural lives. I am your Mother of Perpetual Help, your Queen of Peace, and intercessor before Jesus Christ. I am the Lady of Medjugorje who first began your transformation from possessions of the world to possessors of the Earth. Thank you for inheriting from the Saints the vision and courage to move forward in their likeness. My Special son, it gives Me tremendous pleasure to pray before you as this year moves into its second month. You are indeed accomplishing the goals on a course we plotted together in February 1991. You must surely by now sense the inevitability of your progress in Jesus, and that you feel that your undertakings have been worth the efforts you have invested. Thank you for taking such good care of your brother. As Jesus admires you and remains with you every moment, He was thinking of your brother at His Birth who would be born several hundred years later. Yes, his birthday would be established 33 days after the Nativity of Christ Jesus is celebrated every year. *(I asked Our Lady about the presence of extraterrestrial life in our solar system).* I responded to an earlier question about this by saying that we must concentrate on converting lost sinners here. Now that you have accomplished a great deal toward that goal, I can say without your being distracted that most of the activity you hear about is the playful presence of the Angels. However, there is paranormal life surrounding you, and this life has shown solvency in physical form. Although they supercede primary creatures, they have nothing to do with the Salvation of sinners. They are capable of virtue, transcendent thought, qualitative expression, and objective benevolence. Most of them attempt to discern the origin of the gruesome violence that occurs on Earth on a daily basis. Hypsometrics, explosions, nuclear energy, fires, and natural disasters are quite curious to them. Thank you for your morning prayers, especially for the ending of abortion."

Sunday, February 3, 2008
1:21 p.m.

"Because you are God's chosen ones, holy and beloved, clothe yourselves with heartfelt mercy, with kindness, humility, meekness, and patience." [Col. 3:12]

"It gives Me intense comfort to realize that My children are clinging to their hope for the conversion of their brothers and sisters, and that our prayers together have the remedial influence to redirect them to the fullness of Heavenly Grace. I afford My gratitude to you because you are worthy of praise in light of your faith in Jesus. When Adam and Eve caused the fissure between humanity and Heaven, they did not know about your desire to be one with Jesus to repair it. Indeed, no creature large or small could have foretold your determination to remain steadfast in the righteousness you have inherited from the intercession of the Most Blessed Trinity, to purify, sanctify, and strengthen you for the days when you shall join all the Saints at the Feast Table of the Lord. With this faith, you picture yourselves there, arrayed in the Divine Light of Salvation procured for you by Jesus' Sacrifice on the Cross, sharing your memories, and awing at the loveliness of the Hosts of Heaven. These images are not just vague predictions of an afterlife, My children, they are actualized visions of your relocation into the Father's company where you have yearned to go. They are intricate bands of genius allowing you to know what Eternity is like—no horizons, no darkness, no doubts or fears, no suffering, no death, and no parting. We pray in earnest that you will harbor these things deep in your hearts as you grow older and more reliant on the Cross. It is only through this wisdom that you love Jesus and expect to receive the Crown of Redemption that He has fitted for you. There is no other means to absolution, and this is the Father's Will. This is not magic, it is genuine forgiveness. No potion or elixir can provide the manifest victory over death that you have received in Jesus' Blood on the Cross. Hence, there is no need to search the valleys and catacombs of Earth for added evidence of God, He lives inside your hearts as He is stationed on His Paradisial Throne. When you pray from the heart, you are united with Him. My Special son, when pondering the writing you have planned as the prologue to your 2003-2005 book of My messages, you surely must appreciate the degree of poise you are reflecting upon. The tenor of your language is appropriate, not cynical or sarcastic; it has the proper tone. Yes, your spirit knows what is wrong with the world because Jesus lives in you. The book will be published in late summer, just as last year. The mission to which you were called in 1989 is on course. Please be peaceful inside."

Sunday, February 10, 2008
2:58 p.m.

"I am the light of the world, and no follower of mine shall ever walk in darkness. No, he shall possess the light of life." [John 8:12]

"We coalesce for the common purpose of seeking the Lord's blessing upon your petitions and deeds, and for the brokenhearted who are suffering torment, loss, and deprivation in a world that is fatted with error. When you welcome the Spirit of Christian Truth in your hearts, these things will abate; they will disappear from Earth in the way of the dinosaurs. Today, it is important that you remember your Lenten promises to uphold your faith under the terrible burdens of life and to be strong against your enemies. They will soon be vanquished by God and the prayers of men. There is a reckoning and reconciliation looming, but not before a war has begun. This will be the last great battle for souls between Heaven and Hell, between Jesus' Crucifixion and Satan's evil; and you know by your faith that Jesus has already prevailed. Legions and troops will take sides, and God will give the command for His people to annihilate the adversaries of the Salvation of the world. The Angels will advocate for your potency, the Saints will intercede, the archers will blacken the skies, and the force of God's Justice will overwhelm the whole of Creation. Why must this battle ensue? Because even though you were born essentially flawed, you are not doomed to imperfection. You are to be raised on the last day by the Son of Man to the Glory in which He lives; and whatever is good, just, and excellent, whatever is pure, and whatever is beautiful will remain with Him. What shall become of the rest? Anything that is not of righteousness will be incinerated in the conflagrations of that intense fight. The Lord will send to Earth in justice the fires in which His Martyrs were burned to lap at the souls of the damned until they are forced into the netherworld. The stakes and those who were martyred upon them will rise from the ashes of this war-torn world and reclaim what is right for humanity. There will be gladness and singing for the redemption of men, but not for those who reject the Cross. Theirs will be a hollow existence because they will know that they have been defeated and condemned. There will be no moisture for their lips or consolation for their ears. They will hear only the empty promises they made to themselves that would never come, mimicking the sound of the proverbial one hand clapping. My cherished children, how dearly I hope that you will heed My call for prayer especially as the years expire because the fulfilment of the Scriptures will come. There is an ending to everything ill and the perpetuity of all that is good. Should you lay down your lives in this battle before the Son of Man returns, know that it is for the elevation of the Church, the sanctification of the impure, the restoration of decency, and the lasting peace of the mind and heart for which humanity yearns. I have called you to prayer every time I have spoken, to realize that the Lord hears you with echoing reverberation. You have the capacity to pray extemporaneously in rhythm with the Holy Spirit. You are not unmindful of the courage that Jesus seeks in His flock because you have been subjected to His enemies. Ridding the Earth of corruption occurs one soul at a time, but this does not prohibit the Lord from speaking to the masses in miraculous overtones with lessons and admonishments. We seek more than the conversion of the heart, but that it will translate into a wave of moral uprightness so profound that it will crush any opposition to your Salvation. Wives, husbands, children, and all who call themselves to Jesus must understand that there is little permanence where you live. While the outer realms of Creation seem suspended as if to be indefinite, your time to manifest goodness is now, here in this American nation where men and women have the capacity to teach your successors right from wrong before it is too late to stop them from growing scars on their hearts and callouses over their eyes. Please join your prayers and intentions to Jesus in reparation for those who have yet to accept Him.

My Special son, it is My honor to see the holiness you have made the reason for your life. I need not remind you of the bright beginnings coming to the world. Yes, you see deep sorrow in other families, cities, and regions. There are reckless fatalities and victims of crimes aplenty, but this does not impede your desire to seek the amendment of America to a more civil order. You know that the solution to these problems is Christ Jesus, and that His Sacrifice is the indomitable power that will heal your lands. While there have been countless people who have died with their greatest speeches still on their tongues, you are delivering yours with candor and eloquence. Nary a moment passes by that you do not ponder how to extend to your broken brothers and sisters a guiding hand, well wishes, good will, and material aid. These are the facets of the Spirit of God in you and your brother that you have gleaned from your knowledge of His Messianic Son. This is why your flaws are disappearing; it is the reason you are being perfected in the Blessed Trinity. I reiterate that when someone tells you that it is impossible to be perfect in Jesus, remind them that they are speaking heresy. I sense the jubilation in your heart to know that this is true. I see the anticipation with which you live and the envisionment of the Glory you shall inherit in Heaven. Here in this place, we have built a foundation of trust so invincible that anyone who sees it will not be able to resist joining in. And, in less than two weeks, you will begin another year with Me, praying, hoping, laboring, and encouraging your homeland and close friends. We are on a mission to convert lost sinners so that when the conclusion of the Earth arrives, Jesus will be able to deliver His Mystical Body into the Land of Eternal Ecstasy with swiftness and providential joy. It is imperative that you believe how grateful I am for these things! Just as sure as I have come here, as sure as the Lord gives you signs, it is definite that you will be blessed for your charities of love. You and your brother have outlined a deposit of works from 1991 until 2011, but this does not imply that your goals will end. Most important, your brother wishes to complete this series of books, so let us pray that you both live with healthful longevity, prosperity, peace of heart and mind, and protection from harm."

Sunday, February 17, 2008
3:25 p.m.

"From Heaven the Lord looks down; he sees all mankind. From his fixed throne he beholds all who dwell on the Earth." [Psalms 33:13-14]

"Jesus transfixed on the Holy Cross challenged humanity to become like Him, to follow Him and lift Him up, and to invigorate the whole of the world to strive for Heaven where absolved sinners reside. Now in this age, you see more clearly what He meant about your need for leadership and nurturing, the help you have received from Me. I ask you to put away the materials of the Earth and work for the spiritual perfection that My Son commands. Never mind the vague ideals and arbitrary concepts that compose your psychological curiosities because they are meaningless to the Lord. He requires that you search for the Divine Light that bathes you, even as you appear unaware of the origin of its power. He speaks of overcoming darkness in terms that your hearts comprehend because you know when you are unhappy; your inner-being realizes the difference between the joy of Heaven and the sadness of the netherworld. There is intense sacrifice in the life of a Christian; you have been told this before. With the Holy Spirit inside you, the eloquence and vision you require to overcome the obstacles to all things good lift you to new levels of compassion. You become willing to walk in your brothers' shoes, defer to those whom you know to be close to Jesus through their suffering, and pay due homage to the Mother Church through your litanies and almsgiving. Indeed, adhering to the summons of God is not the life of cakes and ale that some believe, and this is why I am speaking to you. What would your lives entail if you could not see with precision the goal of reaching Paradise? When you become able to stand with humility and declare that your own souls magnify the Glory of the Lord, then you have forded the stream that will take you to the shore of purity. Thank you for allowing Me to uphold you when the world is intent on tearing you down. We have together made great strides in cultivating good will around the globe. We have called humankind to be holy people in the lineage of the Saints. And, before the final remnants of time expire, you shall see that you have indeed complied with Jesus' decrees from the Cross. My Special son, My remarks will be brief because I wish for you to enjoy a time of relaxation, rest, entertainment, and peace of mind. Your Bishop's pastoral, *We*

Implore You on Behalf of Christ, Be Reconciled to God, is a work filled with marvel, truth, peace, and grace. You wonder why he would ponder such things and dedicate them to the written page after this period of time into his episcopate. The impetus for this pastoral came from the Holy Spirit inspiring in him a vision of the Earth that I described in your messages. You are reminded of My call for those in office to utilize their power to propagate the Church. I told you that you do not see everything that is occurring around you, and this pastoral is evidence. You are committing to the American Bishops a corpus of work from which they can discern what must be done to claim the lost and sanctify those who are in need of Jesus' forgiveness toward the goal of final absolution. And, thank you for recognizing the goodness of My other children, and for treating them with gentleness. They are searching for their own role in this life; you have heard their expressions about the gifts you are handing to God. Jesus knows. They all know. My mission is to encourage you during your work and to ensure that you remain steady because of the future manuscripts you will publicize. You know that your next book will be as unique as the former ones, especially in light of your decision to make your prologue a series of brief essays. My child, your writing is sheer genius! You are enduring the life that Jesus has asked you to embrace."

Sunday, February 24, 2008
3:52 p.m.

"A brother is a better defense than a strong city, and a friend is like the bars of a castle." [Prov. 18:19]

"Jesus told you that when you are gathered in His name, He is there among you. And, when you pray with predilection for His Most Sacred Heart, God will bless you with every good thing. Now, we share the brilliance of your inheritance from My Son's Crucifixion and Resurrection that you might know happiness and Salvation, and that Creation will be enlightened through the Wisdom you receive from the Holy Spirit imbedded in your hearts. I often remind you that it is My honor to pray with you and join your petitions so your brothers and sisters will be converted to the Cross. This day is no different. It is imperative that you pray for the end of abortion because the children in their mothers' wombs are precious to Me, and they represent your future in so many ways. God places life in the womb so humanity will exalt His Kingdom and garner the perfection that Jesus teaches. As long as unborn babies are conceived, you are assured that God is pleased that the Earth be fruitful in commending the nations to His Will. I know that you pray with exuberance for the Lord's Grace to overwhelm you with His Sacred Love and the perpetual miracle of faith. My intention is to forever hold you as My children, even as many people are unaware that I exist. The Father guides and informs you through your supplications, and He instills in you the righteousness that blesses your lives and ends your suffering. Can you see that this is important? This is the reason I ask you to pray for expectant mothers and their unborn infants. Abortion violates every instinct known to man, and it is only by the dead of conscience and hardened of heart that it is allowed to occur. There will finally come a time when abortion will cease, but I promise that it is a prospect requiring your daily prayers. Many great people have been killed in the womb, the Holy Innocents who would have been doctors and healers, visionaries, philanthropists, and citizens dedicated to the refinement of the Earth. They are beside Me in Heaven, and they pray that humanity will see their way clear to stopping the abomination of infanticide. My Special son, it gives Me pause to speak to you and your brother on the arrival of your eighteenth year of messages. You have grown so holy during the time I have spoken to you, not that your earlier station in the Lord's peace was not worthy of redemption, but you are now more composed and sure of yourself. Yes, you have become a prolific author by following with obedience the mandates of the Church. The context in which you sense your role in the conversion of humanity extends beyond your immediate proximity and is wider than ever. You have suffered with the Saints, given your heart to the Archangels, and will lend the remainder of your years to the propagation of the Gospel to all the nations. Is this the definition of a prudent Christian? By all means, it is more than an implication or connotation that you have accepted your share in the Cross, it serves as outright confirmation that you partake of the Kingdom of Our Lord while you serve in this earthly exile. Your vision is enhanced by your progress in learning the themes of righteousness firsthand, by deferring to the Holy Spirit and groveling before no man. When you ponder the Fruits of the Crucifixion, you lunge forward and retrieve them for your successors; and this will be the legacy of your life. There are men among you who are embittered, others with a wry sense of humor, and many that perceive religion as a stumbling block to secular paganism. As for the latter, we hope they will fall completely on their knees when approaching the holy shrines that My children are constructing in honor of My intercession. You share all things in common with the Martyrs and Saints, except being slain by the enemies of the Cross; and you know that there is providence in this. The welfare of the whole world depends on the faith of a few, and you and your brother are among them. You were born to serve in the Lord's vineyard for this reason. And, today I urge you to pray for the vocation of parenthood. Can you imagine what it takes to raise four or five children? They must be fed, clothed, housed, physically and spiritually nurtured, educated, safeguarded, and brought to maturity with a responsible conscience. This is why the Lord blesses mothers and fathers with such love and care in their hearts, that they will realize that their own succession resides in their offspring. Not everyone is called to such parenting, and these are the people who must work to refine the order of religious discipline for those who are incapable due to time constraints, mental or physical disability, and those who are only now starting to learn about their duties to Jesus. There is no question that you have created a sterling bequest to My children who hunger for truth and compassion. You are like Jesus helping them; you foster the growth of peace and brotherhood where there would instead be social conflict and animus. What you see as your responsibilities are actually overwhelming gifts to the purification of collective humanity and God's Kingdom on Earth. My little son, can you see that the seventeen years you have devoted to Me are your gift to Heaven? You are the giver, and God is the receiver. You are utilizing your resources and talents for the advancement of the Holy Gospel. The mentally ill and infirm about whom you speak are likewise committing their part toward the conversion of lost sinners. Everyone plays a role that is determined by the Father. Thank you for sending a congratulatory letter to your Bishop upon the occasion of his Pastoral Letter, and thank you for working so dutifully on the opening of your new book."

Sunday, March 2, 2008
2:53 p.m.

"I the Lord have called you for the victory of justice. I have grasped you by the hand. I formed you and set you as a covenant of the people, a light for the nations." [Isaiah 42:6]

"My children, I am drawn here by your enchanting piety and the liveliness of your faith. I bring God's blessings from Heaven, the promise of the ages, and your path to good fortune. Today, I ask you to remember in your Lenten prayers all who are suffering neglect because of civil wars and sectarian strife, and the victims of natural disasters and accidents of all kinds. We pray that Jesus protects His brothers and sisters who are engaged in gainful employment to support their families, and all at leisure and traveling to be with their friends. You see that the winter will soon give way to spring 2008, and the calends and ides of the months pass swiftly into the past. Everything you are achieving for the Lord is recorded in Eternity where you shall find your rest. You have prayed for conversion, and you should anticipate the Salvation to which your souls have been dedicated. I remind you today that you are a favored people in God's eyes because you remain true to the Holy Gospel in word and deed; and everything good that He dispenses to humanity comes at your prayerful behest. I have spoken about the reciprocity between Heaven and Earth and that your lives in Jesus encapsulate God's Will for you. It is never difficult to see that the signature of the Lord is encrypted in the everyday actions of men, that Christians around the globe are cultivating hearts and fields for harvests that will come. We have reviewed My Son's requirements for your conduct according to the Commandments and the Sacred Beatitudes, and how your approach to daily life must reflect everything He told you when He walked the Earth. How is this done? You have inherited the same Wisdom of the Holy Spirit that birthed the Church, and thereby you are descendants of the purity with which the Church still serves the Kingdom of God. It has been My honor to see the billions of souls who were consecrated to My Immaculate Heart and to the Sacred Heart of Jesus given renewal in His Crucifixion and Resurrection. While this blessing is protracted to you, accept the benisons of all the Saints in whose memories you prevail. My Special son, I have come explicitly to speak to you, to thank you for permitting My messages to proceed in this humble home and by your prayers and practical accommodations through which you have established a station for the Holy Spirit to enlighten the world, and for not giving-up on poor sinners. Your trust has the loftiness of eagles and the strength of stallions, and you should remain confident that everything for which you have prayed will be granted to man. Thank you for offering a holy Lent and recognizing how others are either giving freely or fairly reluctantly to bolster the cause of human love. I am pleased that you have included everything you have written in the first part of your next book because it has such appeal to the people who are searching more deeply for theological expressions from the tongue of God. Most Reverend Bishop George Lucas often refers in his weekly editorials to Me. Even though sometimes veiled, you know what he means. Your kind letter of February 23 reminded him that I am always praying for him. I need not repeat every time I come that things are going well, that time is on your side, and that you have at your disposal all the properties and elements to complete the mission that Jesus has assigned to you. This makes Me intensely elated because, as I said in the first part of this century, the beginning and middle of every month force their conclusion, and this is what time does. You will find this year to be no exception; there will be fair days and darker ones. Such is the climate of your mortal exile. Before I close, I would like to add that your beautiful heart and plenteous faith led the media to publish your brother's letter in defense of unborn children in their mothers' wombs. We have never surrendered this message, and we will carry on until the preservation of life is the highest priority to the world. The American Civil Liberties Union refers to abortion as necessary reproductive healthcare. This is Satan's drivel that will be plunged into Hell. My Special son, there are many sinners whose souls will be condemned. As I have said in the past, do not pity them."

Sunday, March 9, 2008
2:51 p.m.

"Every worthwhile gift, every genuine benefit, comes from above, descending from the Father of the heavenly luminaries, who cannot change and who is never shadowed over." [James 1:17]

"There are times when you must lend extraordinary valor to the actions of men, and these are the proper moments. You have been accorded an opportunity to reach untold thousands of people through your petitions and manual actions through your faith in the Lord because He responds to the faith that He implants in human hearts. Were it not for your willingness to comply, the Earth would be poorer in spirit and intent. For My part, I advocate for you before Jesus and invite your trust in His powers. I give you accolades for your work and assure you that the future will be bright. My children, there is no substitute for the constancy of your faith in His Most Sacred Heart because you are called to imitate His life in good times and bad. There is no question that you are asked to be like Him, and you must know that you would not be so summoned if it were impossible for you to accomplish it. I daresay that your holiness induces your desires to reach for attainable dreams that comfort you in the night, ones that you ascribe to chance, but are actually the Holy Paraclete reviving your hopes. There is no question that mental depression is one of your worst enemies in the struggle to unite the world because so many sinners oppose the graces of the Church. If you wish to become giants among men, you must first realize the humility that will take you there, and that upon your shoulders rests the future of your youth. I beg you to give them reason to follow your footsteps. Lend to them your most arduous efforts to show them that the Holy Spirit reigns in your hearts for your sanctification and theirs. The widening avenue that you travel every day to propagate your religious zeal is a gift for your time and ensuing ages. My children, all this is placed into action by your prayers, and not just any prayers. It is not just wishing for good weather or winning the fight against your enemies that you reveal your greatest sacrifices, but in your desire to face-down the devil in places you never expect him to be. It is the lackadaisical approach to holiness of your closest friends that you must address, even at the risk of jeopardizing your relationships. Your prayers must magnify your conviction so they recognize the dignity you have gained by inviting Jesus into your lives. Yes, pray as much for strength during suffering as for clear skies and cool breezes. Your priorities must be aligned in accordance with Jesus' Crucifixion, and He will raise you high beside the Saints in the grandness of His Paschal Resurrection. My children, if you aspire to greatness in themes of secular achievement, you may make this true, but you will eventually perceive them as hollow victories compared to the triumphs of the Church. The question to always return to is whether your intentions and efforts advance everything that fosters the Eternal, that awakens the heroism in other men, that heals the sick and makes peace between nations. The verity of your faith should be evident in loving your neighbors even when they are reckless in their treatment of you, in cases where your most effusive aunt spends an hour speaking to you about nothing but her pet dog, and where you have experienced impatience in your eccentric friends. The point is not whether Jesus is not as apparent in them because they do not suffer like the poor and dying, but shunning them is not a signature of Christian virtue. Again, you must prioritize your actions according to the manifest urgencies of the hour. I appeal to you to make clear to your associates that you are followers of the Cross, and invite them to share in the Cross when they would rather seek leisurely times. Hence, My message is that you consistently make decisions to effect your Christian beliefs according to your station in life, the amount of time remaining in the day, and how you can evangelize the Gospel to the sinners who are most in need. With the ease of communication in this millennium, the Lord has given you plenteous resources to do His bidding. My Special son, I offered the early part of this message for those who see faith as a subpart of life instead of its centerpiece. It is true that you can only do so much; you do not have inexhaustible strength. I invite you to review the quotation of Saint Clare of Assisi that you were given at your workplace on February 25, 2008. Actualize your efforts for Jesus based on the spiritual reason about which she speaks. There is no question that you are doing this. And, thank you for reserving time for your brother. I have said that you are an innate part of his life and his best friend. I know after the passing of so much time and the publishing of many books that you understand. Jesus wants to hold nothing back to convince Americans that He is serious about their conversion. What profound writing you have incorporated into the opening of your 2008 anthology. Did you believe that you were able to see with such theological accuracy? These are the days, My son, that you will look at reflectively and declare with proclamation that the Holy Spirit infiltrated your heart so broadly that you were taken by surprise."

Sunday, March 16, 2008
2:47 p.m.

"Since we have these promises, beloved, let us purify ourselves from every defilement of flesh and spirit, and in the fear of God strive to fulfill our consecration perfectly." [2 Cor. 7:1]

"Gentleness, warmness, piety, and gratitude comprise your holiness with the encouragement of the Lord sufficing your lives. You are close to Him when you embrace these things, when you ponder deeply the struggles of life endured by your forbears who held their faith until death. My dear children, time is of no consequence in your sojourn toward Eternity because the Fruits of the Holy Spirit do not fade with the ages; they stand as your rock in Jesus because it is through them that He recognizes you. The Father forgives you of your trespasses in Jesus' Crucifixion, and you are absolved of everything offensive to Him. You strive for spiritual perfection because Jesus is perfect, but you must not be despondent if you have weaknesses. Every mortal man suffers temptation during his life, and it would seem that this modern age is littered with more distractions to tempt you. When looking at others, do your best to see their nobler attributes, lifting-up their goodness, and never-minding their mistakes. You must never judge someone's life by their weakest moment, for in all souls there is the potential to accomplish good things. A few miscues or mishaps do not nullify an otherwise righteous life of painstaking excellence. Today, I remind you that you might witness in others your own failings, and that you must be as forgiving of them as you overlook your own misdeeds. If you are humble and contrite, and if you search for amendment, Jesus will forgive you. And, this is what He asks you to do for others in honor of the Cross. Please remember that humanity is not inherently corrupt, but you are prone to corruption; you are contaminated by corruption in much the same way that a bacterium infects an organism. The Crucifixion is your antidote to sin and death, and your compliance with the Gospel heals you to all degrees spiritual and temporal. My warning is that you do not be cruel or harsh toward others as you are gentle with yourselves. My Special son, you must know at this juncture that the profound beauty of your life in Jesus will have ripple effects through time. It is not My intention to heap accolades upon you like roses adorning a shrine, but I speak the truth about the impressiveness of your labors. Your brother continues to grow physically weary due to his age and the posture with which he is working. We shall make some adjustments, and he will feel better. He knows that he is glorifying Jesus through his contributions, and he expects these things to happen. You see that he is becoming less opinionated, less apt to argue points that do not matter, and looks toward the humorous side of life. This is something common to many because it offsets issues they face while not feeling well, having a shorter attention span, and wanting everyone to be friends. If you permit it; if you help him dwell on the positive, shying away from combative and divisive topics, these things will have no adverse effect on his longevity. This certainly does not imply that he will not defend the Church and everything important to human conversion. Indeed, he will reserve his best energy and effort specifically for that purpose. Your new writings are beatific expressions that will lend consolation and peace to those who read them. Please remember what the Angels told your brother. Once it is placed into history, no one can destroy it. And, if it seems that I am always thanking you, it is true; and bless you for supporting the homeless woman among you. She has a holy heart; she knows what love is. There are many decent people in the world, hundreds who live in your immediate vicinity, many who suffer egregiously the pressures of life, and others whose agonies are known only to God. You and your brother have been a source of intense comfort for them even without considering your contributions to the Church. One of your fellow parishioners recently read your last book about the little bird that was splayed on the sidewalk beneath a tree branch, and he began to weep that I would mention something of Nature that so intricately describes people's lives. These images and concepts would have had no way into the public domain if you and your brother had not agreed to receive them in private. As I have said on former occasions, you do not realize the moral excellence with which you are living. You uphold the poor and downtrodden; you upbraid the haughty and well to do; you pray for the conversion of the wicked, and you embrace everything that Jesus has taught you. My Special son, please be assured if your conduct was the contrary of these things, I would tell you. I shall be brief today, but I came with My Immaculate Heart overflowing with affection. I promise the intercession of Father Joseph Timothy Murray on his anniversary, and I bless you with Jesus' Eucharistic presence every day."

Sunday, March 23, 2008
2:57 p.m.

"All Scripture is inspired of God and is useful for teaching, for reproof, correction, and training in holiness so that the man of God may be fully competent and equipped for every good work." [2 Tim 3:16-17]

"By receiving Me in your home, My children, you are expressing hope that humanity will change, that hubris will be supplanted by humility, that plenteous goodwill shall overcome the Earth's lack of sharing. I speak to you through the years with the evolving of the seasons, and you respond with your prayers for the conversion of lost sinners. I again tell you that yours is the imperative part; your petitions to Jesus carry the worthiness of Creation refined.

It is My joy to be with you when you pray because you embrace such genuine anticipation of the coming of God's Eternal Kingdom. Humanity will soon witness the collapse of the wall dividing global secularism from Christianity, and with it will come the fulfillment of everything you have ever dreamed. The Lord sees the greatness in you because your loyalties to Him are honed by your consecration to the Cross. In Jesus, your debt to the Father has been retired, and you can rise from your slumber knowing that humanity's fate is elevated to the beatific expressions that you write about in your diaries. Your prayers and holy deeds counteract the ill-conceived ambitions of your enemies. This is why you must remain steadfast in the hope about which I speak! You gladly celebrate the Easter Resurrection of Jesus from the Sepulcher because the Holy Spirit inspires you to believe. Yes, your expectation of being rescued from the obsolescence of your lives gives you reason to walk with joy in your atonement with Heaven! With your dutiful hopes in tow, you have reached the pathway to Paradise that God deigned for you in Jesus' Resurrection. You live the Second Advent with all believers, and your sacred duties are fulfilled when you deny Heaven's adversaries the opportunity to foist doubt upon all who are faithful to the Cross. It is clear that humanity has multiple ailments because not everyone in your company accepts the teachings of the Church. As I have said, this is why I am speaking to you now. We manifest goodness in the face of evil, reflect Light where there is only darkness, and foster healing to everything that is broken. My Special son, with awesome gratitude do I come because it is clear that you are one with the Wisdom that fashioned the heavens. Your supernal obedience is beyond reproach, and your vision about matters of faith and morals cannot be impugned. Truly, it is obvious by your prayers that Jesus inspires you, that the Holy Paraclete infiltrates every fiber of your being, and that your essential existence is given to the Kingdom of God. Please do not misconstrue the intentions of My messages in other cities of the world, but realize how precisely they align with those I have given to you. It is clear that My seers must be expeditious in transmitting them to lost sinners, and you should be scrupulous about where you transfer them. The meaning of My narratives is direct and requires no interpretation. As each day passes, humanity moves through time more closely to the fulfillment of hidden prophesies that I have dictated to My messengers and to the revealing of various secrets that have definitive dates. I urge you today to pray without ceasing for the conversion of prodigals, for the charity of the heart that Christians must practice, and especially for the end of abortion. Pray for the Marian Movements of Priests, for the advancement of the causes of social justice, and for the uplifting of every pauper from the burdens of poverty. This justice is wholly dependent on sharing the Earth's resources and advances in medicine. Jesus knows who has been given the responsibility to heal the sick and house the homeless; and when they do not respond, His wrath follows. He allows the proud to be felled by their own devices, and this is the way that Mercy is spread over the land. When you believe that God is involved with the intricacies of people's daily lives, you stand by Him in setting things right. Your reactions are determined by this framework of prudence that makes amends for the indiscretions of the wicked. And, I see that you are writing your next book with ingenious benevolence. I have attested that you do not realize the magnitude of these things, and this manuscript is no exception. I know that you are thankful for all this, as you have said, but do you recall that it is you and your brother who are living for the Lord? You offer the gift of converted souls to the Messiah who absolves them! Hence, the gratitude comes from Heaven, and the jubilation belongs to God."

Sunday, March 30, 2008
2:53 p.m.

"For a child is born to us, a son is given us; upon his shoulder dominion rests. They name him Wonderful Counselor, God-Hero, Father Forever, Prince of Peace." [Isaiah 9:5]

"Let us be filled with thanksgiving that Jesus affords us the opportunity to communicate through His Sacred Heart to prosper the dignity of His people and work strenuously for the repentance of wayward sinners. You look for truth in a world composed of organisms, chemicals, compounds, wildlife, and spontaneous forces. Today, I speak to My Special and Chosen sons with the auspicious news that I will on December 28, 2008 give My final message as the *Morning Star Over America*. You have grown in paramount ways to receive the Holy Spirit through your faith in Jesus, your adoration of His Eucharistic Sacrament, your veneration of Me, and your holiness that lives forever in the sanctification of every soul. You have become strong in your defense of My intercession through My teachings and pleadings, and you are immune and impervious to the criticisms and persecution that befell you when we first began. My little ones, I am not suggesting that I will cease speaking to you, for I said that I did not come to leave your hope unfulfilled. The Father will decide when My appearances here will end. It is time to allow the Church to begin the arduous task of discernment. The Magisterium declines to assess ongoing private revelations, thus you have heard no official pronouncement about Medjugorje. I remind you that your service, dedication, and generosity are commendable. I once spoke about humanity being poised in holiness to the point that Jesus will take your picture for the final ages. In the Lord's eye, one of these exposures can span a hundred years. When we began your messages on February 22, 1991, we initiated a blessing that will proceed until the end of time. You have in your hearts the seeds of faith that have grown into towering gifts. They consist of parables and images, prayerful contemplations and admonitions, and warnings that are applicable to every creature. Therefore, you will record My purpose today as having freed you to permit wider and more expansive meditations to be drawn through the lessons and teachings of Jesus developing in your hearts. My Special son, let us review what this entails. If you and your brother have good health and opportunity, you will record public messages through the 2008 Feast of the Holy Family. Then, you will publish your final anthology in 2009. You will be able to concentrate on select Scriptural topics or any other manuscript you choose to further enlighten and convert the American people. Such things as newspaper editorials and other public and private writings can be involved in these works, as well as historical references to previous subjects as they apply. I have given you ample messages since 1991 to last an entire lifetime heralding God's Kingdom. My son, does this aptly describe the future we laid out? If the Lord is willing, you and your brother will have longevity to propagate our work that has lasted into 18 years. I regard My announcement today as a liberating and ratifying occurrence, indicating that you have graduated from one level of My intercession into another. I speak today about the events of the next months and years and ask you to acknowledge that you will be responsible for the spiritual awakening of millions of lost sinners. There are times in the lives of Christians when you make an accounting of what the years have wrought, what you have contributed, and how you have grown and been affected by the Wisdom of the Holy Spirit that has descended upon you. Some serving religious vocations take sabbaticals of a year or more to reflect on their service in the Lord's vineyard. We have spoken about how close you and your brother are to your work that you might not realize the magnitude of the miracle. You are feeding the miracle by remaining at peace here at home; you have not lost sight of a goal whose defining moment is upon you. My son, you recognize the larger picture and framework that include a period of time that can cover a quarter-century in human years. You are aware of the sacrifices that I ask of My children that no one knows about, ones that praise God with the suffering of those close to Him, ones whose faith is larger than time and space. Therefore, I offer blessings and gratitude, and My promise of meaningful intercession until the world is through and the final dawn of the Earth arrives. The future will bring many circumstances about which you must ponder, the death of family members, changing of the guard in locations like your workplace and social institutions in America. You must never be an isolationist like some other visionaries. You will stand tall and dignified by your contributions to the Church and to the conversion of humanity when you see them from the other side of life. Yes, you comprehend My intentions completely. Do not forget that this does not imply that I will stop speaking. If there is a most important matter I could request you to consider from this day forward, it would be that you internalize the fact that the Lord is indebted to you. Like Jesus, you are a benefactor for which millions have prayed since the first century. There have been mysteries through the years that will be clear as crystal when the eve of eternity opens."

Sunday, April 6, 2008
2:26 p.m.

"Jesus told him, I am the way, and the truth, and the life; no one comes to the Father but through me. If you really knew me, you would know my Father also. From this point on, you know him; you have seen him." [John 14:6-7]

"It requires a mighty faith in the Lord to withstand the buffets of secular persecution, but you are that strong; you are tall in righteousness because of your trust. My little children, I speak of a determined heart that holds you true to the Gospel because the Holy Spirit binds this in you. You are the mediums for God's Grace to flourish in Creation because your holiness blooms by that same Grace. Thank you for praying with Me, for remembering the ills of broken humanity, and hoping with all your might that your lost brothers and sisters will be found before it is too late. Today, I speak of Grace because this is what sustains you through the perils of darkness. Do you remember that it was Grace that hath brought you thus far? I bring the commendation of the Lord God to you, and His gratefulness, Glory, and divinity abounding across the expanse of the universe to enrich your lives. Jesus uplifts and upholds you through the awesome responsibility that has been placed upon you to defend the Church against its detractors and teach your children the holy path that maintains their corporeal purity. I have spoken about the pluralism that has gripped America in ways that are simply understood. Jesus issues you a consistent challenge to execute your own charter, be your brothers' keepers, and remain true to the Sacred Beatitudes that evoke common good with all people. I guarantee My assistance in guiding you to Him, in preparing you for the tremendous moment when you shall stand before God, and encouraging you when you feel defeated in your everyday lives. It is Jesus who walks with you, who has suffered before you, endured His Passion that humanity might be sanctified, and laid down His life on the Cross to redeem you. He adores you because you are becoming perfected in His ways. Whom else would forgive you for all that has been committed against the Kingdom of Love? Who else would paint the colors of your dreams and dress your wounds? Only the Son of Man who was born to you, who takes you to summits and onto meadows where you see with clarity the intentions of Heaven for your eternal joy. My Special son, it would appear that you are tired this weekend, but not without good reason. You have accomplished benevolent things at home and at your workplace, and you are carrying yourself with real grace through a period of transition. I said last week that I will remain with you because you are My cherished son; you and your brother and the whole of humanity are My adopted sons and daughters whom I love with the intensity of the power of the Lord. You know that Jesus is your Redeemer; the Holy Spirit is your Advocate, and God is the provider of all. When the poet spoke about how grand go the years, she referred to the way humanity treads with gentle dignity to death with trust and admiration for the Kingdom of the Father. Indeed, she spoke about transcending the suffering of this world with supernatural composure that is derived from the peace of Heaven. You are thrice-blessed in your faith, and you see death in the context of the redemption of men. When your forbears spoke a century ago about the disposition of God, they celebrated His capacity to forgive humanity's transgressions in the face of wars and famine, through the good and bad, so that your age can realize that He has always been the same. Even when Jesus was Crucified on Mount Calvary, His Love never died. When you pray the Rosary or the litanies, you stand in this same permanence. These are the reasons I am beholden to you for your allegiance to My Queenship, because you know that I have your best interest at heart. How many times have I mentioned that the Mother of Jesus could not succeed without the dedication of My children? The Angels and Saints are powerful as you have been told, and they speak to God as they have rightly seen Him. It is you on Earth who must work through faith, even with Me as your Maternal Advocate. You must trust Jesus that it is Me speaking to you now! You shall be rewarded for your splendorous willingness to set aside your fears and follow Him to a place you cannot yet see. I promise that what I am telling you is true."

Sunday, April 13, 2008
2:46 p.m.

"Blessed be the name of God forever and ever, for Wisdom and power are his. He causes the changes of the times and seasons, makes kings and unmakes them. He gives Wisdom to the wise and knowledge to those who understand." [Daniel 2:20-21]

"My children, your natural inclinations are imbedded in your atonement and reconciliation with God through His Son, and I have come to facilitate your professions during your prayers. Today, it is imperative for you to pray that Pope Benedict will touch the hardened of heart in America during his Papal visit, and that the healing of old wounds will come to families and severed friendships by seeing the gentleness of his spirit. The Holy Father is aware of your failings and weaknesses, but he also knows of the power of the Sacraments to cleanse you. My whole deposit of messages in America speaks to the easing of societal and racial tensions, a commitment toward righteousness that is unprecedented in your time, the return to purity, chastity, penance and prayer, and the opening of the hearts of your public leaders to stop the mortal sins of abortion and institutionalized suicide. Americans are long on patriotism and woefully deficient in their desire to pray for the coming of the Lord's Kingdom. I speak about a nation that will be visited this week by Christ's Vicar because you must obey his commands and be loyal to the Church. Let us pray during his visit that what happens to him here advances the purpose of Jesus' Sacrifice and elevates the poor and oppressed. We hope for the healing of broken relationships and the enhancement of the spiritual love between America's mothers and fathers, sisters and brothers, husbands and wives, sons and daughters, neighbors, and everyone's love for God. I assure you that Heaven will descend upon the United States this week and broaden your awareness of the Church's mission through a uniquely visionary Pontiff. I also today summon you to remember the sick and elderly, the orphaned, the abandoned and criminal, and all who need the Lord's tender touch. You regularly see the crosses of physically suffering people, but you do not see those borne by those who are hurting inside, the sad, mourning and grief-stricken, the emotionally distraught and spiritually malnourished, and sinners who lack guidance in matters of the conscience. Even in this land of plenty, many children wander the streets in peril of being harmed and exploited because of the breakdown of their family bonds. Pope Benedict will rebuke you for this, and he will demand social justice in a nation that purports to respect the value of individual life. It is important that you place more emphasis on nourishing and housing the poor than exploring outer-space and performing experiments in cybernetics. You have been given ample measure to lend help to anyone who requires it, not just those who know someone of note or are related to partisans in power. In effect, I call you to adhere to the admonishments of the Gospel in your everyday dealings and personal lives. Where America is plagued by atheism, pluralism, relativism and outright evil works, you should realize that the Father will punish you for these things. As I have said, it is not illegal to pray publically for the preservation of human life in your country. You have in your power the ability to sanctify this nation and the entire Earth by your propagation of Christianity. The atonement about which I speak mandates your participation in the purification of the world according to your abilities imparted to you by God. You have modes of communication and transportation that permit you to travel and speak, to teach your lost brothers and sisters about Jesus' Crucifixion that has restored your dignity. It is of profitable consequence that your leaders and former presidents negotiate with your foreign enemies, for what grace is there cohorting with your friends? If a nation is preparing to attack you or your allies, does it not make sense to procure peace where there has been terrorism and atmospheres of war? Anyone who ostracizes Jesus' peacemakers is under the diabolical influence of Satan. As your Mother, I have spoken about the Sacred Beatitudes that Jesus dictated to humanity in His hillside sermon. Many brave men and women have devoted their entire lives defending them while oftentimes being ridiculed by their peers, but theirs is the Kingdom of God.

"My Special son, I am giving you a message that will appear in the final year of your third New Millennium anthology, one in a series that addresses the need to reach-out in faith, search for the Messiah while He can be found, reclaim the innocence of rogue nations and peoples, and seek the Lord's favor upon this new-century world. You have charted your future course to dispense My messages to humanity. This is greater than any one person might do; it is more prolific than constructing a city or lifting skyscrapers; it is more commendable than appointing missionaries to lost acres; it stands in stark contrast to the objectives of capitalist elitists, and it is reminiscent of the Saints in whose shadows you serve. I weep gladly because you and your brother are rarities in America. I have said this over seventeen years. When I tell you that Mine eyes have seen the Glory of the Lord, I recognize it in your actions, in the way you carry yourselves, and the compassion with which you approach the poor. I daresay that you have forged for yourselves a saber of eloquence with which the Holy Paraclete is inspiring the citizens of this republic to take a good look at their lives in reflection of the Christian conscience that Jesus prescribes. While I know that you see an appalling indifference toward the Church, please realize that this is a temporary departure from the norm that existed prior to 1965. Civilization is moving counterclockwise to the inception of the righteousness that God desires in you, swimming against the tides of time, so that when Jesus returns in Glory, all who are dedicated to Him will begin again; not old and worn, but fresh and revitalized, prepared for the youthful rejuvenation that you inherited in Jesus' Resurrection from the Tomb. We have spoken about this. Your AD 2003-2005 book will be as elevated as its predecessor, and your first fifty pages will lift it even higher in ecclesial significance. Do you sense the evocativeness that you are tendering to America? Your brothers and sisters will understand that I am as strong as the Holy Spirit allowed Me to be on Good Friday, the same way the Lord gives you strength and perseverance to witness the dying Earth and the renewal of everything pure about humanity. And, remember that no one who has ever lived, including your Savior Jesus, has loved you more than your brother Timmy. He certainly has his faults, and has made tremendous mistakes to which humanity is prone, but his love for you is of the perfection of God. And, your love for him, your friendship, companionship, spiritual support, and daily advice have been princely, priceless, and indispensable. You extol the holiness of the greatest Saints to have served the Church. I issue My promise that I will never depart your side. I will always hear your prayers and ask Jesus to procure for you the desires of your heart."

Sunday, April 20, 2008
2:55 p.m.

"May the God of peace make you perfect in holiness. May he preserve you whole and entire, spirit, soul and body, irreproachable at the coming of our Lord Jesus Christ." [1Thess. 5:23]

"My children, today is April 20, 2008 and day 111 of the year. I appear as the Holy Father Pope Benedict XVI offers the Holy Sacrifice of the Mass in America for all believers and nonbelievers, for the living and the dead, for all the petitions that the faithful have laid at his feet, for the end of abortion, corruption, and sin of every complexion through the Crucifixion of Jesus Christ. I speak here in your exile about the asylum you have gained in the Wisdom of the Holy Spirit imparted by this Pontiff, knowing that you can trust his homiletics to lead you to the Holy Gospel. This has been a grace-filled week in the United States with the presence of the Lord's Vicar in your nation. The observance of his birthday and anniversary of his election as Pope have taken place during his pilgrimage to the United States as the leader of the Roman Catholic Church. You may take everything you own, all the attributes of your faith and trust, and place them in his care. And, all your faults and failures are his to carry, all the remorse you feel for your transgressions; give all these problems to the Holy Father, Pope Benedict, and God will hear you. This message is about America's penchant for goading others into poor conduct, indecency, impurity, and materialism. Your youth are impressionable souls who must be taught the virtues of discretion and chastity. One of the most grave and troubling aspects of American society is the ideological alarmism that keeps so many living in fear, even those in the Church. The alarmism about which I speak is anything that attempts to frighten you or stir undue, inordinate passions and emotions, that accuses the faithful of zealotry when they fight against violations of the Truth that perplex the wise, exploit the vulnerable, or persecute the innocent. The American secular media are responsible for the alarmism that forces fear into the hearts of the impressionable, and it is perpetuated by false speech on the street and in the marketplace. These issues run contrary to the personal trust you have built into your religious convictions. You are Christians, and the Lord calls you to obey the Sacred Scriptures in your motivations, thoughts, habits, actions, and dispositions. My children, the April 2008 visit of Pope Benedict has brought closure to many who have suffered the atrocities of September 11, 2001, and has given you a clearer understanding of healing and forgiveness. The Pope has made sufficient apology for the weaknesses of the Church that no one or any faction should hold against its priests for any reason. He has brought dignity to a land where dignity is rare. Even as the people of the United States are enduring the rude hustings of another political campaign, Pope Benedict is summoning you to the higher Kingdom of God. His kindness prohibits him from issuing a more stern reprimand and Papal condemnation of the American way of life because he remembers the Fascism and Communism of his youth. This does not mean that he is unopposed to American consumerism and materialism, your rampant crime and atheism, and grotesque culture of death. He prays for you in the presence of the Angels for the conversion of dark American hearts. My little ones, I speak to you today as an ardent admirer of Pope Benedict XVI, as his Mother; and I address a nation that is fractured and splintered not only by what you do, but what you decline to do. Many are worried that the scourge of abortion will not end, and other blind partisans are determined to continue the plague of infanticide. Some are concerned that too much of their money will be shared with poor people whom they believe to be unworthy, while others would like to delve into the pockets of the affluent without completing their rightful chores. Somewhere in the middle of these, My children, Americans will meet, but there is no compromising matters of faith and morals or life and death. There is no substitute for complying with the Lord's proclamation that any life He places in exile must remain there until He determines it to be finished. Hence, when I speak of alarmism, I refer to the unnecessary and unsubstantiated fear that Americans have of people who are different from them, who do not look or sound like them, or are afraid that those who have only little will mount an insurrection against your established economy and holders of wealth. There is no such thing as extorted charity.

My Special and Chosen sons, I have spoken about these matters in other contexts, and you are enjoying another Papal visit by the leader of the Church to inspire the religious zeal of American Catholics. You wonder what non-Catholics feel about seeing the national media coverage of the pilgrimage of the Pope. The answer is that they are divided. Most stand in awe as they witness the primacy of the Holy See. They respect and venerate the Holy Mother Church for everything it proclaims. Other Americans are complacent, and very few are radically opposed to seeing the Catholic Church living and breathing in their midst. To fear an underground movement against the Church or that anti-Catholicism is rampant in America is part of the alarmism that I have spoken about. Alarmism also causes unneeded arguments between parishioners and divisive conversation in the home. It has a false bias based on their lack of self-respect and insecurities. I bid you to shy away from such alarmism, to disavow it, and be more confident in your relationship with Jesus through the Holy Spirit. Do you understand? The 2008 spring has come, and you will see the warmer weather allowing you to spend more time outside. My Special son, the amazing grace about which we speak is the presence of gratitude that God has for His creatures. Jesus knows that His brothers and sisters are confined to a world in which He was cast-out, but their difficult journey will conclude in the mansions of Paradise. Regarding the introductory pages of your book, they are brilliant and stunning, resounding and exalting the power of Jesus with clear terminology and righteous thoughts. Time is on your side, and you hold advantage over anything that might impede you. I know that you understand because I am speaking to the Holy Spirit in your heart. Remember that Jesus looks for conviction and consistency in your faith; and you indicate through your prayers and actions that you approach Him through Me."

Sunday, April 27, 2008
2:38 p.m.

"Our soul waits for the Lord who is our help and our shield, for in him our hearts rejoice; in his holy name we trust. May your kindness, O Lord, be upon us who have put our hope in you." [Psalms 33:20-22]

"It is My high honor to speak to you on this auspicious occasion when you pray with the Mother of God because you are lifting your hearts to Heaven in ways that remake the Earth. It is good that you embrace the exquisite and prestigious Salvation that you have gained in Jesus' Crucifixion because you will be granted Everlasting Life. My humble children, please remember everyone whose hearts are aching and the millions who are shorn of their innocence and without the bare necessities of life. These are dangerous times for humanity not only because of the threats of terror and war, but because only few are addressing the poverty that causes them. You must prepare for the impact on your spirits and consciousness when world events demand your grief. The strength for life is always found in the Sacred Heart of Jesus; this is the reason He solicits your awakening. Whether you know it or not, that for which you pray will come. Every error is expunged when you ask the Son of Man to intervene, and this is also why I augment your prayers. I dare speak of the perfection of humanity because I realize that you are capable of being holy. Indeed, if you do not emulate the Son of God; if you are not reborn in Him, you shall not inherit His Kingdom. Whatever stains and depresses you, what brings darkness where there should be light, and anything that makes you afraid are eliminated through Jesus' Sacrifice on the Cross. How can you not have hope when seeing the millions who have accepted the Messianic redemption that has been accorded to you? This message is the same as always; you need not live on an Earth pervaded by evil and indifference. You belong to the righteousness that has absolved you, and My mission here is to assist your conversion to this eternal deliverance. It is written in the Scriptures and upon the center of human hearts. The reconciliation between Heaven and Earth begins with repentant sinners and will conclude when Jesus reenters His Kingdom in Glory. This is the Lord's plan through the peace and grace of My

Immaculate Heart. The Triumph has begun. My Special son, rare is the occasion when the Lord looks upon His children with as much wonderment as you and your brother. You have participated in a grand opening of human hearts and cultivation of Earth that is unprecedented for your years. As you write in your next book, the purification of humanity resides in the sense of awareness that Divine Love is your power, and in the acceptance of men to tend toward Truth. You have lived in this keenness by exercising your faith as you came of age in the Wisdom of the Father. All the hours; all the effort you have given to Him through your devotion to Me, your dedication to the Cross, and your love for humanity will reap undying benefits. You see the fleeting attributes of life and the purpose for the exile of men. These are preparatory times that esteem the faith you have invested in the Church, your Apostolate, and the future you shall harvest through all of these. Is it possible that a man can see beatifically without opening his eyes? Can someone's spirit be rekindled by images and dreams, by voices in the night, and on journeys to sacred cities? The answer is contingent on their trust in Jesus and their belief in miracles. Reading your prophetic writing proves that miracles can be the basis for practical faith. Anyone who says that you are not a theologian rejects everything the Apostles wrote, effected, and fought for. Yours is an edification that stands on your foundation of service and duty to God through your fealty to His Son, and this cannot be revoked. These are among the reasons that your mission will succeed and the conversion of sinners for whom we have prayed will come to pass. I urge you to never surrender to doubt or despair, and take a lesson from the Martyrs who never wavered in their trust that Heaven embraced them both on Earth and in the presence of the Father. I have given you this promise previously.

It is imperative that you make choices to ease your contempt for the contemptible world. You cannot solve all the problems you see by internalizing their cause. I told you on September 11, 2005 that My call for the conversion of humanity in My messages to you and your brother has given you a false sense that this burden is placed on you; and nothing could be further from the truth. As men grow older, they become more embittered and sarcastic, and this will absolutely take from you the longevity that you have been praying to receive. I am speaking about Jesus' answers to your petitions. His response is that you must reverse the perilous trend where you look only for evil acts of other people, where you dwell on the darkness of the Earth, and where you see no way to purify the world without some catastrophic discipline. I said that there would be chastisements, and this should be sufficient. My son, you share no blame for the way you feel. You are a faithful child of Abba who commands that humanity convert. Your brotherhood alongside Jesus informs your decisions about how others should conduct themselves. I came in February 1991 not to destroy your hope or jeopardize your health, but to enlist your faith and trust that every hint of corruption on the face of the Earth will end. Whatever your frustrations, they will pass. How goes your attitude also goes your health. Your personality traits and reactions to others and life's situations are forcing tremendous stress on you. My Special son, please believe that I am not suggesting this to assign fault, but you have resumed the combative approach that you had earlier eliminated. There is another danger that you will suppress your feelings and harbor your animosities inside. This is more counterproductive than the original problem. You must vent your frustrations when you have them because this is the natural result of being aware. You are completing another anthology that will amend human life as you know it, and this is an inexplicable victory for the people of God. Let us see how your acts nurture your heart and temperament in the future, along with the advice I have given you today. It is an amazing prospect knowing how your brother loves you. *(I had an episode with my condition of heart arrhythmia and had to be taken to the emergency room at the hospital. Timothy dropped me off at the hospital door because there were no parking spaces available. They took me immediately to a treatment room, thinking I might be having a heart attack. When my brother came in, he did not know where they had taken me and could not get anyone's attention to find out.)* I am glad that you did not see the look on his face after he parked the truck and ran into the emergency center and could not find you. And, after another ten minutes, no one would help him. They acted like he was not there. This is a child of the Lord who was violated and criticized as the youngest of his father's sons, who was called a runt by his elder brothers, whom they said would never contribute to the betterment of the world. This is the boy who witnessed in horror his sister killed by the car and how his parents grieved, and the way his siblings were afflicted by illness. This is the one who was poisoned by toxic fumes in his father's repair shop that damaged his nervous system. If he has any dignity, he has received it from you. He took a position of employment where he was abused by the United States government, the Board of Commissioners, slothful tenants, the local and state media, and vendors and contractors of all kinds. All this occurred before the Mother of God appeared and asked for more. This is the boy who loves you, who adores you. This is he who will uphold you before any other mortal, and serve you with the gentleness of the Holy Spirit in his heart. And, this is the one you have loved like Jesus. You have helped him overcome his weaknesses and soften his memories. My Special son, this is the boy you have dignified by feeding, housing, clothing, and telling him that he does not have to drive someone else's used junk. This is what he reminds the Lord that you do for him."

Sunday, May 4, 2008
2:53 p.m.

"For thus says the Lord God: I myself will look after and tend my sheep. As a shepherd tends his flock when he finds himself among his scattered sheep, so will I tend my sheep." [Ezek. 34:11]

"It is My joy to speak about Jesus' Love in comprehendible terms because you come to peace in His Most Sacred Heart. The intention of My messages has always been concise; to unify humanity beneath the Cross in which you become Saints. When the human spirit is converted to Christianity, you make sense of everything, and you know what paths are worthy of pursuit. My children, the final record of the ages will reveal that you have been with Me through your trials and tribulations, that you have understood what it means to be self-sacrificial so your poor brothers and sisters can prosper in the barest aspects of life. The annals will show that when the Spirit of the Lord called on you for help, you came forth. You scrutinized humanity's problems, demanded answers, clarified issues, and offered solutions. You used as your guide the Wisdom of God in all earthly and ethereal matters important to Him. It is with gratitude for your engagement that I appear before you vested in the authority of Heaven to commend and advise you, and to be your Advocate before Jesus who is your Advocate to the Father. Also today, I seek your prayers for modesty, that humankind will know that there is nothing difficult about true holiness, that even those who lack analytical and quantitative adequacies can comprehend what it means to love your brothers in the image of My Son. While there are intricate and specific terminologies for the Sacraments, traditions and attributes of the Church, the faith to which you are called is simple. You are summoned to respond to the edicts of the Holy See this way, and pray for the Vicar of Christ not in some quadragon, but in Saint Peter's Square. We speak in May about the Earth's spring and the New Springtime of spiritual hope that is symbolized by Nature coming to life. There are suffering souls in your company who need prayers for healing, those disposed to depression and physical ailments, and people who are prone to violence. While you are strong in faith, others do not know God; and it is for this reason that I call you to prayer. There is a dismissive air about non-Christians toward the New Covenant that renders them blind to the conditions of the world. We are charged with telling them about a redemption of the highest order that you are given through the Grace of God and Jesus' Sacrifice on the Cross. You know that the Crucifixion is timeless, powerful, and absolving because the Holy Spirit has implanted this in your hearts. Taking this message to the masses who do not believe in Jesus is not as simple as Christian faith itself because you are opposed by Satan's evil factions and the indifference of other less malevolent creatures. How many times have I said that we shall succeed? While it would seem that once is sufficient, I have promised on multiple instances that the Victory of the Cross has been won and the Triumph of My Immaculate Heart is opening. I see how you pity the blind! I know how you pine for the conversion of lost sinners who are led astray by pagans and heathens in the secular void. The suffering that humanity endures is a result of the rejection of the healing balm of Jesus' Blood, requiring the Faith-Church to join His Passion for the sanctification of everyone who declines God's offer to accept Him and all the Hosts of Heaven through that same Crucifixion. Be mindful that time is the venue through which you become inclined to hear the Good News and accept Salvation before the Son of Man returns in Glory. Please pray to stop abortion and uplift motherhood that is celebrated this month. O' how the unborn children yearn to be born into their mothers and fathers' arms! The Lord demands that you remember them, and He will respond. My Special son, this is a fortunate occasion in 2008 because I have the privilege of speaking to you and your brother about the way Jesus provides for you, the health-restoring miracles at My shrines, and how you artfully perceive the way the universe is unfolding according to the decrees of God. What words can I add to these? Intercessory prayers are being said for you by Fathers LaBonte, Murray, Spreen, and Wright at the Feast Table in Heaven as they hear the wisdom of Saint Augustine. There are many Saints who were acquainted with you when they resided on Earth, and tens-of-thousands you never met. But, you soon will. The village of your youth has been transformed into a place you scarcely know because most of your friends have moved away and your forbears are with Jesus. All around, the world is changing, but the Love of God will forever be the same. You are doing better in your perception of fatalism, alarmism, and sarcasm. You will not have the longevity for which you pray if you do not lighten your heart. Remember what you said about choosing wisely the issues you should internalize. And, thank you for praying for your friends from years ago. Some of them have little time left on Earth. I have dispatched the Angels and Communion of Saints to prepare them. Some patients in hospices and nursing homes around the world have been bedfast for years, ones who have laid on their backs, unable to raise their heads. Theirs is the suffering that is sanctifying America and other places around the globe."

Sunday, May 11, 2008
3:26 p.m.

"On one occasion, Jesus spoke thus: Father, Lord of heaven and earth, to you I offer praise; for what you have hidden from the learned and the clever, you have revealed to the merest children." [Matt. 11:25]

"My dear children, while you are suffering America's radical injustices and beleaguered by the solicitations of capitalism, the succession of human events is turning toward the end of the Earth. In this urgency is found your awareness that Jesus is calling you not from afar, but at the center of your hearts. Today, I wish to refresh your recollection about the Holy Gospel message of peace and good will that leads to the coalescence of adversaries. It is peace of mind that you strive to achieve, a time when your conscience is clear from personal indictment, and the entire world is united in Jesus' Most Sacred Heart. You rarely discuss the concept of peace of mind because you are beset by your lack of it. My presence with you is the Lord's gift that you must accept for the cohesion about which I speak. Let us pray for all lost sinners to repent, carry their newfound contrition with them to the foot of the Cross, ask Jesus to tame their wildness, and give them reason to hope. Even as you celebrate Mother's Day, expectant women are preparing to abort the unborn children in their wombs tomorrow morning. This mortal sin is the genesis of your failures, the source of your vexation and lack of understanding of the Will of God. A society that allows the killing of its unborn children is under the influence of evil, and this is the reason you feel forsaken. A fiery dungeon will devour the condemned souls of those who abort unborn children. Why is it true that the Mother of Jesus should tell you this horrific news when I would be much gladder speaking about flowerbeds and rainbows? Because humanity forces its own demise by rejecting the Bible. You have been handed the Holy Gospel, the New Covenant between Heaven and Earth, and yet many choose to do evil. What is the Father's recourse for those who foster the evil scourge of infanticide? How can someone speak of Mother's Day without calling for the end of the atrocity of abortion? When it comes to complying with the wishes of God, there is no middle ground; there are no compromises. You are either with Him or against Him. *Whoever is not with Me is against Me, and whoever does not gather with Me scatters (Luke 11:23).* My Special son, it gives Me intense purpose to speak to you because you are the holy child who has made My revelation as the *Morning Star Over America* possible. You have accepted My presence before you in faith. Yes, you have seen miracles and heard testimonies from the Angels, but so did thousands of your friends who turned another way. This makes you My Special one and your brother My Chosen one, not because he is brought before the world in any magnanimous way, but that he is chosen to be with you. He is My Chosen one because the Lord asked him to help you commit Creation to the Salvation that the sons and daughters of men have found in Jesus on the Cross. You were chosen long before your brother. I share your fatigue in listening to the ranting of nonbelievers who do not receive the Sacraments of the Church. They should have converted heretofore. The religion you were speaking about earlier has been the cause for the defense of the Catholic Church by Jesus' Martyrs for centuries. Please see the following word in your dictionary. Giaour. This is the reason we have not discussed at length the horrendous errors of those who do not share in Holy Christendom. Why? Because it would lead to your own martyrdom before our mission has been accomplished. I wish for you and your brother to focus on the issues that others have in common with Christianity until I tell you otherwise. If you do not, you will become distracted. You will not have the peace of mind that I mentioned moments ago. The blasphemy that comes from some Protestant denominations is offensive to Jesus. Yes, they claim to be led by the Holy Spirit, but are taking the name of the Lord in vain. Never once has any other non-biblical religion referred to the Holy Roman Catholic Church as a great whore or the Antichrist. Do you remember the Sacred Scriptures, warning Christians to beware who has infiltrated their ranks like wolves in sheep's clothing? This is the legacy of the Protestant Church. The reason I have brought this matter to your attention is because Americans should know what I have said about non-Catholics, but not with offensive overtones. And, this is why your first fifty pages of your next book are essential. You have spent hours meditating and concentrating on the opening of your AD 2003-2005 book, and you have struck an appropriate way to relay your thoughts that elevate Me. How can it be true that someone in Texas could state to millions of his followers that the Catholic Church is the great apostate? What kind of evil is this? Hence, you are on the right side of history and in union with the Holy Spirit. In concluding, I remind you today that the Lord prefigured your companionship with your brother from the foundation of the Earth. With your deposit of miraculous works, this must be obvious to you. My son, I adore the covers on your manuscripts. They look like irises that will bloom beyond the skies. What is the sentiment that the Angels dictated to your brother? Let this new beginning mature in truth and live to comb gray hair."

Sunday, May 18, 2008
2:57 p.m.

"Each one of you is a son of God because of your faith in Christ Jesus. All of you who have been baptized into Christ have clothed yourselves with him." [Gal. 3:26-27]

"Dear children, I pray with you as you confidently appeal to Jesus' Sacred Heart with your intentions, and His response is in accordance with the Will of the Father. You have stately souls that are opened wide to receive the Wisdom of the Holy Spirit, and your featly supplications are welcomed by the Hosts of Heaven who intercede for you. I have spoken about the advocacy that is yours through the Legions of Angels and the Communion of Saints, and you have been prudent to enlist their aid as you proceed to the conclusion of time. Today, I refer you to their assistance when pondering the means to mend breaches between nations, and for physical and spiritual healing. You have known that every unseen virtue available to you is encompassing the temporal world; this is why these are such crucial times. Every creature on Earth serves a purpose, and yours as humanity transcends the bonds of mechanical life. The Lord has called each of you to be authors and teachers of your peers so they might inherit greater appreciation for their faith. Remember that nonbelievers are not necessarily your enemies, but the forces that keep them from accepting the Holy Cross are certainly the adversaries of your Salvation. As the dawns come and you tend to your labors, your hearts tell you that you should achieve something manifest, working diligently in the Lord's vineyard to rectify issues that divide the Earth into legions and sects. And, it is not only what you say that is important, but the impressions of your morality and faith you draw forth. The content of your hearts must reflect the constitution of your conscience. This is the moral penmanship that your successors will see for the remainder of their years. Once you introduce the Fruits of Love to your family and friends, they will feed on them; they will return time after time to partake of your imitation of the Son of David. While the Spirit of God is upon you, and He gives you wisdom to speak truly, it is your innate holiness that others want. Your morality prescribes your reputation to the rest of the world. This, My little ones, is why I desire that you look keenly and choose wisely. Once the evensong of the Earth comes, you will be unable to rewind history and begin again. People who attempt to live a belief system that is devoid of Christian virtue are lacking Truth. They make implausible assumptions about the creation of the universe, and are unable to see past the limits of the horizon. Christ Jesus has given humanity the grace of permeating vision, an insight that cannot be gained in any other way. He speaks to His disciples in the parables of Nature and oratories of inspirited souls. The Way, the Truth, and the Life are present in Jesus on the Cross, and these are sacred to your lifeblood by which you are being healed. Thus, the pathway is also your destiny, as I told you years ago. How happy you must be knowing that your departure from this world will initiate your new beginning! Your Christian faith is emblematic of your unity with God through Jesus, and this is the belief that you carry to your death. For My part, I pray that yours will be a glad passing, that you will not fear moving through the veil of exile to reach the height of beatific peace. While change is disturbing, and it is natural to fear the unseen, I implore you to trust Jesus to wrap you in His arms to take you to your heavenly home before the Father. This is what you have been seeking, and it is His Glory that will lead you there. Jesus is with Me when I appear to you, and He urges the faithful to keep your hope alive. I have spoken for centuries to a world that is rife with defiance, but plumbed for perfection. Somewhere between these two extremes is where you live. The hour will soon arrive when the Father will turn everything known to man over to His Crucified Son, every illness that has yet to be suffered, every darkness you could possibly imagine, and all that hails and haunts societies of men. When this Glory unfolds, everyone will succumb to the Triumph of the Cross the way it should have been for 2,000 years. My Special and Chosen ones, My Immaculate Heart is invigorated by the promises you have afforded your brothers and sisters in such lengthy and articulate narrations of beauty in your writing and your lives. You will in the next weeks release another anthology of My messages from AD 2003-2005 that will do more than account for the implications of Salvation I have addressed. The converting instincts that are a normal part of the contrition of the Lord's disciples are elevated by Me and inherited by you. This is what I bequeath to you; it is your inheritance from the Lady of Grace who never died. Thank you for your obedience and loyalty, for your capacity to reach your brothers and sisters with resounding eloquence. We have great hope that all in the world will do the same as your families, that they shall know that you lead your lives in the knowledge that I have given a special benediction to humanity through My messages here. The ones in the book you are about to publish are images from My Heart that will convert masses of sinners."

Sunday, May 25, 2008
2:49 p.m.

"Just as in Adam all die, so in Christ all will come to life again, but each one in proper order: Christ the first fruits and then, at his coming, all those who belong to him." [1 Cor. 15:22-23]

"Welcome into the haven of My Immaculate Heart where you are nurtured by the saving grace of Jesus Christ. When memorializing your friends and loved-ones, I also ask your petitions for sinners who do not know God. My children, it is a blessing when we speak intelligibly because you learn about the holiness that Jesus expects from you. I do not intend to supplant your faith, but to enhance it. Together, we have built a conveyance for humanity's conversion. Thank you for responding to My call. Please pray for the innocents who are exploited around the world, and for those who perpetrate these crimes. It is perplexing that someone's vision is so poor that they cannot see the meekness of children, that they lack the willpower to protect them. These people are under the influence of evil, and you must pray for them. Summon Saint Michael the Archangel to defend the helpless and cast evil spirits into Hell. When I bless you with My Motherly care, the Holy Spirit comes upon you, and the righteousness you seek is implicit in My blessing. You see that the darkness in Creation is expunged by the Divine Light of Heaven. Today, I wish for you to remember the poor souls in Purgatory as you honor those who have died. The years pass quickly, and you carry life's burdens with charity, dignity, poise, piety, and trust. These are gifts of your faith. It is imperative that you see the world through the prism of the Cross because Jesus' Crucifixion is the standard by which all suffering is measured. My appearance today is evidence of His intention to convert wayward souls to His redeeming Blood. Please pray the Rosary devoutly that those who are far from God will repent contritely and amend their lives. This is the reason I have been speaking for so long. Surely you know that the Father dispenses forgiveness upon all who love Him and accept His Son. This is why we pray, My children; it is the service of My messages to the exiled Earth. My Special son, I will be brief because you are tired from your labors, and I would rather you rest. Thank you for receiving Me in this home, for recording My messages, and for your willingness to take them to your families and friends. You and your brother have led lives of holy princes. I bless you during every hour, even when I am silent. Please be wary of the parasites and scavengers who would prey on your work. They are atheists, politicians, media sycophants, and others. You are standing in the Light of Truth by which all men are forgiven. I hope you enjoy the activities in which you are involved because you embrace a simple life while being devoted to completing the manuscripts of My messages. You are in control of the release of your books, and you have said more than once that you have only one opportunity to publish them the first time. Thank you for easing your penchant for jumping to conclusions and dwelling upon issues that have no relevance. I have seen your progress from your childhood, and you have been quiescent at the same time you have wished the world to be right and humanity to embrace justice and fairness. Can you see at this time in your years that these things are happening?"

Sunday, June 1, 2008
2:57 p.m.

"I give you my word, there is no one who has given up home, brothers or sisters, mother or father, children or property for me and for the Gospel who will not receive in this present age a hundred times as many homes, brothers and sisters, mothers, children and property, and persecution besides, and in the age to come, everlasting life." [Mark 10:29-30]

"My children are petitioning at the forefront of Roman Catholicism for the Lord's Kingdom to prevail. My messages have been an inspiration for you to keep preaching, evangelizing, and enfranchising. Never surrender your holiness that is oftentimes unwelcome to those who have no love. I have said many times that the United States prospers detrimentally to the rest of the nations. The call of the conscience requires that you defer to the sense of fairness that Jesus teaches. All the surpluses of America's economic systems must be shared with poor nations with nothing in return. Surely you see that you are farther advanced in amenities, medical services, food and water supplies, communication, and transportation. This is why I call you especially during this month dedicated to the Sacred Heart of Jesus to become like Him. Remember the admonitions of the Holy Gospel that require you to sell what you have and give to the poor. Humanity is one Mystical Body to whom the Father has given much. My Son's Church is prepared to advise you whether you live in joy or mourning versus sickness or health to preserve the dignity of the hopeless. When you consider My prayers joined to yours, we have asked Jesus to help in historical ways. My Son has infinite Mercy for sinners who love Him, but He is swift to scold those who have disdain for the suffering poor. This is My sentiment for the first day of June. I realize that most Americans have been indoctrinated to believe that they are to tend to themselves before reaching-out to those who have sparse means. This is capitalism in motion. However, the Sacred Scriptures mandate that you lend your hearts to the least of God's creatures before satisfying your own needs. I pray that America will comply with the Lord's ordinances of its own volition so forced compliance will not become necessary. The batter is thickening, and the mixture is congealing. Why does it appear that capitalist conglomerates are always in heel-clipping pursuit of their next profitable dollar? My Special son, thank you for welcoming Me so I can speak to the world. You are one of the few who comprehend the urgency of My messages, and you are distributing them according to God's plan. When it seems too toilsome for you, the Holy Spirit always appeals to your sense of innovative truth so the Kingdom of the Lord prospers. When I speak about the Christian conversion of the United States, you know what a massive undertaking this is. Only one in five countrymen claims to be Catholic, and the others are members of Protestant denominations, Eastern beliefs, or have no religion at all. Most of them were not initiated into the faith the way you were. There was a period of enlightenment for you because you were baptized before you reached your older years. However, those who were not must be awakened like the lighting of a torch or lifting of a veil. This is one of the reasons you do not understand why it is taking so long to reach American citizens who are immersed in secularism. I am not demonizing them, I am only citing the bereftness of their spirituality. This is why you remain self-composed during the dictation of My messages and collect your memories and meditations in visitable formats. Your brother says that the Angels speak to him at times during the night to encourage him to stay the course, the same as I urge during My messages. He has told you that My objective was not meant to be as massive as it has become. When I appeared in February 1991, your Diary was to be no more than one-third its size. When the media and American lawyers attacked the priesthood, the book 'White Collar Witch Hunt' came into being. It was a manifest abruption that was not planned in 1991. And, as your brother also stated, his second master's degree was going to be a vocational certificate to prove that he remains in control of his cognitive faculties. Again, your dedication and hard work made it possible for him to earn another degree with awards and accolades from his peers. I have told you that there is unseen depth to My messages that the physical realms occlude, but their knowable dimensions are recorded in your New Millennium anthologies. Can you see that this is done because you are consecrated to Me? The Holy Spirit has been your mainstay and inspiration because you are openly responsive to My call. Everything you have accomplished has been by reason of your compliance with Jesus' wishes, especially your devotion to the Angels and Archangels. While I would never implicate that part of your writings are more prophetic than others, the first fifty pages of your AD 2003-2005 anthology are the Holy Spirit's answer to your petitions in this room. I am joyful that your opening section will have as much impact on the conversion of sinners as the text of My messages. I believe this book will be brilliant, one for the ages. Once you place it into being, it cannot be destroyed. I would be remiss if I did not mention the labors you are placing into your kitchen cabinets and drawers. You are dedicated in your work to make this a place of beauty for Me to appear."

Sunday, June 8, 2008
3:03 p.m.

"Therefore, I am content with weakness, with mistreatment, with distress, with persecutions and difficulties for the sake of Christ; for when I am powerless, it is then that I am strong." [2 Cor. 12:10]

"By the Lord's design, I am in your company to offer the Good News of the Salvation of men, to pray with you for their conversion, and offer My gratitude for your holiness. My purpose is to evoke from your friends the willingness to be like Jesus in purity and offer themselves to Me. Today, I speak of the consecration of the nations to My Immaculate Heart, especially those whose policies allow them to worship Jesus openly. My dear children, the world's democracies are passively imperial and aggressively isolationist, and this has plunged others into poverty. These sovereign states must invite the Holy Spirit to refocus their vision to the mandates of the Gospel so everyone on Earth can share the Earth's plenty. If you seek the truth, the failings of humanity will be eradicated. Do the admonishments of history teach you anything? Did the Lord make this request of the Roman and Ottoman empires, that they should be self-rebuked to be charitable in imitation of Jesus Christ? Do not all governments have the responsibility to construct a new network of diplomacy with the other nations? I am not speaking of meaningless secular commonality, but the unity of hearts in the holiness that Jesus commands. You are equal under Heaven; your plight is ameliorated by the Love of one God, and you are raised to conversion through the Crucifixion of the Messiah. If you call one another to delay the discipline that would mend the ills of humanity, you will never attain the unified oneness that God requires as His disciples of hopeful hearts. I pray that men will reciprocate, that you will see that your Christian duty is to pursue reconciliation with God in the Victim on the Cross. It is imperative that you reach-out to one another to end wars, famine, and disease. My Special son, I extend My appreciation for sustaining an atmosphere in your home that allows the continuation of My messages. The world is blessed by your service to God and obedience to Me. You have given His Kingdom mighty things through the years, and humanity's destiny will prosper. I do not mince My words about My role in the conversion of the wicked. This is a beneficent time for humanity because of the irrevocable goodness that you and your brother have dedicated to their awakening. When you look in hindsight, you will see that everything is as it should be. It was a blessing that you were given the Sacred Heart paintings after Mass last evening at Blessed Sacrament parish. Men will someday refer to the physician David Mack as Doctor of the Church."

Sunday, June 15, 2008
3:09 p.m.

"As long as I was with them, I guarded them with your name which you gave me. I kept careful watch, and not one of them was lost, none but him who was destined to be lost in fulfilment of the Scripture."
[John 17:12]

"Now My little ones, we gather in the effusion of grace from Heaven to pray for the conversion of wayward sinners, and you are prudent to enlist the aid of the Angels. I beseech you to acknowledge the Lord God as your Father, and Jesus as your Brother and Savior. The workings of the world move at such a pace that they distract you from the spirituality to which you are called. To say that the mind is boggled by the whirlwind of actions and prejudices would be to understate the degree to which men are ignoring the higher calling of the sanctifying of the soul. My dear ones, Christianity depends upon its own disciples to survive, and you are the peacemakers who must pray to end the world's indifference and prosper the Gospel of the Holy Cross. The Light of Heaven must be allowed to shine through the darkness to the hardened of heart because this is the only way peace grows. If you ponder all the forces that divide men one from another, and consider the hatred that poisons the relationships between societies, you surely must know that these things are eliminated by the beliefs you profess. I am the Queen of Peace and the Mother of Love, and it is My duty to speak the strains of reconciliation to the warring and those affected by corruption. Today, I summon My children to pray the Holy Rosary for the grueling conditions that are about to come. Does it seem fitting that the Queen of Peace would forbid you to make war? This is the elementary nature of the Earth. I do not wish that men would study war, but that you will pray on bended knee in your churches and homes for the end of human conflict. The Lord requires that you take His message of Peace and Love to your foes who profit by the combats that cost lives. Such things as capitalism, global marketing, and social relativism are means through which the rich and poor are divided. I am not one to espouse elitism or socialism, but I implore you to ensure that everyone has access to the wealth that God provides. It is clear to Christians that the lower classes are beasts of burden for the affluent whose social skills and persuasive techniques allow them to extort anything they want. This is a product of the isolationism that Jesus denounces. I told you recently about the territorial nature of the world's democracies, and there have been hundreds-of-thousands of innocent lives lost in the process of protecting permeable borders. This is also repugnant in the eyes of the Lord who has given the whole world to the family of man. If single persons in remote regions feel helpless to do anything about these issues, they should remember that this is the domain of the Catholic Church. The Holy See is your recourse and agency through which all redressing should start. The Vicar of Christ is God's infallible judge in matters of faith and morals, and it is to these that you are given. With faith in God and a sound moral foundation, humanity will see the universality of His Kingdom. You will realize that there are separate republics, but one Mystical Body of Christ. This is why it is imperative that My children speak privately and publicly to defend the primacy of the Roman Catholic Church for the benefit of all Christians. If someone speaks ill about the Princes of the Church, the laity are responsible to uphold them. This is where you hear the presence of the Holy Spirit. This is the critical essence of practicing your faith. Therefore, I repeat My request that you honor the Father by sustaining the tenets of the faith that He gives you, and adhere to the teachings of the Crucified Messiah in the Grace through which men are saved. Many have spoken of peace in dysfunctional contexts because they fail to mention that unity flows from One God in Three Persons. There can be no peace without perfecting the love of men through the Messiah whom I birthed in Bethlehem.

My Special son, your life with your brother is a component of the conversion of lost sinners because this is the way it was written. Peter and Paul, James and John, and others who have served the Lord's Chosen Son have realized that it is He who lived in them. With all the reckonings that are yet to come, this is the one that matters, that humanity must eventually know that no one serves alone. Jesus is your constant guide and friend in Spirit and Sacrament, and the world cannot be purified without Him. I attest today that your remarks in support of the Most Reverend Raymond Burke harken of the greatest Christian writing of the twenty centuries. Thank you for opening the door for many who will come to know the oneness of the Church, that no one can stand apart or reach the joy of Heaven without aspiring to the unity of men beneath the Holy Cross. And, it is My good pleasure to remind you that Jesus embraces you and your brother as He did James and John, Peter and Paul, and all the Saints. This places you in a royal posture before the Father in whose Judgement you shall be relieved. On this auspicious occasion, I speak about His compassion for His disciples, for the poor and aging, and for all who are doing their best to engage His flock. Your labors have been reflective of the forgiveness that He deigned for humanity when Adam stumbled. Glorious Light consumes you, Wisdom informs you, charity describes you, and Grace delivers you. In the Father's house, there are many mansions. If this were not true, I would tell you. I pray with anticipation of seeing you on the golden streets, riding in the Chariot about which I spoke years ago, waving to Me along your path with Jesus in My arms. I promise that this is the begetting of the most glorious hours you shall ever know. All the gifts of Providence that compose the elements of ecstasy are present there; and this is your peace, it is your destiny. It is your Salvation. I have remarked that there are fascinating images in your manuscripts that will reduce the readers of My messages to tears. Your Bishop is appreciative that you are assisting the making of a deposit of messages that are endearing to the people of the Americas whose origin was founded under his and his predecessor's episcopates. He is not likely to wait until his successor comes to spread the news of My urgent call to repentance and prayer. The Holy Paraclete is your counsel. Call on the Spirit of God to write what He would have you relate to the spiritually-famished world. Humanity is hungry, and you are feeding them."

Sunday, June 22, 2008
2:44 p.m.

"Blessed are you, O Lord, the God of our fathers, praiseworthy and exalted above all forever. Blessed is your holy and glorious name, praiseworthy and exalted above all for all ages." [Daniel 3:52]

"We beseechingly invoke the Blessed Trinity in favor of humanity, that the Lord will honor you with the graces for which you pray. Today, we remember the victims of war campaigns, the survivors of the slain, and those who mourn. Much is said to legitimize warfare after so many troops have been lost because they are not wished to have died in vain. I remind you that the only battles worth waging are those that advance Christianity and find lost sinners. This is the way God is glorified through your efforts for His Kingdom. It is a warm summer's day where I appear to bring the Good News of the Salvation of man, but I realize that it will be winter before most of them awaken to My call. This does not impede our effort or dampen our cause. From the heated desert beds to the Midwestern plains, the Gospel is always rewarding. When we pray together, My children, we make Jesus pleased to intervene for you. The Father is serious about sanctifying the Mystical Body of His Son because it is to His delight when sinners accept the Blood of the Cross. I have witnessed His reaction to righteous wills and purposeful petitions from towering cathedrals to tiny altar rooms. You see the answer to your prayers with My presence. There is evidence that blessings from Heaven are traceable to cenacles and the recitation of the Holy Rosary. You have seen firsthand the link between asking Jesus for miracles and receiving them. I wish you to remember the power of prayer, and that you should turn to God whenever you feel lonely or afraid, whenever someone is ill, or if you believe that the faith of your fathers is waning in your time. A broad, disarming smile appears on Jesus' face when He knows that His disciples are serious about purifying the world, but He expresses disdain toward unholiness with a stern, impeaching stare. I hope you will enlist His satisfaction with humanity by praying without ceasing. My Special son, it would seem that I consistently laud your work with your brother, and today is no exception. You are on the verge of publishing My 2003 through 2005 messages with affection for My Immaculate Heart. The Angels helped you write a narration for the back panel that underscores the vivid substance of My intentions. You have stated that the darkest hour in America is coming, and your fellow citizens will look for the Morning Star to guide them to the Light of God's Glory. I am pleased that you have waited patiently for the proper opportunities to expand your works. Many Americans were touched by the events surrounding the death of Timothy Russert because Roman Catholics spoke so sentimentally about him. They tinctured the hearts of people with memories in the way of good homilists. Several of them spoke about the rainbow above the building where the service was held. This is why your books are so overwhelming. You are unafraid to cite pious poetics about matters that are saturated with mystical grace. Thank you for paying attention to intricacies that appear unobvious to others. And, worship the Father for our loving relationship."

Sunday, June 29, 2008
Feast of SS. Peter and Paul
3:06 p.m.

"Give thanks to the Lord, for he is good, for his kindness endures forever. And say, Save us O God, our Savior, gather us and deliver us from the nations, that we may give thanks to your holy name and glory in praising you." [1 Chron. 16:34-35]

"My children, I have returned for another stanza in the anthem of human life, and I thank you for joining the Angelic Choirs who are singing the praises of God. Today, I want you to remember that stem-cell research is to medical care what perjury is to justice. I exhort My children to heed the edicts of the Pope in Rome about this issue because he speaks infallibly about the ordinances of God. There are so many people who misunderstand His Will because they are not attuned to the Gospel. There is agony and torment all around the globe because of war and greed. The poor are being pushed even further into poverty, and the neglected are forgotten altogether. There are millions whose hopes are in abeyance and dreams in shambles because they cannot compete. My mission for centuries has been the call to simplicity, that Christians will teach non-Christians the meaning of prayer and sacrifice. This is My purpose, My children. I am your Mother who espouses your best interest before your Savior, and I was given these special times to bring you graces the likes of which the Earth has not seen. Your foundation in Jesus is in stark contrast to the rickety boardwalks and shifting sands of nonbelievers, and we must pray that they come to the Church. If you could imagine what life is like for those who do not realize that the Cross is your measure of success, you would see in what darkness these people remain. Our prayers must be centered in God's Love and be strenuously pious. If you help, My children, you will see the reversal of unredressed issues that prevent the brokenhearted from being healed and the lost converted. We implore Saints Peter and Paul to intercede for God's disciples and lead lost sinners to His Eternal Light by their inspirational legacies inscribed beyond the immortal hills. My Special son, it is with favor that you kneel with your brother before Me so we can ask Jesus for His blessings on humanity. The marvels you are seeing in your day are the graces you are given to remain fervent in your devotion to His Kingdom. You are happier than you believe because your mind is often clouded by the burdens of mortality. In a few weeks' time, you will finish your book in which is contained the beatific strains from My Immaculate Heart that will transform the Earth. Can you see that your whole life was meant for this? Indeed, a sense of closure, engulfed by the eternal. Thank you for being affable as you proceed, and remember that Jesus felt everything you have been experiencing during His thirty-three years. Jesus is the Son of the Father, and the Father is in Him. Please never forget the blessedness by which you live because it will be of high import in your later years. The circumstances for which you pray are imminent, and this is why you must finish your work. I have said a number of times that your great gift to the conversion of the world is the generous way you provide for your brother. He tries to be a good friend and not an encumbrance on you. He prays with the fullness of his baptism for the Earth to be turned upside down. Your friendship has aided the thesis of My appearances, and I have built images in My messages that are reminiscent of your childhood experiences and other personal and private recollections. As I say, you have given your heart and treasure to Jesus in untold ways, and you will see souls in Heaven who accepted His Crucifixion because of your life."

Sunday, July 6, 2008
3:09 p.m.

"Be careful to observe the commandments which I, the Lord, give you, and do not profane my holy name. In the midst of the Israelites, I the Lord, must be held as sacred." [Lev. 22:31-32]

"Today, I bless you with the brilliant peace of the Holy Spirit by whom you are welcomed into My Immaculate Heart. I seek from this world the changes that will perpetuate holiness, the amendment of lives in righteousness, the alleviation of suffering, and the interaction between Heaven and Earth that instills in men the desire to imitate the Saints. In order to accomplish this, My dear children, you must have porous hearts, not hearts of stone. You should pray that the Lord will soften hardened hearts and stir the conscience of lost sinners to seek Him. With My intercession to Jesus, you are remade in His image. How Heaven adores you! With what Wisdom are you brought to know that your exile is ending! It is time to act, My children, and accept the fact that 2008 is a pivotal year in the cultivation of the Earth. Your holiness must protrude from the carpentry of the universe like tonic, fulfilling to the forsaken and ameliorative for the suffering. How I hope you will listen! I urge you to pray for the conditions in the Middle East where war is ongoing and battles are raging. Imagine the lives that have been taken due to the aggression of the United States. With what pity you should look upon orphaned children whose limbs have been severed, and the paupers who are wandering the streets, looking for something palatable to eat. It is simple for Americans to sit before their television sets and be entertained by comedies and fabricated news. No amount of sensationalism can justify the invasion of another republic in the name of vengeance. I have said that there may be chastisements for such things as these, but who knows how God will respond? He is a Father of sound principle and fairness, and He calls the same from you. How many prayers should you lift for the suffering? Until your eyes are shuttered in death. This is My message, My children. I summon you to have more than pedestrian faith, but faith that makes positive changes for the plight of the poor. My Special son, this is an awakening time for the West because I have castigated your elected leaders and excoriated the American way of life. I have done so because you are bombarded by evidence every day. However, My goal today is to remind you that you are liberated from secularism by your faith in Jesus Christ. You engage the secular world to pursue fiscal stability and create an atmosphere where My messages can be dispensed. All this was placed into being from the foundation of the world. There have been signs and wonders to give you strength to believe that your work is of God. Yes, I will touch the hearts of the Bishops. You must remember that they are having difficulty disciplining their flock in the United States. What would you have them do when they are ridiculed for considering excommunication of Catholics who foster the scourge of abortion? Should they have the secular police remove these parishioners from the Church? While this is a hypothetical question, I know you understand My point. I have said several times in My messages that the mission of your Apostolate will prevail because it complies with the natural laws of Divine Justice. Just as your brother's family moving to Ashland in 1956 was preordained, so is the fact that the fruits of your labors should be sweet to those who believe in God. How old was Jesus at the Crucifixion? Yes, thirty-three. How many years passed from the time your brother came to Ashland until your 1989 pilgrimage to Medjugorje? Again, thirty-three. The signs are obvious. It matters not that there are many, but that they are the amenities for your service to the Lord's Kingdom. They comfort you during periods of darkness and lead you to the Holy Light. In fact, you do not require signs because you are confident of My presence. I read your books and weep at their beauty. You have been dutiful, and you are blessing your brothers and sisters in ways that must be done by visionaries on your side of the veil. I distribute Rosaries and flowers from the celestial skies, but how would I dispense a dozen miraculous codices from above the clouds? Your mission has become this miracle from God. Please never lose hope, no matter what happens. The entire phenomenon of My apparitions here has been about growing your faith and supporting your heart. I have told you that time is deceptive, and the years expire beyond your control. You learn about eternity when you read My messages anew."

Sunday, July 13, 2008
2:55 p.m.

"Be compassionate, as your Father is compassionate. Do not judge, and you will not be judged. Do not condemn, and you will not be condemned. Pardon, and you shall be pardoned." [Luke 6:36-37]

"Thank you, My little children, for praying with Me for the purification of humanity and the transference of your lives into the Sacred Heart of My Son. I ask you to remember that suffering for the conversion of lost sinners is redemptive and passifloraceous in the likeness of the Crucifixion of Jesus on the Cross. Your sacrifices are as beautiful and your love is as sweet. The world is unified through the bloodline of good faith that you share with your Christian forbears. Today, I request your prayers for everyone who has suffered from the egregious flooding and firestorms across America. Their plight cannot be ignored or overstated, and it is imperative that you remember them even as this message reaches humanity into the future. What are the intentions of the Lord as you endure the catastrophic events of Nature? Is there a chemistry between your conduct and the Will of the Father that must be flushed through your surviving such incidents? Your prayers will answer this question because His dominion remains with you through good times and bad. You should realize that Jesus listens for your petitions for change, and the Father ratifies His response. It is not as though God does not know your every thought and see your every motion. He is not turned away from you when you are not thinking about Him. Heaven seeks a constant line of communication with the temporal world through everything the Church provides. Even as you recite the Holy Rosary in the confines of your homes, you are still praying with the whole Catholic Church. You must seek Jesus' intervention through My Maternal intercession. As I have said, I likewise know your motivations and the good deeds you offer on His behalf. It is not as though the Holy Spirit is eavesdropping while you live because you and the Spirit of God are communing as one. Jesus is your other self, and humanity on Earth is the Faith-Church comprising His Mystical Body in unity with the Church-Suffering and the Church-Triumphant. With this, you know that death does not separate you from your surviving loved-ones, and neither are they who remain distant from you. Humanity is one composite force for fairness and goodness in the Sacred Heart of Jesus when you comply with the tenets of your faith. My Special son, you have arrived at the week when you will begin your final push to publish your AD 2003-2005 anthology of messages. I can attest that you are about to release some of the most evocative and awe-inspiring pages that humanity has ever seen. And, why would the Mother of God not be so serious at the beginning of the 21st century? I need not remind you of the grave condition of the world's morality and the need for the spiritual enlightenment of secular men. What tasteless habits they have, and with what ignoble approaches to problems they take with them from rising in the morning until slumbering at night. What ignorance and shameless neglect they espouse in the face of some of the most cruel suffering that the exiled Earth has ever known! When I speak of admonishments, I refer to the Lord's handiwork in the first fifty pages of your newest book. When I mention chastisements, I draw humanity's attention to the signs that portend that Creation will soon heave a collective gasp of exasperation. Who knows what Jesus will do when He reenters His Kingdom? Therefore, your work with your brother is preparing lost sinners to be purified by fire, a contingent of flames that were ignited by your consent to record My messages in 1991. It does not seem so long ago that we began our mission of inviolate goodness, one in which you have watched people die and nations uprise, where visionaries have prophesied some of the most dangerous circumstances to come upon the world of modern men. My little children have been the sweetness about which I speak because their tears have watered the Passion Flower to which I have referred. Your Christian holiness has been the springtime that has bloomed the redeeming conversion of wayward souls into the sight of the Lord. Can you not see with what Grace you have lived? Now, I give you My promise that My messages will bear all the fruit they were intended to produce, and you will remain united with Jesus through Me until you reach Salvation in Heaven.

    I desire for you to remember that Jesus is always with you during your times of stress at your workplace. God is aware of your anger and conditions of sorrow. Please do not believe that you are immune to the suffering about which I have spoken today. Your position of employment is your part of the sanctification of the world. It is as simple as this. It is your vexation, your cross, and Satan's way of boasting to his evildoers that he can taunt you. I pray for your comfort during these hours as you fight against his darkness. While it is never a fair environment, I ask that you pray for the many elsewhere who are being impugned and shorn of their dignity by superiors in their places of employment. There is victory for you because you have not conceded that others' conduct will always have control over your expectations and emotions. Again, I say that millions of workers in America and worldwide have the same problem as you. If you give in to poor attitudes and helpless feelings, it is because you have decided that this must be your reaction. You have failed to lay your life alongside Jesus' life and declare that evil has no power over you. My little son, this is no sign of weakness in you whatsoever, and it is not an issue that is restricted only to your circumstance. Every single day of the world when you leave your workplace, the followers of the devil celebrate that you might concede to them tomorrow. The competitive mentality in which you were raised, the anxieties you felt during your formative years, and your genetically inherited reluctance to see life's conditions for what they are have all burdened you with a view of life that you must constantly fight something, even if it is something you have to conjure. You have an incessant knack for assuming that every illegitimate issue is worthy of a solution, that courses taken that do not seem amenable to you are derived from untoward origins. Things that differ from your line of thinking are not necessarily always bad. They are not always wrong; and even when they are, they certainly do not stand as matters to which you must respond combatively or as though someone is attempting to wield undue influence over you. As I have said, Jesus knows every minute instance of your days at your workplace. He sees injustices and promises to correct them. Saints Peter, Paul, John and all the rest lived awful circumstances, much like the ones you face every day, and they looked upon those who were causing them with pity, not anger. Even when Jesus evicted the money changers from the Temple, He never lost His nerve; He retained His inner-peace that no person alive or dead could steal. He realized the corruption even in the civilized world, and He allowed room for this in His interpretation of the actions of other people. And, in this, He did not internally succumb to Satan's hatred. If He were sitting in your cubical chair, He would literally chuckle at the decisions that are made, even ones that affect your goals and objectives. He would place the initiatives of perspective and patience into play. He would look with assurance at His colleagues that nothing that happened on any given day or through the trends of time could bring Him to despondence. My Special son, Jesus would do this because He knows that most human decisions are spontaneously made, adjudicated, rectified, and reconciled. This is why He is always the victor in every affair, especially during His trial and condemnation. And, Jesus was submissive so you could be strong. Those who do not perceive the events of life this way must open to the strength and power of the Holy Spirit whose disposition I am rejoicing. I am not saying for a moment that anything in the daily environment in which you are situated is justifiable. After all, there was nothing fair about sentencing Jesus to die. I see your prison. I know that you are confined, and I have compassion for you. This has been a lengthy, terrible process, but we have more work to do, and you cannot permit the evil around you to become a distraction. I will protect you in richness and poverty, sickness and health, and anything else that befalls you. There are no words to describe the seriousness in which I take the insults leveled against you. Jesus' wrath has been poised to strike defeat against those who are guilty, but He knows you will feel poorly at the end of time if He punishes them now. I am speaking to you because your goodness invites Me here."

Sunday, July 20, 2008
2:49 p.m.

"Therefore say: Thus says the Lord God: I too will take from the crest of the cedar, from its topmost branches tear off a tender shoot, and plant it on a high and lofty mountain." [Ezek. 17:22]

"The Mother of the Lord has come to pray with you for a nation that is rife with vulgarness and obscenities, and that ignores the suffering of the poor and the needs of its elderly. Today, I beseech you to pray for the people who have no one to fight for them or provide the dignity they rightly deserve. They are helpless to do anything for themselves because they have no access to America's vast wealth, and they remain enclosed behind the social barriers that keep them from gaining the food, housing, clothing, and health care they require. My children, while they are impeded by the hourglass, this does not mean that their situation is hopeless. We must pray for change in the United States, that your government will care for those who cannot deign for themselves around the globe. You have celebrated many triumphs and victories over challenges, even as you have hailed the Greek figurehead Apollo in your search for new beginnings in the arts, poetry, music, the growing of human intelligence, and the exploration of outer-space. America has spent enough resources going to the Moon and other cosmic adventures that not a single child had to die from starvation. It is this misalignment of priorities that I continue to address in My messages, and this same decree is shadowed from the pulpit and in homilies from the world's most visionary leaders. The Holy Father exhorts the youth to dismantle their penchant for material pursuits, and a former prisoner who was innocent all along reminds Africa and the whole of humanity to remember the poor. Why must the Spirit of the Lord always chastise people when men have had 2,000 years to get it right? The answer is obvious, My children. It is because there is tepid faith in the world; only few are willing to become self-sacrificial in the face of so much hunger and widespread war. Only few in many countries are concerned about the condition of the spiritual health of the billions who inhabit the Earth. This is why I am speaking to you, My holy children, that America will become a shining city on a hill not with diamonds and pearls, but with Divine Light emanating from inside your hearts. This is My plea today, My darlings; it is My request and prayer. My Special son, you must be wary about not becoming too exhausted. I am overjoyed that you slept as many hours as you did last evening. I am pleased by your initial pages of your new book because you write as a theological genius about the mission of the Church, the role of the faithful as the Mystical Body of Christ, the error of everyone who protests against the original Apostles, and how My intercession effects the changes that humanity needs in order to comply with the Will of the Father. Thank you for preserving your strength and realizing that the Holy Spirit is alive in you to keep your spiritual vision clear. You are a strong warrior for Jesus, and you may tell the world that you are coming, and the Blessed Virgin Mary is coming with you! Your honorable years have been a constant vigil for peace and hope for humanity, and your books will achieve the ends that I intend for them. *(At the close of a Sunday news program, they ran an exclusive about a man who dedicated himself to making sure every living World War II veteran was taken to the WWII Memorial in Washington, DC as a gift of his thanksgiving for their sacrifice and service. He began to cry as he recalled how the veterans were humbly thanking him when all the gratitude belonged to them.)* Do you remember this morning that there was a young pilot who was taking World War II veterans to see their memorial? And, what was said that made him weep? Yes, that they thanked him, when those aging men endured the selfless mission of freedom for America. Every time you thank Me, it is the same. I am not the one to be thanked. I am only delivering you and your brother, real heroes for Jesus, to the shrine you have created in the collective human heart, where the Son of Man waits to receive all whom He loves. While I accept your appreciation, yours has been the sacrifice. I beg you on bended knee to remember this."

Sunday, July 27, 2008
2:17 p.m.

"Those who love me, I also love, and those who seek me find me. With me are riches and honor, enduring wealth and prosperity. My fruit is better than gold, yes than pure gold, and my revenue than choice silver." [Prov. 8:17-19]

"My children, now comes your Immaculate Mother to pray with you for the conversion of lost sinners to the Holy Cross, and for everything you look forward to regarding the refinement of the world. You live in America where there is such defiance and lack of peace in cities and families, where darkness and danger loom to conscript your children into depravity and sin, where there is such contrast between rich and poor, and where secular relativism is making a mockery of your relationship with all things eternal.

Your countrymen have defied gravity and have set their sights on defying the Will of God. There is growing despair where orchids should be blooming, and death and destruction instead of life and peace. Given these conditions, you should have no question about My presence here or the Lord's intentions for dispatching the Angels and Saints to intercede for you. My Special son, I would be remiss if I did not bless you for your understanding and compassion. And, I would be equally negligent if I did not tell you how beautiful is the photograph you plan to give your Bishop at My behest. Thank you for investing the effort of procuring it and having it framed for presentation. All these things reinforce the fact that I am speaking as a caring Advocate, and your Bishop will be moved that the Mother of God has given him such a gift. I will speak to you upon the opening of August, and we will pray for the purification of wayward sinners."

Sunday, August 3, 2008
2:53 p.m.

"Beloved, let us love one another, because love is of God. Everyone who loves is begotten of God and has knowledge of God. The man without love has known nothing of God, for God is love."
[1 John 4:7-8]

"My humble children, the Mystical Truth will prevail on Earth by the sheer volume of itself. There is nothing you can do to enhance the Love of God, but you must assuredly propagate it among the nations and take the Holy Gospel to the wicked. You should do this to maintain your oath to Jesus from when you were baptized. Remember that faith is an ocular tool that permits you to see Creation from the perspective of Heaven. In your rigorous defense of the Holy Cross, you witness the unfolding of the universe from beatific realms that your unbelieving brothers and sisters cannot see. Even when praying in the privacy of your rooms, you sense the vastness of the Kingdom of God as though you were situated on a plateau, high above the flatlands. In your meditations, you pray for the refinement of humanity in the themes of Christian righteousness. And, you can stand on the highest elevations of the Earth and peer into the cleavage of the mountain ranges, knowing with peace and confidence in your hearts that Jesus has walked there. My call for you today is to remember to search for this peace, to reach deep within your psyche and focus your sights on the simpler life, on prosperity in the virtues of grace, and the healing and protection of your families and friends. As August matures, be cheerful in the faith given you as a blessing from the Father. To My American children, I urge you to fight for the unborn to be delivered to birth, to denounce the selfishness that causes mothers to abort them, and admonish your lost brothers and sisters who live in contradiction to the teachings of the Church. There can be no true independence if your hearts are not imbedded at the center of Truth, the New Covenant of Christianity. Every gift from the Throne of God comes through Jesus, and all graces flow from My Immaculate Heart. My Special son, I speak to you after your depressing week at your workplace. I know you are maintaining your composure, and this is commendable. You care deeply about defending goodness in the presence of their error, and the struggle is never easy. I understand your suffering, and I am not unmindful that you struggle with your feelings. I shall pray for you during this difficult time. If you focus on your books with the fidelity of the Holy Spirit in your heart and the knowledge that the documents you are completing will alter the face of the Earth, you will be happy. Thank you for your goodness and holiness, and especially for taking such gentle care of your brother who often becomes a burden upon you. I share your hopes that you have longevity and success with your Apostolate. It is a function of positive thoughts and motivations."

Sunday, August 10, 2008
3:44 p.m.

"In everything you do, act without grumbling or arguing; prove yourselves innocent and straightforward children of God beyond reproach in the midst of a twisted and depraved generation—among whom you shine like the stars in the sky..." [Phil. 2:14-15]

"My dear children, we have spoken of the complexities and complications of life on exiled Earth, and of your weaknesses and propensities to commit sin, even with your guard made strong by your well-intentioned faith. Through your membership in the Church, you receive the power of the Holy Spirit to combat the forces that attempt to diminish your holiness. And, I remind you today that Jesus is with you to guide your footsteps and promote your way of spiritual perfection to which every Christian is called. There is nothing simple about facing-down the perils of the world because the secular void has such a ranging reach through the lack of faith of those with influence. There is wholesale goodness in every person if only you will allow the Glory of the Lord to be manifested through you. Man is an enduring mixture of iron and silk, a vastly genius creature with untold instincts to do good, to live intuitively through the Holy Spirit as your mentor, and with the heroism that comes from your belief in everything Jesus demands. He commends you into My open arms and the Wisdom that becomes Me, and His righteousness defends you in every battle that is fought in His name. Remember that you must forever practice love over hatred, and you should never cede any measure of His Kingdom to the wicked. God mandates that you obey His laws of forgiveness, but not that you should ever surrender either your standing or dignity to anything that contradicts His Will. With these thoughts in mind, I pray with you today for the conversion of lost sinners, for the peace and protection of every Christian, for the end of war and infirmity, and for the cessation of the abortion of unborn children. These continue to be auspicious times because they contain extraordinary graces from Heaven. I have spoken about the blessings of God that are irreplaceable for those who believe in Him. And, My Special son, it is My honor to remind you and your brother that you are adored by Jesus, and you know precisely what I mean. For the sake of the defense of your faith and the charities of the Church, I exhort you to remember in your petitions all who need comforted and strengthened on their journey through life. Thank you for having responded to My call. And, as you recognize that I am being brief in these present weeks, it will suffice that I say that you are well on your way to experiencing the profound gift of releasing more of My messages through your AD 2003-2005 manuscript. You have witnessed the dictation of its text that conjoins your own essays, and you must surely know how powerful it is. There is sufficient time to do everything you wish to accomplish with this new book, and likewise with the next. You do whatever is necessary to publish My messages; this is what you have always done well. Thank you for raising your petitions, and I will intercede to Jesus for you in these desires. I shall remain with you in your endeavors in the Sacred Heart of Jesus as we hand everything over to the Will of the Father. If you live slowly and prayerfully, you will have a pleasant summertime and a new fall of happiness. You must place your heart in the peace of the Holy Spirit who brings you this joy. I am mindful of the issues that hinder the sustainment of your sense of peace, and I pray that you permit God to be your stability as Jesus is your Rock of Salvation. Remember that you and your brother are Jesus' darlings in a world filled with fools. Your beauty is undescribable, just as Heaven cannot be placed into words."

Sunday, August 17, 2008
3:01 p.m.

"But the Lord's messenger called to him from Heaven, 'Abraham, Abraham.' 'Yes, Lord' he answered. 'Do not lay your hand on the boy,' said the messenger. 'Do not do the least thing to him. I know now how devoted you are to God, since you did not withhold from me your own beloved son." [Gen. 22:11-12]

"For all the glory you might imagine for the future, we have assembled in your prayer room to offer God our prayers for the conversion of lost humanity. As I have asked, what does this mean? Certainly you know that it is the inclusion of the will of man with the Will of the Father, that you seek His Son and become His likeness. My children, it is imperative that you are humbled by this process, and encouraged that you are capable of achieving the holiness to which you are led. Jesus told you that you would have power when the Holy Spirit descended upon the Church, and I implore you to open yourselves and receive the conduit of new life in Him. Today, I appear before you to assist your thoughtful contemplations of the way Creation ought to be, to advise you in matters dear to you, and remind humanity that there awaits a vast Kingdom of redemption for those who convert to Christianity. The primacy of Eternal Truth rests in Jesus Christ. And, for what should we petition the Father through Jesus? Fairness, justice, prudence, peace, and Wisdom must come to you. Your children and grandchildren must be reared in the faith that was bequeathed to you. You must remain loyal to the death to the Sacraments of the Church, its Sacred Traditions, and in the defense of priests and religious. The Lord has placed the Church under the capable leadership of Pope Benedict because He knew that this Pontiff would be best for these times. Please tender yourselves to the Holy Father's infallible teachings; follow his commands by holding to the principles of your beliefs, and pray as he requires for things that will make this world a better place. You will enter in a matter of weeks the month of September, and autumn, and the sleeping of Nature. You must not allow your faith to fall into stagnation like the Earth turns from summer to winter. There is much work to be done in planting, cultivating, and harvesting Christians for the Lord. I promise that I will be with you and alongside you, praying for your earthly labors, encouraging your intentions, and asking Jesus to bless you every day. My Special son, I am pleased that you are praying with Me for the finding of prodigal sinners. With Me, you help open their hearts to discover new life, and you assist their enlightenment in discerning fact from fiction, seeing with spiritual eyes the differences between secular error and religious truth, and approaching the Living Fount of Jesus' Mercy for the expungement of their sins. Do you see that you are worthy of the accolades that the Holy Spirit heaps upon you? Today, therefore, I pledge to remain in your presence through the whole life of the Church. I will speak to exiled humanity as the Morning Star Over America through you and your brother four more months, and then to you and your brother as long as God wills. What shall I speak about in the latter? My Special son, you will discover that you will enter the most enjoyable time of your life. I will have delivered My messages to the world, and I will help you and your brother draft your memoirs, bring you peace that you have never known, teach you how to approach those whom you consider to be your enemies, generate discussion that brings the Sacred Truth to bear on the masses, help you contemplate matters that we have heretofore not had time to address, give you prayers of healing for the infirm, and many more gifts, blessings, signs, and graces to lend support to your mission. In some ways, your work will begin anew in January 2009. I promise that you will enjoy entering this new corridor, and you will see why I waited almost 18 years before completing My messages to the Church. You are capable of seeing the face of peace without your eyes. You will be better prepared to approach lost sinners with the confidence of kings once our objectives are through. Upon reading your next book that you are about to release, they will see without question the reason I appeared in 1991. You are attesting to the fineness of Christianity that has been addressed by the Doctors of the Church, and you are publishing a framework of spiritualism that should be in the homilies of priests and deacons. Most important, you will see that you have dedicated your life to this, your whole being; all your days and years that comprise your spirit are found in your devotion to Jesus on the Cross. Thank you for having responded to My call. You have wrought the conversion of uncountable numbers of souls with whom you will share the bounty of Heaven. The world is starved for your new book, and you will feed them the knowledge required to become one in Jesus the way the Father has planned."

Sunday, August 24, 2008
3:06 p.m.

"In you, O Lord, I take refuge. Let me never be put to shame. In your justice rescue me and deliver me. Incline your ear to me and save me. Be my rock of refuge, a stronghold to give me safety, for you are my rock and fortress." [Psalms 71:1-3]

"Now, My children, your Mother has appeared before you to pray for lost sinners in a special way because these are amazing days of grace. It is good that you join Me in asking Jesus to invoke His Sacrifice in favor of the Salvation of His lost sheep so they will come to His embrace. The world is a bitter place for those who do not know Him. They have no sense of direction or means to achieve true peace. Even as humanity is sightless, you cannot know that you are living inside a bell unless someone else rings it. This is what the Holy Paraclete does for God's creatures. Jesus is rousing you from your sleep and asking you to embark on the journey of holiness to which the Saints enlisted. While there are wars around you, and poverty stings the Earth, you overcome them by inheriting the legacy of your ancestors. You have within your grasp the ability to change the face of the globe by inviting Jesus to be one with you by encouraging your steps and refining your conscience, and giving you hope that nothing for which you yearn is ever in vain. My prayers supplement these aspirations when you pray in Jesus' name, and you have known since you were babies that He hears and blesses you. Paradise sees the intentions of your hearts and the motivations of your leaders. There is such injustice and inequality in America. When on September 11, 2001 the wealthy lost their friends and families to horrific terrorism, even here, the American president sent the sons and daughters of the poor to die for his vengeance. Is there fairness in this, My children? Did those who enlisted in brigades and companies expect that they would be deployed to protect the lifestyles of the rich and famous? This is the corruption that Jesus promises to rectify to the demise of the sinners whose limousines and airliners are driving them deeper into damnation. Hence, I call you to defer to the Will of the Lord in examining the actions of your country and the misguided mandates it promulgates. I have attested that the United States is among the most corrupt nations in history, and you are seeing the evidence now. My Special son, I will be brief in speaking about matters of the future because of the time allotted for the preparation of your manuscript. I should make special mention that you gave Jesus glad thoughts when you and your brother visited the imprisoned. They are trying their best to be strong through their trials. It must be a consoling feeling to know that you are making a difference in the cultivation of lost sinners. You are generous beyond description, and you are honest with the societies of Earth about what Jesus demands from those for whom He surrendered His life. God loves you and your brother beyond all telling."

Sunday, August 31, 2008
4:16 p.m.

"I see how true it is that God shows no partiality. Rather, the man of any nation who fears God and acts uprightly is acceptable to him. This is the message he has sent to the sons of Israel, the good news of peace proclaimed through Jesus Christ..." [Acts 10:34-36]

"I bring you well wishes from Heaven on this anniversary of My message five years past when I urged you to muster in yourselves the trust and courage to manifest heroic faith in a dreary world that reeks with recklessness and nonbelief. Today, I ask you to pray for those who are fleeing from another coastal disaster, that they will find safety and harbor in their strength of numbers. Inside everyone there exists the potential for peace in their exile, to avoid the gnarling disquietude that turns into such anxiety when lost sinners decline to share the Love of God. I speak about the Peace of Christ the King in whose arms you are nurtured and caressed, comforted and blessed. Through His Passion and Crucifixion, you are cleansed and renewed, awakened from your slumber of indifference. My children, the Holy Spirit affords Me the opportunity to say that prayer is the solution to your problems; it is your guidance in the darkness and strength when you are weak. Your connection with the Holy Spirit is prayer to the Father for His intervention and My intercession. To this end, I come calling My children to live prayerfully on behalf of those who cannot fend for themselves, to sanctify the Earth in ways you have never known, and be healers of the sick and dying. My Wisdom is your encouragement to speak the truth where it is unpopular, to call your brothers and sisters to holiness in the face of their apostasies. As I said five years ago, you have the ability to strengthen your bonds with Heaven, and to see clearly the paths you must choose to unite with the Will of the Father. You have the capacity to amend the affairs that frighten you, ones that cause pain, and conditions that place you at odds with the Sacred Scripture. Dignity, scrupulousness, and liberty are found in the righteousness brought into this century by the teachings of the Church and the advocacy of the Spirit. This is My call for My children; it is the reason I hope that men will open their hearts to the Sacred Gospel summoning them to the Holy Cross. My Special son, are you all right? Thank you for taking your brother to see his siblings and Josephine Parsons who has outlived the other members of his parents' generation. There are memories of tragedy imbedded in her heart, but she has strength in the vigor she owns through her faith. Yes, there is tremendous dysfunction in your brother's family that is apparent in millions of others. What you see them do is not rare among those who have suffered the pains of mortal life, who have broken families and multiple marriages. They are sinners,

but they are trying to do better. They see you in a good, holy light because they know you and your brother are close to God. They are aware of your mission for Jesus, and they support you in ways you do not know. Your new book in all its glory will be another tremendous catalyst for the transformation of America. It uplifts Me as the Morning Star Over America, and you know what this means to Jesus. Let us see what God does in the future. I will come to you in September, and we will enjoy speaking about the prosperous days ahead when My children accept Jesus and enter the Church. I offer you My holy blessing in the name of the Father, and the Son, and the Holy Spirit. Amen.
✞ Please remember to pray for the precious unborn!"

Sunday, September 7, 2008
3:04 p.m.

"Thereupon the Lord heard my voice, he listened to my appeal. He saved me from evil of every kind and preserved me in time of trouble. For this reason, I thank him and praise him; I bless the name of the Lord." [Sirach 51:11-12]

"Today, My little children, I come to pray with you as the Church offers its intercessions for the unborn innocents and those who are suffering the deficits of poverty around the globe. My Immaculate Heart overflows with pity for them, and Jesus intends that we seek His intervention in these regions. I have spoken broadly about the horrible conditions in war-torn nations and other undeveloped, Third World countries where most of the poor people do not have running water. They sleep in grass huts and rusty buildings as shelter from the elements. These families suffer diseases and pestilence because the Western world will not help; Americans are too rapt in politics and materialism. When Pope Paul VI spoke of finding peace, did he not call for social justice, for caring and empathy for people in need? Did not John Paul the Great remind humanity that you shall be judged by how you treat Jesus' presence in the poor? Did not Mother Teresa of Calcutta prove that to be perfectly human means to perfectly nurture the Lord's creatures, great and small; to feed and house them, tend to the dying, and defend the young even before their birth? Is this not the reason you became Christians? There are blessings aplenty for all people on Earth to share wealth, and this is what I seek. The rite of tending to the poor runs pervasively through the Church; it is heralded and made compulsory by the Scriptures. My children, I have spoken during the leap years since 1992 about the extra day that seems to overshadow your concern for the pitiable souls about whom I speak. Why has the United States fallen into such isolationism? Why have secular Americans become so focused on election day in November every leap year with such stark emphasis? If there was equality among Americans and in your view of the poor in other parts of the world, you would not be as concerned about how many of your assets will be redistributed to foreign shores to feed and house those who are still suffering. My children, the mission of the Church is to lead unrepentant sinners to the Cross. However, Jesus taught you not only how to be redeemed, but how to live. Does the Holy Gospel not reconfirm that fairness is defined more by what you sacrifice than the profits you collect? Time after time, parable after parable, and moment by moment, the Son of Man showed your ancestors the meaning of righteousness by being their example. When you put the question before humanity as to what Jesus would do, provide the answer yourselves. I have rebuked and admonished the hypocrisy of America time and again, and it is to this that I dedicate today's message. You will in two months' time choose your new leaders, what policies will best preserve your wealth, how deeply the Church will be permitted to influence the secular debate, and how you will define the beginning of life and the audacity to take it at your whim. In a form of national paranoia, you will discuss how to shield yourselves from the wicked around the globe who would see your destruction, not noticing that it is you who are destroying yourselves. I remind you that the issues to which Americans must look are those mandated by the Church and dictated by the Holy See. Take upon yourselves the mantle of Christian sacrifice, the Commandments and Beatitudes, and Jesus' admonition for you to remain defenders of the just and servants of the poor. When the Lord God said that men should be stewards of the Earth, that you should be fruitful and multiply, He anticipated your stature before the heavens as having the capacity to love. This is the precursor to your Salvation in the Cross. Nowhere does the Father condone your interpretation of the Sacred Scriptures not in alliance with His Vicar in Rome. It is reckless and perilous for humanity to ignore the decrees and encyclicals of Pope Benedict and his predecessors. It is repulsive before Jesus for you to impugn the Pontiff's good name and insult his character. When this Pope blessed the site where thousands died on September 11, 2001, he prayed that you will accept the Christian holiness that would have precluded the catastrophe in the first place. My children, I do not envy the future America has chosen. The Holy Spirit pines to infiltrate and enlighten your hearts with Truth, but you reject it. You remain callous and embittered. Millions of Americans plot their next move to capture greater wealth at the rising of the new dawn. Can you believe that Jesus will have Mercy on them for this? I compliment My priests and missionaries who heed the request for generosity that My Son commands, and I implore the West to be more dedicated to the proposition that all men are created equal. Millions of you have neither listened nor adhered to the requirements of your own stated freedoms. This message consists of the same censure that I gave America before, but I promise that it is not too late for change. There is still time to repent, even though the hour is more than half-spent before the Cross makes everything beneath the sun reflect the beauty and consonance of Heaven. For many, all the warnings in the universe do not matter. Others take notice only after their families and friends become involved. Your idea of freedom has little to do with the liberation of the heart that Christ Jesus is demanding. This is why I have come, to tell you about His imminent response. My Heart is your gift; and in this, I resonate the divinity of God. When I travel the globe and see My children kneel before the Crucifix and the Monstrance containing Jesus' Eucharistic Body, I am confident that the entire world will someday pray. I have said that I have seen the end of your exile, and I know how blessed you are. If you invoke My intercession, you will see as I see, and you will inherit My hope for the healing of every ailment that has befallen the human race.

My Special son, bless you for allowing Me to speak about My intentions. You and your brother have consecrated yourselves in mighty ways to bring the justice of Heaven to bear on those who are lost in sin. We have come together for this reason, and to receive from Heaven the Lord's reaction to the ills of faithless men. You have prepared an exceptional letter to your Bishop when you deliver your book. He will be amazed by the picture of the child. Pope John Paul the Great sees how you weep when you remember his papacy, and he blesses you with the Father in Heaven. I have compassion for the tension you undergo. I know that you are strong and will prevail over anything that tries to dampen your spirit. It was gracious that you attended the Holy Sacrifice of the Mass at Blessed Sacrament Church to receive Holy Communion. Please remember those who have lost loved-ones, young and old, because their mourning is intense. I will speak to you again next week and celebrate the power of the Cross."

Sunday, September 14, 2008
3:46 p.m.

"I am the Alpha and the Omega, the Beginning and the End. To anyone who thirsts I will give to drink without cost from the spring of life-giving water. He who wins the victory shall inherit these gifts. I will be his God, and he shall be my son." [Rev. 21:6-7]

"My dear little children, your Immaculate Mother comes from Heaven to pray with you for the spiritual sanctification of humanity, even as the Lord inspires your conversion to Jesus' Sacred Heart through as many miracles as imaginable to your faith. You have heard Pope Benedict's condemnation of humanity's pagan worship of wealth, materialism and immorality; and you must know that he speaks on behalf of Heaven. The Father would have the United States remember that there are messages of conversion imbedded in the acts of Nature, that you must learn that your discomfort fosters the uprooting of corruption from within you. Your lives are changed in ways that turn your hearts closer to the Sacred Love of Jesus embracing you in times of such loss and sorrow. America must see that He is reaching-out to you so you will understand the purpose of mutual sacrifice, and that you will realize that you have no life without the Holy Spirit thriving in you. When you suffer and witness the agony of others, you coalesce in the shared brokenness of your human state. You become united by the themes that are common with the Saints, and you create in your time ways to react to world conditions that will lead you to enter their presence at the conclusion of your lives. My little ones, I have told you that there is much work to be done before then. As I give you this message, the world is rocking and groveling, churning and unraveling. Creation is prone to shuddering when its inhabitants do not embrace the divinity of Heaven through your Salvation in Jesus on the Cross. And, what comprises the elements about which I speak? All across the North American continent, and from high and low, there is evidence that your citizens are distant from Holy Truth. Your meandering Atlantic seaboard broils with night-lights from towering skyscrapers, and with crime, brutal violence, lust, prostitution, drunkenness, and the shameless rejection of the teachings of the Church. Tens of millions of dollars are wasted wagering on games of chance, extravagant sprees, glitter, pomposity, and gluttony. Countless paupers live in the streets and beneath railroad bridges while snow-bird millionaires take flight from the wintry cold to the sunny beaches of the south. Your national government sits like a giant carbuncle festering on the flesh of a dying beast. My children, America is corroding from its own excesses and addiction to pride and capitalism, leaving in its wake a trail of death and destruction that no natural disaster could rival. You shirk your responsibilities to the dignity of human life from the womb to the execution chamber. You create corporations that cheat and steal the wages and old-age savings from unsuspecting people, and you proudly call it freedom. You make war for profit, and kill enemies for entertainment. You have fashioned an arsenal of military armaments unlike any the world has ever seen, and you are willing to unleash it against anyone who impugns your patriotic pride. You have created a network of deception to lure your foreign neighbors into your traps, hoping to increase your profits and embellish your worldly stature. In the lethal snake pit of Nevada, you propagate gambling, sloth, marital infidelity, substance abuse, child exploitation, staged idolatry, and the stunning influences that perpetuate crimes of inexplicable devastation. Your Pacific coast is the epicenter of choreographed socialized propaganda, the destruction of gender identity, licentiousness, the annihilation of human innocence, and an unmitigated tinderbox for creating false impressions through the evil promises of power and fame. Your airwaves reek with profanity; your atmosphere and rivers are dying from waste; the bucolic forests are being shaved from the Earth like whiskers, and all you do is boast about what a great country you have. The stony faces of four secular idols have been hewn into a mountain to commemorate your conquest of a continent that once stood with silent eloquence, and with beauty and art, with such a benign reflection of the brilliance of its Creator, resting peacefully until the Son of Man returns to renew all things. Somehow, the concept of America has become perverted from the pious intentions of your ancestors, although you inherited your corruptibility from them, just as you fell from grace with Adam when he declared his disobedience to God.

My children, the Great Reckoning about which the Saints have spoken is in the offing. Your forbears and friends have died from their ancient mortal calling, from disasters, famine, disease, wanton neglect, and all the random etceteras by which the human flesh expires. But, their spirits are still alive. They have come to be with Jesus inside the New Jerusalem that is hailed by Revelation, while you are still in the dark. Your framework of instability is a cross of your own making, your own lack of love and wholesomeness, your crassness, isolationism, incivility, and stubborn pride. I have come speaking to humanity as the *Morning Star Over America* to teach you right from wrong, to wake you from your paranoiac coma of indifference against the Kingdom of Eternal Love. My Immaculate Heart is filled with that Love, but also with desire—a driving force that keeps Me here in this place, pulling on your heartstrings like fishermen harvesting their nets, reminding you that at the end of time, you shall recognize that your years have all along been about discerning God's Truth from your lies. You have fabricated a nation that is founded on pluralism and fiendish disbelief, both of which the Son of Man will cast into the flames of the Netherworld. Do you fear His Judgement? Are you unaware that your eternity hinges on your compliance with His Sacred Word? My children, My compassion for you is unprecedented, even by the Messiah about whom I speak! Your Salvation not only implies that you reverse the wrongdoings that I have mentioned today, it demands that you rectify them with honest expedition. Call upon the Holy Spirit to be your guiding Light. Renounce your sinful nature and your propensity to ignore Heaven's warnings. Approach the Cross in contrition, repentance, and with a firm purpose of amendment, and the Lord will set you free. Jesus will rescue you from the pit and lift you from the mire in which you have soiled the dignity of your souls. My children, thank you for caring about the dire conditions in your country. I commend you for working where prudence is shunned, and for feeding the poor, visiting the captive, praying for the wretched and forsaken, and shining like gems in the Lord's vineyard so His Kingdom will prevail. It is fitting that I reprove your American neighbors because they practice a culture of possessionism and lack of charity. These things have created a nation that is reluctant to look into the plight of strangers, even those living next door. Greed and impurity are the key enemies of fairness and goodness, and I am reprimanding those who are responsible. My Special son, My mission is being fulfilled; the world is being warned that there is much remaining for redression.

Problems that adversely affect humanity must be ameliorated if sinners are to receive Jesus' pardon. I will in the next three months make your final New Millennium anthology one to shake the globe, a manuscript to give your friends reason to hope in their faith. As I said, your participation after January 1, 2009 will uplift your spirit because you will understand that *Morning Star Over America* will be complete. I will speak to your viewpoints about faith and the Church, the glowing light that enlivens your happiness in the Kingdom you will soon inherit, and many other issues to help you and your brother be stronger witnesses for Christ."

Sunday, September 21, 2008
1:59 p.m.

"I love you, O Lord my strength, O Lord my rock, my fortress, my deliverer, my God, my refuge, my shield, the horn of my Salvation, my stronghold! Praised be the Lord, I exclaim, and I am safe from my enemies." [Psalms 18:2-4]

"My darling children, I cannot overstate My joy in speaking to you about the holiness of the Catholic Church, the sacredness of its intentions, the beauty of its service, and the promptness of its obedience. Only the love of a mother can comprehend the closeness in which I hold you in My Immaculate Heart. You are the conquerors of the indifference that has brought such corruption to the world because your motivations come from God. Jesus, the Fruit of the Sacred Altar, is your strength and righteousness. He is the reason for your faith, the brilliance in your truthfulness, and the Divine Light safeguarding your footsteps through the land mines of the Earth. The Holy Sacrifice of the Mass is your conversion and Salvation because you are joined there to the Father by the Crucifixion of the Son of Man, the Savior who has healed and justified you, the Maker of Saints who enlightens you in the way of justice. I have told you about His goodness, that He is the slayer of your enemies and bastion of hope during periods of doubt. When you fight against the evil forces of secularism, Jesus stands beside you and the Holy Spirit within you. All your knowledge about Heaven springs from Jesus, My children. Your petitions and meditations are bound and ratified through Him. When I speak about the Fruit of the Altar, I refer simultaneously to the Fruit of My Womb who is blessed, as I am blessed. Jesus is your springtime and autumn, the initiation of your piety, the intuition with which you recognize the difference between goodness and evil, and the uprightness of your moral posture amidst the elements of the world. It is My distinct honor to be the Mother of the Messiah, the Matriarch of Creation, the Queen of Peace and Love, the Mother of the Most High, the Lady of Perpetual Help, and the Handmaid of the Lord.

My little ones, I come of My own volition even as I am dispatched by the Father to touch you. I do not speak to prove the existence of Heaven, but to pronounce the urgency of its calling. You are creatures of the world who are being summoned to higher things, to beatific Wisdom, to the faith that was given your fathers in their most crucial times. My cherubs, your most valuable gift from God is the Holy Sacrifice of the Mass. There, you are rescued from the poverty of human ignorance. You overcome the burdens of your ineptitude in matters of truth and service, and you are edified in the ways of the New Jerusalem where the Saints celebrate their own resurrection in the Most Sacred Heart of Jesus. Genuflecting, bowing, kneeling, praying, singing, petitioning—all of these things compose the physical aspects of your acceptance of the ethereal graces that have absolved you. When a priest pronounces the Presence of your Crucified Savior, you are joined by Heaven that you might be sanctified. I implore you to proclaim the Good News to all men of peaceful will that Jesus Christ inhabits the Earth with trueness and holiness. He brings healing and peace that no one can steal from you. My messages have been a brief encapsulation of the overwhelming awakening that you have found in your faith in Christ because they are derived from the same salvific intent of the Father to restore your genesis. He desires that you join Him in Paradise and bask in His Glory, leaving behind your brokenness and the disingenuous pride that felled Adam and Eve from the Garden. And, once you have reclaimed your innocence by partaking of My Eucharistic Son, you will receive the radical reorientation that the Church celebrates before princes and paupers, among the leagues of nations, around the universe, to the Dominions and Principalities, and all over Creation where spirits have flown. I commend you to Jesus' Divine Mercy during the Holy Sacrifice of the Mass because I have seen its efficacy. Yes, I have witnessed to the delight of My own eyes the lame walk again, the guilty kneel before the Cross, the haughty defer to the meek, the mourning dance with joy, the holy raised to their reward, and the jubilation of the Hosts of Heaven that these things have come. My Immaculate Heart has glowed with happiness knowing that My children have accepted their portion of the divinity of God by becoming one with Jesus, and I have realized that His Sacrifice and My Sorrow were worth the cost.

Henceforth, I beseech you to be reminded of the beauty of the Church. In its holiest hour, it outshines the sun and moves mountains. It forces demons into the grasp of Saint Michael the Archangel where they are cast into the fires of Hell. I have seen baptisms that have brought the cold-hearted to tears, weddings that have united societies, new orders of things that have sprung from the unifying prayers of enemies who willed-away their differences by passing down the nave of churches built on cliffs overlooking huge crevasses. God has sent Me to bless you in more ways than you could capture in manuscripts and picture books. I have touched hearts in places that most Americans have never seen. My legacy of intercession has brought Love and Truth to peoples whose trust has been breached by centuries-old hatred based on little more than the tides of history. I have asked the mute to speak volumes about the Triumph of My Immaculate Heart, the young and the old, the valorous and the afraid, the outspoken and the timid—all who have come to the realization that the miracle of faith is more than something to be novelized by the curious for fortune and fame. Mine is the beauty that is emulated by brides and benefactors, by queens and princesses, by Nature and the eminent. And, we have done more than men can reminisce about for the conversion of the world. We have touched centuries of common souls who wondered what their pains were for, what God meant when He gave them life, what happiness is for if it cannot be savored, and those who for too long groveled beneath the oppression of their kings' unchecked pride. We have tamed stallions to carry the justice they sought into the dance of ordinary life, where pawns and magnates unite in faith to see the Providence of the Christ who has brought them to reconcile as one and all. My children, please do not dismay at the misgivings of the Earth because you have overcome them all. They cannot enslave you any more like they did your ancestors. These words are My blessing for your hearts today, that you will remember with all your might that the Lord loves you without end. My Special son, I am charmed to be with you to speak about the Church that we honor, and about humanity who is refined by your own confessions, healed by your belief in the power of God and the hope that I ask you to espouse until the conclusion of time. Do you see that Satan has tried to impede this message? *(There was distracting illicit pandemonium surrounding my residence as Our Lady spoke to me.)* This means that everything is good; all I have been telling you will be transmitted to humanity through the Will of the Father. Satan can only heckle while we pursue your mission, one where he has already been plunged into the darkness that souls like yours will never be subjected. There are flames in Gehenna, but they emit no light."

Sunday, September 28, 2008
1:03 p.m.

"The fruit of the Spirit is love, joy, peace, patient endurance, kindness, generosity, faith, mildness, and chastity. Against such there is no law! Those who belong to Christ Jesus have crucified their flesh with its passions and desires." [Gal. 5:22-24]

"With overwhelming grace, I am present with you to pray for this world, for everything that requires amendment and reparation, for the finding of lost sinners, the healing and protection of the weak and disenfranchised, and that Divine Love floods Creation with the Lord's definitive Truth. My children, I will three months from this date complete My public messages to the Church as *The Morning Star Over America* because you have seen the reason I have come; and it is time that My children take action, all of you, that the wishes I have set forth are enacted. The United States has changed for the worse in the past quarter-century because Americans are still embroiled in selfishness and greed. I previously told you that western capitalism would soon begin to cannibalize itself, and the events of the past week are tangible evidence of this. What would you have Jesus do with the consumerism and possessionism of the United States? You spend billions of dollars for war, billions in exploring the cosmos, billions for failed investment frameworks, billions for communication, billions for health services for your pet animals, and even more billions for cosmetics and entertainment. Is this not the corrupt work of a society that is headed for its demise? You claim to be interested in helping the poor in lands distant from your shores, and you take your economic systems there to make patrons of them for your own imperial gain. Millions of children are being aborted from the womb. Millions are dying in the streets from starvation and neglect; untold numbers are being sacrificed to false gods and violence, and yet most Americans turn their eyes away, believing that this is the normality of the world. I remind you that you have the responsibility to address these catastrophic conditions not only as a matter of principle, but due to your human conscience in the oath you have taken to Jesus. How can the Father be pleased when I have been impelled by your conduct to speak in recent weeks about the excesses in your country, when He sees that you are withholding wealth from the poor as a resource for the pilferers at the top? Indeed, I have spoken of reckonings and chastisements, and you have chosen to ignore My pleas. Common sense about human life has been supplanted in great part by cronyism and spiritual blindness. My little ones, the Lord would rather be merciful than filled with wrath toward the Earth. However, He demands that your repentance precede Jesus' Mercy. This change of heart is required if you are to become ingrained in the issues that matter to the growth of the Church and the avoidance of sin. If you refuse to communicate with Jesus in prayer, you are effectively declaring that you do not need Him. And, this is the obstinance and disobedience that has led to the downfall of the institutions in your government and society that once protected your children and provided for their future. I have come speaking to you as the Patroness of this nation because I love you. My Immaculate Heart is filled with affection for your potentials that you are not realizing because you will not listen to Jesus. There is only one God, and He is present in the Father, and the Son, and the Holy Spirit so you can be enlightened by the trebled power of the Holy Cross in this immediate hour. My messages have been a pressing initiator for your reaction, and the future is yours to comply. Please take My pleadings seriously and know that Jesus is waiting for your response. When I speak about the trillions of dollars you spend and plan to expend for your own use, does this implicate that you will continue to ignore the plight of the rest of the world? Can you hear their groaning and see their pains that are crying-out for relief? Do you believe it necessary to waste so much money on things that have nothing to do with the redemption of men? I detest that you spend billions of dollars that could be used for eradicating crippling diseases, but you squander them instead to enhance your carnal abilities and for automobiles speeding in circles to see who finishes first. My children, this is not a country devoted to God, it is one that worships at the altar of extravagance and idolatry. And, it is one that in no way looks forward to the Kingdom that Jesus promised to establish when He returns in Glory. My Special son, I take great delight in your prayers, and I know that you see their effects. I remind you that nothing that you and your brother have done or failed to do has anything to do with the waning of America's esteem. It is absolutely not related to you at all. I know that you work extremely hard to protect My messages and your mission, while at the same time striving to force defeat upon the devil. You must not allow your composure or standing as children of God to be defined by others as being within the parameters of sinful Adam, but in the liberating power of Jesus Christ Crucified. It is an exercise of divine power to confront and triumph over any sinful definition that a person may attempt to level against you. I know that you share the Light of the Holy Spirit with all who mourn and suffer this week and always. And, please remember to tell your Bishop that I love him. The Lord requires tested faith, firm faith, not just the faith of shallow followers."

Sunday, October 5, 2008
3:07 p.m.

"Say to those whose hearts are frightened: Be strong, fear not! Here is your God. He comes with vindication; with divine recompense he comes to save you. Then will the eyes of the blind be opened, the ears of the deaf be cleared." [Isaiah 35:4-5]

"My Special and Chosen ones, you have witnessed the greatness of humanity in the power of your faith; you have exalted Truth, ascended mountains, engorged valleys with the fullness of your fears, overcome adversities that would vanquish mighty kings, and brought to the feet of the Lord your obedience, that He might reforge the Earth into the likeness of the Cross. All the imagining you might do to wish-away the darkness, every dream that you have ever pursued; all of this is found in the righteousness of the heart. And, you must not only see this, My children, you must actively pursue everything you know to be the Will of the Father that greets you by tragedy and sorrow, by joy and prophesy, by beatitude and grace. We have for many years prayed together and wished for the atonement of societies who do not know

Christ. We have been to the mountaintops of elation and the pits of despair. When all is said upon the end of time, let it be clear to God and all His creatures that we bade humanity well. We strived to achieve their holiness; we sought the healing of their ills. With your hands in Mine, we walked through the darkness and shadows in which you trembled with uncertainty, and we prevailed, My little ones. You have given to Me what you could have afforded no other—My opportunity to be your Mother as Jesus said. Now, when you kneel to pray and He looks down with hope, He sees your flourishing image of Himself. He feels all the agony that the world has heaped upon you. He recognizes that you have accepted the Holy Spirit as the thoroughfare of commitment between your souls and Heaven. It is all about Salvation, My little children, through the power of His Sacrifice. For anyone who desires to know, this is the essence of Glory. Of course it means that you wish to be delivered. Beyond any doubt, it is the end of your torturous years on an Earth saturated by pain. But, it is preeminently about Glory that we speak. This is the origin of the righteousness at the center of your being. It is the transformation of your existence into unending life. My cherished ones, when you look to the heavens with faith-filled inquiry, Jesus already knows what you are seeking from Him. He anticipates your cries in the night and the needs of your hearts. As you raise your spirits skyward, He desires that you sense His eminence with the innocence of little children. And, He does this because you are the beneficiaries of His Sorrowful Crucifixion, a Sacrifice that has enabled you to be dignified in sight of the Father, a suffering so profound that it is inexplicable to those who refuse to hear. Indeed, My Son desires that you will shade your eyes with your palms and stare into the brightness of Eternal Truth, knowing that you will someday see. Anticipate your redemption by yearning for this Glory. Do your best work with His Kingdom in mind, with your trust in the Angels and Saints, with stouthearted and straightforward determination that you shall succeed in Him, conquer the night, sail the distant shores, climb the highest peaks, rescue the dying, find the lost, feed the starving, admonish the erroneous, and give your entire assets to the fulfillment of the Gospel. He asks not only that you accept His Holy Will, but that you become entrenched in it, propagate and exalt it, bring to the Feast Table your immersion in it, and be drowned with plenteous Absolution affirming your oath to His Will. Can these years pass without the Mother of God inviting you to rest beneath My Sacred Mantle? The answer is definitive in that I not only invite you, I command you as the Queen of Creation to be subservient to the same Glory that will crown you in Heaven. Jesus came to serve and not to be served, and you are called to be His servants according to the prefigured Will of the Father in all things. I have spoken in past years about flickers that became flames, droplets that turned into floods, notions that grew into movements, and little souls who became Doctors of the Church. I have called your faith into being through the Passion of My Son. And, you have seen both with and without your eyes that it has all been worth the fight. You embrace high hopes because of the promises that Jesus made. You have more confidence because He has lifted you beyond the stars. I promise that you will be elated to see the ending of the world that He is waiting to unleash. The faithful will prosper anew, and the faithless will perish. Those who have been true to the Cross will prevail through its Light. The ones who have cursed it will be cast into Hell. My children, the return of Christ the King will be as clear as this. And, My summons rings with equal clarity.

Therefore, you see what your exile is for. Deep in the faith you profess, you know that you have been preordained for conversion. After all, the Son of Man was born that you may also have life. You focus too much on the things of Earth, and on commodities, and all the terrible matters that I mentioned in the past two weeks. Your thrust toward the Eternal City has already been pronounced in your commitment to the Church and the daily prayers you recite from the heart. You feel your ascendance to this beauty by trusting, by knowing in advance the Glory that has come before you were born. You embrace the artistry of Nature because you know the Author of Life. You welcome the clemency of His forgiveness by being fair toward your brothers, by caring for the poor, being good stewards of everything under your charge, teaching your children about the Bible, healing anything and everything that seems fractured, and enlisting in the Army of Marian Catholics who will finally put this world behind them. I pray today that you will respond to the overtures from Heaven, to the miracles that God dispenses, to the signs and wonders of the Angels and Saints, to the legacies of the great servants of the Church, and even to your own conscience when the future seems unclear. There is no way you can do too much good; this is simply impossible. Likewise, it cannot be said that you have not tried to be the best and brightest of the ages in your imitation of the Lord. I honor you for this, My children, and I offer you My assurance that I will be with you beyond the conclusion of time. I am a Mother who is filled with Truth; undefiled, perfect, and Immaculate. My Special son, I remind you that I have not the words to tell you how you are appreciated by the Hosts of Heaven. You have afforded Me a venue to dictate to humanity My messages that are unprecedented in this age. All your works will be read; they will be hailed as uniquely from the genius of God. It may not be tomorrow or next week or next year, but they will be taken in hand by every creature known to the universe. As you know, your mission has been completed outside the element of time. The Saints have read your manuscripts and wept over the harmonies of My parables. All the heavens have poured-out its power on those who have believed. And, you and your brother have been humble; you have given your noblest selves to impoverished humanity, to the millions starved for Truth. Jesus knows this, and the Father is beaming with joy. There is delight in His Kingdom, My Special son. His creatures on Earth, you and your brother, have fought the good fight and have won. I will speak to you more about personal issues, about decapitating the head of evil, prospering your apostolic mission, and harboring gladness when you might feel oppressed. In the meantime, you must know that everything I have given humanity will also bloom. It will thrive through the Will of God about which I spoke earlier, by the good faith of His flock, by the sacrifices of those who believe, and for the conversion of the sinners whom the Holy Spirit is pining to captivate. Whereas you have been dignified in your devotion to Me, the Lord will reward your faith. And, thank you for being so deferential to your Bishop, and giving him your book and the other gifts you delivered. You addressed him with a mixture of poise and innocence, and confidence, and strong vision for a better world. And so, you see after the service of your years to the Church and to Me, and to the transference of God's citizens into the vestibule of redemption, you have given Jesus the gift of your life. *(I told Our Lady that all that I am and all that I have is at Her service, and let us begin anew as on the first day She came.)* Then let us tender your work to the Father's hands and pray for many more souls. Let us commend broken humanity to the charities of His Love, and to the dutiful work that He would have them do on His behalf once they are healed."

Sunday, October 12, 2008
2:16 p.m.

"Thus, may a season of refreshment be granted you by the Lord when he sends you Jesus, already designated as your Messiah. Jesus must remain in Heaven until the time of universal restoration which God spoke of long ago through his prophets." [Acts 3:20-21]

"The constellations are like granules of sand in the palms of those who summon the Holy Spirit to strengthen and guide them in the passing of their ordinary lives. Jesus gives this to you because He loves you, as do I. My children, you must adhere to the faith about which we have spoken, and the Lord will ratify your actions in Him. Today, I remind you that you are My adopted children to whom I have given My life. It is good and proper that you call upon Me for help, as Jesus did during His earthly years. And, you should remember that I am the most beneficial intercessor for your needs, both personal and social, because I bore to you the Savior. I told you explicitly on April 22, 1994 that you are part of Me. It is important that you remember what this means. Everything that I have to offer from Heaven belongs to you, especially My Son whose Crucifixion is your Salvation. I am escorted here by the Orders of Angels who speak to the Father of miracles. This is how your petitions are magnified. We have joined in this place to pray for the ills of this American nation which so woefully affect many other parts of the world. It is because of your overages that millions around the globe are suffering. You must turn to the spiritual arts and Nature to see God better, and discard your penchant for the distractions of materialism and secularism. Even as you take the message of Christian conversion to the masses, remember that they are as indifferent as stones on your pathway to the seas. God knew that your evangelization of His Word would be difficult, that there would be countless stumbling blocks keeping you from being heard. If you proceed lifting My role in human redemption to them, they will listen to you. I will provide the impetus for them to awaken from their sleep, and you will have the venues you have always wanted. Christians realize that it is not enough just to know that you are saved, but that all with whom you live must be given knowledge to seek their Salvation too. While you are confident in your station, it is not always simple when taking the Truth of the Cross into the world. When you peer across the expanse of the architecture of the Earth, you see the beauty of God's handiwork. You see sky-scraping mountains with foggy tips wailing to humanity to look aloft. From the depths of the seas, the sonic appeal of its inhabitants remind you that there is an entire underworld yet to explore. You see evergreens and flat lands, marshes and meadows, crevasses and gorges, and awesome spreads of wildflower woods. Even the bitter winter winds remind you that the spring cannot be long in coming. And, as the Lord created the environment, He gave you creatures of all kinds to accompany your transformation into the perfection of His Son. This is why the cardinals and whippoorwills sing to you, why the eagles fly and seagulls sail. It is the reason you see deer running to the brooks and foxes to their lairs. You have been accorded a clement planet of plenteous grace to give you peace inside. This peace comes in your knowledge that if the Earth can be this beautiful, imagine the breathtaking presence of Heaven. I implore you to remember that Jesus has trekked this life with you in all ways imaginable. He has shared your joys and borne your griefs. His Sacred Heart is your tangible union with the Creator of the Nature you seem to worship from morning until dusk, and in the pit of the night, and when you dream sleepily of better things to come, and after they are granted to you from the Father who deigns to fashion life. Rose buds and wheatfields all belong to Him. Craters and cliffs are some of His best artwork. Everything you can imagine that connects you with His desire to be pleasing to His creatures is a manifestation of His Love.

  This, My children, is why you must be awakened; it is the purpose of your purification, to prepare you for the ultimate gift of Eternal Life. Here in America, you feel the ocean breezes that tell you that the infinity of His freedom is yours. The summits of the Appalachians heave you toward the pinnacles of Heaven that will someday uplift your souls. The rolling rivers filling the southern gulf remind you that life ends in the bay of Truth about which I have spoken. Indeed, when I said in 1994 that you are part of Me, I was referring to My intonation of praises for God, for His only begotten Son, for the Grace by which you are saved, for the Blood in which you are cleansed, and the Resurrection that has overcome your death. I pray that you will come to Me, My children, and hold Me as I embrace you with the power of the Cross. I beg you to permit Me to be your Mother, to show you the dignity that is yours in the Church, the redemption you find in the Holy Eucharist, the liberation you gain in the Rite of Reconciliation, and the Light that has shined your greatest images on the backdrop of immortal time. I spoke that day about promises and deliverance, of the unique bond you share with Jesus in the Father's house. My little ones, before this year is ended, you must remind even yourselves that life is greater than that which you have allowed it to be. It is about holiness and sacrifice, about dodging the piercing arrows of hatred and deceit, of tending to the lost before the gravity of their sins pushes them into the netherworld. Your conversion in Christ is about standing upright in Sacred Truth while holding on to nothing but the Cross, allowing your souls to fall freely into Jesus' waiting arms without inhibition. This is the real definition of valor. I have told you that you may never resurrect a soldiers' line, but this does not stop you from identifying with their cause. It is all about your perception of eternal dimensions, My dear ones. You must consider what such things as plankton and stars have in common, what it means to labor without being rewarded, to walk blindly in faith and still know where you are going. Your Salvation implies that you accept the pressure of bearing the mourning of daily life, of absolving the unforgiving, of feeding paupers at the front doorway, and preaching the genuine profession of your beliefs without concern that you may be spurned. If you wish to be like Jesus, you will enlist His cause like the Saints, as in their best hours in their worst oppression, and like little children who know only matters at hand. Someday soon, Eternity will engulf you. Death will lay you low, and Jesus will raise you up again. The cyclical changes of human endeavors will finally come to a conclusion and reveal the void from which they have all been derived. Then, My darlings, you will see. You will label the enemies of the Church for who they are. You will watch the light emitting from the cracks in the Earth, just as I told you long ago. Rose petals will rain from the skies; the chanting of the Saints shall give you strength; the winds will blow where they will, and everything you have always prayed for in this life and the next will be handed to you. I tell you that I have seen every kindness you wished to have been afforded. I have seen the mending of the social breaches that divide you one from another. I have heard My children speaking in one tongue from battlefield and cenotaph, from hollow to pulpit, and from the pew in the Church to the Seat of Wisdom. This is why you are part of Me. I declare you worthy of grace, exculpation, and redemption. My cause here in this Illinois home has been to seek the repatriation of humanity into the City of Light, from this place where your martyred commander in chief bade farewell to his countrymen to take the reigns of a nation sorely divided from itself. I stood in this very spot on the Earth generations ago and heard the cannons' fire and the eulogies spoken. I saw the stately horses and heard the bells toll. From all the states they came just yards from where I am speaking now to honor a man who set his people free. Now, I return to this avenue of monuments to speak again and finally about a Man who has set all people free, the dignified Savior who gave His fullest measure that all men who were created would be freed from sin, not just Americans, not only the North and the South, but the people of the world. My children, I have wept with you for two-thousand years. I have hoped with you, prayed with you, walked your darkest hours in war and peace, given consolation to the lost, spoken with encouragement, and became your Advocate at the behest of the Messiah. Even in all I have said, My children, these are your finest hours. Thank you again, My Special son, for the gift of your life, for allowing Me to speak to My children with strains that we know will instill in them the desire to begin anew. Your honesty, piety, prayerfulness, and search for Truth have brought you to this moment. You must remember that My messages here would have been impossible without you. I have told you this before. Jesus knows what your heart desires, just as His Sacred Heart yearned to heal the world from His conception in My Womb. You are united with Him, and one with the Father through Him."

Sunday, October 19, 2008
1:21 p.m.

"Toward the faithful you are faithful; toward the wholehearted you are wholehearted; toward the sincere you are sincere; but toward the crooked, you are astute. You save lowly people, though on the lofty your eyes look down." [2 Samuel 22:26-28]

"Wear with dignity your scars from this life, My dear children, because they are translated into the distinction of the Saints in Heaven. My Immaculate Heart is with you during your struggles. My compassion overwhelms your spirit in ways you cannot see. Today, we remember those who are enduring the oppressions of poverty, diseases, wars, and pestilence in regions to which you may never travel. Even so, you must pray for them and fight to eradicate the conditions that plague their lives with torment. And, you surely see the need for the conversion of their oppressors. This is why we are all laboring so diligently to change the texture of humanity and smooth the craggy landscape of human existence. It would seem that your years are filled with crooked edges and faulty footholds because those around you who refuse to accept Christianity cannot see the purpose of their exile. They do not understand that their fractious nature is reparable in the Holy Cross; and this is their infamy. It is their opprobrium. I speak during these important days to help inspirit their hearts with the peace of redemption, the amendment of their consciousness they require to see the spiritual aspects of life. You have been commissioned by the Son of Man to heed the call of the Holy Spirit. Jesus has not promised that you would have flower-strewn walkways in your sojourn to eternity. God the Father has laid the challenge before you to be like His Son, that you will internalize the meaning of Sacrificial Love. When you turn to His ways, you feel in your footsteps the reason for your faith. My children, how many times have I reminded you that prayer is the key to the rejuvenation of the lost? I shall never concede My little ones to the darkness, and neither must you. Your faith is centric through the Apostolic Catholic Church as you obey the edicts of the Holy See. It is universal because it embraces all humanity. It is with fidelity and adherence to the teachings of the Hierarchy that your faith is consecrated; and it should be authentic and active. If you remain beneath the protection of My Holy Mantle, the world's evil cannot defile you. The sordid influences of secularism will never lure you from the purity you have inherited in the Crucifixion of My Son. Today, I again summon your prayers to end abortion. It seems a long time that you have sought from the Father the cessation of infanticide; and He hears your prayers. Add to this, My children, that He will amend the will of those who refuse to obey. Consider everything the Saints do to complement your petitions for the unborn. See in your hearts the millions of babies who have already been preserved by the faithful call of your novenas. No petition is ever in vain, My children. I have told you that the greatest waste in the world is a prayer that is left unsaid. Now, I am imploring you to recite them at every hour for all the little ones who yearn to be born. Let us approach the conclusion of time with the knowledge that you have made the difference that Jesus asks. You have suffered in His perfect likeness and surrendered your passions. Your mission has been about self-immolation, grace, renunciation, peace, love, and charity. Your humanity has been dedicated to the refinement of your personal experiences in perfecting the soul through the virtue of the Cross. This has been My call from Heaven every time I have spoken to you. I bring the good wishes of the Father through the Son, and I offer His blessings in My messages. It is not enough that you concur with what I say, you must be respondent to the inquisition of the Spirit as to why the world is the way it is. You can make the amendments you seek; you have the capacity to alter the course of history; you do not have to accept as inevitable the injustices that have inundated the Earth with the transgressions of men. Your hearts can stand tall as titans in a world of groveling inequities if you will become those remarkable heroes about whom Saint Paul preached. The hours expire for a reason; time is leaning in your favor; the rustic peace that you knew as children still lingers where your innocence was born. I am simply asking you to return to discernment that your government and its people have abandoned for some other way of life, and stop the death knell of relativism that is driving them farther from God. Hear!

I am heralding you to remember all who have come to Jesus, and you will know how to pray. My Special son, I tell you that My Immaculate Heart is with you in the trials you face. I am mindful of the pressure, and I promise My sympathies when you are persecuted. You are doing everything right. You are saying the appropriate things, standing on the side of holiness; and Jesus is pleased that your intention is to protect the pristine excellence of your faith. Whatever you do, never back down. I know that your mind is tired and your nerves are frayed, but you have a hallowed sense for everything Jesus demands of God's creatures who expect to be taken to Heaven. As you watch the war pictures on television, you see how the soldiers died, and their widows and orphans grieved. You sympathize with the plight of the warriors; the suffering, disease, deprivation, and death. It would be appropriate for you to count your blessings that you and your brother have not been among them. You said recently that you have lived your lives in the best of times. This indicates your well-placed vision."

Sunday, October 26, 2008
3:32 p.m.

"The Father himself judges no one, but has assigned all judgment to the Son, so that all men may honor the Son just as they honor the Father. He who refuses to honor the Son refuses to honor the Father who sent him." [John 5:22-23]

"My children, the ethereal vitalism of your religious faith is derived from your apostolic zeal. Today, I bring renewed impetus for that motivation into this room, to your hearts filled with love for the suffering poor, the neglected, oppressed, diseased, and dying. I shall nine more times enter your presence as the *Morning Star Over America* because you are My children. How deeply I have cherished My commission as Eternal Matriarch of the nations! You must be prepared for your redemption, My dear ones, because the finishing of the Earth was inscribed in Eternity by Jesus on the Cross. Although He does not know the hour of His return [Mark 13:32], Jesus is already aware of those who belong to Him. I have asked you to live in perpetual expectation of His Coming in Glory because you have only so much time to be perfected. Although death comes like a thief in the night, your deliverance across the chasm of the ages into the infinity of Paradise will occur with prophetic dissertation. And, when referring to your Salvation into the New Jerusalem, you have been told! The Gospel has been edifying the consciences of earthly men for twenty centuries and enlightening the ignorant, opening eyes, reveling hearts, instilling hope, and transforming the ages into one crescendo of beatific energy. So, when you hear the bells peal and smell the flowers' scent, be sure to call the teamsters to prepare the thoroughbreds because the Lord's chariots will be standing nearby. You will be taken heart and soul to the Judgement that too many have feared and billions have already seen. The seasons are turning, the years have passed, and the almanac rings as true as the tines of a fork. Given the divine potential of men, this is not the time for recriminations; it is an historical opportunity for humanity to become reconciled. You must shed your penchant for corruption and discard the excesses of your possessions. And, your system of corporate feudalism must finally be dismantled. Those who have only half-fledged intentions to share the world's wealth with the poor are found lacking alongside Jesus' Crucifixion. You must remember that in the absence of human holiness, fear and suffering are the primary deterrents to sin. Christians are allotted no respite from their labors for the Lord, no sabbatical from His righteousness, and no furlough from sacrifice. You must tell humanity what I am saying and admonish your friends who have only a raspy understanding of the mission of the Church. You are being watched and adjudicated while you live, even as you pray for full deliverance upon your death. The Lord's invigilation of His creatures was pronounced before the inception of time. Jesus of Nazareth is your hero of Living Truth. God offers an astonishing awakening once you convert to His New Covenant because Eternity is His prerogative for the appendices of the years. The Holy Spirit clings to your petitions, elevates your aspirations, and invigorates your bearings in the themes of Paradise. Why would you wish to be conquerors in Him if you were too timid to engage the fight? God knows that you yearn for love, even as you wonder what might settle over your helplessness like mist lingering in the hollows. My children, how can I be more clear in expressing Jesus' romantic reception of your spiritual honor in claiming you for the Father? Has His Grace been insufficient? Do you not see that your healing is your religious faith, that the broadness of your prosperity is imbedded in your compassion for other men? I have taught long and sincerely about your responsibilities as Christians, especially devoted to Me, invested in the Church, and destined to be one with the Saints through your mystical awareness of your union in the Cross. You cannot enter Heaven unless you accept the Holy Cross. This is My warning to humanity! I am overjoyed that I speak and you can hear. Jesus gives the Angels reason to appeal to a future already foretold. He lightens the burden of the innocent who would otherwise be stricken by the misgivings of the wicked. If you remain with Me in prayer, we will bring the changes to the Earth that I have addressed today. We will light the torches in the hands of those who pray, the millions who wait in joyful hope for the Coming of the Lord.

This, My children, is a day filled with good tidings because you have not surrendered your willingness to fight for the redemption of wicked men. When you rise at dawn, you see that Jesus has brought new hope with the sunrise, with brisk intentions that this might be the hour that He shall flush from your presence everything that opposes your faith. We are hopeful as Mother and children that the Father embraces you with His Divine Love as in times past because you are loyal to Him; your hearts are affixed to His Will for Creation. Indeed, this is your reflection of His Resurrected Son. The year in which you live has moved into 300 days, and I bring His dedicated Truth as your guide to honor what Heaven shall accord you when you die. We pray together so righteousness will overcome the Earth, inundate it with loveliness, and usher Eternity to your doorstep as the Son of Man knocks. I thank and bless you for living in Him because My Immaculate Heart is brimming with desire to greet you in Heaven. My Special son, I wish you to remember that I magnify My intercession for your intentions when you fall into despair. I have seen My children from all the ages bantered by nonbelievers and barraged with the hatred of men. This is not new in your age. Whatever thoughts of depression men endure are not signals of weak faith or an inability to serve My Son. You are all human, and thoughts like these were common among the Saints. How you deal with them, whether you permit them to destroy you, and allowing them to inhibit your work in the Church are other matters. I will not burden you with the false comparisons of the suffering of your forbears, those living in abject poverty, imprisoned, and deprived of the right to practice their faith. What men suffer inside is unique to them, their view of the world, how they were reared, the ways they were abused and exploited, and what they perceive the Kingdom of the Lord to be. Therefore, whatever you do, avoid blaming yourself when you are sad. Jesus has a remarkable plan for you, and I often repeat that it is in the offing. The changes you seek are real because I have planted these images in you. I beg you to believe that I have not given you false hope. Your brother said that he prayed for a stable atmosphere where you can prepare your anthologies, but as I told the world in Medjugorje, the dark influences around the globe have evil intent. You are seeing it closer to you. You must know that conditions of uncertainty led Me to dictate that particular message in Medjugorje yesterday. One of the keys is that you do not descend into despondence. I do not require much, but I pray for the trust you have given Me since you were first aware of My presence in the Church. My hopes are that you will take better care of yourself, not just physically, and not that you want a life of more than simple peace. The Lord did not come to place you under any stress, but when you agreed to comply with My request, you become a target of Satan's egregious attacks. Spiritual darkness, the loss of your jovial ties, and the turmoil are part of his evil. Now you are about to fall ill with exhaustion because you are burdened by that darkness. Alas, you will be forced to take time for yourself and ponder what to do next. We have discussed in times past that you are My prince, My warrior and conqueror of the enemies of the Cross. You are living the Resurrection with the poise that has been given you, and I assure you that you are not called to relinquish your dignity to anyone. It must seem paradoxical that I urge you to be happy when

I have said more than once that I cannot make you happy on Earth. The happiness about which I speak is a determination to succeed in faith and prevail in the likeness of those who preceded you. You are not weak; you have not surrendered, and you never will. You are a child of God who sees Heaven with your heart, like Mother Teresa and Saint Pio. Thus, I give you the peace of God as Mother of the King, and it is you who see that He reigns so you can have hope. Please know that the affronts against My messengers are occurring not only to you. Some seers have even been forced from their neighborhoods, locked in jails, deprived of food and clothing, and committed to asylums. I am not suggesting that anything of this nature will happen to you, but the depression you are feeling is part of your cross. The issues I will speak to you and your brother about in January will give you an initial comprehension of the architecture of Heaven that has no boundaries, how the soul deposes the body and takes flight from the Earth, where the Saints say their prayers, what happens to their memoirs, how the Crucifixion prevails over the metaphysical universe, and so on. In many ways, we will begin afresh with a course of transcriptions that you will cherish more than your previous works. I will take you places and sing ballads that will inspire you, lead you to the brink of ecstasy, direct your attention to the appealing soliloquies that have filled amphitheaters with Angels, and commit you to more enduring sacrifices as a means of prayer. These are My promises because I love you. I beseech you to remember that I buttress your reputation before men, and I pray that you will accept it."

Sunday, November 2, 2008
2:47 p.m.

"Rejoice O young man while you are young, and let your heart be glad in the days of your youth. Follow the ways of your heart, the vision of your eyes; yet understand in regards to all this that God will bring you to judgement." [Eccles. 11:9]

"My dearly beloved children, the situation in America is dire. The lines of moral discretion are becoming blurred, and your traditional family values are being perverted beyond recognition. The future of many among you is becoming lost in the complex network of human diversions that are hidden in the foliage of everyday life. This is why we must pray with emphasis so that a teardrop does not become a deluge or a snowflake grow into an avalanche. The Earth is tainted by the errors of misguided men, and we are called to touch them with the power of the Cross. This is why I am so adamant about requesting the intercessions of the Catholic Church. Remember that shallow faith, impotent hearts, and withering vision mean that you are not praying enough. While I have told you that you stand on the leading edge of redemption through your repentance, you must recognize that its trailing edge is man's personal sacrifice. I intend to consecrate My children to the Blood of the Crucifixion so you will forgive yourselves even as you are absolved by Jesus. I realize that this is a difficult process. You will not be popular among those who do not share your faith. Sometimes even your close friends will betray you to avoid your Christian beliefs, resorting with impunity to anger, hatred, violence, and destruction. They will abandon you as though you had never met. The Lord has purposely warned you that walking the narrow path of righteousness is a spirit-wrenching undertaking, and you must rely on your trust with every fiber of your being. Those who throughout their lives have never brought the sunset to tears with the artwork of their faith have yet to truly live. Your reward will be great if you respond now; and when Jesus pronounces the strains of Matthew 25:21 upon your souls, you will know that your lifelong battles have been worth the fight. Your compassion for those who grovel in poverty is more important than your own self-sustenance. When you set eyes on the soft faces of the brokenhearted, please help them carry their grief. You travel aboard a dying Earth that is perspiring with desperation and brawling with madness. And, you have learned that enduring the torments of life is not child's play. As we near the Feast of Childermas to which I referred, remember what My presence has been about. Never forget why the Morning Star descended from the skies above America. You have searched for ways to convert the world's unfaithful people, often referring to them as brash and uncouth, cowardly and arrogant, pretentious and shallow; and all these things describe the enemies of the Church. By all means, you have been gentle in your reproval. Jesus sees their disbelief as unworthy of humanity, even animalistic and villainous, satanic, derelict, and condemnable. He has a final epitaph for their lives that is almost too disheartening to hear, and this is why we must reach them before it is too late. I have for nearly eighteen years been reminding you about My Son's Divine Mercy for those who accept Him. This is not something that He dispenses lightly. Those who bow before His Sacred Cross must know that they are expected to become new creatures, reborn in His Sacrifice, refined by His Resurrection, and determined to uphold the laws of the New Covenant. They must promise to live compliant with His timeless ordinances and decrees, denying the self, fasting on bread and water, declaring an oath to chastity according to their station in life, and be determined to walk with such contrition that they actually repudiate their former selves. My dear ones, this is the begetting of the dignity they were lacking before they found Jesus. It is the Lord's desire for you; it is Heaven's gift to the lost sinners on whom the Church places so much emphasis. If a man commands respect from his peers, then he must be their servant and thereby their leader in forging new ways to be reconciled with Heaven. You must always examine yourselves in the context of the interrogatories taken from the Sermon on the Mount. Do you feel as though Jesus was identifying you when He was counting the blessed? Have you mourned or been poor in spirit? Are you meek, merciful, and clean of heart? Do you make peace instead of war? Do you suffer for your faith, and are you persecuted for your loyalty to the King of kings? Remember that you are the salt of the Earth and the light of the world.

  My children, from the moment you are conceived, you are growing, developing, and maturing in body and soul. You are born into a world that despises everything about you that reminds them of God. You come upon an age of reason in Divine Truth that comports with your desires for something greater, a way that drives you to see Creation through the lens of perfection from which your existence was founded. Although you do not realize it, you are the product of the Heart and Soul of the Creator who is determined to give you every benefit to know Him in all His fullness. When you begin to recognize physical objects as things familiar to you, your thoughts shape opinions about them, whether they seem pleasing or disquieting to your sense of peace. In essence, you are primordially destined for greatness upon an Earth that impugns your potentials by its own failures. As I have told you, My little darlings, you are better than you would ever believe if you listened only to the ranting of the lost. In Jesus, you are discovered for Heaven and for yourselves. Your new beginning is a testament to your ability to succeed in all the ways Jesus endured. When the Holy Spirit enters your heart, you are destined to prevail over the darkness by virtue of your prefigured enlightenment. When I speak to you, it is not solely from outside the realms of your own sublimity, but complementary to your oneness with the Son of Man. The teachings of the Church in compliance with the Sacred Scriptures are your guideposts to let you know where to turn and what avenues to pursue. Christianity cannot exist in a vacuum, but only through the conviction of the conscience upon whom faith is given. It is to this awakening that the Lord dispenses all His power to deliver you to the Cross. As I speak and you listen, it is as though you have placed your ear upon Jesus' Sacred Heart, and His Love for you outlays the pattern of your conversion beyond the elements of the world. My messages all along have been to invite you to accept this pleading, to sense for yourselves the meaning of His Sacrifice in beatific realms so nothing on Earth can again bring you sorrow. It is as though your consciousness is raised from the depths of the Earth's gravity toward a higher state of being. And, once you have accomplished this, My little ones, nothing can harm you. This is the essential valor that brought the Apostles to become Martyrs and allowed them to believe in miracles. This is the intonation of wisdom that took them walking across the world with faith in hand to lend their allegiance to Christ for the building of His Kingdom. It is the reason they wept, spoke, agonized, and bled. This is also the inspirited nourishment that created Saints and Doctors of the Catholic Church, the evangelists who made the ground beneath their feet their home for the night, and all the anonymous believers in Jesus' Resurrection who vowed to never cower in the wings of the world while non-Christians prospered in wealth. In truth, they knew that fame and worldly possessions do not matter anymore.

I become incensed by people who demand recompense for doing only what Jesus has called them to do. The Holy Spirit will not wait for time to end before summoning them to the Crucifixion that has filled Paradise with Saints. Life is rarely easy; it was never meant to be. However, it is the precursor to your reunion in Heaven. Selfish actions and hellish circumstances abound where unconverted sinners live, and this is the unfortunate environment where you work, sweat, and pray. There is no such thing as an unfaithful Christian. If anyone assumes that he is put upon for being loyal to the Church, he is declaring how great is the Lord who condones it. I have spoken about the Crucifixion of Jesus Christ in so many ways that it has been like a hailstorm to the sinners who have listened. The Light of the Cross is blazing through time and space more powerfully than a billion suns, and your souls can see it according to your willingness to believe. I offer My commendation to all My seers who have known the majestic touch of miracles from the Throne of the Father with welcoming and determination. My Special son, these days are marked by the miraculous for you. You know that Jesus is closest during your darkest moments, and the periods of spiritual despondence that you have suffered over the years are evidence that My intercession is needed. I have appeared to Popes, visionaries dedicated to the Church, and individuals whom the world will not know until the Earth's last days. I will make a difference where others have failed, and I will not relinquish your heart to the confusion attempting to take you from Me. I will do whatever necessary to keep your spirit in flight. I shall raise you to the heavens with regenerative peace, proving that your present despair will be turned against Satan like a dagger in his throat. Jesus will spin the Earth upside down and spread your enemies over the netherworld to grovel in the depths of the Abyss. My mission that began in February 1991 is one of victory, the introduction of the unconverted to the Church, and for the millions who need the Bread of Life. You should recall that I am the most awesome Woman ever given life. My Immaculate Heart basks in your trust, in your awareness that the Lord's Providence is sustaining you, encouraging and uplifting you, watching you while you grieve and weep, and calling you to see the redemptive dimensions that you feel in His Kingdom. If these things were not happening, My son, I would say that I made a mistake, that I did not mean those things I said about the sacrifices of the Saints. I would beg you to forgive Me for presuming that you would slay those who violate your heart, and remind you that it is only through the orthodoxy of the Church that humanity is changed. My Special son, you would never want Me to say this because you believe in miracles. You know that you are practicing a living faith that accepts the current-day interaction between Heaven and Earth, just as you wrote in your recent book. There are no hidden conspiracies against your right to exist.

You see every day an assemblage of secular events that lack righteousness, that do not lend to the sanctification of humanity or discovering the lost. Even parishioners in the sanctuary pews beside you have become numbed by the erratic instabilities of the United States. They wonder what is happening to its faith, to the hundreds of thousands who joined them in celebrating the Traditions of the Church, to the voice of the spiritually motivated who stood against the onslaught of perversions that Satan is leveling across this land. Millions of westerners and foreigners worldwide are seeing the reckless abandonment of everything decent, making a mockery of discretion and the desire to live in peace. Their families and friends are falling apart at the seams, causing disruption, violence, and infighting reminiscent of the ancient times. They want to know even more about the Divine Grace of God and the intercession of the Holy Spirit. Heaven's answer is that we are still here. Grace abounds and holiness lives. We did not abandon humanity, they left us! The tides of unscrupulousness have cloaked the young in immorality, and you know the rest. I invite you to broaden your vision to see how many have suffered because of meanness and impurity. Can you tell that all this is coming to an end? This is why the Church must be perseverant. You prayed for this; you practically demanded that Jesus do something to defeat the enemies of the Cross and elevate His Bride above their corpses. His answer from the Scriptures is that it is always darkest just before the dawn. This is where you are going; this is what humanity will make of these opening decades of the 21st century. It is by design. Therefore, let your detractors wander into death's valley and see that they are sinking into the dust. It is with reassurance that I ask you to be strong. The beauty of your heart cannot be put asunder. The callousness of the Earth is trying to destroy the child you have become. My little son, when you see what the future holds; when people close to you begin to die and lose their loved ones; when the world as you know it begins to fade away, you will put your problems in larger perspective. I beg you to enlist the strength that brought a nearly 80-year-old Roman Catholic Cardinal to accept his final role in the conversion of the wicked, Pope Benedict, who has walked in your shoes, who declared that the cold, stale darkness of the Earth would never force his vocation into obsolescence. And, most important, I ask you to pray. Feel grateful that the Lord allows your country to choose its public leaders by the ballot instead of blood. Whomever is elected Tuesday can be converted, and things will suddenly change. What would happen if someone was chosen from Illinois where the Morning Star has appeared blocks from your capitol, where two lives converged, yours and his. Who says that Jesus will not make this event the leading salvo in the final battle for lost souls? Anyone can be converted by the Mother of God. Their eyes can be opened and heart remolded. It will require more than overturning laws to urge expectant mothers to give birth to the children in their wombs. After all I have said, the United States is sprawling with potential, with communication systems to crack the shell of silence keeping so many in the dark. Pray for whomever your citizens elect to lead you into the next decade. Do not worry. If you believe that a door is closing, God will open a hundred more."

Sunday, November 9, 2008
2:57 p.m.

"Let the children come to me, and do not hinder them. It is to just such as these that the Kingdom of God belongs. I assure you that whoever does not accept the reign of God like a little child shall not take part in it." [Mark 10:14-15]

"Your lordly obedience is worthy of the Salvation you seek, My children, because Jesus' holiness is exemplified by your lives. You are uniquely devoted to your faith and embrace the responsibilities of the Church as a compelling imposition and community sacrifice. Remember that you do not just adapt to Christianity, you are completely reconstituted by it from the core of your being. Please understand that the Lord did not create any impenetrable hearts, and it is possible to reach the battle-hardened if your love excels in leading them to Heaven's quieting peace. I ask you to keep your spirits elevated despite the darkness in the world. There are untold numbers of embittered sinners around the globe, and it is your duty to tenderize their perspective about the ultimate purpose of human life. Unfortunately, most Americans will engage only in dialogue that patronizes their own vengeance. And, My children, you are a better country than this. What honor is there in human judgement if the Lord must strike you with infirmity or slash of the sword to comply with His sacred commands? If you do not heed the call of the Holy Spirit, you will be disenfranchised from speaking your piece about how you feel because of your infidelity to Jesus. When the great tragedies come and you wonder what to do next, there is still consolation in what you must believe as sanctified men. When turbulence threatens and night falls across the fruited plains, you are not lashed to your anxieties. The cardinal rule for growing your spiritual courage is to remember that life is for pursuing faith and redemption when the years seem so tattered by confusion and fear. Your open-heartedness to the Cross valorizes your determination to succeed in the introduction of Christian morality in the public domain. I will help as best I can, as much as you will allow. The Father has girded you with plentiful grace for the conquest that will capitalize the eternal triumph of the Roman Catholic Church. You need not feel insecure about the future or defend yourselves from a point of weakness as though you are locked into a fetal position. The Holy Cross is your interior assurance that the Lord sustains you through the suffering heaped upon you by your adversaries, and even the threat of martyrdom. I have told you that His Triune Advocate will help you speak when you are silenced during the fight for your lives. You will next month celebrate the anniversary of Jesus' birth in Bethlehem, and will be taken in mind and heart to the Creche where the world was introduced to Heaven's Divine Light. Some people speak of relative obscurity as though it is a disadvantage, but they should never forget that the Crucifixion of a King born as a pauper has redeemed the entire human race. Before that grand celebration arrives, you should be praying about the inundation of your souls in the waters of your baptism and the Blood of that Holy Sacrifice. These blessings are dispensed by God to vouchsafe your absolution so that you are cleansed, renewed, and fully prepared for your entrance into Paradise. Today, I urge you to think about what this means for the long-term consequences of your life's actions and destination after death. This is not something that you do not already know. We have spoken about exemplary faith, courage that transcends the worst calamities the world has to offer, brilliance that can solve any mystery, and peace that flows like a river. Even as you wake in the morning and know not what the day will bring, you cling to the thread of hope that connects your past and present, forbears and descendants, and time and eternity to the Truth of God calling you like warriors to take up your arms for the common good. Those who oppose you could not defeat the Spirit of Love in you if they tried for the next ten-thousand years. They cannot remove from your spiritual conscience what God has seeded there no more than they can intercept your soul from its journey to His Heavenly Throne. When you speak of inevitability and irrevocable destiny, you refer to your oneness with His Kingdom that reclaims you alongside Adam who has been forgiven through the Blood of the Cross. What the Son of Man has preordained, no creature can destroy; and no misfortune, insurrection, bloodletting, or inferno could ever reverse what the Lord God has fixed in stone.

  Thus, the emergence of your holy presence on the earthen floor has come; this is your moment in the history of man to leave your mark on the doorpost of Creation, and you shall know when you have done it. Your hearts will bleed the affection of the Angels and fill those loving cups about which you have written for every Abigail and their fathers. My children, our mission will not conclude until you have reached the summit of perfection in Jesus' Resurrection. We are making grand strides toward the sanctification of the Earth through His Crucifixion, and we are now attempting to lift humanity to that understanding in accordance with the Lord's plan. How many times have I said that He cannot tell you a falsehood? Jesus cannot lie because His Sacred Heart is the center of Truth. For all the years you have read the Sacred Scriptures, you have sought the meaning of life from its pages; and the Holy Spirit has revealed it to you. Your prayers are the genesis of your deliverance because they connect you heart and soul to the Gospel. This is why I have asked you to pray for the living and the dead. Indicate to the Lord that you belong to Him by giving yourselves to His Will. In all things, be the keepers of your brothers and practitioners of the faith handed to you from your fathers. When all is done, My little ones, you will see the rising of the sun simultaneously with the finishing of the Earth in the Sacred Mysteries by whose graces you have been upheld. Life wears on you; it stings and causes you to weep in sorrow and anxiety. This is why Jesus calls you out of the world to place your heart and faith in the things of Heaven you cannot see. Miracles are composed of this, but also is your evidence that goodness is worth seeking. Jesus suffered perfectly for your redemption, and He beckons you to become perfect sufferers in His likeness for the conversion of the lost. As the Glory of Paradise shines on you, it is necessary that the authenticity of your Christian tenacity shine toward the skies. My Special son, let no one record that you ever conceded a day to defeat. All your struggles are working for the crescendo that I mentioned before, the pinnacle of reasoned excellence given by the power of the Holy Spirit. It is ordained that you shall join the Son of Man on the Cross that you might have everlasting life in Him. You and your brother will one day count among your fondest memories the hours that you wondered whether you would finally prevail in your work. It is not the winningest moment that contains the transforming energy of your Marian Apostolate, but the heaviest times when you are closest to the Lord, when you thought His Grace was farthest from you. He imparts signs and wonders to signify that you are winning, and He saves His best accolades for the final outburst of freedom you shall see in time. History has cited the decisions of contests that mattered as much to you in previous times as your success today. Do you remember when you used to place a **W** or **L** on your basketball schedule when you were a young athlete to indicate whether you had won or lost a contest? There is a **W** at the end of the road you are traveling that Jesus borrowed from your Bible. Please look at Revelation 13:18 and tell Me the first word. *(I looked at the passage in my Bible, and the publisher erroneously omitted the letter W from the word Wisdom, and the text said 'isdom' instead. Our Lady continued).* Where is this **W**? It is waiting at the end of your life; it is the Lord's proof that eternal victory is yours. Now, you must guard your self-confidence, never worrying about the toll of the darkness, disregarding your reputation, and always telling yourself that all things work for good for those who believe in God. Even in the last months and years, you are given signs that victory is at hand. In the battles for lost sinners, there are no reversals of fortune, there are no bulges like that of the Second World War. Your progress is toward the origin of Eternal Love, and there is no retreating or backsliding. Everything you have been doing will help you remember this; all your prayers, your dedication to Me, your desire to overcome your perceived weaknesses, and all the rest. And, bless you for remaining with your brother whose own despair comes and goes. You have seen this since he came to be with you. He worries about failing not because of anything you might do, but because he knows that Satan expects him to retreat. He is a fighter, and he will not desist in his work on behalf of this broken world. There are benisons aplenty for all who shall savor the fruits of your lives. I have said that you must approach your faith from a position of strength. And, you and your brother have worked tirelessly to do so. You will someday see thousands of blessings because of your love. This is why you must be strong, much more reassured than you were reared to be. Stop wringing your hands about the future and live one day at a time. You are a child of God who has prayed for longevity. If you receive it, then the years must pass. Actualizing your faith means walking on water and not fearing falling in. It means commanding respect from those you venerate. It means never cowering to your emotions over your knowledge of prudent events. Realizing your faith means taking everything that has ever haunted you and throwing it into the Abyss. You can do this if you take life one day at a time, and you should be since I summoned you to refocus humanity's sights toward Heaven. I have trained your attention on everyday life that precedes Eternity looming before the creatures of Earth. I am not speaking in contradictory or paradoxical terms, rather I am suggesting that you are taking these days for granted. Being a servant to your faith does not imply that you must surrender your dreams. There are languishing people around you, in all the cities and states across the globe. Lead them to the Cross as the Holy Paraclete speaks of their plight when you pray the Rosary."

Sunday, November 16, 2008
2:54 p.m.

"Love justice, you who judge the Earth; think of the Lord in goodness, and seek him in integrity of heart because he is found by those who test him not, and he manifests himself to those who do not disbelieve him." [Wisdom 1:1-2]

"My children, I speak with urgency today because you are about to receive my final messages to humanity. I call the whole world to Christianity, to the Holy Eucharist of the Catholic Church, and to the Crucifixion that is imperative for your transfer to eternal bliss. Nowhere in America will I speak again at such length or with such definitive instructions as I have in this diocese consecrated to My Immaculate Conception. I plead with you to respond to the intercession of the Holy Spirit. Please do not settle for some other persuasion just because you are desperate to find meaning or you dislike the road being charted. Become a community of believers who are striving together to achieve moral righteousness in your day. Listen to your brothers who are lent to the power of the Cross, and remember that you rarely oppose any one person in all things. Yes, it is true that even your own detractors make an occasional agreeable statement. Find common ground in the Gospel of Jesus Christ, and anything that divides you will become insignificant. You have been handed the gift of intuition, of an unusually prudent capacity to discern right from wrong. The only reason why the idea of a mastermind has such a negative connotation is because keen intelligence is rarely utilized for the public good. Material wares always lose their luster once you tender your souls to God, and only the promises of the next world seem good enough to pursue. If you do not remain focused on the mission of the Church, you will soon discover that the years are exhausted, your resolve depleted, and your pledges broken. Become absorbed in this holiness; enter the arena, share the heaviest burdens, grow the coffers, and increase your personal sacrifices. Do not measure your steps too quickly, but mark your words with emphasis when speaking about the outcome of the Earth. All of you comprise the Mystical Body of Christ which has many parts; and while there are multiple roles to play, not every part is suitable for all, even as ambidextrous as your spiritual convictions are. You must stand on the solid ground of Christianity during the darkest hours and know that the cold, gray winter always gives way to the garish sunlight of spring. I have addressed the people of the United States specifically since the turn of the millennium. You have been battered by the forces of evil from the outside and within. Sadly, you often measure success by air strikes, cannon fire, insults, and accusations. Your definition of freedom and the rule of law mutate as each growing segment of society discovers a new way to scandalize their peers. This is unworthy of a nation that calls itself blessed. Many citizens of the United States are more concerned about their wallets than defending sound morality. They exercise their franchise based on fiscal averages and indexes, on trends of financial loss, profits in the marketplace, and apathy in issues of faith and orthodoxy. This is how abortionists are elected public leaders. To claim that human life is an exercise in exceptions is not to understand the constancy of Deific Truth. Jesus will help you in your periods of discernment if you humbly call on Him. He knows that you are yet imperfect in a far less perfect world. The Lord provides a valance under which He conceals your mistakes that oftentimes appear as weaknesses. You have watched your ancestors die like waves washing out to sea, and you miss their influence upon the affairs of the day. They have gone to be with Jesus, and He is much more your wise counselor than anything they could say. Your loved-ones and friends who have died adore Him, and their sentiments resound the voice of the Holy Spirit. I implore you to come to the Catholic Church to be in full communion with Christianity, to see the Cross with distinction and receive the Bread of Life, the Holy Eucharist, the Most Blessed of the Seven Sacraments, so you will be seamlessly united with the Kingdom of the Father. There is no clearer way to say it. What the Protestant religion calls communion is no more than an artifice, a fraudulent misrepresentation of the true Manna from Heaven spoken about in the Scriptures, consecrated and dispensed by the priests of the Roman

Catholic Church. The exquisite fineness of the Body, Blood, Soul, and Divinity of Jesus Christ is brought into the world only upon these sacred altars of Sacrifice.

I urge humanity to recognize where you have been hiding in Creation to avoid exposure to your sanctifying rehabilitation. It seems an endless process that you have been observing, dissecting, and analyzing everything on Earth that is chemical, mechanical, and behavioral in nature. And, you base your opinions on impulses over which you have little control. I say again, this is your time for change. You must invite peace into your hearts; you must create a more stable environment between yourselves that coincides with the spiritual holiness you have found. Believe it or not, there can be a perfect combination of dominion and practicality that elevates you beyond the callousness of the Earth. The Gospel tells you that God will in due time force the reconciliation of all men; and when He does, you will be so afraid to say another negative word and so swift to find peace that your handshakes of agreement will sound like freight trains colliding in the night. You will finally realize that the world's unfairness was created by the greed of impious men, and this caused the atmosphere in which social instability took rise and incurable diseases were imbedded in the flesh. My children, this must be your reminder that you cannot survive either spiritually or physiologically without the Holy Cross helping you through the perils of life with all the peace the Lord has to offer. And, you arise by giving your hearts to Him. He does not Will a world that is filled with sickness and defeat. His compassion shields you from everything that stains your lives, and Heaven is prepared to receive you when you open yourselves to Divine Love. My messages are of the ordinances of Truth by which you must live, and they are your succor in times of trouble spoken about in the Sacred Scriptures. As much as any previous wars or annihilations, more than any prior degradation of the moral fabric of America, these are your times of trouble. You have been handed perseverance, some call it steadfastness, to make in life good things for the world, especially for those who deserve a better fate than has been dealt to them. My Special son, you must see from My words that I have not surrendered the fight against evil. I have told you on numerous occasions that human beings are not inherently evil, but they are corrupted and attacked by evil legions whom they may have never seen or heard. Whenever you perform pious works and declare Jesus the King of the nations, you are derided in the way of the Apostles. And, when you pray for the end of war, those who are farthest from God heighten the stress that causes such wars because Satan attempts to defy you. *(For several weeks without a moment of respite, all day and through the night, I have been enduring a definitive mystical mental oppression. It is satanic, diabolical and horrific. All heavenly consolation has been overshadowed and replaced by a relentless mental scourging that I cannot banish from my thoughts. It is as if a menacing force is not allowing my vision to be lifted to Heaven, but is instead thrusting me down at every moment like a colossal weight placed upon my spirit. I can no longer see the future as before. It is as if I have lost all my spiritual senses while the devil is standing right next to me soliciting my surrender. I live a constant invocation of perseverance, a requirement that is almost too difficult to sustain. Satan is even mimicking miraculous signs like those Our Lady has guided me with through the years in order to sow further confusion within me. But, I know where he is at, and can still discern the difference. I have simply invoked a very patient cadence to my discernment in order to winnow our Virgin Mother's guidance from his chaff. Our Holy Mother told me this mystical onslaught was coming as a punishment from Satan who is infuriated by my essays in my previous anthology.)* As your brother told you, the assaults against you over the past month have been the vindictive reprisal of Satan for your fifteen essays in the book containing My 2003-2005 messages. Yes, you see signs, and you must distinguish their origin. Are they blessings from Heaven or temptations from Satan? This is the question that every decent man must answer when seeking guidance in his spiritual life. There is no weakness in your faith. I am not saying that it is not tested or that darkness never assaults you. The lessons and teachings of Jesus Christ are filled with the battles He fought against the sins of the world, against the evil that causes them, and the indifference of sinners who do not care. This is a campaign that was not limited to His earthly years because everyone born in the flesh inherits the sin of Adam. You know the process by which they are cleansed in the Sacraments that keep you pure. There is nothing new in telling you this. However, what you must understand is that the evil about which I am speaking changes venues according to the weaknesses of those involved; evil does its worst when sinners do not know how to avoid its snares. Dubiousness pervades the consciousness of those who live in the United States about matters of religious faith because they believe that democracy exempts them from the laws of God. Some believe that they are free to indulge in whatever depravities they desire without consequence. What you do about this depends upon how much you are willing to be criticized. And, in that prospect, welcome to the flock of Christians.

The principles I have taught through the years lift you from temptation, but they have yet to spare you the punishment inflicted by the enemies of the Cross. Your heart and daily meditations inform you that there is no greater power than the Crucifixion, but such is little consolation in the heated battle. It takes a great deal of time, it would seem, for your enemies to realize that they are on the wrong side of the fight. And, your spiritual fortitude can lose a tremendous amount of blood while you wait for them to change. The darkness you have felt is not the same as the void that I spoke about in earlier messages. In this darkness, you are closer to the Father than you know. This is also something you have always been told, but again, little comfort when you feel alone. When all is said and done, you are given the task of judging yourself, not only about the things having to do with right and wrong, but how you entered the fight. There is no question that I have always been with you, and surely you understand that the Holy Spirit has been your guide. But, these are quiet interventions, like huge steamers crawling across the seas. The sovereignty of the Lord hovers above you as would a giant zeppelin, watching your every move with admiration. You are adored because you will not leave the Church, because you enrich the Earth with your prayers when you would rather see it destroyed, and because you maintain your poise and self-dignity under the most excruciating conditions. Whatever evil comes toward you cannot condemn you because your soul is marked with the Sign of the Cross, and Satan knows it. The only way he can ultimately touch you is force your surrender under duress, while he attempts to make you believe that God is no longer your friend. I do not speak casually about this because I stood at the foot of the Cross on Good Friday and wondered why the sorrow. However, I remembered what the Father told humanity from the lips of My own Son. He spoke of darker days to come, of persecution and ridicule, the martyrdom of believers, of poverty and depression, of indignity and infighting, and all the other effects of the reckless conduct of Old Adam that would hinder the Church. Let there be no mistake. I knew that your Savior would prevail because I lived and walked with Him alongside the Apostles and disciples, and you are required twenty-centuries later to believe this in faith. I pray deeply that I can instill in you a sense for the timelessness of what I saw, how important it is for you to comprehend that the persecution of Christians did not end at the Ascension! What did Jesus say that day; what would happen from On High? That you would not be left orphaned. Living in you now is the same Holy Spirit that came upon the Church, the same Light and Truth in which you have loved and will exalt before these days are through. There is little I can say to help you rise in clearer comprehension of the magnitude of this victory until I begin My personal messages after the first of next year. You and your brother have been suffering many things at the same time. These will not injure you, but you must fight the good fight referred to by Saint Paul in a world that contradicts most everything I have said. And, you are here with Me, winning the bread, facing the same struggles, seeing the degradation of society in your nation, praying for your countrymen to awaken from their slumber, and reading the signs before you. You have become saintly messengers, even doctoral in your determination to succeed. By the time I make My 2009 appearances, most of your questions will pass because I will take your role to a new plateau that has simply been impossible to ascend until now. How can hopes be true hopes if you have seen their outcome? Bringing miracles into being is what we are doing for humanity."

Sunday, November 23, 2008
2:58 p.m.

"Blest shall you be when men hate you, when they ostracize you and insult you and proscribe your name as evil because of the Son of Man. On the day they do so, rejoice and exalt, for your reward shall be great in Heaven." [Luke 6:22-23]

"This is your time to make a difference for the eternity of the Church in reveling the human spirit in the themes of righteousness. There are countless matters left for you to complete, and men who have a healthy conscience realize that they not only lack all the answers, they do not even know the questions. My children, you sit around your kitchen tables, wondering why life must be this way. I will tell you if you listen. While Heaven is not a physical location, your station in exile sits adjacent to its verge with a permeable veil through which I am speaking. It is true that life is oftentimes what you make of it, but you must remain humble even in your successes. Proud men live in a state of emblematic envy, always searching for ways to memorialize themselves in a forgetful and transient world. You have learned that the typical Christian life is not a storybook filled with art prints and ribbons, and you spend far too much time battling secular pandemonium, gorged with foggy initiatives and vague ideals. My dear ones, the clock is marching forward, and you must heed My call with earnest. You have nearly passed the 21st century aughts, and are about to embark on its second decade. I remind you that you have the capacity to reach for Eternity from this place; you can even say the words today, tomorrow, and forever in a single breath. America boasts to the nations of being the cradle of freedom, and yet you are a democracy whose capitalism is paralyzed by the nausea of greed. This is why Jesus came among you, to seek your hearts in the name of holiness. Repentance does not mean throwing yourselves away and starting over, nor does it call for suppressing everything good you wish to achieve in this life. I pray that you will begin to comprehend God's Love so uniquely that you feel as though you have entered another dimension, and that you will eventually grow so accustomed to His righteousness that anything less you see will not matter anymore. Every human conscience is a breviary of reflections, meditations, and hopes that allow you to denounce the hideous sensationalism that is distracting you from seeing the destabilizing effects of a life without Truth. You learn from Christianity that the Holy Spirit induces the human heart to secrete redemptive compassion for those who suffer, and it allows you to know where you are and where you are going. History constructs eras and prohibitions that separate you from the past; the good and the bad, and all of them are eclipsed by what is yet to be disclosed. A child becomes a statesman, a path a thoroughfare, and an idea a movement. A nickel loaf of bread is now a dollar, and a doctor's house call is out of the question. You see falling stars, and trawlers and steamers that sink to the depths, books losing their leaves, echoes that die out, and memories fade. The seasons duck their heads in the door and are gone again; and with pleasant surprise, you unexpectedly discover that you have all along been in the presence of greatness. You have witnessed the refining of humanity during an hour in time when all the glorious potentials of men have reached their peak and receded back to the present that itself is ingrained in the perpetuity of the universe. It is the honor of these proceedings that keeps you whole, that saves you from crossing life's unseen forbidden lines. So, do not let your impending departure from the physical Earth make you believe that you no longer own the innocence of your youth or the strength to rise for the ovation of the years, thanking you for staying strong, keeping the faith, and never losing sight of the Kingdom to come. Remember that I told you in My final December 1996 message that this is a time of renewal for the world, a time of baptism in faith and an epiphany in conviction to Love. The days are short, the years are fleeting, and the world is passing away. With what true urgency does the Father requisition your prayers! He sees what the Church already knows, that there is a catapulting resurgence of the spirit of faithful men that is about to overcome every form of evil I have ever mentioned. You must be part of this charge! The Son of Man needs you, the Kingdom of the Blessed sustains you, the Holy Spirit invigorates you, and the period of renewal about which I have spoken must never be impeded.

  My Special son, I pray for the demise of everything that opposes you, all the rancorous attempts to impugn your faith, the idiocy and blasphemy, the brainless distractions, and every enemy whose lack of honesty and fair play will ultimately fail. I find it reprehensible that they might believe that they have approached the holiness you have achieved. Theirs is a legacy of corruption and disdain against anything to do with the Kingdom of Jesus; and they shall be judged accordingly. Please do not pity them. My child, I speak not only about the adversaries of the Church, but the shark-infested framework of the American government and the institutions of Western capitalism. They will all be devastated to know upon their deaths that they have for generations worked in diametric opposition to the Will of the Father. Every sense of reason says that I should be telling you this, that you must take My messages to the farthest corners and enlist the conversion of every foreign land. If we wait for another generation, it may be too late. I have spoken about the miracle of the human heart blossoming as a flower to receive the Lord's Grace like sunshine in the middle of the night. We have prayed that all will heed My call because the hour is urgent, and wayward sinners are still wandering in the darkness. Thank you, My Special son, for praying like Jesus. I have more to say, so please be attentive. I have reserved today to tell you again that the Holy Spirit comes into the world to reach the heart. The heart communicates and transfers God's

Will into discernable action. The reason I have said this is so others will not refer to My messages as something that has been manifested uniquely by you. Please open the dictionary to a word that some in the Church will use to describe your circumstances. The term I will give you is a difficult one. It is oneiromancy. What does it say? Yes, divination through dreams. You should know that the Catechism discusses divination as being something cult-like that is not attuned to the Holy Spirit. This is somewhat ambiguous because the Scriptures mention dreams as the means by which certain people heard instructions from God. The point I am making is that it was easier to describe this communication as dreams because the information was transferred without the will of the person involved. Being inspirited directly by God is also without one's will, although it cannot be described as dreaming. I have brought this to your attention to make you aware of one type of attack that will be leveled against your work. The Holy Spirit will convince your detractors that your faith and conscience were fully awake when you received My messages. You were not dreaming, and you were not asleep. I implore you and your brother to be aware of the power of your dedication to the Cross by acknowledging that your lives since 1991 are about to change, not end, but being amended so the Church can begin the process of discernment. My precious son, I know what you have suffered all the years since you were a boy. I was there, keeping an eye on you, watching your successes and defeats, asking My Son to bless you. You kept telling Him in your heart that you wanted to help bring Light into the world and make every moment count for ushering His Kingdom into being. Indeed, all through the years, you have remained devoted to Him, not conceding to peer pressure, not taking the easy course, not entering temptation and sin, and not surrendering to the popularity that could have been yours in some extremely propitious times. This is why Jesus adores you, My son, in reflection of His unconditional Love. How could He not ensure that everything for which you have yearned makes the Glory of the Father apparent to all who are exiled on Earth? It is you who welcomed your brother's proclamation that I first spoke to him in 1991. You did not have to do this; you were not required to do so. But, look at your bountiful works! You are kind to your brother as Jesus is with you."

Sunday, November 30, 2008
2:47 p.m.

"I have always pointed out to you that it is by such hard work that you must help the weak. You need to remember the words of the Lord Jesus Christ himself who said that there is more happiness in giving than receiving." [Acts 20:35]

"There comes a time, My dear children, when everything has a reckoning with the ages, the plants and animals, all the species that are seen and unseen, humanity from all walks of life, and even the moons and stars above you. Creation is being raised toward its reconciliation with the Creator who framed it, and you are involved in that process. Even as dying wolves cry foul and the rocky arches break, many souls among you have gone adrift in the backwaters of spiritual darkness. They must be found, and you are required to search for them. You have tried with valor to enlist the service of the American people, but they are much too self-absorbed and bent on making money than playing any part in supporting the Church. The pursuits and positions of the secular media are contentious, smug, imprudent, and immoral. They are a profit-seeking vendor that tends to attract consumers who are steeped in partisanship and atheism. And, they are enabled by a colonial First Amendment that mandates their right to speak, but not to tell the truth. It is clear that the media see the persecution of the Roman Catholic Church as America's only allowable prejudice. They regularly use the word *alleged* to justify their slander. And, they have been so ingrained in the American culture that addressing their corruption is something akin to stopping a rockslide with a silk-laced handkerchief. When given absolute power, unholy men behave like monsters; and this is how fascist empires are built and gated communities with ivy-covered walls marginalize the lives of the poor. Impressionable children become indoctrinated in the lies of angry men, and the airwaves are polluted by persuasions of the elite. Subcultures hold on to their biases as though they are the synthesis of life. All this is done while there are still multitudes so plagued by homelessness, starvation, and disease that they see their only relief in having an early death. What can you do about the callous indifference that batters them every day? What must be done to reach the hardened of heart? How do we touch the heartstrings of burly, stone-faced men upon whom you would have to chisel a smile? The answers rest in your allegiance to Christ. You must employ every attribute of your identity to glorify the Cross. If you can see and speak, you should read aloud the strains of the Holy Scriptures; and if you can sing, melodize the pleadings of the Psalter. Remember what I told you about Heaven's miracles and your willingness to believe them. What if you could smell gravity and measure the cubic feet of the skies? Welcoming the

Spirit of God in your hearts is more supernatural than these. Forgiveness is the irresistible fragrance of your Christian sanctification. When your brokenness astringes your ability to move, breathe and have your being, turn to Christ Jesus for help. It is obvious that you wish that you could splice life's best moments into a continuous ribbon of joy, but there can be no peaks without the valleys below. And this, My little children, is why I am speaking to you now. I ask you to recognize that you are already standing in the Grace of the Father, and all you must do is look away from yourselves. He speaks of the poor, and I have openly scolded the wealthy about spurning those who have only little for themselves. You see by the sadness in their eyes that the light of compassion seems distant from them. These broken paupers are often so exhausted from the trials of indigence that they rarely fall asleep at night; they sleep where they eventually fall. They are subjugated by mindless politicians with an agendum of self-interest who bear a partisan grudge. All I ask is that you rebuke these leaders according to the ordinances of the Gospel. No one complains about the role of the Church in reaching-out to the poor, but Christianity is carrying a disproportionate share in bringing charity and equality to the nations, far from the affluent regions of the Earth. Recall deep inside your hearts Myself and Saint Joseph as we tended to God's Messianic Son. We were so in love with your Eternal Salvation that we ignored the inclemency of the Earth. We did not fret whether it was too frigid or hot, or high noon or the darkness of night. We acted according to God's Kingdom, never impulsively, but heeding His signs for the purification of the world. My children, My messages are manifested from those years.

    My Special son, you have enjoyed a splendid life with your friends of your generation, and you have seen your labors for Jesus grow from buds to branches in only a few years. I have made true promises to humanity that must be kept, but they are dependent upon the faith and actions of the disciples in whom Jesus has placed His trust. The Will of the Father is amendable by your petitions; and even in this, they must reflect His desire that humanity be brought to perfection in the Holy Cross. Certain matters are immutable, meaning that prayers are often raised while petitioners do not always recognize the purpose of particular conditions that purify the Church. Every manifestation to which you are called in either gladness or pain brings joy to the outcome of the Earth when Christ is elevated before the nations; for only in Jesus is there Salvation. You have witnessed much evil in your time, all the horrific wars and devastation that have been handed to humanity on bitter platters of hatred and deceit. Tell your countrymen that their scourges and battles have taken them nowhere near the truth, but are marginal catastrophes to fill their history books with the irrelevance of their misplaced pride. We have been playing a role in the finishing of the world because it is through your best hours and nobler angels that you have prepared for the Coming of the Lord. What value is placed on your faith? At what profit would you part with it? Truly, it is not for sale. With all the holy acclamations that the Saints have echoed through the ages, humanity has been enlightened because the Spirit of the Messiah informed them. If you calculated their sacrifices in measures of torment and pain, do you reckon you would see the shadow of the Cross? You know that the Saints bear with them the blessings with which they lived, though they no longer suffer; and you are heir to their lives of sacrifice, all the holy men and women. You share their submission to the Cross by which you have lived. I therefore commend you and your brother as the final month of My messages to humanity arrives tomorrow. I shall in the next four weeks reaffirm the reason I came on February 22, 1991 in the context of the events of these times. You are nearly two decades beyond those days, and you are clear about the Divine Mercy of Jesus in ways for which you are more thankful than before. Never forget that He did not come only to bring peace, but to divide and cultivate, upbraid and absolve. Jesus is the Man of His Word, and you shall know why He set out to liquidate everything that inhibits the propagation of the Church. One might have thought that there would be thousands of Popes in the span of 2,000 years, but the Holy Roman Catholic Church is so edifying, pure, and efficacious that those Vicars who led it did so to their dying days. Imagine all the prayers and encyclicals that have been offered throughout the centuries. They are recorded in Heaven and on Earth as proof that the Wisdom of God prevails. Your life is both a gift and a burden because you sense His Glory in your heart, and yet your flesh reminds you that your exile is heavy. However you feel and whatever you perceive life to be, it has never been anything less than the sublime beginning of your Salvation in Heaven. Your brothers and sisters will eventually see what I have revealed to you; they will learn every lesson that the Holy Spirit has taught. They must, My son, lest they reject the Kingdom they will see when they die. Yes, these days are difficult, confusing and severe, but you are not prone to follow the distractions of the world. For this, Jesus and all the heavens are grateful for your faith. I speak softly as you ponder life, and it is obvious that you are determined to complete the tasks that Jesus has given you. Satan is so assaulting you and your brother at the last of My public messages that it is indescribable. Most of your sorrows are caused by the actions of other men, but you will not surrender to anything that Satan does. All spiritual gifts come through the diminishment of the flesh. Are you sure you can dismiss the uncertainties about which we have conversed? If you convince yourself that you are strong, you will not be weak. Thank you for being so holy in an obscene world that does little to dignify the disciples of Jesus. I have nowhere on Earth spoken so effusively as I have as the *Morning Star Over America*, and every word is by design. I will give a message next week to stir the spirit of humanity and bring stoic hearts to tears. I cannot do anything without the help of My children. You are the reason I am here."

Sunday, December 7, 2008
2:57 p.m.

"My brothers, if someone is detected in sin, you who live by the Spirit should gently set him right, each of you trying to avoid falling into temptation himself. Help carry one another's burdens; in that way you will fulfill the law of Christ." [Gal. 6:1-2]

"Now, I appear before you in advance of Christmas to remind humanity that you are never whole when separated from the Grace of God, but your lives in Jesus connect you with Him. Even in all I have said to upbraid My American children, I love you beyond all understanding. Everything that is good in you, the Lord has made. And, you have enlisted Him during hours of intense personal grief. From your eastern lighthouses to western sequoias, you have given Jesus your troubles. You have known that your lakes are more than great; they are grand, and so is your ability to be righteous in the lineage of the Saints. From your northern skies to the south river deltas, your ambitions are keen of heart, and your faith deserves God's commendation. You are pilgrim voyagers on a sea crest of natural marvels, given to conversion by your soul-cleansing strife. I warn you to safeguard your reputation and remember that anyone who tells you untruths will eventually speak falsely about you. The attitude of many in the United States is to concede submission to no one, especially to the Father; and you particularly deplore your government lording over your affairs. While the latter is a practical expectation, the former is a recipe for condemnation. Atheists in the world cite the Sacred Scriptures only when they believe that Christians are not living-out their faith, specifically in the matter of reproving others' sinful acts. However, admonishing someone for embracing moral depravity is not being pretentious, it is a function of God's Wrath. The Earth is a multi-tiered spectrum of matter, energy, growth, interaction and organization, but the miracles that are flowing from the heavens into your daily lives are confounding even to the most astute theologians. You must know that the Lord is serious about your trust in His intervention. This is why I have come seeking the hearts of those farthest from Him. I pray that He gives Me the appropriate strains to enunciate how deeply you are loved. You are a better people than to be attracted to the swagger that strips you of your scrupulous judgement, drowning you in such brazen arrogance. There is no question that your exile is not easy. Many of you look upon the past as if to have conquered a formidable foe, but you approach the future with recurring consternation. This is the way you live in a country where civility is wrecked, chivalry is near extinction, your best gladiators have gone missing, the unborn are discarded like litter, and your discretion is impaired by your irrational emotions. While many societies cling to their icy indifference with their cold hearts biting like razors, you as Christians have a potential for heroism that is simultaneously sweet and pungent, piercing the universe with an aroma of self-denial, aspiring to the bequeathal of legends. And, you know that earthly materials have nothing to do with the spiritual welfare of your holiness. Such things as trinkets, medallions, trophies, and ornaments are no substitute for the bedrock of your faith. You discover in Jesus that life places you into a rhythm and harmony with the outermost stars, synchronized with all things beatific, and at odds against everything that opposes the Calvarian Cross. He transfers you by unconditional amnesty to the parlours of redemption, clean and pure, so that you may look with foresight at the gladsome brilliance of His Holy Sacrifice and see your reflection in it. While you plod through the passing years, there is a sarcophagus waiting to receive your mortal flesh that cannot imprison your spirit when given to My Son. Clearly, Jesus will not accept neutrality in response to this call. You are either for Him or against Him. Through the Crucifixion of the Son of Man, there is no stopping the clutches of Heaven from reaching into the tombs of deceased mortal men. When His final clarion is heralded from above the skies, what will it take to ignite the Earth? A flicker of hope? A spark of genius? A flaming arrow? Whatever it is and whenever it does, God will shine His glorious Light on every glade and hollow, every brick facade and stony fortress, reveling to the nations the reason for life and justification for your pain. As I have said, the journey is laden with this; but unless night falls, there can be no sunrise. And, without the wintertime, there will surely be no spring. This is how you must see your interior sorrows. I implore you with emphasis not to grovel before the things you fear.

Therefore, My children, you see that I have given you reasoned justification to invest your trust in the assurance that the blessings for which you have prayed will come. It is according to the Will of the Father because He knows what is best for you and the glorification of His Kingdom. I hope Americans do not perceive their Patroness as having disdain for what you do, rather that I come to enlighten you about the Wisdom of God and your entry into Paradise, beginning with your admission that you have sinned, that humanity must reconcile with the Father through the Crucifixion of Christ Jesus. This entails your spiritual repentance and amendment of life that makes you like Him in all ways, that you must willfully do what He commands through the Holy Scriptures and the teachings of the Church. While time changes global cultures, the Cross is unchanging. Customs and habits have no effect on the means through which you are purified and branded with the mark of redemption by your baptism. If you must know, My dear ones, there are times when I wished not to have addressed humanity so coarsely because it tends to make you believe that you will always be wrong. I confirm that you are capable of leading exemplary lives in the image of the most austere Saints and monks to have breathed the air of life. It is impossible for you to imagine all their sacrifices that brought the Earth to this place in time. Where would the Church be without their faith? Who would have preserved the relics and reliquaries through which so many Christians gained strength over the years? It was your predecessors, your Roman Catholic forbears, who gave you the gifts that keep you strong in the Holy Gospel when you might have otherwise believed no man. You are all capable, My children, of attaining the status of princes and princesses before the Throne of the Father through the Cross, and Jesus will soon return and stand you before Him. My Special son, My messages have been maximally candid when you might have preferred to hear something else. By presenting three more messages, remember that I have come to open humanity's heart as much as embrace and comfort you. Let no one believe that My efforts will be in vain. We have spoken about the Lord who can do anything, all that embarks Creation on the journey about which His Son preached. His succinct reminders to the people of His day apply to every age because all sinners are stained by Adam. You have been redeemed with Adam in the Crucifixion, and all who comply with the sacredness for which Jesus died will inherit Eternal Life. This is not news to you; it is a fact you have known since you were a boy. I will discuss in the next three weeks My intentions for the remainder of the exile of man, a reproaching of the United States, themes for celebrating the Feast of Christmas, and a parting message to My children that will send them to their knees in expectation of the Second Coming of My Son. I shall remain with you as long as the Holy Spirit gives earthly creatures minds and tongues to speak, and beyond the expiration of the world. My attention to your desires remains full, and you are welcome to imbibe in My Wisdom as have all the Apostles and Popes. We will do as you have stated; stare down the world together, bind-up the wounds of humanity, seek-out sinners who have yet to hear the voice of God, and relate everything Jesus told you while He lived on Earth. This will be My privilege, and you shall realize before your mortality is complete that there were no unprovided hours of darkness, none without some reason, and not a single sorrow that did not glorify the Cross. We pray for this earthen domain, you in the realms of the world, Me in Heaven and on Earth. We have interacted through the charity of the Lord to strengthen your knowledge about the reward you will receive in Jesus' Sacrifice because He knows that you will share it with your friends. Your station in life has been of high import; you were given this mission years ago. And, whoever comes into your life, they were led there because they needed Me. Wherever you go, I will follow. You cannot stray from the path of righteousness; your spirit cannot escape the blessings you have been given. The cornerstone has been laid for your brothers and sisters to learn from you as you have taken lessons from the Saints. Each day is a number, and you do not know where you are in them. I have stayed at your side to assist your journey to the City of Light, and you have carried the sightless with you. Their alliance with everything I have said is imbedded in your published works, and mostly in the prayers from your heart. You have given them more than you will ever receive, but reciprocity will come when you enter Heaven. If you wish, you may recall your life as an image of the splendor once regaled, the divineness of the Sacred Heart who espouses your petitions to reverse the terrible scourges that have plagued the Earth since the downfall of man. I know that you and your brother are trying your best to finish your work under intense pressure from Satan. You are correct in your assumption that evil is attempting to divide you precipitously and permanently. Your brother's purpose here has been to remain united with you in Jesus to deliver the Gospel of Salvation to the masses. However, this does not imply that he is not one with you in every other way. The prayers you have said and sacrifices shared have been unique and powerful. You have amended the course of human history and made reparation for those who have turned away from God."

Sunday, December 14, 2008
2:58 p.m.

"My brothers, count it pure joy when you are involved in every sort of trial. Realize that when your faith is tested this makes for endurance. Let endurance come to its perfection so that you may be fully mature and lacking in nothing." [James 1:2]

"My children, it is imperative that your conscience be shaped by the New Covenant Gospel of Jesus Christ and by nothing else, no other religious persuasion, tendency, philosophy, indoctrination, or belief. You must do more to rid the Earth of avarice, genocide, heretical inclining and ghastly pride; and humanity must learn the difference between reckless rebellion and constructive dissent. As Christians, you are struggling to uphold the dignity of a grace-filled Church in an extremely unstable secular atmosphere. I urge you to intensify your daily prayers to mitigate humanity's perversions and excesses, and be sure to use Holy Water to bless, consecrate, and purify everything surrounding you, and to ward-off evil spirits from violating the chaste and innocent. The motivations of Christ's archenemies are so entrenched in delusion that it may require a chastisement of Biblical proportion to break them from their sins. They despise the traditions and doctrines of Roman Catholicism and hate everything about the Holy See. Their obstinance and hedonism are already pronounced as dead as their ability to enter Heaven when they draw their last breaths. They are so blind to the vision of Truth that they cannot distinguish between Satan's baited hook and the Lord's message in a bottle. Those who enter the Eternal City were preordained to be redeemed because the Father imprinted the Crucifixion into their spiritual identities. He has known all along whom would be His apostles and disciples. Your lives here in America are affected by the aspects of your culture, as advanced and developed as it is. Sadly, it has become one of social isolationism and peer disconnection. You are prone to conducting faceless interaction using technological devices devoid of human expression; and civility and unity cannot survive in such a vacuous environment because it is easier to issue insults and provocations without reprisal. Moreover, we have spoken about kindness and forgiveness. Many American states and commonwealths routinely execute convicted criminals with no uprising from their people, but when someone suggests that abortion should be illegal, their voice is submerged by the clamoring indictment against their religious values. Such censorship is discouraging for those who are trying to propagate the Lord's Will. The Heavenly Father is incensed by the unscrupulous tactics of the detractors of the Church who take no time to understand the Sacraments it administers. Much to their dismay, the Holy Gospel compels you to interject the splendorous proclivity of redemptive Wisdom into the public discourse. Remember that your conveyance into the realms of Eternity was guaranteed when Jesus was transfixed onto the Cross on Good Friday. In that pursuit, you must not live your faith lightly or with shallow gestures, but with a deep and abiding oath to holiness and sacrifice. Many have seen that there is no entitlement associated with Christianity other than the reward of posthumous resurrection. My children, go to your Salvation heart in hand! Praise Jesus in speech and song, with oblation, self-denial, charity, and servitude. Your devotion to the Cross is a precursor to your sanctification. If you in America truly wish to become the land of the noble free, you must rein-in your addiction to everything that binds you in the chains of human sin. You must forego your elaborate plans for expanding your capitalist empire beyond your shores because a fairer share of the world's plenty will soon arrive in other countries by the dissolution of your own economy. This is why, My little ones, you must reassess your priorities. You tend toward giving piccalilli to your friends, hemlock to your enemies, obsequies for the departed, and the frost from your shoulders to strangers in the dark. Jesus will someday inquire what you did on Earth while it was in your custody. Did you feed and house the poor, clothe the naked, and make the leprous comfortable? Did you mentor the young and befriend the old? Were your resources shared equitably among those who slept on the street? What kind of human beings spend a million dollars a thousand times over for a sports stadium when there are people dying in city parks? What justification can a nation give whose citizens are trampled to death stampeding into the secular marketplace? And, while United States explorers have exhausted a fortune launching complex flying machines into the void of outer-space, there are people in other regions too weak from starvation to even raise themselves to their feet.

Here, I have told you about conditions, deprivations, and circumstances that are traumatizing the spirit of your land, and we know how to ameliorate them through your prayers. Can you sense that America has a far distance to travel to stand in good stead before Jesus? He does not wish to punish them for the things they have done wrong. His intent is to change them, to give them Wisdom about what alterations should come into their lives from the inside. I will one fortnight from now tell you why I came, and you will remember everything I brought from the Sacred Heart of your Savior. This has all along been My pleasure because you are deserving of the blessings you harvest by your willingness to hear. The Earth and its creatures are being bruised by the ill motivations of humanity; much has been suffered, and gross misfortunes have befallen you. We rectify this by asking Jesus to remake you by His Sorrowful Crucifixion. Everything you will ever learn about Christianity will elevate you to a clear understanding of the mind of God, the bounty of Heaven, and your place there. Your exile is not a permanent home or resting place; this is why you feel discomfort here. It is the reason you cannot find the enviable position about which many have spoken when you realize that everything around you is absolutely perfect. This is your role in the Church, My children. You are reclaimed by the Lord God who gives life in your profession of faith, and He responds to your desires once you have consecrated yourselves to Jesus. What He wills and allows is for Him to know, but you can be sure that He is aware of everything that is best for you. I have been with you, and I shall never leave your side. I have made promises that are not only mandated by God, but to reecho My Fiat to the Archangel Gabriel as Mother of the Redeemed. My Special son, it is an honor to affirm that I pray with you for those you love. Your bountiful heart is touched in affectionate ways, ones that invoke your emotional memories; and these are good for your sense of perspective. It is indicative of your sensitivity to everything beautiful that God created, all that encompasses your physical and social environments. Indeed, you see in other people the same awesomeness that is inherent to sunsets and rainbows. This plays to your spiritual strength; they are definitely not signs of weakness. Every time you open your discussions with your brother about these things, the world is shaped more concisely into what you wish to see. He loves you; he desires to be your soundboard to whom you can turn for counsel and support. You will have a bright future if you believe it can be, if you do not presume that negative events are preordained. Obviously the Grace that sustains you is prefigured, and so is your place in history and eternity. Your openness to receive My messages is unprecedented even for the other shrines I have created around the globe. You render to the Lord what He craves, and that is the flock from whom Jesus has required true sacrifice through the ages. I have given them a holy message today, and I will do so twice more."

Sunday, December 21, 2008
3:19 p.m.

"I proclaim good news to you, tidings of great joy to be shared by the people. This day in David's city a Savior has been born to you, the Messiah and Lord. Let this be a sign to you: In a manger you will find an infant wrapped in swaddling clothes." [Luke 2:10-12]

"My children, the solstice has come; the light will soon linger, and I shall lift humanity to My humble breast for comfort. You will this week celebrate the Christmas Feast, your remembrance and awakening that everything in Creation that is tarnished can sparkle once again. You have known that My messages in America have been about reproval, cultivation, nurturing, maturity, and harvest. Even in the correction I have administered, I have had compassion for your trials while righting humanity's faults. And, I have said that Christians will be sent into places that are not predisposed to embracing God's Sacred Word. Some people allow life to come to them, while others openly pursue it, creating new circumstances and reacting to change, funneling their power and energy toward all charitable good. I have told you that there are too many passive pedestrians who feel that their birth into the world was a setback in their inexplicable journey through universes unknown. Whatever interface they experience is based solely upon their need to survive. My children, I have never given up on their destiny. I have always spoken of them as stars in search of a cosmos, orators looking for a lectern, and prodigies in waiting. When they finally accept what the Catholic Church has to say, they will come alive in every way a creature was meant to live. They will strike keys and sound horns; they will perpetuate the purpose of the Lord's affection, and all who ever dreamed of prevailing over their weaknesses will be hoisted arm and heel onto the crest of valor for their maiden voyage to the core of modern genius. Yes, this is Advent; and I urge you to turn away from yule logs and garland in favor of Jesus the Christ Child reigning inside your hearts. The luminaries overhead and the Star of Bethlehem guide you to the poverty of Jesus' Nativity, reminding the lost that the Kingdom of righteousness hovers in your presence, descending every moment into the exiled world with prophecy, healing, and foresight about the New Earth yet to come. The Lord God Most High who was accused of not making Himself prevalent to the slant-hearted and doubtful was born as an infant through His only begotten Son. And, He knew that everything flawed about you would be ultimately perfectible. My apparitions and locutions throughout the ages have been private revelations for your shared public faith. I have warned that there are demons and warlocks conspiring outside your doors to prey upon your hearts and devour your innocence like nest eggs in the spring. There are signs to help you along the way. You hear the canyon echoes of head-butting rams to remind you that there are opposing forces to everything you believe, but the defiance of your adversaries glances off your steadfastness like sleet impacting stone. You remain in the Lord's good graces when you agree to concessions, that Jesus is the Author of Life, and humanity is His opus. You have the free will to write the storyline of the years, but Jesus finishes your faith with Salvation. I beseech you before My valedictory message next Sunday to obey all the Commandments, especially the Fifth and Sixth. There are so many human actions born from tragedy that there seems hardly any time for spontaneity. Your blueness and melancholia are symptoms of your frustration with the blunders of the flesh. In response, God gives you faith in a hierarchical Catholic Church. Do not allow any foes, heretics, or nonbelievers to rewrite the account of events that have brought us to this day. When the Father created Me, He gave humanity hope that you would be snatched from the flames of perdition in time to be saved from the netherworld. And, in the life and Crucifixion of Jesus, He fulfilled that hope. Those who would try to deny this fact would be no more successful in tearing down His Church than if they could breathe under water or conceal the skylines of the New Jerusalem beneath the Rocky Mountains. Even with a Gospel that seems so unnatural to human logic, nothing better articulates the causes and effects of your thoughts and reflections, the differences between right and wrong, and the ability to see the Light in a world so filled with darkness.

As My messages conclude in seven days, I end them at a time when the United States exhibits all the elements of a republic at the precipice of moral insolvency. Many among you have forgotten that Jesus did not innoculate you from damnation to give you license to sin. You are still held accountable for the consequences of your behavior. I warn you that if there is anything whatsoever lacking in your moral armor, it could become an insurmountable breach on your way to the Promised Land. Yet in light of this, I implore the Church to never forget that the Father in Heaven has incorporated in His plan of Salvation all the exculpating apparata you will need to be free from guilt when you stand before His Son in judgement. For today, and as long as your tumult of corruption remains, you will have much more suffering and disappointment to endure. This is the reason I have tried to make clear the contrasts between sin and holiness. My messages have been about the sheen of Paradise versus the dullness of the exiled Earth. Those who are responsible for keeping the world in turmoil must know that Christ Jesus was born to either convert them or destroy them, and their amorality is as intrinsically evil as their immorality. As I say, you stand with the Lord or against Him. This is why there is heroism lying dormant inside every man, and dreams are abounding in the mysteries of your faith. As you shape your Christian identity, you are constantly purging, excavating, refining and rebuilding; and your thoughts become reflective of the apogees of invisible worlds. Heaven knows that you have witnessed your share of heartaches. Humanity has seen pandemic stress, families uprooted, vultures feeding, children exploited, tender ships sunken, vows broken, comrades felled, maestros silenced, virginity impugned, aspirations slain, veins bled dry, and hopes extinguished. Why is this so? What desperation came upon your homeland to make these things occur? For what enrichment have you been so insolent? What profit is found in being so unholy? You discover that the violence of the world and the peace of the Church cannot coexist, but your reluctance to enter the arena feeds your indiscretions. This is the reason I have spoken here for so long, My precious ones. I have provided answers to questions for men who constantly question the answers. My hope is that I can convince them that the Kingdom of God is always more attractive than humanity's facades. My Special and Chosen ones, it brings Me lasting peace to know that we have come near the completion of My messages to humanity. I will repeat as many times as necessary that I will speak to both of you into the future according to the ordination of the Father. You have taken My messages to the world, and I will soon say that you may go outdoors and play. It began with the Love of God that He asked Adam and Eve never to violate, not to partake of the fruit of the tree in the Garden. And, while nothing good ever came of their error, God reconfigured it in your favor on an Earth that is beaming in the afterglow of Jesus' Resurrection. It was likewise to a tree that Jesus was impaled, as He is the Fruit of the Cross whose Love cannot be matched by any sinful man. You have recorded My messages for the Church that they can hold in their hands and be enlightened, consoled, and inspired. The fruits of your efforts are the keys to a holier life. You will next week receive My final words to humanity to end My years of instruction with a humble Amen. There will be little needed beyond this simple acclamation of 'Let it be.' I have told you on several occasions that human life marches toward the future in eras, epochs, and phases; and you have accorded Jesus the best of all possible gifts during your time on Earth. You have both lived more decades than you have remaining, but this does not imply that your years cannot be better than any you have seen. You have become honorable emeriti in the college of visionaries and locutionists who have tread the world with hope and service, and especially with holiness and sacrifice. Whatever I tell you in the years to come, with Jesus prepared to return, can be transmitted to your brothers and sisters in your own terms, giving humanity your best rendition of Jesus' most endearing peace that the Holy Spirit provides. While in no way wishing to sound as though I am departing a millimeter from you, I reaffirm that it has been My joy to have spoken to you through the years. My Special son, you have given the most between the two of you because your brother was 37 when we began. You were much younger, and you have consecrated your days from age 29 until now to the conversion of the people with whom you will share eternity in Heaven. Of all the things I wish you to know, I do not take lightly your holy blessings to the Church and the Kingdom of God. You have endured the loneliness of being isolated from your friends, and you will reap the rewards from this sacrifice. You must continue working here in the Lord's vineyard, anticipating the Earth's conclusion. Thus, it has come to this. You will next week place My final message to humanity in your 2008 manuscript, and I will proceed with matters dominating your spiritual health. I ask you to remember the tremendous contribution you have made to the Faith Church, the huddled masses, consolation for the Church Suffering, and joy for the Church Triumphant. Not a moment has been wasted since we began our journey on February 22, 1991. You will always celebrate the Christmas Feast with hope, even in times of sorrow, so others will enter Paradise from their torment in Purgatory. The message that I have given today which you will describe as the most preeminent of any words I have said in the history of the world is meant to stir the hearts of mortal creatures for the grand things that come when they search for Salvation instead of the treasures of Earth. Your compliments and sentiments are priceless; they always have been. I cannot explain how humbled I am that My children confide in Me. You will have a meaningful life, many memorable times. You must make decisions from which you will never turn back. I have always said that confidence is your greater trait. We will assemble next week to bid farewell to this year of suffering, prudence, revelation, virtue, and sureness; and your days will go on.

    This means we shall begin anew to grow your faith in the Father's Will by praying as all the faithful have prayed throughout the ages. Your lives are on the course that was laid at the foundation of the world. You are the Lord's emissaries, helping purify all that has become compromised and enlighten all men great and small about the indignities you endure for the magnification of His Kingdom. I want you to know that this is an enhancement of the relationship about which you have written. There will be more time to discuss your concerns and increase your knowledge about Jesus' intentions for the Church. I will dictate detailed analyses about My experiences with the Archangel Gabriel and Saint Elizabeth. I will open wide My Immaculate Heart so you may infuse your faith with My perfection, and you will become closer to the eternal being that the Church is making of you. Of course, I shall continue giving you lessons and teachings about human life, all of which you may paraphrase to assist your brothers and sisters to comprehend the meaning of Holy Love. You should always remember that it is for this Love that I came, and it has been to spread this Love from the Heart of the Father that Jesus lived and died. Thus, we look into the future with more than fragile hope because you know that certain events and circumstances are inevitable. Among them is the fact that lost sinners will come to perceive and live by the Grace that gave us life. They will understand that it is by this same Grace that you are saved. All in all, as I have said, you are more than mortal men. You are more than heroes and conquerors, and your destiny does not lay in doubt. Saint

Alphonsus knew what I am teaching you about My power. All the Church Doctors have known it; all My seers and locutionists have witnessed it, and soon the entirety of the Mystical Body of Christ will become aware that the Mother preceded the Son in ways that have been overlooked for centuries. My plan is embedded in the Plan of Salvation according to the Gospel, comporting with the Son and the Holy Spirit, and with deference to the finest prayers ever said by the people of the Church. Why would God spread fair skies across Creation if He did not intend His flock of believers to soar there? We have given them plenteous seeds to grow their lives in Jesus by the content of My messages, and you must accept this as Truth; you cannot allow suffering to cast a pall over your happiness, no matter how many years remain. I implore you to never let self-pity consume you, and especially do not give in to sarcasm or bitterness. You have been handed a diamond crown of sanctified men through everything you have given to God, and He will place it where it belongs in time. I am heartened that Jesus chose to place the Biblical passages upon the pages of your 2008 messages because it leads everyone to the Scriptures that are being fulfilled. And, My Special and Chosen ones, you will find peace knowing that you will be free to write, speak, and express yourselves unencumbered by the formalities you have known. My Special son, it was My honor to have awakened you and your brother to the miracle of My intercession in ways that you did not know prior to 1991. Do you understand that I have a great deal more to teach and share with you? I have taken you into My confidence for the same reason Jesus approached Sister Faustina, and you have seen that certain days can be taxing. Please do not allow this feeling to become a self-fulfilling prophecy. And, know that Satan will try to divide you and your brother by any means available because what I will relate in the future will mean more than all the messages I have given thus far. You must avoid pettiness and bitterness. You should remember that you are free to enter each other's heart to resolve conflicts before they begin. You have never been selfish. I ask that you share whatever has been unknown before now. My messages will change the world, even before the Church's apostolic mission has been completed. As we move onward, know that your lives are on a course toward wholesome success. I will speak as long as the Father allows. The length of your messages is according to your capacity to receive them. This is expressed by the peace in which you remain and openness of heart about each other's needs. In essence, you are entering a new era next week because My messages to humanity will be ended. You might be tempted in moments of anger to separate yourselves. Satan will employ any avenue to divide you, and whether he succeeds is according to you. Leave no stone unturned in safeguarding yourselves against pain, danger, injury, and death. Yes, this is a good day, but your finest hour has been to present your first fifty pages of your last book to a world that is starved for holiness. Do you remember when we agreed that it is difficult to describe the Blessed Trinity? And, you realize that there is only one single Truth? Perhaps you might in future years refer to what I have described as Triune Truth. How can anything that is single have three parts? I am not saying goodbye because I am not leaving. I will simply say what I have told you for years, that I will speak to you next week. I love you! You will be given a special Messianic benediction now.

Well done, My good and faithful servant. Your Jesus.

Sunday, December 28, 2008
Valedictory Message of the *Morning Star Over America*
2:29 p.m.

"To the one who wins the victory, who keeps to my ways till the end, I will give authority over the nations, the same authority I received from my Father. He shall rule them with a rod of iron and shatter them like crockery; and I will give him the Morning Star." [Rev. 2:26-28]

"Glory to God in the highest, and peace to His people on Earth! Thus goes your true reason for living and the foundation upholding your faith. My children, you are standing on the fossils of an ancient world created especially for you, but your future is severed from its roots. The time has come. My appearances as the *Morning Star Over America* will conclude today. Why has the Lord superimposed My messages across the landscape of the years? Would your joy have been as complete and your crimsons as bright? Does your gold weigh more heavily on your conscience than it did before? You are invited by the Roman Catholic Church to draw every conceivable parallel between your suffering and the Crucifixion of Jesus Christ because everything that torments you has been sanctified by Him. The Father sent Me to garden your potential to become like the Son of Man in every way and by all means, granting you the Grace to know it and the venue to achieve it. It is important to remember that I am not leaving today, I am simply falling silent before the masses so you may internalize with perspective everything I have said here since February 22, 1991. My communication with My pious Illinois sons will proceed as long as God allows. I request that humanity look to the early days of My presence when I began opening your hearts like web-covered vaults beneath the earthen floor. I have always believed that you would spring from that captivity, from that darkness, if only your freedom would arise. I am the Handmaid of the Lord bearing the Savior of the world whose Passion and Sacrifice have pulled you from those depths. Like lightning, the Holy Spirit has set the globe afire while searing, gutting, cleansing, mortifying, and purifying everything in its path. The Father has mandated peace through the destruction of everything opposed to His Will, and My Immaculate Heart is the mainstay of that movement. I birthed the Messiah whose Cross has absolved you. I uttered the refrains of righteousness when others were voiceless. I procured miracles from a Man whose time had not yet come, the sanctioner of believers and the nemesis of the impure. My children, I am seeking miracles from Jesus to this day; and I beseech you to be open to scepter and violin with heartsongs and eloquence so you will long for redemption, live in His service, and die in the faith you profess. I came to you in the Year of Pope John Paul II at a time when humanity was rending at the seams, and I have tried to unify you through the Crucifixion of My Son. It is a mathematical certainty that I will succeed. We have spoken of exaltation falling from your lips like honey, of imminent winds of change, principles predating the pooling of the oceans, and Triune Love that will never wane. I have taken your hearts to places where kings could never travel and shown you signs of eternal reason in the form of simple piety. Where you go from here is according to your aptness to follow the Gospel, your willingness to fight, and what you make of your gifts from God in the blessings He has sown. With sunlight sabering through your windows and winter on the ground, you have seen that the Church has prevailed. You are your fathers' descendants who will leave in your wake a brilliance unforetold, a bright and shining honor to which your children will be drawn. I have delivered you to this excellence at the behest of the Christ for whom you have lived. You share a sacred brotherhood with Him that cannot be deposed, and His Paschal Resurrection inundates you with Heaven's deluge of life-giving waters. It is there that your thirst will be quenched and your soul bathed in His Beatific Light, christened by Eternal Glory. Heaven is an appealing dwelling place into which you are invited but never conscripted, as much as My Fiat to the Archangel Gabriel was a voluntary response. Our Father God is with you in your most perilous hours. Yes, when Nature speaks, humanity should listen. One of the most terrifying places on Earth is to be standing in a gorge and hear the roar of an approaching avalanche. If you leave your hearts out in the cold, this is what will happen. Remain in the Church until you die, and preserve its dignity at all costs. You have discovered that it is practically impossible to engage secular men and women when broaching matters of faith and morality, but you need not worry because they will eventually come to you. As your Mother, I have fledged your lives with Wisdom so you may soar among the eagles, caroling the Gloria In Excelsis Deo to which I have referred. You bask in the aureoles of the Angels and Saints whose company you will join sooner than you know. Thank you, My children, for forestalling your anxieties while lending Me your prayers. God bless you everyone! I will see you in Heaven. And, may Christ Jesus grow your love, hasten your Salvation, embolden your resolve, and enshrine the holiness in your hearts. Amen."

**The Morning Star of Our Lord, Incorporated
Other Available Titles**

*In Our Darkest Hour
Morning Star Over America
February 22, 1991 - December 31, 1992
Volume I*

*In Our Darkest Hour
Morning Star Over America
January 1, 1993 - February 22, 1997
Volume II*

*Morning Star Over America
Twentieth Century Anthology
February 22, 1997 - December 31, 1999*

*At the Water's Edge
Essays in Faith and Morals*

*When Legends Rise Again
The Convergence of Capitalism and Christianity*

*White Collar Witch Hunt
The Catholic Priesthood Under Siege*

*Babes in the Woods
With a Little Child to Guide Them*

*To Crispen Courage
The Divine Annihilation*

*Supernal Chambers
A Resurrection Prayer*

*Morning Star Over America
The New Millennium
AD 2000-2002*

*Morning Star Over America
The New Millennium
AD 2003-2005*

See copyright page for ordering information.

www.ingramcontent.com/pod-product-compliance
Lightning Source LLC
Chambersburg PA
CBHW070715160426
43192CB00009B/1193